An Infinity of Nations

EARLY AMERICAN STUDIES

Series editors:
Daniel K. Richter, Kathleen M. Brown, Max Cavitch,
and David Waldstreicher

Exploring neglected aspects of our colonial, revolutionary,
and early national history and culture, Early American
Studies reinterprets familiar themes and events in fresh
ways. Interdisciplinary in character, and with a special
emphasis on the period from about 1600 to 1850, the series
is published in partnership with the McNeil Center for
Early American Studies.

A complete list of books in the series is available from the
publisher.

AN INFINITY
OF NATIONS

How the Native New World
Shaped Early North America

MICHAEL WITGEN

PENN

UNIVERSITY OF PENNSYLVANIA PRESS

PHILADELPHIA

Published by
University of Pennsylvania Press
Philadelphia, Pennsylvania 19104-4112
www.upenn.edu/pennpress

Printed in the United States of America on acid-free paper
10 9 8 7 6 5 4 3 2 1

Library of Congress Cataloging-in-Publication Data
Witgen, Michael J.
An infinity of nations : how the native New World shaped
early North America / Michael Witgen. — 1st ed.
    p. cm. — (Early American studies)
Includes bibliographical references and index.
ISBN 978-0-8122-4365-9 (hardcover : alk. paper)
    1. Indians of North America—Government relations—To
1789. 2. Indians of North America—Colonization—History.
3. Indians of North America—Social life and customs. 4. North
America—History—Colonial period, ca. 1660-1775. I. Title.
II. Series: Early American studies.
    E91.W58 2012
    970.004'97—dc23   2011030913

CONTENTS

═════════

Contents

===

The Long Invisibility of the Native New World

Eshkibagikoonzhe felt anger, betrayal, and a deep sense of disappointment. He sat behind a table in his home at Gaazagaskwaajimekaag (Leech Lake), an immense lake with nearly two hundred miles of shoreline. Five medals, several war clubs, tomahawks, spears, all splashed with red paint, lay on the table before him. Eshkibagikoonzhe painted his face black for this council session. The Bwaanag (Dakota) had recently killed his son and he mourned his loss. All of the people, the Anishinaabeg (Ojibweg), felt the pain of this death, the loss of a future leader. Eshkibagikoonzhe summoned the man he held responsible for his son's death to join him at council in his home. Now he waited.

The man he waited for came from a new power that had risen in the east. It had been a little over three decades since Eshkibagikoonzhe (Bird with the Leaf-Green Bill) began to hear about this new people. They were called Gichi-mookomaanag (the Long Knives/Americans), and they had a reputation as ruthless killers with a hunger for Native land. The Long Knives had been part of the Zhaaganaashag (British), but they shape-shifted, and now the Gichi-mookomaanag and the Zhaaganaashag formed two rival peoples.

The new people, the Gichi-mookomaanag, began to travel into Anishinaabewaki, the lands of the Anishinaabeg. Shortly after they had separated from the Zhaaganaashag, a young warrior from the Gichi-mookomaanag named Zebulon Pike visited Eshkibagikoonzhe at Gaazaskwaajimekaag. The young man came to find the source of the Gichi-ziibi (Mississippi), the massive river that flowed from the heartland of the continent all the way to its southern shore. He also wanted to establish a relationship between his people and the Anishinaabeg in this region. He sat at council with Eshkibagikoonzhe and gave him a Gichi-mookomaanag flag.[1] Shortly after Pike's visit, a few of the Long Knives managed to insert themselves into the fur trade that was an integral part of Anishinaabe life. These Long Knife traders wanted what the Zhaaganaash and the Wemitigoozhig (French) before them wanted—to claim a place in the villages of Anishinaabewaki where they might forge relationships and live among the hunters and traders who brought pelts out of the western interior. In spite of their fierce reputation only a few of the Gichi-mookomaanag moved through Anishinaabewaki, and they brought valuable trade goods that sparked a healthy competition with the Zhaaganaash traders who manned posts in the north.

Along with their trade, however, the Gichi-mookomaanag made demands, insisting the Anishinaabeg end their conflict with the Bwaanag. They promised to be the arbiters of this new peaceful relationship, which they promised would improve hunting and trade for both the Anishinaabeg and the Dakota. The man summoned to council by Eshkibagikoonzhe had been chosen to live among the Anishinaabeg. He was to be the voice of the Gichi-mookomaanag. The Americans called Eshkibagikoonzhe Flat Mouth, a translation of Gueule Platte, the name by which he was known among the French-speaking traders. Flat Mouth had been waiting patiently as the American Indian agent for the Anishinaabeg slowly made his way west.

The agent, Nawadaha (Henry Rowe Schoolcraft), finally arrived at Flat Mouth's village on July 17, 1832, after an arduous journey. He departed from his post at Bow-e-ting (Sault Sainte Marie), an important Anishinaabe village at the eastern end of Gichigamiing (Lake Superior), the greatest body of water in Aishinaabewaki. He traveled along the southern shore of the great lake for approximately five weeks, and then made his way inland by a series of river systems. Schoolcraft traveled with a small party of ten American soldiers, Methodist missionary William Boutwell, and a mixed-blood fur trader. The trader, named George Johnston, operated out of the American post at La Pointe on the southwestern end of Gichigamiing. The son of a British-born Canadian fur trader and a prominent Anishinaabe woman, Johnston acted as guide and interpreter for the Americans. He was also the brother-in-law of Schoolcraft, who had married his sister. It was rare for any American official, even an Indian agent, to make his way this far into the west. It was even rarer for American soldiers to travel this far into the northwest interior of the continent. American missionaries, similarly, were unheard of among the Anishinaabeg in the west.

The violence between the Anishinaabeg and the Dakota that took the life of Flat Mouth's son prompted Schoolcraft's 1832 expedition. He had made a similar journey the year before to promote peace. And he along with the governor of Michigan Territory had held two treaty councils—one in 1825 at Prairie du Chien on the Gichi-ziibi and another at La Pointe in 1826. When the treaties and the 1831 expedition failed to stem the violence between the Anishinaabeg and Dakota, Schoolcraft wrote to the secretary of the U.S. Office of Indian Affairs proposing the second expedition. "Events growing out of the political condition of the Indian tribes on the headwaters of the Mississippi," he argued, "call for the continued interposition of the friendly influence of the government on that remote part of our northwestern frontier."[2] The secretary responded favorably, informing Schoolcraft that "it is no less the dictate of humanity than of policy . . . to establish permanent peace among these tribes."[3] These expeditions, along with knowledge appropriated from his wife and her Native relatives, provided Schoolcraft with a literary career. He published accounts of his travels in Indian country and wrote several historical and ethnological studies focused on the Anishinaabeg.

Schoolcraft's publications described the United States' exploration and claims of discovery in the Great Lakes and upper Mississippi valley. They also revealed the existence of an intact, and unconquered, Indian social world in the heartland of North America. Though it was claimed by the United States as the Michigan Territory, Flat Mouth and his people controlled this space that they knew as Anishinaabewaki. When Schoolcraft left La Pointe—short for La Pointe du Chequamegon (Shagwaamikong), a hybrid French-Anishinaabe designation—he made his way west across a landscape dominated by Native place-names, Native people, and Native politics. He passed through Anishinaabe villages at places he could only identify by their Native designations: Ga-mitaawaa-ga-gum (Sandy Lake), O-Mush-ko-zo-sag-aii-gum (Elk Lake), Miskwaawaak-zaaga'igan (Red Cedar Lake). As the Americans traveled they met with ambivalence, even though they dispensed gifts from the U.S. government. They also learned that the people of Red Cedar Lake were raising a war party to raid the Dakota in retaliation for the death of one their warriors. In an attempt to stop this war party and fulfill his mission, Schoolcraft made his way to Leech Lake—the seat of Anishinaabe political and military power in the west.

The Americans arrived at nightfall, and at first light they received a summons from Flat Mouth. The Anishinaabeg of Leech Lake were known as the Pillagers because of their habit of looting the traders who came among them. Lieutenant John Allen, the man in charge of the American soldiers who traveled with Schoolcraft, described Flat Mouth in his journal as "the principal chief of his band, and perhaps one of the most powerful and influential men of his whole nation."[4] Flat Mouth lived in a large frame house with a stone chimney, more substantial than the building occupied by the resident traders. When the Americans entered they took note of the décor. Flat Mouth greeted them from behind a table covered with the paint-spattered weapons. The walls of his house were lined with warriors wearing red war paint starring fiercely at the Americans. The missionary William Boutwell wrote in his diary that "their countenances were full of a wildness such as I never saw before. They look some of them as fierce as the tiger, and as bold as the lion, and may be well denominated 'Pillagers.'"[5] On the wall behind Flat Mouth there were two flags, one British and one American. The flags, the war paint, the weapons, and simulated blood were meant to send a not-so-subtle message to Nawadaha.

Flat Mouth rose and addressed his visitors; he complained about the stinginess of the American traders, and the American government's failure to restrain the Dakota as they had promised. Then following the protocols of the council meeting Schoolcraft gave the Pillagers presents, which were immediately distributed by the civil chiefs under Flat Mouth. "I called their attention to the subjects named in my instructions," Schoolcraft later wrote, "the desire of the government for the restoration of peace, and its paternal character, feelings, and wishes in relation, particularly to them." He also "reminded them of their solemn treaty of peace and limits with the Sioux, at Prairie du Chien in 1825."[6] The Americans and Europeans considered warfare endemic to the savage state of being, rather than strategic or political in nature, and Schoolcraft called for an end to a conflict that he believed derived from the Indians' inherent aggression.

In addition to ending hostilities with the Dakota, Schoolcraft sought to promote America's "civilizing mission" among the Anishinaabeg. Broadly speaking this facet of U.S. Indian policy aimed to alter both the culture and the political economy of Native peoples. In addition to ending intertribal conflict Schoolcraft was charged with helping the Anishinaabeg convert to Christianity and adapt to commercial agriculture. After reminding Flat Mouth and his people of their treaty obligations with the Dakota, Schoolcraft asked them to listen to the word of the gospel, delivered by Reverend Boutwell, on behalf of the United States. The missionary spoke about the work of his fellow Christians among other Indian tribes in North America and expressed a desire to provide similar instruction to the Anishinaabeg.

Flat Mouth called on his warriors to listen to his response to the Gichi-mookomaanag. He began, the missionary noted in his diary, by announcing "that he was sorry that Mr. S considered them as children, and not as men." The diplomatic language of the Anishinaabeg relied on the use of kinship terminology to signal the nature of a relationship between two peoples, and indicated the relative power and responsibility that animated any such connection. In making his opening statement, Flat Mouth rejected American paternalism. He also asserted that the Anishinaabeg stood in relation to the Americans as brothers, that is, as equals—not as children seeking the protection of a more powerful father.

Flat Mouth proceeded to harangue Schoolcraft about the failure of the United States to meet its treaty obligations. According to Boutwell's diary the leader of the Pillagers not only ignored the missionary's message about Christianity but spoke with a sense of bitter disappointment about the failure of the American government and its traders to adequately provide gifts and trade goods to relieve the poverty of their country, and alleviate the pitiful condition of the Anishinaabe people. Pity and a poverty of resources demanded relief from those with power. Once again, using ritual language, Flat Mouth evoked the failure of the United States. To point to your own pitiful condition in council was a demand for generosity, for gift giving. The Americans compounded this failure to provide for the Anishinaabeg by failing to constrain the Bwaanag, the Dakota. Staring at Nawadaha with a blackened face, Flat Mouth expressed contempt for the Americans' call for peace: "He had before heard the Americans say peace, peace!" In response, Flat Mouth said, "he thought their advice resembled a rushing wind. It was strong and went soon. It did not abide long enough to choke up the road." Every year since 1825, when his people signed a treaty with the United States pledging to end their war with the Dakota, they had been attacked. They kept their word while the Americans failed to keep their promises. According to Schoolcraft, "He then lifted up four silver medals attached by a string of wampum, and smeared with Vermillion. Take notice, he said, they are bloody. I wish you to wipe off the blood." Flat Mouth recalled the scalps they had taken and declared that he was not satisfied, nor were his warriors. "Both they and I," he declared, "had heretofore looked for help where we did not find it." He gestured to the American flag. "We are determined to revenge ourselves. If the United States does not aid us, I have in mind to apply for aid elsewhere." Flat Mouth gestured to the British flag. He concluded by telling Schoolcraft that when the Dakota killed his son, "I resolved never to lay down the war club."[7]

Lieutenant Allen noted in the journal he kept during this expedition that the Pillagers exhibited a disturbing independence. They traded with both the

American Fur Company and the British at the Hudson's Bay Company post to their north at Rainy Lake. He also complained about their "impudence," and "total disregard of, and disrespect for the power and government of the United States." Allen lamented the fact that the nature of their territory, its remoteness and inaccessibility, made the Anishinaabeg impossible to punish. "The traders have, in vain, to threaten with the power of the government to check their excesses," he wrote, and then noted, "their reply is, that they have not yet seen that power." Allen concluded in his report that "It is probable, however, that our visiting them with such apparent ease may have the effect of lowering their ideas of their inaccessible position."[8] The day after this council the Americans began the long journey back to Bow-e-ting. On this leg of their journey they were again dependent on Native guides. They would not move unaided and on their own power until they reached the American post at La Pointe on Lake Superior.

Perhaps Lieutenant Allen felt compelled to express confidence in the power of his country, but he must have realized that sending ten soldiers into the west under the command of a junior officer was not that intimidating. These men literally could not travel without a Native escort, and in truth they could not have mounted an independent military campaign in the western interior. The Americans were tolerated, even welcomed in some places. American traders introduced an element of competition that gave the Anishinaabeg an edge in dealing with their British rivals, and vice versa. There were, however, only two powerful social formations of any consequence in the northwest interior and both were Native. The Dakota and the Anishinaabeg were the dominant military and economic powers in this region.

Flat Mouth addressed the American Indian agent as a prominent leader of one of those powers, the Anishinaabeg. At council he forcefully informed Schoolcraft of America's failure to meet the obligations of its conditional relationship with his people. In doing so, Flat Mouth operated within a political tradition that had shaped Anishinaabe councils for nearly two hundred years. Violence with the Dakota, as well as peace and alliance with them and with European empires (France and England) and now the United States, structured the political relationships that shaped the social world of the Anishinaabeg. Flat Mouth was particularly adept at negotiating the boundaries and obligations of these relationships. This made him a great leader, and a leading political figure in early nineteenth-century North America. His possession of three names—Eshkibagikoonzhe, Gueule Platte, Flat Mouth—spoke to his political sophistication and the cosmopolitan nature of the Anishinaabe social world. His people controlled a vast territory and a transcontinental trading system that circulated significant resources between the indigenous west, the settler colonies in the east, and the larger world market economy. Flat Mouth was not a simple son of the forest. Neither was he a conquered Indian chief, nor the leader of a dying people dependent on American hand-outs. And yet, in 1832 this was exactly what most Americans, including Henry Rowe Schoolcraft, John Allen, and William Boutwell imagined when they thought of Native peoples.

In his official reports and his published books Schoolcraft asserted a pa-ternalism and sense of cultural superiority over Native peoples that was com-monplace in nineteenth-century America. He held onto this view in spite of the fact that through the strategic use of military confrontation, trade, and diplomacy Flat Mouth managed to shape the nature of his relationship with the Gichi-mookomaanag in a way that was largely beyond his country's control. Flat Mouth created an ongoing relationship with the Americans that required the republic to treat with him on a regular basis, and forced its rep-resentatives to continually promise to work harder to provide for the political and material needs of the Anishinaabeg. The truth of Anishinaabe power and independence is revealed in various Anishinaabe encounters with officials and missionaries recorded by men such as Schoolcraft, Allen, and Boutwell. These men, however, could not comprehend the Native New World that the Anishinaabeg had created for themselves in the two centuries since their first encounter with the peoples of the Old World.

For the Americans the New World was a place of European discovery, conquest, and national reinvention. Schoolcraft, Allen, and Boutwell sim-ply could not imagine that there were Native peoples in the interior of the continent who had made the same transition and transformation, and in the process created a distinctly Native New World. Perhaps the deepest irony stemming from this cognitive dissonance would come from the role these men played in creating an inverted, literary version of Flat Mouth and his world. The encounter between Flat Mouth, Boutwell, and Schoolcraft would become the template for Henry Wadsworth Longfellow's *The Song of Hi-awatha*, an epic poem about vanishing Indians and the fantasy of a wild and unpeopled continent.

From the brow of Hiawatha
Gone was every trace of sorrow,
As the fog from off the water,

As the mist from off the meadow.
With a smile of joy and triumph,
With a look of exultation,
As of one who in a vision,
Sees what is to be, but is not
Stood and waited Hiawatha[9]

Hiawatha, the protagonist of *The Song of Hiawatha*, woke up from a dream. He had seen the future, and it was a new world—a world without Indians. He stood at the threshold of his wigwam on the shore of "Gitche Gumee," or more accurately Gichigamiing (Lake Superior), and waited. He felt joy, relief, even exultation. He could see the object of his dream moving across the lake toward his village, but he could not yet make it out. At last he saw the flash of paddles, and spied a birch bark canoe. "And within it came a people / from the distant land of Wabun." From waaban, or dawn, from the land of dawn, "Came the Black-Robe Chief, the Prophet, / He the Priest of Prayer, the pale-face, / With his guides and companions." Hiawatha stood on the beach, his hand held aloft in a gesture of welcome, waiting until he heard the crunch of the canoe sliding onto the pebbles of the beach.[10] There would be no place for Indians, no place for simple children of the forest in this new world. The future belonged to the people from the land of dawn, "the land of light and Morning!"

Hiawatha saw this future even before he heard the words of the Black-Robe chief, the prophet. He did not turn away from his destiny. He embraced it. The world he had known and ruled over was about to change. He did not resist this change, because it meant progress, and it was inevitable. The people from "the land of light and morning" were a people of progress. There was still hope for his own people left behind to face the coming of a new day. They could heed the wisdom and learn the ways of the Black-Robe and his companions, or they would share a darker version of his destiny. Another character in the poem, Iagoo, a bit of a trickster figure, also dreamt of the future. He too saw the "shining land of wabun." A marvelous place, "All the land was full of people, / Restless, toiling, struggling, striving, / Speaking many tongues, yet feeling / But one heart in their bosoms." And he saw a dark future for Native people, if they fell upon savage ways, "Weakened, Warring with each other; / Saw the remnants of our people, / Sweeping westward, wild and woful."[11] A true Indian, noble and proud, Hiawatha would not succumb to this fate, but then neither would he give up the ways of the forest. Instead Hiawatha would share the fate of the setting sun. He would fade away, a blaze of red on the horizon of America's past, a reminder of the noble race of men who solemnly bequeathed their continent to the new peoples of North America.

This was the American fantasy at the midpoint of the nineteenth century. The two faces of savagery—brutality and nobility—explained the disappearance of the Native peoples of North America, and the triumphant rise of the United States. The brutal savages who haunted the backcountry during the French and Indian War, and during the Revolution, sowed the seeds of their own demise. To the Europeans, these Indians were mean, low people, who would turn on themselves like vicious dogs, because that was their nature. These savages could only destroy themselves.[12] They would find no place in the industrious, teeming, and dynamic America that called on its many peoples to abandon their old ways, and embrace one another in their new life together. They were people from a darker time in North America's history. Fortunately, with the arrival of Europeans in North America a new day had dawned.

The real point of *The Song of Hiawatha*, however, was to give expression to the other face of Indian savagery, the noble savage. This Indian forefather was all that was good and beautiful about America, and Hiawatha was the noble savage personified. He turns over possession of his lands to the new Native peoples of North America, the people of the future, the citizens of the United States. In this version of the fantasy the land itself shares a destiny with the American people. The United States of America, a new form of civilization, can be called into existence only when its people are able to transform the land, to improve it, by making it into farms and cities, and converting the wealth of nature into property. This is the true legacy of *The Song of Hiawatha*, read by generation after generation of schoolchildren. The poem gave concrete expression to an understanding about the meaning of America so familiar it was almost invisible.

The Song of Hiawatha made Longfellow a famous man. To be fair, in some circles, it also made him an object of ridicule. Even though many literary critics found this poem to be nothing more than romantic trifle, it was wildly popular. What are we to make of this success? Longfellow's poem clearly resonated with the American public. The most likely explanation for its popularity is that the epic poem articulated a story about the fate of Indian peoples that easily tracked onto what most Americans thought they knew about their history. Ruthless savage or noble savage, Indians were literally fading away in the face of American progress and civilization.[13] Their fate, their history, would be an act of disappearance not unlike the disappearing act performed by Hiawatha at the end of the poem. In this sense, *The Song of Hiawatha* provided Americans with an ideological justification for the dispossession of the Native peoples of North America.

If the peoples of the United States regarded themselves as the newest, most dynamic form of civilization, many also harbored doubt that a country so new could match the artistic and intellectual greatness of the Old World. Thomas Jefferson had published a vigorous defense of all things American in his *Notes on the State of Virginia*, including the power and beauty of the continent's Native orators. In a similar fashion, Longfellow hoped to draw from the oral traditions of Native peoples to create a distinctly American vernacular, a Native folk tradition. He constructed the template of his epic poem from the publications of Henry Rowe Schoolcraft, amateur ethnographer as well as Indian agent at Sault Sainte Marie, the village in the upper peninsula of Michigan Territory that his wife's people called Bow-e-ting. The poet and Indian agent corresponded with one another, and Schoolcraft advocated the idea that incorporating Native legends and oral tradition could provide something unique to American literature.[14]

Longfellow shared this belief in the idea of using Native storytelling to create a uniquely American folk tradition. In this manner, Americans would inherit the storied landscape of North America, and make it their own. The literary critic Christoph Irmscher describes Longfellow's adaptation of Schoolcraft as "a carefully contrived performance," and "an elaborate play on the notions of authorship and authenticity." Longfellow, Irmscher argues convincingly,[15] had so completely internalized the idea of Noble savagery that he became convinced that these stories were not products of Native culture, but were the literary artifacts of the landscape itself. *The Song of Hiawatha* was the story of the American wilderness. Longfellow was not alone in conflating Native storytelling and culture with the natural world, and a sort of universal primitive humanity. Schoolcraft echoed these same sentiments in his publications. In a book titled *Oneota; or, The Characteristics of the Red Race*, he wrote, "The poetry of the Indians is the poetry of naked thought." And he suggested that "tales occupy the place of books with the red race. They make a kind of oral literature, which is resorted to, on winter evenings, for the amusement of the lodge."[16] Stories like *Hiawatha* simply reflected the "naked thought" of natural man, and in this sense were universally accessible, and universally available for production and consumption.

Longfellow acknowledges Schoolcraft's influence on his work, albeit in veiled fashion, when he tells the reader he learned Hiawatha's story "from the lips of Nawadaha." Few readers would realize that this was the Indian agent's Ojibwe name. Longfellow asserts that Nawadaha had merely repeated these stories, not unlike himself, and not unlike an Indian sitting in his lodge on long winter nights telling stories to amuse the children. The fact that School-craft gave voice to this fantasy, however, is more puzzling. Not only did he live in Michigan Territory at a time when Native peoples still outnumbered American citizens, but he was also married into a prominent Native family. Schoolcraft had married Jane Johnston, the sister of George, his interpreter on the 1832 expedition to the Mississippi. George and Jane were the children of the educated and aristocratic fur trader John Johnston and an Ojibwe woman named Ozhaawshkodewikwe (Green Prairie Woman). Their grand-father was an Ojibwe chief, or ogimaa, named Waabojiig (the White Fisher), who had been a war leader in his youth and became a civil chief as an elder in his community.

Jane Johnston Schoolcraft was a product of the world created by the an-cestors of her parents. Theirs was a polyglot, cosmopolitan social world that emerged during the course of nearly three centuries of ongoing encounter and interaction between the agents of European empires and North American nation-states and the Native peoples of the Great Lakes and western interior. The focus of much of this interaction was the fur trade, which had evolved into a complex combination of diplomacy, politics, and economic transac-tions. People, manufactured material goods, processed natural resources, in-formation, and ideas had long flowed freely between the centers of this trade in Paris, London, Montreal, and New York, and the principal villages of the Great Lakes and western interior. The two primary sources of wealth for Eu-ropeans who came to North America during the seventeenth and eighteenth centuries had been the profits made from this vast inland trade, and land. Access to both of these things required interactions with the Native peoples. As a result, imperial politics and the politics within Native social formations had become deeply entangled.

Succeeding in the Native social world of the Great Lakes and western in-terior, a world created by this long history of cultural encounter, required a great deal of political and cultural sophistication. Men like John Johnston spoke French, English, and Ojibwe, the lingua franca of the fur trade in the Great Lakes. And they understood Native culture and politics through the families they created within the Native social worlds where they worked and lived. This was the world that Jane Johnston Schoolcraft had been born into, and her husband had profited by her knowledge of this place that seemed so foreign to most Americans. Certainly, what Henry Schoolcraft knew of Native peoples came from her, and his scholarship relied heavily on the appropriation of her knowledge and literary talent.[17]

What made Schoolcraft's collaboration with Longfellow so strange was not merely that he ought to have known better, but that he had actually made a voyage into Ojibwe country that paralleled *The Song of Hiawatha*. His 1832 expedition to the Ojibwe villages at the west end of Lake Superior, and out west in the headwaters region of the upper Mississippi valley, oddly mirrored the arrival of the Black-Robe prophet in Longfellow's poem published in 1855. In the poem the "Priest of Prayer" arrives at a Native village on the shores of Gichigamiing "with his guides and companions." In 1832, however, when Schoolcraft accompanied the first American missionary into the territory of the people depicted in the poem, the Anishinaabeg were not a people on the verge of disappearing. In fact, they were expanding from the Great Lakes into the prairie west. Schoolcraft identified twenty-seven Anishinaabe villages in the upper Mississippi valley in a report prepared for the American secretary of Indian affairs in 1831. "The population is enterprising and warlike," he wrote. And he concluded that "they have the means of subsistence in comparative abundance. They are increasing in numbers."[18] In short, the experiences of Schoolcraft and Boutwell ought to have been a revelation. Indian peoples were not vanishing, and they were not eager to adopt American culture and social practices.

Schoolcraft's 1831 and 1832 expeditions reflected the reality of the autonomy and political power of Anishinaabewaki as a social formation. The expeditions, in effect, represented an attempt by the United States to establish its authority in a territory it claimed, but where it did not and could not actually exercise sovereignty. Flat Mouth's rebuke of Schoolcraft demonstrated this reality. If Flat Mouth was unintimidated and uninspired by his encounter with American officials, perhaps it was because he and his people had been dealing with Black-Robes, traders, and various other peoples from "the land of light and Morning" for the better part of three centuries. He disregarded Boutwell because the missionary had nothing new to say. There had been missionaries among his people preaching Christianity as a pathway to "civilization" since the first days of contact with the peoples of Europe. More to the point, from Flat Mouth's perspective, it was the American who needed instruction. The republic had failed to meet its treaty obligations, and their failure cost the ogimaa the life of his son.

If Longfellow appropriated from Schoolcraft, who in turn appropriated from his wife's heritage and the culture of the Ojibwe people at his agency, the New England poet also took liberties with his story that stripped it of any historical or cultural accuracy. The story of Hiawatha did not come from Ojibwe tradition as the poem suggests. Hiawatha was in actuality the culture hero of the Iroquois confederacy. The Iroquois, who called themselves the Haudenosaunee (People of the Longhouse), consisted of five (and later six) linguistically related peoples who came together as a confederation to bring an end to chronic warfare. Hiawatha was the advocate of the Prophet Deganawida, who brought the Great Law of Peace to the Iroquois during a time when they were tearing themselves apart. They re-created their collective identity as a people around the law given to them by Deganawida, and disseminated among them by Hiawatha, actual historical figures.[19]

The true culture hero of the Ojibwe peoples was a shape-shifting hare called Nanabozho, a trickster figure. Apparently, Longfellow found both the name and the character of Nanabozho to be out of sync with the protagonist he imagined at the center of his epic Indian poem. Nanabozho was a mischievous persona, not prone to self-sacrifice, whose misbehavior frequently landed him in trouble. Once, for example, in seeking revenge for the death of his wolf-brother he killed a creature whose death flooded the world. Selfish acts, revenge killings, and world destruction were not the qualities of a noble savage. Clearly, Longfellow's Hiawatha was not a product of the Ojibwe imagination. Neither was it a genuine adaptation of the Iroquois story, or even an accurate reflection of Schoolcraft's ethnographic description of Native peoples. In the end, Hiawatha was simply a literary cultural production that captured the European fantasy about the discovery of North America. This was a story about people who found a wilderness continent, and made it their own, benignly transforming people and place into a New World, and creating a new form of civilization—the United States of America.

The story of the Ojibweg, who also called themselves Anishinaabeg, like the story of Nanabozho, involved a lot of shape-shifting. *Ojibweg* is the plural form of the word *Ojibwe*, a name that nineteenth-century Americans mispronounced as *Chippewa*. This was, however, only their most recent appellation. The Ojibweg entered the historical record in the midseventeenth century as the Sauteurs, the French word for "people of the waterfalls" used to describe the people resident at the village they called Sault Sainte Marie, or the falls of Saint Mary (Bow-e-ting). The term *Anishinaabeg* could be translated as first or original human beings, but by the nineteenth century speakers of

Ojibwe translated this word more simply as Indian.[20] The Ojibwe language, or Anishinaabemowin, was spoken with mutually intelligible dialect variation across the Great Lakes and its hinterlands. Anishinaabeg was a collective identity shared by a number of peoples, speakers of Anishinaabemowinan, who inhabited the Great Lakes and upper Mississippi valley including the Odawa, Boodewaadamii, and Mississagua, as well as numerous smaller groups living in the interior north of Lake Superior and west of Hudson's Bay. The French referred to these linguistically related peoples collectively by the designation *Algonquian*.

The history of these changing names unfolded through the evolution of a complex indigenous social world in the Great Lakes and western interior of North America. The history of the Anishinaabeg was, in fact, an epic story in its own right, and one that had as much power and drama as Longfellow's poem. It was a history that saw the emergence of a Native New World in the heartland of North America. This was the real history of discovery. It was a process of encounter and mutual transformation where the outcome was not always one sided or unidirectional. Native peoples did not go the way of Longfellow's Hiawatha. Some people, like the influential Anishinaabe leader Flat Mouth, not only survived, they thrived in this new world of their own making. The one thing that Longfellow got right was that the story of the Anishinaabe people and the landscape they created was epic, and it needs to be told because it is an important part of the history of North America.

Nineteenth-century Americans believed without question that Indians were destined to fade from history while the United States advanced across the continent it was destined to occupy. This is the certainty of an ideology that equated American expansion with the idea of human progress. The funny thing about the misplaced certainty of nineteenth-century Americans, other than the certainty itself, is that it has blinded us to the history of the Native New World. Until the middle of the nineteenth century autonomous Native peoples occupied the vast majority of North America. The continent's settler colonies possessed very little influence in much of this Indian-occupied territory. The United States, for example, possessed a very limited influence in the region it claimed as the Michigan Territory. Moreover, this limited power derived from the fur trade, which was largely detached from the colonial ambitions of the American nation-state. This does not mean that this Native space was void of political struggle. Attempts to control the fur trade encompassed European imperial politics as well as a complicated social world where Native peoples vied for the power that came from dominating the exchange networks of the inland trade. The combination of violence and diplomacy that shaped this power struggle was anything but the tit-for-tat raiding between "traditional enemies" that Schoolcraft and many other American officials imagined. The Anishinaabeg and the Dakota were two of the largest, most successful, and politically diverse Native social formations to dominate the western interior. And yet for the most part Flat Mouth is a little-known historical figure, and not generally regarded as a political leader who was at least as important as his contemporaries in British Canada and the American republic.

The evidence capturing the Native perspective of this ongoing colonial encounter, however, is often readily available. This is not necessarily a matter of reading European texts against the grain. It is, rather, more simply a matter of reading texts written by Europeans without privileging the fantasies of discovery. *Hiawatha*, of course, is all fantasy, even though it borrows elements of the ethnography of Henry Rowe Schoolcraft. But Schoolcraft's ethnographic work, and the texts of people like Reverend Boutwell, actually described the distinctly Native social space of the northwest interior of North America as it existed. These men recorded their encounter with an autonomous and evolving Native world where only a handful of non-Native peoples lived as interlopers, and where the institutions of North America's settler colonies were nonexistent. The descriptions of this world produced by Schoolcraft and Boutwell were laced with biases and misplaced certainty. And yet the story of Flat Mouth and his world is also present in these texts. He speaks to us through word and gesture, and with his refusal to meet American expectations about what it meant to be an Indian.

The key to reading these texts, and others like them, is figuring out how to disentangle expectation from reality. The ghosts of Flat Mouth and Hiawatha fight for your attention, struggling to assert their opposing perspectives. Reading Boutwell's diary, for example, it is important to understand both his expectations about Native North America, and the world he actually encountered once he arrived in that place. The missionary expected to find a Native world very much like the one Longfellow imagined. That is, he expected to find the noble savages of the northern forests, people who awaited instruction from the people from the land of morning and light. At the very least he seemed to anticipate finding people who understood they were wards of the American state. What America's first missionary to Anishinaabewaki found instead was another world altogether. More to the point, this was a dynamic and evolving world with a very long history—a history that has been rendered largely invisible because of the mythology of discovery and conquest.

Thinking about the New World as a place created by European discovery and conquest has resulted in a very particular, and peculiar, Indian history. There are some Native leaders who figure prominently in this history. Witness the popularity of American Indian warriors such as Metacomb (King Phillip), Pontiac, and Tecumseh, who battled English and American settler colonists to preserve the independence of their people. In the late nineteenth century when the United States and Canada fought for control of the Great Plains, Sitting Bull and Geronimo emerged as iconic figures in the popular culture due to their heroic resistance and tragic defeat. Louis Riel, leader of the Red River Rebellion in 1870 and an emblematic figure in Manitoba, similarly became a founding father, although he never quite reached the status of his nineteenth-century counterparts in American popular culture. All of these warrior figures proved themselves ready to fight to the death to preserve their autonomy, marking them as capable of the sort of virtuous behavior required by the freedom-loving citizens of republican government. Once they were vanquished they could enter civil society, at least in iconic form if not as actual citizens. In other words, once conquered they could become the symbol of the new nation's indigenous national heritage.

Most early American college-level survey courses would include some discussion of Metacomb, Pontiac, and Tecumseh, but Flat Mouth and his contemporaries among the Anishinaabeg and Dakota remain conspicuously absent. They reached the height of their power during the era of removal in the United States, when Indians were conveniently taken out of the national narrative, even when they managed to refuse actual physical removal. There are, of course, many excellent histories of Native peoples in the nineteenth century. There are too few histories of nineteenth-century North America that tell the story of the numerically significant and politically independent Native peoples who controlled the majority of continent's territory, and who helped to shape the historical development of the modern American, Canadian, and Mexican nations.[21]

This book is divided into four parts, each with two chapters. Part I, titled "Discovery," focuses on the ideology behind the notion of a European discovery of the New World. These chapters examine this concept, but also seek to provide a Native counternarrative to the idea of European discovery, which was a largely discursive process. Part II, titled "The New World," examines the social worlds created by the arrival of people from Eurasia and Africa in the Americas. These chapters seek to uncover the emergent social worlds formed by this encounter, specifically focusing on the Atlantic World of settler colonies and the Native New World that formed in the interior of North America. Part III, titled "The Illusion of Empire," explores the political reality created by the existence of two emergent social worlds in North America rather than a singular New World. These chapters outline the limits of imperial influence in the Native New World, and trace the collapse of French influence in the indigenous west in the period leading up to the Seven Years' War. Finally, Part IV, titled "Sovereignty: The Making of North America's New Nations," offers an examination of how acknowledging the existence of a Native New World changes our understanding of the encounter between the American nation-state and the autonomous Native peoples who occupied territory claimed by the republic in the west. This part also explores how the collision of the Native New World and the American republic affected the relationship between Native peoples and British Canada.

Infinity of Nations begins with an exploration of the idea of discovery. The concept of discovery functioned as the expression of an ideology by which Europeans divided the world between civilized and savage peoples. Civilized peoples lived within sovereign societies of their own making. Savage peoples lived as part of the natural world rather than as members of a society. Virtually all Europeans who produced a written record of their encounters with the Native peoples of North America understood their contact with the indigenous Other through the lens of discovery.

Of course, in reality discovery unfolded as a mutual process where the peoples of the Eastern and Western Hemispheres came to know each other. The teleology of the European idea of discovery was fraught with fear of the savage, but ultimately ended with the idea of conquest—the triumph and expansion of the civilized world.

On the ground, however, the reality of European conquest varied. The French created an empire in North America where their colony remained deeply intertwined with and mutually dependent on Native peoples. The Spanish conquered some Native peoples, but found others unconquerable. They also treated some Native peoples as political vassals, and intermarried widely with the indigenous populations in the territory they controlled politically. The English similarly conquered some Native peoples, but also formed political alliances with others for the purposes of trade and warfare. In each of these empires the monarchy imagined that at least some of the Native peoples living in or near their New World settler colonies had become subjects of the Crown. And in spite of this more nuanced reality, each monarch claimed sov-

ereignty over these colonies, their hinterlands, and the Native peoples who
resided in both by right of discovery and conquest.

The existence of Flat Mouth and his world stand in stark contrast to the
false history created by the idea of European discovery. If Europeans began to
discover Anishinaabewaki in the mid-seventeenth century, and then came to
possess this people and place in the decades that followed, then there would
have been no need for Indian agents and treaties when American officials
made their way onto this same territory two centuries later. Only by recovering the story of the process of mutual discovery and encounter that created
Flat Mouth's world can we begin to know the true history of North America.
The simultaneous existence of Anishinaabewaki and the imagined world of
European discovery and conquest that created the political fiction of empire
and cultural production like *The Song of Hiawatha* make sense only if we
recover the still largely invisible history of Native North America. My exploration of the idea of European discovery in this book proceeds with a simultaneous telling of the Native history of encounter with the peoples and things
of the Atlantic World.

After narrating the history of Anishinaabewaki during the era of discovery, this book explores the world that emerged in the indigenous western
interior of North America. Encounter created an Atlantic New World that
brought together the peoples of Eurasia, Africa, and the Americas, but this
New World had its limits. It did not extend into the indigenous west, although its peoples, ideas, and things circulated between the interior and the
settler colonies at the coast. Historian James Merrell wrote that "we should
set aside the maps and think instead of a 'world' as the physical and cultural
milieu within which people live and a 'new world' as a dramatically different
milieu demanding basic changes in ways of life."[22]

Merrell's work explored the ways in which Native peoples were forced
to reimagine their social place and identity in the New World created by the
expansion of Atlantic World empires onto North American soil. But what
about all of those indigenous peoples in the vast interior of the continent
where the institutions and peoples of empire were largely absent, or arrived
only in disembodied form such as disease, metal, cloth, or ideas about racial,
cultural, and social differences? In the Great Lakes, the northern Great Plains,
and the northern boreal forests that swept inland from the great bay Europeans named after Henry Hudson, another New World emerged when the two
hemispheres collided. This other "new world" was a Native New World. It
was the transregional space at the heart of the North American fur trade. This

inland trade would connect Native peoples with little or no direct contact with Europeans to an emerging world market economy. This connection demanded change. It brought both opportunity and tragedy. And it demanded that Native peoples, like the peoples of empire, reimagine their social identity in the wake of the epic encounter that brought their two old worlds into contact.

Anishinaabewaki, the social formation of the Anishinaabe peoples, emerged at the heart of this Native New World. Unlike the Great Lakes Indian world imagined by Longfellow, Anishinaabewaki was not an ahistoric and pristine wilderness that could only fade away when exposed to civilization. The story embedded in the poem reflected the logic of the ideology of European discovery. In reality, the Anishinaabe people suffered from the effects of encounter, but they also figured out how to benefit from this experience. During the course of the seventeenth, eighteenth, and nineteenth centuries the Anishinaabe peoples evolved as a multipolar social formation. The social organization of European empires centered on the nation, which provided a unified and hierarchical structure for organizing collective social identity and mobilizing political power. The Anishinaabeg, in contrast, mobilized political power through a variety of social structures formed according to a seasonal cycle linked to their political economy and ritual calendar.

Political power and social identity took on multiple forms among the Anishinaabeg. This capacity for change and adaptation mirrored an ability to shape-shift, a concept that was pivotal to the worldview of Anishinaabe peoples, and reflected in the behavior of their trickster figure Nanabozho. This fluidity allowed the Anishinaabeg to function as part of a transregional collective social formation, or to detach from this larger formation and mobilize political power and identity on a microlevel as members of a doodem, or clan with claims to particular hunting territories, watersheds, rice beds, and so on. This flexibility allowed the Anishinaabeg to weather the vicissitudes of a fur trade that was at once a function of their political economy, essential to intergroup diplomacy, a means of connecting to European empires, and the product of an evolving global market economy.

The expansive and diffuse nature of Anishinaabewaki as a social formation also allowed the Anishinaabe doodemag (clans) to bridge the Atlantic and Native New Worlds. As they moved between these distinct social worlds, their ability to form relationships (peaceful and violent) with both the peoples of empire and the peoples of the indigenous west like the Dakota made the Anishinaabeg a powerful political force in North America. Similarly, their connection to the numerous bands of Ojibwe, Cree, and Ojibwe-Cree speaking peoples that the chief financial officer for the colony of New France would identify with great trepidation as "an infinity of undiscovered nations" in the heartland of the continent made the Anishinaabeg indispensible to the fur trade.[23]

The French official's fear stemmed from the ideology of discovery, and the corresponding belief that the heartland of the continent was dominated by an infinity of Indian nations whose allegiance and territory might be discovered and claimed by a rival empire. While this fear involved the meaningless political fiction of European discovery as a form of conquest, it also demonstrates the truth of the existence of a Native New World. In effect, the continent was not an unsettled wilderness inhabited by savages. It was instead an autonomous Native social world, "an infinity of nations," and it would survive as such into the lifetime of Flat Mouth in the early nineteenth century. Of course, this was not actually a world of indigenous nations, but rather a world of bands, clans, villages, and peoples. In the Native New World land was not the exclusive dominion of a single individual or nation. It was instead a shared resource where use rights were claimed, negotiated, and exercised as part of the lived relationships that people forged with one another in the process of creating landscape and social identity.

After describing the formation and function of the Native New world, and the evolution of Anishinaabewaki within this space, *Infinity of Nations* returns to a consideration of the claims of empire. By the middle of the eighteenth century the chain of outposts that sustained the political interests of European empire in the Native New World would become increasingly ineffective. The evolving power of the British and French Empires, and the changing interests of Native peoples, produced a fundamental change in the way that the peoples of the Native and Atlantic New Worlds related to one another. Europe would lose much of its fragile political influence in the indigenous west. The fur trade would continue, and even thrive, but it became divorced from imperial politics. The Anishinaabeg and the Dakota would become increasingly oriented to life in the west, and they would become largely disengaged from the world of empires.

This historical trajectory, explored in Part IV of the book, helps to shed a new light on the nature of the relationship between the United States and the peoples of the Native New World. The cognitive dissonance experienced by Reverend Boutwell and the confrontation between Flat Mouth and Schoolcraft occurred because the United States believed that the republic was the inheritor of a legacy of European discovery and conquest that had, in fact, never happened. As a result of this disconnect the United States would be forced to work hard as an expanding settler colony. The illusion of American expansion as a dynamic and natural process would give way to reality in the region that the United States labeled the Northwest Territory. It would take serious political work to plant the institutions of the American nation-state in Anishinaabewaki. American officials would be forced to undergo constant negotiation over fundamental categories that defined the republic such as the meaning of race, nation, and sovereignty. It was this long history of encounter between the two emergent and constantly evolving social worlds in North America that produced the modern world of the nation-state on this continent. *An Infinity of Nations* attempts to tell the story of the parallel development and eventual convergence of these two emergent social worlds—the Atlantic New World and the Native New World.

PART I

Discovery

This book begins with a simple premise, that it is possible to write a history of Native North America in the seventeenth century. Of course, any history of Native peoples during this time period must also be a history of the encounter between the indigenous peoples of this continent and the European empires that brought settler colonialism to the Western Hemisphere. And so one might expect that this Native history of North America is also a book about the discovery of the New World.

The idea that Europe "discovered" the Americas is obviously flawed as a historical concept. The two continents existed before Europeans arrived and began to interact with the peoples they found living there. From a European perspective, however, the Americas were a New World because they had been conspicuously absent from the Old World that they had known for millennia. This place and its people were not in the sacred texts and origin stories of Europe, Asia, or Africa. They were absent from maps, and even from the historical imagination. Given this absence, it makes sense that colonists thought of this place as a New World even though it was occupied by people who had a long history in the Western Hemisphere.[1] It also makes sense that they relied on a language of discovery to describe their experiences in a place so completely unknown to them.

These are the biases that encode virtually all of the textual evidence that historians must rely on to write the history of seventeenth-century North America. Stephen Greenblatt has argued that narratives of discovery, as historical artifacts, actually teach us about the writer rather then the New World. What we witness is not the discovery of The Other—be it place, person, or thing—but rather the experience of the author confronting a radically different world. It is that experience, that confrontation with the unknown that the writers describe.[2]

The discovery of the New World, in other words, was a discursive act. Europeans used the tools at their disposal—particularly written narrative and cartography—to reveal this unknown world to the peoples of Europe. These texts were an attempt at translation. They described and labeled the New World so that it could be observed, understood, and ultimately possessed by the peoples of the Old World. "The ritual of possession," Greenblatt argues, "though it is apparently directed toward the natives, has its full meaning then in relation to other European powers when they come to hear of the discovery."[3] In this way narratives of discovery and claims of possession went hand in hand.

Thus, much of what Europeans had to say about the New World had nothing to do with the reality on the ground, but rather was directed toward a European audience. The English, French, and Spanish Empires, for example, all claimed possession of vast territories in North America by right of discovery. This was particularly true for the French Empire. With a small number of settlements situated along the bank of the Saint Lawrence River, the colony of New France laid claim to territory stretching deep into the interior and encompassing the regions we now think of as the Great Lakes and the northern Great Plains. In reality, European colonies in seventeenth-century North America consisted of a small number of settlements on the east coast, except for Spain, which controlled the former territory of the Aztecs at the southern tip of the continent. The vast interior of North America remained indigenous. The empires of Europe could, at times, influence the peoples and events in the interior, but most of the continent lay beyond their control, even beyond their comprehension.

To dismiss the idea of discovery as mere political fiction, however, leaves untold a crucial part of the epic story of encounter that defined the early modern world. The New World was, in effect, created through a process of mutual discovery. Just as European empires confronted the implications of discovering a New World, indigenous social formations like the Anishinaabeg were forced to comprehend and incorporate new peoples, animals, tools, weapons, and countless other material artifacts into their social world. In North America these adjustments altered the social relations of production by which human communities sustained themselves. But this encounter had the same effect on the peoples of Europe and Africa. Increasingly, the people, things, and ideas that circulated between their homelands connected human communities on each of these continents. This was the true meaning of the New World: a place of mutual discovery that forced human beings to imagine themselves and their place in the world anew.

To understand the New World and the process of discovery in this way, however, demands a fuller accounting of the history of Native peoples. This, in turn, requires that we rethink the historical archive. If the language of discovery constitutes a literary convention that privileges a European perspective and European social, cultural, and political categories, how do we make sense of the Native peoples that appear in these records? We can begin to answer this question by taking indigenous social formations seriously. This will require that we think about the self-representations of Native peoples as political and diplomatic actors in the era of discovery. And we must recognize that some of the social, political, and cultural constructs and categories used by Native peoples will have no easily translatable equivalent in the social world of Europeans.

Historians of early North American history, like the agents of the English and French Empires, have treated the Iroquois Confederacy as a significant social formation and important political power. This has occurred in large measure because the Iroquois presented European observers with a recognizable social formation. The Iroquois or Haudenosaunee consisted of five culturally related social units, easily recognizable from a European perspective as Native nations, linked as allies in a political confederation governed by commonly accepted laws and religious customs. The political, economic, and military power mobilized by this confederacy resembled the social formations of Europe.

The indigenous peoples of the Great Lakes and the northern Great Plains, however, presented European empires with a different kind of social formation. The peoples of these regions lived largely as hunter-gatherers with a habit of seasonal migration. The patterns of this movement and the social structure that made it possible resulted in a social adaptability that European observers interpreted as politically unformed and culturally primitive. The interactions between these peoples and the empires of Europe have been more difficult to historicize, in large part because European observers struggled to make sense of their social organization and political identity. Nevertheless, the peoples of the Great Lakes constituted a majority among the Native peoples allied to New France, and they constituted a demographic majority in the region they occupied and controlled by virtue of a sophisticated and interlocking system of diplomatic and economic relationships. Throughout the seventeenth and eighteenth centuries no European empire managed to establish more than isolated outposts in this region.

The fact that Native peoples maintained a demographic majority in the Great Lakes throughout the colonial era makes this region unique. What does this demographic fact say about European claims of discovery and possession? Certainly it raises questions that ask us to go beyond an interrogation of the discourse of discovery. The idea that large Native confederacies like the Iroquois influenced the development of North America permeates most of early American history. But what should we make of the idea that the vast heartland of this continent was occupied and controlled by Native peoples, rather then being possessed by European powers? Should we consider the seasonal migrants of the Great Lakes and the Great Plains to have been political, economic, and military powers in their own right? If so, should this change the way we think and write about the discovery of the New World, and the colonial period in North American history?

In the aftermath of the discovery of the New World, or rather the arrival of European explorers and settlers in inhabited lands, Native peoples nonetheless remained in control of the vast majority of the North American continent. They were not conquered and dispossessed. This stunning fact means that during the colonial era the settler regimes of Europe were surrounded by autonomous Native communities that governed access to the vast majority of the continent's land and resources. If we acknowledge that the possession of large portions of Native North America by the empires of Europe never occurred, changes must be made to the national narratives of Canada and the United States. But in order to realize the full impact of this history, we must tell it as part of a continental history that traces the simultaneous development of Native and colonial settler social formations in the early modern era.

CHAPTER 1

Place and Belonging in
Native North America

In the spring of 1660 the Anishinaabeg converged on a central location below Gichigamiing (Lake Superior), the largest freshwater lake in North America. They came to a village at another smaller lake, Odaawaa Zaaga'igan (Ottawa Lake, which the French designated as Lac Courte Oreilles). This lake connected two important watersheds, one flowing north into Gichigamiing, the other southwest into the headwaters of Gichi-ziibi (Mississippi), a massive river system that flowed from the heartland of North America into a large ocean gulf that framed the southeastern shoreline of the continent. This village was situated at a crossroad of sorts. It linked the vast grasslands that spread across the interior of North America to the watersheds and lakes that connected the center of the continent to the eastern seaboard (Figure 1). The Anishinaabe bands that lived at the west end of Gichigamiing sent word to the peoples of these regions—other Anishinaabe bands, the Wyandot (Huron) to their east, Muskekowuck-athinuwick (Lowland Cree) peoples from the north, and the Dakotas to their west—that they planned on hosting a ceremony in the spring.[1]

In the spring people arrived at the Anishinaabe village burdened with the things they valued most in the world. They carried food, animal skins, and peltry fashioned into clothing. They brought wampum, beaded belts made from purple and white shells exchanged as a signifier of alliance or a declaration of war, and used as a ritual gift to mourn the dead. They brought trade goods manufactured by the Europeans who had settled on the east coast of North America. They also carried the bones of their dead ancestors. These things represented the building blocks of a potential exchange network that would link the peoples together in an alliance relationship. This was why they

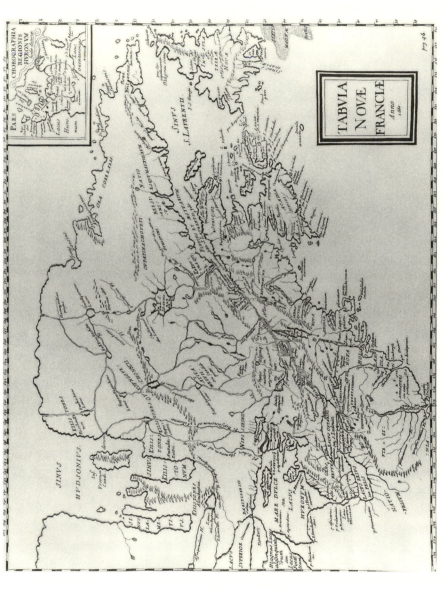

Figure 1. Tabula Novae Franciae [Pere Creuxius] Anno 1660. Hudson's Bay Company Archives, Provincial Archives of Manitoba, G. 5/24 Plate 16 (N15248). This detailed map created from information obtained from Native informants presents the western interior, or Anishinaabewaki, as a complex social space mapped according to Native place-names and self-designations.

had come together. The Anishinaabeg of Gichigamiing wanted to end the bitter warfare between their community and the Dakota and the Muskekowuck-athinuwick, and replace it with a new relationship. They wanted to end the cycle of raiding and counterraiding that killed off their young warriors, and saw their women and children taken into the villages of their enemies as slaves. To do this they needed to find a way to transform their enemies into allies. In the world of the Anishinaabeg there were two categories of people— inawemaagen (relative) and meyaagizid (foreigner).[2]

The Anishinaabeg needed to find a way to transform their enemies into relatives. To create this new relationship they borrowed a ceremony from the Wyandot, a form of the athataion, or a Feast of the Dead. This Feast of the Dead lasted fourteen days; each filled with dancing, games, gift exchanges, ritual adoption, and arranged marriages between members of the different bands in attendance. The ceremony culminated in a massive eat-all feast where the living dined alongside the corpses of their dead relatives, consumed all the food in the village, and then gave all of the goods that they had accumulated to their guests as gifts. Following the feast, the dead were interred in a common grave.[3]

The Feast of the Dead ceremony inscribed the past with a new meaning. With the bones of their ancestors joined together, the Anishinaabeg, Muskekowuck-athinuwick, and Dakotas could imagine a shared history of kinship and alliance. Their pasts were buried together. Their futures, in the form of their children—now intermarried—also joined them together as an extended family. Enemies literally and ritually had been transformed into allies by being made into kin. They were now inawemaagen, relatives.

In this way, the Feast of the Dead represented a rebirth. It represented the possibility of uniting a landscape divided by violence and warfare. Relatives shared a sense of responsibility for one another. Along with this responsibility came rights to trade, hunt, fish, harvest rice, and generally sustain the life of the community, all of which were negotiated among the composite parts of a social formation that operated as an extended family. The social relations of production for any Anishinaabe community involved the recognition of reciprocal rights and responsibilities between the different beings (human and other-than-human) occupying a given territory. Alliance expanded the scope of these relationships to include new people and spaces, effectively expanding the physical and social world of the Anishinaabeg.[4]

In effect, the Feast of the Dead refashioned the rights and responsibilities that defined the relationship between people and landscape. It linked the peoples from the north and south shores of Gichigamiing together, and tied them to the people from the region of Gichi-ziibi, the enormous river valley that drained the forests and grasslands of the interior west. The political and economic integration of these peoples represented a significant reconfiguration of power and space. Joined in alliance, the combined social formations of the Anishinaabeg, the Muskekowuck-athinuwick, and the Dakota possessed the ability to control the circulation of people, animal pelts, and trade goods throughout the heartland of North America. This ceremony, in other words, created an indigenous sociopolitical formation that could, potentially, rival or surpass every other power—Native and European—vying for control of North America's fur trade. And control of the fur trade translated into power; the power to determine the fate of the Indians and European immigrants struggling to make their place in the New World.

The New World was born of this struggle between Natives and newcomers over place and belonging, and over the rights and responsibilities owed to one another. On a continent that came to be defined by the mass immigration of outsiders, and the wide-scale displacement of the indigenous population, understanding who belonged where, and by what right, are among the most fundamental questions that can be asked or answered. This was what made the Feast of the Dead hosted by the Gichigamiing Anishinaabeg significant in 1660, and this is what makes the story of this event important now.

This ceremony was an act of political self-determination that redrew the boundaries of Anishinaabewaki, Indian country, the homeland of the Anishinaabe peoples. What makes this event remarkable is that it captures a moment of political imagination that represented a rebirth and expansion of Native power and social identity at a time and place usually associated with the expansion of European power. This alone makes the ceremony stand out as a narrative about the history of early modern North America. Reading about the feast we are told a story that cuts against the grain of the usual meanings associated with this period of the continent's history—stories about the death and diminishment of Native peoples and Native power. But perhaps the story of this Anishinaabe Feast of the Dead only seems remarkable because we know the outcome of Native America's encounter with the empires of the Atlantic World. That is the central problem of writing the history of North America, vantage point. How to write a history of the New World where it is possible to imagine a Native present, the possibility of a North America that was not entirely consumed by European and then American, Canadian, and Mexican colonization? Begin with a story that allows you to see how it might have happened otherwise—Native peoples refashioning a New World on indigenous terms—Anishinaabewaki reimagined through the adaptation of a Wyandot ceremony that transformed meyaagizid into inawemaagen.

The 1660 Feast of the Dead shows us this process, Native peoples refashioning their world on indigenous terms, but it also reveals the challenges involved in recovering that story. This ceremony inscribed new meaning onto the physical remains of past lives. Deceased ancestors, both enemies and allies, were buried together to give the living a shared bond in the present. This bond provided the basis for an alliance between distinct and previously antagonistic Native social formations. But how do we make sense of this event from the vantage point of the twenty-first century? We can think of this ceremony as a ritual that allowed participants to reimagine their place in the world by retelling the story of their shared past. And yet this was not the past as history, at least in the western intellectual tradition that recognizes history as the (literal/narrative) representation of past events. Instead, the Feast of the Dead offers us a different kind of narrative, one that used the past to create a political imaginary strikingly different from our own time and place. This is particularly valuable because so many stories about the New World represent the indigenous people and spaces of North America as unknown. This ceremony, in contrast, tells the story of Anishinaabewaki, revealing that North America was not a wilderness inhabited by wild people, but a human place with a storied past.

Following Benedict Anderson, we can think of the social relationships produced by the Feast of the Dead as a cultural artifact that signified a particular form of collective identity. "Communities are to be distinguished," he wrote, "by the style in which they are imagined." The Feast of the Dead speaks to Anderson's idea that social formations, and collective identity, take shape as imagined communities.[5] With this ceremony we are shown how community was created through an indigenous representation of time, space, being, and political self-determination. We are shown the New World imagined from an indigenous point of view.

This was not a New World divided between the savage and the civilized, the known and the unknown, Indians and Europeans. This was a world divided into meyaagizid and inawemaagen, and new people entered this world according to these categories. They became relatives of the Anishinaabeg, taking on the rights and responsibilities that this relationship implied, or they remained outsiders who could expect to be treated as such. Accordingly, Anishinaabewaki changed in terms of territory as people negotiated place and belonging within this imagined community. This was not political self-determination (sovereignty) expressed through the possession and exclusive control of physical space. This was, instead, a territory created by the relations between people.[6] As such, the 1660 Feast of the Dead represented a significant expansion of Anishinaabewaki, and an increase in Anishinaabe power. Contemplating the New World from this vantage point, we can clearly identify the Anishinaabeg as an emergent power expanding into the heartland of North America in the same manner that we might describe New France or New England as emergent powers expanding inland from the Atlantic seaboard.

The introduction of new power, and new powers, to any social world brings change. The adaptation of the Feast of the Dead ceremony by the Anishinaabeg was a response to the massive change brought on by the arrival of Europeans in North America. With this ceremony, the Anishinaabeg used the past to alter the meaning of present-day events and relationships. Because this happened by way of a ritual where dead and living human beings comingled over a shared meal, this particular representation of the past seems wildly exotic, perhaps even something that must remain unknowable from the perspective of modern North American history.

This brings us back to the question of interpretation. How do we make sense of this ceremony, both as a construction of the past and as the representation of an imagined community? We can, as Benedict Anderson suggests, think of this ceremony as a cultural artifact, and then try to understand how this artifact came into existence as a historical phenomenon. With this exercise, however, we return to the problem of vantage point. All of the information we have about the Feast of the Dead comes to us in the form of written documents produced by Europeans. A French man, one of the few non-Native participants at the 1660 Feast, subsequently wrote about his experience in an attempt to demonstrate knowledge of Native North America. He produced this text hoping to convince English benefactors, including Charles II, king of England, that he could open the interior of North American to English commerce. To make his case the author placed himself at the center of a story about the discovery of an exotic place populated by exotic people. In this story the author offers himself as both expert and master of this strange New World.

This is the work of history, to sort out the different ways that Natives and newcomers inscribed meaning onto events, and explained their place in the New World. This is the other important lesson of the 1660 Feast of the Dead: history comes to us from the biased narratives of others. Sometimes those others share a biological or intellectual heritage with the historian. Sometimes not. But the historical others, those producers of past meaning, are separated from us by time. In this case by centuries of time, and their stories reflect their lives in that other past place. This, in fact, is what we hope to recover—their understanding of that past world. This is also the challenge of writing about the meeting of Natives and newcomers in North America. For the most part, only the newcomers left behind written documents describing their experience.

Narratives of Discovery

In 1667, seven years after witnessing the Anishinaabe Feast of the Dead, Pierre Esprit Radisson, a French voyageur, produced a manuscript describing the ceremony in vivid detail. In this manuscript Radisson offered himself as the architect of the alliance ceremony, and as an expert in the North American fur trade. Written in a garbled Francophone English, Radisson described four separate voyages into the interior of the continent. The fourth voyage chronicles a harrowing two-year journey that took Radisson west beyond Gichigamiing, and into the Dakota country where he supposedly orchestrated the Feast of the Dead uniting "eighteen several nations."[7] The French called Gichigamiing Lake Superior, an approximation of the meaning of the Anishinaabe name for this body of water, and they called the Great Lakes region the "pays d'en haut," or the upper country. The country of the Dakotas, in the region of Gichi-ziibi, or as it would come to be known, the Mississippi River valley, was (from a European perspective) the edge of the known world. This is what makes Radisson's manuscript so significant; there are very few written documents that describe the Anishinaabeg and their country during this time.

This fact also makes Radisson's manuscript a very problematic document. How do we judge the veracity of this text? It was written as a form of self-promotion, and in a style that positioned the author as the "discoverer" of new lands and new peoples. In terms of style and content Radisson's manuscript closely paralleled *The Jesuit Relations*, an extensive collection of published texts that circulated widely among the reading public in both New France and Europe. *The Relations* were published accounts of the missionary experiences of the Jesuit order operating out of New France.[8] These texts, along with Radisson's manuscript, constitute almost the entire written archive concerning the peoples and places of Anishinaabewaki and the Dakota country at the midpoint of the seventeenth century. They also represent a distinct literary genre that can best be described as narratives of discovery.

Narratives of discovery represented a very particular form of literary and cultural production. These texts performed discovery, and advanced claims of possession, by identifying, naming, and describing the people and places of the New World. The discourse of discovery, in effect, appropriated indigenous people and space by placing them under the gaze of Atlantic World empires. In this way Anishinaabewaki became the pays d'en haut and part of the known world through a simple act of textual representation.[9] Both *The Jesuit Relations* and Radisson's manuscript paid special attention to mapping the place and identity of Native peoples. The Jesuits sought souls for Christ, Radisson beaver pelts to enhance his own personal wealth. Both endeavors required knowledge of and a relationship with Native peoples.[10]

In 1660 French voyageurs and missionaries were just learning to navigate their way through this landscape of Indian peoples and place names. Radisson's manuscript described this transitional moment when fur traders and priests began to move into the west in search of furs, trading partners, and converts, instead of waiting for annual caravans to descend on Montreal in search of trade goods. In his narrative, Radisson wrote that he and his brother-in-law Médard Chouart Des Groseilliers offered to undertake a voyage of discovery on behalf of New France: "we made our proposition to the governor of Quebec that we were willing to venture our lives for the good of ye countrey, and go to travell to the remotest countreys wth 2 hurrons that made their escape from the Iroquoits."[11] The remote country they promised to explore was Anishinaabewaki, or from the French perspective the pays d'en haut. To reach the Anishinaabeg in their homeland, however, they would rely on Huron guides described in Radisson's text as refugees from the Iroquois.

The ravages of the Iroquois and plight of refugee Hurons figure prominently in the narratives of discovery produced by agents of the French Empire. In many ways the stories of these two peoples represented the battle between good and evil that missionaries especially used when describing their attempts to bring "civilization" to the New World. Huron was the name that the French had given to the Wyandot, an amalgamation of Khionontateronon or Petun and Wendat peoples. Once part of a confederacy of Iroquoian-speaking peoples thirty thousand strong, the Wyandot had many converts to Christianity, but had been devastated by smallpox epidemics and internal divisions over spiritual practices. Thus weakened, they fell victim to brutal attacks from another rival confederacy of Iroquoian speakers who occupied and controlled territory below the Saint Lawrence River valley.[12] Europeans called this rival confederacy the League of the Iroquois. The confederacy called itself the Haudenosaunee, the People of the Longhouse.

Confederation, and the collective identity that came with it, was the source of Haudenosaunee power. This self-designation evoked the dwellings and villages that protected the peoples of the confederacy. The longhouse was a tall framed building covered with elm or cedar bark siding. These long rectangular buildings housed multiple extended families, and were situated within palisaded villages that Europeans described as castles. This mode of habitation provided shelter from the elements and enemies, and in this sense also served as a conceptual model for the confederacy, which imagined itself as if it were a longhouse. The Haudenosaunee consisted of five communities, each speaking a distinct Iroquoian dialect, but each closely related through intermarriage, and through a system of shared clans and rituals that governed social relationships within and between villages. The Mohawk (Keepers of the Eastern Door), the Oneida, the Onondaga (Keepers of the Council Fire), the Cayuga, and finally the Seneca (Keepers of the Western Door)—five peoples who constituted a single extended family, inhabiting a single living structure—the People of the Longhouse. They controlled a vast territory identified by the European colonial powers as beginning in the east at the Hudson valley corridor and stretching west along the length of the Mohawk River valley to the southern shores of Lakes Erie and Ontario.[13] For the Haudenosaunee this territory was the embodiment of their collective being, the longhouse. Their occupation of this territory and their way of life were integral to Haudenosaunee identity.

The People of the Longhouse were the perpetual enemy of the French Empire and their Native allies in North America. Samuel de Champlain, the founder of New France, ensured this enmity by attacking Haudenosaunee villages in a series of raids by which the French staked their claim to belonging in the New World—as allies of the Huron, and their partners in the fur trade.[14] The People of the Longhouse controlled the waterways that connected Dutch and English colonies in the east to the peoples and resources of the interior. They had ambitions to extend their influence into Anishinaabewaki, and over the waterways connecting this space to Montreal and Quebec via the Ottawa and Saint Lawrence Rivers. The merchants of New Netherlands and subsequently New York fueled this ambition by arming the warriors of the Haudenosaunee, and encouraging them to aggressively pursue the fur trade by raiding for plunder and to extend the northern range of their hunting territory. New France, in effect, came into being as part of a power struggle centered on the control of territory that facilitated the circulation of animal pelts and trade goods between the east coast and the northern interior of the continent of North America.

Narratives, such as those written by Radisson and the Jesuits, or even Samuel de Champlain, described this struggle from a very distinct perspective. They tell the story of New France and its founding as part of a larger story about the discovery of the New World. We are introduced to peoples, like the Wyandot and the Haudenosaunee, in the language of empire as the Huron and the Iroquois. And what we learn about them in these narratives is similarly encoded with the meaning and perspective of immigrants struggling to make sense of a new land, while they simultaneously claimed this space as their own. In these stories, the imagined communities of Native peoples exist only in relation to empire.

This was appropriation at its most elemental level, writing a New World into existence by claiming North America as a homeland for the peoples of Europe. These narratives represent no less than the discursive dispossession of Native North America. Native peoples existed as part of the French Empire, either as refugees fleeing a savage enemy, or as antagonists threatening the colony. Either way their history becomes subsumed by the story of European powers fashioning a new homeland in a wilderness devoid of civilization, where Native peoples lived as *les Sauvages*, that is, as "wild men."

Discovery narratives, in addition to describing unknown peoples and places, also recorded the arrival and establishment of European settlements in North America. Part of the process of "Discovery," in effect, was to provide a chronicle of the making of the New World. This genre of writing relied on a political imaginary that divided the world into domains of savagery and civilization. This was an essential part of the ideology that justified settler colonialism. The indigenous peoples of North America were identified as living in a state of nature (as wild men), or as barbarians (that is, nomadic and non-Christian). Their condition was inconsistently described by European jurists, but was generally linked to the idea that Native peoples had either not transformed their lands into private property, or to the idea that their lands were not permanently occupied.[15] As such they had not exercised dominium, or sovereignty, in constituting their communities. Similarly, some Europeans argued that the absence of the Christian faith among Native peoples placed them outside of civil society, which left them without rights in a civilized world. Whatever the specific formulation, the logic of discovery meant that

North America was, from a European perspective, uncivilized and therefore unsettled land.[16]

Thus emptied of meaning North America and its indigenous inhabitants entered the historical record compiled by Europeans only in relation to the founding of their New World empires. Native peoples were not described as culturally distinct and politically sentient beings with social formations that functioned according to their own logic and imagination. Rather, they became Indians, the uncivilized peoples of the New World. In this fashion, the idea of discovery created by the European colonization of North America dispossessed Native peoples of both land and political identity. But it is important to note that this was a discursive dispossession. It is possible to dig beneath these new names and to look beyond the language of discovery to recover an understanding of the indigenous New World. At the time Radisson made his journey the peoples of Anishinaabewaki not only controlled their homeland but were also engaged (along with the French, the English, the Haudenosaunee, and the Wyandot among others) in a struggle to control the fur trade. They were not the occupants of an unsettled land, but an autonomous people, fighting to defend and even expand their territory.

A Landscape of Relationships

Although most Native peoples in the seventeenth century remained politically autonomous and controlled at least some territory, the colonization of North America produced brutal and wide-scale social disruption. Both Natives and newcomers must have struggled to make sense of the calamity visited upon indigenous peoples—some of which, at least, seemed to be of their own design and some of which Jesuit missionaries interpreted as acts of God. When disease ripped through Native communities the missionaries often regarded it as an act of providence, an opportunity to baptize the departing souls and guarantee their existence in the next life.

In recording these episodes the Jesuits provided evidence of a time of remarkably violent change. *The Relation of 1640*, part of *The Jesuit Relations*, for example, recorded the arrival at the French town Trois Rivières of "a band of Algonquins dragging with them many poor widows and orphans, come to throw themselves into the arms of our charity." *Algonquian* was a general designation that the French applied to all speakers of Anishinaabemowin, the Ojibwe dialects of the Algonquian language family spoken by the Anishi-

naabe peoples. In the language of empire, *Algonquian* emerged as a broad descriptor of political identity that encompassed multiple communities bound
together by language, culture, and a shared interest in the French fur trade.[17]
This identity, and the associations that came with it, made the "Algonquians"
bitter rivals of the Iroquois. The Algonquian band that arrived at the Trois
Rivières mission in search of French charity offered a poignant example of
how colonization was reshaping Native lives in the New World. The members of this band were destitute, possessing only a single bag of corn. Their
community had been reduced largely to widows and orphaned children who
managed to escape death when disease swept through their village. The Jesuits took these people into their mission and recorded the story of one of
these widows who, they wrote, "seems to have been reserved for Heaven by a
special providence of our Lord."[18]

This widow, who remained nameless in *The Relation of 1640*, grew up
among the people of the Haudenosaunee. She had been born a child among
the Anishinaabeg, however, and taken captive by Haudenosaunee raiders as
a youth. She entered captivity at an early age and forgot her natal language.
The widow was recaptured by the Anishinaabeg on a raid into Iroquoia led by
the founder of Quebec, Samuel de Champlain, meaning that she most likely
would have returned to her people sometime between 1620 and 1635. Her life
was spared because she remembered one word of Anishinaabemowin, *niin*.
She shouted this word, *Niin! Niin!*, or "Me! Me!," over and over again until
one of the raiders recognized her as an Anishinaabe captive. She returned
to Anishinaabewaki, the land of her original people, and lived another life.
When she arrived at the Jesuit mission at Trois Rivières in 1640 she had been
spared yet again. An undescribed illness struck her village, and according to
the Jesuits "she saw her husband, her children, and a great many of her relatives die."[19] Now an old woman with no food and little hope she gathered up
the orphaned children of her village and removed herself to a Jesuit mission
attached to New France.

This unnamed woman belonged to many places in the New World that
emerged after the peoples of Europe and Africa began to arrive in North
America. And the story of her past provides a record of the ways in which
Native peoples forged new relationships with one another, and with different
places in the wake of European colonization. For the Jesuits this was a story
of salvation, perhaps even a story of their own redemption given the obvious
brutality that followed European immigration to the New World. For this
woman, however, her life history told a story of family and the obligations of

kinship. Redeeming and revenging lost relatives, and replacing population lost to disease, was at the root of much of the warfare raging across North America in the mid-seventeenth century.[20] But this was not only a story of death and destruction; it was also a story of life and preservation. In this brief story about a remarkable woman, the Jesuits tell a story of self-preservation, and illustrate how indigenous communities survived in spite of horrific loss and violence.

For the Jesuits the horrors of Native suffering seemed to be matched by their own horror at finding themselves charged with the task of converting such a barbaric people to Christianity, and to a civilized life. In 1642 Jerome Lalemont wrote about the mission in the country of the unnamed widow, in the Lake Nipissing region at the eastern edge of the territory that the French called the pays d'en haut. Lalemont described the Nipissing Anishinaabeg as "peoples who do not differ from us more in climate and in language then they do in their nature, their way of acting, and their opinions, and in everything that can exist in man except body and soul." These "Algonquins," in other words, possessed a body and soul just like the peoples of Europe. And yet, at least to Lalemont, they appeared to be different in the very nature of their being. The Wyandot, in contrast, with their bark longhouses and fixed fields of corn, beans, and squash, seemed barbaric and heathen but comprehensible. They were more proximate, literally and in terms of lived experience, to the French colonists. With regard to the Nipissing Anishinaabeg, however, Lalemont wrote in *The Relation of 1642*: "It must be confessed that we are still very much in the dark as regards these Algonquians who live in these countries that are more remote from the fort of our French people."[21]

For Lalemont the remoteness of the Algonquians, spatially and at the core of their way of being, represented a form of barbarity that proved especially resistant to conversion. "They live a wandering life of people scattered here and there, wherever the chase or the fishing may lead them," he complained. They lived he wrote: "without a house or fixed residence, without gathering anything from the earth, beyond what it yields in a barren country to those who have never cultivated it. It is necessary to follow these people if we wish to Christianize them; but as they continually divide themselves up we cannot devote ourselves to some without wandering from the others." Lalemont described the mission among these wandering peoples as a grueling physical and emotional hardship.[22]

In writing about the Nipissing Anishinaabeg the Jesuits described a way of being that they believed to be the antithesis of civilization. They described the seasonal migration of the "Algonquins" as random and chaotic—a wandering life following wild game that left people scattered and separated from one another. These nomads constantly dissolved into small groups that moved across a landscape that seemed especially harsh to the Jesuits because it was (from their perspective) uncultivated, a wilderness. This explanation of "Algonquin" life was shaped by the ideology of empire, which was predisposed to see the world as divided between the savage and the civilized. *The Relation of 1642*, and other related texts like Radisson's manuscript, failed to connect Algonquian migration to the fact that animals moved according to cyclical patterns linked to reproduction and the availability of food resources.[23]

The migration patterns of Anishinaabe peoples actually required a sophisticated understanding of the seasonal availability of resources and the carrying capacity of the land. The movement of nomadic peoples in North America was not random, nor was this life a result of the lack of social development. On the contrary, this way of being required a sophisticated social structure, one that facilitated the expansion and contraction of community. Mobility and the variability of community, in turn, required a relationship to land that was not fixed and restrictive like the property regimes of settler colonialism and European empire. Instead, the landscape of Anishinaabewaki was created by the relationships between people. Place was not created as a possession or as the occasion for the exercise of dominium, but resulted from the recognition of mutual rights, obligations, and responsibilities shared by inawemaagen (relatives) living within an extensive resource base.[24]

Lalemont experienced the creation of this kind of Native space firsthand when he witnessed a Feast of the Dead ceremony hosted by the Nipissing Anishinaabeg in 1642. The record of this ceremony, like the life experiences of the unnamed widow, told a story about the meaning of family, the obligations of kinship, and preservation of ties to a landscape shared by many different Native peoples. A location was chosen for the ceremony, he wrote in *The Relation of 1642*, at "a bay of the Great Lake," most likely along the shore of the extensive bay in the north of Lake Huron. Invitations were sent to "all of the confederated nations." Lalemont estimated attendance at approximately two thousand persons. His description of the ceremony resembled Radisson's description of the feast he witnessed in 1660. Participants played games. Rituals were danced and sung. Enormous quantities of gifts were exchanged: "Beaver robes, skins of Otter, of Caribou, of wild Cats, and of Moose; Hatchets, Kettles, Porcelain Beads, and all things that are precious in the country." This, of course, also included tremendous quantities of beaver skins distributed by the Nipissing ogimaag, the chiefs hosting the ceremony. Lalemont seemed astounded by the extent of the giveaway, and guessed that the gifts "would have cost in France forty or even fifty thousand francs."[25]

After the giveaway, the people sat with their dead and feasted throughout the night. The following day the dead were interred in a common grave. At the interment, yet more gifts were exchanged and two councils were held. The first council, according to Lalemont "consisted of the Algonquians who had been invited." The other included the Nipissing and the Wyandot.[26] In 1642 as in 1660 Anishinaabeg used this borrowed Wyandot ceremony in order to reach out to non-Anishinaabe peoples in a gesture of kinship and alliance. In a sense, these ceremonies serve as counternarratives to stories recorded by the Jesuits that focus on depopulation and refugees forced to flee into the arms of French charity. Depopulation certainly occurred and disease and warfare ravaged Native communities. These things were true. But also true was the fact that Native peoples found ways to preserve their communities and keep alive connections to a shared cultural landscape.

The Jesuits, in fact, relied on these connections as they attempted to expand their missions into the pays d'en haut. The expansion of the missions, and similarly the expansion of the fur trade, relied on a process where Jesuits and traders set out to discover unknown Indians. Lalemont wrote that he attended the Feast of the Dead in large part to "win the affections of chief personages."[27] To accomplish their mission the Jesuits, in Native fashion, gave gifts with the explicit goal of creating new social relationships. "In consequence," he reported in *The Relation of 1642*, "the Pauoitigoueieuhak invited us to go and see them in their own country." He described these people as "a Nation of the Algonquian language distant from the Hurons . . . towards the West whom we call the Inhabitants of the Sault." Traveling with a party of Wyandot or Huron guides, two Jesuits made their way to this village in the early fall, where they found an estimated thousand people.[28]

The Relation of 1640 provided a similar, brief description of this village. In this volume the Jesuit Paul Le Jeune wrote an enumeration of Native peoples that read like a cultural geography of the pays d'en haut as the French understood it. This document begins at the Gulf of Saint Lawrence, and then moves inland tracing the water route that took the Jesuits to the so-called village of the Sault in 1642. In this description the reader moves across a landscape defined not so much by its physical geography as by the names and descriptions of indigenous peoples. Writing about the place where Lake Superior drains into Lake Huron, Le Jeune named the "Amikouai" and the

"Oumisagai" as residents of lakeshore villages below a river connecting the two bodies of water. The river connecting the lakes formed a rapid, or a sault in French, and Le Jeune called the residents of the village at this location the "Baouichtigouian" (Lalemont's Pauoitigoueieuhak). Later Jesuits would record this name with more phonetic accuracy as something that sounded like "Batchewana Irini." This, in Anishinaabemowin, would translate as the people of Bow-e-ting, or as the French transcribed it in *The Relation of 1640* and in *The Relation of 1642*, the people of the Sault.[29]

In French records the people of the Sault became the Sauteurs. The residents of the Sault, like the people of Lake Nipissing and the people from the west end of Gichigamiing who hosted the Feast in 1660, however, also called themselves the Anishinaabeg. The term *Anishinaabeg* can be translated as "human beings," or "original people." In fact, all of the peoples that the Jesuits identified as living in the immediate vicinity of the Sault would have identified themselves as Anishinaabeg, as would virtually all of the peoples the French identified as Algonquians, or people of the upper country (*les nations supérieures*).[30] The "Amikouai" people identified by the French as residents of a village below the Sault, for example, would have called themselves "Anishinaabeg." "Amikouai," or more properly "Amikwas," meant "beaver" in Anishinaabemowin and represented doodem, or a clan identity. The "Oumisagi" people identified as living in this region were also Anishinaabeg. This term, more accurately spelled Mississauga, meant "mouth of the river" in Anishinaabemowin and like Bow-e-ting signified an identity tied to a village location. Thus, Anishinaabeg, as a self-referent, connected speakers of Anishinaabemowin living in communities identified by village location and clan identity as fellow human beings; that is, as part of an extensive, kinship-based, indigenous social formation.[31] This was, to borrow Benedict Anderson's terminology, an imagined community.

According to the Jesuit Charles Raymbault, the people of the Sault invited the Jesuits to come and live among them. The missionary renamed this place Sainte Marie du Sault (present-day Sault Sainte Marie) after the Virgin Mary, an important figure in the Catholic faith. In 1642, however, this place was simply too far beyond the reach of the colonial officials and institutions of New France, and so it remained for all practical purposes Bow-e-ting. It would be twenty-six years before the Jesuits established a mission at this village. And until that time the only French people to visit this location would be men making their way into the west as traders. Anyone making their way into the pays d'en haut had to portage the rapids of Bow-e-ting, making this village a vital link in the circuit through which people and things moved between the indigenous interior of North America and the Atlantic World colonies on its eastern seaboard.

This was, in fact, how the Jesuits learned of the Sauteurs and their neighbors described in *The Relation of 1640*. Paul Le Jeune received his description of the Native peoples of the western interior from Jean Nicolet, the interpreter of the Compagnie de Nouvelle France, who lived for a brief time in a village of the Nipissing Anishinaabeg. Like the Jesuits, Nicolet gained his information in part by traveling with Native guides, and in part through Native informants who periodically traveled great distances to trade with other peoples. Thus borrowing from Nicolet who borrowed from unnamed Native sources, *The Relation of 1640* described the "Kiristinon" or Cree who called themselves "Muskekowuck-athinuwick," and lived to the north and west of "the Great Lakes of the Hurons." This text also described the "Naduesiu" or Sioux, who called themselves "the Dakota," and lived west of the place that the French thought of as Green Bay on the western shore of Lake Michigan. Nicolet had even learned from an "Algonquin" about the trade fairs held by the *Si'pucka nu'mak* or Mandan in the very heart of the Great Plains that attracted people from all across the interior of the continent.[32]

And so by 1640, all of the peoples that Radisson would describe as participants of the Feast of the Dead he claimed to have organized in 1660 had entered the historical record compiled by the European discoverers of North America. The Jesuits who visited Bow-e-ting in 1642 were also given descriptions of and directions to the Dakota and Muskekowuck-athinuwick, or the Sioux and the Cree in the lexicon of the French Empire. These peoples, they were told, engaged one another in "continual wars."[33] This information made it into print and circulated in texts read throughout the known world, or at least the portions of the planet controlled by Europeans. And yet while agents of European empire began to know at least approximations of the Native peoples of the interior of North America, they still did not know how these people related to one another, exactly where they lived, or what categories they used to define their relationship to a physical landscape.

This, however, was the way that discovery worked. Written records, such as those compiled by the Jesuits, offered readers a narrative description of the relationship between New France and the peoples of the New World from the perspective of empire. What they did not do, at least directly, was offer a description of the indigenous New World. Instead, this form of knowledge production sought to make the indigenous people of North America legible

to the peoples of Europe. It described the seasonal migration of the Anishinaabeg as mindlessly nomadic, their land as uncultivated (and therefore not
truly possessed), and their humanity as savage. They were a wild people living
in a wild space. Discovery was the process by which Europe claimed this wild
people and space for God and civilization, by making them known.

Warfare as the Fur Trade Moves West

Just as violence and disease compelled the band of the unnamed widow in
The Relation of 1642 to seek temporary refuge in the east at Trois Rivières,
these same processes compelled the Wyandot and many Anishinaabe bands
to seek refuge in the west. In 1650 the Wyandot left their homeland in search
of trade opportunities, and in search of relief from the relentless raiding of the
Haudenosaunee. Through ceremonies such as the Feast of the Dead, they had
forged a connection with the peoples of Anishinaabewaki. These connections
gave them a right of residence, as well as the right to trade and travel in the
country of their "Algonquian" allies.[34]

Radisson entered Anishinaabewaki in much the same manner as the
Wyandot, in pursuit of Algonquian trading partners. Unlike the Wyandot,
however, Radisson and his brother-in-law did not belong in the west, at least
from the perspective of the French Empire. They made their 1659–60 voyage
without a congé, the license to trade among the Indian allies of New France.
In his manuscript Radisson claimed that the governor demanded to be made
a partner of any trading venture undertaken in the pays d'en haut. Not wanting to share either their expected profits or their hard-won knowledge of how
to navigate the trade routes of the interior, Radisson and Des Groseilliers left
without licenses.[35]

Radisson's illegal journey into the western interior of the continent was
not a unique experience. The French had a name for men who traveled inland
to trade with Native peoples without a license from the governor. These men
were called *coureurs de bois*, or runners of the woods. Around the time of
Radisson's voyages they began to enter the west in significant numbers. They
went, according to one colonial official, because "it was a Peru for them."[36] In
French documents the coureurs de bois entered the west chasing a multitude
of Native peoples moving west in search of riches and respite, as traders and
refugees, simultaneously fleeing the Iroquois and searching for beaver pelts.

By the mid-seventeenth century, this reorientation toward the interior caused by continual warfare with the Haudenosaunee and population shifts due to epidemic disease began to severely disrupt the political economy of New France. In 1653 a Jesuit missionary named François Le Mercier lamented: "Never before were there more beavers in our lakes and rivers, but never have there been fewer seen in the warehouses of the country." Before the devastation of the Huron, he wrote, a hundred canoes came to trade every year. Now, he complained, "the Huron fleets no longer come down to trade; the Algonquians are depopulated; and the more distant nations are withdrawing still farther fearing the fire of the Iroquois."[37] Le Mercier asserted that the Algonquian peoples, like the Huron, had been devastated and dispersed by the Haudenosaunee.

In *The Relation of 1653* the missionaries lamented the collapse of the fur trade economy, but also reported a rumor that New France had successfully negotiated a truce with the Haudenosaunee. "But now," Le Mercier wrote, "if God bless our hopes of peace with the Iroquois a fine war will be made on the beavers." As if to confirm his hope that the French might once again wage war on the beaver, the Jesuit reported the arrival of three canoes at Trois Rivières in the spring of 1653. They came he wrote, "from the former country of the Hurons—or, rather from the depths of the most hidden recesses of those regions, whither several families have withdrawn, out of all communication with the rest of mankind." These canoes contained people "from four different nations" who brought news that they were gathered together with two thousand warriors, and living approximately 150 miles to the west of the former country of the Huron. They informed the French at Trois Rivières that they planned to come next spring "to bring a large number of beaver skins for the purpose of doing their ordinary trading, and furnishing themselves with powder, lead and firearms, in order to render themselves more formidable to the enemy."[38]

The next spring the colonists of New France watched the waterfalls above Montreal with trepidation. "We were suspended between fear and hope," Le Mercier wrote, waiting for the return of their Native friends, and fearing the return of their Native enemies. When at last a fleet of canoes appeared, fear gave way to relief as they recognized their allies returned in large numbers, as promised, to trade. The people of Montreal, he wrote, "experienced a double joy upon seeing that these canoes were laden with furs, which those nations come to exchange for our French products."[39]

The return of Native allies to Montreal, at least in French records, was not exactly triumphant. Le Mercier described this trading party as a mixture

of peoples "who speak the Huron language, "and those "speaking the Algonquian language," and he identified them with an unusual precision as Khionontateronon (Wyandot) and Kiskakon (Giishkaanowed Odawa). "All of these
peoples," he wrote, "have forsaken their former country and withdrawn to the
more distant nations." He placed them at a location the French came to call
Green Bay on the western shore of Lake Michigan. "The devastation of the
Huron country," Le Mercier wrote, "having made them apprehensive of a like
misfortune, and the fury of the Iroquois having pursued them everywhere,
they thought to find security only by retreating to the very end of the world."
The Jesuit concluded by noting: "They live there in large numbers, and form
a greater population than before occupied all those countries; several of them
have different languages, which are unknown to us."[40]

These unknown Indians, as much as the animal skins they produced, represented the wealth and future of the colony. They were souls to be claimed
for God. Even more importantly, they were the source of the only riches that
the French had discovered in their corner of the New World—beaver peltry.
And as Le Mercier implied, from this relationship sprang all of the wealth of
the colony. He compared the trade in beaver hides to a bountiful river system
that provided life to the colony, and complained that "the Iroquois war dried
up all these springs."[41] In the relationship that the subjects of New France had
formed with Native peoples fur trade exchange, political alliance, and warfare
were completely and irrevocably intertwined.

The return of their Native allies promised a return to the prosperity that
war with the Haudenosaunee threatened to steal away. "In a word," Le Mer-
icier wrote, "the country is not striped of beavers; they form its gold mines
and its wealth, which have only to be drawn upon in the lakes and streams."
Toward that end, he noted "all our young Frenchmen are planning to go on a
trading expedition, to find the nations that are scattered here and there; and
they hope to come back laden with beaver skins of several years accumulation."[42] Many of these young men, like Radisson and Des Groseilliers, would
make their way into the western interior of North America as coureurs de
bois. In doing so, they became part of a transformation of the French Empire
in North America that began to occur when the fur trade moved from met-
ropolitan cities like Quebec and Montreal into village centers throughout the
Great Lakes.

Le Mercier described this transformation as a retreat "to the very end of
the world." And so it might have been for the French traders who ventured
into the west in search of another Peru. The more traders and missionar-

ies learned about this other world, however, the more it became apparent that Anishinaabewaki, the land that French colonists thought of as the pays d'en haut, was not a wasteland rapidly filling up with refugees. It was instead a rather sophisticated arrangement of social relationships organized around village centers, trade routes, ritual ceremonies, hunting territories, and resources like fish runs and rice stands.

From the Jesuit mission at Tadoussac, east of Quebec, the missionary Gabriel Dreuillettes began to amass information about the peoples who lived at "the very end of the world" in the hope of bringing them into the Jesuit mission system of New France. In the mid-1650s he began to publish information about the identities and trade networks of Native peoples in the western interior in *The Jesuit Relations*. Dreuillettes interviewed people—both French and Native—who participated in the inland trade. He wrote that the Algonquian language was spoken across the region stretching north and west from New France for a distance of fifteen hundred miles. "I know well there are some slight differences among these Nations," he reported, "but they consist in certain dialects, which are soon learned."[43]

In subsequent writing Dreuillettes described New France and the interior of the continent north and west of the colony as divided into three language groups. The peoples of this part of North America, he wrote, "all speak either pure Algonquin, or pure Montagnais, or pure Abanquois." By Montagnais, Dreuillettes referred to the Naskapi or eastern Cree, and here at least he seems to have substituted "pure Montagnais" for the Cree dialect of the Algonquian language family, which is closely related to Ojibwe. By "Abanquois" he referred to the language of the Abenaki, or Wabanaki, another imagined community of Algonquian speakers similar to the Anishinaabeg occupying territory between northern New England and the Saint Lawrence River valley. Dreuillettes wrote that, "Some confuse these three languages, which much resemble one another, so that these missions as a whole may be called the Algonquin Missions."[44]

This, in effect, was the Jesuits' understanding of the cultural geography of the social world in which the French colony was embedded. It was, as far as the Jesuits could tell, a world built in large part by overlapping languages and dialects. The other thing that connected the peoples of these language communities to one another was trade. Exchange, the circulation of both animal peltry and manufactured goods of indigenous and European origin, and ritual gift giving defined the social landscape described by Dreuillettes in *The Jesuit Relations*. Following the Nipissing and other "Algonquian" peoples they met at the Feast of the Dead ceremony, or come to trade in French towns, the Jesuits recorded no less than six widely traveled trade routes that traversed the length and breadth of the Great Lakes and connected this region to the Mississippi Valley in the west and Hudson's Bay in the north.[45]

This was not an empty land populated by scattered nomads and desperate refugees. It was instead a cosmopolitan world occupied by a great diversity of peoples. The two thousand people that the Jesuits counted when they visited Bow-e-ting, for example, would not remain in that location throughout the year. Instead, they moved through a landscape marked by the periodic abundance or restriction of resources. Village communities actually consisted of multiple named bands, doodemag such as the Amikwas. These units, in turn, were composed of winter bands that consisted of two to three lodge groups. Extended families, usually led by a senior male, and including his adult male children, and one or two other male relatives, and their families, formed winter bands that dispersed from their lakeshore villages into the interior to hunt.[46] Or they combined hunting with long-distance travel in order to trade with their allies and raid their enemies. The expansion and contraction of Anishinaabe social units, and their seasonal mobility, depended on a complex web of social relationships that constituted an extensive imagined community of Native peoples.

Onontio and His Children

In the summer of 1656 Gabriel Dreuillettes recorded the arrival of two French men, licensed traders returned to the settlements of New France after a two-year voyage into the west. "Their arrival," he wrote, "caused the country universal joy for they were accompanied by fifty canoes, laden with goods which the French came to this end of the world to procure."[47] These two voyageurs, one of whom was Médard Chouart Des Groseilliers, traveled with a party of Odawa traders. Their arrival signaled not only a resurgence of the French fur trade but also a reaffirmation of the alliance between New France and its Native trading partners.

This fleet of Odawa canoes met with a grand celebration, including the firing of canon in salutation when they arrived at Port St. Louis in Quebec. Their presence in New France, or more accurately their desire to trade with the French, was key to the survival of the colony. This was especially true after the majority of the Wyandot, their accustomed trading partners, moved into the west. After building temporary shelters to house themselves during their visit to the city, Dreuillettes wrote, "the Captains ascended to Fort saint Louys to salute Monsieur our Governor, bearing their speeches in their hands." They gave the governor two presents, Dreuillettes noted, "which represent words among these peoples." With the first they asked for Frenchmen to winter in their country, and with the second they asked for Jesuits to live among them. According to the missionary, "They were answered in their own way, with presents, and were willingly granted all that they asked."[48]

The French, who had witnessed ceremonial events such as the Feast of the Dead, understood that gift giving created relationships between peoples. Thus, as Dreuillettes reported, the French accepted ritual gift exchange as an aspect of diplomatic protocol. When the Odawa asked that traders and priests come to live among their people, they asked for a living connection to New France. This request came with gifts that signaled the debt they owed the governor in creating such a connection. At the same time these gifts created an obligation on the part of the recipient. They represented a kindness, a show of material support that needed to be answered in kind. Accordingly, to signal his desire that French colonists live among the Odawa, and to thank them for their gifts, the governor responded with presents of his own. In this manner gift exchange created mutual obligation, which became the basis for an ongoing social relationship.[49]

The exchange of material goods, in other words, made it possible for different peoples to join together as part of a shared community. Using gifts to structure social interaction required people to meet one another's needs. And a means of ensuring ongoing peaceful interaction was a necessity within a community that defined itself, in terms of social relations, as an extended family. In order to facilitate this kind of family- or kinship-based connection to the French, the Odawa, Wyandot, and other Native allies positioned the governor of New France as the father of their alliance. In accepting this responsibility each successive governor took the name of Onontio. This was a title, and a social persona, that represented the governor's status as the father of an extensive family of Native children.[50]

The children of Onontio, the Indian allies of New France, represented power for the governor. They hunted and traded the furs that constituted the lifeblood of the colony. They were souls to be claimed for God. They were an auxiliary army of Native peoples who guarded New France from the Haudenosaunee. This relationship also played an increasingly important role in opening the territory and people of the pays d'en haut to French voyageurs.

In finding a common metaphor to express the form and function of their alliance, however, Onontio and his children were forced to try and reconcile very different understandings of the role and responsibility of fatherhood. The French presumed that they would accrue an inherent power in accepting their status as father of the alliance. They wanted to be the sole arbiter of their New World family, and they assumed that this role, in European fashion, carried the absolute power of a patriarchal monarch. The status and influence of an "Algonquian" father, however, came from his role as a provider and peacemaker. Any position of power in the social world of the Anishinaabe peoples, which the French thought of as the Sauteurs, Ottawas, Nipissing, Mississauga, and Amikwas, placed the empowered person in a position of responsibility. Accepting their role as children—the weaker and more dependent family members—Native peoples assumed a position of ritualized humility, which demanded kindness and intervention. In effect, an Anishinaabe father did not exercise power over his children; he wielded power on behalf of his children.[51]

In relationships of unequal power the Anishinaabeg and other Algonquians sought to make themselves appear pitiful. Essentially, they wanted to compel those with more power to meet their needs. Pity did not evoke scorn or ridicule, but rather represented a condition or status that deserved positive intervention and protection. Power, or in Anishinaabemowin *manidoo*, represented the capacity for the extraordinary. Manidoo represented the ability to make things work in the world in a way that an ordinary human being was not capable of doing on his or her own. Metal axes, for example, split wood in a way that material objects of Native manufacture could not. Guns, knives, hatchets, and like objects similarly possessed manidoo, that is, a capacity to control or manipulate the natural world in an extraordinary way. "Generally," the Jesuits remarked, "whatever seems to them either helpful or hurtful they call a Manitou, and pay it the worship and veneration which we render only to the true God."[52]

People too could possess manidoo in the sense that they controlled access to a source of this extraordinary power. Then again, a being—human or other-than-human—might also control access to something ordinary like particular game animals. In either case, whether manidoo rested in a material object or in providing and denying access to things that helped human beings to survive, it represented a power of control exercised over the world at large. Onontio possessed this kind of control power. As governor of New France, Onontio provided access to the empires of Europe in the form of trade goods.

And Onontio, as the French father, represented a potential means of augmenting the power and scope of the kinship-based alliance-and-exchange network that bound people like the Nipissing, Odawa, and Wyandot together.[53] When the Odawa presented the governor of New France gifts and asked that he send traders and Jesuits to live among them, they asked for exactly this kind of intervention.

The governor willingly obliged his children, because this request reaffirmed their commitment to one another. Equally important, sending his people out into their homeland represented an expansion of French power into the pays d'en haut. Accordingly, the governor outfitted thirty traders (including Des Groseilliers) to winter with the Odawa who were preparing to move inland with a small party of Wyandot for their winter hunt. He also sent two priests, Gabriel Dreuillettes and Leonard Gareau, who would establish the first Jesuit mission in Anishinaabewaki, or as they called it the upper country. Their brief sojourn in the west, however, underscored the limitations of Onontio's power and the vulnerability of New France.

The French-Odawa-Wyandot caravan that left Quebec for the interior was a formidable force. The warriors carried newly acquired French firearms. Traveling in sixty canoes filled with trade goods they returned to their people with the manidoo of the Atlantic New World. Better still they moved west with a large party of French traders, a living testimony of the kindness of Onontio and their alliance with New France. Soon after they set out, however, they met with a single canoe piloted by two French soldiers sent to warn them about a Haudenosaunee ambush farther up the Saint Lawrence River. Upon learning that the commander at Trois Rivières had decided not to meet this intrusion with military force, the traders sent west by Onontio turned back for Quebec.[54]

The Odawa and Wyandot pressed forward confident in their numbers, 250 warriors, and their new weapons. With the exception of the Jesuit priests, however, the French abandoned their allies to meet their fate against the Haudenosaunee alone. A party of approximately 120 Mohawk warriors waited for the caravan in an entrenched position overlooking the river. Father Dreuillettes later recounted that when the Odawa-Wyandot caravan reached this location they "received so prompt and furious a shower of lead, that many were killed without knowing who dealt the blow." They had rushed toward their enemy recklessly, he complained, and the advance guard of six canoes was quickly overwhelmed: "The Iroquois had no sooner fired their pieces then they burst from their ambush like lions from the lair, rushing upon those who were still alive, and dragging them into their fort. Father Leonard Gereau, who was in this advanced guard, was wounded by a musket shot which broke his spine."[55]

The Odawa and Wyandot warriors recovered from this initial setback, and laid siege to the Mohawk fort. The battle lasted until nightfall and ended in a standoff when the Odawa and Wyandot retreated to their own hastily built fort. The lateness of the season compelled them to move on, however, and so they entered into negotiations with the Mohawk who were given presents to persuade them to withdraw. The warriors of the Haudenosaunee were divided; some favored retreat and some vowed to continue the fight at dawn the next day. While they deliberated the Odawa and Wyandot used the cover of darkness to slip away. As Onontio had abandoned them, they abandoned his servants to their mutual enemies. The caravan departed without Dreuillettes. *The Relation of 1655–56* reported that in spite of the violence he experienced, the priest wanted to continue his mission but, as he later recalled, "no one would take him into his canoe."[56]

This story was more than a tale of martyrdom, it was also a parable about the founding and fate of New France. If beaver peltry represented the "gold mines" and sole source of wealth for the colony as the Jesuits claimed, then preservation of their Indian alliance network was indispensable to its survival. This alliance threatened to collapse whenever Onontio failed to protect his children. If the Haudenosaunee raided their allies with impunity, the allies might abandon the empire. Left unprotected by their father, they abandoned the French trade and fled to "the very end of the world." Dreuillettes's story presented a frightening caveat to the Jesuits' standard description of Iroquois violence and Algonquians scattering into unknown territories as refugees. The children of Onontio might seek a truce with the Haudenosaunee on their own terms, essentially negating their alliance with the French. Either way, the beaver peltry that fed the colony like springs of water dried up, and French cities became vulnerable to attack by hostile Indians. These twin fears of abandonment and betrayal in the face of their own weakness would haunt French colonial officials for as long as their empire lasted in North America.

The Inland Trade

The people and things of the Atlantic World were becoming increasingly integral to the alliance networks of indigenous social formations in the western interior of North America. They augmented the practices of self-determination among Native peoples by providing new sources of power, or manidoo, in the form of trade goods. Exchanged ritually these goods created new identities, as in the case of Onontio and his children, and allowed for the expansion of existing alliance networks, as with the of the Feast of the Dead in 1642 and 1660. By the same token, items of little value to Native peoples, such as worn-out beaver robes, drew Europeans and the material artifacts of their empires—glass beads, mirrors, wool cloth, brass kettles, axes, knives, guns, shot and powder, and so on—into spaces that colonists still thought of as the very end of the world. The narratives of Dreuillettes and Radisson captured the moment when these old networks and new identities began to overlap.

Both Native and European traders learned to exploit the overlapping circulation of indigenous and European goods to become power brokers. This was not a role that allowed individuals to wield a coercive form of power. It was instead the power of mediation, the ability to reconcile enemies, and forge alliances across increasingly larger networks of Native peoples. Multivillage and even multiethnic alliances represented the ability to control access to resources in multiple and widespread locations. Manidoo in Anishinaabewaki derived from the ability to transform strangers into kin, meyaagizid into inawemaagen, creating the social space of alliance and making it safe to hunt, trade, and travel. This, in effect, was the potential power represented by the fur trade. This was the central lesson at the heart of the narratives of discovery produced by the agents of the French Empire like Dreuillettes and Radisson.

In these narratives, however, the power represented by the fur trade was mischaracterized as evidence of European dominance and superiority. Tales of discovery were meant to convey the power of Europe in the form of an imperial gaze that reached into the unknown territories of the New World, and made this space and its peoples comprehensible to outsiders. But they were also meant to illuminate the superiority of European ways of being—governance, sacred practices, means and methods of economic production, material goods, and so on—and the corresponding inferiority of New World peoples whose advancement (civilization) depended on acquisition of the artifacts and knowledge of their discoverers.

Because of this bias, these documents also serve as cautionary tales about the ways in which both individual travelers and traders, and the empires they served, claimed to exercise power. Dreuillettes's 1656 voyage ended in failure, and no new missions were established in the pays d'en haut. This turn of

events revealed the limitations of Onontio's manidoo in the world beyond the
colonial cities under his direct control. This weakness was underscored by the
willingness of Onontio's licensed traders, including Des Groseilliers, to forgo
a season's trade rather than risk a confrontation with Haudenosaunee raiders.
Des Groseilliers's second attempt to travel into the pays d'en haut the following spring met with success, but the tentative nature of his enterprise hardly
suggests that Europeans dominated fur trade exchange.

And yet Radisson claimed that the power represented by European trade
goods not only allowed him to dominate the trade but, more importantly,
allowed him to control the Native peoples with whom he interacted. The successful relaunching of Des Groseilliers's trade expedition became the "Third
Voyage" in his travel narrative.[57] This was the voyage that set in motion the
Feast of the Dead ceremony that Radisson claimed to orchestrate. In this
sense, the third and fourth voyages represented a triumph of European manidoo. Radisson, the agent of empire, used trade and the promise of continued
exchange as an instrument of power. In the process, he placed himself at the
head of a dramatically expanded network of Native allies. The common de-
nominator in the stories told by Dreuillettes and Radisson, however, was not
emergence of European power in the pays d'en haut, but the incorporation of
European people and things into the existing power structures that defined
Anishinaabewaki. The traders and missionaries who entered this space were,
quite literally, powerless. Far from being independent agents, they traveled,
communicated, fed, and defended themselves only with the assistance of Native guides.

Underscoring the reality of this dependence, the narrative for Radisson's
"Third Voyage" begins with the brothers-in-law waiting at Trois Rivières,
along with scores of other men, for the arrival of Native traders. At the midpoint of the seventeenth century, any French trader—licensed or not—who
wanted to participate in the inland trade needed to first find Native partners
willing to take them back to their home communities. Radisson's narrative
described "severall companies of wild men Expected from severall places,"
arriving in the French settlements that spring. In the early summer, he wrote,
"before setting forth we made some guifts & by that means we weare sure
of their good will, so that he and I went into the boats of the wild men."[58]
They then made their way west to Manitoulin Island in Lake Huron with a
mixed party of Odawa, Wyandot, and French traders. "But," Radisson wrote,
"our mind was not to stay in an island, but to be knowne wth the remotest
people."[59]

The desire of Radisson and Des Groseilliers to meet with the most remote people seemed to coincide with their hosts' intention to travel further inland to trade. "The time was come of their traffick," he wrote. And so, after yet more gifts, the two voyageurs persuaded the Odawa and Wyandot to take them to Green Bay on the western shore of Lake Michigan, where their Native companions planned to trade the goods they had acquired in the French settlements. From this location they moved into the region west "of a lake called Superior," to find the "people of the Sault." According to Radisson, "Since the destruction of so many neighboring nations they retired themselves to the height of the lake. We knewed those people well. We went to them almost yearly, and the company that came up wth us weare of said nation, but never could tell punctually where they lived because they make the barre of the Christinos from whence they have the castors that they bring to the French."[60]

This passage in Radisson's manuscript reveals the significance of the third voyage: he and Des Groseilliers were to travel to the source of the peltry that Native peoples traded with the French. The region at the northwest end of Gichigamiing was the best and most abundant source of winter coat beaver, or *castor* to the French, in all of North America. But this convoluted explanation also presents the reader with a mystery. At least some Sauteurs it seems were traveling with the two Frenchmen, although Radisson had not mentioned them until this point in the narrative. Moreover, he accounted for their presence in the west by suggesting that they retreated into this region as refugees. Radisson also wrote that French voyageurs traded regularly with the Sauteurs, but then claimed that they never knew exactly where to find them. This statement suggests that these people migrated frequently throughout the Great Lakes region in a pattern that French traders could not readily comprehend.[61]

As an added complication, Radisson asserted that the Sauteurs' mobility derived from the fact that they traded with the Christinos, also known to the French as the Cree. In an earlier passage he described the Cree as "confederates" of the people he traveled with "by reason of their speech, wh is ye same." He also noted that the Sauteurs "make the barre of the Christinos." It is difficult to know what Radisson meant by the word "barre." Was this an anglicization of the French word *la barre*, meaning a bar or line, and implying (figuratively) that the Sauteurs were connected to the Cree? This awkward sentence construction might also imply that the Sauteurs barred the Cree from direct trade with the French, but then this sort of adversarial relationship would not seem to fit with his categorization of the two peoples as "confederates." In this section of the narrative he also noted that the Cree and Sauteurs "joined together & have had companies of soldiers to warre against the Nadoneceronon" (more commonly spelled Nadouesioux or Sioux).[62]

In spite of the awkward writing, a clear pattern emerges in the connections between Native peoples described by Radisson. The relationship between the Sauteurs and the Cree fits within the pattern of Anishinaabe alliance making. So too did their relationship with the Sioux, who were outsiders and therefore enemies. The Sauteurs waged war against the Sioux not because they intruded onto their territory as newly arrived refugees, but because violence generally characterized relations with nonkin. In contrast, according to Radisson, the Cree hunted this region with "skill in yt game above the rest." In addition to hunting, they made their way inland from Hudson's Bay to this region, he noted, specifically to trade with the Sauteurs. Both of these details suggest peoples with an intimate knowledge of the area north and west of Gichigami-ing.[63] All of these descriptions, in fact, fit exactly within the pattern of social relationships that defined territoriality and identity in Anishinaabewaki.

The acquisition of European weapons, however, made warfare more deadly and as a result all the parties who occupied this territory began to think about the expansion of peace and kinship. The Dakota presence in this region was significantly larger than their Anishinaabe and Muskekowuck-athinuwick enemies. Radisson claimed they had thirty times the population.[64] And yet, as he explained it, "now seeing that the Christinos had hatchets &knives, for that they resolved to make peace wth those of the Sault. . . . They would not hearken to anything because their general resolved to make peace wth those of the Christinos & an other nation that gott guns."[65]

According to Radisson, this desire for peace increased following a great battle that resulted in heavy losses on all sides. In the voyageur's narration of this event, a war party of a hundred Sauteurs joined "those that lived to-wards the north," and an even larger party of Cree warriors, in an attack on the Sioux. Radisson's "People of the North" were described as expert hunters from the region north and west of Gichigamiing whose seasonal migration brought them into alliance with the Sauteurs, and therefore into the conflict with the Dakotas. When this battle came to an end the warrior leading the Sauteurs gave a speech to all the combatants. In the fight, this man had lost an eye. This loss, he proclaimed, sapped his courage, but with his remaining eye the warrior could foresee what he must do: "he himself should be an ambas-sador & conclud the peace."[66]

This offer of reconciliation brought an uneasy peace to the region. Radisson wrote that "we retired ourselves to the higher lake nearer the nation of the Nadoneceronons, where we weare well received, but weare mistrusted when many weare seen together." Here as in other French texts the Dakota were identified with a variant of the Anishinaabe phrase *na-towe-ssiwak*, most often spelled phonetically, as noted earlier, as Nadouessioux or shortened to Sioux. This phrase meant "alien or foreign people," and signified an enemy. Thus the designation *Sioux*, like *Sauteur*, applied Anishinaabe categories of identity in a way that came to reflect the coded language of empire.[67] Radisson's story, in fact, was written to suggest the potential power that empires could exert by controlling trade, which would allow a small number of Europeans to dominate the diplomacy that governed peace and warfare in the pays d'en haut. Accordingly, before returning to the French settlements, Radisson wrote that "att last we declared our mind first to those of the Sault, encouraging those of the North that we are their brethren, & that we would come back & force their enemy to peace or that we would help against them."[68] In other words, Radisson and Des Groseilliers pledged their support to the one-eyed Sauteur with the hope of gaining access to the castor-rich territory controlled by his people.

The 1660 Feast of the Dead

Pierre Radisson produced the only written description of the 1660 Feast of the Dead hosted by the Anishinaabeg. In this narrative, Radisson's "Fourth Voyage," the author placed himself at the center of the ritual process initiated by the one-eyed Sauteur. Like the texts of his other voyages, this was written in garbled Francophone English, and it is a flawed and deeply biased document. In this narrative Radisson made himself the lead actor in a story in which he was, in reality, only a minor character. For all its pretense, however, Radisson fully grasped that this ceremony and the increasingly violent conflict that precipitated it represented a struggle over manidoo. This attempt at a realignment of social relations related directly to the circulation of new people and things moving between the indigenous west and the colonial east of North America.

The narrative of Radisson's "Fourth Voyage" begins with the two brothers-in-law, once again, loitering in the French settlements waiting for Native guides to take them inland. They waited discreetly, the governor having interjected himself into their plans to become rich by taking control of the inland trade. Finally, "a company of the Sault" arrived at Trois Rivières in August. "We made guifts to the wildmen," Radisson wrote, and he asserted that they "wished with all their hearts that we might goe along wth them." The leader of this party was the one-eyed Sauteur, trading peltry from the interior in order to acquire sufficient goods to host a Feast of the Dead ceremony, which required elaborate gift presentations.[69] They agreed to wait upriver for two days for Radisson and Des Groseilliers to join them. That night, the two men left the colony, embarking without a license to trade. Radisson wrote that they traveled west as "Discoverers," but they were more than that. They were coureurs de bois intent on finding another Peru—a land where beaver peltry would provide wealth like the gold mines of Mexico and South America.

Radisson's "Fourth Voyage," like the narrative of his "Third Voyage" or the Jesuit account of Dreuillettes's failed inland voyage, unfolds as a series of encounters with different Native peoples. Once again, these encounters fit within the pattern of social relationships that defined territoriality and identity in Anishinaabewaki. Making their way up the Saint Lawrence River, Radisson's party met the inevitable Iroquois ambush. After a fierce battle, they captured, killed, and beheaded fourteen of their Iroquois attackers, and pressed on to the Anishinaabe village sites at Lake Nipising and Bow-e-ting.[70] As they made their way inland they met a variety of allies—a party of Odawa traders returning from New France; a "small nation" of "confederates" head-ing to their winter hunting territory south of Gichigamiing; "a company of Christinos," in fact the same Cree they had wintered with during their last voyage; and finally, additional small parties "of the nation of the Sault."[71] By the time they arrived at what the French called Fond du Lac, the region at the southwest corner of Gichigamiing, a place crisscrossed with rivers, streams, and marshes connecting the lake to the watershed of the Gichi-ziibi (Missis-sippi), their caravan had swelled from a small party to twenty-three canoes.

Soon after their arrival, fifty Anishinaabe warriors and a crowd of four hundred onlookers escorted the voyageurs to a large palisaded village. They were met with great celebration. "We weare Cesars," Radisson wrote, adding that the people "admired more our actions than the fools of Paris to see enter their King."[72] In response the voyageurs gave gifts, including a kettle, desig-nated "to call all the nations that weare their friends to the feast wch is made for the remembrances of death." They gave two hatchets for "knocking the heads of their enemies," and they gave six knives "to shew that the Ffrench weare great and mighty, and their confederates and friends."[73] After the gift giving, their hosts called a council, which Radisson claimed to control. "We knewed their councels," he wrote, "and made them do whatsoever we thought best."[74]

Following the council, and a three-day-long feast, messengers were dispatched calling the peoples of Anishinaabewaki, the Athinuwick peoples, and Dakota to the ceremony in five months' time. Immediately following their council the village dissolved into small bands that ascended the forested watersheds that drained into the lake for their winter hunt. At this leave taking, Radisson offered a subtle clue that his authority was overstated, or at least rivaled. "We weare lodged in ye cabban of the chiefest captayne," he wrote, but then proclaimed, "We liked not the company of that blind, therefore left him."[75]

The one-eyed Sauteur, although identified by Radisson as the "chiefest Captayne" and the original architect of the 1660 feast, virtually disappears from the narrative at this point. In his place Radisson offered himself. The presence of two French men in the territory of the Anishinaabeg was, apparently, well known as they received frequent visitors throughout the winter, and were the first camp visited by Dakota emissaries at the time of the ceremony. This advance visit occurred as part of a ritual where the Dakota clothed and fed the voyageurs, and then cried over them, allowing their tears to fall onto the heads of the Frenchmen. Like the Anishinaabeg, the Dakota sought to make themselves appear pitiful and deserving of protection and assistance. Following these acts of ritual humility, they offered Radisson and Des Groseilliers a calumet, a pipe ceremony that signified peace, and created a social bond in the same manner as gift giving. For their part, the Dakota were all too aware of the manidoo, or in their language the *wasicun*, of French trade goods.[76] Their visit to and treatment of Radisson and Des Groseilliers signaled recognition of the status of the voyageurs. They were not only representatives of the French colonial regime but beings who controlled access to the things that had made their enemies so formidable.

This status, and the fact that the Dakota peoples had no existing relationship with the French colony, explained their visit and ritual interaction with Radisson and Des Groseilliers. The voyageurs, however, understood the gesture represented by this ritual as a sign of political and cultural submission. In response to the calumet Radisson informed the Dakota through an interpreter: "Yee are called here to know our will and pleasur," and then reassured them that "we take you for our brethren by taking you into our protection."[77] That two men representing a colony of a few thousand people offered to protect a village of seven thousand, who were in turn part of a social formation of approximately thirty thousand people, seems either delusional or wildly overconfident.

In reality, the voyageurs presented the Dakota with an opportunity to establish a relationship with the beings that controlled access to a new source of power, or wasicun, affecting their world. But this opportunity occurred through their participation in an ongoing social relationship and ritual process that the French understood imperfectly. In the days following the calumet that introduced them to the Dakota, Radisson noted, "the considerablest of our companies went and made speeches to them." In other words, the Feast of the Dead opened with a council where prominent Anishinaabe ogimaag (leaders) spoke to the ritual participants. In response, Dakota "Elders" announced that they "weare come the morrow to renew the friendship and to make it with the French."[78] The feast would reaffirm the peace initiated by the one-eyed Sauteur, and it would be expanded to include the French.

Radisson's narrative offers a glimpse of this reality, although it must be viewed through a lens that magnifies the significance of French power. When the Dakota delegation arrived, Radisson noted dismissively that "our Captayne made a speech of Thanksgiving, wch should be long to writ it."[79] Again, Radisson suggests a council meeting centered around Native orators, but he quickly turns the focus of this encounter to his own presence at the ceremony. Called to attend this council, he wrote that the Dakota had come "to make a sacrifice to the Ffrench, being Gods and Masters of all things, as of peace, as warrs; making the knives, the hatchets, ye kettles rattle. Etc." They gave the voyageurs four gifts, the last "ffor being the masters of their lives." They were then presented with another calumet by an old man who disrobed after presenting the pipe, and gave them the animal skins that served as his clothing. Standing naked before the two French traders this man, according to Radisson, proclaimed: "Yee are masters over us; dead or alive you have the power over us, and may dispose of us as your pleasur."[80] This ceremony concluded with a call to arms, as the Dakota asked the voyageurs and their Anishinaabe hosts to join them in war against the Cree.

Radisson and his brother-in-law answered the Dakota gifts the following day, and made clear that they came west as life-givers and peacemakers. Over a series of gifts, they claimed that "we weare come from the other side of ye great salted lake, not to kill them but to make them live; acknowledging you for our brethren and children." After positioning themselves as both brothers and fathers, they described themselves as similarly related to the Cree. "The Christinos weare our brethren," Radisson declared "we adopted them for our children, and tooke them under our protection." The voyageurs then pledged that they would make the Cree come to the Feast of the Dead, and "conclude a generall peace."[81] They declared that they "would see a universall peace over all the earth," and promised to destroy the people "that would not submit to our will and desire wch was to see them good friends."[82] This odd mixture of the kinship terminology associated with alliance making signaled Radisson's imperfect understanding of the role he played in the ceremony that he claimed to control.

Whether delusional or wildly overconfident, however, Radisson's claim to power and offer of peace worked. The voyageur's threat to use coercive force must have been interpreted as hyperbole, or at least been regarded as a rather hollow gesture. It seems far more likely that the Athinuwick and Dakota agreed to enter into a new relationship brokered by their mutual allies the Anishinaabeg. The presence of French traders at this ceremony, however, would have been strategically important. By including the voyageurs in their ceremony the Anishinaabeg offered access to the manidoo of New France. And this power resided not only in trade goods but, equally important, in the way that traders and trade goods facilitated peacemaking. This was the life and death power that the Dakota elder recognized in Radisson and Des Groseilliers, rather then the imagined God-like attributes that they ascribed to themselves.

After the opening council, people began to arrive in great numbers at the Anishinaabe village to witness the ceremonial joining of the Anishinaabe, Athinuwick, and Dakota dead. Many came, Radisson noted, to witness "those two redoubted nations . . . to see them doe what they never before had." Here, he seemed to indicate that the novelty of an Anishinaabe-Dakota alliance caused excitement throughout the region. Over a thousand people participated in the ceremony. "We made guifts for that while 14 days' time," the voyageur wrote. And then he described the ceremony as "the renewing of their alliances, the mariages according to their countrey coustoms, are made; also the visit of the boans of their deceased ffriends, ffor they keep them and bestow them upon one another."[83] Imagine giving the remains of a loved one to your enemy, accepting the remains of theirs in return, and then burying them in a common grave. This act of mutual sacrifice and shared mourning created a social bond by ritually creating a common ancestry and a shared past. Meyaagizid into inawemaagen, this was the power of the Feast of the Dead. This was how Anishinaabewaki was imagined.[84]

No doubt, Radisson and his trade goods helped to mediate an end to the warfare between the Dakota and the Anishinaabe and Athinuwick peoples. This new relationship, however, evolved as a part of the existing social world that defined Anishinaabewaki, rather than as the outcome of a process of discovery and expansion on the part of the French Empire. Following the ceremony Radisson traveled with "a company of people of ye nation of ye Sault" to the principal Dakota village at the headwaters region of the Gichi-Ziibi. They stayed in the region for six weeks and returned "loaden wth booty," meaning they acquired a large store of beaver peltry.[85] This conclusion to the feast was significant, not because it produced wealth for the Anishinaabeg in the form of animal skins, but because it represented a significant change in the way that Native peoples in the heart of the continent of North America imagined place and belonging. Just as the Wyandot had created social relationships that gave them the right to reside in Anishinaabewaki, the Anishinaabeg had created a relationship that allowed them to live among the Dakota in their territory. That bond would prove fragile, but it also proved to be a long lasting and critical bridge between the world of empires and colonies in the east and the world of autonomous Native social formations in the interior.

Babylon

In August 1665, five years after the Anishinaabe Feast of the Dead, the Jesuit Claude Allouez returned to the west end of Gichigamiing to establish a mission. French traders frequented this region, but the mission would be the first real outpost for the French Empire in the west. Allouez departed Trois Rivières with six other French men and "in company with more than four hundred Savages of various nations."[86] His journey was not easy. One of the French canoes broke apart at the first rapids they met, and the Natives refused to stop and help them make repairs. When the French caught up to the caravan Allouez chastised his Native companions. "Do you forsake the French?' he asked, and then added: "Know you that I hold Onontio's voice in my hands, and that I speak for him, through the presents he entrusted me, to all your nations?"[87]

The caravan readily absorbed the voyageurs, but declared their intention to leave behind the priest, whom they regarded as feeble and useless, even though he called himself the voice of Onontio. Only when Allouez agreed to paddle did they consent to carry him. The voyageurs with their trade goods constituted a real connection to Onontio and New France. The priest represented something altogether different. Missionaries would become important figures in the alliance, and would come to represent the manidoo and voice of Onontio as much or even more than the traders and their merchandise. In 1665, however, they had not yet made a place for themselves in Anishinaabewaki.

Allouez produced an account of his passage through this country that mirrored those produced by Radisson and Dreuillettes, and revealed a cosmopolitan world that revolved around travel, trade, and the harvest of seasonal resources. His caravan ascended the Saint Lawrence and Ottawa Rivers, passed through Lake Nipissing and Bow-e-ting (Sault Sainte Marie), and then began to coast westward along the southern shore of Gichigamiing. "This Lake," the Jesuit wrote, "is the resort of twelve or fifteen different nations." They came from the north, south, and west "to the best parts of the shore" for fishing and "to make their petty trading with one another, when they meet."[88] After two months of travel Allouez and his party arrived at a place the French called La Pointe du Chequamegon, which he described as "a beautiful bay, at the head of which is situated a great village of Savages. . . . They number eight hundred men bearing arms, but are gathered together from seven different nations, living in peace, mingled with one another."[89]

Like Sault Sainte Marie the name of this village was, in part, a geographic description rendered into French by missionaries—La Pointe du Chequamegon. La Pointe referred to a small peninsula that stretched across the top of a bay at the southwest end of Gichigamiing. *Chequamegon* or *Shagwaamikong* was an Anishinaabe place name that meant "soft beaver dam." This description was, in turn, linked to a story about Nanabozho, the trickster figure who played a prominent role in Anishinaabe origin stories. In this story, Nanabozho, himself a human-sized shape-shifting hare, created the peninsula to trap a giant beaver. The beaver escaped, breaking the dam and creating the bay. Any narrative that people tell about themselves and their past is instructive, and this story, encoded in a place name, was particularly meaningful. Like Nanabozho, the Anishinaabeg came to La Pointe du Chequamegon to hunt beaver. For the Anishinaabeg the story of the origin of this village signified a connection to hunting territory in the marshlands that drained into Gichigamiing from the west.[90]

The sheltered bay at La Pointe provided a perfect refuge for hunters who wanted to travel west to hunt during the winter months. Coasting the shoreline below this village it was possible to travel up a number of rivers into a swampy terrain dotted by small lakes. At an elevation of approximately four hundred feet, this network of lakes drained into northeast and southwest flowing river systems that emptied into Gichigamiing and Gichi-ziibi, respectively. These watersheds, which connected the Great Lakes to the Boreal forests and Great Plains of the north, were choked with beaver dams.

Thus Chequamegon, like Bow-e-ting, was an important part of the inland trade that gave shape to Anishinaabewaki by virtue of its location, connecting the east coast and western interior of the continent. "This part of the Lake where we have halted," Allouez reported, "is between two large villages, and forms a kind of center for all the nations of these regions."[91] The Jesuit described the main village, "which embraces forty-five or fifty large cabins of all nations, containing fully two thousand souls." Several satellite villages further inland ringed the two central lakeshore communities, with people moving between various sites to trade, attend ceremonies, or hunt and fish. The Jesuit called his mission Saint Esprit, and he described the place where he found himself struggling to explain the Christian faith as "this Babylon."[92]

This New World Babylon, like its biblical namesake, drew visitors from throughout the known world, that is, the world as the Anishinaabeg knew it. In *The Relation of 1669*, the Jesuits claimed: "More than fifty Villages can be counted, which comprise diverse peoples either nomadic or sedentary, who depend in some way on this mission."[93] The missionaries noted "the Illinois peoples" from the lower Mississippi Valley, identified as occupying five villages with two thousand residents, "go to this place from time to time in great numbers as merchants."[94] The Jesuits reported that "the Illinois are warriors and take a great many slaves whom they trade with the Outaouaks for Muskets, Powder, Kettles, Hatchets, and Knives." These people had a history of conflict with the Dakota, "but made peace with them some years ago . . . in order to facilitate their coming to La Pointe."[95] The Jesuits described the Dakotas, or "The Nadouessi," as "the Iroquois of this country, beyond La Pointe."

Significantly, in the 1660s the Dakota also came to La Pointe to trade. Their history of warfare with the residents and visitors who frequented the villages of this region, however, according to the missionaries, "obliged them to come here only in small numbers and as if on embassy."[96] The Jesuits also wrote of the Dakota: "They fear the Frenchman because he brings iron into this country." And in spite of the recent peace, they noted that "all the nations of the Lake make war on them." Iron, or more accurately the weapons manufactured and traded by the French, gave added wasicun to the "nations of the Lake" who were the enemies of the Dakotas.[97] In the summer of 1669, however, the Dakotas accepted a gift from the mission and agreed to come to

La Pointe in the fall to attend a general council with the peoples connected to Saint Esprit and the French fur trade.[98]

The Jesuits benefited from this movement toward peace as it allowed them to establish Saint Esprit in the midst of a multitude of Native peoples, many of whom were connected to New France only indirectly through peoples known to the French as Ottawas, Hurons, and Sauteurs. In addition to the Illinois and the Dakota, they noted, "of all the nations toward the north, there are three, among others, who come to trade here," arriving in caravans as large as two hundred canoes.[99] Presumably, these were the same Ojibwe-speaking people of the north described by Radisson. The Jesuits also identified "The Kilistinaux" or Cree, as "nomadic people," who lived "toward the Northwest of the mission of Saint Esprit," as frequent visitors.[100] And they recorded visits from peoples who had migrated to Green Bay seeking refuge from the Iroquois, specifically identified as the Pottawatomi, Fox, and Sauk, coming to La Pointe for trade and ceremony.[101]

When these diverse peoples arrived at La Pointe they found a large community of people speaking Anishinaabemowinan, the Ojibwe dialects of the Algonquian language family. These were the Anishinaabeg, the people of Anishinaabewaki. The Odawaag (Ottawa) and the Wyandot were the most recent additions to this village. Having left their home territories around 1650, they had resided with other refugees from the east in the Green Bay region, until moving north to La Pointe around 1660 in the wake of the Feast of the Dead. Their migration into the west had contributed to the conflict between the Anishinaabe and Dakota peoples. Frequent intrusion onto Dakota hunting territory precipitated a cycle of hostile encounters and retaliatory raids that made the western interior a dangerous place to live, hunt, and trade. The Feast of the Dead had created a fragile peace, however, that allowed trade to flourish at La Pointe.

The Jesuits appeared poised to expand this peace when the complex diplomacy of La Pointe unraveled. Their mission was a failure in terms of converting the peoples of La Pointe to Christianity. They had, however, successfully reached out to most of the peoples of the west and in this manner played an important role in maintaining peace in the region.[102] And then, the Odawaag and Wyandot who were the focus of mission Saint Esprit breached the tentative peace with the Dakota. A Wyandot party hunting in the Dakota territory was captured. A Dakota elder secured their release, and then escorted his new allies back to their village at La Pointe to ensure their safety. Once there, he was imprisoned, tortured, and ritually cannibalized.[103] Fearing the onslaught of retaliation from the region's largest military power, the Odawaag and Wy-andot fled into the east, returning to their homelands.[104] The missionaries abandoned Saint Esprit, leaving the remaining Anishinaabeg to negotiate the intricacies of peace, warfare, kinship, and alienation that would be demanded of them if they were to maintain their place and manidoo in the Babylon that was Shagwaamikong.[105]

The world the Jesuits left behind at La Pointe du Chequamegon was complex and cosmopolitan, and with so many different peoples competing to control territory and trade, diplomacy was often a life-and-death affair. This was the lesson offered by the ritual of the Feast of the Dead, which brought peace and created kinship, and also by the act of cannibalism that brought a return to enmity and the destruction of the French mission. The northwest interior, the heartland region that connected peoples throughout the continent, was not "the very end of the World" as Father Le Mercier had once lamented. This region was not a wilderness inhabited by a scattered population of nomads and refugees. Instead, this place was a Babylon—a dynamic crossroads of interconnected villages that linked several massive indigenous social formations.

CHAPTER 2

The Rituals of Possession
and the Problems of Nation

On June 14, 1671, Simon Francois Daumont le Sieur de St. Lusson claimed the interior of North America for the king of France. He voyaged west from Quebec to the Anishinaabe village that the French originally called Sainte Marie du Sault, under orders from the intendant of New France, and "summoned the surrounding peoples" to witness the possession of their country by the king of France. According to the Jesuit Claude Dablon, who provided a written account of this event, "fourteen nations" responded to St. Lusson's call. The French emissary then convened a public council, bringing together all of the Native peoples who had gathered at the village they knew as Bow-e-ting. A party of approximately twenty French traders and Jesuit missionaries from the newly established mission at this location also attended the council. While the council watched, St. Lusson climbed a height of land that overlooked the village, planted a cross and a cedar pole bearing the king's coat of arms, and took possession "in his place and in his Majesty's name, of the territories lying between the East and West, from Montreal as far as the South Sea" (Figure 2).[1]

With this grandiose gesture a handful of French men stood before an audience of a few thousand Native people, and claimed the continent of North America from Montreal to the Pacific Ocean for the king of France. Intendant Jean Talon, the man responsible for initiating this ceremony, served as the chief financial administrator for the colony of New France. He had returned to the New World in 1670 for a second term in office. Talon's orders, according to the Jesuits, were "to work strongly for the establishment of Christianity, promote our missions, & make known the name and domination of our

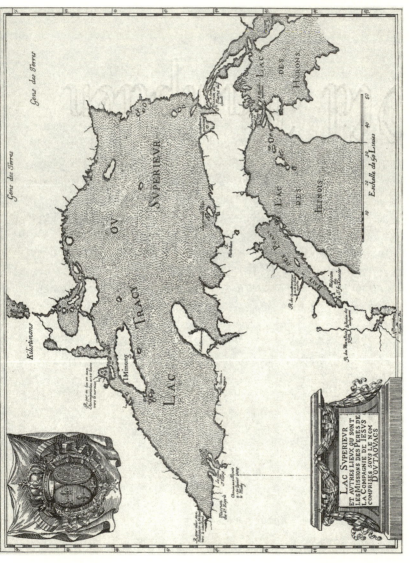

Figure 2. Jesuit map of Lake Superior and parts of Lake Huron and Lake Michigan, from *The Jesuit Relations and Allied Documents: Travels and Explorations of the Jesuit Missionaries in New France, 1610–1791*, ed. Reuben Gold Thwaites (Cleveland: Burrows Brothers, 1898), 55: 95. This map published along with Père Dablon's narrative description of the "Outaouac Territories" empties Anishinaabewaki of any Native peoples or place-names in regions served by the Jesuit missions. They are situated on the map and in the text within the missions themselves.

invincible monarch among the nations even the most unknown & the most remote."[2]

Talon, however, hoped to discover more than remote Indians unaware of the power and glory of Louis XIV. "I have made le Sieur de Saint Lusson leave to push toward the west," he reported, "to search carefully if there are lakes or rivers which connect with the southern sea that separates this continent from China." Europeans believed that an inland waterway linked North America to Asia. This waterway, called the Northwest Passage, was a geographic fantasy. The idea of its existence, however, was enough to motivate officials of both the French and the English Empires to finance quixotic expeditions to search for the passage. The prize was simply too great to resist. Any empire that controlled such a waterway would dominate the global market economy that emerged in the wake of Europe's colonization of the Americas.[3]

St. Lusson's ceremony and the related search for the Northwest Passage were, in fact, efforts to control the trade and resources of North America. The region to the north and west of Gichigamiing (Lake Superior) was the primary source of the winter coat beaver coveted by European traders and merchants. Upon his return to New France, Talon learned of the establishment of an English post on the seacoast of this territory. This information came from "Algonquins" who wintered in the French settlements. "I learned that they saw two vessels that capsized (this the term of the Savages) near Hudson's Bay," he wrote to his superiors.[4]

This region, like Shagwaamikong (La Pointe de Chequamegon), served as a hub for the inland trade. The English set up their operation under the guidance of someone intimately familiar with both regions, and with the Native peoples that connected them. "I can not then shut down the English who," Talon reported, "under the conduct of one named Des Grozeliers, one time habitant of Canada, were able to take the resolution of trying this navigation."[5] Des Groseilliers and his brother-in-law Pierre Radisson tried to convince French officials to reimagine the fur trade. The French transshipped their goods at Montreal from sailing vessels to birch bark canoes and made the arduous inland journey to trade with Native peoples in the west. The brothers-in-law wanted to bring their goods to the interior by sea. They wanted to establish trading posts on the western shore of the great bay to the north of the French colony in order to gain direct access to the peoples and resources at the heart of the continent. Radisson and Des Groseilliers failed to get the political and financial support from New France that they needed to make this idea work. Undeterred, they crossed the Atlantic to convince King

Charles II that they could transform the fur trade and open the American west for England.

Radisson and Des Groseilliers won the king's support. In 1667 the two voyageurs secured a royal commission for an expedition to the region known to the English as Hudson's Bay, and they sailed for North America the following year. Outfitted and financed by Prince Rupert, cousin of Charles II, and several other prominent members of the king's inner circle, the expedition was a success. The voyageurs returned to London with a valuable cargo of castor gras (fat beaver), the most sought after beaver pelt, and a claim to have purchased a river and territory at the bottom of the bay. The English called their river Rupert River, and their newly acquired territory Rupert's Land. In 1670 they returned and established a post, and King Charles II declared Rupert's Land an English possession.

The English, however, had gained their knowledge of Rupert's Land entirely from coasting the shorelines of Hudson's Bay. They had, in fact, named this territory after Henry Hudson, the English navigator who explored the region in search of the Northwest Passage. With the establishment of the Hudson's Bay Company, the English proceeded to "discover" and rename the rivers that discharged into the Bay—the Churchill, Nelson, Hayes, Severn, and Albany Rivers among others. The watersheds were given new names so that the map of the coastline, at least from an English perspective, appeared to be an English space. Discovering this territory from the sea, however, yielded no understanding of the interior or of the Native peoples who lived there. Thus, although they had mapped and renamed the coastline, the English knew next to nothing of the territory opened up by the rivers that drained into the bay other than what they learned from their French defectors. Nevertheless, Charles II granted the newly formed Hudson's Bay Company title to "the lands and territoryes" of all the "streights, bayes, lakes, creeks and soundes" that drained into the bay.[6] The company's charter, in effect, claimed possession of the interior of North America from Hudson's Bay to the Rocky Mountains.

The French disputed this claim. They called Hudson's Bay simply le Bay du Nord, because of its location north of the French settlements in the Saint Lawrence River valley. And the French argued that this bay was, irrefutably, a part of New France because "the English have always stopped at the Seaside making their commerce with the savages who came to find them there." In contrast, they argued, "the French have not ceased to travel through all the land and the rivers that lead to the Bay, taking possession of all these places."[7]

For the French, discovery and possession in North America could not be separated from social relationships. To claim a particular landscape meant, in some way, to claim a relationship to the people who inhabited it.

When St. Lusson staked the king's coat of arms into the earth he claimed a formal, and physical, possession of the western interior of North America for France. He declared Bow-e-ting, renamed Sault Sainte Marie, along with the surrounding territories—imagined rather expansively as extending from the Great Lakes to the Pacific Ocean—to be part of the French Empire. This gesture, however, was interpreted and ceremonially enacted as the creation of an alliance between New France and its Native allies by the Jesuit missionary Claude Allouez. The superior general for the Jesuit missions of New France, Dablon, in providing the narrative account of the ceremony performed by St. Lusson and Allouez, published in *The Jesuit Relations*, represented France's claim to possess the western interior of the continent. The documents produced by these missionaries also served as an alternative spatial history. That is, they represented the heartland of North America as part of the French Empire, rather than representing it as a largely unknown Native space, or worse still, as the territory called Rupert's Land on English maps of the New World.

Both the English and French Empires in North America came into being as part of a process of territorial expansion where their respective monarchs claimed new territory by right of discovery and conquest. These overlapping claims to the western interior, through purchase and political ritual, revealed the fiction of this conquest. North America was not New Spain, and neither St. Lusson nor Henry Hudson was Cortes. The possession of North America by the great powers of Europe in the seventeenth century was an event that occurred in Europe, on maps and in correspondence between royal courts. On the ground North America continued to be an almost overwhelmingly Native space, particularly in the heartland of the continent. On the ground these competing claims of possession represented attempts to make weak claims appear strong, and to create the idea of Native acquiescence to mask Native strength. This was how the fantasy of discovery played out in the reality of the North American New World. And yet French and English claims to possess the heartland of this continent are highly significant precisely because they represent founding moments from the perspective of the legal and cultural traditions of these colonial powers and their political descendants, the United States and Canada.

Laying claim to possession of the western interior in this fashion was, for all practical purposes, an act of political fiction. The geographer David

Harvey argues, however, that "the discursive practice of 'mapping space' is a fundamental prerequisite to the structuring of any kind of knowledge." In other words, mapping represents a form of knowledge production, a way of creating information to describe the world. "The power to map the world in one way or another," he asserts, "is a crucial tool in political struggles."[8] Following Harvey's line of thinking, we can see how the English and the French used mapmaking, ceremonies, and other rhetorical strategies as part of their political struggle to control North America. In this sense, both powers relied on cartographic texts to define and defend their western empires on the continent.

These claims of possession may have been cartographic fiction, but the texts that made them had real political consequences in that they represented the New World as a European space. Rupert's Land, le pays d'en haut, or even L'Amerique Septentrionale (Northern America) existed as places in relation to the discovery and possession of their territory by the empires of Europe. Mapping naturalized this claim of possession even when, in reality, the map was not really the territory.[9] The metaphorical representation of a place is not, in fact, the place itself. Nevertheless, the maps produced by England and France represented space and place in ways that were familiar to a European audience, organizing territory into national units controlled by monarchies.

St. Lusson's ceremony, in a similar fashion, represented an attempt to constitute the allies of New France as nations in order to claim sovereignty over them as subjects, and incorporate their territory into the French Empire. According to Talon, St. Lusson, through an interpreter, "declared to the upper nations that henceforth, from the present, they were to be answerable to his Majesty, subjects to submit to his laws and follow his customs, they were promised all protection and assistance from his part against the incursion or invasion of their enemies." Neither were they to allow "other potentates, princes or sovereigns" to take possession of any part of their country.[10] In this manner, the French relied on a familiar political construction in order to incorporate an unfamiliar people into their empire. Conceiving of the Anishinaabeg as subject nations, and mapping their identity and territory as part of the French Empire, made the indigenous landscape legible to the powers of Europe.

This was the purpose of the maps and narrative description of St. Lusson's ceremony published in *The Jesuit Relations*. To make their claim of possession the Jesuits wrote for a European audience. On the ground, however, the Jesuits needed to speak to a Native audience. On the ground, the map was not the territory. To claim their place in this space, to make the case that they belonged, the French used ritual and ceremony to bind themselves to Native people as inawemaagen—as relatives. Increasingly, the colonial officials of New France learned from experienced traders to think of le pays d'en haut, or the upper country, not so much as a physical space belonging to a particular Native nation, but rather as a set of relationships that bound Native peoples to one another. Political alliance was expressed as kinship. Trade, as a form of peaceful exchange, was the outcome of interaction between people who were related to one another. One shared with relatives, provided for their needs when there was want, and expected a reciprocal kindness in return. On the ground, the purpose of St. Lusson's ceremony was to create the conditions that would make it possible for the peoples gathered at Sault Sainte Marie to imagine the French people who came among them as inawemaagen.

The idea of nation, as either a political construct or as a descriptor of collective identity was the misapplication of a European social category onto a Native social formation. The historian David Bell argues, like Benedict Anderson, that the idea of the nation as a social structure constructed through political action emerged only in the eighteenth century. Before that time, he asserts, "in European usage, nations were facts of nature: they signified basic divisions of the human species, not products of human will." He notes that the first dictionary of the Académie Française defined the term *nation* as "the inhabitants of a common country, who live under the same laws, and use the same language." Applying such a singular category of collective social identity to a place such as Anishinaabewaki, however, misrepresented the social structure that produced space and identity in this region.[11]

The Algonquian bands that hunted in the western interior and traded at posts in the region that the French called the pays d'en haut were central to a new and evolving set of situational identities that lay at the heart of this relationship between the people of New France and their Native allies. When these bands of mobile and highly adaptive hunter-gatherers entered villages with Jesuit missions and contingents of French traders, as at Sault Sainte Marie, they assumed identities that signaled their connection to the alliance that had created these newly hybrid communities. That is, they identified themselves as children of Onontio. By the late seventeenth century, in the "upper country," being identified as children of the French father was increasingly linked to peoples that the French identified as Ottawas, Sauteurs, and Cree. Even as these "national" identities took shape in the context of the alliance, however, the Anishinaabe peoples retained a more flexible sense of social identity. Individuals and extended families lived in social formations as small as hunting bands associated with a senior male relative, but also identified as members of a dodeem or clan, and as part of named bands or villages—associations that might change during a person's life time. Collective identities such as Ottawa or Sauteur increasingly functioned as situational identities linked to the places where the French alliance system worked, on the ground, transforming Natives and newcomers into inawemaagen.

These collective identities, however, were more ambiguous in the western interior. Native peoples who identified as children of Onontio at places like Sault Sainte Marie did not assume this identity in places where the alliance did not work. People who identified with the Sauteurs in the pays d'en haut might assume a more appropriate designation to signal their identity when they passed the winter hunting in the muskeeg, or swamplands to the northwest of Gichigamiing. In this space they might identify themselves as Awasse, Monsoni, or Ni-ka, as members of dodeemag with a right to hunt in this region. These designations would make them more legible to other Anishinaabeg, and would signal their place among the constellation of Native peoples who made up Anishinaabewaki as a territory and as a social formation that predated the French alliance.

The maps and written records produced by the Jesuits worked to erase this ambiguity, and replace it with narrative descriptions of the ceremony that transformed the peoples of the western interior of North America into subjects of the French king, and then claimed formal possession of their territory. There were additional narratives produced by licensed traders and colonial officials that recorded the events surrounding this ceremony. Intendant Talon wrote descriptions of this ritual, and discussed the policies and events that prompted him to send St. Lusson into the west in his reports to the minister in charge of France's overseas colonies. Colonial official and historian Claude Charles le Roy, Bacqueville de La Potherie, and the voyageur Nicolas Perrot also wrote accounts of St. Lusson's ceremony as part of larger narratives about the relationship between New France and its Native allies.

This collection of documents, in spite of their intent, actually subverted the simple logic behind French claims of discovery, possession, and sovereignty over the interior west. Instead, they provide a picture of identity, space, and cultural contact in North America that imposes the perspective of empire onto places where empire did not reach. These records, in fact, provide differently situated accounts of a complex Native social organization that defied easy categorization and suggest a world where power and identity constantly changed form and function. They suggest a world dominated by an expansive, multiethnic, and distinctly Native social formation, rather than a world dominated by nations and empires. They provide another glimpse of the world that Father Claude Allouez, five years earlier, described as Babylon.

Speaking to Natives

St. Lusson's ceremony represented a conversation about power, the French Empire, and the meaning of alliance. This conversation was meant to influence two different audiences—one, the royal courts of France and England, and the other the children of Onontio. When Claude Dablon wrote about this ceremony he addressed a European audience. His narrative, however, revealed how the meanings that Europeans attached to this ceremony held little or no meaning among the Anishinaabeg. Le Sieur de St. Lusson literally could not speak to the Native peoples he addressed when he claimed possession of their territory on behalf of the king of France. To communicate the meanings of his actions he needed a translator. This task fell to the resident Jesuit at Sault Sainte Marie, Claude Allouez, the man who established and then abandoned the Jesuit mission at La Pointe. By the time of St. Lusson's ceremony, Allouez had been among the Anishinaabeg for six years. Although he had few converts, he had learned how to speak about power and the meaning of rituals well enough to be able to translate this ceremony in a way that made sense to his Native audience. Accordingly, Allouez did not speak to the people gathered at Bow-e-ting about becoming subjects of the French king. He spoke to them about their identity as children of Onontio. The ceremony, in its retelling, changed meaning. It became less about the transfer of land and sovereignty, and more about the power of the French father and the mutual obligations of family.

Allouez's performance, unlike St. Lusson's, drew upon the conventions of an Anishinaabe council. He used Anishinaabe categories of identity, and relied upon Anishinaabe conceptions of power in order to tell a story. For St. Lusson the ceremony culminated in his claim of possession, followed by shouts of "Long Live the King!" and the discharge of muskets by his fellow Frenchmen. But when the crowd quieted down, Allouez began a performance of his own. "My brothers," he declared, "Cast your eyes upon the cross . . . this is where JESUS-CHRIST, the son of God, making himself man for the love of men, was pleased to be fastened and to die, in atonement to his Eternal Father for our sins." Then he proclaimed: "He is the Master of our lives." Next, Allouez directed his audience to regard the post bearing the king's coat of arms. The king, he explained, "is the Captain of the greatest Captains, and has not his equal in this world." Onontio "that famous captain of Quebec," and their father, was but a child to the king—an obedient soldier of the greatest of captains—the king of France.[12]

Allouez translated St. Lusson's ritual into something tangible to the peoples of Anishinaabewaki—a claim of kinship, and an assertion of power. The Anishinaabeg used the term "Master of Life" as a variation of the concept of Gichi-manidoo (the greatest of spirit beings). It was also a variation of the term used to designate spirit beings that controlled access to a particular game species, or to a particular source of manidoo (power). They often characterized such spirit beings as grandfathers, a way of claiming a relationship to these other-than-human persons.[13] The term "captain" likewise served as the French translation for ogimaa in Anishinabemowin, a word that meant leader and signified a person skilled in diplomacy, warfare, trade, or hunting—someone with access to manidoo and the willingness to use such power and resources on behalf of the people of the leader's community. The Jesuits knew about these concepts. And so, when Allouez described the French king as the greatest of captains, a person whose standard was placed ritually alongside the standard of the Master of Life, he described a leader with access to the ultimate source of power in the world. When he then proceeded to describe Onontio as a child of the French king, he implied that St. Lusson's ritual gave the Anishinaabeg, as children of Onontio, access to a very powerful grandfather.[14]

Having established this connection, Allouez described how the manidoo of the French king worked in the world. "When he attacks," Allouez declared, "he is more terrible then thunder, the earth trembles, the air and the sea are set on fire by the discharge of his canon." The priest told his audience that in battle the king appeared amid his warriors "all covered with the blood of his foes, of whom he has slain so many with his sword that he does not count their scalps, but the rivers of blood which he sets flowing." The king, he said, took endless numbers of prisoners and slaves and possessed a countless supply of trade goods—"warehouses containing enough hatchets to cut down all your forests, kettles to cook all your moose, and glass beads to fill all your cabins."[15] Allouez offered a powerful message. Onontio represented access to the manidoo of the French king, a powerful grandfather with access to the Master of Life, and a being who controlled access to the weapons and trade goods that were transforming Native North America.

In *The Jesuit Relations* the missionaries paired themselves with Native peoples as opposites, Christian and civilized as opposed to les Sauvages, the wild men of the New World who lived without knowledge of the one true God. And yet when Allouez spoke, his words resonated with his Native audience because he spoke to them in the ritualized language of spiritual power. The Jesuit account of this ceremony reveals the point at which the worldview of the missionaries and the Anishinaabeg overlapped—a point too easily overlooked because of the biased nature of these narratives. The Jesuits and the Anishinaabeg believed in a world that was animated by spiritual power. The worldview of the Jesuits centered on bodily resurrection and the ability of God, the Master of Life, to first sacrifice his son, and then restore him to life. The Jesuits, as Catholics, brought the Eucharist and the doctrine of transubstantiation to North America. Priests transformed unleavened wafers and wine into the body and blood of Christ. Christians ritually, and in Catholic minds literally, consumed the body of Jesus in recognition of their redemption through the bodily sacrifice of the son of God.[16]

When Allouez described the French king to his Native audience, he described a father drenched in the blood of his enemies, capable of making the earth tremble with a power greater than thunder, and in possession of an unending supply of captive slaves and trade goods. Allouez described a father endowed with a spiritual power that both Christians and Indians readily understood. Ritualized violence—the power to destroy the bodies of his enemies and restore the bodies of his allies—defined the power of the Master of Life, the very power by which he kept his children alive.

These concepts had a parallel in the world of the Anishinaabeg in the form of the ritual of raising the dead. Families, and communities more generally, replaced loved ones whose lives had been stolen by death. With the passing of an important ogimaa, a family member or a well-regarded person from the same doodem might assume this identity, taking on both the name and persona of the deceased so that the important role the ogimaa had played in that community did not die out. Families who lost children to illness or young warriors in battle took captives and adopted them. Human persons were lost but the self—that subject position that signified a son or daughter—was kept alive by this form of ritual adoption and social resurrection. The family and community then socialized this adopted person to become a restored version of their lost relative. This form of kinship was considered as real as biological kinship. And this way of imagining or socially constructing kinship was how ceremonies like the Feast of the Dead worked. Alliances were imagined politically and socially as the creation of kinship relations.[17]

The idea of metamorphosis or transformation was central to rituals like raising the dead, ceremonies like the Feast of the Dead, and the creation of new alliances like the one between Onontio and his children. Metamorphosis, the idea that beings could shape-shift—take on the physical form and social persona of another being—was, in turn, central to the worldview of the Anishinaabeg. From an Anishinaabe perspective the concept of shape-shifting could be used to describe the relationship between different categories of beings, and between different categories of social identity. In this sense, shape-shifting reflects a particular habit of mind or worldview; but it also served as a metaphor for the potential for interconnection between different groups of peoples.

As a habit of mind, shape-shifting started with the supposition that the world is made up of spiritually animate beings. Some of these beings were human and some were other-than-human. Everything that is animate possesses some degree of manidoo, or power; this is what makes the person or thing a living being. It is what makes them animate. To live a healthy life in this world people must establish proper relationships with the other animate beings that share the earth. In this way, all living things are potentially connected.[18]

It was from this perspective, this habit of mind, that Anishinaabe peoples made sense of the world, and it was how they understood their particular place in that world. Shape-shifting was frequently a part of the trickster stories that the Anishinaabeg told to explain the origin and evolution of life on earth. These stories also served as a way of telling people the proper way to behave. In these stories Nanabozho, the trickster figure who was himself a hare, might become another creature or change shape and size. The capacity to shape-shift, that is the ability of animate beings to take the shape of other animate beings, also explains the relationship between human communities and niinwidoodemag, the animal totems that represent a distant ancestor from the time when human beings first began to live on earth. These animals were understood as blood relatives who were the progenitors of extended families of human beings.[19]

Shape-shifting, as a habit of mind, meant seeing the potential for beings to transform themselves, and to be transformed by others. This transformation was at once literal and metaphorical. Ceremonies like the Feast of the Dead, and rituals like raising the dead, allowed people to transform strangers into kin. The relationship was metaphorical rather than biological, but it was considered a literal creation of family ties in the same way that marriage created a new family. When Allouez translated St. Lusson's actions to his Native audience, this was the explanation he gave; the French ceremony created and affirmed the kinship relations between Onontio and his children.

Writing for Europeans

If the Jesuits knew how to speak to a Native audience, they also knew how to write for Europeans. Before presenting his account of St. Lusson claiming possession of the western interior of North America for France in *The Jesuit Relations*, Dablon took his readers on a narrative journey through this territory. "It is good to give a general knowledge of all of the Outaouacs country," he wrote in *The Relation of 1670–71*. A map that pictured Lake Superior and the northern parts of Lake Michigan and Lake Huron preceded his narrative. This was clearly designed to serve as a visual guide for the written text, and it was labeled "Lake Superior and other places where there are the Missions of the Fathers of the Company of Jesus included under the name of Outaouacs."[20] The narrative itself followed the literary conventions of the discovery genre, bringing unknown people and places to the attention of a European audience.

To emphasize the idea of discovery Dablon used a narrative voice that placed his reader on the ground, moving across the territory revealed by his text. "By a glance that one can cast on the topography of the lakes and the lands, on which are settled the most part of the peoples of this region, you will have more light on these missions than by a long discourse," he wrote. Then he told his reader: "You can first cast your eyes on the mission of Sainte Marie du Sault three leagues below the mouth of Lake Superior." This place he described as "the great resort of most of the Sauvages of this region & the most common crossing of all that go down to the French settlements." And Dablon noted, it was here "that all these lands were taken possession of in his majesty's name."[21] Leaving this central location, the narrative moves along the rivers and lakes traveling to the Jesuit missions attached to the principal villages of Anishinaabewaki, revealed to the reader as "the Outaouacs country." This particular marriage of map and text, in effect, used the Jesuit missions to frame this space as part of New France, rather than representing it as Native territory. In this sense, Dablon's act of possession was perhaps more complete then the ceremony enacted by St. Lusson and translated by Allouez.[22]

In effect, Dablon's act of possession was the invention of the "Outaouac country" as a coherent national space that might be attached to the empire in the same way that the province of Breton or Languedoc became a part of France. This gesture made the region that the French more commonly called the pays d'en haut legible for a European audience. Dablon literally provided a picture of the children of Onontio that fused Native social identity with the European category of nation, a construct generally associated with a social formation that shared a common language and culture and exclusive claims to a national territory.

In part, this sort of representation of Ottawa identity reflected French confusion about the nature of Anishinaabe social organization and categories of identity. Writing about the Ottawa mission in *The Relation of 1666–67*, Father Allouez noted: "The Outaouacs claim the great river belongs to them and that no nation can navigate it without their consent." As a result of this claim, he wrote, "all who go to trade with the French, although of widely different nations, bear the general name of Outaouacs, under whose auspices they make their voyage."[23] The "great river" described here became known to the French as the Ottawa River. This was the principal waterway linking the "upper country" to their settlements. Dablon himself echoed this understanding of Ottawa identity in *The Relation of 1669–70*, writing: "We call these people the Upper Algonquins. . . . They are commonly given the name Outaouaks; because of more than thirty Nations that are found in these countries, the first to come down to the French settlements were the Outaouaks whose name afterward remained with all the others."[24]

This confusion of people, place, and river was compounded by the many different ways that people, both Natives and colonists, used the term Odawa—most commonly transcribed as Ottawa. The Jesuits' use of the word Outaouacs represented a phonetic approximation of the term Odawaag, the plural form of the word Odawa that might be used in reference to any of the four doodemag (clans) of the seventeenth-century Odawa peoples. Like most of the peoples who resided in Anishinaabewaki, they spoke a dialect of Anishinaabemowin. This language consists largely of verbs; however, adding the suffix -win transforms a verb stem into a noun. Adding this suffix to the verb stem for the word to buy or trade adaawe, such as adaawewin, and then adding the word for a man or person, inni, to this noun, forms the word adaawewininni or "trader." This term applied to all Anishinaabe peoples participating in the inland trade, and was easily conflated with the Odawa identity.[25]

Even if we set aside the semantic difficulties associated with this national designation, the problematic nature of representing the "Outaouac country" as a national space is revealed in the details of Dablon's narrative journey. After describing Sault Sainte Marie, Dablon wrote: "Toward the other end of the same lake is found the mission of Saint Esprit, covering the district known as Chagaouamingong point, and the neighboring islands." He described the residents of this mission as the "Outaouacs" and the "Hurons," who he suggested lived at this location "in the seasons suitable for fishing and raising corn." But then he informed his reader that "it would be easy to recognize the rivers and routes leading to various nations, either stationary or nomadic, located in the vicinity of this same lake, who are somewhat dependent on this mission of Saint Esprit in the matter of trade."[26] Dablon provided a sketch of these "dependent" nations that included peoples called the Illinois in the lower Mississippi valley, the Nadouessi (Sioux) in the upper Mississippi valley, as well as a nation "of an unknown language," the Assiniboine, the Cree, and finally the "Inland peoples of the North Sea," all living northwest of Lake Superior. On the map and in the narrative Sault Sainte Marie and Saint Esprit framed the east-west borders, and the northern limits, of the "Outaouac country." Clearly, however, a multitude of "nations" that the Jesuits saw as distinct Native peoples inhabited the northern and western range of this territory.

Dablon next framed the southern boundary of the Outaouac country. "After having traveled by eye all of Lake Superior with the nations surrounding it," he wrote, "let us go to the Lake of the Hurons." Dablon identified the mission of Saint Simon on Manitoulin Island in northern Lake Huron as the true country of "some nations of the Outaouacs." He described this region as "ravaged by the Iroquois," and newly restored to peace by the governor of New France. Dablon wrote that "part of the Outaouacs" along with "the peoples of the Missisaugué, the Amicouës, and other surrounding neighbors" had since returned to this country. He located the mission Saint Ignace farther to the south at Michliamackinac Island, in the straits dividing Lake Huron and Lake Michigan. Dablon described this territory as a famous fishery occupied by the Ottawas, Hurons, and "various peoples."[27] Then, he wrote, "one enters the Lake called Mitchiganon," and he traced the western shoreline of this lake to a long bay that the French called either the Stinking Bay or Green Bay. Here Dablon located the mission Saint François Xavier situated among a number of villages—many populated by refugees from the east, but mixed with long-time residents of the region—situated at river mouths, and inland, along the banks of watersheds draining into the bay. He catalogued the peoples of this cluster of villages as the Pottawatomie, Sauks, Mascouten, Miami, Menominee, Fox, "and other peoples" driven south by the Iroquois.[28] These Native peoples, supposedly attached to mission Saint François Xavier, and those at the other missions described by Dablon were the children of Onontio.

Dablon's map and narrative description, like St. Lusson's ceremony, were designed to simplify a complex political and cultural landscape. And it was written for a European audience rather than to reflect the reality that existed on the ground. The map was central to this project. This cartographic text replaced the suggestion of Babylon, still evident in the written narrative, with a blank Cartesian space largely void of Native content. The map not only reduced Allouez's thirty-plus "nations" to one "Outaouac nation," it also visually contained the component parts of this identity within the missions, which provided the sole representation of their existence in this territory. Entering the territory of the map, as Dablon asked his reader to do, one could discover the Outaouac country, inhabited by the children of Onontio, and witness its possession and their subjugation by the king of France.

Actually witnessing the ceremony translated by Allouez, on the other hand, would have communicated an entirely different set of meanings. On the ground St. Lusson's actions did not reconfigure the relationships between people and space according to the logic of empire. The peoples of the "Outaouac country" did not become one nation bound to the king of France through their father in Quebec. This ceremony may have allowed New France to exercise some influence in the cosmopolitan world of Anishinaabewaki. It certainly did not confer dominion over this territory, or represent any legitimate claim to the western territories stretching toward the Pacific Ocean. Instead, this event suggested how the French learned to use ritual in order to speak to Native peoples—to communicate their desire to forge a relationship.

Reading the documents created to chronicle this event we see the French Empire in the New World in the way that the French wanted their audience in Europe to see it. Paying careful attention to how this ritual was enacted, we see the French struggling to make sense of the New World as they actually found it. At the same time, we can begin to understand the contours of Anishinaabewaki as a territory and as a social formation. Allouez's preceremony description of this place as Babylon was particularly telling. With the performance of St. Lusson's ceremony, we are shown a picture of the world as it existed after the collapse of the tower of Babel—a complex, polyglot space of political intrigue, diplomacy, warfare, and trade. Reading Dablon's description of this world we can also see the tower for what it really was—an allegory about a fantasy place designed to represent a simple world that never existed.

Shape-Shifters and the People of the Sault

Through a combination of text and ritual the French sought to impose a categorical clarity onto Anishinaabewaki. In order to be a father to his children, Onontio needed to be able to name the Native nations that made up his New World family. To maintain the fiction of his possession of the pays d'en haut or "Outaouac country" for a European audience, the governor of New France needed to represent his allies as subordinate Native nations. But this naming process served a purpose beyond the claims related to discovery. The colonial officials of New France wanted to impart identity and social structure onto their allies in such a way that they could be compelled to act with the collective will of a European nation. Accepting and inhabiting this form of collective identity provided stability, from a European perspective, to the otherwise confusing array of communities that existed as part of the larger Anishinaabe social formation.

The need to interact with so many different kinds of social units at times seemed to overwhelm French diplomacy, and undermine French officials' ability to influence their allies. Villages that appeared united about participation in the French trade and alliance system fragmented all too easily and, at least in part, defected to the English at Hudson's Bay. A significant aspect of Talon's discomfort at learning about the English post in the north derived from the fact that he came by this information from Native traders supposedly allied to New France.[29] This sort of defection meant more than a loss of trade. The inability to control the children of Onontio revealed the fiction of St. Lusson's ceremony, which, in turn, jeopardized French claims to sovereignty and possession over the territory occupied by their allies.

What Europeans perceived as instability, however, was simply the cultural logic of a different kind of social formation. This was particularly true for the peoples who lived in the northern range of the territory described by Dablon. In his narrative description of the "Otaouac country," the Jesuit wrote, "the Kilistinons are scattered through all of the lands north of the Lake Superior, without having any corn, nor fields, nor any fixed residence, but incessantly wandering among the great forests living there by hunting." In addition, he noted, "there are other nations from this region, who are called for this reason

peoples of the interior [Gens des Terres], or of the North Sea." The Gens des
Terres and the Kilistinons or Cree situated to the north and northwest of Lake
Superior on the map were the only Native peoples actually designated in writing on the Jesuit's representation of the "Outaouac country."[30] According to
Dablon these people lived as hunter-gatherers, and occupied no permanent
village. They were described, however, as "having some dependence on the
mission of St. Esprit for trade," implying that they were habitual visitors if not
residents of the Anishinaabe village at La Pointe du Chequamegon.[31]

This assertion contradicted an earlier written description of the same
peoples provided by Dablon in *The Relation of 1669-70*. In this volume the
Jesuit attached two unnamed "nations" from the north, presumably the same
people he subsequently identified as Gens des Terres, to the village of Sault
Sainte Marie. He also identified "six other nations who are either people
from the North Sea, like the Guilistinons & the Ovenibigonc, or wanderers of the lands around this same North Sea," as also connected to the Sault.
"The greater part of them had been chased from their country by famine," he
wrote, and then asserted that they came to Sault Sainte Marie periodically
because of the abundance of the fishery. Dablon labeled all of these northern
people nomads, and described "their way of life" as "incessantly going about
the depths of the woods & assembling only rarely for some trade fair, or some
feast according to their custom."[32] In reading Dablon's description, we find
an echo of the Jesuit missionary Jerome Lalemont, who complained in 1642
that the Nipissing Anishinaabeg were impossible to minister to because "they
continually divide themselves up," wandering the woods and lake country in
pursuit of fish and game.[33]

In both instances the Jesuits described nomadic peoples with no permanent home, and yet they also described these nomads as participants in a
ritual process that connected them to peoples throughout Anishinaabewaki.
Just as Lalemont witnessed a Feast of the Dead in the Lake Nipissing region
in 1642, Dablon more vaguely described these peoples coming together for
trade fairs and feasts at Sault Sainte Marie in 1670. A decade earlier Pierre
Radisson described meeting the Cree and "the People of the North," in the
country west of "La Pointe du Chequamegon," and later converging on the
Keweenaw Peninsula on the southern shore of Lake Superior for the summer
season. Similarly, additional French sources place people identified either as
Cree or Gens des Terres as trading in the colonial settlements of Tadoussac,
Montreal, and Quebec.[34] The picture that emerges here is not of a singular
people, a nation, attached to a single village. Instead, we see a constellation

of peoples with an extensive territorial range, and access to multiple villages, both Native and European, where they participated in trade and ceremony.

The mobility of these northern peoples, and the social flexibility of Anishinaabe village communities, however, suggests why the French had such difficulty attaching a singular identity to the Cree and Gens des Terres. In spite of their prominence on the Jesuit map, the French also frequently found it difficult to determine who was a Cree, who was a Gens des Terres, and how both groups related to the Ottawas and the people of the Sault. La Potherie, the French colonial official and historian of New France, merged the two identities, writing: "Those who occupy the north are scattered widely. They are the Christinaux, Monsoni, gens des terres, Chichigoueks, Otaulibis, Outemiskamegs, Outabytibis, Onaaouientagos, Michacondibis, Assinipoels, and several others. All these people are known under the name gens des terres, because they are always wandering."[35] In addition to the Christinaux or Cree, La Potherie counted the Siouan-speaking Assinipoels among the Gens des Terres. The Assinipoels, or Assiniboine, who call themselves *Dakota*, a word that translated as "the Allies," separated from the Dakota peoples that the French identified as the Sioux sometime between the thirteenth century and sixteenth century. Closely allied to the Cree, they were the only non-Algonquian speaking people included in La Potherie's list, and they were situated farthest to the west in the prairie parklands region of the northern Great Plains.[36]

Christino or Cree emerged as a "national" identity in the context of the fur trade rather than as a form of self-designation for the indigenous peoples of the Hudson's Bay region, and related bands living in the parkland-plains region of the western interior. The name, in fact, was Ojibwe in origin. It was the designation applied to speakers of what would become known as the Cree dialect by speakers of Anishinaabemowin, the closely related Ojibwe dialects of the same Algonquian language family.[37] The English traders at Hudson's Bay Company posts adopted this name as well. Dablon's alternate designation in *The Relation of 1669–70*, the "Ovenibigonc," was actually closest to the name that at least some of the so-called Cree people gave to themselves. This phonetic approximation for the term *Winipeg*, a term designating foul-smelling salt water, was used by the residents of the coastal marshlands of the western shore of Hudson's Bay as a signifier of both place of residence and identity, as in Winipeg-athinuwick (coastal marsh people).[38] Thus while both the French and the English applied the term Cree to Natives on the coast, they also applied this term more broadly to all the Native peoples who traded at the coast, but lived in the watersheds throughout the interior—many of whom the French called "Gens des Terres." In this sense, the name *Cree* functioned as a situational identity applied to Native peoples from the northern interior that traded along the western shoreline of Hudson's Bay.

Although the Jesuit map suggests a territorial division between the Cree and Gens des Terres, French records clearly indicated that no such division existed. The term *Gens des Terres* was a literal translation from Anishinaabemowin into French of the phrase *nopiming daje inini*, which meant "Inland Peoples." This name, however, implied a pejorative connotation that might be more accurately translated as "Backwoodsmen" or "Bush People." In effect, this designation referred to people who chose to live in the bush as migratory hunters, and suggests a category of identity that signaled a division between these "Inland Peoples" and the semipermanent residents of the larger more cosmopolitan lakeshore communities like Sault Sainte Marie and La Pointe.[39] Like the peoples that the French identified as Sauteur, Nipissing, and Ottawa, the Gens des Terres were speakers of regionally varied but mutually intelligible dialects of the Ojibwe language, or mixed dialects that blended the closely related Ojibwe and Cree dialects of the Algonquian language family.

The Gens des Terres were clearly not a Native nation, but rather a large interrelated Native population that consisted of named bands, or doodemag. In addition to their clan designation these people, like their relatives to the south, would have also referred to themselves as the original or true people, the Anishinaabeg, or in a northern dialect variation such as Anishininii.[40] These peoples hunted and lived in the watersheds that connected the north shore of Lake Superior with the western shore of Hudson's Bay. But they also relied on real and socially constructed kinship connections that they had forged with the bands that controlled places like Bow-e-ting or Shagwaamikong for purposes of trade and ceremony. In fact, these connections between the large lakeshore villages and the western interior were integral to the political economy of Anishinaabewaki in that they made the inland trade possible.[41]

In French records the distinction between the Cree and Gens des Terres often appeared as a rather arbitrary distinction based on trade patterns. Cree people traded at Hudson's Bay, the Gens des Terres traded in villages attached to the French fur trade. In effect, the distinction between these terms as national designations reflected an attempt to apply Anishinaabe categories of identity onto peoples whose habit of seasonal migration made them nearly indecipherable to the French as a collective social entity. In this way, the term *Gens des Terres* functioned as a situational identity linked to the French fur trade, just as the term *Cree* came to signify inland peoples trading at posts on the western shore of Hudson's Bay.[42]

The peoples of the interior in particular, and Anishinaabe bands more generally, fit poorly into European national categories even though the named groups associated with summer village communities, like the Sauteurs and the Ottawas, became increasingly important to the French fur trade and diplomacy. These communities expanded to incorporate a broad range of peoples, each with different claims to hunting territories in the interior, many with trade ties to other villages. These interconnections made Anishinaabe-waki, as a territory, into something that might be said to have resembled a web as opposed to a national territory.[43] Real and socially constructed kinship established through trade, ritual, language, and intermarriage crisscrossed over a vast space connecting peoples to one another, but not in such a way that territory could be considered a bounded space. Anishinaabewaki was not a national identity with exclusive claim to occupy a particular physical space. It was instead a constellation of lived relationships.

Dablon's map and narrative, like St. Lusson's ceremony, represented an attempt to transform these relationships into something recognizable to a European. Reading national identity onto these Native peoples, however, imposed a static representation onto their identity that failed to account for the dynamic and fluid way that they constructed imagined communities. Thus, Dablon's invention of the "Outaouac country," like the idea of an all-encompassing Outouac nation, made no sense on the ground. The fact that French colonial officials, missionaries, and traders could not agree about what it meant to be an Outaouac as opposed to a Sauteur, a Gens des Terres, or even a Cree reflected the problem of imposing a singular category of identity onto people whose sense of corporate identity was inherently flexible.

It was not that the Anishinaabeg had no sense of themselves as a people, but rather that to be Anishinaabe could mean different things in different places. Just as the trickster Nanabozho might shape-shift to fool an enemy or to hunt down game, Anishinaabe bands accepted the need to transform their collective identity to fit the circumstances on the ground. The doodemag of the interior could be traders (adaawewininni) descending the Ottawa River with their relatives to exchange goods with the French, or they might join with their relatives at Bow-e-ting to harvest the resources of the fishery. Similarly, the doodemag of Bow-e-ting might disperse into the interior to hunt or trade with their inland dwelling relatives who controlled the beaver rich watersheds of this region. These doodemag, or even smaller social units consisting of two to three extended families, might even undertake an extended sojourn to trade with the Winipeg-athinuwick at the sea coast, or relocate to the Shagwaamikong region to take advantage of the opportunity to hunt and trade at this vital crossroads village that connected to a transcontinental trading system. Any attempt to attach fixed identities to these peoples as members of a Gens des Terres, Ottawa, Sauteur, or Cree nation was bound to create invented, and unreliable social and political categories.

For the Anishinaabe peoples the reality of lived experience revealed the necessity of metamorphosis. Any animate being might shape-shift, or assume another life form, in order to make its way in the world. This same logic applied to human beings gathered together to form a collective social body. Communities came together, and they came apart. At each such instance the people collectively inhabited a social identity formed by the creation of community in a particular place. When the season changed the people moved and formed new communities, or resurrected dormant ones in different places according to the necessity of the season and the conditions of the physical location. The people of this world, the Anishinaabeg, recognized a shared sense of identity that linked people and territory. This was Anishinaabewaki—their homeland, Indian country—a physical and social landscape created by their connection to one another. But the Anishinaabeg recognized that were many different ways of making these connections, and many different ways to imagine themselves within this space.

The mobility of various Anishinaabe peoples in the north-northwest interior and the social flexibility of Anishinaabe villages situated at strategic points throughout the Great Lakes created a diplomatic challenge for New France. The constant metamorphosis within these communities made it extremely difficult for Onontio to speak to his children, let alone command their obedience, engage them in trade, or protect them from enemies. St. Lusson's ceremony represented a claim of possession, but this aspect of the ritual was intended for a European audience. On the ground this was an attempt to provide structure and stability to the relationship between New France and its Native allies.

This ceremony, in seeking to impose structure onto the alliance, imagined all Anishinaabe peoples to be "Outaouacs," even if only for the purpose of inserting these children of Onontio into the hierarchy of empire. The French

saw these so called Upper Algonquins as a confusing amalgamation of nomadic hunter-gatherers and seminomadic villagers who came together out of
a shared interest in acquiring French trade goods and to defend themselves
from the Iroquois. Underlying this assumption was the idea that the people
of the pays d'en haut entered the western Great Lakes and Mississippi valley
as refugees from homelands in the east.

In other words, the Ottawa and related peoples moved into the west in
search of beaver pelts, and in flight from the Iroquois. This made them relative newcomers to the region. This idea, in turn, created a political imaginary
that explained the relationship between Onontio and his children. From this
perspective, that is, from a point of view created by the westward expansion
of the French Empire, the alliance brought unity and cohesion to a world
the colonizers perceived to be chaotic, disordered, and largely composed of
refugees.

This narrative, so central to the origin story that New France created for itself, was undermined by the fact that the numerous peoples of the north were
not firmly attached to Onontio, and they were not traveling west as refugees.
Neither were they permanently attached to a particular village, at least from
a European perspective. The French were both right and wrong in assuming
that refugee immigrants populated the space they thought of as the pays d'en
haut. Many peoples, such as those gathered at Green Bay, entered the west as
refugees. Many others, such as the Peoples of the North and the closely related people of the Sault, moved through this territory as seasonal migrants.
These patterns of migration, even among the refugees, evolved from trade and
kinship ties that predated the French alliance system. Both the Cree and the
Peoples of the North, for example, appeared loosely attached to the Sauteur
villages at Bow-e-ting (Sault Sainte Marie) and at Shagwaamikong (La Pointe
du Chequamegon). The uncertainty of these relationships, however, posed
a problem from the perspective of New France. So long as the People of the
North remained unnamed and or little known, they might be "discovered" by
a rival power. The English claim over the territory they called Rupert's Land
would be strengthened in the courts of Europe as they named and claimed
the Native peoples of the western interior as subjects of their empire. Even
more dangerous, with the growing trade on the ground at Hudson's Bay, they
might actually shape these peoples into a rival alliance, perhaps even drawing
the Ottawas and Sauteurs into the English sphere of influence.

The strategic necessity of attaching the peoples of the north more clearly
to Onontio, coupled with the idea that these people lacked a permanent resi-

dence, made the French relationship with the peoples of the Sault vital to the success of Saint Lusson's ceremony. This was the only village with a strong connection to the peoples of the north where the French had an institutional presence in the form of a Jesuit mission and licensed traders. They needed to attach a coherent national identity onto the peoples gathered at Sault Sainte Marie in order to claim them as children of Onontio, and subjects of the French Empire.

Describing the residents of the village of Bow-e-ting as members of a single nation, however, proved to be extremely problematic. In *The Relation of 1669–70*, Claude Dablon wrote, "we have been obliged to establish a permanent mission here, which we call Sainte Marie du Sault." The fishery at this location, he noted, "attracts the surrounding nations here during the summer." Dablon then went on to describe seventeen different groups of Native peoples as seasonal residents of this village. He ascribed a distinct national identity to each group, providing some names that were familiar to the French such as Sauteurs, Amikwas, Mississauga, and Cree. Dablon also described two nations resident at the Sault as "entirely nomadic," and offered no name or other marker of identity for these people other than to suggest they "go towards the lands of the north to hunt during the winter." Finally, he described six nations of "wanderers" who came to Sault Sainte Marie seasonally from "the lands around this same North Sea." He suggested that these wandering nations were Cree.[44]

With so many different Native "nations" living in this village, what made the Jesuits identify it as belonging to the Sauteurs? "The first and natural inhabitants of this place," Dablon explained, "are those who call themselves Pahouting dach Irini." This was a rough phonetic translation of the self-designation for the people of Bow-e-ting, which the French translated as people of the falls, or Sauteurs. "They live at the falls," Dablon asserted, "as in their own country, the others being there as borrowers." The Sauteurs, he claimed, "have united themselves with three other nations . . . to whom they have made as a cession the rights of their native country." Dablon identified these nations as the "Noquet" (Bear), "Marameg" (Catfish), and "Outchibous" (Loon), in effect, providing phonetic approximations for named Anishinaabe bands or doodemag. In the winter these bands, like all the other "nations" at the Sault, moved onto their hunting grounds. According to Dablon, the Bear, Catfish, and Loon clan peoples all traveled to territories in the region west of Gichigamiing during the winter to hunt. People with these same doodem identifications, in fact, continued to be identified in European records hunting and trading at Shagwaamikong and to the north and west of this village well into the nineteenth century.[45]

The people that the French thought of as Sauteurs understood their identity as rooted both in the village community at Sault Sainte Marie and in a pattern of western migration. In the early nineteenth century the descendants of the Sauteurs resident at Shagwaamikong described the origins of their community to officials representing the government of the United States. By that time, that Anishinaabe people called themselves "Ojibwe," or in the plural form "Ojibweg." William Warren, a mixed-blood Anishinaabe serving as translator for this council, later recorded their story as part of an ethnographic history of the Ojibwe people. The American agent had been sent to the village known to Americans as La Pointe to negotiate a treaty. Looking for a singular source of authority, he asked the council which chief among them spoke for the Ojibwe people. In response to the American's question the ogimaag offered a series of stories to explain the history of their village communities on the lakeshores of Gichigamiing.

The elders at this council, Warren observed, spoke of the Ojibweg as interconnected family groups, each identified by a doodem designation. The Ojibweg understood their origin as a people as the history of the migration of these family groups to Bow-e-ting, and then further west to "Shaug-ah-waum-ik-ong." The ogimaa of the Crane doodem explained that the families of the Ojibwe people first came together at Bow-e-ting. He told the story of the Crane's arrival at this site as an allegory. Gichi-manidoo made a bird and sent it to live on earth. This bird settled on a hill overlooking Bow-e-ting, and chose to live at this place because of the abundant fishery. "Satisfied with its chosen seat," the ogimaa explained, "the bird sent forth its solitary cry; and the No-kaig (Bear clan), A-waus-e-waug (Catfish), Ah-auh-wauh-ug (Loon) and Mous-o-neeg (Moose and Marten clan), gathered at his call. A large town soon congregated, and the bird whom the Great Spirit sent presided over all." The Crane family repeated this pattern, migrating west along the shoreline of Gichigamiing. The bird admired the fishery at Shagwaamikong and once again called the families together. With this story, Warren later wrote, the Crane doodem claimed "to have been the first discoverers and the pioneer settlers at Sault Ste. Marie, and again at Pt. Shauug-ah-waum-ik-ong." They were, in this sense, the first among the Ojibwe people to call the families together, but they were a first among equals as the doodemag and the Ojibwe were one and the same.[46]

In providing this explanation of the origins of these two strategically important villages the ogimaa described the pattern of relationships that defined his community. Anishinaabewaki, as a territory, was a constellation of social relationships. The connection between Bow-e-ting and Shagwaamikong did not entail the movement of a people or nation into a new territory, but rather the movement of a collective identity. We can follow this migration by comparing Dablon's description of the Sauteur identity to the story recorded by William Warren. The Crane people, identified in Anishinaabemowin as the Bus-in-aus-e or Echo-makers, were the people Dablon identified as the original inhabitants of Bow-e-ting. They incorporated Anishinaabe bands from the west—the Bear, Catfish, and Loon families—into their community, making these people Sauteurs even though they periodically returned to live in their western territories.

These doodemag identified themselves with the original inhabitants of the Bow-e-ting, and regarded this place as their home territory, but this Sauteur designation fit within the larger world of Anishinaabewaki. In this sense, the Sauteur identity, like Cree and Gens des Terres, represented a situational identity. When the French identified these categories of identity as representing Native nations it was not because any of these designations could actually be translated as the word for "nation." There is no such word in Anishinaabemowin.[47] More to the point, Anishinaabe as a self-designation encompassed multiple forms of identity. Anishinaabeg, Marameg (Catfish), Amikwas (Beaver), and Sauteur, for example, were interlocking categories of identity. Each designation signified a link in a chain of social relations that made it possible to come together, and move apart, in order to create different kinds of communities in different places.

The social relations of production required to sustain a winter band in the bush were quite different than what was needed to sustain a summer village. The village was a composite community where several named bands came together seasonally. Bands such as the Marameg, Noquet, and Outchibous gathered in the summer to visit, trade, participate in ceremonies, and forge marriage alliances. They might also come together in order to harvest fish runs in the fall and spring. This activity demanded significant labor resources, and therefore required the mobilization of a large-scale alliance network.[48] In contrast, usufruct rights that determined winter migration and hunting patterns were exercised by the winter band and the lodge group, component units of the named band. The composition of these smaller social groups often changed on a yearly basis. Similarly, their dispersal along watersheds and into the forested interior did not follow a set pattern, but reflected strategic decisions designed to allow the maximum harvest of seasonal resources within a given territory.[49]

The relationship between place and identity for the Anishinaabeg was grounded in kinship, but that kinship was not static, and it was not necessarily biological. Named bands might decide to establish themselves at an entirely new winter territory, or summer village, in response to changes in animal populations or habitat or to respond to new trading opportunities. Such a change necessarily involved a reconfiguration of social relations. In effect, the creation of new situational identities occurred when named bands such as the Marameg, Noquet, and Outchibous entered into an alliance with the Bus-in-aus-e, expanding the seasonal population of Bow-e-ting. The integration of these Anishinaabe bands as a collective social unit at Sault Sainte Marie represented a reconfiguration of kinship and identity that facilitated seasonal migration between the forested interior and an important summer village.[50]

The people resident at this village, the Sauteurs, did not however, live together exclusively or permanently as a community at this location. In 1670 Dablon noted that the Marameg or Catfish people migrated from territory in the west to become Sauteurs, even though he also indicated that the people of this doodem continued to hunt in their original territory during the winter. This pattern of seasonal movement apparently continued in spite of the assumption of a Sauteur identity as French traders identified the "Malamac," which they translated as "Gens de la Barbue" or Catfish people, as a distinct Indian nation residing in the interior region northwest of Shagwaamikong in the 1690s.[51] The Marameg doodem or possibly smaller units from this community may have periodically lived at the Sault, and even assumed an identity as Sauteurs. The members of this doodem, however, were Anishinaabe people from the west. And while they may have periodically migrated east to the Anishinaabe village at the place they called Bow-e-ting, it seems that French records marked their return to Shagwaamikong as a western migration of the Sauteurs.

Thus, in French records, the Sauteurs entered the west as immigrants—just like Europeans. The story of this migration was, in effect, a story of empire building in the Atlantic New World. Large numbers of Native peoples moved west as refugees, and in pursuit of animal peltry. The expansion of New France entailed a westward movement of French traders, missionaries, and allied Indians. Similarly, the Sauteur identity, as a designation for Native allies of New France and children of Onontio, moved west as part of this empire-building process. Paying attention to the Native narratives interwoven into French records about their alliance, however, reveals a history where Native immigration and migration overlapped considerably. Clearly, Anishinaabe bands lived in the west before the French and the institutions of the alliance made their way to La Pointe du Chequamegon. It was the name *Sauteur* that moved west with an expanded French alliance, not the people. Nevertheless, the French witnessed this migration and feared that this constellation of Native peoples, which they found so difficult to identify let alone control, might shape-shift and give their trade, kinship, and alliance to the English posts at Hudson's Bay unless they could be held together as children of Onontio—that is, as Indian nations allied to New France.[52]

Reaffirming French-Native Alliances

St. Lusson was sent into the west to attach the peoples and territory of the pays d'en haut to the French Empire. The ceremony that he brought to Sault Sainte Marie represented a claim of discovery. But it also represented an attempt to bring order to the world of the Native peoples allied to and trading with New France. The ceremony was a remedy for the confusion of refugees, immigrants, and seasonal migrants whose constant movement and changing social identifications left the French in fear of losing their allies to the English.

On this errand St. Lusson was merely a vessel, an aristocrat who embodied the hierarchy of the French Empire, but he was delivered to the upper country by the voyageur Nicolas Perrot. This man, in his person, embodied the manidoo, or power, of the French Empire. Perrot and his fellow voyageurs delivered the trade goods into the interior that facilitated the exchange process connecting bands in the west to the large lakeshore village communities of Anishinaabewaki, and increasingly connected these villages to the French Empire. Perrot was one of the most astute voyageurs to enter the trade, and over the course of a career that spanned nearly four decades, he learned that diplomacy and trade functioned as an extension of kinship ties and the obligations that came with them.

Perrot knew how to read the landscape of Anishinaabewaki. At the end of his life the voyageur wrote a memoir about his experiences in this Native world. This narrative included a brief account of his role in St. Lusson's ceremony. The text provides a different perspective than the narratives produced by the Jesuits. Perrot offered little detail about the actual ceremony. Instead, his narrative focused on the diplomatic negotiations required to bring the ritual participants together at Sault Sainte Marie.

In this narrative, Perrot's diplomatic mission closely paralleled the experience of Pierre Radisson, who as noted earlier participated in a Feast of the Dead with Anishinaabe people he identified as Sauteurs in 1660. Both men produced narratives that chronicled the seasonal round of Native peoples moving through Anishinaabewaki, and demonstrated how ceremonies that created kinship made this life possible. Perrot departed Montreal with St. Lusson in the fall, and passed the winter in the pays d'en haut among the Anishinaabeg on Manitoulin Island in Lake Huron. The voyageur hunted with winter bands he identified as Amikwas and Sauteur, and at the end of the season he asked them to make their way to Bow-e-ting in the spring to hear St. Lusson deliver a message from the French king. "I also sent some of the savages," he wrote, "to make it known to those of the north not to miss returning to their country."[53] Perrot not only grasped the connection between the peoples of the north and the people of the falls but also identified this village as being "their country." In effect, Perrot sent word to people living in the bush north and west of Gichigamiing, bands connected to Bow-e-ting, but who may have chosen not come in to this village in the springtime. He asked that they come this year for a ceremony, demonstrating a knowledge of the seasonal rhythms and kinship connections that made this village community.

Perrot understood how the villages of the pays d'en haut connected people to one another. He also understood how the manidoo of Onontio, and the power of French trade goods, could be used to connect these villages to New France. These relationships, however, required constant maintenance. Ceremonies like St. Lusson's made sense less as an imperial discourse then as part of a larger conversation about the mutual obligations of family. Perrot recognized that kinship was the key that opened and closed the spaces of the physical world that he thought of as the pays d'en haut. Kinship placed people either inside or outside of a shared social identity. Unlike empire, however, these relationships could not be mapped as an abstract space. They were instead made on the ground through lived relationships that placed different peoples together as members of an imagined community.

St. Lusson's ceremony offered the Native allies of New France the possibility of reaffirming their kinship and connection with their French father. And so when virtually all of the peoples living at Green Bay signaled their intention to stay away from the ceremony, Perrot must have been filled with apprehension. These communities were largely composed of refugees seeking relief from decades of Haudenosaunee raids against their peoples, and should have been eager to find security in their collective identity as children of Onontio.

Perrot immediately set out to make sure these villages remained open to the French, and part of the alliance. In his narrative, however, the voyageur offered no real explanation of the problems that compelled him to make this trip. La Potherie, in contrast, in his *Histoire de l'Amérique Septentrionale* offered a more complete account of this expedition to Green Bay based on information he obtained from Perrot and from various traders and missionaries. He suggested that tensions with the Jesuits and French traders had created disaffection among the peoples of the bay. La Potherie claimed that the dispute arose over the price of French merchandise. He implied that the Indians behaved arrogantly toward the French in demanding a better rate of exchange. La Potherie also noted that the Dakota had recently attacked a village community at Green Bay.[54] Neither Perrot nor La Potherie linked the quarrel with the French to the Dakota raid. The Dakota, however, traded with the French at La Pointe.[55] This trade armed an already formidable enemy with weapons of European manufacture. From the perspective of the peoples of Green Bay this was a betrayal, a signal even of their abandonment by Onontio.

Evidence of the role played by the Dakota in causing this tension between the refugees of Green Bay and their French allies was conspicuously absent in Perrot's narrative. The Jesuits, on the other hand, provided a vivid account of the peoples of Green Bay pleading with the French for help in this conflict. At the time of the ceremony Allouez had just returned from a winter sojourn in this region, and it was he who warned Perrot of the people's discontent. As the priest traveled among the cluster of villages at the lakeshore, and further inland along the Fox and Wisconsin River watersheds, he heard about the ferocity of the Dakota. When Allouez arrived at a pallisaded village of Mascouten and Miami peoples, he found them preparing for war. The French were called to a council where the man leading these preparations spoke to them: "You have heard of the peoples called the Nadouessi. They have eaten me to the bone and not left a single member of my family alive. I must taste of their flesh as they have tasted of my relatives. I am ready to set out against them in war, but I despair of success there if you who are the masters of life and of death are not favorable of me in this enterprise."[56]

The Jesuits heard similar tales of despair, and a sense of abandonment by the French among the Mesquakie peoples whom they identified as the Sauk and Fox nations. "Black Robe," they pleaded with Allouez, "take pity on us." They asked the Jesuits to come and live among them "to protect us from our enemies and to teach us to speak to the grand Manitou (Gichi-manidoo) the same as you do with the savages of the Sault." They met with a similar call for help and protection at each village they entered.[57] The peoples of Green Bay may have been angry at the hard trading of the voyageurs that came among them. They may have despaired when these representatives of New France passed through their villages en route to trade with the Dakota. But they still saw alliance with the French as the best hope of securing the manidoo from Onontio that would protect their people.

Perrot arrived at Green Bay to find this potent mixture of anger and desperation, but also a willingness to use the proposed French ceremony as an opportunity to reanimate their identity as children of Onontio. After a friendly reception by the Boodewaadamii Anishinaabeg, refugees from the northern peninsula below the straights of Michilimackinac, the voyageur was greeted with a show of force at the Miami village. All of the warriors of Green Bay's mixed villages turned out to meet the French party with weapons drawn, though after a mock battle, they invited their guests to smoke the calumet. With peace reestablished on Native terms, Perrot returned to Sault Sainte Marie with representatives from the various peoples living at Green Bay to enact the French ceremony. In his narrative he noted that the "principal chiefs" of the Pottawatomis, Sauks, Puans, and Menominees accompanied him. Perhaps signaling their lingering frustration, the peoples identified by the French as the Fox, Mascoutens, Kickapoo, and Miami declined to send their own leaders to the ceremony. Instead, they asked the Pottawatomie, or more accurately Boodewaadamii (Keepers of the Fire), to represent their interests. This choice was significant because these people had once taken refuge at Bow-e-ting, and they were closely connected to the people identified by the French as Ottawas and Sauteurs.[58] Most importantly, from the perspective of Perrot's narrative, by sending a delegation to the ceremony, the leadership at Green Bay signaled their consent to French possession of their territory, and they accepted their status as subjects of the French king exchanging their allegiance for his protection.[59]

While Perrot carefully identified all of the Indian nations from Green Bay who attended or sent representatives to signal their consent at St. Lusson's ceremony, he described the Anishinaabe peoples with active ties to Bow-e-ting with far less specificity. "I found, at my arrival," he wrote, "not only the chiefs of the north, but also all of the Kiristinos, Monsonis, and entire villages of their neighbors." He also noted the presence of the chiefs of the Nipissing, Amikwas, and "all the Sauteurs who have settled in the same place." La Potherie simply noted the attendance of "all the chiefs of the bay, those of

Lake Huron, of Lake Superior, and the people of the North, not counting several other nations who found themselves at the Saut at the end of May."[60] Both of these accounts included a variety of unnamed Native peoples from the country north and west of Gichigamiing. Apparently the Sauteurs who hunted with Perrot on Manitoulin Island sent word of the French ceremony to peoples scattered throughout the northwest interior, suggesting an extensive territorial range for doodemag with ties to this village.

St. Lusson's report describing the outcome of his ceremony, in contrast with Perrot's narrative, actually provided a clearer picture of both the people of the Sault and the unnamed people of the North. He identified Sainte Marie du Sault as "the actual residence" of "the savage nations named Achipoes (Loon), Malamechs (Catfish), Noquets (Bear), and others." Here the ubiquitous unnamed "others" might be construed as the Crane doodem, the first inhabitants of the Sault and the people who called the families together. St. Lusson then named the peoples of Green Bay in attendance, more or less matching Perrot's and La Potherie's narratives. But he also described the "habitants of the north country and their close neighbors from the sea," describing the Assiniboine, Cree, Monsoni (Moose and Marten), the Ni-ka (Goose), and Muskegoe. These last two bands, like the Moose, Loon, and Catfish doodemag, came to the Sault from the region west of Gichigamiing. The Goose doodem, in fact, was common among the northernmost range of Anishinaabe peoples who spoke a mixed Cree-Ojibwe dialect, and were called the O-Mushke-goes (swamp people). They lived in the country north of the headwaters of the Mississippi River valley, a territory of lakes, swamps, and boreal forest that bordered the northern plains.[61]

For the peoples of Green Bay, and for the multitude of Anishinaabe peoples with ties to Bow-e-ting, St. Lusson's ceremony was a negotiation about the meaning of empire. This negotiation, however, was not about the physical borders of New France or the possession of the pays d'en haut as a territory. Instead this ceremony signaled the creation or reaffirmation of a set of social relationships that would connect the French, in Europe and Canada, to the Native peoples who lived in the interior of North America. Of course, the colonists who produced a record of this event wrote for a European audience. They argued that the pays d'en haut had become a part of New France, signaling an expansion of the power and territory of their empire. The French, however, wanted their ceremony to create something more concrete then a claim of sovereignty over the ephemeral shape-shifting identities of Anishinaabewaki. They wanted the peoples of the interior to take shape as nations allied to New France, and they wanted these nations to take on the persona and obligations of children of Onontio.

Two Views of a Native Conversion

Intendant Talon sought to transform the shape-shifters of Anishiaabewaki into coherent Native nations with St. Lusson's ceremony. But he also recognized that the social relationships that gave order to this world were too complex to be reorganized by a single ceremonial encounter. Even though New France claimed sovereignty over their allies in the western interior, Talon knew that many of these people moved freely between the English at Hudson's Bay, and the French colony and posts in the pays d'en haut. Accordingly, after he sent St. Lusson west, the intendant began to search, in his own words, for "some men of resolution to invite the Kilistinos who are in great number in the neighborhood of this bay, to come down among us." Talon informed the minister of marine, who oversaw administration of France's colonial possessions, that in the past, the Cree traded with the Ottawas, who carried their furs to the French. He complained to the minister, however, that for the last two years the Ottawas from the north had traded instead with the English at Hudson's Bay.[62]

Talon found his men of resolution, and sent them on a mission to end the English trade at Hudson's Bay, and erase English claims to the interior northwest. While St. Lusson claimed possession of Anishinaabewaki from Sault Sainte Marie, a Jesuit named Charles Albanel voyaged north in August 1671 to reclaim Hudson's Bay. En route to the bay, Albanel duplicated St. Lusson's ceremony, though with less grandeur. Talon, in effect, wanted to create a narrative of discovery that would overturn English claims to possess the northern interior. This alternative narrative, like St. Lusson's ceremony, needed to be legible to both a European and Native audience in order to have any chance of actually ending the English presence in this region. Talon began by asserting in writing "these lands have been anciently discovered firstly by the French." To make his argument on the ground, he sent Albanel "to repeat" the ritual possession of this territory by New France.[63] With these gestures Talon hoped to erase the English claim to possession of the western interior by writing a new spatial history. He intended to rediscover this space, still blank on British maps, and make it and the Indians who lived there French.

Albanel traveled north along a known trade route that had previously connected the Wyandot to Anishinaabe and Muskekowuck-athinuwick peoples in the interior. Talon selected Albanel because of his association with the mission at the village of Tadoussac at the mouth of the Saugenay River. This watershed drained into the Saint Lawrence above Quebec from a lake in the northern interior renamed Lac St. Jean by the French. Twelve different river systems drained into Lac St. Jean from the Hudson's Bay region. The village at this lake, much like the village at Sault Sainte Marie, was an important gathering place for Native peoples. "This was formerly the place," the Jesuits wrote, "where all the nations who were between the two seas, from the east and from the north, went to make their trade."[64]

The same combination of disease and conflict that sent the Wyandot into the west ruined the trade relationships that once defined this landscape. Now, however, these relationships began to form again as trade goods circulated inland from the French colony and English posts at the bay. Albanel identified this lakeshore village as the territory of the Kakouchac, or Gaagwag people. This designation signified the Porcupine doodem. The missionary noted, however, that the inhabitants of this village "are beginning to repopulate by the people from foreign nations who come there from various directions since the peace."[65] Shortly after arriving at this location Albanel began to encounter a number of different named bands generally identified by the French as Gens des Terres or People of the North. "Five canoes of Attikamegues, or *poissons blancs*, & of Misstassirinins came and joined us," he noted. These people brought news of English ships trading extensively at Hudson's Bay. They came by this information not directly, but through trading with yet another Gens des Terres band identified by the French as the Papinachois.

Examining the meaning of these various Gens des Terres names suggests that Albanel was not, in fact, witnessing a repopulation of the Porcupine nation. More accurately, he recorded evidence of the restoration of the social relationships that gave shape to the muskeeg—the swampy lowlands that stretched inland from the Hudson's Bay region and north shore of Lake Superior. This landscape formed the northern range of Anishinaabewaki as a territory and a social formation. Mistassirinins or Misstasini represented a geographic location, Lake Misstassini to the French or Great Rock Lake to speakers of the Montagnais-Naskapi dialect of the Cree language. Similarly, the self-designation *Mistasini-wiyiyu* identified the people of the Great Rock. Their territory bordered the watershed that the English claimed to have purchased and renamed the Rupert River.[66] The Attikamek or Whitefish people inhabited watersheds to the west of Lac St. Jean, and were linguistically related to the Cree speakers at the Hudson's Bay coast.[67] The Papinachois, likely a derivative of a Cree term for wandering people, ranged over territory from the Michipicoten River draining into Lake Superior to the tributaries of the Moose River that emptied into Hudson's Bay. They spoke a mixed Cree-Ojibwe dialect suggesting a pattern of intermarriage and cohabitation shared by all of the seasonal migrants who moved between villages and hunting territories at the lakeshore and seacoast.[68]

The English posts at Hudson's Bay could potentially play a significant role in restoring the social relations of production that allowed the peoples of these watersheds to sustain themselves. The interplay of village, doodem, and watershed shaped the social identity of the various "peoples of the north." Trade facilitated the integration of these peoples into a larger social formation. This was not a Gens des Terres nation, but it was a collective social body oriented toward the harvesting, trading, and processing of natural resources on a scale that exceeded the requirements of self-sufficiency. In other words, this was a social formation capable of engaging the world market system dominated by the empires of the Atlantic World. Albanel was sent into the north country to make certain that these inland or bush peoples looked toward the pays d'en haut and New France when they sought trade goods and allies.

As Albanel traveled he claimed the country he passed through for New France. He was forced to describe his journey, however, using Native place names—making for locations such as "Pikousitesinacut" (The place where shoes are worn out) and "Makoumitikac" (The bears' fishing place)—which only underscored the fact that this country was Native space and not functionally a part of any empire. Nevertheless, he told the Native peoples at Lake Mistassini that Onontio had saved them from the Iroquois. "Your country was dead, he has brought it back to life," Albanel told his audience, "Fish, hunt, and trade in all directions without fear of being discovered by your enemies."[69] And finally, while presenting a series of gifts, he admonished the villagers to "abandon the plan of having commerce with the Europeans, who trade toward the North sea . . . retake your old path from Lake St. Jean." The following day the leadership of this village gave Albanel a gift in return, asserting: "The French oblige us strongly, in giving us peace, he brings us back to life."[70] The Jesuit then planted a cross and a staff with the king's coat of arms, claiming the people of this village as subjects of Louis XIV, and declaring their territory a part of his empire.

Perhaps Intendant Talon believed that these simple transactions signaled the acquiescence of local populations to French rule. At the very least, he recognized that French claims of sovereignty in the interior depended on the creation of an ongoing social relationship between Native peoples and the colony of New France. Onontio had been absent too long from this region. Talon knew this, and a careful reading of the record of Albanel's journey suggests that the priest knew this as well. He may have claimed possession of this region for his European audience, but his encounters with Native peoples on the ground revealed a complex negotiation over the meaning of place and identity.

When Albanel finally arrived at the recently named Rupert River, a place he identified as "Meskoutenagasit," he found the English post abandoned. The Hudson's Bay Company ships had returned to England for supplies, carrying a significant cargo of peltry. Albanel described this region as home to the Mattawagami people (Montagnais-Naskapi speakers), the Cree, and the Monsoni, all of whom occupied river systems that drained into the bay. He described the coast itself, Meskoutenagasit, as the home territory of the People of the Sea (Winipeg-athinuwick). The Jesuit began to move north along the shoreline in search of the people living at the coast who had accommodated the Hudson's Bay traders. He quickly found them and approached with caution. "These people," he wrote, "were likely to take umbrage at our visit & our pretensions, our intention being unknown to them."[71]

The Jesuit and his companions, however, received a friendly welcome. The "Captain" of the People of the Sea waded into the water and guided Albanel's canoe to shore, then escorted the priest to his cabin. This man, identified by Albanel as "Kiaskou" or Gayaashk (the Gull), accepted a gift of tobacco and a calumet. The priest then called the Winipeg-athinuwick to council. He presented Gayaashk with a present, and then spoke to him as the embodied voice of the French father: "It is me, Onontio says to you, who made peace." Speaking in the first person, as Onontio, the Jesuit declared that he had snatched the war club from the Iroquois and rescued their daughters from the fires of their enemies. "I give you back your country," he concluded.[72] Albanel then presented the council with a second present, and informed him that the French wanted the People of the North to convert to Christianity. According to the Jesuit, for the next three days he and Gayaashk negotiated in earnest about the meaning of the two presents.

The narrative of Albanel's journey published in *The Relation of 1671–72* emphasized the spiritual rebirth of Gayaashk. The captain of the People of the Sea asked the priest to baptize his people. Albanel refused, they possessed only a tenuous grasp of Christianity, he argued. "You are so wavering," he told

Gayaashk, "and so unstable in your belief in a Sovereign spirit who governs all things."[73] He asked the ogimaa to wait until he returned next year, when he could provide further instruction. According to Albanel, the Winipeg-athinuwick barred his departure while he sparred with Gayaashk at council over the meaning of baptism and Christianity. They refused to accept and ritually answer the gifts he had offered as the voice of Onontio in order to make clear to him what was at stake. At last, after wrestling with these issues for three days, the missionary relented and agreed to baptize Gayaashk.

Though presented as a triumph of the faith by Albanel, the baptism of Gayaashk was a striking blend of French and Native ritual practices and meaning making. Both men attempted to manipulate this ceremony in order to gain a measure of control over the meaning of the relationship between New France and the People of the North. After Albanel promised to baptize Gayaashk, the ogimaa passed the entire day before calling his people together. "It is not the difficulty of speaking that has made me defer holding this council," he told the Jesuit, "but the answer that you must make to the French that troubles me." Albanel was anxious to leave, Gayaashk noted, and giving him presents would only add to the burden of the arduous journey that lay ahead. On the other hand, if the Jesuit left without presents, he feared "they will say at Quebec that I have no mouth—that I am a child unable to speak." Gayaashk then proposed a remedy for this dilemma. The priest would depart with a few otter skins to acknowledge Onontio's gifts, and "my young men will carry my words and my thanks to Lake St. Jean the following year."[74] Before Albanel left the next morning he baptized Gayaashk and gave him the Christian name Ignace.

Albanel's account of this encounter managed to skillfully intertwine stories of spiritual rebirth with the discovery narrative's usual trope of European political domination and territorial possession. To resonate with his European audience, Albanel allowed the ogimaa to remain dead to God for three days before his redemption. Then Gayaashk, reborn as Ignace, transferred his allegiance to the French king and "the sovereign spirit governing all things," and Albanel claimed the territory of his people for New France.

By accepting a new name, however, Gayaashk actually subverted the logic behind the story of his conversion and dispossession. He did not want to be a child who was "unable to speak." Becoming Ignace gave Gayaashk a voice. It enabled him to speak as a child of Onontio, and an ally of New France, even though he had traded virtually all of his peltry with the English. Taking a new name or a temporary identity in order to secure your place within a new community made sense to Anishinaabe and Athinuwick peoples. Through the ritual of baptism Gayaashk gained access to Onontio, who, in turn controlled access to the manidoo of the "Sovereign spirit who governed all things." By shape-shifting between Native and Christian identities he created a relationship with the governor of New France, and with the traders who carried the manidoo of empire into the interior. He also gained access to the most powerful grandfather of the spirit world, Gichi-manidoo.

This encounter offered a remarkable contrast between the ideologies that framed the interactions between Native peoples and the French and English empires. The English bestowed a name, the Rupert River, onto the watershed that they claimed to have purchased in order to make Hudson's Bay recognizable as an English space. And then they built a lonely outpost to trade with the Native peoples whose cultural and social identity meant very little to either their business enterprise or their kingdom. The English made expansive claims of territorial possession, but imagined the relationship between their empire and the Native peoples of the western interior as largely mercantile. The French chose not to rename the territory, but rather to rename the Native leader they associated with this place. Then they engaged this man in a ritual process where they claimed his soul on behalf of their god, claimed his political allegiance by changing his social identity, and claimed possession of his country as part of their empire.

The story of Gayaashk's transformation, in effect, reads like a parable about the founding and expansion of New France. Unlike the English, the French actually imagined Native peoples as part of their empire. This inclusion was the basis for their ambitious political and territorial claims. For Native peoples, however, the price of their political inclusion was political and cultural rebirth as children of Onontio. In this sense, the metamorphosis of Gayaashk into Ignace was more than a religious conversion. His rebirth meant the assumption of a new identity as a child of the French father. This transformation obligated the governor of New France to meet the needs of his people by supplying them with trade goods and military protection in exchange for their exclusive allegiance and trade. The problem with this parable, however, was the transitory nature of social rebirth in the minds of people like Gayaashk.

The ritual focus on the physical redemption and social reanimation of both individuals and whole communities by Intendant Talon's Jesuit ambassadors would have resonated with the Anishinaabeg and Athinuwick peoples. The practice of assuming a new name and status made sense to seasonal migrants with a fluid sense of social identity. The movement of people up and

down watersheds, out into the muskeeg, and back into trading villages required an ability to interact with and even become a part of many different
kinds of social units. This kind of social mobility, however, made it virtually
impossible to organize the Anishinaabeg into a Native nation—that is, a collective social body with a fixed territory and an exclusive social and political
identity. Their life as a people, or rather as interrelated peoples, required that
they assume multiple identities as their community changed size and location to hunt, fish, harvest rice, attend ceremony, trade, and do all of the things
that they needed to do in order to live. This way of being defined the Anishinaabeg as a people and Anishinaabewaki as a social space. It also posed a
fundamental challenge to the way in which the French tried to organize their
empire in North America.

The French sought to expand their empire by discovering Native nations
that could be attached to their colony as subordinate political units. This idea
of discovery and attachment, however, proved impossible to realize in any
meaningful way. The French used ritual skillfully enough to establish relationships with the peoples that dominated the trade relations that gave shape
to the political landscape at the heart of the continent. These shape-shifting
social formations, however, could not be held together as nations and the
French Empire certainly did not control them as political entities.

In reality, the process of mutual discovery that brought the French and
English Empires into contact with the peoples of Anishinaabewaki and the
northwest interior did not end in conquest, or even in political subordination. The English trading posts did not represent permanent occupation, and
even though the English had begun to rename this territory on their maps,
travelers and traders still needed to know Native place names to navigate
this landscape. The French claim of possession was equally weak. The ritual
that renamed Gayaashk represented political expediency rather than political transformation. One might even argue that in taking the name Ignace,
Gayaashk and the Winipeg-athinuwick laid claim to New France, while their
continued control of the seacoast ensured an on-going relationship with the
merchants and traders of the English Empire, thus making them a significant
regional power. This was the reality of discovery in the heartland of North
America. Encounter with the peoples of Europe did not necessarily diminish
Native autonomy and political power. It could, in fact, enhance them. This
was discovery, not a one-sided revelation that ended in European possession,
but a process of cross-cultural encounter that left some Native peoples in a
position of power as they faced the dawn of the early modern era.

PART II

The New World

THE NEW WORLD was born when the Atlantic World empires arrived in the Western Hemisphere. The discovery of North America in the early modern era did not, however, result in the conquest and dispossession of all of Native America. In fact, in North America, conquest, rapid depopulation, and total dispossession occurred only in pockets of territory along the east coast of the Atlantic. This historical fact contradicts the mythology of discovery, particularly for America where the stories of Squanto and Pocahontas (the Native cofounders of the Plymouth and Virginia colonies) serve as origin stories for the genesis of an Atlantic New World. La Malinche, a Nahua slave, similarly provided a story of Native complicity in the Spanish conquest of Mexico in the south of North America.[1]

The French also produced a narrative tradition of discovery that made Native peoples complicit in their colonization. Unlike the Spanish and the English, however, in New France Native peoples did not facilitate the birth of a New World order that guaranteed their disappearance in the face of advancing modernity. In place of the tragic figures that ushered in a new era, which could only bring death to their people, the French delivered a Native regenesis. In New France Native peoples would be born again as the Children of Onontio, the French father. This story, so different from its English and Spanish counterparts, retained some of the moral uplift that infused the initial calls for colonizing the Americas—providing salvation for the primitive peoples of the New World.

These stories, particularly the stories of La Malinche and Pocahontas, are powerful. They are more than the narratives of historical figures. La Malinche and Pocahontas became metaphors that explained the fate of Native peoples in the context of the history of North America during and after the era of discovery. Native peoples, embodied in the form of these two young women, see the future and recognize that there is no place in this New World for their people. At least there is no place for them so long as they exist as indigenous peoples living a savage or uncivilized life. Their future exists only in their subordination, indeed their sublimation or assimilation to the New World created by their Atlantic World conquerors. The children these women bear for the men bringing civilization to the New World, the mixed-blood–meztiso/a, become a tangible, embodied signification of the fate of Native North America. It must become a part of the Atlantic World to survive in the New World created by Europe's discovery of the Western Hemisphere. And in doing so, by assimilating into this new social world, the Native peoples encountered at discovery are destined to fade away—to disappear physically, spiritually, and socially into the world of the new Americans.

The French imagined a startlingly different New World. Native peoples need not disappear; they might be reborn as the children of empire. Their French father would not only give them a new life, he would also nourish them as only a mother could. Onontio would make himself a mother/father figure, and suckle his children—providing mother's milk in the form of life-changing trade goods, metal weapons, firearms, and physical protection from rival empires and Indians in exchange for their loyalty. Owing to their demographic and geographic limitations the French could imagine their place in the New World only alongside the Native peoples who continued to live in large numbers on the territories they claimed as part of their colony—in spite of disease, warfare, and exposure to the supposedly advanced cultures of Europe. They imagined a mutual dependence, but they demanded political subordination from their Native children. The undercurrent in the French narrative, however, was the fear that many of the children of Onontio could actually choose to assert their independence, rejecting their French family entirely.

This hint of Native independence, of survivability, suggests the flaw in all of these New World origin stories. They are meant to explain the discovery of the New World and its incorporation into the emergent Atlantic World system. And yet simply reflecting upon the demography and geography of North America during the colonial period demands a rethinking of concepts such as the Atlantic World/New World. As late as 1750, most of the continent was occupied exclusively by politically and culturally autonomous Native peoples. Clearly the lives of Native peoples were dramatically affected by the introduction of new plants, animals, peoples, and material artifacts into their social worlds. But that does not change the fact that European claims of discovery, conquest, possession, and sovereignty over the entirety of North America, while true in enclaves at the coast, were meaningless in the vast interior of the continent.

Rather than imagining people like the Dakota, or even the Anishinaabeg, as subordinate peoples within an Atlantic World system we need to imagine how they saw their place in this New World. Undoubtedly they experienced a radical transformation of their social world following first contact. But they remained autonomous peoples and so we must ask how they would express their own self-determination, and how they would explain the history of their encounter with the peoples and things of the Atlantic World. In short, we need a history of the Native New World that developed in the west alongside the Atlantic World that emerged on the east coast of North America.

The structure and function of social formations that dominated the western interior, like the Anishinaabeg, Dakota, and Muskekowuck-athinuwick, remained indigenous in nature even after exposure to the peoples and things of the Old World. Social identities evolved after contact with this other world, but then the same was true for the immigrants who established themselves on the east coast of North America. Success in the New World demanded change. At a minimum, people were forced to imagine their communities in new ways when they encountered people who acted on entirely different ways of being in the world. With a habit of mind that readily transformed outside peoples into insiders in order to facilitate long-distance trade and travel, the Anishinaabeg easily accommodated French fur traders into their existing exchange-based diplomatic and social practices. The Dakota made similar adjustments, and with the adaptation of an equestrian political economy would see their power and territorial range expand exponentially. Distance from settler colonies and physical as well as social mobility made people like the Anishinaabeg and the Dakota elusive targets for empires that wanted to exercise control over easily identifiable, politically subordinated, Native social units.

The stories of La Malinche, Pocahontas, and Onontio are meant to explain the new human geography created when peoples of the Americas like the Anishinaabeg and Dakota came into contact with the peoples of Europe, Africa, and Asia. This encounter unfolded from the moment of first contact across a transoceanic circuit that began a new and worldwide system of exchange, circulating people, plants, goods, and ideas in a way that would transform humanity. This process created a unique social system that scholars identify as the Atlantic World.

The geographer D. W. Meinig has described the Atlantic World as a place of dynamic interaction, rather than as a site of transfer where people and things moved from one hemisphere to another. Meinig argues that the discovery of the Americas was, more accurately, "a harsh encounter between two old worlds that transformed both and integrated them into a single New World."[2] The Atlantic World in this conceptualization emerged as a site of encounter, a transoceanic network that we can envision, in his words, "as a single vast spatial system."[3] This singular geographic field was rooted in Europe, but expanded relentlessly into African and American hinterlands. Native peoples became a part of this emergent imperial social formation, but they were locked in a system where meaning and order were determined by colonial powers with homelands in Europe. In effect, Meinig imagines the New World as a multifaceted spatial system created by the encounter and integration of the different peoples of the Atlantic World.

Thinking about the Atlantic World in this way has enriched our understanding of the history of encounter in the Americas. It is far better than simply imagining encounter as Europe's discovery of an undeveloped, primitive world. Nevertheless, Meinig still imagines the New World as the periphery to a European core, where social and political systems operate along a spatial axis between a European homeland and Indian country, essentially signifying the developed and underdeveloped, and more importantly dominant and subordinate worlds.[4] To be fair, Meinig recognizes that this construction carries with it the teleology of thinking about encounter as a meeting of Old and New Worlds. To compensate for this bias he emphasizes the historical agency of Indian peoples.

Thinking about the Atlantic World/New World as a singular spatial system, however, seems problematic even if we recognize Native agency. The historian Richard White has changed the way scholars tell the story of encounter by introducing the idea of the middle ground—the spatialized, hybrid cultural world of the French alliance. The middle ground convincingly presents the story of encounter in the Great Lakes of North America as the meeting and merger of distinct Native and European social worlds.[5] In order for there to be a middle ground there must have been a Native New World that developed alongside the Atlantic New World. In other words, Native homelands did not cease to exist, nor did the majority of Native peoples forfeit their autonomy in the immediate aftermath of the establishment of European colonies on North American soil.

The essential fact of the continued existence of autonomous indigenous social formations in North America throughout the colonial era demands that we rethink the meaning of the New World. The collision of these two Old Worlds transformed the social systems of the communities that encountered and sustained relationships with people from another hemisphere for the first time. The cultural geography of this ongoing encounter, the New World, was simultaneously rooted in indigenous and European homelands. To fully tell the story of early America we must explore the Native regenesis that developed out of the integration of these two Old Worlds. As historian Pekka Hämäläinen has argued, "we must turn the telescope around and create models that allow us to look at Native policies toward colonial powers as more then defensive strategies of resistance and containment."[6] We must look to the history of the vast majority of Native North America that existed as autonomous social formations. Their history is the story of the Native New World.

CHAPTER 3

The Rebirth of Native Power and Identity

By the last decades of the seventeenth century new peoples and things moved between the colonized east coast of North America and the indigenous western interior. The settler colonies on the coast developed as part of a larger Atlantic World. The European powers at the center of this world system claimed the western interior of the continent as part of their empires. Some of these claims overlapped, but they also ignored the political realities of the New World in other more important ways. The vast interior of North America was occupied and controlled entirely by Native peoples, making any imperial claims over this landscape nothing more than fiction. Peoples of the indigenous west struggled to control the circulation of people and things moving between the coast and interior, and they became entangled with French and English diplomacy, trade interests, and imperial ambitions. But the story of this struggle is not a story about empire. It is not even truly a story of the Atlantic World. The struggle to control the movement of people, things, and ideas between the Atlantic World and the indigenous west was instead a story about the creation of a Native New World in the heartland of North America (Figure 3).

England, France, and Spain each claimed all or some portion of the western interior of North America as part of their empires. The settler colonies established by each of these imperial powers depended on regular trade with Native peoples of the western interior. And yet these claims of possession and dominion were a political fabrication. Trade in the west occurred outside of the institutions and control of empire, but not beyond its influence. Europeans and their microbes, animals, and material goods circulated in the interior, and new social formations emerged in response to the opportunity and the tragedy that came with these new things. In other words, people and things from the Atlantic World made their way into the indigenous heartland of North America through exchange relation-

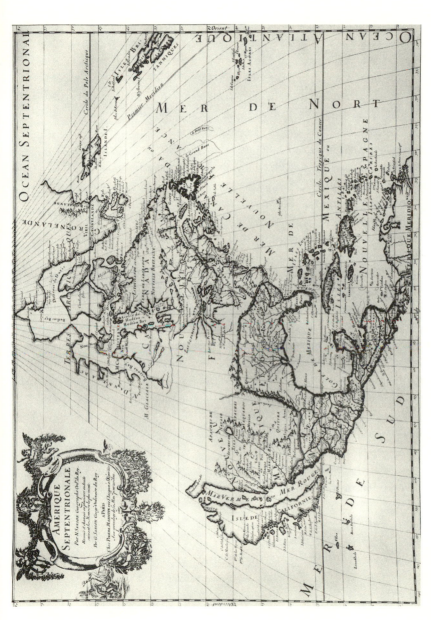

Figure 3. "Amérique Septentrionale," by Nicholas Sanson, in *Mappe monde, ou, carte du globe terrestre, representee en deux plan-hemisphere, revue et changée en plusieurs endroits suivant les relations les plus recentes* (Paris: chez Pierre Marriette, 1669). Courtesy Hudson's Bay Company Archives, Provincial Archives of Manitoba, G. 5/24 Plate 5 (N15246). The western shore of Hudson's Bay suggests the existence of the Northwest Passage, while the interior west remains blank space revealing both the fantasy and the reality of empire.

ships created by an emergent world economy. They acted as catalysts, prompting transformations of existing kinship and exchange relations to produce new spatially reconfigured alliances between different Native social formations. The Native peoples of the western interior of North America, however, maintained their political, economic, and cultural autonomy.[1]

French trade goods, for example, entered the upper Mississippi valley, but the colony of New France lacked the resources or infrastructure to extend its empire into this region. In similar fashion, English trade goods, though not English traders, reached into the Great Lakes and western interior from posts on the western shore of Hudson's Bay. Dynamic, constantly shifting networks of Native peoples routinely circulated people, animals, and goods of indigenous and European manufacture between the colonial east and the indigenous west. The result of this flow of people and things was the creation of a vast Native heartland connecting the northern Great Plains, the Mississippi valley, the prairie parkland northwest of the Mississippi River headwaters, and the boreal forest that arched across the top of the Great Lakes and drained into the marshy lowlands of Hudson's Bay. This was a vast indigenous space knit together by multiethnic Native alliances and exchange networks. It was not a Native empire, but then neither was it part of any European empire.[2] This was instead a Native New World created by indigenous social formations in response to the emergence of a global market economy, and the expansion of the Atlantic World empires onto North American soil.[3] For the peoples of the western interior discovery did not result in conquest, but it did alter identities, requiring Native peoples to imagine themselves in new ways in order to preserve their power and autonomy.

Understanding this Native New World will require historians to decenter European empire as the focal point of early American history, and look instead at this other locus of political and economic power in North America. This would necessarily change the way we think about space, social identity, and even narrative trajectory. It might, in effect, offer scholars of early America an alternative way to conceptualize the history of the New World. Such a reimagining would require historians to take serious account of the autonomous Native social formations that controlled the vast majority of North American territory. This would mean more than adding a Native perspective to the history of early America. It would mean treating the Native New World as an analogue to the Atlantic World—a space that formed in response to the expansion of the world market economy, but that remained independent of the European empires at the core of that system.[4]

We need to tell the story of these indigenous peoples if we are to truly write the history of early America. First and foremost, historians must re-think the language of empire, and start thinking in terms of the relationship between Native categories of identity and social structure, concepts such as Anishinaabeg, doodemag, and Anshinaabewaki. These concepts deserve the same consideration that scholars have applied to the designation Indians (and the various names given to them), and to categories like tribe and nation. At the very minimum scholars need to pay attention to the way that Native peoples named themselves, and explained themselves and their environment, as the key to understanding how they related to the new people and things entering their world. It is important to remember that indigenous intellectual traditions and cultural practices continued to shape the social and political identities of the vast majority of peoples living in North America during the seventeenth and eighteenth centuries, even as they were being transformed by the collision of two hemispheres jarringly connected after millennia of separation. Their history must be at the core of any history of early America. Failure to account for the evolution of this Native New World elevates the Eu-ropean fantasy of discovery to the level of history, making the North Amer-ican continent into an empty wilderness populated by indigenous peoples fated to disappear rather than enter the modern world.

Modern North America was shaped by the clash and ultimately the coex-istence and parallel development of the Atlantic World and the Native New World. Complex and shifting alliance and exchange relationships connected autonomous Native social formations from this territory in the west to Euro-peans, and European-allied Indians in the east. But these relationships were fluid and often volatile. Anishinaabe peoples, identified in a variety of ways by the French—as Sauteurs, Ottawas, Nipissing, Mississauga, Amikwas, Po-tawatomie, or Gens des Terres, for example—were longtime trading partners and allies of New France. The Dakota peoples identified as Sioux Indians by the French were neither, but their territory in the upper Mississippi valley was crucial to the French fur trade. There were no permanent French posts in this region until the eighteenth century, and those were tenuous and short-lived establishments. For the most part only unlicensed French traders, the coureurs du bois, carried goods to the Dakota.[5] The Anishinaabeg lived in summer villages in the central and western Great Lakes, but they migrated seasonally into the Mississippi valley and northern boreal forest to hunt and trade. This pattern of seasonal migration overlapped and was amplified by the migration of displaced Native peoples from the east into the western margins of the Great Lakes beginning in the middle of the seventeenth century. They came as refugees seeking relief from Haudenosaunee raiders, the expansion of European settler colonies, and epidemic disease; and, they came in search of prime winter coat beaver. As the refugees and the fur trade moved into the west, the Dakota, the Anishinaabeg, and the French found themselves entangled in a web of relationships that turned increasingly violent. The story of this violence was the story of the overlap and collision of the Atlantic and Native social worlds that made up the New World in North America.

The birth pangs that went into the fashioning of this New World were famously destructive and constructive. Native America, at times and in places, seemed on the verge of obliteration. Europeans freed of the constraints and traditions of the Old World reinvented themselves on a new continent. Too often, however, these standard tropes of early American history overlook the extent to which Native peoples survived this process of mutual discovery and, like Europeans, imagined themselves and their world anew. Not all Native peoples were destined for tragedy just as not all European colonies were destined for success. The Anishinaabe and Dakota peoples entered modernity having successfully navigated this collision of epic proportions. For two centuries after the first settler colonies were established in North America it would have been self-evident to any observer, Native or newcomer, that the Anishinaabe and the Dakota peoples held their destiny in their own hands as free peoples. Both peoples held onto their land base until the second half of the nineteenth century, and both still maintain communities in these homelands. In the seventeenth century they not only exercised political control over their homelands but were also embarking on a process of western expansion. This process involved migration and social reinvention, would come to define who the Anishinaabeg and Dakota were as people, and guaranteed their autonomy into the era of nations and nationalism that would begin to transform the New World yet again at the end of the eighteenth century. Their story, like those of many people in the New World, would be shaped by violence as much as it was by ingenuity, and the courage to do new things, and dream in new ways. In the beginning this process would require the Anishinaabeg and Dakota to embrace new allies and attack old ones; and, to use violence to gain a measure of peace and prosperity in a dynamic but dangerous New World.

Worlds Collide

In 1681 a massive raiding party of eight hundred Anishinaabe and Dakota warriors, unified by a recent alliance, launched a devastating attack against a Mesquakie village allied to New France. They killed fifty-six men from this village, including the principal ogimaa. And although French records offer only indirect evidence, it seems that they carried away women and children as captives.[6] This attack struck at the heart of the relationship between New France and its Native allies in the west. The alliance imagined the governor of the colony as Onontio, the French father, and imagined the Native allies as his children. Constructing the alliance as a familial relationship placed both sides under obligation to meet their responsibilities to one another as members of a family. The French father was foremost charged with protecting his children. The Anishinaabe-Dakota attack revealed the limitations of the governor's protection and authority, and the military weakness of the French in the west. This weakness, and the violence that resulted from it, threatened to collapse the fur trade by destroying the social nexus that made the trade possible. In other words, this raid was not only a brutal assault against a vulnerable people but also struck at the very idea behind the French alliance system—that all of the peoples inhabiting the territory that the French called the pays d'en haut were bound together as kin, as the Native children of Onontio, the French father.

This attack, however, originated from outside of the physical space and social world of the French alliance. Anishinaabe warriors, identified as Sauteurs by the French, formed a war party with the Dakota and entered the pay d'en haut from the west.[7] They descended the Mississippi River moving along a known war road that connected refugee villages at Green Bay with the Native peoples of the western interior. From the Mississippi the warriors moved east following the Wisconsin River to its source, and then made the portage to the Fox River, which drained into Green Bay. Traveling from west to east the Dakota in particular faced great risk. They moved through enemy territory, and would have been forced to stop and carry their canoes overland at least a dozen times to avoid rapids, exposing their party to counterattack each time. The Anishinaabeg faced different risks. Traveling from territory they occupied jointly with the Dakota in the west, they returned to country that they identified as part of their homeland—Anishinaabewaki. Close allies such as the Boodewaadamiig (Pottawatomie) and Odawaag (Ottawa), Anishinaabe peoples with a shared language and social identity, were or had been residents of villages in the Green Bay region. They lived among the Mesquakie (Red Earth People), called the Fox by the French. The Mesquakie made their villages among closely related peoples known to the French as the Sauk, Kickapoos, and Mascoutens.[8] Widely intermarried and speaking dialects of the same Algonquian language, all of these closely related peoples, like the Anishinaabeg, were trading partners and allies of New France. Attacking the Mesquakie, who became enemies of the Dakota when they migrated to the west of Lake Michigan, the Anishinaabeg risked the enmity of Onontio and his children—many of whom were relations they had been tied to through ceremony, trade, and intermarriage since long before the arrival of Europeans. They risked becoming outcasts in a world defined by the status of inawemaagen (insider) and meyaagizid (outsider).

The Anishinaabeg may have counted on their relatives in Anishinaabe-waki to keep them safe from the consequences of their actions, but if this was the case it was a miscalculation. A Mesquakie war leader convinced thirty men to forgo their winter hunt and follow him into the west to avenge their losses. He led a party of Mesquakie survivors, joined by a small group of Western Abenaki warriors, refugees associated with the St. Francis mission in Lower Canada. They traveled up the war road and into the Dakota country. Their counterraid was a deadly success. They apparently destroyed an enemy band and carried away a dozen women and children as slaves, including the daughter of a prominent ogimaa from the village community at Shag-waamikong (La Pointe du Chequamegon).[9]

The captives would have been given to the grieving families among the Mesquakie. These families might adopt the slave, forcing that person to assume the place and persona of the deceased. This ritual process, called raising the dead among Algonquian peoples, was widespread throughout Native North America. It depended on a coercive socialization that rewarded the captive with kinship status in exchange for this social metamorphosis. Grieving families might also simply choose to incorporate captives into their families as slave labor. Then again, captives could be ritually tortured and killed to atone for the emotional pain and spiritual loss caused by the violent death of an important community member. The daughter of the Anishinaabe ogimaa, because of her social status, was marked for just such a death.[10]

The looming death of this Anishinaabe captive resulted from the reimagination of her social world. Her presence in the upper Mississippi valley represented a significant reconstitution of Anishinaabewaki as a social space. The people of her village at La Pointe du Chequamegon at the west end of Lake

Superior had forged an alliance with the people of Mde Wakan, or Sacred Lake, the principal village of the Dakota in the Mississippi headwaters region. The presence of Sauteur families in the upper Mississippi valley, hunting together with Dakota families, represented something more than economic cooperation. This was nothing less than a reconstitution of family.

In this sense, the capture and fate of this young Anishinaabe woman told the story of that alliance. Her presence among the Dakota represented a turn away from the social world and obligations of the French alliance by the people of her village at La Pointe. The fact that the raiding party from Green Bay found Anishinaabe and Dakota people together at this time of year suggests that they had come together as single band to hunt during the winter months. These winter bands, composed of approximately seventy-five people, hunted as a single residential unit while game remained sufficient, and dissolved into lodge groups of three to five families when necessary.[11] The mobility and flexibility of the winter band enabled migratory hunters to maximize the seasonal harvest of resources without overtaxing the carrying capacity of the land. Separated from the extended kin of their village communities, however, band and lodge groups were vulnerable. When the Mesquakie attacked, small bands of Anishinaabe and Dakota peoples would have been hunting and trapping beaver in the marshlands and watersheds that connected the upper Mississippi valley to the west end of Lake Superior.[12] Some of these bands comprised both Dakota and Anishinaabe peoples, reflecting the kinship and alliance forged between their respective village communities. The existence of these multiethnic bands reflected a social innovation—a collective response or adaptation to the violence sweeping into the west following the establishment of settler colonies on the east coast, and the rapid expansion of the trading of furs for European manufactured commodities that connected the peoples of the coast and interior.[13] The story of this Anishinaabe girl, her capture in the Dakota country, and ultimately her redemption by a prominent French trader represented a moment when the Anishinaabeg, who moved between the Atlantic World and Native New World, began to withdraw from the colonial east to reinvent themselves in the indigenous west.

The conflict that enveloped the Anishinaabeg, Dakotas, and Mesquakies was not the mindless violence of uncivilized peoples, although this was often the explanation Europeans attributed to indigenous warfare. Instead, these raids reflected a struggle to determine the meaning and obligations of family, and the boundaries of kinship and social space in the Native New World. The French Empire expanded its influence into the territory it designated as the pays d'en haut by virtue of an alliance system that combined French diplomacy with Algonquian kinship rituals. For the alliance to work, however, it needed to operate on indigenous terms. That is, the allies needed to recognize one another as family, as inawemaagen. The French placed themselves at the head of this family by assuming the persona of Onontio, the French father. Their Native allies, in similar fashion, became the children of Onontio.[14] Constructing their alliance in this way, the allies created a social and political relationship based on the obligations that members of an extended family owed to one another.

The anthropologist Marshall Sahlins has characterized this sort of relationship as positive reciprocity, a situation in which allies were obligated to provide for the needs of their partners in the same way that they met the needs of the members of their extended family. This sort of relationship hinged on the peaceful exchange of staple commodities, ritual goods, and marriage partners. The French fur trade evolved to meet the needs of this relationship. In other words, trade relations between Onontio and his children functioned as something more than a mechanism for the exchange of material resources. Fur trade exchange mirrored the practice of gift giving that was central to ceremonies like the Feast of the Dead. The unequal exchange represented by the gift created obligation, and acceptance of a gift item signaled recognition of the need to repay this social debt. In this way, exchange served as a means of creating an ongoing social relationship, and as affirmation of an existing alliance.

This sort of reciprocity was not only for important rituals like the Feast of the Dead but also for council meetings, and even as an aspect of everyday life. Giving and receiving gifts at a formal council established boundaries and obligations between the participants. In similar fashion, peaceful exchange was part of the give-and-take of everyday life among members of an extended family. In both the formal setting of the council and the more intimate and mundane context of daily existence, exchange practices signaled the recognition of a mutual obligation to sustain the life and well-being of the community. In effect, ritual exchange made fur trade exchange possible by creating a social nexus that facilitated the peaceful transfer of goods and people between different social groups, across a jointly occupied territory.[15]

The fur trade was more than a mutually beneficial exchange process, it was a commitment to provide the material and social resources that made both life and alliance possible. In the context of the French alliance system, fur trade exchange provided Onontio and his children with the opportunity to establish a proper relationship with each other, as a father and his children. The rapid expansion of the fur trade, however, also resulted in conflict that frequently erupted in violence when the French failed to meet their obligations, either by trading too hard, by trading with enemies like the Sioux, or by failing to keep the peace among Onontio's children as they pursued separate interests to enhance or protect their respective village communities.

The Dakota remained outside the French alliance system, and therefore had no relationship with Onontio and his children, but the territory they occupied overlapped territory occupied by the Anishinaabeg. This jointly occupied territory was one of the most abundant sources of castor gras, the fat winter coat beaver coveted by French traders. The juxtaposition of new social formations, like the French Empire, and older social formations of the Native New World (the Dakota, the Anishinaabeg) meant that exchange relationships in this region were volatile. The Anishinaabeg, seeing all spiritually animate beings as potentially connected, readily embraced opportunities to forge relationships with new peoples and places, accepting that they might be transformed in the process. Creating relationships with other beings (human or other-than-human) could be a source of new power as well as a cause of metamorphosis. It also meant that shape-shifters like the Anishinaabeg who moved easily through the territory of these parallel social worlds might feel compelled to forge a cooperative relationship with the Dakota when their interests merged.[16]

The rapid economic transformations and massive social dislocations that accompanied the emergence and evolution of the New World made this capacity to adapt socially and culturally to new peoples and new ways of being a necessity for survival. Both the Anishinaabeg and the Dakota moved through the marshy terrain that connected the Mississippi River valley and Lake Superior in search of beaver that provided a valuable seasonal resource base. The use value of this animal increased exponentially during the course of the seventeenth and eighteenth centuries as Europeans scrambled to exchange life-changing trade goods for the processed skins of beavers. Hunting these creatures in winter, however, remained a small-scale operation. Thus it was at the band level, in small winter camps in the swampy interior west of the Great Lakes, that the Anishinaabeg and the Dakota forged an alliance. One Anishinaabe ogimaa instrumental in negotiating this peace described the process as a "rebirthing."[17] This rebirth allowed the Anishinaabeg and the Dakota to act collectively as a newly reconfigured social formation—hunting a jointly occupied territory; exchanging food, trade goods, and marriage partners peacefully; and fighting together to avenge and defend one another as inawemaagen.[18]

The Anishinaabe-Dakota alliance was a dangerous development for the French Empire in North America. In creating this relationship the Anishinaabeg effectively turned away from their French father. By attacking the Mesquakie they signaled that they valued cooperation with the Dakota more then they valued their relationship with the French. Onontio, as the embodiment of the French Empire, demanded that all of his children recognize one another as allies—as family living peacefully together and providing for one another's needs. He also demanded that they act collectively in pursuing the fur trade and defending the alliance that made trade possible. The manidoo of Onontio, and the survival of New France as a colony, depended on the capacity of the agents of empire (the governor, licensed traders, military officers, Jesuit missionaries, etc.) to hold their Native children together in an alliance. Far more so than in the case of their English rivals, the success of Canada as a settler colony depended on diplomacy and the forging of mutually beneficial political relationships with Native peoples. This was both the genius, and the Achilles heel, of New France as an Atlantic World colony.

The rebirth of the Anishinaabe and Dakota peoples as allies was dangerous precisely because it was not part of the imagined world created by the French Empire and alliance system. It was instead an example of indigenous people reinventing their identity as part of a Native New World. This social-political transformation, in turn, underscored the contingent nature of the French Empire in the Great Lakes. Without their Native allies the French Empire did not exist beyond the transportation corridor where the Saint Lawrence River valley connected to the Atlantic Ocean. If the children of Onontio shape-shifted, becoming people of the western interior rather than children of empire, the French would lose everything—their Indian allies, access to beaver peltry, their claims to the west.

The Middle Ground

The French alliance required the ritual performance of social identities that allowed colonists and Native peoples to identify one another as inawemaagen, that is, as kin. In this way, social identities attached to the alliance were embodied. They were lived relationships connecting people to one another as members of a community, in this case, imagined as an extended family. The fur trade facilitated this process because it provided a way for Onontio and his children to establish proper relations with one another. Exchanging peltry for goods of European manufacture, the French and their Native allies practiced reciprocity. Thus, in Algonquian fashion, alliance not only represented the creation of an imagined community but also represented the means by which that community kept itself alive.

In other words, the social relations of production for Native communities engaged in the fur trade literally produced the social world of the French alliance system. Richard White, as noted earlier, has described this social world as the middle ground. This evocative designation described a process where Natives and European immigrants were forced to fashion a "mutually comprehensible world." This was the place, he wrote, where "the boundaries of the Algonquian and French worlds melted at the edges and merged." This merger of French and Indian categories of meaning, and ways of knowing the world, produced a new hybrid space—a middle ground between the Atlantic World empire of New France and the Native New World.[19]

White described the middle ground as a process of mutual invention where French and Native allies attempted to adapt the cultural forms of their partners to their own purposes. This was something more than a process of mutual accommodation. According to White's formulation the middle ground was created during the course of formal ritual encounter, and through the daily lived experience of the fur trade when French and Native peoples figured out how to solve the problems that came from their need to live with one another. Attempting to borrow the cultural logic of the Other in order to justify a belief, action, or expectation, Onontio and his children often ended up creating entirely new cultural constructs.[20] In this fashion, the mixing and frequent (mis) interpreting of cultural forms and practices that made the alliance work had the effect of creating a hybrid space bridging the Atlantic and Native New Worlds.

The middle ground brought the French Empire into the pays d'en haut by transforming Anishinaabewaki into a place where the French and their Native allies recognized one another as Onontio and his children. The social world of the alliance, however, was circumscribed by the relationships and identities that brought it to life. Just as these lived relationships created an embodied social identity, they also created an embodied social space. If the alliance fell apart, the French Empire in the western interior came apart as well. And so when Anishinaabe people like the Sauteurs joined western Indians like the Sioux to strike at the Fox, it was a threat to the entire French alliance system.

Violence in the west, however, presented the French with a paradox. It revealed the weakness of Onontio in the upper country, but it also provided Native peoples with a key rationale for allying with New France. The French used conflict opportunistically to forge a relationship with Native peoples in the western interior. Violent conflict with the Dakota, like the war against the Iroquois, presented the French and their allies with a shared problem—an enemy they could not defeat on their own. Stepping onto the middle ground as Onontio and his children, the French and their Native trading partners were able to shift the balance of power in their favor. They fought their enemies as a unified social formation rather than as isolated village units comprising bands that might choose to migrate to avoid conflict instead of fighting a formidable enemy. This was what made the Anishinaabe-Dakota alliance in 1681 so potentially devastating. Up to this point the children of Onontio had created periods of temporary truce with the Dakota, but not lasting peace. As long as the Dakota remained na-towe-ssiwak, foreign people, and not in-awemaagen their relationship with the Anishinaabeg and other Algonquian peoples would be defined by episodes of violence that characterized relationships with outsiders. It was this history of violence, in fact, that allowed the French and the Anishinaabeg to forge a middle ground and inhabit the social personae of Onontio and his children. Violence, in short, allowed the French to extend the influence of their empire into the west.

Warfare with the Dakota helped the Jesuits consolidate their missions among the Anishinaabeg. When violence erupted between the Odawaag and the Dakota in 1670 the Jesuits abandoned mission Saint Esprit at La Pointe du Chequamegon (or Shagwaamikong). They retreated to Sault Sainte Marie and formed a new mission, using the conflict in the west to establish a more cohesive social identity among the doodemag of the Anishinaabeg as children of Onontio. "The war that all of these peoples have with the Nadouessi," they wrote in *The Relation of 1672–73*, "has obliged them to leave Lake Superior and to come settle on Lake Huron where the peace they have with the Iroquois makes them a refuge against their new enemy." The Jesuits described this migration as an act of God—"Divine providence seeming to want them to gather thus almost in the same place and render them less wandering in order to make it easier for the missionaries to go find them to show them the path to heaven."[21]

The Jesuit Gabriel Dreuillettes wrote about the growth of Christianity at the Sault Sainte Marie mission, but what he really described was Anishinaabe people adapting the cultural practices of the French to their own interest.

When the Jesuits came to this village they built a fortified church, and the doodemag that converged at this location seasonally chose to settle next to the French building because they feared an attack from the Dakota. This same fear caused them to shelter their families at the Jesuits' mission before they made their annual voyage to Montreal to trade. According to Dreuillettes, before the departure of the trade caravan he called the people together for religious instruction. At this time "one of their oldest Captains," a man named Iskouakite, covered with scars earned fighting the Dakota and the Haudenosaunee, rose to address the assembly. First, he noted that the priest had brought the women and children into the safety of their fortified church. Because of this kindness on the part of the Jesuits, he declared, "They are truly our fathers." And then he told the village: "These black robes . . . guard us and . . . give life to the Sault receiving our women and children at their house and by praying for us to JESUS, the God of war. Although the Nadouessi must come to attack us (as we have learned) we place all our confidence in the King of Heaven and the earth." Iskouakite then proclaimed that Jesus, the god of war, protected their young men when they traveled for trade or went to war, and cured them when they fell ill. He concluded by admonishing his people, "let no one be slow in going to The Prayer."[22]

The Anishinaabeg took prayer and the son of God and dragged them onto the middle ground. In Jesus they found a god of war—a grandfather with the manidoo to keep them safe. With the Jesuit missionaries they found the personification of the French father, beings that could intercede on their behalf, calling upon the manidoo of Jesus, and providing physical protection for the women and children of the village. The Jesuits, for their part, were perfectly willing to see this attempt to secure protection from the Dakota through the spiritual power of their mission as a "Divine providence" leading the Anishinaabeg onto the path to heaven.

The path to heaven apparently also included warriors who took Jesus with them on the warpath against their Dakota enemies. When the Odawaag arrived at the Sault on the heels of their conflict with the Dakotas at La Pointe, they gave presents to the elders of this village and to an individual that the Jesuits identified as the chief of the young men, a war leader. They asked the people of the falls to leave the mission and form a village with them. In response the war leader called a council. Addressing all of the Anishinaabe doodemag, he declared that "the enemy had killed one of their relatives." And then, he told the council, "it would be their honor to revenge this death." He asked, however, that the Odawaag join the community living at the mission.

They agreed and the war leader led a raiding party against the Dakota. Before they left he visited Father Dreuillettes at the church and informed the priest "that he acknowledged Jesus alone as the Master of War."[23]

Dreuillettes wrote about this council as part of a larger story about the response of the Anishinaabeg to creation and expansion of the Jesuit mission during a time of warfare with the Dakotas. In *The Relation of 1672-73* he framed this story by noting that "*Les Sauvages* had never been better disposed to receiving the gospel then they were at present."[24] This was not, however, the gospel of Jesus the son of God who accepted his own death so that the sins of humanity could be forgiven. Nor was this the Jesus who preached forgiveness at the Sermon on the Mount, telling his followers that if struck on the right cheek their response should be to offer the aggressor the left as well. This was an altogether different gospel, one forged on the middle ground. The Anishinaabeg seemed willing to accept Jesus as a savior who brought them bodily redemption, but not from a life of sin. The Jesus that the Anishinaabeg found at the Sault mission was Jesus, the Master of War, scourge to the Dakota.

The Jesuits celebrated the martial victories of this new Jesus, reimagined on the middle ground as the Master of War. *The Relation of 1672-73* included a section titled "Some Marvels that God made at Sault Sainte Marie." The missionaries noted that the Anishinaabeg needed to learn about God not only through instruction but also "by the sight of some effect beyond the usual course of nature."[25] The Jesuits recognized that their power, and the power of their God, needed to be recognizable to the Anishinaabeg. Accordingly, they celebrated victory against the Dakotas secured through the intercession of Jesus as proof of the will of God and "evidence of truth of the Gospel."[26] In making this claim, however, they took a Christian concept, the will of God, and made it resemble manidoo—the ability to cause "some effect beyond the usual course of nature."

In 1672 the self-evident truth (or manidoo) of the gospel came to the Sault in the form of yet another successful raid against the Dakota. A party of Zhiishigwe (Rattlesnake) warriors came to the Sault from the region northwest of Gichigamiing (Lake Superior) that the French called lac des Bois or Lake of the Woods.[27] The people of this Anishinaabe doodem, often identified as Gens des Terres but here identified as people of the Sault, had come to the mission seeking religious instruction. The Jesuits counted the outcome of this visit as one of the "marvels made by God" in the Native New World: "A Band of Chichigoueks, composed of ten or twelve warriors, had taken care to go and be instructed at the Sault and to ask the blessing of the God of Armies before leaving to go to war against their nadouessi enemy; God so blessed their undertaking that after embarking in three canoes they not only took thirteen enemy scalps, they brought away two little girls as captives."[28] The warriors were ambushed on their return but escaped injury and returned to the mission at Sault Sainte Marie. Their families, overjoyed at their success and safe return, brought the captives to the missionaries for religious instruction. Thirteen people dead and scalped. Two children enslaved. Marvels made by God.

The ogimaa of the Zhiishigwe told the missionary Gabriel Dreuillettes that he knew the "marvelous effect" of prayer. This man, Gaa mii Chi ziidid (the One with Many Toes), told the Jesuit that he no longer acknowledged the manidoo of dreams as a source of revelation—a common belief among the Anishinaabeg. But he also told the priest that the previous winter he offered the heads of all of the animals he killed to "the great Spirit, the master of men and the master of war." He declared that it was this new god of war who had revealed to him the location of the Dakota, making their victory possible.

Gaa mii Chi ziidid was perfectly willing to accept divine revelation in place of dreams as the source of manidoo that delivered him from his enemies.[29] Dreuillettes was perfectly willing to count the sacrifice of animal heads as prayer, and victory against the Dakota as evidence of the truth of the gospel. It was exactly this sort of manipulation of the cultural forms of the Other that brought the middle ground into existence. Gaa mii Chi ziidid and Dreuillettes found a way to communicate with one another about manidoo, spiritual power of the Christian God and his son Jesus, and how these things worked in the world. As a result, the community at Sault Sainte Marie was revitalized and unified during a time of war. This was the middle ground created by the alliance between the French Empire and the peoples who inhabited the villages of Anishinaabewaki—a world of shared meaning created by the misappropriation of the Other's cultural categories and practices. Neither could simply dismiss the Other as a signifier for all that was good, bad, or missing in themselves, but instead had to find a way to interact with the seemingly alien beings who had become a very real presence in their lives. Everyone was searching for a way to turn outsiders into insiders.

The problem with the middle ground, however, was that it did not produce a permanent, material, expansion of the French Empire. It did not function as an extension of the Canadian settler colony. Rather, the middle ground was the culmination of social practices that drew from the hybrid cultural logic of the alliance. It functioned as a shared understanding of how the world ought to work, allowing French colonists and Native peoples to imagine themselves in a relationship defined by their kinship to one another. When Onontio and his children could not make the Other meet their expectations, that shared understanding of the world diverged, and the middle ground ceased to exist.

The Hudson's Bay Company and the Autonomy of the Indigenous West

While Jesuit missionaries mastered the intricacies of ritual, ceremony, and meaning making that structured the social world created by New France and its Native allies, the fur trade brought this world to life. French voyageurs delivered trade goods into the west, facilitating an exchange process that amplified the ability of the Anishinaabe doodemag to form large cosmopolitan lakeshore communities. These villages incorporated bands and territory from throughout the northwest interior, providing people from remote regions access to the manidoo of the Atlantic World. At the same time, a shared village identity expanded kinship connections, leading to increased possibilities for hunting and trading in the hinterlands of Anishinaabewaki, where winter coat beaver was most abundant. The diplomacy, rituals, and exchange practices that bound these village communities together easily incorporated French traders. In this way, the social relations of production that sustained both the French Empire and its Native trading partners fostered interdependence. This, in turn, resulted in the creation of the middle ground, the social nexus that linked the colonists of New France and the peoples of Anishinaabewaki together as Onontio and his children.

The establishment of the Hudson's Bay Company, however, brought instability to the French alliance system. The possibility of increased access to English trade goods created a dynamic push and pull that resulted in a continual rearrangement of the social relations of production among the Native groups that hunted and traded in the west. Anishinaabe doodemag from the interior continually changed the ways that they connected to one another, shifting labor, resources, and allegiance to adjust to changes in game populations or new trade opportunities. Direct access to European trade goods at the seacoast expanded the possibilities that came with this sort of social mobility. Anthropologist Patricia Albers has argued that it was possible for distinct populations of Native peoples to be integrated within a regional political economy that allowed them to move between cycles of symbiosis, merger, and war. This process, she argued, utilized "exchange mechanisms to adjust labor and resources in a jointly held territorial space." Groups moved either toward warfare and raiding or various merger relationships that involved temporary periods of shared resources, labor, and identity.[30]

The French alliance system, in contrast, depended on the creation of stable social relationships characterized by the ongoing sense of mutual obligation that family members shared with one another. The presence of English traders to the north meant that at least some Anishinaabe bands could chose to maintain their independence from the French without sacrificing their access to the manidoo of the Atlantic World. In 1673 the Jesuits at Sault Sainte Marie wrote to the governor of New France warning that the English presence at Hudson's Bay "will cause a notable prejudice to the Colony." In fact, the missionaries feared that trade with the English would cause the alliance to unravel in spite of St. Lusson's ceremony, and in spite of the fact that French traders now lived permanently at the Sault and at other regional villages. "The English," they wrote, "have already diverted a great many of the inland savages [sauvages des terres] who have come to Lake Superior, and drawn them to themselves by their great liberality."[31] The Jesuits who brought the voice of Onontio into the Native New World, who gave "life to the Sault" by bringing Jesus the god of war to Anishinaabewaki, reported with trepidation that "some of the savages of this region have seen inland savages during the winter who made their trade last autumn with des groseilliers and the English."[32]

In other words, the Hudson's Bay Company had capitalized on the experience of a disaffected French trader to build their own exchange network reaching into the Native New World. Did the establishment of English posts at the bay signal the emergence of an English father to rival Onontio? The Jesuits learned that Des Groseilliers planned to hold "a grand council with all the nations that are their neighbors." According to the Jesuits the doodemaag that gathered at the Sault Sainte Marie mission praised the generosity of these new English traders. And yet they claimed that at least some were unsettled by this potential realignment of social relationships in the interior. The Jesuits at the Sault informed the governor that "all of this news upset the savages who are fond of us." They enjoyed the peace won by "the victorious arms of the King," and "the protection of heaven that Christianity begins to bring them, they are in some apprehension that all of this not be disturbed by these revolutions." The Jesuits promised the governor they would work to keep the people of the Sault united among themselves, and united with God and the French.[33] But they feared revolution—a change in the relationships

that brought their Native allies together on the middle ground as children of
Onontio.

The Jesuits were not witnessing revolution, but they were correct in recognizing a readjustment of the exchange mechanisms that shaped social relations and situated identity in the Native New World. The English witnessed
this realignment firsthand, and the journal kept by the governor of the newly
established Hudson's Bay Company post revealed the social and spatial limitations of European power in the western interior. The English traders, like
the French Jesuits, saw the generosity of their imperial rivals as the chief im-
pediment to their success. But that excessive generosity really signified the
power of Native peoples to force the terms of trade in the west.

After establishing themselves at a location they identified as the Rupert
River, at the southern tip of the bay, the English spent a long winter low on
food supplies and with little contact from Native peoples. Toward the spring
a band identified as the "Cuscudidah Nation" made camp near their fortified
post in anticipation of the trading season. The leader of this doodem, identified as King Cuscudidah by the English, called on the governor. Apparently
he had little beaver peltry having "sent their best to Canada."[34] He came to the
fort, however, because he feared attack from French-allied Indians "whom
the French Jesuits animated against the English." According to the governor,
"the French us'd many Artifices to hinder Natives trading with the English;
they gave them great Rates for their Goods," and obliged company traders
to lower their prices in the hope of attracting "the Indians who dwelt about
Moose River, with whom they drove the greatest trade."[35]

The Hudson's Bay Company traders debated moving to the Moose River
watershed but, at least initially, felt too vulnerable to attack to leave their
post. The governor's journal, rewritten into narrative form and published as
a history of the discovery and settlement of Hudson's Bay, provides a rough
outline of cultural geography of the northwest interior. This document mirrored the Jesuits' descriptions of this region, but more clearly revealed the
social relationships that made hunting, trade, and travel possible. This was
not a world of French fathers and Indian children. Rather, it was a social
space formed by complex and shifting alliances among a multitude of autonomous Native peoples. Using vocabulary lists compiled by the governor's secretary, we can identify the "Cuscudidah Nation" that sought refuge
at the English post as the Attikamek, the self-designated Whitefish people
that the Jesuit Claude Albanel had encountered at Lake St. Jean.[36] This band
of Cree-speaking people, linguistically and socially tied to Cree-speaking

coastal dwellers, hunted the lowlands west of the watershed renamed the Rupert River by the English.

For the English the Cuscudidah represented a potential link in a chain of social relationships connecting Native peoples from the seacoast deep into the western interior. So even if King Cuscudidah had traded with the French, his apparent fear of Native peoples closely allied to New France signaled that he was only marginally attached to the French Empire. Unfortunately, however, the spring thaw that opened up the rivers that drained the interior brought only bad news for the English. The brother of King Cuscudidah arrived at their post and reported that "there would be few or no Upland Indians come to trade that season."[37] The French had built a post up the river from the English that intercepted Native traders heading for the coast. These Native traders, the "Upland Indians," were the people that the Jesuits identified as "sauvages des terres."

The sauvages des terres or "Upland Indians" came from the region to the north and northwest of Gichigamiing where castor gras or winter coat beaver was most abundant. These were the peoples most commonly identified as Gens Des Terres or inland peoples, but they also appeared in French records on occasion as Sauteurs. The people of the Zhiishiigwe or Rattlesnake doodem that originated in the territory northwest of Gichigamiing, for example, were described as residents of Sault Sainte Marie and part of a newly reconstituted Sauteur nation that St. Lusson claimed as subjects of the French king. For the English, in similar fashion, the designation *Upland Indians* functioned as a rather loose category that included the peoples living in the watersheds connecting the north shore of Lake Superior to the west coast of Hudson's Bay, but also included the Assiniboine and Cree peoples from the prairie parkland region to the north of the Great Plains.[38] Coming from hunting territories deep in the interior, these upland peoples were distinguished by their ability to forge ties with the peoples of the coastal lowlands of Hudson's Bay. Trade ties and social kinship brought bands together as part of a larger multiethnic social formation. The relative power of any particular band hinged on its status and position within the chain of relationships that made up this entity.

With a French post upriver from their own, the English and the Cuscudidah found themselves rather poorly positioned to take advantage of the inland trade. Consequently they were more vulnerable to violent exchange and less likely to be incorporated into an alliance relationship based on trade and mutual reciprocity. Only a single rather small upland band composed of fifty people and identified as "the Nation call'd Pishhapocanoes" visited the English post. The French identified this band by a Cree dialect term for seasonal migrants, *Papinachois*. In 1671, the Jesuit Claude Albanel reported that these people had traded with the Hudson's Bay Company and with the Attikamek when the English first appeared at Rupert River.[39] But this time the Papinachois, like the Cuscudidah, called on the English after having traded most of their peltry with the French.

Outmaneuvered by the French, the governor of the Hudson's Bay Company sent a ship to the Moosu Sepee, or Moose River, farther up the coast. Des Groseilliers, accompanied by "English Indians," presumably the Attikamek, traded for 250 skins with the Tabitee. This was a phonetic approximation of an Ojibwe designation signifying "Blue-Water people," used to identify Anishinaabe people who inhabited a lake and river system of the same name. Alternatively identified as Gens des Terres and Cree by the French, the Tabitee's watershed was a tributary of the Moosu Sepee.[40] The "Captain" of this band explained to Des Groseilliers that "the French Jesuits had not brib'd the Indians, not to deal with the English, but to live in Friendship with the Indian Nations in league with the French." More to the point, he blamed the English for "trading with such pitiful Nations as the Cuscudidahs and Pishhapocanoes." In other words, they had created a relationship with weak and ineffectual doodemag incapable of helping them to expand their trade. At the same time, the Tabitee captain chastised Des Groseilliers for exacerbating this problem by trading too hard. Finally, the captain advised the Hudson's Bay Company to establish a permanent post on the Moosu Sepee.[41]

This expedition to the Moosu Sepee, in fact, provided the English with trade ties to inland bands that had eluded them at Rupert River, where their operation was more easily disrupted by the French. Des Groseilliers and his associates acquired an additional 1,500 skins from the "Shechittawams" doodem at this new location. This term, *Shamattawa*, represented an Ojibwe dialect designation for "great river Junction," and was used by Hudson's Bay Company traders in reference to a people and a watershed above the Moosu Sepee, most likely a stretch of the soon to be renamed Albany River. After trading with the Shamattawa the English governor followed these people to their home territory to visit with "the King and his son." The governor promised, "to come with a ship and trade with them the next year." The "King" of the Shamattawa, in return, assured the governor "they would provide store of beaver and bring the Upland Indians down."[42]

Read together with French documents, this English text that supposedly describes the colonization of the Hudson's Bay region actually reveals the existence of an autonomous Native social world characterized by the seasonal movement of interdependent doodemag. These bands came together to form a larger multiethnic social formation. The constituent parts of this social formation moved between upland and lowland watersheds linking the western interior to the Great Lakes and the seacoast. This movement reflected a transregional political economy, a vast inland trading system, that connected culturally related peoples occupying overlapping territories. Given this reality, the production and distribution of resources involved both cooperation and competition as interdependent groups vied for power through the control of resources, territories, and trade.

From the English perspective the "kings" and "captains" of Indian nations ruled the western interior of North America. Whether trading at a place with an English name, like the Rupert River, or at the Moosu Sepee, Hudson Bay Company traders moved through a world controlled rather imperfectly by these leaders. The history of Hudson's Bay produced from company journals succinctly described this world: "The Indians of certain Districhs, which are bounded by such and such rivers, have each an Okimah, as they call him, or Captain over them, who is an Old man, consider'd only for his Prudence and Experience." These captains (ogimaag) possessed a limited authority based in large measure on their ability to negotiate advantageous exchange relationships. "He is the speech-maker to the English," but possessed "no authority but what they think fit to give him." The primary role of the ogimaa was diplomatic, not only in speaking to Europeans but in addressing "their own grave debates, when they meet every Spring and Fall, to settle the Disposition of their Quarters for Hunting, Fowling and Fishing."[43] The English described these annual councils as the seasonal adjustment of family boundaries, that is, the negotiation of social distance or kinship ties that could establish conditions leading to either confrontation or cooperation among bands occupying overlapping territories.

The western interior described in this English historical narrative was part of the New World, but it was a Native New World and not part of any Atlantic empire. Like the middle ground, this was a social world created by a political imaginary that envisioned community formation to be the result of the relationships between the members of an extended family. Unlike the middle ground, however, the inhabitants of this social world were not seeking a beneficially dependent relationship with powerful outsiders. In other words, this was not a world of European fathers and Indian children. But then neither was this space the domain of Indian nations and their kings that the English imagined they had discovered, claimed, and colonized. This was instead a world of ogimaag and doodemag, of meyaagizid and inawemaagen. This was a world created by formal rituals like the Feast of the Dead, and by the ritualized meaning attached to the everyday exchanges that made the inland trade work.

The indigenous social formations that forged this New World utilized contact with, alliance to, and the material artifacts of the Atlantic World to shape political and social power and identity while they continued to adapt, alter, and inhabit indigenous categories of being. This world, shaped by indigenous social categories and cultural meaning, lies encoded in narratives written by English traders and French missionaries who set out to write the history of their encounter with the peoples of a new continent. These histories, in spite of their intentions, reveal that the real source of power in the western interior of North America was not empire or even the larger Atlantic World, but rather a Native political imaginary that determined the meanings attached to space, place, and collective and individual identity.

Recognizing and historicizing the emergence of this distinctly Native New World underscores the centrality of Native peoples in the evolution of the emergent world system that came to define the early modern era. The ogimaag were not kings presiding over nomadic Indian nations. They were instead more like diplomats or political mediators, men who used their personal influence to navigate a complex, polyglot world where leaders balanced the interests of hunters, traders, warriors, and families of their own communities with those from the Great Plains, the Great Lakes, the Atlantic coast, and western Europe. Anishinaabewaki, as a social space, was created by the relationships between the peoples living within a shared resource base. Negotiating the boundaries of this community could be contentious, even violent, because the stakes were life and death: to be accepted among the people, inawemaagen, and part of a self-sustaining community with mutual rights and responsibilities, or to be outside, meyaagizid, and cut off from that shared world.

Massacre at Sault Sainte Marie

Violent encounter was perhaps as integral to the inland trade as peaceful exchange. Raiding, after all, worked like trading to foster the circulation of people and things, and could open or close social distance between people in jointly occupied or overlapping territories. The English at Hudson's Bay generally found that violence curtailed the total volume of their trade. The French, in contrast, found that violence played a more complex role in structuring their relationships with Native peoples. Inland posts and missions sometimes allowed the French to manipulate conflict to the advantage of their empire. They used warfare with the Haudenosaunee and the Dakota to unify and even expand their alliance system. Incorporating violence into the social relations of the alliance, however, posed a risk. Armed conflict brought chaos and disruption that all too easily spiraled out of control. If not managed properly from a ritual perspective, violence could bring an end to the shared meanings that allowed French-allied Indians to see themselves as children of Onontio.

For practical purposes such as diplomacy and the fur trade, the social world of the French alliance system, the middle ground, had physical boundaries. It existed in the places where the rituals of the alliance occurred—in the cities of Canada, and more tenuously in the principal villages of Anishinaabewaki, which the French thought of as the pays d'en haut. A combination of formal ceremony and fur trade exchange structured the social relationships that brought the middle ground into existence. The alliance extended into the pays d'en haut so long as these practices worked to transform the Native allies of New France into the children of Onontio. Even after the French and their Native allies created this new hybrid social space, however, a distinct and autonomous Native New World continued to evolve in the northwest interior.

In other words, the fluid nature of social formations in the western interior, moving constantly between merger and warfare, created a multilayered social space. Europeans found it difficult to read this cultural geography, as the form and function of social identity did not directly correspond to their own social structures and cultural categories. Watersheds like the Moosu Sepee that drained into Hudson's Bay served, like Bow-e-ting, as seasonal gathering points that were essential to the inland trade. The seasonal communities that formed at these locales were essential to the lived relationships that made up Anishinaabewaki as a social space. Even as these places acquired European names—like Moose River, Sault Sainte Marie, and the pays d'en haut—and connections to European empires through the French and English fur trade, they continued to be part of the Native New World. In effect, the middle ground allowed the French to enter the Native New World, or at least a hybrid version of this space where the overlapping territories and influence of Anishinaabewaki and the Atlantic World came together.[44]

It is important to remember that the sort of cultural appropriation that made the middle ground possible worked both ways. Like watersheds that acquired European names, trading posts and mission houses could be incorporated into the cultural and political landscape of the indigenous west. In 1674 Anishinaabe bands that hunted in the west attempted to use the manidoo of the French alliance to bring peace to their contentious relationship with the Dakota. Just as they earlier called on the Jesuits to invoke the power of Jesus as the Master of War when raiding against the Dakota, they now asked the missionaries to intercede once again in a matter involving warfare with their enemies in the west. Anishinaabe warriors captured and enslaved an entire Dakota band in the upper Mississippi valley, and removed them to Sault Sainte Marie. They brought them to the Jesuit house not to celebrate this victory, or to seek their conversion as an act of thanksgiving. They came instead to ask the Jesuits to help them transform this act of war into a peace offering. Word was sent to the Dakota. Send ambassadors to the Sault, and their people would be redeemed in exchange for an end to the warfare between the Dakota and the Anishinaabeg. They would come together in the Jesuit house at the falls, a signal that the French would act as guarantors of this new peace.

The Dakota sent ten of their most renowned warriors to negotiate with the Anishinaabeg through Jesuit intermediaries at Sault Sainte Marie. *The Relation of 1674*, which contains a written account of this visit, described the Dakota as enemies of the children of Onontio: "The nadouessi nation extremely numerous and warlike was the enemy of all the savages who are included under the name of outaouac or upper algonquines." The Jesuits also noted that the Dakota had pushed into territory to their north "making war on the Kilistinons [Cree] who live there." According to the Jesuits, the Dakota were fierce warriors known for carrying stone knives into battle.[45] This detail suggests that the large Dakota population west of Gichigamiing continued to have only limited access to European trade goods. It also suggests why these warriors were willing to undertake so hazardous a journey. In redeeming their people through Jesuit mediation at one of the principal villages of the Anishinaabeg they would gain access to the middle ground, the social world created by the French alliance. Peace with the People of the Falls represented alliance with the children of Onontio, and access to iron weapons.

The village at Sault Sainte Marie, however, was not united when it came to creating an alliance with the Dakota. According to the Jesuits, Cree and Mississauga warriors came to the village after learning about the captives, and they "not only expressed their dissatisfaction but also prayed resolutely to prevent the peace from being concluded." Nevertheless, the Jesuits wrote that the Dakota delegation was "received with joy" by everyone else at the Sault.[46] All of the people of the village gathered at the French house, both "the ones for concluding peace with the nadouessi, and the others to prevent that it be concluded." An effort was made to disarm everyone who entered the mission to attend the peace council, but several Cree managed to conceal their knives. Once inside one of these warriors confronted the Dakota. Drawing his weapon he approached a Dakota warrior, blade in hand, and said, "You are afraid," while threatening to strike him. According to the Jesuits, "the nadouessi without being astonished told him in a fierce tone and an assured expression 'if you believe that I tremble strike straight at the heart.'" In response to this defiance, the Cree man plunged his knife into the breast of the Dakota warrior. Struck with a fatal blow, this man, the Jesuits wrote, "cried out to those of his nation, 'we are being killed my brothers.'"[47]

The Jesuit mission erupted in a scene of chaos and death captured in writing by the missionaries. Believing themselves betrayed, the Dakota, who had retained their weapons, "arose and struck with their knives at all the assembled savages without making a distinction between the Kilistinons and the sauteurs thinking that they had all equally conspired with the intention of assassinating them." The people of the Sault had entered the mission unarmed, confident in their power to control the council. They paid a heavy price for their confidence. According to the Jesuits, the Dakota "made a great carnage in a short time." Their fierce counterattack killed several Anishinaabeg, including, presumably, at least some of the political leaders who would have been seated in close proximity to the Dakota delegation. They also managed to acquire guns, shot, and powder and to take over the mission. The Anishinaabeg piled birch bark canoes against the mission walls and set it on fire only to see the Dakota escape to another fortified building. Surrounded by an entire enemy village, the Dakota warriors fought to their deaths leaving behind forty Anishinaabeg dead and wounded in the process. In the end, only a single member of the Dakota delegation was left alive—a woman the Jesuits identified as a slave.[48]

The Jesuits noted the presence of this slave among the Dakota with only a passing reference to her survival. She was allowed to live because "she was of the Algonquine nation." They remained silent, however, about the details of her story. How and when did she become a slave? Was her arrival at Sault Sainte Marie a homecoming? Why did the Dakota bring her to this negotiation? The Jesuits' curious silence about this woman's personal story creates an important gap in their narrative history of this failed peace overture. Female captives frequently played important roles in such negotiations. Often they represented a point of mutual connection. This woman most likely spoke Dakota, and she may have served as a translator. As women were frequently incorporated into their captor's society, she may even have left family behind in the Dakota country, possibly a husband and his extended kin, or even children with bilingual skills and blood ties to both communities. At the very minimum, her life may have been a gift offered by the Dakota—a slave redeemed in exchange for the lives of so many Dakota slaves held captive by the Anishinaabeg at the Sault.[49]

The Jesuits failed to report the fate of the eighty Dakota slaves, another curious absence in their narrative account of this massacre. Instead, they concluded this story by focusing on the fate of their mission at Sault Sainte Marie. The missionaries, they wrote, "saw themselves abandoned by the Savages of the country, who in the fear that the nadoessis, seeing the delay of their people would suspect what happened to them and would want to take vengeance for their deaths, all moved away and left them exposed to the fury of their enemy."[50] The Anishinaabeg melted into the bush, most likely dissolving into doodemag (clans) and moving into their winter hunting territories. Presumably, the Dakota slaves were divided among the families of the Sault and adopted, enslaved for their labor, or traded for commodities among the Native and French traders circulating between the Atlantic coast and the interior.[51] Tragically ripped from their community, these people might someday make their way home like the Anishinaabe slave who traveled with the Dakota, as cultural brokers in a future attempt at making peace. Such a desperate hope, however, must have been overwhelmed by the bleakness and pain of the massacre and their enslavement.

The Jesuits managed to attach some ritual significance to the massacre for their European audience. The missionaries remained at the village site, abandoned by their allies. Their mission had been burned to the ground. They were implicated in the deaths of the entire Dakota delegation, and complicit in the enslavement of eighty people. Still, they wrote in *The Relation of 1674*, "God had not failed to derive his glory from these misfortunes." Several of the wounded asked for and received baptism. Souls claimed for God, a triumph in the face of tragedy.

This was not the sort of intercession the Anishinaabeg had hoped for when they asked the Dakota to join them on the middle ground. With a single reckless act of violence a Cree warrior transformed their bold peace overture into an act of hostility that demanded a bloody retaliation. Now, instead of building ties to the largest and most formidable social formation in the western interior, they would be seen as responsible for a brutal attack against them. The Cree managed to translate ritual violence designed to facilitate reconciliation into betrayal and overt hostility. They made certain that the Dakota remained alienated from the French and from their Native allies at Bow-e-ting. From the Jesuits' description it is impossible to know exactly which Cree band sabotaged the peace council. The suggestion that the Dakota had moved into the region to the north of their own country to attack the Cree, however, suggests the possibility that these were the people identified as Upland Indians by the English at Hudson's Bay. The people from this region would also be the most likely to see a Dakota-Anishinaabe alliance as something that compromised their position in the inland trade.

An Anishinaabe-Dakota Alliance

In the winter of 1678 a prominent Anishinaabe ogimaa named Oumamens (Waamamins/ the White Berry) made his way to the Jesuit mission at Sault Sainte Marie. This man was from the Amikwas or Beaver doodem that occupied a village site on the river below the mission. He would not have been a stranger at this village, called Bow-e-ting by the Anishinaabeg. This community formed seasonally along a stretch of rapids that needed to be portaged when traveling the river connecting Lake Superior and Lake Huron. Anyone entering or leaving the territory that the French described as the pays d'en haut passed through this village. Oumamens, like many Anishinaabe people, would have periodically taken up residence at this community for trade, for ceremonies, and to take advantage of its abundant fishery.

When he arrived at the Sault Sainte Marie mission in 1678 he came as an emissary for the Anishinaabeg at Shagwaamikong. Oumamens approached the resident missionary, asking this man to accompany him on a journey to the region west of Gichigamiing to serve as a mediator at a peace council between the Dakota and the Anishinaabeg. "The Saulteurs who went to the bottom of the Lake," Oumamens explained, "turned to him so that by his intervention he could compel some French to join them, under the belief they have that the peace made between them, would be more strong, supported by their presence." The missionary, father Baloquet, asked for time to consider his response. Surely, he knew of the Jesuits' role in the massacre at the Sault mission four years earlier, and of their complicity in encouraging

raiding parties against the Dakota. After a day of reflection Baloquet told
Oumamens that he could not help him. The priest told the ogimaa that "he
did not know if it was the will of Onontio that the Saulteurs make peace with
the Nadouesioux."[52]

Fortunately for Oumamens, a French military officer named Daniel
Greysolon le Sieur Du Lhut arrived at Sault Sainte Marie intent on launch-
ing an unlicensed trade expedition into the west. Oumamens began to ask
questions about the French officer and his interest in the Dakota country.
When Du Lhut heard about these enquiries he arranged a meeting with the
Amikwas ogimaa. He, in turn, asked the ogimaa to explain his interest in
the Dakota. Oumamens explained the purpose of his journey to the Sault.
Perhaps feeling defensive after the Jesuit rejected his request for assistance,
Oumamens further explained that he had not known that their French father
wanted the Anishinaabeg to continue the war against the Dakota.

Du Lhut assured Oumamens that he was mistaken. In a letter to the governor describing this meeting Du Lhut explained that "far from finding it bad
that the Saulteurs and the Nadouessioux make peace, on the contrary they
would not know how to make you a greater pleasure." He then promised to
leave in the fall with between eight and ten French men to winter in the Dakota country and work for peace. In response, Du Lhut wrote, "at this point
Oumamens did not have any more doubts that I would make the voyage,
and said that the Saulteurs would have an unconceivable joy." Now certain
that he had secured French mediation, Oumamens proclaimed that he "was
born again for giving life to both the Saulteurs and the Nadouesioux." Locked
in a violent struggle for the past decade, the Anishinaabeg and Dakota suffered a kind of social death. By securing a clear pathway to peace, Oumamens brought both peoples back to life, and in the process would be reborn
himself.[53]

After expressing joy and a sense of rebirth at the thought of French mediation, however, Oumamens suddenly fell silent. In his letter to the governor
DuLhut interpreted this silence as reticence. He asked the ogimaa if he worried about the Huron. They had recently sent a large war party from Michilimackinac into the Dakota country. Oumamens responded succinctly, "If
the Huron caused the least trouble, the Saultuers would kill them." Then he
fell silent again. Du Lhut took this as a sign that the meeting was concluded,
but before he could take his leave Oumamens spoke again: "He told me that
he saw something threatening, this was the people of the North, who, not
knowing this and being at war with the Nadouesioux, would be an obstacle to

my enterprise."[54] Du Lhut reassured Oumamens that he would send a French party to the north to tell the Assiniboin "and other nations of this side" about the peace, and to warn them "to be careful of what they do, since they could not kill the Nadouesioux without killing us." According to Du Lhut, the ogimaa told him "that this was the only choice I could take."[55]

In a remarkable turn of events both men agreed that the French needed to create an alliance with the Dakota. Because alliance created ties of kinship, killing a Dakota would become an act of violence against the French. Du Lhut, without authority, motivated by greed, promised to transform these enemies of the alliance into children of Onontio. He knew that in opening a secure trade relationship with the Dakota he would gain access to the only true source of wealth in French Canada—prime winter coat beaver. He also counted on the governor, Louis de Baude le Comte de Frontenac, sharing his interest and his motivation. Du Lhut's gamble paid off. He formed a partnership with the governor and eventually secured a license as a trader, much to the consternation of the intendant, Jacques Du Chesneau, the chief financial officer for the colony.

Unlicensed French traders, in fact, would become an increasing problem in the French relationship with Native peoples in the west. Operating outside of the control of colonial authorities, coureurs de bois destabilized the alliance system by creating social relationships with peoples who were the enemies of their allies. From the perspective of most French-allied Indians, bringing trade goods to the Dakota, especially weapons, increased the power of an already fierce enemy. These unlicensed traders also diverted peltry to the English in Albany. Du Chesneau complained to the court of Louis XIV that "everybody boldly contravenes the King's interdictions." The governor, he asserted, conspired with the coureurs de bois, who no longer even bothered to hide their trading voyages to the west. All attempts to block this trade, he argued, "have been in vain in as much as several of the most considerable families in this country are interested therein, so the Governor lets them go, and even shares in their profits."[56] In a subsequent letter Du Chesneau complained that the widely known "intrigue" between Frontenac and Du Lhut created disorder and "filled the woods with coureurs and vagabonds to the number of eight hundred."[57]

Frontenac responded to the accusations of the intendant by claiming that his actions prevented illegal traders in the west from taking their commerce to the English. In 1673 Frontenac established a French post at Catarcoui on Lake Ontario, ostensibly to stop coureurs de bois from carrying their furs to Albany. It was generally understood in New France, however, that Fort Frontenac at Catarcoui was established to mask the governor's illegal trading in the west.[58] In 1675 the governor sent his engineer from this post, Hugues Randin, to Sault Sainte Marie. Randin brought gifts from Onontio that were meant to signal his desire to open trade with the Dakota. Arriving in the aftermath of the massacre, however, he apparently failed in this endeavor. When Du Chesneau complained about the disorder created by the governor's illicit trade activities and collusion with the coureur de bois, Frontenac sent a response to the minister responsible for the overseas colonies of France asserting that, on the contrary, "one named du Lut . . . had established some sort of order and discipline there, and under the pretext of what I had begun three years ago by le Sieur Randin when I sent him to the Nadouesioux, rendered a considerable service to the colony." Du Lhut, he reported, had placed himself in a position "to make peace of all the Outaouiaise nations with those of Lake Superior, and of the west, where at present is the source of beaver."[59] In other words, Du Lhut had acted independently, but his actions served the best interest of the colony.

Du Lhut calculated correctly that if he made it easier for the French to gain access to "the source of beaver" he would win a pardon for his actions. In the spring he traveled with five coureurs de bois escorted by Oumamens, and a slave purchased as a guide, "to the bottom of Lake Superior, where the Saulteurs and the Nadouesioux were in fact meeting one another."[60] Du Lhut's description of this encounter and its outcome was vague and overly concise. He claimed that he was well received by the Dakota and brought to their village at Mde Wakan, called Mille Lacs by the French, located in the headwaters region of the Mississippi River valley. "July 2 1679," he later wrote, "I had the honor of planting the arms of his majesty in the grand village of the Nadouesioux, called Izatys."[61] As simple as that, Du Lhut claimed possession of the Dakota country for the king of France.

Du Lhut claimed that he mediated this peace because it represented the best interest of both the colony and the Native allies of New France, an assumption clearly shared by the governor. He described the Dakota as "the largest nation with the most people," and he declared "they will bring every year a considerable profit to the people of this region, when they live in peace." Du Lhut's letter to the governor explained that with peace established "they will hunt around the bottom of the lake." At present, he complained, "no one hunts there." According to Du Lhut fear of attack prevented both the Anishinaabeg and Dakota from harvesting and processing beaver peltry. "This place was," he wrote, "following the report of the savages, a nursery for beavers."[62] Du Lhut even lamented that while he gave gifts to create this new alliance, the Anishinaabeg and the Dakota could not properly reciprocate "since all of the beavers which are there are still alive."[63] In other words, the natural order in the country below Gichigamiing had been disrupted. No one hunted. Beaver dams choked the rivers and lakes, making them all but impassable. The people suffered, unable to secure the necessities of life. In this sense, peace, as Oumamens declared, represented a restoration of the natural order—a rebirth for both the Anishinaabeg and the Dakota.

Where Oumamens saw rebirth, and Du Lhut the prospect of making "considerable profit," others could see only political ruin, financial loss, and the threat of violence. Intendant Du Chesneau warned the king that the consequences of Du Lhut's intervention would be an expansion of illegal trading among the peoples of the western interior. René-Robert Cavelier de La Salle shared this concern. La Salle was a licensed trader operating out of Frontenac's post on Lake Ontario. He traded with the peoples of Green Bay and among the Illinois and Miami in the lower Mississippi River valley. La Salle complained that the coureurs de bois associated with Du Lhut "have been and returned several times into the settlements loaded with goods and pelts, they have exhausted Lake Superior which they have besieged from all avenues."[64]

From La Salle's perspective both Du Lhut and the Anishinaabeg sought a relationship with the Dakota in order to gain a commercial advantage in the fur trade. This, he believed, could only disadvantage his own operation. "The Sauteurs," according to La Salle, "are the savages who carry the most peltries to Montreal." And he complained that "the Nadouesiux, invited by presents . . . negotiated a peace to unite the nation of the Sauteurs with the French and to go to trade in the country of the Nadouesioux around sixty leagues west of Lake Superior."[65] La Salle also disputed Du Lhut's claim to have been the first European to discover the Dakota country, and even cast doubt on the assertion that he took formal possession of this territory. Moreover, he disparaged the value of this discovery, arguing that "the region is uninhabitable," consisting entirely of swamps and unnavigable rivers teeming with wild rice to the point of congestion. The only thing Du Lhut and the Sauteurs would accomplish, La Salle asserted, was the disruption of his existing trade network. "The King has awarded us the trade in buffalo hides," which he argued "would be ruined by the going and coming to the Nadouesioux."[66]

In La Salle's narration of this event Du Lhut hijacked a peace process where the Sioux were seduced by presents into opening their country to rogue traders and their Native henchmen, the Sauteurs. Du Lhut acted boldly and defiantly to enrich himself at the expense of the colony. He was a deserter who passed himself off as the envoy of the governor, "charged by his orders to negotiate this peace during which his comrades negotiated the better acquisition of beaver."[67] La Salle's narrative castigated Du Lhut as a coureur de bois, but it also reinforced the idea that the peace he helped to mediate was an expansion of the French alliance system.

Piecing together the story of the Anishinaabe-Dakota alliance from the correspondence of French traders, it is all too easy to adopt their perspective and forget the long and complex relationship between these two peoples. It is also easy to overlook the important role played by Native diplomats like Oumamens. Du Lhut, in fact, responded to an invitation to join an ongoing peace process initiated by Native peoples. "There were many talks with the Nadouesioux," according to La Salle, rather than the singular event described by Du Lhut that ended with him planting the king's coat of arms in an act of ritual possession. These talks were not held at the principal villages, but rather at smaller encampments in their winter hunting territory—in the marshes and rivers connecting the Mississippi River and Lake Superior—a landscape seasonally occupied by both peoples. Council sessions, according to La Salle, moved between these camps; "the Sauteurs had been to and come from among the Nadouesioux several times, and the Nadouesioux among the Sauteurs."[68] In effect, the Anishinaabeg and the Dakota passed the winter like relatives, living together in small winter camps. The French colonial official La Potherie reported that during this time, "they gave their daughters in marriage to one another," creating blood ties to augment the kinship of the alliance.[69] Living in peace, the Anishinaabeg and the Dakota undoubtedly began to hunt beaver for trade.

To describe the Anishinaabe-Dakota alliance in commercial terms, however, would be to misconstrue the social significance of this relationship. This description reflected La Salle's perspective as a licensed trader, motivated by a desire to make a profit. In similar fashion, it would be erroneous to accept the idea advanced by both men that Du Lhut had instigated and presided over a peace process that was effectively an extension of the French alliance system. Du Lhut had been brought into the peace process as a mediator, and as a representative of New France, but the Anishinaabe-Dakota alliance was not forged in the social world of the middle ground. This was instead a relationship necessitated by the political and social imperatives of the Native New World evolving in the western interior.[70]

For the Dakota, the Anishinaabe alliance was a matter of strategic necessity. Of course the Dakota sought secure access to trade goods, particularly
firearms and iron. As Du Chesneau's reports suggest, and as evidenced by
the testimony of La Salle and Du Lhut, traders poured into the west during this period. The expansion of the trade, however, brought instability and
increased competition for resources. When it came to buffalo, for example,
the hunting territories of people in the upper and lower Mississippi valley
overlapped. The Dakota's buffalo grounds on the tall grass prairies stretching west from the confluence of the Mississippi and Minnesota Rivers to the
lower Missouri River faced pressure from western peoples to the south such
as the Iowa, Omaha, and Osage, but also from the burgeoning population in
the Green Bay region where La Salle traded. The Dakota faced similar pressure from the north as the Cree, Assiniboine, and various "upland Indians"
armed by the English at Hudson's Bay pushed into the headwaters region of
the upper Mississippi. In short, the Dakota needed allies; this would be the
key to maintaining control of hunting territory, and securing access to trade
goods.[71]

Alliance with the Dakota was also a strategic necessity for the Anishinaabeg of Shagwaamikong. The country west of Gichigamiing was, as Du Lhut
described it, a nursery for beaver and the seasonal hunting grounds of both
the Anishinaabeg and the Dakota. The rapid expansion of the French and
English fur trades resulted in increased competition for the resources of this
region. A peaceful relationship between the Anishinaabeg and the Dakota
allowed for a coordinated defense of this hunting territory, and enough social
stability to resume the usual activities of their respective seasonal rounds. The
Anishinaabeg-Dakota alliance was, in effect, calculated to reduce violence
and restore stability to the social relations of production. In this sense, it was
much more than a simple commercial relationship; it was a strategic response
to the emergence and evolution of the Native New world.

The strategic thinking behind this alliance was a reflection of this social
world rather than the social world created by Onontio and his children. In
fact, the Anishinaabeg and Dakota forged their new relationship in order to
add to their political power and economic influence in the western interior.
Accordingly, this new relationship would undermine the strategic position
of the peoples who resided to the north and northwest of Gichigamiing. Like
King Cuscudidah, people such as the Cree, Monsoni, and Zhiishiigweg would
now face rivals to their south connected to the French trade who could intercept bands of Native traders coming from the interior. It was fear of exactly

this political realignment that prompted Cree warriors to preemptively attack the Dakota delegation that came to Sault Sainte Marie to negotiate an alliance in 1674.

The violence that sparked this massacre, however, was endemic to the inland trade, where doodemag with little or no attachment to Onontio were both more vulnerable to attack and freer to raid. Oumamens had skillfully pressured Du Lhut to broker a peace with the peoples of the north that would protect the new alliance. Du Lhut apparently saw the need to protect his new trading enterprise among the Dakota. He also grasped the vast potential of the northwest interior, and the threat to the French trade posed by Hudson's Bay. In his correspondence with the governor in 1678, Du Lhut claimed that "if some French had not gone to the north at the end of last year, all the savages of said place would have brought their peltry to Hudson's Bay, like the Kristinos and Monsonis did last summer, in the number of 120 canoes, loaded with beaver."[72] He asserted that these inland bands brought their trade to the English because they had been "pillaged" by the Odawa the previous spring. Perhaps more important, Du Lhut described the Native inhabitants of this region as "foreign nations" that did not trade with the French. He concluded by arguing that "if the French are excluded from the trade on the North coast, before three years from now, not one beaver from these places will come down to the French settlements."[73]

Du Lhut seemed to grasp the political and economic autonomy of Native peoples in the western interior. The French claimed these peoples as subjects and allies through rituals such as the one conducted by St. Lusson. Raiders like Gaa mii Chi ziidid, however, more accurately reflected the reality on the ground. If Du Lhut, like St. Lusson, overreached in terms of the political claims that he made, at least his experience with the Dakota seemed to have taught him that French power could be extended into the west only by creating and sustaining social relationships. Therefore, in the early fall, he kept his word to Oumamens and called the Assiniboine "and all the other nations of the north" to grand council—"a rendez-vous at the bottom of Lake Superior to make peace with the Nadouesioux, their common enemy." At this council, Du Lhut wrote, "so that a longer peace would be made among them, I believed that it could only be better cemented by making reciprocal marriages of the nations with one another." This process, he reported, required extensive gift giving on his part. Du Lhut also wrote that during the following winter he "made them meet in the woods . . . so that they could hunt together, feast one another, and by this means, build a more intimate friendship."[74]

Du Lhut claimed that the Dakota and the other "nations" from the west that attended his rendezvous promised to send delegations to Montreal in the spring. This never came to pass. Du Lhut claimed that false rumors about an outbreak of smallpox in the French settlements caused these new allies from the west to stay home. This was certainly plausible. The more likely explanation, however, was that the alliances he mediated represented attempts by Native peoples to alter their power and status among other peoples of the interior—rather than create a relationship with Onontio. Considered from this perspective, Du Lhut's intervention represented a diplomatic triumph for Oumamens and the Anishinaabeg of Shagwaamikong.

The Misunderstood Adoption of Father Hennepin

In the early spring of 1680, when the ice broke up and opened the rivers and lakes, a Dakota war party made its way south. Fifty birch bark canoes carrying 120 warriors moved rapidly down the Mississippi River, heading toward the watersheds that flowed east into Green Bay. The warriors came from several Dakota communities including Mde Wakan, the village that had forged an alliance with the Anishinaabeg. One man from this village, Aquipaguetin, carried the bones of his deceased son—killed by the Miami—wrapped in an animal skin. With these bones he carried the pain of his loss into battle. Aquipaguetin was an itancan, the leader of a Dakota band, and many of the warriors followed his lead in seeking revenge against the Miami and their allies at Green Bay.[75]

Before reaching the bay villages, however, the Dakota surprised a party of three French men camped on the riverbank. The Europeans scrambled into a dugout canoe and paddled toward the advancing war party. One of these men held a calumet pipe and called out in a language the Dakota did not understand.[76] Young warriors stripped to the waist and painted for war leapt out of their canoes and surrounded the dugout, dragging it to shore. One of the young men ripped the calumet from the hands of the European stranger.[77] This same European began to offer pieces of tobacco to the warriors swirling around him. Accepting this tobacco and seeing its fine quality, four elders began to call out, settling their young men. The Europeans used signs to explain that the Miami and other bay peoples had already fled south into the Illinois country. Following a brief uproar at this news, the elders placed their hands on the European who carried the pipe, and began to cry and sing over him until his head was wet with their tears.

The Dakota moved the Europeans to the opposite bank of the Mississippi and began to unload and sort through their equipage. They made camp, and the Europeans offered them food, three turkeys caught earlier in the day. The European pipe carrier then gave hatchets, knives, and additional tobacco to the elders. They responded with a ritual gesture of hospitality, presenting the Europeans with a platter of cooked beaver. The elders cooled the meat with their own breath and placed three morsels into each of their mouths. Satisfied that a mutual respect had been established, the Dakota returned the calumet to the Europeans before bedding down for the night. Their enemies had discovered their war party and fled, but wakan tanka, the powers that animated the universe, presented them with a new opportunity.

At the break of day, the itancan who attempted to communicate with the Europeans, a man named Narrhetoba, asked the European pipe carrier for his calumet. When it was given to him he filled the pipe with Dakota tobacco and presented it to each of the warriors who followed him. Then he circulated the pipe among the warriors from the other Dakota bands. With peace between the Dakota and the French ritually affirmed, Narrhetoba indicated by sign that the strangers, now recognized as friends, should accompany them on the return to their home territory. Three warriors were ordered into the wooden dugout with the Europeans to help them keep up with the faster birch bark canoes of the Dakota. They began to move north at a pace the Europeans found exhausting, paddling from sunup until sundown.[78]

We learn the details of this encounter from the written narrative of the French pipe carrier, Louis Hennepin, a recollect Franciscan priest who accompanied La Salle into the west. Hennepin produced a text that was part discovery narrative and part captivity narrative. He described the intercession of Narrhetoba and the anguish of Aquipaguetin as part of a dramatic struggle to determine his fate. The issue at stake in this struggle was his life or death. Should the Dakota kill the priest and his comrades to avenge lives lost to the French-allied Indians at Green Bay? Or should the French be taken into captivity with the hope that the Dakota could leverage their lives into some sort of trade relationship with New France?

This struggle was, in effect, a question about what kind of relationship the Dakota wanted with the French Empire. According to Hennepin the Dakota were divided on this question. "Those who took us," he wrote, "were of divers Villages, and as much divided in their Sentiments, in regard of us."[79] Every night, Hennepin claimed, Aquipaguetin lamented the loss of his son and exhorted the Dakota to kill their captives to assuage his suffering. "But the other

Savages," he wrote, "who were very fond of European Commodities, thought it more adviseable to protect us, that other Europeans might be encourag'd to come among them."[80] In his narrative Hennepin and his companions traveled north under duress, not as guests, but as slaves taken in lieu of Miami captives. As such, he believed they were in constant danger of being martyred.

Hennepin was correct in thinking that there was tension among the leaders of the Dakota war party about their relationship with the French. But he exaggerated or misinterpreted the threats to his life. In part, this was because Hennepin interpreted the actions and behavior of the Dakota through the lens of what he perceived to be his impending martyrdom. When the elders wept over him Hennepin believed they cried tears of rage—an expression of their desire to take his life. Time and again he made this assumption as the itancan of the Dakota smoked the calumet and shed tears onto his head as he made his way deeper into their territory. On these occasions Hennepin often gave away trade goods thinking that he had purchased his salvation, at least temporarily. When Aquipaguetin tried to force the French to camp among his warriors they believed he meant to kill them. And when Narrhetoba came and physically dragged them over to his side of the camp circle, they believed they had narrowly escaped death. After this incident, Hennepin wrote, "they separated, and gave us to three of their chiefs, instead of three of their sons which had been kill'd in the War: Then they seized our canou, and took away all our Equipage."[81]

Fearing for his life and ignorant of Dakota customs, Hennepin misunderstood the actions of the Dakota. What the priest described as tears of rage was actually ritual practice. The Dakota wept in order to appear pitiful and in need of assistance whenever they encountered beings that possessed or controlled access to wasicun. Like manidoo, wasicun was anything with sacred or extraordinary power. For a person or thing to be wasicun meant that it was infused with wakan—the creative force that animated all living things in the universe.[82] Weeping over Hennepin the itancan of the Dakota demonstrated their humility, their need for the wasicun of the French. When the priest responded to this ritual practice by giving away trade goods he unwittingly acted in an appropriate manner. Aquipageutin and Narrhetoba were not arguing over whether or not to kill Hennepin. They were both trying to establish a relationship with Hennepin and his companions in order to gain access to the wasicun of New France.

In other words, the Dakota leaders were competing for the right to take the Europeans back to their home villages. Once they reached the Dakota territory in the headwaters region of the Mississippi valley, they stopped at a small village. After a feast, and after more heated discussion, Aquipaguetin presented his calumet to Hennepin and asked the priest for his pipe in return. They smoked, and Hennepin was made to understand that he would become the adopted son of Aquipaguetin. Narrhetoba adopted the remaining two French men, and both leaders departed for their own villages.[83]

From this point on Hennepin lived a relatively autonomous existence among the Dakota, and he seemed to realize that he faced no real threat of death at their hands. He was ritually incorporated into Aquipaguetin's lodge group. They performed yet another and more elaborate calumet, provided Hennepin with a beaver and buffalo robe, and began to address him using kinship terminology. In his narrative, however, he complained of being poorly treated. The Dakota withheld food, he complained, and they had taken his possessions, including his priestly vestments. Hennepin seemed to feel vindicated when a man named Ouasicoude, or the Pierced Pine, chastised the warriors who had offended him, sayng publicly "in a full council, That those who had robb'd us of our Things, were to be compar'd to famish'd Dogs."[84]

Hennepin described Ouasicoude as "the wisest and most considerable of all the chiefs of the Issati." This term derived from the designation "Camp at Knife" made reference to a pipestone quarry, and was originally used by Dakota-speaking peoples living in the west along the Missouri River to identify allied peoples from the east in the upper Mississippi valley. The name *Issati* encompassed all of the people from "divers villages" who had taken Hennepin while raiding to the south, including the Mdewakanton, or the people of Sacred Lake village. Hennepin's narrative contains very little discussion of the political structure of the Dakota, and his analysis of their diplomatic practices consists mostly his various misinterpretations of the cultural meanings associated with the calumet ceremony. Here, however, he makes a fleeting reference to a "full council" of the Issati where their principal itancan harshly criticized warriors who made "unworthy affronts upon men, who brought them Iron, and other Merchandizes." Ouasicoude concluded his speech by telling the council, which included the newly adopted French men: "That for himself, he shou'd one day have an opportunity of being reveng'd on him, who had been Author of all our Sufferings."[85]

In other words, Ouasicoude, speaking to a full council of the Issati as the leading itancan, expressed an interest in cultivating a relationship with the men who could bring "iron, and other Merchandizes" into their country. Such a meeting would have included leaders from all of the bands living in the upper Mississippi valley, and on this occasion it seems that ambassadors from the western bands were also in attendance.[86] Twenty years earlier when Pierre Radisson traveled southwest of Gichigamiing he found traders operating in this region. And ten years earlier the Jesuit Claude Allouez at mission Saint Esprit wrote about parties of Dakota hunters coming to the village at La Pointe to trade. Hennepin's experience, however, matched the observations of the Jesuit missionaries at Sault Sainte Marie in 1674, who described the Dakota as armed with stone knives. Hennepin made note of the fact that the Dakota and their allies in the west cooked with clay pots and expressed a desire for iron goods and guns, neither of which they seemed to possess.[87] Clearly, violence between the Dakota and Native peoples allied to the French had curtailed trade in this region. Ouasicoude's council speech, like Oumamens's diplomacy, signaled a desire for peace—for some sort of alliance to restore productive social relations among the peoples of the western interior.

With this desire clearly expressed at council, Ouasicoude led his people onto the prairies west of the Mississippi for their summer buffalo hunt. Their newly adopted French relatives made this journey as well, and they were encouraged to seek out La Salle once they reached the lower Mississippi region where he traded. The hunt was a success, but the effort to find La Salle and his men failed. At the end of July, when the Issati prepared to return to the upper Mississippi valley, they received information about a small party of French traders who had made their way inland from Gichigamiing. "The Savages," Hennepin wrote, "press'd us to go with them; promising to conduct us as far as the Nations that inhabited at the End of the Upper-Lake." According to the priest, "they said they had a design to make an alliance with those people through our Means."[88]

Here Hennepin seemed to give voice to a desire among the Dakota for an alliance with the Anishinaabeg. It is difficult to know what to make of this shift in emphasis, but it seems likely that Ouasicoude was aware of the emerging alliance between his people and the doodemag of La Pointe and Sault Sainte Marie. He would also have been aware of the role of French influence—promoting both peace and violent confrontation—in this evolving relationship. The appearance of a party of French traders in the Dakota country one year after council sessions between the Dakota, Anishinaabeg, and the French was not a coincidence. The man leading this party was Daniel Du Lhut. He traveled with four French men and a Native guide—the Dakota slave purchased at the Sault to serve as an interpreter and to show them the water route connecting Gichigamiing to the Mississippi. At the confluence of the Mississippi and a river the French called the St. Croix, Du Lhut encountered a small band of Dakota hunting the marshlands. From them he learned of the capture and adoption of La Salle's men, and requested a meeting with his countrymen.

When Du Lhut arrived at the camp of Ouasicoude, he claimed to be the older brother of Father Hennepin, and then asked that he be allowed to accompany the Dakota to their village at Mde Wakan. He too wrote that the priest "had been robbed and taken into slavery."[89] When they arrived at the village, Ouasicoude, identified by Hennepin as "the first Captain of the Nation," invited Du Lhut to attend a feast where the priest was honored for having covered the dead relative of the itancan. Du Lhut, according to Hennepin, was chastised for failing to act with comparable generosity. Du Lhut, however, later wrote that it was he who called the council to chastise the Dakota for their "bad treatment" of the three French captives. "I gave back two calumets that they danced," he wrote, and then claimed that he informed the full council of the Issati: "I take no calumets from people who, after having received my presents of peace, and having been, for a year, always with the French, robbed them when they go to see them."[90]

Both Hennepin and Du Lhut imagined themselves as the chief protagonist in the stories they recorded. Hennepin reveled in his near martyrdom. Du Lhut presented himself to be a skilled diplomat and sought to justify his illegal voyage to the west. In the end, however, both men produced narratives that revealed that they had been swept up in a wide-ranging and complicated diplomatic negotiation between the various bands of Anishinaabeg and the Dakota peoples. After spending several weeks at the village of Mde Wakan the French decided they were not well enough provisioned to winter among the Dakota. According to Hennepin, their decision to leave sparked a debate about the nature of the relationship that had been created with the French.

In Hennepin's narrative Du Lhut wanted to set a rendezvous at a point midway between the Dakota country and the French settlements. And he wanted two Dakota warriors to make the journey east with them. This idea was rejected by the Dakota, who proposed instead that the French join them in destroying their enemies in the east, "that then their Men shou'd go and return with us to fetch them Iron, and other Commodities which they wanted." From this dialogue Hennepin concluded that the Dakota were hopeless barbarians consumed by "Thoughts of Revenge," and not ready "to receive the meek Doctrine of the Gospel."[91] Du Lhut's narrative omitted these council deliberations. Instead, he focused on his rescue of the French captives and the discovery and possession of the Dakota country. In his story, the council ended when he admonished the council for this act of betrayal. While he had not learned to speak as the voice of the French father this early into his career, Du Lhut implied that the Dakota accepted his authority as a soldier of the French Empire.[92]

Hennepin, however, concluded the narrative of his captivity among the Dakota with a vignette that revealed the true source of power and political authority in the upper Mississippi valley. Ouasicoude called a final council, or otiyotipi, a formal gathering of the leading men of the Issati. He celebrated the return home of their newly adopted French children. He provided provisions for their journey and even drew a map showing them the best route east. It seemed that Hennepin, in spite of his many miscues in reading Dakota behavior, correctly perceived that there had been some disagreement about the status of the French. While the Dakota warriors seemed to universally admire French goods, not everyone felt this way about the French themselves. To some they were inferior and troublesome outsiders.

A few days after their departure a canoe with three Mdewakanton Dakota warriors caught up to the French as they made their way down the Mississippi River. They came on embassy, according to Henepin, "to acquaint us that their Grand Captain Ouasicoude having learnt that another chief of the same Nation had a Design to pursue and murder us, he came into the cabin where Said Captain and his Associates were consulting about it, and gave him a Blow on the Head with so much Fury, that his brains flew out upon those that were present at the consult."[93] This news apparently left Du Lhut unnerved. According to Hennepin, he remained distressed and apprehensive until they left the Dakota country. Ouasicoude proved willing to act with force and violence to preserve his new ties to these French traders who were allied to the Anishinaabeg. He had literally crushed the head of dissension among the Issati, and he wanted Du Lhut to know this, and to know his ability to wield power.

A Parable of the French Alliance

In 1681, one year after the Mdewakanton Dakota ritually adopted Louis Hennepin, the Anishinaabeg of La Pointe joined them in the devastating raid against the Mesquakie that killed their ogimaa and left fifty-six people dead. In the last council with their adopted French sons, the Dakota expressed a desire to clear a path to the east by destroying their enemies in that direction. Sending eight hundred warriors from the west to raid the refugees of Green

Bay was a forceful demonstration of the potential power of the Anishinaabe-
Dakota alliance. Any of the European colonies in North America would have
been hard pressed to raise a militia of this size. This raid was a demonstration of the increasing independence of the Anishinaabeg, and their growing
detachment from the French alliance and the imperial politics of the Atlantic
World. Joining the Dakota attack against the Mesquakie signaled a rejection
of the middle ground and an abandonment of their identity as children of
Onontio. Taking on a new identity as western Indians, however, was not without its consequences. When the Mesquakie sought revenge by raiding the
Dakota for slaves they carried away Anishinaabe captives who had been living among them. The struggle to redeem these captives would reveal the cost,
to both the French and the Anishinaabeg, of turning their backs to Onontio.

In spite of rather extravagant French claims of sovereignty and territorial
possession, the social world of the French alliance in the region they called
the pays den haut was contingent on the relationship between the French and
their Indian allies. This meant that the French Empire in the west functioned
as an extension of these relationships, or not at all. And yet the imperial foot-
print of New France in the region remained quite small. The infrastructure of
the alliance—the missions, military garrisons, and trading posts—consisted
of structures that were not permanently occupied. French traders, in fact, had
not been in the west when the Anishinaabe-Dakota-Mesquakie raids took
place. When they returned to their posts in 1683 they found an alliance on the
verge of unraveling as a result of the conflict between the Mesquakie, Dakota,
and Anishinaabeg.

The experienced voyageur Nicolas Perrot led a party of twenty men
charged with the responsibility of preserving the frayed alliance, and expanding the trade into the Dakota country claimed by Du Lhut. When Perrot arrived at Green Bay in the spring of 1683 he found the villagers of this region in
turmoil. He first met the bereft father of one of the captives, an Anishinaabe
ogimaa who had traveled to the bay to redeem his daughter. According to
Perrot, "all the nations of the bay carried a great many presents to the Outagamis to buy back this girl," only to be rejected. "They even feared," he reported,
"that she would be sacrificed to the soul of the great chief the Sauteurs had
killed." With his crew of twenty voyageurs he made his way inland to the
Mesquakie village, and found the community shaken and angry. The entire
village approached the French trader, "melting in tears, telling him the story
of the betrayal of the Sauteurs and the Nadouaissious." They expressed their
rage at the killing of their most preeminent leader. Perrot called a council to

respond to their protests, and he promptly demanded the redemption of the captive Sauteur.[94]

At council Perrot assumed the voice of Onontio. Perhaps even more striking, he claimed to embody both the French father and his Sauteur children. Two accounts of the voyageur's testimony exist, both written by Bacqueville de La Potherie in his *Histoire de l'Amérique Septentrionale*. La Potherie based his narrative on the experiences and published memoir of Nicolas Perrot. Each account focused on the successful redemption of the Sauteur slave and on the restoration of peace and a sense of mutual obligation among the children of Onontio. The Dakota are noticeably absent in these stories. For both Perrot and La Potherie they remained outsiders in the social world of the alliance. The abduction and redemption of the captive Sauteur girl, however, was written as a morality play about the regenesis of the alliance itself.

In one account Perrot transposes the body of the Sauteur captive with his own. In this version of the story the voyageur tells the village, "Listen, Outagamis, to what I am going to say you. I have learned that you have a strong desire to eat the flesh of a Frenchmen. I have come," he declared "to satisfy you." Gesturing to his fellow voyageurs, Perrot told the Mesquakie, "put us into your kettles, and fill yourself with the flesh you have been wanting." Their war chief responded in horror, "What child is there who would eat his father, from whom he has received life?" This man continued by asserting that Perrot, their father, had given birth to his people when he first brought iron to their village. Perrot then chastised the war leader, saying that in return for the life he gave them the Outagamis brought trouble to the country by "killing the Sauteurs" whom, he noted, "I adopted before you." Perrot then issued a command: "Vomit up your prey; give me back my body, which you wish to put into your kettle." He then warned the Mesquakie that if they tried to cook him, the vapors from his body would create a storm and destroy their village.[95]

In this story the Mesquakie, identified as the Outagamis, gave up the Sauteur captive and in doing so saved themselves and also the alliance. "Believe your father," Perrot concluded, "who will not abandon you until you compel him to do so." The Outagamis listened and responded immediately. La Potherie then described how the French, shortly after this incident, prevented the Sauk from raiding the Dakota. The Sauk were also residents of Green Bay and intermarried among the Mesquakie in great numbers. Though these events were not explicitly linked, they were written as part of a single narrative about the restoration of peace in the western pays d'en haut and the rebirth of the alliance, and in this way the Dakota entered the story, if only indirectly. The Outagamis nation, birthed by the French father, restored the alliance by vomiting up their father, whom they had eaten in the form of a Sauteur captive.[96]

In the second version of this story it was the Outagamis who were in danger of being eaten. In this account, when Perrot addressed the council he told them: "I have known that, in order to make a good peace between the Sauteurs and the Nadouaissous, through a meeting which we had together, the former had invited the latter to put you and your families into their kettles."[97] He then told the Outagamis, "She is mine I demand her from you, I am your father . . . swallow your desire for vengeance, if you want to live." Perrot reminded the Outagamis of their recent victory over the Sauteurs. He gave credit for this victory to "the Spirit who created all." This was a reference to Gichi-manidoo. Perrot, in effect, claimed that the ultimate source of power in the world wanted peace among the children of Onontio. He then demanded that the Outagamis redeem the Sauteur slave. Perrot offered the calumet three times to the warrior who held the girl. This man, the brother of the prominent chief slain in the Sauteur-Sioux raid, refused to smoke.[98]

In this telling of the story the Outagamis ultimately saved themselves, while Perrot again offered up his own body to save the alliance. The leader of another Mesquakie band called a second council to discuss the Sauteur captive. This man convinced the village of the need to give up the slave, and then tried the calumet once again. He collected trade goods and gave them to the warrior to cover the death of his brother. The warrior at last relented, and he and his relatives smoked the calumet. The Outagamis then admonished Perrot to protect them against the Sauteurs. The voyageur sent the Sauteur girl to her relatives with the message that he planned to live among the Mesquakie peoples of the bay. If they attacked again he warned, "they would break his head."[99] If he was slain, Perrot promised the Sauteurs that the French would avenge his death.

In these stories Onontio, the French father, gives birth to Native children who begin to kill each other. The children eat one another until their father commands them to stop, and to regurgitate their siblings so that he can restore them to life. In the process of resurrecting his lost children, Onontio risks death; he offers up his body to his children for their consumption. Eating one another, they are killing him, literally eating his flesh because they, being his children, are born of his own flesh and blood. These gruesome tales of cannibalism and patricide make one thing abundantly clear—for Onontio and his children it is alliance or death. Either they acknowledge their relationship as members of a family, a father and his children, as siblings, and live together; or they will die merciless deaths surrounded by enemies who mindlessly seek their destruction. On one path empire, alliance, and salvation, on the other Indian savagery and inevitable death.

This tale of the life, death, and resurrection of a French father and his Native children is the story of the French Empire. It is both allegory and description of the relationship between New France and the Native peoples allied to the colony. In telling the history of the events surrounding the Sauteur-Sioux raid against the Outagamis, La Potherie and Perrot created what was essentially a founding myth for the colony of New France. This was not like the stories that the English (and later Americans) told about Pocahontas, Squanto, and Hiawatha. That is, it was not a narrative about Indians who acted like midwives to usher in a New World where Europeans become in some fashion reborn as the new Native peoples of North America. Rather, this was a story of Native regenesis. It was a story that explained the working of the alliance system that became synonymous with New France. The alliance functioned in a state of near perpetual crisis, a tension that forced the French to fulfill their role as fathers to their Indian children. This process, in turn, made them the guardians of a collective identity that bound Native peoples together as nations allied to a European empire. Here the French Empire, through the person of Onontio, gave birth to New World children who continued to exist as Natives, but only in relation to their French father.

In La Potherie's narrative about Perrot's experiences in the west we can see where the French struggled to make sense of the Native New World. This was an alien place filled with strange peoples practicing strange customs. This was a place frequently rocked by violence and death that seemed inhuman, savage. The answer to this savagery was rebirth, a regenesis that could come only when the savages were turned into the children of empire. This was a story that explained how the French Empire worked, but it was also a heroic story about the triumph of empire. At one time or another all European colonial powers claimed they came to the New World to save the Indians from their own savagery, and yet they all had to contend with the fact that their settlements brought them only death and destruction. Unlike in the English stories in Jamestown or New England the Natives were not required to give their lives in the birthing of a New World. In New France they were themselves reborn as part of that world.

The story of this rebirth is literally encoded in the texts that record this history. *Sauteur* and *Nadouesioux* were both misapplications of signifiers of identity in Anishinaabemowin. *Sauteur*, a Francophone designation for a person from Bow-e-ting, or Sault Sainte Marie, was applied broadly to speakers of the Ojibwe dialect. This application assumed a permanent residence at the falls, and therefore regarded all "Sauteurs" in the west as recent immigrants or displaced persons. The identification of Dakota as Na-towe-ssiwak, Sioux, or foreign peoples placed them outside of Anishinaabewaki and the French alliance. In the lexicon of New France this marked them as the Iroquois of the west—savage outsiders. Similarly, *Outagamis* was the phonetic Francophone spelling of the Ojibwe dialect expression *agaaming*. This phrase signified the other side of the lake, and in this case indicated the Mesquakie who lived on the west side of Lake Michigan. The widespread use of this designation among French traders and missionaries suggests, perhaps, an acceptance of the tendency among the Anishinaabe peoples who dominated the alliance to regard these people as social outliers and refugees.

Part of the problem with stories written by men like Perrot and La Potherie is that they were produced within the framework of European discovery and colonization of the New World. Names for people and places more often than not reflected moments of discovery when Europeans gained a partial and imperfect understanding of the people and places of this Other world. In this sense, La Potherie's account and similar colonial texts assume a narrative point of view. The peoples of the Native New World enter the historical record as they enter into a relationship with New France or some other empire. In effect, they are literally and figuratively brought into existence by virtue of their relationship to empire and the Atlantic World.

There is a historical trajectory encoded within this narrative viewpoint, and it moves across time and space from east to west with certain teleology. Indians step onto the historical stage as empire makes them known to the world. They become either enemies marked for destruction or savages destined for oblivion as colonial settlement advances through the wilderness, or they are conquered—politically subordinated as subjects of a European sovereign. Death, diminishment, or rebirth as subalterns on their own continent, this is the framework that narratives of discovery impose on the Native peoples of the New World.

A New Constellation of Native Power

We could, however, read this story differently. What if we viewed this sequence of events from the perspective of the Sauteur girl and her father? Why did the Anishinaabe ogimaa place his daughter in harm's way, living among the Sioux? To answer this question we would need to tell the part of the story that La Potherie and Perrot avoid, in part through constraints of language, but also because it does not unfold as a narrative of discovery. This tale of captivity and rescue tells the story of the evolving relationship between the Anishinaabeg and the Dakota. The emergence of the Anishinaabe-Dakota alliance is a story of Native regenesis, but it was a rebirth that took place in the Native New World, and this story cannot be told using the social constructions of the French alliance.

We should not simply accept that the collective identities assigned to Native peoples to explain their relationship to empire actually ordered their existence, or accurately expressed their political will and social identity. If we accept that the peoples of the Native New World were free and politically autonomous, then we must assume that this self-determination was more accurately expressed through indigenous categories of being, collective association, and social identity. The narrative trajectory that best explains why this young Anishinaabe woman became entangled in the violent conflict between her community, the Dakota, Mesquakie, and the French Empire moves across time and space from west to east.

This alternate narrative trajectory begins with an explanation of how the Nadouesioux understood themselves and why they, as a Native social formation, wanted to extend their political influence into the colonial world to their east. Dakota was the signifier of a collective identity shared by multiple, named bands of Siouan-speaking Native peoples who referred to themselves as the "Oceti Sakowin," or the Seven Council Fires. The Oceti Sakowin consisted of seven oyate—a word best translated as "people"—the Mdewakanton, Sisseton, Wahpeton, Whapekute, Yankton, Yanktonai, and Teton. Members of these oyate referred to themselves as Dakota, a designation that signified "ally."[100] In the Teton dialect the *d* sound corresponds to *l*, and becomes Lakota. This term could also be interpreted to mean "real people," as opposed to *tokayapi* or "enemy peoples." Additionally, *Dakota* serves as a root verbal construct that can be used to designate categories of social identity, such as *dakota* (meaning "she or he is a Dakota"), and *dakotapi* (meaning "they are Dakotas").[101]

Oceti Sakowin, essentially, served as an overarching designation for the Dakota peoples. It was not a reference to an actual governing structure for the alliance. Rather this self-designation reflected the sense of connection—of shared language, intermarriage, kinship, and alliance making—that linked the Dakota peoples together. The oyate of the Oceti Sakowin, in fact, were modeled on the lodge group, or the tiyospaye. This term designated a band composed of between five and twenty families that chose to form a camp circle.[102] Each of the Dakota oyate, such as the Mdewakanton or the Teton, comprised several tiyospaye, whose internal composition changed frequently. Band members regarded one another as kin whether or not they were biologically related.[103] In this sense, the social relations of production that allowed the camp to reproduce itself were understood in terms of the prerogatives and responsibilities of family life. Accordingly, the kinship system of the Dakota provided order to the social interactions that set the pattern of day-to-day existence. In this manner, the *tiyospaye* served as a model social organization, one that showed the allies how to relate to one another—that is, how to act as and be kin.[104]

Similarly to the Anishinaabeg, Dakota identity was produced via an interlocking network of social relations that connected bands organized as extended families to larger and larger social units. These larger units were mobilized periodically for diplomacy, warfare, and perhaps most significantly for hunting buffalo. Archaeological evidence suggests that the Dakota emerged as a distinct social formation in the forested marshlands at the head of the Mississippi River valley in the fourteenth century. Dispersed throughout this region in small bands during the winter months, the Dakota mobilized large-scale hunting parties during the spring and summer.[105] These hunting parties moved onto the grasslands to the southwest along the lower Mississippi to hunt buffalo when the herds congregated in large numbers to mate. The large size of the herds necessitated communal hunting, which meant that bands that lived apart during the winter needed to come together as a larger social unit. These larger tribal units also needed to move with the herds, a process that entailed disbanding into smaller groups that tracked the buffalo, and then reformed when herds were located. Emphasizing the tiyospaye as the model for organizing this collective social behavior provided a kinship-based structure for intergroup cooperation. This, in turn, allowed a vast multitude of autonomous Dakota bands to come together periodically to hunt, trade, and raid their enemies.[106]

This fluid linkage between social units—the tiyospaye, oyate, and Oceti Sakowin—allowed the Dakota bands to migrate deep into the west, into the heart of the buffalo country, until the territory controlled by the allies stretched from the Mississippi River to the Missouri River. Thus, while French colonial officials recorded the incursions of Sioux raiders east into the pays d'en haut, the more significant story was their migration into the west. This migration occurred gradually and as a response to the emergence of extremely large buffalo herds during an especially wet period on the Great Plains, followed by the contraction of the bison range and the withdrawal of the herds deeper into the west.[107] The allies moved west in pursuit of this abundance.[108] At the time of their alliance with the Anishiaabeg, the Mdewakanton remained a powerful presence in the upper Mississippi valley, but fully two-thirds of the Dakota bands lived in the west year-round. By the end of the seventeenth century the French estimated that the Dakota-Yankton/Yanktonai-Lakota alliance network encompassed at a minimum twenty-four thousand people, making this social formation significantly larger than New France with a population of approximately twelve thousand settler colonists during this same time.[109]

The Dakota bands, of course, represented a mobile nonstate entity that functioned as a multipolar social formation. They were not an empire or settler colony, and their expansion occurred as the amplification of a pattern of seasonal migration. They were, nonetheless, the constituent parts of an imagined social collective. As a collective social body the Dakota peoples evolved to adapt to a changing world, and this meant a more permanent emphasis on what had once been only a part of their seasonal round. But even as the west and the buffalo presented the allies with the opportunity of a new way of being, the emergence of a global market economy demanded similar attention.

The creation of Atlantic World empires along the eastern coastline of North America resulted in the circulation of new peoples and things into the indigenous west. The Dakota needed to determine how to incorporate or exclude the people and material artifacts of this other emergent social world into their own. In reality, of course, exclusion was impossible. The presence of established European colonies and the mutual attraction of Natives and Europeans to the resources and material goods of the other made interaction and exchange inevitable. The real issue at stake was control. Who would control the circulation of people and things moving between the parallel social worlds of the Atlantic and the indigenous west?

The cycle of raiding, trading, and captive taking described by Perrot and narrated by La Potherie reflected this struggle for control. More significantly, the story told by these men also reveals the complex interdependence that linked Native and European social formations in North America from the time of first contact to the formation of the continent's nation-states. Just as the Dakota are the unspoken presence in Perrot's tale of loss, redemption, and regenesis, so too are the French and other Europeans a ghostly presence in the evolution of Native identities in the western interior.

Thus while the Dakota became a buffalo people in the west, the Mdewakanton used their villages in the upper Mississippi valley to become specialists in the fur trade and diplomacy. In doing so they were able to defend their prairie hunting grounds from the refugees at Green Bay. They also controlled access to the western interior and the western Sioux bands. The emergence of the allies in the west as buffalo people was facilitated by the increased circulation of guns and trade goods that gave them a distinct advantage when it came to acquiring horses, and defending and expanding their access to the buffalo herds of the Great Plains.[110] Throughout the seventeenth and eighteenth centuries the Mdewakanton bands effectively policed the flow of people and goods between the indigenous west and the colonial east at annual trade fairs in their territory that brought together allied bands from the west and east, and traders from Louisiana, St. Louis, Hudson's Bay, Michilimackinac, and Montreal. The sheer size of the alliance, and its control over the flow of people and goods between the Atlantic World and the indigenous west, made the Dakota one of the most dominant social formations on the continent.[111]

Similarly, the Anishinaabeg associated with La Pointe village and the country west of Gichigamiing were themselves part of an extensive multipolar social formation. Like the Dakota they were linked to a network of culturally related peoples. The political organization of both of these social bodies changed composition to adapt to different political, economic, and military needs. The hallmark of the Dakota and Anishinaabe peoples as social formations was their multipolar power structure, as well as their capacity to absorb linguistic and cultural outsiders through a social nexus that imagined community as kinship.

The Anishinaabe-Dakota alliance represented a marriage of two of the most dominant indigenous social formations in the Native New World that emerged after the reconnection of the Eastern and Western Hemispheres. Aligning themselves with the Oceti Sakowin, the Anishinaabeg of Shagwaamikong repositioned their community within a globalized network of exchange relationships that was transforming North America. Reborn as people of the indigenous west and as kin and allies of the Dakota, they exercised a degree of autonomy denied to the children of Onontio. Nicolas Perrot's story of redemption was, in fact, an attempt by the French to contain this social transformation. The Anishinaabe-Dakota alliance represented a new constellation of Native power in the west that undermined the French alliance system. This reconfiguration of Anishinabe identity secured their access to the fur-rich upper Mississippi valley and northern Great Plains. And it provided them with a military capability that exceeded the power and reach of the French Empire.

CHAPTER 4

European Interlopers and the Politics
of the Native New World

In 1685 the governor of New France, Jacques-René de Brisay Denonville, prepared a memoir on the state of affairs in Canada for the court of Louis XIV. He delivered a dire warning. The English presence at Hudson's Bay threatened the very existence of the colony. "For if their establishments continue as they have begun in the three places of this Bay," he warned, "we must expect to see all of the best commerce from beaver in quality and quantity to go into the hands of the English." Denonville feared more than just the loss of trade. He feared the collapse of the economy of New France, and the unraveling of the alliance system by which the French had staked their claim to empire in the New World. "If we do not chase them away," he predicted, "they will have all of the fat beaver [castor gras] from an infinity of nations who are to the north that are discovered every day, drawing the greatest part of the peltries that come to us at Montreal from the Outaouas and Assinibois and other neighboring nations" (Figure 4).[1]

This was the true threat posed by the English at Hudson's Bay. They might discover the infinity of Native nations residing in the western interior of North America. French claims to possess the west, of course, rested on prior discovery and on the supposed subject status of their Native allies who occupied this region. And yet Denonville admitted the existence of a Native heartland beyond the control of either the French Empire or the English Empire. This was the reality of the Native New World. A seemingly endless number of autonomous Native peoples occupied the western interior of the continent. Their allegiance remained undetermined. Their trade represented the only means by which the mercantile empires of France and England could hope

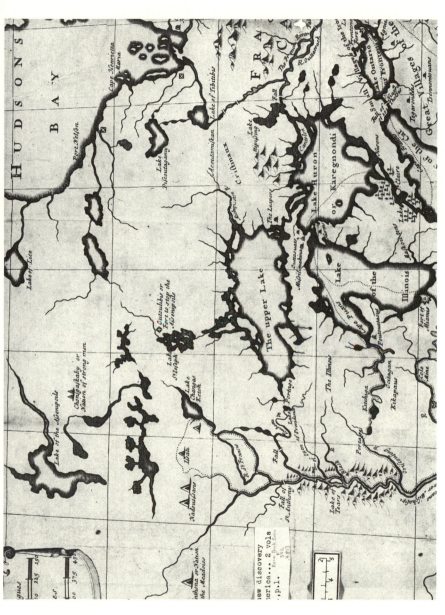

Figure 4. From Father Louis Hennepin, *A Discovery of a Vast Country in America*, Vol. 1, ed. Reuben Gold Thwaites, 2nd ed. (London, 1698; repr. Chicago: A. C. McClurg, 1903). This map designates the Dakota village at Mde Wakan or Mille Lacs and maps the water routes connecting this territory to Shagwaamikong and the northern borderland with the Western Cree and Assiniboine.

to acquire the most profitable and most easily extractable natural resource in this part of the New World—animal furs and hides.

The establishment of posts at Hudson's Bay had changed the fur trade by providing the English with direct access to the people and resources of the west. They also made it possible for Native people from this region to assert a greater degree of autonomy in their exchange relationships with Europeans. English traders made no effort to attach their Native trading partners, politically and socially, to a larger imperial regime. They did not present themselves as the servants of an English father, and the Indians with whom they traded were decidedly not the children of the English Empire. As a consequence, exchange relationships at the bay remained fluid and dynamic, involving a multitude of Native peoples who shifted their trade between the different English and French posts at the seacoast, in the Great Lakes, and at Montreal. The Hudson's Bay Company governors worked to attach their posts to these indigenous exchange and alliance networks from the western interior, but they did not become an English version of Onontio. They did, however, grudgingly recognize the social implications of exchange—at the insistence of their French partners Radisson and Des Groseilliers—who had been hired, in effect, to guide them through the social meanings and cultural practices of the fur trade in the Native New World.

The presence of these veteran French traders only compounded Denonville's fears about the threat posed by the Hudson's Bay Company. The country inland from Hudson's Bay and north of Lake Superior remained largely unknown, and the difficult terrain allowed French traders to carry only limited amounts of merchandise into the region. "Some pretend that they can go there by land," Denonville wrote, "but the river to go there is not yet discovered." So long as they were forced to rely on an overland route, the governor argued, New France would lose the inland trade to the English at Hudson's Bay. Native traders from the western interior—Denonville's undiscovered infinity of nations—"will find a double advantage" at the English posts where, he argued, they would find a better rate of exchange at a shorter distance from their home territories.[2]

Denonville was not alone in recognizing the social implications of English traders inserting themselves into the exchange networks that sustained the political economy of their allies, and by extension the economy of New France. In 1679, five years after Des Groseilliers established an English presence in the Moosu Sepee watershed, the intendant of New France, Jacques Du Chesneau, informed the minister of marine, "This will eventually ruin our trade with the

Outawacs, which is most considerable, and constitutes the subsistence and wealth of the colony."[3] In 1681 Intendant Du Chesneau wrote another memoir to the king, "to make known to my Lord the Savage nations from whom we draw our peltries." This document traced the contours of the fur trade, and the relationship between Native peoples and the French Empire.

Du Chesneau's memoir provided yet another descriptive map of Anishi-naabewaki, or from the French perspective the pays d'en haut, which mirrored the cartography and written description produced by St. Lusson's ceremonial possession of this territory. Various Anishinaabe peoples were identified as the principal trading partners of New France. "The Outaouacs Savages who are divided into several nations and who are the nearest to us," the intendant wrote, "are the most useful to us because they have the beaver." Du Chesneau claimed that these Odawaag nations did not hunt but, "they go searching in the most far away places" to exchange French merchandise for processed bea-ver peltry. He then identified the "Outaouacs Savages" as "the Themistamens [Temiscaming], Nepisseriens [Nipissing], Missisakis [Mississauga], Ami-coues [Amikwas], Sauteurs [Ojibweg], Kiscakons [Gishkanokwad-Odawa], and Thionontatorons [Wyandot]."[4]

These were the children of Onontio imagined as a multinational Native social formation that the French designated alternately as the "Outaouacs" or the "Algonquians." In Du Chesneau's description the "Outaouacs savages" were identified more as trading Indians than as the self-identified Odawa peoples. In this sense, the intendant's memoir reflected the problematic na-ture of applying European social categories to Native peoples, as well as the multiple ways that speakers of Anishinaabemowin used social identity. The Anishinaabeg, or for that matter the composite social units identified by the French as the Ootaouacs, Sauteurs, Nipissing, and so on, were not sin-gular Native nations but rather members of a multipolar social formation. As such, they skillfully used trade relations to expand the social boundaries of their world. Du Chesneau noted that their "Outaouac" trading partners "draw the peltries from the north coast from the Gens des Terres [Inland Peoples], from the Kislistinons [Cree], from the Assinibbouels [Nakoda], and from the Nadouessioux [Dakota]." He also claimed they carried the furs from the peoples of Green Bay and the lower Mississippi River valley to Montreal. The Anishinaabe peoples, according to Du Chesneau, were the most dominant traders in the western interior, and the primary conduit of exchange between the peoples of the Native New World and the colonists of the Atlantic World.

The result of this dominance was the expansion of Anishinaabewaki, which created both problems and opportunities for the French Empire. Creating social relationships with the peoples of the western interior the Anishinaabeg expanded the French fur trade. French traders, and the countless coureurs de bois who ventured west annually, were complicit in this expansion. In spite of records left behind by people like Du Lhut, Frontenac, and Radisson, however, the French played only a subordinate role in Anishinaabe diplomacy in the west. Du Chesneau's memoir on the fur trade underscores this reality, and stands in stark contradiction to the documents produced by traders like Du Lhuth, La Salle, and Radisson who presented a veneer of European dominance as a means of self-promotion.

The intendant stressed the importance of trading generously with the Anishinaabeg in order to maintain their trade and goodwill. "These peoples never negotiate any business without making presents to represent and strengthen their words," he wrote. And Du Chesneau warned that if these gifts were not met reciprocally with kindness and fair trade, the peoples of Anishinaabewaki would make alternate alliances and exchange relationships among themselves. "Our interests are to hold these peoples in unity," he argued, "and to make us in all things their arbiters, their protectors and to bind them by a great dependence and by the gentleness with which we trade with them and caress them and give them presents." The intendant concluded that the Anishinaabeg, or les Sauvages Outaouacs, "must be made to understand that their happiness consists in being attached to the French."[5]

As Du Chesneau's memoir made clear, however, the Anishinaabeg were fiercely independent, and from the French perspective at least, socially incoherent. Ritually the alliance was supposed to serve as a disciplining mechanism—a way to impose order onto Native people making them both legible and accountable to empire. This was the underlying motif of La Potherie's story about Nicolas Perrot, the redemption of the Sauteur slave, and salvation of the Outagamis nation. Through the alliance Onontio gave birth to his children, the Native nations of the French Empire. Onontio brought iron and order so that his children could hunt, live in peace, and when called upon join together to make war on the enemies of New France. But the unspoken story at the heart of Perrot's tale of redemption was the independence of the Anishinaabeg and the existence of an autonomous Native social world in the western interior that was not part of the French alliance.

The presence of permanent and well-supplied European posts on the west coast of Hudson's Bay had changed the geography of the fur trade. More significantly, these posts were also changing the social geography of the western interior. This is what alarmed governor Denonville and Intendant Du Chesneau. Hudson's Bay Company posts gave the indigenous peoples of Anishinaabewaki and the western interior an alternate source of trade goods. For the French, who claimed possession of the west but still conceived of this region as populated by "an infinity of undiscovered nations," this was a frightening prospect. This unknown infinity of nations could become English. Equally problematic, these people, armed and outfitted by both English and French traders, could take whatever shape they wanted. Like the Sauteurs they could reject their father Onontio and the family of nations allied to New France. They might instead embrace new identities in the west, shape-shifting into kin and allies of the Dakota. Expanding the social boundaries of Anishinaabewaki into the northwest, the doodemag of Shagwaamikong and Bowe-ting fractured the social world of Onontio and his children. English posts, in similar fashion, would allow the peoples of Anishinaabewaki to abandon the middle ground of the French fur trade, changing the boundaries of the alliance and the French Empire.

The French Reassert Claims at Hudson's Bay

Intendant Du Chesneau's 1681 memoir called for a diplomatic policy aimed at making New France the agent and guarantor of Native unity in the western interior. This had also been the purpose behind St. Lusson's 1671 ceremonial possession of "the Outaouacs country," imagined as a territory stretching from Sault Sainte Marie to the Pacific Ocean.[6] In both instances the call for unity came from fear of the English at Hudson's Bay, and the corresponding threat of disunity brought about by their presence. When De Chesneau wrote that the English "are still at Hudson's Bay on the north coast and are very much harming our trade in peltries . . . because they attract the Outaouacs nations," he gave voice to the fear that the Anishinaabeg would dissolve, socially and politically, into that undiscovered infinity of nations that dominated the western interior of North America.[7] If their principal trading partners refused to accept their role as the children of Onontio, the French alliance system would collapse, and along with it the fur trade, and any hope of a military counterweight to Iroquois aggression.

The only way to avoid this fate, Du Chesneau concluded, was to drive the English from Hudson's Bay and reassert French claims to this territory or to expand French posts in the west and intercept Native traders heading for the coast. Governor Denonville shared this sentiment. He proposed "to find the means to sustain la Compagnie de la Baie d'Hudson formed in Canada." That is, Denonville called for the empire to fight for control of the inland trade, and their alliance, by establishing French posts at Hudson's Bay.[8]

Fortunately for Denonville and New France, the officers of the Hudson's Bay Company drove Pierre Esprit Radisson and Médard Chouart Des Groseilliers from their employ, and back into the service of the French Empire. The company decided to end private trading, no longer allowing employees to trade from a personal store of supplies for their own profit. Perhaps more importantly, they rejected the idea of establishing a new post at the watershed of the Hayes and Nelson Rivers advanced by Radisson and Des Groseilliers.[9] This watershed represented a direct connection to the prairie parklands in the far west, the home territory of the upland peoples. Located above the English posts at the bottom of the bay, and west of the rivers that connected these posts to the north shore of Lake Superior, this trade route would outflank French traders operating from the western edge of the Great Lakes. The brothers-in-law believed that whoever controlled the mouth of this watershed would dominate trade relations in the western interior. Denied the opportunity to trade on the side, and the possibility of dominating the market for winter coat beaver through a new post at the Nelson River, Radisson and Des Groseilliers joined the French Compagnie de la Baie.[10]

The prospect of great wealth rather than great power politics motivated Radisson and Des Groseilliers, but the establishment of a post on the Nelson River watershed represented an unprecedented possibility to exert European influence on trade relations in the western interior of North America. In recognition of this potential, Jean Baptiste Colbert, the influential minister of marine under Louis XIV, cleared the brothers-in-law of their existing debts, granted them a generous salary, and secured them letters of pardon from the king.[11] In exchange, they were, in Radisson's words, "to employ the greatest of our skill and industry with the natives for the utility and advancement of the beaver trade in the French colonies."[12] Their new post would provide France with direct maritime access to the peoples and resources of the western interior.

Radisson and Des Groseilliers sailed two ships into the Hayes-Nelson watershed in early September 1682 and quickly established French dominance over the western shore of Hudson's Bay. Before the winter hunting season concluded, Radisson had been adopted by the ogimaa of a Cree band that descended the Hayes River to trade at the coast. He also managed to isolate and then take captive two parties of English traders. Radisson had literally embedded himself within a kinship network that stretched from Hudson's Bay onto the prairie parkland of the western interior. Equally important, he excluded the English from this trade.

Following the defection of Radisson and Des Groseilliers, the English recognized the importance of establishing a post at the mouth of the Hayes-Nelson watershed to defending their posts at the bottom of the bay. Accordingly, company directors sent two ships to establish a rival post at this new location. One of these ships arrived within days of the French. The captain had been ordered by the Hudson's Bay Company to set up his post on the "rivers that goe doun into Kennedy," and instructed to "make contacts with the Natives of the River in and above Port Nelson as may in future times ascertain to us a right and property therein and the sole liberty of trade and commerce there."[13] The captain and his crew, however, had no experienced traders and no one who spoke a Native language.

The French, already established at the Hayes-Nelson watershed, possessed immense advantages over their English competitors. Des Groseilliers had been to this region before and had a sense of the geography of the two river systems. Four members of the French company spoke Cree and Ojibwe dialects and possessed considerable experience trading with the peoples of Anishinaabewaki and the interior west. The day after Des Groseilliers selected a site to construct a fort, Radisson went upriver in search of Indians. He quickly encountered a Cree band. A party of nine canoes approached Radisson's camp. One of the eldest men from this group armed with a lance stood in his canoe. He took an arrow from his quiver, signaled to the four directions and then broke the shaft. According to Radisson, this man told his people: "Young men, be not afraid. The sun is favorable unto us. Our enemies shall fear us, for this is the man that we have wished for ever since the days of our fathers."[14] In response Radisson asked this group to identify their leader. They indicated the elder who had spoken words of thanksgiving. Radisson took this man by the hand and declared: "Your friends shall be my friends, and I am come hither to bring arms to destroy your enemies. You nor your wife nor children shall not die of hunger, for I have brought merchandise. Be of good cheer. I will be thy son, and I have brought thee a father."[15]

Unlike the English, Radisson made no pretense of buying the land for his post, a meaningless gesture in the Native New World. Instead, following his speech he gave out tobacco and pipes, and smoked with the people he now claimed as relatives. When Radisson saw a man cut his tobacco with a piece of flat iron, he grabbed the metal and flung it into the fire. Radisson made a show of weeping, dried his tears, and told his companions, "I was very much grieved to see my brethren so ill-provided of all things." He then promised "they should want for nothing whilst I was with them." Radisson then gave his sword to the man who had carried the piece of iron. He ordered his men to pass out knives as presents, and provided his new father with a gun, shot, and powder.[16]

The elder accepted Radisson's claim of kinship. He took off his cloak and placed it on Radisson's shoulders. Two decades earlier at the Feast of the Dead Radisson had claimed to dominate his trading partners, and his writing extolled the superiority of European beliefs, customs, and social mores. Now he wept to show pity, described his gifts as an attempt to relieve want and provide for his new relatives, and placed himself in a subordinate position as a son. In short, Radisson acted in an appropriate fashion for someone who wanted to establish a proper relationship. His new relatives responded in kind. All of the people traveling with his adopted father took off their furs and placed them at the voyageur's feet along with a quantity of peltries. After this exchange Radisson and his Cree relatives parted, but the Cree sent three more canoes loaded with beaver later that same day. For the remainder of the trading season a shifting number of band members stayed with Radisson and his men.

The band that adopted Radisson had clearly come to the coast to trade. It had, however, come seeking the English, not the French. Word seemed to have spread from English forts on the Albany, Moose, and Rupert Rivers that the English intended to trade at the mouth of the Hayes-Nelson watershed. When the Cree met the voyageur they carried an ample supply of processed beaver pelts, and after establishing a relationship with Radisson, they brought him even more. These people were lowland Cree who spoke what came to be known in the eighteenth century as Keskachewan, a dialect subsequently identified as Western Cree by English-speaking traders. The Lowland Cree, who identified themselves in terms of their residence in the river valleys that drained into the bay, were linguistically related to the Upland Cree bands that the English identified generally as Keskachewan, Western Cree, or more simplistically as Upland Indians.[17] Radisson's new relatives put him in contact with a range of lowland and upland bands that arrived at the Hayes River, a place that the Cree called Penesewichewan Sepee, to trade.[18]

The Penesewichewan Sepee was both a place and a social identity. That is, Radisson met and was adopted by a Lowland Cree band that identified itself by its residency in the Hayes River. This identity, however, would have been fluid. Like Anishinaabe doodemag, the lowland Cree referred to themselves both by band designation, and by the term *Athinuwick*, which translated as "people" or "human beings."[19] *Athinuwick* was a term linguistically related to the Ojibwe dialect word *Anishinaabeg*. Unlike the Anishinaabeg, however, Athinuwick bands attached an additional modifier onto their self-designations. By the eighteenth century Hudson's Bay Company traders had mapped out these divisions. Coastal dwellers identified themselves as Winipeg-athinuwick. *Winipeg* literally translated as foul water–salt water, and *Winipeg-athinuwick* as "people of the seaside." Lowland bands that lived in the marshlands created by inland rivers that drained into the coastal plains of Hudson's Bay referred to themselves as Muskekowuck-athinuwick, or "people of the swamp."[20] The Penesewichewan Sepee, in other words, identified themselves linguistically to other Western Cree speakers as human beings, or athinuwick, from the seacoast.

Athinuwick implied a shared collective identity formed by the migration of individuals and extended family units between bands associated with the watersheds of the Nelson, Hayes, Severn, Moose, and Albany Rivers. When Des Groseilliers traded at Rupert River in 1674, for example, he interacted with individual hunters he identified as Moosu Sepee (Moose River people), Washeo Sepee (Severn River people), the Eastern Cree or Naskapi Innu band that wintered next to his post, and two Gens des Terres doodemag identified as the Cuscudidah and Tabitee. Similar patterns of migration occurred between the river mouths on the western sea coast and the muskeg or swamplands that demarcated the Hudson's Bay lowlands.[21] Lowland Cree bands expanded and contracted seasonally, and moved between river basins, and between the coast and interior to hunt and trap as game populations shifted.[22] The Athinuwick peoples, in other words, were part of Du Chesneau's infinity of nations and their ability to shape-shift into different composite social units created the illusion that the west was full of new peoples yet to be discovered by the empires of the Atlantic World.

Like the Anishinaabeg, the Athinuwick constructed relationships with other bands that migrated between the western interior and coastal (as opposed to lakeshore) trading villages. Many of these interior or upland bands were also Western Cree speakers, the Nehiyaw-athinuwick. *Nehiyaw* translated as "those that speak the same language." Upland Cree bands also referred to themselves as *Saka-athinuwick*, or "bush people." Like the Lowland Cree,

Upland Cree peoples also identified themselves by band designations, usually associated with place names or animal totems.[23] The Upland Cree were
also closely identified with the Siouan-speaking Assiniboine, with whom
they forged an intimate relationship centered on military alliance and long-
distance trade. The Assiniboine called themselves *Nokoda*, a dialect variation of the word *Dakota* signifying "allies." Though linguistically linked to the
Siouan-speaking peoples identified as the Nadouessioux or Sioux by Europeans, the Nakoda were a distinct population occupying territory stretching
west from Lake Winnipeg to the Saskatchewan River region of the northern
prairie parkland. Their designation *Assiniboine* in European records came
from a phonetic transcription of the Anishinaabemowin identification *assini-
pwa-n*, or stone enemy.[24] In addition to the Cree and Assiniboine, there were
also Anishinaabe bands that spoke Ojibwe or mixed Cree-Ojibwe dialects
that English traders classified as Upland Indians.[25] All of these peoples migrated between interior hunting grounds and summer trading villages. By the
late seventeenth century these trading villages were increasingly associated
with either the French or the English.

    Kinship facilitated this pattern of migration and exchange among the
Athinuwick in the Hudson's Bay lowlands. It also determined what peoples
or groups had access to the river mouths where the English, and now the
French, set up their trading posts. Upland Cree bands, or the Nehiyaw-
athinuwick, and inland Anishinaabeg bands descended these watersheds to
trade at the coast by negotiating directly with the Lowland Cree. This negotiation took different forms ranging from raiding and theft to the creation
of socially constructed kinship bonds that frequently involved intermarriage
between social groups.[26] Among the Lowland Cree an ogimaa determined the
nature of this relationship with outsiders. The English translated *ogimaa* as
"captain" or "king," and they appealed to these captains to attract Upland (inland) Indians to their posts on the coast.[27] Radisson's adoption fit this pattern.
By attaching himself to the ogimaa of the Penesewichewan Sepee, Radisson
positioned himself to begin expanding kinship and exchange relationships
from the western interior to his post on the Hayes River.

    The complicated latticework of identity that connected the Athinuwick
to one another, to Anishinaabeg and Assiniboine bands, and to particular
landscapes did not fit European categories of social identity. The mobility
and flexibility inherent in social relationships designed to facilitate migration
made it difficult, if not impossible, to impose the hierarchy of empire and
national identity onto the western interior. Radisson's experience, however,

allowed him to recognize that identity and authority could expand laterally to encompass the seemingly infinite peoples that lived in the west. Moreover, this network could retract, reform, and reexpand time and again to allow traders and hunters to adapt to changes in environment and population. Radisson offered the ogimaa of the Penesewichewan access to a European father. But at least in his narrative, he did not attach this father figure to Onontio and New France, and neither did he offer himself as the voice of this distant father. Instead, Radisson chose to become a child himself. The role of the father was not so much attached to a person or institution as to the post itself, and the commitment to keep it supplied with European commodities. Radisson would not be the head of a vast alliance of Native nations. Rather, he would become an extension of a shifting kinship and exchange network attached to the Penesewichewan Sepee, and to his post in their watershed.

Radisson's post at the mouth of the Hayes-Nelson watershed would be a gateway to the Native peoples of the western interior. The Hayes and Nelson Rivers converge on the west coast of Hudson's Bay, separated by a spit of tidal marshland approximately seven and a half miles wide. From this point the Nelson, arching to the north, connects the bay, via the Saskatchewan River, to the prairie parklands and northern Great Plains. The Hayes, sweeping to the south, connects the bay to Lake Winnipeg and to the upper Mississippi valley via the Red River valley. People, pelts, and goods flowed south along these watersheds either to French posts or to Native peoples who traded at French posts. Trading from the mouth of the Hayes River gave Radisson the potential to redirect the flow of people, furs, and goods that made up the inland trade.[28]

European Competition for Native Allegiances

Within days of Radisson's adoption, the voyageur discovered that not one but two separate parties of English traders had arrived to compete for the allegiance of the Penesewichewan Sepee, and to launch their own bid to capture the western fur trade. The two groups of English traders, however, were initially unaware of one another. Unlicensed traders from New England and a Hudson's Bay Company ship had entered the Nelson River within days of one another. The New Englanders had established themselves farther inland while the company ship remained near the mouth of the river. Radisson encountered the New England traders first and learned that the crew was inexperienced, did not speak any Native languages, and was deeply afraid of being discovered by the Hudson's Bay Company post commander. Radisson proceeded to inform the New Englanders, and later the Hudson's Bay Company men, that he had taken possession of the Hayes-Nelson watershed for France. He also claimed that the Native peoples in this region were attached to the French and hostile to the English. Radisson cautioned both parties to remain in their forts, and he guaranteed their safety if they promised not to trade with the Natives.

The English, although they did not know it, outnumbered the French, but they lacked language skills and the resolve to risk their lives in an unknown country. Radisson easily convinced both groups that they were vulnerable to attack, and they quickly consented to his conditions. Hiding in their posts, the English never learned that they might have overwhelmed Radisson's small trading party. During the winter the voyageur frequently visited the two encampments. Through bold maneuvers like this, he gained valuable intelligence about the English forces and their provisions. When the Nelson River iced over and crushed the Hudson's Bay Company ship, killing the ship captain and stranding his crew, Radisson recognized that this catastrophe presented the French with an opportunity. He immediately captured the surviving commanders of the two English trading parties, and removed them to his post. Leaderless, and isolated in a harsh environment of which they had no knowledge, the two English crews surrendered to the French. With the English eliminated as a threat, Radisson then sent Des Groseilliers's son Jean-Baptiste inland to winter with the Penesewichewan Sepee, "to go along into the country to make the several sorts of Indians to come traffic with us."[29]

Toward the spring Jean-Baptiste returned with Native peoples that promised to bring their peltries to the French fort. Again, Radisson did not identify these people by name. He did write, however, that in addition to the Indians brought in by Jean-Baptiste, "a good company of Indians, our old allies," also sent word that they would trade at the Hayes River post.[30] It seems likely these "old allies" were Native peoples that traded with Radisson and Des Groseilliers at either their Rupert River or Moose River posts, when the voyageurs worked for the Hudson's Bay Company. It also seems likely that Radisson's old allies were Lowland Cree bands, because the groups that he mentioned in his narrative moved easily, and frequently, between the various river valleys that drained into the bay. When spring arrived and the rivers opened up for travel, Winipeg-athinuwick and Muskekowuck-athinuwick bands gathered at Radisson's post to negotiate their place and status in the composite social formation that made the inland trade possible. As they came together they began to debate among themselves about whether they should trade with the French at the Penesewichewan Sepee or migrate south to trade with the English at their posts on the Albany, Moose, and Rupert Rivers.

The Native traders who came to the French fort in the spring complained that Radisson and Des Groseilliers traded too hard. These people, including the band of Radisson's adopted father, called a council. They laid out presents for the brothers-in-law consisting of a variety of foodstuffs. A single man addressed the French traders, comparing them unfavorably to the English: "You men that pretend to give us our lives, will not you let us live? . . . You style yourselves our brethren, and yet you will not give us what those that are not our brethren will give. Accept our presents, or we will come see you no more." The council offered Radisson gifts of food, a gesture that signaled their desire to feed the French and fulfill their obligations as kin, but with a new understanding about the rate of exchange. They asked Radisson to accept these new conditions of reciprocity, and give more generously to his relatives. Radisson at first refused to speak, and when prompted to respond he asked: "To whom will thou have me answer? I heard a dog bark."[31] Radisson's angry response told his adopted relatives that their gesture was an insult. They spoke to him like a dog snarling at a stranger, not like a brother.

A complicated negotiation ensued where Radisson and various Cree band members argued about the nature of their obligations to one another. The voyageur drew his knife, grabbed his adopted father by the hair, and demanded to know who he was. The ogimaa responded, "Thy father," to which Radisson proclaimed, "If thou art my father and dost love me, and if thou art chief, speak for me. Thou art master of my goods."[32] He then released his father, and taunted the council, telling them if they wished to see the English they could visit the traders held captive at his fort. Radisson concluded this harangue by giving the man who spoke against him a sword. "Here take this," he said, "begone to your brethren, the English. Tell them my name and that I will go take them." Radisson indicated to his brother-in-law that it was time to leave the council and return to their fort, but his adopted father stopped them. The ogimaa, he wrote, "encouraged us saying we were men; we force nobody; everyone was free; and that he and his nation would hold true to us." Then, according to Radisson, he promised, "that he would go persuade the nations to come unto us, as he already had done, by the presents we sent them."[33]

The Indians gathered for the council, however, had not reached a unanimous agreement about the kinship status of the French, or the desirability of inviting Upland Indians to trade at this post. In defiance of both Radisson and his adopted father, the man who spoke out against French prices threatened to kill any Assiniboines who came to trade among the Penesewichewan Sepee. Radisson threatened this man, in turn. "I answered him," he wrote, and declared "I would march into his country and eat sagamite [meat broth] in the head of his grandmother."[34] As he spoke this insult, Radisson simultaneously presented gifts of tobacco to the council members who supported him. They accepted his gift, and by extension his terms of exchange. Radisson had effectively disgraced his opponent and together with his adopted father convinced the bands gathered at his post to accept the notion that trading with French, no matter the rate of exchange, left the Athinuwick peoples in the most powerful position.

This was power envisioned in terms of the politics of an Algonquian social formation. In other words, Radisson and the ogimaa of the Penesewichewa Sepee demonstrated their ability to fashion a coalition of lowland bands so as to guarantee the circulation of people and resources between the coast and interior. The council ended in a feast where Radisson exchanged trade goods for the pelts that the Winipeg-athinuwick and Mushkekowuck-athinuwick brought him. He accepted the gift of food offered by the council, and responded in kind by feeding his trading partners and their families. With this series of exchanges Radisson and his adopted father stifled their opposition, and connected a network of Lowland Cree bands to the French and the Hayes River post.

In his narrative describing these encounters, however, Radisson wanted to emphasize his power in terms that would make sense to a European audience. He wanted to demonstrate his ability to enforce a fixed trade regime, and he wanted to demonstrate mastery over his Native trading partners. Thus, he insisted on a particular rate of exchange that was, evidently, less generous than the English offered at their posts at the bottom of the bay. This strategy was largely rhetorical.

Insisting on a fixed rate of exchange sounded good to a European audience, but it was a risky strategy to pursue with the autonomous Native trade networks of the interior west. This sort of trade regime represented a form of balanced exchange that was very fragile. Standard rates of exchange depended on a consistent production and supply of pelts, and this level of consistency was rare in the North American fur trade. Game populations shifted. The desire and ability of Native groups to participate in the fur trade shifted as well.[35] Moreover, as Radisson indicated in his narrative, he faced considerable competition from English posts to his south, and from French posts in the pays d'en haut and coureurs de bois trading in the bush.

To compensate for competition and instability Radisson gave gifts generously. He insisted on a fixed rate balanced exchange, but he created imbalance by giving presents. This put a large quantity of goods in circulation to stimulate additional production, and at the same time created obligation, an expected return of his generosity in one form or another.[36] This strategy, deftly exploited by Radisson's adopted father, persuaded the lowland bands to trade with the French in his territory. Radisson's gift giving and exchange practices represented diplomacy, however, and not a method of political control. In his narrative he implied otherwise. This document was written to demonstrate that Radisson could set the rate of exchange, and ensure profitability, by exerting control over his Native trading partners. In reality, Radisson, a highly skilled trader, could at best hope to influence his kin and allies—just as his adopted father and other ogimaag led through the power of their influence rather than through coercion.

This, in fact, was the true arena of European competition. Europeans were not locked in a struggle to be the first power to colonize, and control, the western interior. They were, instead, struggling to find a way to influence autonomous Native social formations already connected to a wider Atlantic World economy. Radisson's alliance with the Penesewichewan Sepee represented one such possibility. This indigenous social formation connected the bay and interior. The lack of consensus that Radisson faced at council, however, revealed the problematic nature of exchange networks that connected migratory Athinuwick bands at the seacoast and muskeg with upland peoples. The Muskekowuck-athinuwick, that is people from the marshlands upriver from English and French posts, could choose to block the descent of upland bands like the Assiniboine if, for example, they felt excluded from the alliance formed between Radisson and his adopted father.[37] The Muskekowuck, or Swampy Cree bands, historically traded at both the Nelson and Severn Rivers, and during the time of Radisson's narrative only the English were able to maintain well-supplied posts in this region. Similarly, the Anishinaabeg or Gens des Terres from the Moose River region might persuade the Assiniboine and their Upland Cree allies to trade with the English at James Bay, or at French posts on the northwest shore of Lake Superior. The threat presented to Radisson at council was not that one or more individuals might defect to the English. It was, rather, that while the Lowland Cree shared a sense of collective identity, they did not possess a singular national identity.

Bands routinely shifted their trade relations between different river basins controlled by people who were their kin, or with whom kin ties could easily be reanimated.

In truth, the French and the Penesewichewan Sepee had constructed a mutually dependent relationship. As kin they reconstructed themselves socially into a network that served as a conduit of exchange between commodities manufactured in Europe and animal pelts that were, for the most part, trapped and processed in the western interior. The ability of Radisson and his adopted father to unify the lowland bands around an exchange network centered at, and among, the Penesewichewan Sepee, was only a minor victory. The more significant challenge would be for this alliance to connect itself to the Upland Indians that controlled the resources of the western interior. And that was a problem that had plagued both the French and the English since the beginning of the fur trade.

This problem took two forms. On the one hand it was structural. The French consistently failed to deliver a sufficient quantity of trade goods to forge a lasting alliance network in the western interior. Radisson and other voyageurs such as Du Lhut frequently benefited from the ambitions of Native leaders who co-opted their trading ventures in order to expand an alliance network, or strengthen their position in the inland trade. But ogimaag commanded respect and authority only so long as they provided for their people and allies. Alliance relationships collapsed, became strained, or even turned into violent conflict—particularly between different ethnic and linguistic communities—when the circulation of material goods faltered.

On the other hand, this problem was also political. The peoples of the Native New World were autonomous polities, and creating an alliance between lowland and upland peoples was a complicated political and territorial negotiation. While Radisson's adopted father promised he would "persuade the nations" to trade with the French, he also reminded the voyageur "everyone was free." Read carefully, the ogimaa of the Penesiwechewan Sepee clearly linked the power of his persuasion to the presents or trade goods the French had sent to them following their arrival at the bay.

Radisson needed to keep Lowland Cree traders, and their upland allies, attached to his post and his adopted father. Accordingly, he used trade like an Algonquian to expand and solidify the network of bands attached to the Penesewichiwan Sepee. After forging a consensus among lowland bands at council, Radisson learned about a dispute between the family of his adopted father and "another great family of the country." He identified this other family, or doodem, as the Martens. Radisson's new father had recently killed a member of this band when they came to the coast to trade. Apparently he killed to defend his family, but the death remained unresolved. The ogimaa had not raised or covered the dead, breaching any alliance relationship with the Marten band, and leaving the Penesewichewan Sepee vulnerable to attack. Radisson recognized that this situation jeopardized his adopted father's status among the lowland Cree, and he gave the man a large supply of trade goods to cover the dead and restore his social position. The French traders and the Penesewichewan Sepee then hosted a "feast of unity" to reestablish the relationship between these peoples.

The fact that Radisson identified the Marten doodem by name presents an intriguing puzzle. He designated only one other Native group by name, the Assinibone. Why name these bands when he failed to differentiate among the other Native peoples he encountered at his post? The answer seems to lie in the fact that the Martens, like the Assiniboine were "Upland Indians" from the western interior. In the mid-nineteenth century, the Anishinaabe historian William Warren identified the Marten or Waabbizheshiwag doodem as closely connected through intermarriage and alliance to the Monsoni or Moose doodem.[38] These two Ojibwe-speaking bands were connected to and often identified as Sauteurs by the French.

The Marten and Monsoni were connected politically and socially to the people of Bow-e-ting, or Sault Sainte Marie, but they were from the western interior. The Marten doodem hunted and lived in the watersheds that connected Gichigamiing (Lake Superior) to Gichi-ziibi (the Mississsippi) and the Dakota country. The Monsoni occupied territory northwest of Gichigamiing and they were allied with people identified by the English as Lake of the Woods Cree, peoples who spoke a mixed Ojibwe-Cree dialect reflecting their history of intermarriage among the Anishinaabe doodemag.[39] The Monsoni and Cree traded with the English in 1678 at their Hudson's Bay posts, and may have been among the upland bands trading with the English in 1673–74 in the Moose River region.[40] As traders with the English, their presence within the exchange network created by Radisson and his adopted father was vital. New France was increasingly losing the trade of the peoples from the western interior to the English.

As in past narratives, Radisson presented this sort of complicated diplomatic wrangling as evidence of his expertise. He wrote this manuscript after he had returned to France, and he showed it to courtiers in both England and France to highlight his performance and to demonstrate the importance of the Hayes-Nelson post.[41] Read carefully, however, this narrative styled by Radisson as his fifth voyage reveals an ogimaa who was himself a skilled leader. This man effectively used his relationship with Radisson to secure access to French goods and mediation. This access allowed the ogimaa to connect his band to upland peoples, an important connection that brought the pelts into his river valley that would, in turn, keep the French at this location, maintain his social status, and protect his people.

Together, Radisson and his adopted father had managed to activate a kinship and exchange network that brought trading Indians from across the lowland watersheds, and from the western interior, to the French fort. Their success was mutually dependent. By late summer, however, the French found themselves in a rather perilous position. Spring breakup had been particularly harsh and both French ships had been destroyed by the surge of shifting ice flows. Radisson and Des Groseilliers cobbled a new ship together from the wreckage. They took their prisoners and the New Englanders' ship and set sail on July 27, 1683. They left Jean-Baptiste Des Groseilliers behind, in charge of a mere seven Frenchmen, to maintain their post and the French claim to Hudson's Bay.

Native Ambitions and French Vulnerability

Once again Radisson and Des Groseilliers's pursuit of wealth in the New World became entangled in the politics of the Old World. The voyageurs became embroiled in a conflict between the court of Louis XIV and colonial officials over taxes, trade licenses and policy, and the exercise of political power in New France. La Compagnie de la Baie d'Hudson collapsed and was reformed with the appointment of a new governor. The brothers-in-law lost their claim to a share of the peltries they had acquired at the bay as a result of the bureaucratic infighting surrounding this new company.[42] They returned to Europe bitter and alienated from the French Empire. The new governor failed to resupply Jean-Baptiste Des Groseilliers and the skeleton crew left behind by the French at the mouth of the Nelson and Hayes Rivers for the 1683 trading season. Perhaps more significantly, the English managed to keep their posts at the Nelson, Albany, Moose, and Rupert Rivers well supplied.[43]

It is easy to think of the history of Hudson's Bay in terms of this rivalry between the English and French Empires. The Europeans engaged in this struggle, however, remained stranded on the beach until the end of the eighteenth century. Although rather slim and narrowly focused on trade and empire, the historical archive for the Hudson's Bay region during this period offers a revealing glimpse of the dynamic politics and evolving social formations of the Native New World. The way that Native peoples connected to one another at the coast and to peoples in the west had a far greater impact on the inland trade than imperial rivalry. This was where the real power struggle for the control of Hudson's Bay took place. The creation of a new European outpost in the Hayes-Nelson watershed, and its sudden collapse, created a political vacuum that resulted in a violent attempt to change the social order among the peoples of the coast and between those of the coast and the interior.

The ogimaa of the Penesewichewan Sepee was not the only man with ambitions among the Winipe and Muskekowuck-athinuwick. Just days after the departure of the French ship Jean-Baptiste Des Groseilliers and his men heard the sound of cannon shots coming from the Nelson River to their north. They set out to investigate and discovered a party of "14 or 15 savages loaded with merchandise." According to Jean-Baptiste the members of this trading party identified themselves as Muskekowick-athinuwick from the Washeo Sepee, or Severn River Cree. Their leader bluntly informed the French "that they came to trade with their brothers who were established at the bottom of the bay." In other words, they came to trade with their English allies, their "brothers" from the bottom of the bay, who had established a new post at the mouth of the Nelson River.[44]

The Washeo Sepee, that is the Severn River Lowland Cree, visited the French fort at Jean-Baptiste's invitation, and they signaled a willingness to realign themselves with the French. They accepted gifts of tobacco, and claimed that they would have been just as happy to trade with the French had they been aware of their presence. The Washeo Sepee remained outside the French post, however, entering one man at a time only, and their ogimaa returned to the English under the pretext of recovering a forgotten item. When he returned, it seems he had struck a deal with the English. Together they would decapitate the French connection to the Penesewechiwan Sepee, and take control of the inland trade flowing into the Nelson River.

The ogimaa of the Washeo Sepee spread word of his plans to the Muskekowick-athinuwick gathered around the French fort. Then he waited until he found Jean-Baptiste alone inside his post. He seized the voyageur by the hand, and as Jean-Baptiste later explained the incident to Radisson, declared the French were of "no value," and he complained, "I had not paid him by a present for the possession of the country." This man asserted that such tribute was owed to him "who was the chief of all the nations and the friend of the English at the bottom of the bay."[45] Still grasping the hand of Jean-Baptiste, the ogimaa struck at him with his war club. The voyageur blocked the blow with his free hand, and wrestled his attacker to the ground. He drew his sword and stood over the ogimaa, realizing too late that Indians carrying war clubs surrounded him. One of these warriors cried out: "Do not kill the French, for their death will be avenged by all the nations from above upon all our families!"[46] The Washeo Sepee panicked and threw down their weapons. Jean-Baptiste let them depart unharmed, hoping that he could preserve an alliance among the Muskekowick-athinuwick families through this act of generosity.

The ogimaa of the Washeo Sepee, however, had clearly chosen to develop his relationship with the English to enhance his status as a trading captain. This man's attack on Jean-Baptiste was not only a challenge to the French but also a challenge to his group's Penesewichewan Sepee relatives. When Jean-Baptiste's adopted brother-in-law learned about this attack he led a war party to track down the Washeo Sepee traders. They caught up to the ogimaa and his men, and invited them to a feast. This act of generosity was an attempt at reconciliation. The adopted brother-in-law fulfilled his obligation as kin, and asked the ogimaa to repair his relationship with Jean-Baptiste. This man responded with contempt, asserting that he would return in the spring and the Frenchman would die by his hands. The adopted brother of Jean-Baptiste then stabbed the ogimaa, and struck him in the head with a hatchet. He died immediately. They spared his followers, but proceeded to the English posts and killed two employees of the Hudson's Bay Company.[47]

In spite of the ferocious defense mounted on his behalf, Jean-Baptiste's adopted relatives could not change the dire circumstances that made the French trader vulnerable in the first place. Jean-Baptiste could not fulfill the social obligations created by Radisson and his adopted father. He had no trade goods, and his alliance network depended on the exchange of pelts and goods to maintain generalized reciprocity, or peaceful exchange, among the many different peoples moving between the coast and interior. A few months after the attempted assassination another party of Mushkekowuck-athinuwick traders "from the south coast" arrived at the French post to trade for guns. Jean-Baptiste had to turn them away and they went to the English. The Hudson's Bay Company traders not only supplied this party with guns, they gave them presents, and promised even more presents if they killed Jean-Baptiste. Fearing to act directly this band appealed to warriors among the

Penesewichewan Sepee to abandon the French. There was apparently some ill feeling toward the impoverished traders. Jean-Baptiste complained of being spied on, and one warrior shot and wounded a voyageur when he traveled to a remote location away from camp. Growing increasingly desperate, Jean-Baptiste was forced to ask the ogimaa of the Penesewichewan Sepee to arrange a truce with the English in order to trade the pelts he had acquired for English guns.[48] This was the only way that he could resume trading, and maintain his precarious relationship to his uncle's disintegrating alliance.

While Jean-Baptiste traded with the English to arm the Penesewichewan Sepee, his Native relatives fought to resurrect the alliance. Radisson's adopted father, the ogimaa, sent word, according to Jean-Baptiste, "to entreat all nations who had sworn friendship to my father and my uncle to come make war upon the English and the savages on the southern coast."[49] In this narrative Radisson and his nephew switch between the terms families and nations to describe the social units vying for political power at the coast. The interweaving of kinship ties and community based identities tied to the watersheds that drained into the coast created confusion for Europeans trying to sort out these politics. What at times seemed like an infinity of nations to Europeans, an endless number of autonomous native peoples, periodically revealed itself to be an intimately connected multipolar social formation. This became most obvious when Europeans became involved in and tried to make sense of events such as the murder of the Washeo Sepee ogimaa. This murder reflected the mounting tensions between the lowland bands from the southern and northern coasts of Hudson's bay as they struggled there to make their communities into a nexus of trade, alliance, and kinship that linked Europeans at the Hudson's Bay coast to the western interior.

In the midst of this growing crisis the Assiniboine arrived at the French post. This was what the Muskekowuck-athinuwick fought for—to be the link that connected Upland Indians to European traders in coastal river valleys. Radisson's generous gift giving had brought large numbers of the Assiniboine to the Penesewichewan Sepee. According to Jean-Baptiste, four hundred Assiniboine men plus their families came to trade. They expected to find a well-supplied French post. Instead they found chaos. Jean-Baptiste, already low on provisions, could not sustain such a large population of trading Indians at his post. The Assiniboine immediately sent half of their people back into the west to avoid starvation.[50] The rest resolved to stay and march against the English and the Washeo Sepee. Jean-Baptiste managed to maintain the allegiance of these upland and lowland bands, in spite of his lack of trade goods.

This war party, however, was a Native initiative and should be seen as part of the larger pattern of raiding and trading that shaped social relationships and identity in the indigenous west. The Assiniboine, according to Jean-Baptiste, had decided to gamble on Radisson's return and his promise to connect them to a steady supply of French goods.

Cree Mothers and English Fathers

Radisson set sail for Hudson's Bay on May 17, 1684, once again in the employ of the English. With the merger of the French and English posts at the Hayes-Nelson watershed, peace was restored to the alliance and exchange network of the Muskekowuck-athinuwick. As soon as the company ships arrived at the river mouth, Radisson made his way upriver with a small party of men. He feared a conflict with the French voyageurs who had remained at the bay, and he immediately set out to find Jean-Baptiste Des Groseilliers. Radisson quickly encountered ten canoes of Indians descending the river to trade. He asked if Jean-Baptiste had any relations among them, and one man replied, "He is my son." Radisson sat this man down and called over the English captain who followed him ashore. He told Jean-Baptiste's adopted father, "I have made peace with the English for love of you. They and I from henceforth shall be but one."[51] Then he made this man embrace the English captain, and sent him off to find his nephew. Jean-Baptiste arrived the next morning. Radisson pulled him aside and in a private conversation told his nephew, "I come to inform you that we are now Englishmen."[52]

In truth, the distinction between French and English influence at the bay was minimal. The kinship ties that connected Jean-Baptiste to Radisson and Radisson to the Hudson's Bay Company made it possible for both men to become English.[53] In the social world of the interior west, a world constructed by the interplay of individuals and groups with multiple identities, this transformation was not unusual. Radisson's narrative and Hudson's Bay Company documents represented these events as part of a larger struggle between the English and French Empires over possession of the west and its resources. It was, more accurately, a struggle between different Europeans stranded on the beach at Hudson's Bay to position themselves within an autonomous and economically powerful Native exchange network that stretched from the coast deep into the west. In this struggle Europeans changed loyalty, and identity, as readily as their Native trading partners. Identity formation, and in particular national identity, was a new and often unreliable category in North America, even among European immigrants.

Radisson's return, and his rebirth as an English trader, resulted in a quick dissipation of tensions among the many different peoples gathered at the coast. The structural weakness of the French fur trade and the autonomy of the Native networks of the western interior resulted in the ready acceptance of this transformation. Radisson and the English supply ships and reinforcements arrived literally on the eve of battle. The Assiniboine-led raid was halted and the French voyageurs shape-shifted into "Englishmen." With a crisis averted, Radisson immediately set out to repair and expand the trade network he had built with the Penesewichewan Sepee.

Again Radisson produced a narrative, titled his "Sixth Voyage," which described events following his return to Hudson's Bay in 1684. Radisson arrived at a time of social turmoil, and as a consequence the voyageur asserted a public persona alternately as a son, brother, and, perhaps most intriguing, as a father. Immediately after his meeting with Jean-Baptiste, Radisson proceeded to a rendezvous with thirty canoes of Upland Indians. Again, he failed to name these people but they were most likely some combination of Assiniboine and Western Cree, or Nehiyaw-athinuwick, possibly traveling from as far away as the country west of Lake Winnipeg.[54] According to Radisson's narrative these people traded with French traders in the Great Lakes as well as with the English at Rupert River. When Radisson arrived they had been mobilizing for war against the English, and they were reluctant to accept them so suddenly as allies and trading partners.

In response to this reticence, and following Native custom, Radisson called a feast of unity to unite the upland peoples in an alliance relationship with the people of Penesewichewan Sepee and the English. In his narrative, Radisson explained that he began this ritual in the manner expected of an ogimaa, with a speech. He expounded upon the strength of the English, and he spoke of his own desire to provide for the needs of his relatives. Radisson described in vivid detail the superiority of English sea power, and their capacity to increase the flow of trade goods into the west. He then provided a generous feast from English provisions to demonstrate this power. At the conclusion of the meal, and in a reversal of standard conventions for European traders, Radisson demanded of "the chief of the savages, in the presence of those of his nation, that he should make me presents."[55]

The Upland Indians spoke among themselves at some length before presenting Radisson with a gift of thirty beaver skins. They asked Radisson to accept this "as a sign of our ancient friendship." The Assiniboine and Upland Cree apologized for giving such a small gift, but they noted, "the French of Canada made them presents to oblige them to open their parcels." They also indicated that they had traded with the English at the bottom of the bay because of the generous rate they offered, "3 hatchets for a beaver."[56] With this dramatic reversal of convention, Radisson confirmed the hard truth about his place in the inland trade and the status of his alliance in the Native New World. He faced competition from both the French and from the Hudson's Bay Company posts to his south. This competition was more than a matter of supply and demand, however; it was a reflection of the social relations that made up the inland trade. In order to bring such a diversity of Native peoples together across such a vast space, a lot of goods had to change hands. Native peoples traded to acquire desired goods, but also to establish and maintain social relationships that enabled them to make the trip from the prairie west to the seacoast.

In this narrative Radisson presented his demand for gifts as a show of English strength. In reality, Radisson asked for gifts in order to establish the social context for the generous terms of trade he was about to offer: "I replied to them that I had compassion for their condition," and he declared, "I would do all in my power to relieve them." Radisson then noted that trading at the bay "spared them the trouble of going to Quebec," an arduous journey for peoples from the west. Then he stressed the advantages of trading at his post, saying, "as to the difference in the trade of the English at the bottom of the bay with ours, I told that each was the master of that which belonged to him." Radisson echoed his adopted father, who noted that in terms of trading and alliance, "we force nobody; everyone was free."[57] They were free to trade where they wanted, but he declared, "I had for my friends all the other nations; that those were the masters of my merchandises who yielded themselves to my generosity."[58]

Radisson, in effect, presented himself as a pivotal point in an exchange relationship that linked Native peoples in the western interior to Europe. He concluded this council by noting, "that there were 30 years I had been their brother," and he hinted "I would be in the future their father if they continued to love me." This was a declaration of the strength of his trading network, and an intriguing promise. Radisson declared himself and the English brothers in relation to their native trading partners. He presented the idea, however, that he could become an English father. Radisson told his audience, "I would cause all the nations around to be called, to carry to them my merchandises," and he noted that this increase in trade "rendered them powerful." The voyageur then offered the upland peoples ten knives for one processed beaver, and a gun for twelve, more generous terms than the posts to the south.[59] With these concluding gestures to his feast of unity, Radisson offered himself as part of an extensive kinship and exchange network where his relatives, in true Algonquian fashion, could demand his goods to meet their needs. He was a brother who might yet become the head of an extensive Native family.

This was exactly what Denonville feared. The undiscovered infinity of nations in the western interior might be discovered; that is, they would be transformed into subjects of their English rivals. This fear was misplaced. Radisson succeeded because he worked to integrate French and English traders into the social world of the Muskekowuck-athinuwick, not because he turned the Cree nations of Hudson's Bay into English subjects. No sooner had Radisson concluded the feast of unity with the upland peoples when, he wrote, "I also saw plainly the need the English had of being succored and the necessity the French had for provisions."[60] He promptly set about arranging a second feast of unity aimed at reconciling the Europeans at the coast. This was the antithesis of the middle ground. This was the wholesale adaptation of Native cultural practices to assimilate European peoples into the social world of Native North America.

Radisson brought together six of the most important leaders among the Muskekowuck-athinuwick. He then brought his nephew and the English governor before this council. In their presence he asked Jean-Baptiste to remain behind while he returned to England. His nephew at first declined, but then the governor promised to divide his authority with the French trader. The council of ogimaag told Jean-Baptiste "that they regarded him as the nephew of the one who brought peace to the nations and made the union of the English and the French." After listening to their testimony the voyageur consented to stay, "and the savages on their part burst out in cries of joy." A feast followed this council where the Muskekowuck-athinuwick wept over Radisson, lamenting the loss of their French father. Then they lavished Radisson and his nephew with presents while they cried: "We have lost our father. We have lost our children." The voyageurs accepted their gifts and Radisson responded, "Here is the nephew of your father, who will be your son. He remains with you and he will have the care of his mothers."[61] With this ritual the Muskekowuck-athinuwick gave birth to new family, and a new alliance. They became mothers and partners to English fathers who accepted their responsibility to use English sea power to care for their relations in the Native New World.

The manuscripts of Radisson's "Fifth Voyage" and "Sixth Voyage" offer a brief and rare recognition in European records of the vast, independent, Native social formation that dominated the interior west and the western fur trade. Here, even more so than at the western edge of the country the French called the pays d'en haut, Europeans were forced to treat with a multiethnic social space, an "infinity of nations," that defied patterns of national identity and territorialization emerging in Europe and European America. At times localized historically specific forces altered the social arrangements that governed identity and interethnic relationships in this space. The intrusions of French traders, or the possibility of increased access to English goods that came with the development of Hudson's Bay Company posts, created a dynamic push and pull that resulted in a continual rearrangement of the social relations of production among Native groups in the interior west.[62] This readjustment was reflected in the shifting patterns of raiding, alliance, and kinship that forced Radisson to become a brother, son, and father in order to stay connected to Native peoples who clearly existed outside the boundaries of colonial power in North America.

The readjustment of local identities within this social formation also suggested the extent to which the western interior remained part of a Native New World. The ability of lowland bands and individuals to move between overlapping identities such as Winipeg-athinuwick, Muskekowuck-athinuwick, and Penesewichewan Sepee, for example, facilitated the movement of people, pelts, and goods along the coast and through river valleys. These identities named the relationship of Native peoples to particular landscapes.[63] They also structured the relationship between the Penesewichewan Sepee, the Washeo Sepee, and other lowland peoples with various bands of Nehiyaw-athinuwick and Anishinaabeg, who were, in turn, connected by name or identity to landscapes in the west such as the prairie parkland and the boreal forest and to villages at La Pointe or Shagwaamikong in the Great Lakes and Mille Lacs or Mde Wakan in the pper Mississippi valley.

The Europeans at Hudson's Bay, in contrast, remained stranded on the beach. They migrated between the river mouths, their North American colonies, and European port cities. They claimed possession of an interior of which they possessed very little knowledge, and over which, practically speaking, they exercised very little influence accept when they operated on indigenous terms. The French, in fact, learned of Radisson's defection only when they finally showed up to reinforce his post in September 1684. When Radisson claimed possession of this country for the French they had renamed the Nelson River the Bourbon River. Radisson's reinforcements, however, discovered the English in possession of this space, which they insisted was Port Nelson. The two monarchies argued about the name and possession of this river basin for the next twenty-five years. The inability of either power to access the people and resources of the interior without the cooperation of the lowland Cree peoples, however, suggests the extent to which Native peoples continued to frame the social relationships that mattered in this region. And while this space became increasingly visible on European maps and in colonial records as Port Nelson of Hudson's Bay, it continued to be Penesewichewan Sepee on the ground.

French Efforts to Influence "an Infinity of Nations"

French colonial officials remained divided about the importance of Hudson's Bay, but they agreed about the significance of the west, and the western trade, to the French Empire in North America. Even before he learned of Radisson's defection, Frontenac's successor, Governor Jacques-René Brisay de La Barre, was focused on denying the English access to the west. His involvement in la Compagnie de la Baie represented one aspect of this strategy. But La Barre also wanted to find a way to control the flow of Native peoples from the interior west trading at the bay. More specifically, he wanted to make certain that Native peoples allied to New France were not pulled into the orbit of the exchange networks that reached into the west from the Hudson's Bay coast.

To implement this policy he turned to Daniel Greysolon Du Lhut. In 1683 he wrote to the minister of marine and complained that "the English of Hudson's Bay have attracted this year many of our savages from the north who are no longer coming to trade at Montreal." La Barre then informed the minister that he had sent Du Lhut among these peoples "in the hope that he send them flowing into Michilimackina," and to convince these inland bands to "join him in preventing all of the others from going there." In effect, the governor hoped that Du Lhut would counter the success of Radisson. "The English at the bay," he wrote, "excite the Savages against us and le Sieur Du Lhut alone can bring calm."[64]

Du Lhut had long asserted that in order to control trade in the western interior the French needed to be able to influence the seasonal migration patterns that connected inland peoples to summer trading villages. He also argued that the French needed to do more than make a ceremonial claim to this space, as they had with St. Lusson's ceremony and Albanel's expedition to the Hudson's Bay coast in 1671. Accordingly, Du Lhut secured permission to build posts at Kaministiquia on the northwest shore of Lake Superior and at Lake Nipigon. He described posts in this region as "a grand necessity for the colony of Canada," which could "easily attract a good part of the peltries that go to Hudson's Bay."[65]

Du Lhut's post at Lake Nipigon, Fort La Tourette, became the focal point of this effort to disrupt the flow of people and pelts to the bay and to assert French control over the interior west. In the fall of 1684 he wrote to Governor La Barre and outlined his plan to attach the people and resources of this region to the French trade-and-alliance system. Du Lhut's brief letter lacks the rich detail of Radisson's narratives. Read alongside of Radisson's manuscript, however, it provides another look at the expansive multipolar Native social formations that dominated trade and alliance making in the interior west.

In this letter Du Lhut claimed that he had won the loyalty of the various peoples from the interior trading at Hudson's Bay. He reported from his post at Lake Nipigon that "I have made in June the necessary presents to prevent the savages from carrying more of their beaver to the English." He also wrote: "The savages of the north have plenty of confidence in me, and that's what makes me promise that before two years they will not go down to the English, at Hudson's Bay. They have all promised me and committed themselves by the gifts that I made them. The Cree, the Assinipoulacs, the Gens de la Sapinière, the Opemens d'Acheliny, the Outouloubys and the Tabitibis, who compose all of the nations who are west of the North Sea, have promised me to be, in the next springtime at the fort I have made . . . at the bottom of Lake Nipigon." Du Lhut then informed La Barre that next spring he planned to go to "the country of the Cree." He promised to stop these bands from trading at the bay, or die trying.[66]

Du Lhut had been working to create some measure of political organization among the peoples of the western interior centered on himself, and at least nominally on New France, since he entered the trade illegally in 1679. In spite of his efforts, however, all of the bands named in Du Lhut's letter continued to appear in both French and English records as trading at various locations in the Great Lakes and at the Hudson's Bay coast. It seems likely, for example, that the Nehiyaw-athinuwick and Nakoda who visited his post in 1684, and were identified by Du Lhut as the Cree and Assiniboine, were the very same peoples who traveled to the Hayes-Nelson watershed to trade with Radisson later that year. Du Lhut claimed he bound these peoples to the

French with gifts, and they candidly informed Radisson that "the French of Canada made them presents to oblige them to open their parcels." Du Lhut had also tried four years earlier to forge an alliance between the Assiniboine, unnamed "nations of the North," and the Dakota through arranged marriages and a ceremony similar to Radisson's Feast of Unity.[67]

In his 1684 correspondence with the governor, Du Lhut named the Gens de la Sapinière, Opemens d'Acheliny, the Outouloubys, and the Tabitibis as "Peoples of the North" committed to trading in the future with the French. This later designation was generally used without the specificity of band names, village locations, or any assertion of national identity. In the case of the Gens de la Sapinière, he provided a name that was a French translation of the Anishinaabe designation *Sugwaudug-aawininiwag*. In the mid-nineteenth century the Anishinaabe historian William Warren translated this expression as "men of the thick Fir Woods." At the time he wrote his *History of the Ojibway People* in 1852 the Anishinaabeg also referred to this doodem as Muskegoes or Swampy people, and French-speaking Métis traders called this band the "Bois Fort" ("Strong Woods"). These people spoke a mixed Ojibwe-Cree dialect, resided in the Lake of the Woods region northwest of Lake Superior, and were often identified as Cree Indians by French traders in the seventeenth century. Du Lhut, in fact, earlier identified these people as the Cree allies of the Monsoni, and he cited their decision to trade with the English at Hudson's Bay in 1678 as one of the reasons behind his attempt to forge a peace between the Anishinaabeg, "the people of the north," and the Dakota.[68]

Their presence at his fort on Lake Nipigon in 1684 suggests that the Gens de la Sapinière or Muskegoes were part of the nexus of Anishinaabeg and Athinuwick peoples that constituted the Canadian governor's undiscovered infinity of nations. Their alliance with the Monsoni meant that the Muskegoes would also have been closely connected with the Marten doodem and the larger Anishinaabe village community of La Pointe (Shagwaamikong), which included doodemag most often identified as Sauteurs, including the Marameg (Catfish), Ne-ka (Goose), and several other peoples that participated in St. Lusson's ceremonial possession of the "Outouac Country" in 1671.[69] And yet like the other "savages of the north" that traded with Du Lhut in 1684 these peoples usually appeared in French records with the generic designation *Gens des Terres* or "inland peoples." The Outabiti and Tabitee fit into this category, and it is worth noting that both of these bands traded with Des Groseilliers and the English in the mid- and late 1670s. Similarly, the *Opemens d'Acheliny*, or more accurately *nopaming deja inini*, was actually the designation for inland people (or more pejoratively Bush people) in Anishinaabemowin, and in this instance may have referred to any number of Ojibwe-, Ojibwe-Cree-, or Cree-speaking bands.[70]

The hold that Du Lhut claimed to exercise over these people was clearly weak. His relationship to this network paralleled the relationship between Radisson and his trading partners at the Hayes-Nelson watershed post. In fact, these two networks obviously overlapped. For Du Lhut the different Anishinaabe bands that might be described here as fitting into the category of inland peoples worked like the Penesewichewan Sepee and various other Lowland Cree or Muskekowuck-athinuwick to link his post to the peoples of the western interior. The doodemag that the Anishinaabeg identified as "Bush people" shared an identity linked to the watersheds that arched across the top of Lake Superior and drained into Hudson's Bay. Lake Nipigon represented an alternate summer village location for these bands, and a point of connection with Upland Indians that lived farther west.

Du Lhut's new allies, however, proved even more mobile than the peoples of the Hudson's Bay coast. They could find trade at any post or village in Anishinaabewaki, in their home territories, along the inland watersheds, and at the mouths of rivers draining into the ocean at Hudson's Bay. Moreover, the Anishinaabeg of the northwest interior made a habit of shape-shifting between identities linked to the French alliance and the middle ground and band designations that identified them as people of the western interior and the Native New World. The Gens de la Sapinière, for example, appeared in French records at one time or another as Sauteurs, Ottawas, Cree, Gens des Terres, Bois Fort, and Peoples of the North. They were also called Swamp people and Bush people and were identified by various self-ascribed doodem designations by people who considered them to be, like themselves, Anishinaabeg, which might be translated as "original human beings," or even "Indian" or "Native." In other words, not only did Du Lhut face the problem of asserting French influence in a region where the institutions of empire did not yet exist but he also had to align himself to people whose identity was so fluid that they were known by more than a half dozen social designations.

Du Lhut needed to find a way to make these peoples legible to the French Empire. He needed to do what St. Lusson had failed to accomplish; that is, he needed to make the Anishinaabeg of the western interior behave like children of Onontio. Ceremony and gift giving alone would not work to bind these people to New France. Du Lhut's newly formed alliance network would depend on the circulation of goods, pelts, and people. Recognizing this fact,

Du Lhut requested that the governor grant his brother, Claude Greysolon Du Lhut, a license to trade in the country northwest of Nipigon in the spring of 1685. This request was granted, and Du Lhut's brother made his way into the interior during the next trading season with two canoes full of trade goods. The Du Lhut brothers needed to reconfigure kinship and exchange relationships in the interior in order to attach the inland peoples to their post, and to Onontio. This effort failed miserably, however, and underscored the structural problems New France faced in controlling the western trade and attaching western Indians to their alliance system.

Daniel Du Lhut's Native trading partners fulfilled their social obligation. They honored the gifts that Du Lhut gave them; they came to his post to trade in the spring. The French, however, failed to meet their obligation. Claude Du Lhut made his way inland with two canoes, and was confronted with over fifteen hundred Native people who expected to trade. They informed the voyageur that they regularly traded with the Hudson's Bay Company at Port Nelson, and expressed their anger and disgust at the failure of the French to provide an adequate quantity of trade goods. Moreover, even while a large number of western peoples had promised to trade with the French, there were yet more people from the interior who continued to trade with the English at the bay. Some of these western bands, perhaps even Du Lhut's disgruntled trading partners, made their way to Radisson's Hayes River post in the spring of 1685. The French post at Nipigon was for many trading Indians just a stop on the way to the coast. In his report to the governor, Claude Du Lhut concluded that in the country stretching west from Lake Nipigon, "there are an infinity of peoples, and there is only hope to trade with them by sea."[71] In short, Du Lhut had reached the same conclusion as Radisson.

The French failure to structure their exchange-and-alliance network in the interior and the English inability to move beyond the shores of Hudson's Bay revealed that French and English claims of sovereignty and possession in the west remained only claims. Although these two colonial powers represented this region in maps and memoirs as part of their national territories in North America, this space was, in fact, beyond the institutions of either empire. The western interior of North America was for all practical purposes beyond their direct influence.

The social formations of the western interior frequently assumed new shapes and configurations as they continuously transformed their relationships to one another to cope with the opportunity and the adversity caused by the new peoples and things entering their world. Radisson's alliance at the Hayes River, for example, linked the Winipeg-athinuwick through the Penesewichewan Sepee to the Nehiyaw-athinuwick and Nakoda, and to various Anishinaabe doodemag. This network, in effect, operated as a composite multipolar social formation. Power might shift within this social formation, as it did when the ogimaa of the Penesewichewan Sepee was able to use Radisson's trade goods and mediation to repair his relations with the Marten doodem in the west, and place the Washeo Sepee in a subordinate political role. But social relations constantly evolved, and people like the Muskegoes might just as easily shift the balance of power within this network by joining with the Monsoni and giving their trade and military support to the Anishinaabe village at Shagwaamikong (La Pointe) redirecting power and resources away from the seacoast.

For the most part, self-aggrandizing European traders produced the historical archive that described this dynamic social world. These men invariably placed themselves at the center of their stories about the western interior, and at the head of complex political and diplomatic relationships that they only vaguely understood. Their adopted Native relatives, who more often than not acted on their behalf and served as their guides in the Native New World, are very present in these narratives. A careful reading of this archive, in fact, reveals that the multipolar social formations of the western interior were not created by European colonial powers on the blank canvass of the North American wilderness. Rather Europeans and the material artifacts of the Atlantic World acted as catalysts, prompting transformations in existing kinship and exchange networks that produced new spatially reconfigured alliances between different indigenous social groups.[72]

Murder, Native Consequences, and French Justice

In 1683 two voyageurs made their way toward Michilimackinac from the Dakota country. As they traveled along the southern shore of Lake Superior they came to the Keweenaw Peninsula, where they were forced to make a long and difficult portage. At some point during this overland trek the two men were killed. This was not an isolated act of violence. During the following year French colonial officials recorded the deaths of thirty-nine Frenchmen in the Great Lakes region of the pays d'en haut.[73] This violence flowed directly from the expansion of the French fur trade into the west. The two men killed at Keweenaw were not killed because they found themselves in the wrong place at the wrong time. They were targeted for death to send a message to Onontio, the French father, and to those who carried his voice into Anishinaabewaki.

These murders represented an act of political violence, and they were partially directed at the French Empire. They were committed, however, to impact the struggle among the Anishinaabe doodemag for control of the inland trade. The story of these murders and how they were resolved reveals how the social world of the French alliance created an intersection between the Atlantic World and the Native New World. This intersection, described by Richard White as the middle ground, resulted from the efforts of the French and their Native allies to fashion a mutually comprehensible world. The social world of the middle ground, however, was frequently a violent place. The French most often worked to mediate this violence and, as White has argued, the alliance worked best when they assumed this role.

A party of Anishinaabe warriors murdered the two voyageurs at Keweenaw in 1683 in order to force the French to step into their role as fathers of the alliance. The problem, as always, with demanding that the French accept this responsibility was that Onontio and his children had different expectations about what that meant. A year after this murder Daniel Du Lhut decided to act like a father. In doing so he wanted to discipline his allies for daring to kill the voyageurs, but he also acted to secure his trading operation in the western interior. The identity of the killers was widely known among the peoples living in Anishinaabewaki, including the French. Du Lhut learned that one of the killers, a Menominee, "had arrived at Ste. Marie du Sault with fifteen cabins of Sauteurs who were fleeing from Chaouamigon because they had struck conjointly with the gens des terres on the Sioux." The other killers were identified as the sons of Achiganaga, an ogimaa of the Noquet, the French appellation for the Makwa or Bear doodem, also referred to by the cognomen *No-ka*.[74]

The identity of the killers suggests clues to their motivation, as does the fact they had joined warriors identified as Gens des Terres on a raid against the Dakota. When the Jesuits first identified the Sauteurs as a Native nation they noted that the people of the falls were, in fact, at least four distinct nations joined together as one.[75] The Makwa doodem originated in the west along the southern shore of Lake Superior in the Keweenaw region. They were allied to doodemag with homelands or hunting territories at the falls, but also farther west in the region that the French called La Pointe du Chequamegon (Shagwaamikong). All of these peoples identified themselves as Anishinaabeg and spoke the same Ojibwe dialect of Anishinaabemowin.

All the peoples described as Sauteurs in French records had both sacred and political connections to Bow-e-ting, the village the French called Sault Sainte Marie, but they were not all permanent residents of this community, and they did not function politically as the equivalent of a European nation. The social structure of indigenous political identity was at once much more expansive and much less hierarchical. Indeed, the fact that the "Noquet" were forced to flee Shagwaamikong after "striking at the Sioux" suggests they were not cooperating with the doodemag from this region who had formed an alliance with the Mdewakanton Dakota.

The Anishinaabeg were not united in their desire for peace with the Dakota. Killing the two voyageurs was a bold and violent political maneuver not unlike killing the Dakota emissaries in the Jesuit house a decade earlier. In both situations the killings signaled a refusal to accept the new alliance forming in the west. The Makwa doodem were keepers of the war pipe among the Gichigamiing Anishinaabeg. They would have advocated against peace with an enemy people such as the Dakota. Raising war parties and killing traders would have been considered highly aggressive, but socially appropriate behavior for the leaders of this doodem.[76] Du Lhut did not identify the Gens des Terres by name, and so these raiders could have come from any number of bands from the interior that might also have regarded the Dakota-Anishinaabe alliance as damaging to their interests in the inland trade. The Menominee, with a homeland in the Green Bay region, similarly had a recent history of conflict with the Dakota. And the Menominee warrior involved in the murder had a brother, a sister, and an uncle married into the village of the Giishkaanowed Odawa, a doodem that initiated a conflict with the Dakota when they resided at the west end of the lake in 1670. Thus, all the men identified as the killers of the two voyageurs came from communities that continued to regard the Dakota as enemies, wanted to stop the French from trading with them, and wanted to destroy the alliance between the Dakota and the Anishinaabeg of Shagwaamikong.

In October 1683, Du Lhut traveled with a contingent of six Frenchmen to Sault Sainte Marie intent on arresting the killers. He quickly captured the Menominee and placed him under guard at the Jesuit mission. Du Lhut then called an impromptu council of all the peoples gathered at the Sault and told them that "they must declare themselves." While the people deliberated he sent an experienced coureur de bois to arrest Achiganaga (the Bass) and his sons at Keweenaw, where he was rumored to be gathering warriors for another raid against the Dakota. The council at the Sault deliberated for three days during which they exonerated the Menominee prisoner, and blamed the absent war chief. The council also warned Du Lhut that they feared the men sent to arrest Achiganaga might be killed. "This did not burden me," he later wrote, "since I doubted that the allies nor any of the nation of Achiganaga would want to have a war with us." However, with some warriors openly talking about taking his prisoner away from him, Du Lhut returned to Michilimackinac.[77]

A few weeks later Achiganaga and his sons arrived at Michilimackinac with the man Du Lhut dispatched to find them. What unfolded next was a strange, ad-libbed, hybrid cultural production that combined elements of a European legal trial with an indigenous tribal council. Du Lhut described this event in detail in a letter written to justify his actions to the governor. The youngest son of Achiganaga was sent to spread the word among the Makwa doodem and the neighboring "Sauteur" peoples of the reason for his father's captivity. "I informed all of the chiefs and elders," he wrote, "that they must come to a council that I wanted to hold."[78]

Du Lhut attempted to place the killers on trial for murder using the conventions of European law. He told the Menominee and the sons of Achiganaga to choose "two relatives to sustain their interests." He then proceeded to interrogate his suspects before the council, which he had called to act as a jury. The Menominee and the two oldest sons of Achiganaga readily admitted to the killings. They blamed one another for instigating the attack, but all three took responsibility for their actions. Following this interrogation the elders proclaimed: "It is enough you accuse one another, the Frenchman is now the master of your bodies."[79] This was where Du Lhut began to run into trouble.

Neither the accused nor their advocates nor the council saw this ritual as an adversarial process designed to punish the killers if they were found guilty. Instead they recognized the need for a ritual reconciliation between the French and the Anishinaabeg—a repairing of the relationship that bound the two communities together as family. The killers admitted their wrong and in so doing Du Lhut became the master of their bodies. A benevolent father would raise up his dead brothers with the bodies of these wayward children, giving them a new life by taking the place of the departed, a situation in which they might expect to live and work among the French traders living within their own community in Anishinaabewaki. The loss suffered by the French would be rectified, and the bond between the two peoples would be strengthened.

Du Lhut, however, would not meet these expectations because he wanted the council to determine the fate of the accused by pronouncing their guilt. He quickly discovered that an Anishinaabe council was ill suited for playing the role of a jury. Du Lhut expected swift justice and met instead with arduous deliberations. Exasperated, he told the council "there was no longer any doubt that the French had been assassinated and robbed, that the murderers were known, and they knew their practice on similar occasions." His request apparently dumbfounded the council. They had, in fact, responded according to customary practice. The killers' lives were forfeit to their father. Now they waited for his response. And yet when Du Lhut responded he only complained about what he perceived to be the council's failure to render a verdict: "To all of this," he wrote, "they answered nothing."[80] Operating with entirely different understandings about the appropriate actions, modes of conduct, and responsibilities required for settling conflict, the French and the Anishinaabeg stared mutely at one another across the council fire.

To resolve this impasse they would have to meet one another on the middle ground. Du Lhut initiated this process by trying to apply what he believed to be Anishinaabe cultural logic to what was a European social practice—the murder trial. First, he called another council in the cabin of Ginoozhe (the Pike), an important Odawa ogimaa. It seems that Du Lhut thought this gesture might signal his desire to see the leadership of Michilimackinac decide a punishment. At council he heard no pronouncement about the fate of the killers. "Seeing," he wrote, "that all my councils came to nothing but the reduction of tobacco to ash I began to speak telling them that since they did not want to declare anything . . . the next day I would make known to them what myself and the French had resolved." The next day Du Lhut called the council together again and proceeded to shock and horrify the assembled ogimaag. Rather than act as a benevolent father, he took the path of an enemy warrior. He called for Anishinaabe blood.[81]

Du Lhut had reconvened the council in the cabin of Ginoozhe. He identified the representatives from the three Odawa doodemag, the Sauteurs, Mississauguas, Huron, Amikwas, and a people he called "d'achiliny" as present for this meeting. The term *d'achiliny* was either an abbreviated version of the Anishinaabe phrase for bush people or the French Gens des Terres or it signified the Ne-Ka or Goose doodem, identifying this band as Muskegoe. In either case, this was most likely the Gens des Terres band that fled to the Sault following the raid against the Dakota led by Achiganaga. According to Du Lhut, "All of the elders" for these doodemag entered the lodge, and he specifically identified Oumamens, "chief of the Amikois." Du Lhut chastised these men. They knew of the murders at Keweenaw. They knew the identity of the murderers. And yet they did nothing. "I was surprised," he declared, "that no one dared to declare themselves for us." Then, like an enemy warrior, Du Lhut called for revenge: "Onontio had lost his blood that was still warm and . . . there must be other blood to satisfy it."[82]

In the letter that Du Lhut crafted to explain this event he asserted that his call for European-style justice for the killers of his men was, in fact, supported by Anishinaabe cultural practice. In this document he explained that he had simply asked the council "to give us the same justice they make between themselves. . . . When the nation of those who have killed do not want war with the one that has been offended, the nearest relatives of the murderers kill them themselves, that is to say man for man."[83] In other words, he justified his call for blood revenge by appealing to what he believed was the Anihsinaabe way of resolving murders peacefully.

The French traders who lived among the Anishinaabeg were apparently as horrified by this demand as the ogimaag. Neither they nor Du Lhut had the military power to prevent retaliation for a ritual killing that they knew would be understood as a declaration of war. There were eighteen men wintering at Keweenaw who begged Du Lhut "to treat this affair with all the gentleness possible." In response to their concern, he wrote, "I believed that it would be expedient for the security of all their companions who wintered in Lake Superior that I put to death only two." And again, he asserted, "only killing man for man they would have nothing to say since this is their way of doing things." Du Lhut then decided that he would execute the Menominee and the eldest son of Achiganaga. "This was why I made known to them," he wrote, explaining his speech to the council, "that two would be killed by two different nations, that one of each would die, and that the same death that they had made the French suffer they would suffer."[84]

Du Lhut then explained to the assembled ogimaag that his pardon of the third killer was a gift from the governor, their French father. He suggested this act of benevolence was a concession to the cultural logic of his allies. Unimpressed by this supposed act of generosity and accommodation, the Odawa ogimaag pressed Du Lhut to show mercy to all the killers. They reminded him that they had recently given up Iroquois captives at the request of the French. Du Lhut countered that those captives had been prisoners of war and not criminals. This social distinction, however, made no sense to the Anishinaabeg, who thought in terms of inawemaagen (relatives) and meyagaazid (foreigners) when deciding the appropriate response to a killing. But Du Lhut went so far as to blame the impending execution on the assembled elders for allowing their young men to believe "that to kill the French is not a matter of great consequence as it would appear, since for a slave or a packet of beaver one would get away with it."[85]

It was Oumamens who finally urged the council to move beyond their consternation with Du Lhut's outrageous demands. The ogimaa of the Amik-was joined Du Lhut on the middle ground, and he called on the council to follow him. He spoke after hearing the Odwawag protest Du Lhut's demand for punitive justice, and hearing the Frenchman's rebuttal. According to Du Lhut, Oumamens "thanked me for being content with so little." Then he praised the voyageur for releasing Achiganaga and three of his children. Historian Richard White has noted that "Oumamens chose to emphasize those of Du Lhut's actions which conformed to Algonquian custom." In other words, Oumamens sought out the middle ground by focusing on the one aspect of Du Lhut's behavior that made sense to the Anishinaabeg. He had taken pity on Achiganaga. By allowing the ogimaa and two of his sons to go unpunished he gave them back their lives, even though he inexplicably insisted that two of his own children must die. After Oumamens offered public recognition of this concession, Du Lhut brought his two prisoners in front of an audience of approximately forty Frenchmen and at least four hundred Native warriors where, he wrote, "I broke their heads."[86]

As Achiganaga watched a French soldier crush his son's head with a war club, he must have realized what a terrible miscalculation he had made. His adopted French son was among the half dozen voyageurs that came for him at his winter camp. The Makwa ogimaa initially tried to end this conflict by dancing the calumet for these men, and offering them slaves to raise the dead.[87] When they refused the pipe and he agreed to accompany them to Du Lhut's post, perhaps he expected a more elaborate peace ceremony. Whatever he expected, the fact that Achiganaga willingly traveled to Michilimackinac signaled his confidence in his own power, not his fear of French power. We cannot know what the ogimaa felt when he found himself forced onto the middle ground to watch a cruel father take his son's life. But we can see in Du Lhut's own testimony that the political implications of these deaths reverberated throughout Anishinaabewaki like an earthquake.

Two days after the executions ritual feasts and elaborate gift giving began in earnest among all of the parties involved in this affair. The Odawa doo-demag invited Du Lhut to a council where they presented him six belts of wampum, "two from each nation to cover the French killed and to dry their blood."[88] They then preformed the exact same ceremony for Achiganaga and the relatives of the dead Menominee. The Wyandot resident at Michilimackinac followed suit, disseminating Wampum belts among the French and among the Anishinaabe doodemag. The following day Du Lhut held a feast in the cabin of Ginoozhe. He wrote that he wanted "to take away the heart ache" he had caused the ogimaa by pronouncing his verdict in the man's wiigiwam. Du Lhut invited elders from all the peoples he had gathered for his trial to this feast. In short order, all of the peoples that gathered at Michilimackinac for the trial, including Du Lhut, began to cover the dead and to ritually reaffirm their kinship and alliance.

In effect, after the execution Du Lhut's murder trial began to morph back into a condolence ritual. This transformation culminated with the decision by Du Lhut to provide Achiganaga with enough gifts to outfit his family for the winter season. "I told them that you were not content with giving them life," he wrote the governor, "but that you wished to preserve them in furnishing all that would be necessary to prevent them from dying of hunger and cold." Du Lhut then gave Achiganaga and his family guns, powder, shot, blankets, leggings, shirts, tobacco, axes, knives, netting, and wheat. For all practical purposes Du Lhut atoned for the death he brought upon Achiganaga's family. He covered the dead. Du Lhut concluded his report by asserting that the ogimaa left for Keweenaw "the most happy of everyone."[89] This assessment seems highly unlikely, but at a minimum Du Lhut could assert that his improvised combination of French and Anishinaabe cultural practices resolved this string of murders in a way that managed to preserve the alliance, though clearly it did not establish the authority of French law.

This is what Richard White meant when he described the middle ground as a space created by the mangled interpretations of the cultural logic and practices of the Other. Du Lhut wanted European justice, biblical justice even. He wanted an eye for an eye. He justified this demand, however, by making reference to the Native practice of avenging a death by retaliatory killing. Grieving relatives sought revenge for their dead relatives by taking a life of comparable social standing from the enemy community that caused the death in their own. The Anishinabeg, however, reserved this practice for outsiders, for meyaagizid, not for their relatives. When a death occurred among allied peoples the community of the killer covered their dead relative, offering gifts to the grieving family, which might include a slave to raise the dead. In this manner the social position occupied by the deceased could be restored to the community in the person of the adopted slave, assuaging their loss, and reestablishing proper relations between the allies. This had been the logic by which Nicolas Perrot was able to redeem the captive daughter of the Anishinaabe ogimaa taken by Mesquakie warriors seeking revenge for the loss of their ogimaa in battle. This had been the logic that led the elders at the earlier council to tell the killers "Le Francois est maintenant Maistre de vos corps." Claiming a right of revenge and exercising that right was, in contrast, an act of overt hostility.[90] Du Lhut ignored this distinction in order to justify his desire to impose a European value—the just punishment of the guilty and the rule of law—onto the social relations that governed the alliance.

In this social situation the Anishinaabeg valued mercy and compassion, not violent punishment. These qualities restored order, healed grievances, brought balance. The French, in contrast, valued authority and power. This was not the power that came from giving gifts and creating social obligations. This was the power that came from imposing order and obedience, by command when possible, and by force of violence when necessary. These were two very different understandings of how political leaders brought order to social relations under the stress of violent conflict. When neither side could impose the logic of their worldview onto events on the ground, the ensuing deadlock produced a new hybrid worldview, a middle ground.

In trying to assert French standards of justice for the punishment of his murdered men, Du Lhut initially placed the alliance at risk to advance his own trading interests. No doubt, he acted from a sense of cultural superiority. But he also acted out of a sense of self-preservation. Du Lhut's trade operation depended on his ability to access the prime winter coat beaver from the peoples of the western interior. This meant that he needed to trade with the Dakota, as well as with the doodemag from the north and northwest classified as bush people by the Anishinaabeg. The relationship between these peoples and between French-allied Indians was contentious to say the least. The murder of his men was, in effect, a shot across the bow—a warning by the Makwa doodem not to take his trade into the territory of their enemies. Du Lhut met this challenge by claiming to speak for Onontio, and then demanding revenge as a condition for preserving and reaffirming the alliance. A vengeful father was an oxymoron among the Anishinaabeg, but they too were forced to improvise in order to preserve their place in the inland trade. This improvisation reflected the struggle for power among the social formations of the Native New World.[91]

Why else would Achiganaga surrender himself and his sons to French fur traders at Michilimackinac? This war leader was certainly not compelled to act out of fear. The few dozen French traders scattered about the villages of Anishinaabewaki would not defeat his people in a military confrontation, and the French Empire could hardly disentangle itself from the fur trade. Submitting to the will of Onontio, however, provided an opportunity to restore proper relations with the French. Achiganaga gambled that he could control the terms of this reconciliation.

To the minds of some among the Anishinaabeg, such as Achiganaga, the Dakota were outsiders. There had been consistent opposition to the faction among the Anishinaabeg seeking peace and alliance with these people. The murder of Du Lhut's men was a reminder to Onontio and the French of their obligation not to trade with the enemies of their Native children. As a war leader Achiganaga could not stop the doodemag of Shagwaamikong from forming an alliance with the Dakota. But he could sabotage that alliance by forcing the French to end their trading relationship with these people, identifying them as outsiders, as meyagaazid. By killing the traders, figures of little political or military stature, and then consenting to a ritual reconciliation the Makwa Anishinaabeg of Keweenaw would force the French to reaffirm their relationship, while tacitly accepting the fact that the Dakota were not children of Onontio, and therefore not allies of either the French Empire or the broader imagined community of Anishinaabe peoples.

Achiganaga's violent intervention into the politics and diplomacy that connected the peoples of Anishinaabewaki to the western interior backfired. Du Lhut's erratic behavior proved problematic, but not impossible to overcome. After all, in the end Du Lhut backed away from his aggressive posturing, and resorted to accepted condolence practices. The war leader and the Makwa doodem were undone, however, by Oumamens and his allies among the doodemag of Shagwaamikong. By improvising a resolution that recognized the loss suffered by the French and the Anishinaabeg in terms that both could recognize, Oumamens joined Du Lhut on the middle ground. In doing so he shifted the focus of the condolence rituals. Achiganaga lost the opportunity to focus the ritual of reconciliation on the breach of obligation that occurred when the French traded with the Dakota. Instead the ritual focus centered on repairing the destructive acts committed first by the Anishinaabe warriors against the French, and then by the French against the Makwa doodem and the Menominee and his relations.

Engaging Du Lhut on the middle ground made this an extraordinary event, rather than something that could be expected to follow a predictable pattern according to Anishinaabe cultural practice, and the social norms of the Native New World. This was where Achiganaga lost control of events. Not only did he lose his son in Du Lhut and Oumamens's bizarre murder trial/condolence ritual, but he also lost the initiative in trying to sabotage the emerging Anishinaabe-Dakota alliance. The Amkiwas ogimaa forced Achiganaga to "restrain" his warriors from taking any further aggressive action in the west with a gift of wampum that served as the final ritual exchange that marked this event. According to Du Lhut the "Sauteurs," for whom Oumamens spoke collectively, gave these belts of wampum to the Makwa doodem, "in order that they take good care to stir up nothing on the subject of the death of their brother, and that in case some one had an evil intention, to stop them by these collars." With this gesture the resistance of the Makwa doodem to the emerging Dakota alliance was effectively contained.[92] Achiganaga accepted the gift of these wampum belts, or collars as the French styled them, and returned to Keweenaw.

This reaffirmation of peace among the Anishinaabeg and the French also brought a respite for the peoples of the Oceti Sakowin. The allies of the Dakota in the west were still largely without firearms and vulnerable to attack from Native peoples trading directly with Europeans. Anishinaabe raids were not limited to small-scale attacks against winter camps on the eastern edge of the upper Mississippi valley. Achiganaga's raid in the winter of 1682–83, for example, apparently reached into the heart of the allies' territory, striking the lower Yanktonai. A firsthand account of this raid was recorded on the pictorial winter count kept by the band of the nineteenth-century Yanktonai leader Drifting Goose, marking this battle as the most significant event to occur that year.[93]

At the time of the raid the Yanktonai were already moving farther out onto the northern plains, occupying territory between the Red River in the east and the Missouri in the west. The Jesuits described the allies, identified as the Nadoussioux, as living in forty villages extending into the west from the Mississippi River valley. Father Louis Hennepin similarly described social formation of the Dakota as a world of interconnected villages capable of mobilizing in significant numbers for hunting and combat. The Yanktonai, situated at the center of this massive social formation, played a crucial role in the diplomacy and trade that kept the families of the Oceti Sakowin connected as a people.[94]

In attempting to disrupt trade and social relations of this network of families and peoples (tiyospaye and oyate), Achiganaga sought to advance his place within the other significant social formation that dominated the western interior—the alliance of Nehiyawa-athinuwick and Nokoda, or Western Cree and Assiniboine peoples. Achinganaga's association with people identified as Gens des Terres by the French suggest that he was allied to the Anishinaabe doodemag from the region north-northwest of Gichigamiing who shifted their trade between English posts at Hudson's Bay and French posts in Anishinaabewaki. This network of Native families had been revitalized by their success in forging a stable alliance linking the coast through the Penesewichewan Sepee to the prairie parklands to the north of the Yanktonai territory. Viewed from the rather limited perspective of empire, the conflict with Du Lhut and his men represented a struggle between Onontio and his children to control the terms and conditions of their relationship. The murders and their resolution were, in fact, a product of this struggle. Achiganaga and Oumamens, however, were simultaneously playing at a larger game. They were engaged in a fierce political battle to determine the place of the Gichigamiing Anishinaabeg within a Native New World being reshaped by the inland trade and connection to the world economy.

PART III

The Illusion of Empire

MAKING SENSE OF the relationships between European empires and the Native peoples of the Great Lakes and western interior of North America requires recognition of an important fact. Namely, the Native social formations within these overlapping territories were not, in spite of European claims, the subjects of European empires or their settler colonies. Neither was their territory meaningfully incorporated into any of the empires with colonies on North America soil. The French occupied a thinly garrisoned string of posts in the major village centers of Anishinaabewaki. Their presence farther west was even more ephemeral. And as Du Lhut's murder trial revealed, the French wielded political power in this region by occupying a middle ground with their allies, not by imposing their sovereignty over them. The Native peoples in these territories remained autonomous and independent political actors throughout the colonial period.

This was also true for the peoples of the Haudenosaunee, who were in the politically precarious position of being at the western edge of a particularly avaricious array of British settler colonies. They remained, however, politically independent and in possession of much of their land base until the national era in North American history.[1] This was perhaps even truer for the majority of the peoples of Anishinaabewaki. The upper Great Lakes were far removed from the population centers of North America's settler colonial regimes. The upper Mississippi valley and the northern Great Plains and prairie parklands at the heart of the continent were even farther removed from colonial settlement. Moreover, these regions in the western interior were the homelands of a Native population that rivaled or surpassed the populations of European immigrants settled along the east coast of the continent. The western interior and the upper Great Lakes were fully integrated politically and economically as the peoples from these regions engaged one another, and European interlopers, on a routine basis. With the fur trade so easily adapted to the political economy of the Native seasonal round in these territories, the social formations of the Great Lakes and western interior were also integrated within the emergent global market economy. In other words, these Native homelands were not isolated wilderness, they constituted a Native New World.

Neither should these Native homelands be defined or understood exclusively though their relationships with European empires. The claims of the French and the English to the sovereign possession of Anishinaabewaki and the western interior were an illusion. Given this fact, the Native social formations in these territories ought to be considered as political powers in their own right. Jeremy Adelman and Stephen Aron, however, argue that the social world of the French alliance, the middle ground, "rested on the contingencies of imperial rivalry."[2] In their formulation, the historical trajectory of the colonial powers and nation-states shaped and defined the contours of early American history as a whole. Native peoples, in contrast, are conceptualized as "the peoples in between," and the late eighteenth century, they argue, "was the twilight for the Great Lakes" as the defeat of the French Empire saw the dawn of an a era of declining imperial rivalries.[3] First the French and then the British abandoned their Native allies for the sake of political expediency, leaving the peoples of the Great Lakes without the power to fend off the European social formations lurking at the borderlands of their territories.

Richard White offers a different historical trajectory for the collapse of imperial alliances in the Great Lakes. He has argued that New France began to lose control of the pays d'en haut because of the French victory over the Iroquois that resulted in the Great Peace of 1701. With their enemies subdued the allies found themselves increasingly unwilling to find accommodation, dissolving the middle ground. Other scholars have interpreted the outcome of the conflict between New France and the people of the Haudenosaunee, and the Peace of 1701, as a victory for the confederacy. There is yet another scholarly perspective that asserts that the diplomatic triumph that produced a peace treaty in 1701 between the French, the Native allies of New France, and the peoples of the Haudenosaunee ushered in an era of Pax Gallica—a period of French hegemony when the sovereign Native nations of Iroquoia and the Great Lakes coexisted peacefully under a regime of political arbitration administered by New France. All of these authors struggle to understand how the relationship between Native peoples and the European empires of the Atlantic World shaped North American history.[4]

Defining the history of the Great Lakes in such an imperial fashion, however, is problematic given the demographic dominance of Native peoples in this region. Such claims are even more problematic for the regions of the western interior like the upper Mississippi valley and Rupert's Land. Aron and Adleman, for example, describe the social world of the Great Lakes as a borderland, which they define as "the contested boundaries between colonial domains."[5] The problem with this definition is that Indian peoples are empowered and autonomous only so long as they have rival European colonial powers to exploit—hiding, it must be presumed, their inherent social and political weakness. According to this logic, without competing colonial powers

Native peoples become politically irrelevant. Why should this be the case? If Native peoples constitute the demographic majority of a particular territory why are they not relevant political powers in their own right? In the Great Lakes Native social formations were important, and their impact on the history of early America amounted to more than the history of their relationship with empires that were often marginal at best to their internal politics and political power.

As the French were losing their North American empire the Anishinaabe peoples were, in contrast, approaching the zenith of their power as a social formation. Their population was increasing significantly, and they were expanding their territory and influence into the west.[6] The same was true for the Dakota-Yankton/Yanktonai-Lakota peoples. When the French transferred their claim of possession in the Great Lakes to the British how much did it matter? What they gave their rivals was a few posts where the British would, like the French, garrison a few soldiers and struggle to manage relations with Native peoples who greatly outnumbered them, and who largely ignored their laws and customs. In other words the British did not gain sovereign possession of the Great Lakes, they simply inherited the illusion of empire.

The departure of the French, for example, made no difference to the Anishinaabeg of Shagwaamikong at the west end of Lake Superior. Perhaps the most important political relationship for the doodemag of this region, and really for most of the peoples of Anishinaabewaki and the western interior, was their deteriorating alliance with the tiyospaye and oyate (bands and peoples) of the Dakota. The French had been unable to influence this Native alliance, and they had struggled to keep the Anishinaabeg in the west at Shagwaamikong, Keeweenaw, and northwest of Lake Superior attached to their own alliance system. More than two decades before the outbreak of the Seven Years' War, they would find themselves powerless when the Dakota challenged and forced the removal of French imperial forces from their territory. Cut off from the Dakota, the French would become pawns in the expanding alliance of Anishinaabe peoples who were asserting themselves as one of the dominant political powers within the inland trade.

In a complete inversion of the middle ground the Anishinaabe doodemag of the western interior would force the French to abandon the protocols of the alliance, and enter into the politics of the Native New World. The price of this engagement sealed their fate in the Dakota country, but it made them partners with an extensive network of Anishinaabe peoples in the lucrative inland trade. When the British halfheartedly took on the mantle of Onontio,

French traders stayed on at places like Sault Sainte Marie, Michilimackinac, La Pointe, and Grand Portage. In other words, the social world of Anishinaabewaki and the inland trade continued largely unaffected by the imperial crisis in Montreal, New York, London, and Paris. Like the evolving social world in the colonial east, the western interior continued to evolve as part of the emergent world market economy of the early modern era. Anishinaabewaki was a sophisticated composite social world with important cosmopolitan population centers. At the end of the eighteenth century it was not at the twilight of its history. On the contrary, the Anishinaaebeg and Dakota had survived over a century of encounter with European empires without being colonized. They had absorbed the people, material goods, and cultural and political influences of the Atlantic World and either rejected these things or made them a part of their own autonomous, postcontact, Native social world.

Some of the peoples of Anishinaabewaki would be pulled into the political turmoil of the Ohio country, and they suffered in the maelstrom of violence unleashed by the Seven Years' War—the first true world war. This would include some of the peoples that the French called Sauteurs, Ottawas, and Huron from the more populous villages of the Upper Great Lakes. But by and large, the migrants to the Ohio country came from the refugee centers in the Green Bay region and the adjacent Illinois country. They would forge an alliance with other refugee peoples that Europeans called the Shawnee, Delaware, and Mingos who would bear the brunt of the pressure from a land-ravenous British settler population. Richard White argues that this conflict resulted in the collapse of the middle ground.[7]

In truth, it could be argued that the middle ground, a hybrid cultural creation of the village world of the Upper Great Lakes, never really mapped onto the Ohio country. Greg Dowd has instead described the new social world created by this convergence of Native refugees—some with claims to an Ohio homeland, others new arrivals—as a contest between the seekers of accommodation and Nativists. At times working together and at times at odds, this confederation of Native peoples confronted an invasion of Anglo-American settlers who had little interest in finding a common ground with the indigenous peoples who fought them for control of the new territory beyond the established borders of European settlement. They regarded this land as unimproved and therefore unsettled. The middle ground, to the extent that it survived, did so in the form of hereditary chiefs who used the ritual, protocols, and the patterns of political and military cooperation of the old alliance to mobilize an opposition to stanch the western flow of Anglo-American set-

tlers. The Nativists, in contrast, emerged as part of a broad multiethnic revi-
talization movement that formed a north-south axis running along the length
of the borderland with America's settler colonies. This was the first explicitly
"pan-tribal" Native social movement, and it represented a militant rejection
of the tradition of compromise and misappropriation that had defined the
middle ground. In a sense, Dowd's work suggests that the social world of
the middle ground did not move east into the Ohio, and south along the
Appalachia backcountry to the gulf coast. At best, some migrants from Anishinaabewaki, that place the French thought of as the pays d'en haut, brought
the cultural legacy and social practices of their alliance with them when they
migrated east.[8]

They tried and failed to adapt these traditions to the politics of the new
world order created by expanding Anglo-American settler colonialism. The
Nativists suffered a comparable failure when their resistance to this expansion gave way to military confrontation and defeat. This is the legacy that
Reginald Horsman details in his history of the origins of America's Indian
policy, which he situates in the Old Northwest Territory. He chronicles how
the newly formed United States dispossessed Native peoples in this region
through a series of treaties linked to the conflicts with militant Nativists and
culminating in the 1795 Treaty of Grenville. With this treaty the United States
paradoxically relinquished claims to the territory west of Ohio and what
would become southeastern Indiana, but it reserved the right of preemption.
In exchange for this admission of Native independence, the United States
reserved the exclusive right to purchase Indian lands. In other words, the
federal government not only planned to reclaim these lands by purchasing
them outright but also planned to break the back of future Native resistance
to American expansion by systematically reducing the land base they would
require to continue living as unassimilated Indians.[9]

Horsman rightly asserts that these policies would prove disastrous to Native peoples living in country contiguous to American territories. The Chero-
kee, Choctaw, Creek, Chickisaw, and Seminoles, the so-called Five Civilized
Tribes, would feel the full effect of this cruel history and experience removal
from their homelands by the 1830s. Horsman traces a similar and more rapid
pattern of dispossession in the regions that would become Ohio, Indiana, and
Illinois. In the process, however, he constructs his history of the Old Northwest through the experience of peoples like the Sauk, Fox, Wea, Miami, and
Pottawatomies living at the southern edge and hinterlands of the Great Lakes
region. The majority of the peoples of Anishinaabewaki would never be re-

moved from their homelands. And while a small segment of these communities living in the Ohio country and what would become southeast Michigan were party to the Treaty of Grenville, the vast majority of the Anishinaabeg were not.[10] This was, in part, because of the expansive and nonnational nature of Anishinaabewaki and Anishinaabe collective identity.

The majority of the country claimed by the United States as the Northwest Territory remained part of the Native New World until well into the nineteenth century. This region, the upper Great Lakes and the upper Mississippi valley, remained demographically, culturally, and politically indigenous long after the ink had dried on the Treaty of Grenville. The Hudson's Bay Company claimed the region northwest of Lake Superior. Other than the small fur trade colony of Red River, which was largely occupied by the Métis or mixed-blood participants in the fur trade, the company operated trading posts at the coast, with a few additional inland locations in the nineteenth century. There was no colonial settlement, and the laws and institutions of colonial Canada were never imposed on this region and its people.[11] The border between British Canada and the United States was, for all practical purposes, a part of Anishinaabewaki, and the idea that a border existed had no impact on the social lives or political economy of the Native peoples of the region.

In spite of the disaster of Grenville and America's rapacious appetite for Native lands, when the British finally turned over their forts in the Great Lakes to American forces all they really accomplished was a changing of the guard. The Americans would become the latest caretakers of the illusion of empire in Anishinaabewaki. Unlike the rapid conquest that took place on lands farther south, the Old Northwest would not be deluged by American settlers intent on improving Indian country in order to turn it into American soil. The United States would have to work hard to colonize this space. It would have to work at being a colonial power if it wanted to truly end the autonomy and self-determination of Native peoples in this part of North America.

American authorities quickly realized that any hope they had of colonizing the country they thought of as the Northwest Territory depended on their ability to co-opt the peoples of the middle ground. The social world of the French alliance was long gone, but the middle ground continued to exist as a living culture. It was quite literally embodied in the Métis peoples who were the heart and soul of the fur trade. These communities surrounded the forts that the Americans inherited from the British. American officials found they would need to turn to these peoples if they wanted to make their way in this world of Native peoples, Métis voyageurs, and Canadian traders.

Not only were the Great Lakes and western interior not colonized, but these territories remained in the control of autonomous Native peoples whose mode of self-determination and collective identity were at odds with the world American treaty makers tried to inscribe on their new country. In 1809 the American Indian agent at Prairie du Chien at the juncture of the Wisconsin and Mississippi Rivers, Nicolas Boilvin, wrote the newly elected president of the United States, James Madison, in French, to warn him about the independence of Native peoples in this region. "I solicit your consideration," he wrote, "that you may, from time to time, cast your fatherly gaze upon the Indians who surround me." Boilvin expressed concern that Native peoples from the west crossed between territory claimed by the United States and British Canada to trade with their "English father." British Canadian traders at Michilimackinac, he wrote, "seek to sow discord in their hearts to turn them against the principles and administration of our government." Boilvin concluded by asking for presents to be distributed annually, and a company of soldiers to eject or at least control Canadian traders operating within territory now claimed by the United States. Without these measures, he warned, "it will not be necessary to maintain an agent here, because instead of attaching the savages to our government, it will turn them from us and give the British subjects triumph—and God knows what may be the result of that."[12]

Writing to colonial officials on the east coast from his post in the upper Mississippi River valley, Boilvin described a social world that would have been remarkably familiar to Nicolas Perrot more than a century earlier. The fur trade dominated the political economy of the region and all interactions between Native and non-Native peoples. As in the past, trade and diplomacy could not be disentangled, and kinship structured exchange relationships and political alliance. Boilvin, like Perrot, spoke on behalf of a distant father struggling to make his voice heard among the peoples of the western interior. And even when that father was American, the language he spoke was some combination of Anishinaabemowin, Dakota, or French.

The message of Boilvin's letter to the American president was essentially the same message that Perrot delivered in his memoir about life in Great Lakes region, and what it meant to enter into a relationship with the peoples of Anishinaabeawaki. If the president wanted to assert the political authority claimed by the United States, he needed to begin acting like a father. That is, if the Americans hoped to exert any influence in the upper Great Lakes and western interior they needed to negotiate their entrance into this world in the same way that any Anishinaabe ogimaa (leader) would. They needed to negotiate their place among the network of Anishinaabe doodemag (clans) and Dakota oyate (people) that knit these western regions together as a coherent social space. Not only were the American claims of sovereign possession meaningless in the space they knew as the Northwest Territory, but if they wanted to begin to have some influence here they would have to learn how to adapt to the politics of the Native New World.

CHAPTER 5

An Anishinaabe Warrior's World

The hybrid murder trial/condolence ritual staged by Du Lhut preserved the French alliance in the heart of the Great Lakes, but it did not extend the alliance into the west. In fact, Oumamens successfully co-opted the trial in order to stifle opposition to the Anishinaabe alliance with the Dakota among the doodemag of Anishinaabewaki. This success provided the peoples from the village La Pointe and the region west of Gichigamiing (Lake Superior) with secure access to the Native New World emerging in the western interior (Figure 5). The Anishinaabe-Dakota alliance also offered some refuge to French traders who carried goods into the Mississippi valley and beyond, but even after the trial they faced fierce opposition among the peoples of Green Bay.

When European traders entered the west they entered another New World, one that was filling up with new peoples as the native inhabitants of the interior of North America began to reimagine their social worlds. Voyaging onto the prairie parklands of the northwest from their post at Lake Nipigon, Daniel Du Lhut and his brother Claude caught glimpses of this other Native New World, and of the "undiscovered" infinity of nations emerging on this landscape. Farther south on the northern and central Great Plains Native peoples began to experience a rebirth that was perhaps even more dramatic. In the last decades of the seventeenth century a combination of guns, metals, and horses brought social, cultural, and political changes to this region that were at once dynamic, transformative, and ferociously destructive.

In 1684, while Daniel Du Lhut dealt with the deadly consequences of his intrusion into the Native politics of the inland trade, Nicolas Perrot made a similar intervention. La Potherie, the chronicler of New France, incorporated Perrot's efforts to extend the French fur trade into the west within his *Histoire de l'Amérique Septentrionale*. In this narrative he described the trader's attempt to establish a post among the Dakota, and he narrated French ambition

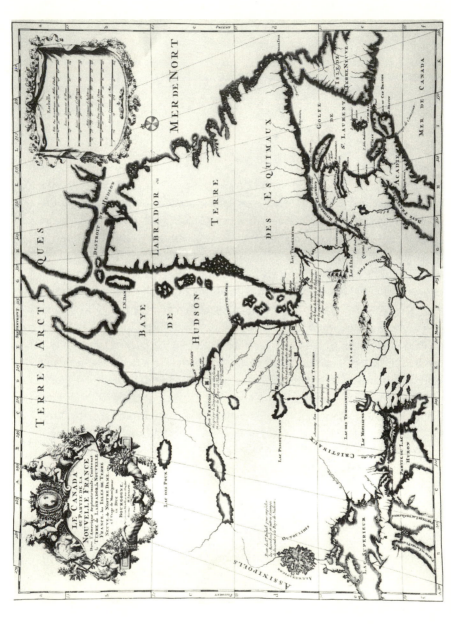

Figure 5. Hubert Jaillot, "Le Canada ou Partie de la Nouvelle France dans l'Amérique Septentrionale . . ." Paris, 1696. Courtesy Hudson's Bay Company Archives, Provincial Archives of Manitoba, G. 5/24 Plate 6 (N15247). The map details the water routes connecting northern Lake Superior with the Hudson's Bay coast.

to claim the peoples and resources of the west as part of New France. "The north was known, and the south gradually revealed," he wrote, but "it was still necessary to penetrate the west where it was known that many Nations lived."[1] Nicolas Perrot, like Du Lhut, would attempt to "discover" and more importantly open trade with the unknown infinity of nations residing in the heartland of North America. And like Du Lhut, he would discover that the alliance system that served the French so well in the east could become a dangerous political liability in the west.

Shortly after Perrot helped to restore a sense of calm to the villages of Green Bay by redeeming an Anishinaabe captive from the Mesquakie, his men began to hear stories about the western interior from their Native allies. According to La Potherie, Perrot and his men became "greatly excited by all the speeches the savages made to them, they only heard talk at the bay of the new nations that were unknown to us." Some living at Green Bay had traveled to the southern plains where they met men on horseback and traded for turquoise. Others had traveled across the northern plains to the junction of the Red and Assiniboine Rivers where they acquired hatchets from the Upland Indians who traded at Radisson's Hayes River post in the country of the Penesewichewan Sepee. "All these reports," La Potherie wrote, "gave birth to an attempt to do something considerable."[2]

Encouraged by stories of intercontinental trade, Perrot decided to lead his small party of Frenchmen into the country west of the Mississippi River valley. He moved inland from the French post at Green Bay in the company of a band of Western Abenaki Indians, refugees from the brutal conflict with the English in western New England. This band had a history of raiding in the Dakota country, and had recently returned from raiding with the Illinois along the southeastern edge of the plains. As Perrot traveled west word spread of their journey and a leading man among the Miami invited the voyageur to a feast at his village, a mixed community composed of Miami, Mascouten, and Kickapoo peoples. At the feast this leader informed Perrot "that his nation wanted to establish themselves next to his fire, and he begged him to show him the place." Perrot responded "that he was going to establish himself on the upper Missisipi this side of the Nadouaissioux, where he would serve them as a barrier, because he knew they had made war together." Perrot then gave the peoples of this village presents, "twelve braces of tobacco" and some kettles. These gifts reaffirmed peace and alliance between the French and the peoples of Green Bay. With these gifts Perrot also promised to restrain the Dakota. In return, he asked his allies to be cautious; if they attacked the Dakota, they would implicate him.[3]

Perrot then departed with the Abenaki and made his way to the Mississippi River, where he stopped and sent his Native guides out onto the plains
"to try to discover some nations." According to Perrot this was a difficult voyage to make "because in this region, beyond the Missisipi, there are plains of a
vast extent, all deserted, in which one can only find beasts."[4] To European eyes
the Great Plains were wastelands, the physical equivalent of a trackless desert.
At this point the narrator reveals that a party of Puans, the French identification for the Winnebago people who called themselves the "Ho-Chunk," or
"People of the First Voice," was selected by Perrot to search the plains for potential trading partners. The Ho-Chunk were not refugees, and their territory
at the edge of the plains, as well as linguistic and kinship connections with
peoples in the west, made them ideal intermediaries for the French.[5]

After five weeks on the plains the Ho-Chunk returned, and communicat-
ing by signal fires, made their way to the makeshift French post with emissaries from the west. According to La Potherie, "There came about eleven days
from the signal some deputies from the Ayoes, who gave notification that
their village approached with the intention of establishing themselves with
us."[6] The "Ayoes," or Iowa, were speakers of a Chirwere dialect, a Siouan language closely related to the dialect spoken by the Ho-Chunk. By their own account they had separated from the Ho-Chunk at Green Bay and moved west
of the Mississippi River, eventually forming three distinct Chirwere-speaking
peoples, the Iowa, Otoe, and Missouria. When they encountered Perrot the
Iowa migrated seasonally between the floodplains of the Iowa River southwest of the Mississippi and onto the tall grass prairies to the northwest of this
river where they hunted bison.[7]

The Iowa shared a ritual complex and material culture similar to the Dakota and other plains peoples. Their ambassadors performed a greeting ritual:
"They approached the French weeping hot tears," which they rubbed onto the
heads of the voyageurs. Perrot, as the French leader, was wrapped in buffalo
robes and carried into the cabin of their chief who repeated the weeping ritual
before feeding the Frenchman buffalo tongue (a favorite food for many plains
peoples), and smoking the calumet. The Iowa leaders demonstrated their humility with the ritual weeping, and signaled their acceptance of Perrot as an
ally by feeding him and performing the calumet. The voyageur was familiar
enough with the elements of this ritual process that he knew how to respond
appropriately to his initial encounter with the Iowa. As a result, he was able
"to engage them to hunt beaver during the winter, they went for this effect
into the depths of the land."[8] In other words, in exchange for trade goods still

rare in the west the Iowa traveled far onto the plains, which the French had not learned to navigate, providing Perrot access to a new resource base.

The problem for Perrot, however, was that while he knew enough to manage this initial encounter with peoples of the west, he was not particularly skilled at managing the politics of the Native New World. The voyageur was a master diplomat on the middle ground, but as Du Lhut had discovered, the French alliance did not extend into the western interior. Similarly, he would also learn that the children of Onontio were adept at using the politics of the French alliance to advance their influence and position within the vast intercontinental trade networks that connected the resource-rich interior to the Atlantic World colonies on the east coast. As a result, the politics and alliances of the west, predicated on a combination of raiding and trading and centered on two rival social formations in the northern prairie parklands and central and northern Great Plains, frequently brought violence and political tension into the social world created by the French alliance. In the far north the Assiniboine-Cree alliance and below those peoples the Dakota-Yankton/Yanktonai-Lakota alliance were emerging as the dominant trading and military powers in the northwestern interior. Both social formations maintained only a marginal and informal relationship with New France, and were increasingly in contact with the Comanche in the south and the Mandan-Hidasta in the north—Native trading powers who provided an alternative access to food stores, trade goods, horses, and slaves that were fueling the transformation of western peoples.[9]

Like the French, the peoples of the middle ground saw opportunity in the evolving social world of the western interior, a place of abundant and increasingly accessible resources. The Anishinaabeg had managed to forge peaceful connections among peoples of both of these powerful social formations. The peoples of Green Bay, though, particularly the refugees, largely shunned attempts at forging new alliances and focused instead on raiding and expanding into western hunting territories. When Perrot returned from his visit to the Iowa he found two men from the bay waiting for him. A Mascouten and a Kickapoo from the village that feasted the voyageur on his way west informed him that part of their village had relocated upriver from the French. Once again they asked Perrot to name "the place where he wanted them to light their fire." Perrot traveled to their campsite and was feasted in the lodge of the village ogimaa. According to La Potherie's narrative, "This chief asked him for possession of a river that watered a beautiful country that was not far from the place where they were."[10] In effect, the leader of the Mascouten and

Kickapoos village asked Perrot to assume the role of ogimaa, and to assign the families a hunting territory in the country of the Dakota.

The people of Green Bay heard Perrot's declaration that he would carry the standard of New France into the west, into the country of their enemies, and they decided to follow their father onto this new ground. The leader from Green Bay asked Perrot to be a father to his children. He asked the voyageur "to protect all of the families of their nations and to prevent the Nadouaissioux from insulting them." The Mascouten claimed to be in the process of negotiating a peace with the Dakota. Their leader also said that he had received a promise from a large village of Illinois that they would join him in the west at the new French post. Perrot, with good reason, feared that the Illinois planned to raid among the very western Indians with whom he wanted to develop trade relations. He denounced the Illinois as cannibals, questioned the intention of the Mascouten/Kickapoo villagers, and suggested he had not decided whether or not to prevent the Dakotas from harassing them.

In response to this challenge, the Mascouten leader retreated to the language, protocols, and obligations of the French alliance. He told Perrot "that he was surprised he mistrusted his children. You are our father," he declared, implying that they intended to maintain peaceful relations with the voyageur's new trading partners. The ogimaa explained that "the Ayoes were their youngest children, thus they could not strike them without striking himself, since he had placed them at his breast, and that they had sucked the same milk that they would want to suck again." Accepting the Iowa as younger children of their French father, the Mascouten then asked Perrot to provide them with weapons. Called out by the children of Onontio, the voyageur had no choice but to follow the protocols of the alliance. He presented his calumet to the leaders of this community. While they smoked, Perrot "told them that this was his breast that he had always presented for them to suck, and that he was presently going to suckle the Nadouaissioux." If the Dakota refused to obey him and "came in war against them," Perrot pledged, "he would declare them an enemy."[11]

The Mascouten leader placed Perrot in a precarious position, sanctioning the Mascouten expansion into the west, and making him responsible for providing a diplomatic answer to any opposition from the Dakota. Ironically, using the language of the alliance, the Mascouten-Kickapoo villagers forced the French to make a place for them in the west out of fear that their presence would otherwise sabotage the French trade among the "newly discovered nations" of this region. The Mascouten and Kickapoos spent the winter on the plains hunting large game for food, but the Abenaki dispersed into the tributaries of the Mississippi to hunt for beaver. Shortly after the calumet ceremony with the bay peoples, Perrot's men encountered a party of forty-eight Dakota canoes "delighted to see the French." They returned with this party to their village to inform the Dakota of the new peoples from the east and west they had brought into their country, and to ask them to show restraint toward these outsiders in exchange for the trade they brought to their people.

Even as Perrot pledged, tentatively, to incorporate the Dakota into the French alliance he must have realized that he lacked the resources to do so. The French simply did not have the resources or the manpower that would be required to fold such a large and non-Algonquian social formation into the social world of the alliance. Indeed, the only children of Onontio with ties to the Dakota, the Anishinaabeg of Shagwaamikong, were becoming increasingly detached from the French alliance. As a result, traders voyaging into the west now traveled almost exclusively through Green Bay, creating considerable anger among the allied villages in this region. This fact was not lost on the Jesuit missionaries at the bay, who wrote to the governor that Daniel Du Lhut had found "it necessary to open and make secure" the road between the bay and the Dakota country by showing a willingness to use military force. In addition, following his murder trial/condolence ceremony, Du Lhut visited the Boodewaadamii and chastised them for their past involvement in murders committed against the French. At the time of the trial, the Jesuits informed the governor that this series of interventions might "prevent the rupture of the Outagamies with the Sauteurs," which was at the heart of the violence engulfing the children of Onontio in the west.[12]

Du Lhut's intervention fell short, however, and Perrot's formal establishment of trade relations with the Dakota left the Mesquakie antagonized even as he managed to appease their Mascouten and Kickapoo neighbors. According to the post commander at the bay, Du Lhut had promised to redeem Mesquakie captives taken by the Anishinaabeg during their recent conflict. He promised to undertake a mission parallel to the one taken by Perrot when he redeemed the daughter of the Shagwaamikong Anishinaabe ogimaa. Eager to resume his trade in the country northwest of Lake Superior, Du Lhut apparently failed to honor this pledge.

As a consequence the Mesquakie raided the Dakota to raise their dead. Striking a winter camp in the Mississippi valley, however, they killed six Anishinaabe men and took nine women and children captive. These people were from the family "of one of the more considerable Sauteurs whom they found among the Sioux."[13] In the aftermath of this raid, the Jesuits at the Green Bay mission reported that their allies continued "to fall out with one another from the murders between the Outagamies and the Saulteurs." And they noted "that there were some rumors going around that the French had gone to the Nadouescioux . . . and had been killed there." The Jesuits fought to counter these false rumors, but they acknowledged that these accusations and the ongoing conflict between their allies signaled discontent over the growing relationships between the Anishinaabeg and the French with the Dakota.[14]

La Potherie's narrative of Perrot's time in the west struck an entirely different tone than the letters of the Jesuits, who openly worried about the collapse of the alliance. He returned to the themes that animated his stories of Perrot among the peoples of Green Bay. For La Potherie the story of New France and the French alliance with the peoples of the pays d'en haut was a story of redemption and rebirth; it was the story of a French father giving birth to Native children, literally creating and suckling Indian nations into existence. Unlike their English rivals, the French imagined the fate of New France to be tied to the fate of the Native peoples bound to their empire. The French, however, would never have the capacity to expand their alliance system into the indigenous west. The powerful imagery of a French father nursing his Native children with a mother's milk of cloth, metal tools, guns, and other manufactured goods created by the peoples of the Atlantic World was more rhetoric than reality. In truth, they struggled to maintain their status as fathers on the middle ground, in the pays d'en haut, from the establishment of the colony until the time when they surrendered Canada to the British.

More accurately, Perrot's performance and La Potherie's narrative represented the theater of empire rather than the reality on the ground. Perrot had gained the stature of an ogimaa of the French alliance. There was real-world power in this status, and he wielded that power effectively, but only within the confines of the alliance. In the west, far away from French posts and missions, there was no middle ground, and Perrot would find himself surrounded by demanding children eager to carve a space for themselves in this new territory. And all too often, he would confront angry trading partners in the west interested in his goods, but wary of his presence, and hostile to the Native intruders who followed in his wake.

The limited collection of letters from the Jesuit missionaries and licensed traders stationed at Green Bay that record this 1684 raid against the Dakota, and the capture of yet more Anishinaabe captives, lacks the power of La Potherie's narratives. But those letters reveal an important shift in Native politics linking Anishinaabewaki to the west. The "Sauteurs" taken captive by the Mesquakie were not trespassers on Dakota territory. They were living with Dakota families, members of a winter band, a tiyospaye. Living with the Dakota in this fashion represented a political transformation for the Anishinaabeg. This transformation entailed shape-shifting from cultural outsiders into a single kindred, tákukic 'iyapi, or a people "related to each other."[15] Dakota kinship terms specified the social roles of band members as if they were an extended family. As a semantic domain, *wótakuye*, or "kinship," did not distinguish between biological and social kinship. Both categories of social relations were expressed by the term *mitakuyepi*, or "my relatives," a general category of kinship that signified "relatives with whom I live" or "close relatives."[16] For members of a tiyospaye, the act of relating to one another provided structure to all social interactions.

For both the Anishinaabeg and Dakota this alliance was more than a shift in political obligation; it would have entailed a fundamental reshaping of their social world. For both peoples kinship represented an interrelated spiritual and moral bond. Just as the use of kinship terminology specified behavioral and moral responsibilities between individuals, it also signaled a shared sense of social values, rights, and obligations for the residential community as a whole. The Dakota ethnographer Ella Deloria wrote that to address a relative was the equivalent of smoking the calumet. The Dakota language, she noted, implicitly linked kinship and prayer. The verb stem for the words signifying "to address a relative" and "to pray" is the same, *wac 'ekiya*.[17] Writing about this semantic connection, the anthropologist Ray DeMallie has suggested that "in a linguistic sense prayer evokes kinship with the universal powers."[18] In other words, for the allies there was a direct connection between kinship and spiritual power, or wasicun, a term understood as "manidoo" by the Anishinaabeg. Kinship was the expression of a proper relationship, between individuals and with the universal powers.[19] In this sense, DeMallie argues, "Sioux culture had no prescribed boundaries." It worked as a system of potentialities that structured and made sense of all human interactions. This means of social adaptation was particularly important to migrant peoples like the Anishinaabeg and the Dakota.[20] Outside this circle of kinship there were only outsiders and potential enemies. For the Anishinaabeg connected to Shagwaamikong, alliance with the Dakota increasingly translated into exclusion from the rights and obligations that bound the children of Onontio to one another and to their French father. Alliance with the Dakota signaled a withdrawal from the middle ground, and a political and cultural reorientation to the Native New World evolving in the western interior. In short, this new alliance represented a reimagining of the Anishinaabe social world to embrace the possibilities, as well as the potential dangers, of the indigenous west.

An Attack on the Miami

When the Mascouten and Kickapoos migrated to the Mississippi region to hunt for Perrot, the Miami decided not to follow them. The Jesuit missionary Claude Allouez invited them to move to the bottom of Lake Michigan at the edge of the Illinois country near the Chicago portage so that he could minister to them. Many families joined the missionary while others remained at the bay. In the fall of 1686, a party of Miami hunters from Green Bay scouted signs of a large encampment at the bottom of the Lake. They had discovered an Iroquois army on the march. This was not a raiding party. The Seneca, Keepers of the Western Door of the Haudenosaunee, had mobilized an army of warriors that would have rivaled the armed forces of any of North America's colonial powers in numbers. In terms of their ability to place such a force in the field and march them across what the English considered the backcountry, and the French the pays d'en haut, the Haudenosaunee were unmatched.[21]

The Miami hunters fled, bringing the news of this army to their village at Green Bay. Some villagers believed that this bold attack from their Iroquois enemies signaled a betrayal by New France. Believing their father had abandoned them, the peoples of the bay fled into the west. The Seneca found and destroyed the Miami who had relocated to the bottom of the lake. They let the handful of Frenchmen at the nearby post live, but as these men and the few Miami survivors later reported, "The Iroquois . . . generally took all of the women and children."[22] The Seneca enslaved five hundred Miami women and children, and began to march them back to their homeland. Their attack sent a brutal political message to the children of Onontio. The Haudenosaunee laid claim to new territory in Anishinaabewaki—the territory north of Lake Huron and to the west across the peninsula of land above Lake Erie, stretching as far as the southern shores of Lake Michigan. But this attack also signaled profound problems within the Haudenosaunee. Decades of vicious fighting to consolidate their territorial control over the Dutch and English fur trade, combined with exposure to devastating European diseases, took a heavy toll on the population of the Peoples of the Longhouse. They desperately needed captives/adoptees to stabilize their population losses. The capture of an entire enemy village was a sign of both their strength and their weakness.[23]

The brutal attack against the Miami came after a series of successful Iroquois diplomatic and military encounters with their enemies that emboldened members of the confederacy. Following significant victories against the Susquehannocks to their south and the Wampanoag, Mohican, and Abenaki peoples to their east, the warriors of the Haudenosaunee turned their attention toward the Native allies of New France.[24] The children of Onontio were their main rivals in the fur trade. At the time of their attack in 1686, the Iroquois claimed this disputed territory by right of conquest. Two years earlier the Seneca plundered a party of voyageurs trading for the governor of New France, Joseph-Antoine le Febvre de La Barre. The traders were overtaken in the Illinois country on their way to resupply Fort Saint Louis. The attackers pillaged the governor's traders, and then laid siege to the fort for six days before retreating.[25] La Barre personally led a military campaign against the Seneca to punish the confederacy. He marched French troops to Fort Frontenac where they waited for their Native allies to join them. Influenza spread through the camp leaving the majority of the troops at the post on the edge of the Iroquois country incapacitated and vulnerable. When an Iroquois delegation arrived to determine if the French came to their country to make peace or war Governor La Barre, dangerously exposed, accepted peace on the confederacy's terms.[26]

Five hundred Native allies of New France arrived on the scene to fight for their father, only to discover the battle was conceded before it had even begun. Learning that Onontio had ceded territory to the Iroquois, his allies returned to the west in despair. The English took advantage of French weakness and Iroquois aggression to expand their trade into Anishinaabewaki. The governor of New York advised his Haudenosaunee allies "to strengthen themselves by alliance Offensive & Defensive with the Ottowaws & Twich Twicks [Miamis] & farther Indians, lay the path open for them to come & trade with us." To help open the path to Albany for the peoples of Anishinaabewaki, the governor also recruited and licensed French voyageurs to carry the English trade to Michilimackinac. Following La Barre's capitulation, these men entered Anishinaabewaki with a Seneca escort, and traded with French-allied Indians in the villages attached to the French post.[27]

English ambition, however, combined with Iroquois expansion put added pressure on the game populations in the disputed territory to the west of Lake Erie. The Iroquois regarded the French trade in this region, at Fort Frontenac and at Detroit, as an affront to their treaty with Governor La Barre. Perhaps even more significantly, they believed that these forts encouraged the Miami and the Illinois to overhunt beaver in this region. As a result of this perceived transgression, and in spite of the New York governor's call for alliance-making diplomacy, the Iroquois began to attack the allies of New France to assert their territorial claims in the west. Following their attack at Fort Saint Louis in the Illinois country in 1684, they struck again at Michilimackinac in the early summer of 1686, carrying off 106 Odawa and Wyandot captives.[28]

When the warriors of the Haudenosaunee struck at the Miami later that year, killing all of the men and carrying off all of the women and children, they destroyed the Miami village. This attack eclipsed the more selective targeting of a traditional mourning war raid, and instead aimed to destroy the Miami as a people. Killing all of the adult men, they denied their enemies the capacity to define and defend the social boundaries of their community. By absorbing the women and children into their own families they robbed their enemies of a future, claiming their ability to reproduce themselves as a people for the Haudenosaunee. This aggressive military strategy not only destroyed their enemies but actually consumed them whole. Claiming the life and lands of their enemies in this fashion, however, strained the social structure of the confederacy as young men died in alarmingly high numbers. In the Haudenosaunee push to take control of the fur trade centered in Anishinaabewaki, their fighting strength would be reduced by as much 50 percent during the next two decades.[29] The warriors of the confederacy made this grim sacrifice in order to try to control a western hinterland that they believed was vital to their social and economic integrity as a people.

The French also believed that this space, for them imagined as part of the pays d'en haut, was vital to the survival of their colony. In fact, both New France and New York claimed possession of and sovereignty over this border region between Anishinaabewaki and the territory of the Haudenosaunee.[30] They sent trade and traders into this region, and the French stationed armed forces at a few scattered posts, but imperial influence was feeble and fragile. Their competing claims of sovereignty were a fiction that mattered only on European maps, and not at all on the ground. The struggle to control this borderland, a vital gateway linking the Native New World in the western interior to colonial cities on the Atlantic coast, was part of a broader struggle to control the interconnection between these two social worlds. The English and French fought to position their empires so that they could take maximum advantage of this intersection. Neither European power was capable of extending their settler colonial regimes into this territory. More accurately, they sought to attach this space and the Native people who controlled it to their empires. This was, from a European perspective, part of the discovery process—finding, claiming possession, and profiting from the peoples, places, and things of the New World. But the discovery process was mutual, and on the other side of this encounter were Native social formations who fought in similar fashion to control access to the peoples, things, and new places of the Atlantic World that were fueling political, cultural, and economic transformation in the west.

The expansion of the French trade into the west, to the Mississippi and beyond, benefited individual traders and merchants, but actually destabilized French alliances in the Great Lakes. Trade in the west had an effect similar to the opening of English posts at Hudson's Bay in that it created instability among the different village communities allied to New France. Voyageurs like Perrot and Du Lhut traded with western Indians without really integrating them into the alliance, and they brought their allies into new territory where they competed for trade, hunting territory, and political dominance. As a result, social interactions in the west were not easily governed by the protocols of the alliance. Equally problematic, violence in the west threatened to undo the social ties and sense of mutual obligation that served as the foundation of the middle ground, the social world created by Onontio and his children in the Great Lakes region.

When the Iroquois attacked the Miami in 1686 the latter were especially vulnerable because Nicolas Perrot, the French commandant, had taken his post and his people off of the middle ground and into the west. The French were caught unprepared to meet the Iroquois threat because they had, quite literally, turned away from the world of the alliance. News of the Miami's devastation reached Perrot at his fort in the Dakota country where he and a party of French officers and traders engaged a multitude of Native peoples, many without any diplomatic relationship with either Onontio or his children. They spent all of their energy and resources trying to prevent hunters drawn to their new post from Green Bay and the Illinois country from clashing with the Dakota and the Iowa. Along with news of the Seneca attack, they learned "that one hundred Miamis, Maskoutechs, Pouteouatemis, had pursued the Iroquois to whom they had given the axe by hand with such fury that they killed one hundred, took back half of their people, and routed the Iroquois."[31] Along with this news, Perrot also received orders from the governor to rally the allies for a retaliatory attack on the Haudenosaunee.

A new governor had replaced La Barre, and the assault on the Miami gave him the chance to act like a father, unifying his children in the face of a common enemy. Perrot left the plains and returned to the Miami village at Green Bay. The voyageur presented the surviving Miami bands with a war club and presents. He told them, "The cries of your dead have been heard by Onontio your father, who wanting to have pity on you has resolved to sacrifice his young men to destroy the cannibals who have eaten you." Speaking for Onontio and as the voice of the alliance, Perrot told the people that their children cried out for revenge. He called on the Miami to redeem their loved ones, and to bring the same atrocity to the Seneca that had been visited upon them. "They must be made to disgorge and vomit by force your flesh that is in their stomach," he declared. Equally important, he called for retribution: "If your children have become his dogs and his slaves you must make their women become ours."[32] To rally his allies Perrot spoke like an alliance chief, and speaking as the French father, he selflessly offered to give up the lives of his young men in battle to restore the lives of his children. He promised his allies that together they would turn the Iroquois into their dogs and slaves.

The Seneca attack presented the French with an opportunity to erase the string of humiliating defeats that the Iroquois had inflicted upon New France and its Native allies. The Miami promised to take up the war club. Shortly after this council, however, Perrot learned that his other children at Green Bay had already turned against him. As he spoke to the Miami, a war party of fifteen hundred Mascouten, Kickapoo, and Mesquakie warriors advanced into the west. An army three times the size of the one that had rallied to fight for Governor La Barre marched toward the Dakota country in defiance of Perrot himself. "I learned," Perrot later wrote, they "were going to war against the Scioux, would pillage my merchandise knowing I was not there; and that they would do the same to the French farther up and slit their throats."[33] Believing themselves betrayed by Onontio, the people of the bay planned to kill and pillage the French traders in the west, and then use their newly acquired weapons to raise their dead among the Dakota. Like the warriors of the Haudenosaunee they fought to secure a western hinterland, and to punish the French interlopers who stood in their way.

Rushing back to his post ahead of the main body of warriors Perrot scrambled to defend himself, and the French Empire, against claims of infidelity by the peoples of Green Bay. What made this situation so delicate, of course, was the fact that his own trading interests did in fact compromise the security of peoples like the Miami, Mesquakie, Mascouten, and Kickapoos. With only seven men to face down an army of fifteen hundred Perrot would need to do everything in his power to make the approaching army see him as the kind of father they wanted at the head their alliance. Recent experience, unfortunately, made him and his fellow Frenchmen seem like the self-centered agents of an empire no longer capable of protecting its own isolated outposts, let alone its Native allies. Perrot managed to arrive at his post ahead of the war party from the bay. He sent messengers calling for the ogimaag leading these warriors to join him at a council in his post. When the leaders arrived Perrot reproached them for their plot to murder the voyageurs trading in the Dakota country. He expressed his disappointment only after feeding the ogimaag, and after giving them presents and a gift of tabacco, which they smoked together. After a discussion where Perrot complained, among other things, that his children wanted to eat him, the voyageur managed to persuade these men to call off their raid against the Dakota.[34] In short, he treated them like family, and while he scolded them for their cruel intentions he also gently reminded them that he spoke in the name of their father.

Perrot blunted the anger of the war leaders with the promise of Iroquois slaves to raise their dead. The next day when the main body of warriors arrived, Perrot kept the ogimaag locked in his fort while they addressed the war party together.

The voyageur later wrote that "I made them understand that they were dead at the first sign of violence made by their people." This was bluster intended for his European audience. The real give-and-take here was reflected in Perrot's statement that "they begged me to trade their peltries for ammunition so that they would be able to hunt buffalo."[35] He allowed the entire war party to enter his post in small groups to trade, after which, they dispersed in winter bands out onto the plains to hunt. In effect, Perrot derailed the war party by generously providing provisions for the winter. La Potherie's narration of this event makes this fact more obvious. He wrote simply that "the shortage of supplies oppressed them, we took pity on them . . . we gave them some." In his version of this encounter, Perrot then gave a final gift of tobacco and firearms to the war leaders. This gift, he told the departing warriors, "closed for them . . . the door by which they would enter the home of the Nadouaissioux." While he closed one door, however, Perrot sought to open another. He admonished the warriors of Green Bay to "turn their weapons henceforth against the Iroquois, and . . . they would serve as the bow that Onontio pulled on his enemy, and the war club for his hand to bring down upon their families."[36] Drawing on the conventions and protocols of the alliance, Perrot sought to redirect the violence of his allies for the benefit of their father and his empire. The problem, as always for the French, was that their allies expected much in return for meeting the demands of their father. These expectations included a successful resolution of the threat posed by the Iroquois. But they also included an increasingly more urgent desire to see their father destroy the threat posed by the Dakota.

Leaving the Middle Ground for the Western Trade

The Iroquois attacks on the peoples of Anishinaabewaki underscored the weakness of New France in the west. French posts were strung out across a vast territory at the edge of the region they called the pays d'en haut. They ranged from Du Lhut's undersupplied posts at Lake Nipigon and at Kaministiquia northwest of Lake Superior to Perrot's new post on the Mississippi River and his old post inland from Green Bay at the mouth of the Wisconsin River, and as far south as the newly refortified Fort Saint Louis on the Illinois River. These posts anchored French claims to the pays d'en haut and to the western interior. French voyageurs and military officers enacted the alliance at these locations. They traded with the children of Onontio and forged a middle ground. The alliance worked when everyone recognized their kinship to one another, and accepted the obligations implied by the status of this relationship. Under these circumstances, the fur trade allowed the French to mediate disputes between their allies, and to keep them united against common enemies such as the Iroquois. These posts, however, increasingly served as jumping-off points for voyageurs engaged in the lucrative trade with the unallied Indians of the west. Bypassing their allies to trade with western Indians, the French ignored the needs of their children in the pays d'en haut. They all but abandoned the middle ground and brought trade goods, including weapons, to outsiders or even worse to the enemies of their allies. This expansion of the French fur trade into the west left the allies divided, poorly provisioned, and vulnerable to attack. Now, Onontio seemed incapable of stopping the Iroquois from raiding his children and claiming their hunting territory.

By attacking the children of Onontio at Detroit and in the Illinois country the Haudenosaunee threatened to reconstruct the boundaries of Anishinaabewaki. Equally important these attacks signaled the increased ability of the English to influence indigenous exchange and alliance practices in the west. Increased demand for pelts at Albany fueled Iroquois aggression, and after facing down the French for control of this territory the Haudenosaunee claimed it by right of conquest. Iroquois warriors were willing to go to war to secure this space as their hunting territory, and they would claim the women and children of their enemies as slaves in compensation for the lives they lost in the process.[37] While Iroquois aggression began to cause the alliance to unravel, the English posts at Hudson's Bay increased the autonomy of Anishinaabe peoples in the west who hunted the prized winter coat beaver that underpinned the French fur trade.[38] This increased competition spurred French expansion into the west, which proved so destructive to the alliance. French voyageurs and military officers focused on the western trade neglected the rituals and obligations that bound their allies together as children of Onontio. As a consequence, both they and their allies were disorganized and ill prepared to fight off Iroquois advances.[39]

When his own allies from Green Bay attacked his post on the Mississippi, Nicolas Perrot was forced to divert his resources from the west, and refocus on meeting the needs of the children of Onontio. Forced to act like a father, Perrot was subsequently able to rally three hundred Boodewaadamii, Menominee, Mesquakie, Mascouten, Kickapoo, Miami, and Ho-Chunk warriors from the villages of the Green Bay region. They traveled to Michilimackinac where the Odawaag, and the Wyandot, somewhat reluctantly, agreed to march with the French against the Seneca. The Sauteurs remained conspicuously absent from this army, which joined forces with Governor Denonville, who commanded a force of approximately two thousand regular troops, Canadian militia, and mission Indians from Lower Canada.[40]

Denonville managed a limited victory against the peoples of the Haudenosaunee. The victory put an end to the English trade expeditions entering Anishinaabewaki through the Seneca country.[41] The Seneca sustained only a few casualties, but the French and their Native allies routed them from their villages, which were then looted and burned along with their agricultural fields. The loss of food crops caused some suffering, but the Seneca found sanctuary among the other peoples of the confederacy. Reprisals against the French for this rather anemic victory, however, began immediately. French settlements were raided and colonists carried off into captivity. In spite of its limited success and negative consequences, however, Denonville's campaign did bring a temporary sense of cohesion and purpose to his alliance.[42]

Denonville successfully rallied his Native allies, but his campaign ultimately undermined the security of the French Empire in North America. The Iroquois retaliatory assault on New France occurred at a time when the colony was particularly vulnerable. In the year following Denonville's campaign, a smallpox epidemic decimated the colonial population, and the governor learned that a looming conflict between France and England in Europe meant that he would not receive the troop reinforcements he expected.[43] Fortunately for the governor, the Haudenosaunee Confederacy was wracked by internal divisions between Christian and non-Christian political factions who could not agree on the best course of action for dealing with New France. Within a few short months, Denonville's campaign and the Iroquois counterattacks had morphed into a protracted negotiation between the colony and the confederacy over the terms and conditions required by both sides to make peace.[44]

The merchants and traders of Canada took advantage of the reduction in violence that accompanied this diplomatic wrangling between the governor and the leaders of the Haudenosaunee. Voyageurs recovered the backlog of peltry stored at Michilimackinac since the outbreak of violence. The licensed traders mobilized to lead the warriors of Anshinaabewaki in battle were similarly able to return to the west to resume the operation of their posts. These men, skilled agents of empire like Perrot and Du Lhut, realized the need to keep their allies unified. They had watched in horror as their allies prepared to abandon their identity as children of the French father, leaving them to face the Iroquois alone. They witnessed firsthand how their push to expand the trade into the west contributed to violent quarrels between their allies and undermined their relationships with the peoples of Anishinaabewaki. Even so, they all but ignored the children of Onontio as they rushed back to their posts.

If the Seneca campaign provided a temporary cure for the troubles of the alliance, the Dakota trade acted as an even more potent poison. Men such as Perrot and Du Lhut, who functioned as alliance chiefs, traveled east at the head of an Indian army to fight for New France. But they left behind men of lesser rank to mind their posts, and the continued presence of French traders among the Dakota and other western peoples was regarded by some of Onontio's children as an abject betrayal. As the voyageurs returned to the west they received reports that the Mesquakie had burned the Jesuit mission at Green Bay to the ground, and let it be known that they planned to block the water route to the Dakota country. Nicolas Perrot's cache of furs, stored inside the mission, was destroyed, leaving the voyageur deeply in debt and even more dependent on the success of his post in the Dakota country.[45] When he and Du Lhut reached the bay they did not stop, but pressed on to their posts in the west.

Before he could move on, however, three Mesquakie men intercepted Daniel Du Lhut and asked him to join their people at council. The voyageurs learned about Anishinaabeg taken captive in the Dakota country. They quickly discovered that "all the people of the region were greatly alarmed by an attack the Outagamis had made on the Sauteurs."[46] The Mesquakie appeared to be asking Du Lhut to make good on his earlier pledge to mediate their ongoing dispute with the Gichigamiing Anishinaabeg. This had been the true strength of the alliance; it had provided a way for refugees and seasonal migrants to forge new communities together. Du Lhut, however, chose to ignore his responsibilities to the people of Green Bay in order to pursue his own interests as a trader. He declined the Mesquakie request, and instead let it be known that he planned to make his way to his posts via the Mississippi River. The soldier turned voyageur threatened to open fire on anyone who attempted to stand in his way.

Their pleas for intercession rejected by Du Lhut, the Mesquakie sent additional messengers to beg Perrot to come to their village and reprise his role as redeemer and mediator of the alliance. This time they sent five ogimaag, who approached Perrot's canoe "with feelings so penetrated with grief" that the man recently appointed as commandant of the west could not refuse them.[47] They admitted to Perrot "that it was true that a party of their young men going to war against the Nadouaissioux, had met some Sauteurs in their enemy's country." The Mesquakie explained that they had been waiting for the French to come and redeem these captives. They made it clear that they wanted only to cooperate with the French because without the benefit of their trade "they could only expect to be disgraced and the victims of their neighbors."[48] In short, the Mesquakie begged Perrot to act the part of their father and take pity on his children.

Once again, conflict between the peoples the French identified as the Sauteurs and the Outagamis would be used as a morality play in which Perrot prevented his children from eating one another and destroying the alliance. He entered the cabin of the principal ogimaa to find this man sitting before a boiling kettle filled with venison. When it was cooked the ogimaa placed the kettle and some raw meat before Perrot. The voyageur refused to eat. "This meat," he said "did not please him and only when the Outagamis became reasonable he would have it." The ogimaa then had three Sauteur girls brought into the cabin. "This is how reasonable the Outagamis can be," he said. "He vomits the meat he had intended to eat because he remembered that you had forbidden it to him." The ogimaa then "begged him to put it back from where he had taken it." Perrot praised the Mesquakie for sparing their captives' lives. He told them to "remember the war club they had been given from Onontio their father, who had declared to them that they were given it only to use henceforth on the Iroquois." Perrot admonished the Mesquakie, telling the elders gathered before him they had used their war clubs "to strike his own body and to mistreat the families of the Sauteur." Then he told them to go hunt beaver, and wage war only against the Iroquois. Finally, in recognition of their mutual obligations to one another, Perrot "left behind some Frenchmen to maintain the trade."[49]

This particular conflict emerges as the set piece of La Potherie's narrative history of New France. This ongoing drama between the Outagamis and the Sauteurs distilled the essence of the alliance, at least as the French wanted to see it. Only a strong French father could keep his querulous children united so that they could fend off the marauding Iroquois, and become prosperous hunters. More accurately, however, La Potherie's narrative demonstrated the diplomatic brilliance of the Mesquakie as much as it highlighted Perrot's skilled diplomatic performance, suggesting the real give-and-take that went into creating the middle ground. The Mesquakie managed to transform a botched mourning war raid into leverage, forcing French traders to pass the winter in their village instead of moving on to the west as they intended. This vignette, in effect, reveals both French fantasies about their role in the alliance and the underlying truth of the relationship between Onontio and his children. But unlike La Potherie's previous narration of crisis and redemption involving the Outagamis and Sauteurs, this story contained a second act. While Perrot made the concession of leaving some men behind, he did not abandon his post in the Dakota country. He left the Outagamis and ascended the Mississippi River where Dakota warriors met him, and La Potherie attempted to describe the impact of this new relationship on the politics of the French alliance.

When he returned to their country the Dakota met Perrot on the Mississippi, wrapped him in beaver robes, and carried him to their village at the end of a procession of warriors singing ritual songs associated with the calumet. According to La Potherie they brought him to the lodge of the chief, presumably Ouasicoude, the leader who orchestrated the adoption of Louis Hennepin to create a relationship with the French. After receiving this ritual welcome and affirmation of their alliance Perrot learned that the post he established near the main Dakota village had been pillaged in his absence. La Potherie's narrative noted of the Dakota that "they are at war with all of the nations, with the exception of the Sauteurs and the Ayoes."[50] The fact that so many enemy peoples came to trade with Perrot at his post in their country must have caused considerable consternation among the Dakota, although it was also possible that the French post was pillaged as a result of tensions among the Dakota oyate (peoples) about access to the French, or as part of a disagreement about whether or not to incorporate the French into an alliance relationship with the Oceti Sakowin (Dakota-Yankton/Yanktonai-Lakota peoples).

Whatever the cause, a single war leader at the head of one hundred warriors stole Perrot's trade goods, and according to Perrot and La Potherie, nearly paid for this act of aggression with his life. According to the Frenchmen, "The chiefs who had not been involved came close to killing this chief; they regarded him as a result of this with great contempt."[51] And yet even after settling this affair and ritually renewing their alliance with Perrot, the Dakota stole "a crate of merchandise" from the voyageurs. Angered by what he considered an affront, Perrot threatened to set fire to the marshlands surrounding the Dakota village. To underscore his demand the voyageur threw a cup of brandy onto the fire, and the resulting burst of flame so frightened the Dakota that the missing goods were immediately returned. This, at least, was how La Potherie described this encounter.

At the time Perrot established his post on the Mississippi, and when La Potherie wrote his narrative history of North America, French expansion into the west was controversial. The influential minister of finance to Louis XIV, Jean-Baptiste Colbert, wanted to consolidate the colonial development of New France in Lower Canada. It would have been important for proponents of a western empire to demonstrate that the French could easily control autonomous western peoples like the Dakota who remained clearly outside of the alliance. Narratives like those written by Perrot and La Potherie made this case. They dramatized the discovery of Native North America by the agents of the French Empire, and they told the story of the peoples and territories of the New World, showing how French immigrants made this country into their own. That is why, after startling the Dakota into submission with the flash of fire from a cup of brandy, Perrot took formal possession of the west before returning to Montreal with his furs. In May 1689, he assembled a small party of Jesuits and traders at his post on the Mississippi and "took possession, in the name of the King, of all the places, where he had been in the past and where he was going to go." With this rather ambiguous declaration Perrot reclaimed Green Bay, and claimed anew the country of the "Nadouesioux," the west coast of the upper Mississippi, and "other far away places." With the recording of this ceremony Perrot created on paper what he could not create on the ground. Namely, he made a unified physical and social space in the indigenous west where the Iroquois and the English were excluded, and where Native peoples recognized French sovereignty, authority, and power.[52]

It seems unlikely, however, that the thousands of Dakota peoples moving through this village site would be unsettled by the pretense of Perrot's show of power when he threw his cup of brandy on the fire and demanded obedience. In fact, this narrative marks a point when the Dakota became a more distinctive presence in the records of New France. For much of the history of the colony they seemed to lurk at the edge of French influence. Dubbed the Iroquois of the west by the Jesuits, they are portrayed as a vaguely menacing but largely unknown people in French records. This would begin to change by the end of the seventeenth century, when the French would find, as La Potherie did, that the Dakota could no longer be ignored.

This encounter on the Mississippi River was clearly not the story of a powerful father commanding over wayward children, and demanding they recognize his authority. More accurately, Perrot found himself entangled in the internal politics of Dakota society. The war leader who pillaged Perrot's fort was, most likely, not from the Mdewakanton oyate that had initiated a relationship with the French. The Yanktonai made a record of the plundering of Perrot's post in one of their winter counts, suggesting that they had traveled east to trade with their Dakota relatives, possibly even seeking access to the French traders. The Yanktonai were in the process of expanding their territory deeper into the west. Shortly after Perrot reestablished his fort, they fought the Omaha for control of the Great Plains river valley that would come to be called the Big Sioux River. The winter count, when read alongside French records, provides a picture of the Oceti Sakowin as an expanding power in the Native New World. These events reveal that the Dakota oyate were simultaneously expanding onto the plains, where they gained access to buffalo and horses, and extending their reach into the east, where they gained access to metals, weapons, and other trade goods as well as Native allies with long-standing ties to both English and French traders.[53]

The Dakota's Devastating Loss

In the summer of 1695 two war leaders made their way east to Montreal from the marshlands at the bottom of Gichigamiing. One was a Mantanton Dakota named Tiyoskate (Plays in the Lodge). The other warrior was

Anishinaabe and named Zhingobiins (the Little Balsam Fir). The country they left behind was crisscrossed with rivers and creeks that connected their peoples to one another and to a shared resource base. In the spring and early summer months the Mantanton and other Dakota bands converged on the prairie region along the Minnesota River to hunt buffalo. In the winter this band, a subdivision of the Mdewakanton, returned to the headwaters region of the Mississippi River. From their principal village site at Mde Wakan, the place the French called Mille Lacs, the Mantanton and other Mdewakanton bands dispersed into the network of tributary rivers that drained into the Mississippi River basin from the marshlands above. It was here that they met Anishinaabe doodemag moving inland from the western lakeshores of Gichigamiing.

The Anishinaabeg ascended watersheds that the French called the St. Louis, the Bois Brulé, and the Mauvais into the marshy interior that arched across the top of the Mississippi River. Like the Mdewakanton, the Anishinaabeg moved through this landscape on a seasonal basis. Bands that hunted in relative isolation in the winter coalesced at maple stands forming sugar camps in the early spring. When the ice broke up on the lakeshores they moved back east into the mouths of rivers and streams that drained into Gichigamiing to harvest sturgeon and sucker fish entering the lake to spawn. These bands formed small seasonal villages that periodically came together in the Shagwaamikong region at lakeshore villages identified by the French as La Pointe and Fond du Lac for ceremony and to trade. In late fall the large number of people gathered at these village sites made it possible to harvest enormous quantities of whitefish and lake trout spawning on offshore reefs. When bands hunted for the fur trade this was also the time when they took their presents, or later their credit, before moving back into the interior.

Tiyoskate and Zhingobiins traveled together because the Anishinaabeg and Mdewakanton Dakota had formed an alliance in the interior region between Gichigamiing and the Gichi-ziibi, that is, Lake Superior and the Mississippi River on European maps. Bands from both communities periodically hunted, traded, and raided together. This alliance, in fact, represented a nexus of two powerful Native social formations. It facilitated the movement of Anishinaabe and Dakota peoples in the west. In a world of episodic violence the alliance made hunting safer. It allowed the Dakota and the Anishinaabeg to move between the village, riverbeds, and forest edge. In other words, the alliance made life possible. Traveling east to Montreal, however, was an entirely different matter.

For Zhingobiins, this meant moving through space that was at once Anishinaabewaki but also connected to the French Empire. Anishinaabeg from the west frequently moved between La Pointe and other important lakeshore village sites at Keeweenaw, Michilimackinac, and Sault Sainte Marie to trade and for ceremony. Occasionally, they even passed through the Great Lakes and descended the Ottawa River to Montreal. This trade and travel was an integral part of being Anishinaabe. But it had also become an important part of the ritual process that animated the alliance between the Anishinaabe doodemag and the French. For Zhingobiins, traveling east meant that the French traders, priests, and government officials he encountered expected him to be and act like a Sauteur alliance chief. That is, they expected Zhingobiins to be a child of Onontio, and to act accordingly. For Tiyoskate, however, the voyage east represented a journey into the land of his enemies.

The expectations Tiyoskate faced would be entirely different. No Dakota had ever traveled to Montreal under his or her own power. When the Dakota entered the the pays d'en haut they came to make war, or they arrived as slaves from the west. And even though Zhingobiins traveled through the country of his kinsmen, doing so in the company of a Dakota warrior placed him in danger. Many of his relatives would see Tiyoskate as an enemy combatant who needed to be either killed or enslaved. Moreover, they exposed themselves to Iroquois raiders who frequently stalked the roads between the Great Lakes and Montreal in search of peltry and slaves. Why, then, did these two warriors undertake such a hazardous journey? Tiyoskate and Zhingobiins traveled east, beyond the physical spaces and the social world of their alliance, to call the governor of New France to council. They came east to demand no less than a new social order linking the indigenous west and Anishinaabewaki to New France.

The indigenous west and New France were linked, not as constituent parts of the French Empire, but as two autonomous regions connected to a larger Atlantic World. These connections overlapped in Anishinaabewaki in a way that made any boundary between New France and the western interior—that is, the middle ground between the indigenous and the colonial—difficult to control or even define. This space where the two social worlds came together was particularly dangerous. Moving seasonally between their territory in Anishinaabewaki and western interior, the Anishinaabeg forged new social ties that weakened their connections to the French Empire, and strengthened their position in the west. Native peoples living at Green Bay and in the Illinois country, in contrast, entered the west to hunt peltry and slaves to trade with the French. In doing so, they leveraged their position within the French alliance system at the expense of western Indians who were, after all, not children of Onontio.

Native social formations in the western interior controlled enormous territory and resources. They exercised far less control, however, over their access to the market resources of the Atlantic World. This is what brought Tiyoskate and Zhingobiins to Montreal. Anishinaabeg in the west wanted to revitalize their connection to New France, mobilize the French alliance against their enemies at Green Bay, and renegotiate their access to French trade goods. The Dakota wanted to extend the power and influence of the Oceti Sakowin into the east. They wanted to extend their reach into Anishinaabewaki, where they might, in turn, influence people and politics of the French Empire. They wanted trade goods, particularly iron and weapons. Standing in their way were the peoples of Green Bay who wanted to control French access to the western interior, and sought to deny the resources of the French Empire to western Indians.

This space at the edge of two distinct social worlds was a place of violence and intrigue. The French found themselves caught between competing Native social formations, blocks of regional power that wanted to control the nature of exchange relationships between the indigenous west and the colonial east. In the year before Tiyoskate and Zhingobiins made their journey to Montreal, this conflict spiraled out of control. Sometime between 1693 and 1694, Mesquakie peoples identified as Outagamis and Mascouten by the French raided a large Dakota village encamped below Nicolas Perrot's fort at Lake Pepin on the Mississippi River. French accounts of this incident suggest that the raiders carried away the majority of this village's women and children. More ominously, the Mascouten put to death approximately two hundred of these captives in retaliation for the deaths of fifteen warriors killed during the raid. Several French traders went to the Mascouten village hoping to redeem the remaining captives, only to be rebuffed. They quickly departed fearing for their own lives.

The details of this massacre, and the events that unfolded in its aftermath, are narrated in La Potherie's epic *Histoire de l'Amérique Septentrionale*. The story of this event, like much of La Potherie's history was written in collaboration with Nicolas Perrot, and unfolds through the eyes of the veteran voyageur. For more than a decade Perrot had struggled to reconcile the peoples of Green Bay with the Dakota bands. While he did not put an end to this conflict, his mediation tempered the violence that occurred between these opposing networks of Native peoples at the western edge of Anishinaabewaki. Raiding persisted, but on a scale where mediation frequently resulted in the redemption of captives and covering of the dead. The atrocity committed by the Mascouten represented a massive escalation of the level of violence in this ongoing conflict. The peoples of Green Bay braced for retaliation.

The Miami immediately sent word to Perrot asking for his intervention. They expected an equally brutal Dakota counterraid, and wanted to avoid being pulled deeper into the conflict. The Miami entrusted Perrot with a calumet, and he set off to offer peace to the Dakota. He quickly discovered a scouting party from the upper Mississippi valley on the war road to Green Bay. Perrot called these warriors to council at his fort, and they agreed to send a delegation to meet with him. Traveling together they passed through the ruined village, and found utter devastation. The entire village had been destroyed, eighty lodges reduced to smoldering ash. The wailing of grief-stricken survivors pierced the air, lamenting the devastating loss of life suffered at the hands of French-allied Indians. And yet Perrot welcomed the Dakota to his post next to their destroyed village, calumet in hand, to hold a council seeking peace.[54]

Perrot found his task complicated by the presence of another Frenchman, a rival trader. La Potherie's narrative never identified this man by name, but wrote of him dismissively as someone "who called himself a great captain." This man evidently represented himself as an alliance chief, and he offered to provision the Dakota "in order to bring death on those who had devoured their families." Perrot accused this man, most likely a coureur de bois, of wanting only "to more easily get rid of his merchandise." He countered his rival by offering the Miami calumet to the Dakota.[55]

Perrot warned the Dakota that the Mascouten and Outagamis waited for them in entrenched positions. He also cautioned that the Outagamis still held many of their loved ones alive, and any counterattack placed them in jeopardy. With the grieving Dakota gathered at his fort to attend his council, Perrot proclaimed sadly, "Chiefs I weep for the death of your children that the Outagamis and Maskoutech have robbed from you deceiving me." But he also cautioned these grieving warriors, "This blood is still too fresh to undertake revenge for it so soon." Instead, he told them, "I cover your dead." And then he presented the Dakota with a gift of two kettles to sustain them during their time of loss. He declared that the Dakota dead were not buried deep, merely covered for their own protection. When Onontio heard of their loss, Perrot promised that he would "cause the restoration of your children who are slaves among your enemies."[56] Onontio provided consolation, and even greater still, he possessed the power to bring the dead back to life.

Did the Dakota hear the voice of the French father? Did they trust in his power to restore their dead? They listened to Perrot's words, and they accepted the Miami calumet. But as they sang their death songs, and ritually burned their flesh to mourn their dead and captured relatives, Perrot must have doubted. He approached the Dakota war party a second time. "Smoke chiefs, smoke warriors," Perrot declared, and in an effort to influence the ritual meaning of their mourning he placed tobacco before them and admonished: "Smoke peacefully, in the hope that I will send back some of your women and children, that I will withdraw from the mouth of your enemies, give all your confidence to Onontio who is master of the land." Finally, Perrot gave the Dakota additional gifts—several packages of knives "not for lifting the scalps of men," he noted, but "for skinning beavers."[57] Like children of Onontio they would hunt beaver for the French, and wait patiently for the intervention of their father.

This, at least, was the meaning that Perrot wanted to attach to the mourning ceremonies and ritual exchange of goods that transpired at this fort. The Dakota, it seems, did not share in this interpretation of events. They approached Perrot's rival, the other "great captain," and declared their intention to sing "funeral calumets." Rather than abandon their dead to be buried, they planned to carry away an entire village of French-allied Indians in order to raise them. The goods he traded earlier, they explained, would bring death to their enemies. They wanted the two French captains to smoke with them. The rival agreed, so long as Perrot accepted the war pipe as well.

The Dakota made it clear to Perrot's rival that they intended to attack only the Mascouten. The Mesquakie had already tried to distance themselves from the extreme violence of their raiding partners. They killed none of their captives, and even allowed ten women to escape their custody without giving pursuit. These women returned to the ruined camp carrying the message of the distress felt by the Mesquakie over the cruel behavior of the Mascouten. Everyone appeared ready to abandon the Mascouten to their fate. Everyone that is, except for Nicolas Perrot.[58]

What the Dakota proposed, in effect, was a new constellation of power in the west that would simultaneously reshape Anishinaabewaki. By offering the funeral calumet to the French captains they sought to align French traders in the upper Mississippi valley to an existing alliance of Dakota and Anishinaabe peoples, now joined by the Miami, and possibly even the Mesquakie. At a minimum the Mesquakie and other Green Bay peoples seemed to pledge neutrality. The French, by siding with the Dakota, would guarantee their place in this network by providing access to trade goods. Smoking the funeral calumet—that is, singing a death song for the Mascouten—the French would abandon their role as mediators. They would cease to be a father to their allies and become something else—a link in a chain of social relations that connected the people of one world to the people and resources of another. They would be allies, kin even, but like the members of a tiyospaye they would be equal partners in a social relationship that existed only so long as it was mutually beneficial. Like the individual tiyospaye that collectively made up the oyate of the allies such as Mdewakanton or the Yanktonai, they would be interdependent but autonomous parts of the imagined community of the Oceti Sakowin.

With so much experience in the west, Perrot knew his place among the Dakota. He did not assume the voice of the French father. Instead he entered the cabin of the Dakota war chief and took his place in the calumet ceremony. The Dakota smoked, they called on wakan tanka, and then they passed the pipe to Perrot, who refused to take his turn in this ritual performance. "Being only a child," Perrot confessed, he "could not do anything without the consent of his father." He came only to weep over their dead. But Perrot insisted that the Dakota needed to recognize the wasicun of Onontio, and wait to hear his counsel before deciding how to act. According to Perrot and La Potherie, the "Nadouaissioux admitted that he was right." They promised to "hang up the war-club" until the governor was informed of all that had passed.[59]

With the cycle of violence set off by this catastrophe suspended, Perrot and the other licensed French traders made preparations for their seasonal return to Montreal. There remained, however, an impending sense of disaster. The Dakota may have extinguished their funeral calumet at Perrot's fort, but then they immediately conspired with the Miami to destroy the Mascouten. A village of the Miami had moved west of the Mississippi River when Perrot began to trade in the upper Mississippi valley. Now that they seemed poised to ally themselves with the Dakota, Perrot complained "that they were of no use for supporting Onontio in the Iroquois war." He threatened to cut off their supply of trade goods unless they relocated to the Miami village at the Saint Joseph's River on the eastern shore of Lake Michigan.[60]

Whenever the alliance threatened to unravel in the west, it simultaneously lost the ability to contain the Iroquois in the east, leaving Onontio and his children vulnerable on two fronts. The precarious status of the Outagamis, once again, heightened this instability. In spite of their tacit truce, they continued to fear retribution from the Dakota, and abandonment by the French. As a consequence, they acquired two Iroquois prisoners in the hope that, if necessary, they might redeem them and ask to resettle in the territory of the Haudenosaune.[61] In this tense atmosphere, when the French finally left for Montreal, all of the French-allied Indians in the Mississippi Valley returned to villages in the Green Bay region.

A New Relationship with Onontio

All of the children of Onontio moved east of the Mississippi River. Only the Anishinaabeg remained in the west. And now, after growing increasingly detached from the world of the French alliance, they sent Zhingobiins to Montreal. His ally, the Dakota war leader Tiyoskate, traveled with him to the seat of French power in the New World, to establish proper relations with Onontio. Zhingobiins would have known the perils of this journey, but he also would have known the safest way to navigate this landscape. He and Tiyoskate traveled as part of a larger party, twelve canoes in all. Five French traders made the voyage with them, including Pierre-Charles Le Sueur, the man sent west by the governor to "manage the peace between the Sioux and the Sauteurs."[62] More accurately, Le Sueur, like Perrot, represented French interests in the indigenous west where Onontio wielded very little real power. He was a supplicant seeking access to the resources and trade networks that produced some of the best winter coat beaver peltry in all of North America. His presence on this voyage to Montreal, however, sanctioned Tiyoskate's journey in search of an audience with the French father.

Zhingobiins and Tiyoskate made their way east as part of a larger procession. Hundreds of French-allied Indians converged on Montreal in the summer of 1695. Louis de Baude le Comte de Frontenac managed to get himself reinstated as governor of New France. Frontenac was a narcissist who often seemed more interested in enriching himself than governing the colony, but he knew how to inhabit the persona of Onontio. With escalating conflicts in both the east and the west straining their alliance, Frontenac was well suited to meet the diplomatic challenges facing the French Empire. In their summary report of the year's events French colonial officials suggested that their allies had rallied to fight the Iroquois, and that they came to Montreal to demonstrate their loyalty and unity, and to receive the counsel of their father.[63]

The records of their council meetings with the governor, however, indicate that war with the Dakota played at least as important a role in bringing the allies to Montreal in such large numbers.

While warfare with both the Haudenosaunee and the Dakota served as the backdrop for this series of council meetings, the issue at the forefront was power. Attending this council was a bold move on the part of both the Mdewakanton Dakota and the Anishinaabeg of Shagwaamikong. They were, in effect, using their power as allies in the west to demand a reworking of the French alliance system. French records identified Zhingobiins as "Chin-gouabe, Chief of the Sauteurs."[64] Presenting Onontio a gift of beaver robes, Zhingobiins said, "I came to greet you on the part of the young men who are at la pointe de Chagouamikong." He then thanked Onontio for sending his people "some Frenchmen to live with them." When Le Sueur arrived at La Pointe in 1693, it had been twenty-two years since the French had occupied a post at this village site.[65] Presenting another gift of beaver pelts Zhingobiins announced the real purpose of his visit: "We come to ask you a favor; that is to let us act, we are Allies of the Sioux: they have been killed by the Outagamis or the Maskoutechs, the Sioux came to mourn with us, let us act my father, let us take revenge."[66]

Zhingobiins called on Onontio to act like a father. Mediation had become the cornerstone of French power in the social world of the alliance. Accordingly, when the Anishinaabeg brought their grievance against the Masquakie and Mascouten to Montreal, it fit within the pattern of the French alliance system. But when Zhingobiins claimed the Dakota as allies, and then asked that Onontio grant the right of revenge to both their peoples, he forced the governor to formally reveal the nature of his relationship with the Dakota. The French traded among the Dakota. The Anishinaabeg of Shagwaamikong, children of the French father, claimed them as allies. Were the Dakota allies of the French? Were they children of Onontio, or not?

Zhingobiins, in effect, demanded that Onontio provide diplomatic sanction for the expansion of Dakota-Anishinaabe power. Name the "Sioux" children of the French father, and then recognize their right, along with the "Sauteurs," to seek revenge among their enemies. Calling on Onontio to abdicate his role as mediator in this conflict, Zhingobiins asked the governor to deny his alliance, kinship, and responsibilities as a father of the Outagamis and Mascouten. On the other hand, this shrewd bit of diplomacy also left Onontio the option of playing the role of mediator. He could claim the Dakota as kin and then act like a father. This would require the French to take responsibility for raising the Dakota dead, and establishing regular trade relations in the west. This, in turn, would necessarily involve maintaining peace between his children at Green Bay and in the upper Mississippi valley.

When Zhingobiins finished speaking, a prominent Odawa ogimaa from Michilimackinac, Ginoozhe, addressed the governor. "We have come from the elders, who have given us some robes to trade for powder," said the ogi-maa whom the French called "Le Brochet," a French translation of the Ojibwe designation for "the Pike." He informed Onontio that all of his people's young men were at war with the Iroquois. They would be pleased to find the means to continue on the warpath when they returned. Then Ginoozhe offered the governor his opinion of the Sioux. They would be formidable allies. "This is a bellicose nation," he declared; "it is rare to see them fall into the hands of their enemies." According to Ginoozhe, the Sioux preferred to die, even at their own hands, rather than accept a life in captivity.[67]

By invoking les anciens, the elders, Ginoozhe made a strong statement about the Dakota and the Odawa Anishinaabeg to the governor of New France. He claimed to represent a consensus among the Anishinaabe leader-ship at Michilimackinac. They hosted Tiyoskate for two weeks at their vil-lage as he made his way down to Montreal. Feasts were held in his honor. A Dakota slave, the wife of an important Mdewakanton leader, was given to Tiyoskate. Ginoozhe and the Anishinaabeg at Michilimackinac claimed no allegiance to the Sioux. They made this clear to the governor, asserting that "the Sioux . . . had not yet made alliance with us."[68] The Odawaag fought with the Dakota when they lived at the west end of Gichigamiing. More recently, they were indirectly brought into this conflict by the murder trial/condolence ritual held in the wiigiwaam of Ginoozhe by Daniel Du Lhut. But now, their presence at council, the redeemed captive, their kinship and close connection to the Anishinaabeg at Shagwaamikong, and the fact that they spoke with a unified voice signaled a willingness to accept the Dakota into the family of their relations. Equally important, as they negotiated the shape of the alliance in the west, their warriors marched against the Iroquois in the east.

Following an introduction by Ginoozhe, Tiyoskate spread a beaver robe before the governor. He layered another beaver robe on top of that, and then placed a tobacco pouch and an otter skin on these garments and began to weep, "crying bitterly, saying have pity on me." After this act of ritual humil-ity, Tiyoskate dried his tears and spoke to the governor. "All the nations had a father who gives them his protection, and who has iron," he proclaimed, "but me, I am a bastard in search of a father."[69] He then placed twenty-two arrows on the robe spread before the French father. With each arrow, "he named a village of his Nation that asked the protection of Onontio, and wanted him to regard them as his children."[70]

It is impossible to recover the full meaning of Tiyoskate's spoken words in Dakota. And yet it is almost certain that he would have described the communities represented by the arrows as oyate, or peoples, in the same way that he would identify the principal divisions among the Oceti Sakowin. As in Ojibwe, there is not an equivalent word for *nation* in seventeenth- and eighteeth-century Dakota. Le Sueur, translating this speech into French, would likely have chosen "nation" rather than "people" because in a European context this term designated the sort of culturally distinct, politically organized social formation capable of conducting diplomatic negotiations. But here it represents a specific discursive practice employed by the French rather than an accurate characterization of Dakota identity.

Tiyoskate came to Montreal on behalf of the allies, or the Dakota oyate, in search of trade and mediation. This account suggests that he spoke for all of the principal villages of the alliance, bands on both sides of the Mississippi River. In other words, he claimed to represent the Oceti Sakowin, the Seven Council Fires, and by extension all of the Dakota peoples. Tiyoskate described the nature of their relationship with the French. They were bastards in search of a father; they wanted to become children of the French father. Tiyoskate then placed this request in context, informing Onontio: "I learned from the Sauteurs that he wanted for nothing, that he was the master of iron, and that he had a big heart in which he could receive all nations." Knowledge of Onontio's generosity learned from his Anishinaabe allies "compelled me to abandon my body to come ask for his protection." Finally, he begged the governor "to receive me among the number of his children." And he concluded: "Take courage great captain, and reject me not; despise me not, though I appear poor in your eyes. All the nations here present know that I am rich and that the little they offer is taken on my lands."[71] Rather than speaking for the Oceti Sakowin, what Tiyoskate really offered the French was access to the Dakota bands, including those in the west, through the Mdewakanton village in the upper Mississippi valley.

In accepting this connection to the indigenous west, the French pledged to change the nature of their relationship with the Native peoples that they continued to think of as the Sioux. A formal alliance would allow the French to extend their political influence and trade into the interior in a way that was far more meaningful than the hollow gesture of possession performed by Perrot in 1689. Accordingly, Frontenac informed the Dakota warrior that "he received them among the number of his children on condition that they would hear only their father's voice." Both Zhingobiins and Tiyoskate asked Onontio to allow Le Sueur to return to the west to live with them. Again the governor agreed. Then, with Frontenac seated before him, Tiyoskate began to weep again. He grasped the governor's knees, and with Le Sueur acting as translator told him, "Have pity on me; I know well that I am incapable of speaking to you, being yet only a child." But he promised that next year Le Sueur would be able to tell Onontio "what the Sioux nations, that you see here before you, turning toward his arrows, will be able to do, when they have the protection of so good a father, who will send them Frenchmen to bring them iron, of which they only begin to have knowledge."[72]

Again Tiyoskate described his relationship to the French, but this time he offered a caveat. Being "only a child," Tiyoskate and the Dakotas could not properly speak to Onontio. With access to the power of New France, however, the allies would change. They would learn the power of Europeans—the wasicun of iron—and they would no longer be children. In other words, with access to iron and Onontio came the potential for the Dakota and the French to enter into a proper relationship. They would form a voluntary association, autonomous and equal social units bound together as allies and, necessarily, as kin. This was the model provided by the tiyospaye, and Tiyoskate's speech suggests that the Dakota assumed it was the social form that they and the French should aspire to achieve. In this relationship Onontio would become a man of influence, or an itancan, among the Sioux.[73] But Tiyoskate, Zhingobiins, and other leading figures among the dakotapi, or "people who are allies," would remain itancan as well.

In other words, what Tiyoskate offered Onontio was access to the indigenous west and the Dakota-Yankton/Yanktonai-Lakota peoples, by virtue of an alliance with the Mdewakanton. The governor, however, wanted to transform the Dakota into children of Onontio. He wanted to extend the influence of New France into the indigenous west, transforming the "Sioux" into a subject nation that recognized his authority. At the very least, he wanted to transform the Dakota country into something like the village world of the pays d'en haut—where the French and their allies created hybrid Native/colonial spaces to enact their alliance. This was how the French claimed sovereignty over territory that they did not control politically. In this sense, the Dakota and the French had conflicting political and territorial ambitions.

Speaking to one another through interpreters, Tiyoskate and Frontenac negotiated categories of language, kinship, and identity that would determine the social boundaries of Anishinaabewaki and the indigenous west. Would the Dakota and the Dakota country become nominally a part of the French Empire in the same way that the Outtouac, the Sauteurs, and the pays d'en haut were? Or would French traders begin to act like dakotapi—that is, as a people allied to the Dakota, like the Anishinaabe doodemag from the west end of Gichigamiing? It is clear that neither Tiyoskate nor Frontenac understood the subtleties of one another's language. But they did understand that they were negotiating to determine what categories of knowledge and identity mattered in the west. They were, in effect, negotiating about the meaning of kinship, social obligation, and political authority. Would the governor of New France be a father to his Dakota children; or would he become itancan, a leader who commanded the respect of the many tiyospaye that made up the Mdewakanton, and who could, therefore, presume to speak to the other Dakota oyate?

The Mdewakanton wanted to expand their alliance network into the east to include regular trade with the French. In fact, this adaptation had already occurred to a significant extent. Dakota bands interested in the fur trade used the village at Mde Wakan in the headwaters region of the Mississippi Valley as a seasonal base of operations. This village was attached to wild rice stands and beaver habitat; it was also connected by the Saint Croix River and Mississippi River watersheds to French posts. Itancan among the Mdewakanton routinely policed the behavior of Dakota bands that arrived at this village to trade.[74] In 1680, Ouasicoude, the Mdewakanton leader who had captured and adopted Father Hennepin, as related earlier, bludgeoned a rival band leader to death when he threatened to raid the French traders who redeemed the priest. Perrot witnessed a similar, though less brutal, use of police power to ostracize the man who had pillaged his fort.[75] In both cases itancan of the Mdewakanton acted to ensure cooperation among the various tiyospaye who came east to trade.

This pattern of enforced intragroup cooperation and seasonal migration to acquire an important resource was the hallmark of the Dakota peoples. In this case, trade goods were the important resource. This pattern had evolved, however, in order to secure access to the buffalo. This animal was the primary food and trade resource for all of the Dakota bands. By the end of the seventeenth century the buffalo were concentrated west of the Mississippi River. During the summer months the herds congregated in large numbers to mate and the Dakota bands converged on the prairies and plains to hunt.

The itancan ensured the coordination of male hunters used to operating in-dependently as part of autonomous tiyospaye. If individual hunters struck the herd before all of the Dakota bands were in position to hunt, the buffalo would scatter, and the consequences would be disastrous. Alliance, leader-ship, kinship, and social identity had evolved among the Dakota peoples as an adaptation to secure access to this vital, and in Dakota eyes, sacred resource.

Trade goods were not sacred, but they represented a source of power, or wašicun. That power, like any other, was linked to wakan tanka, but access to trade goods, or iron, was controlled by the French. To the Dakota, Onontio was the "Master of Iron." And what Tiyoskate asked for was the intercession of Onontio, the Master of Iron and a powerful being, on behalf of his people. By giving the Dakota access to this resource he would, in turn, increase their spiritual power.[76] Tiyoskate made it clear that with access to iron the Dakota would become more than children. They would become capable of fulfilling their social obligations as kin and allies. This was a remarkable adaptation among the Mdewakanton, comparable to the expansion and specialization of western Dakota bands as equestrian buffalo hunters.

This sort of specialization would reorient the Mdewakanton bands to-ward the fur trade as opposed to subsistence hunting, effectively expanding the reach of the Dakota alliance network into the east. At council Tiyoskate suggested to Onontio that while the Dakotas appeared poor, their land was rich. By acknowledging his "poor appearance" Tiyoskate signaled that trade goods did not circulate widely among the allies. By the end of the seventeenth century only Mdewakanton and Yankton-Yanktonai bands maintained vil-lage sites east of the Mississippi River. The French often engaged people they identified as Sioux to hunt beaver during the winter months, but this oc-curred at the level of the tiyospaye. The buffalo hunt remained the primary focus of large-scale cooperation and social organization among the Dakota. Thus, while the allies occasionally participated in the fur trade, they remained oriented toward the prairies. Tiyoskate offered the Mdewakanton as a bridge between the prairie country of the indigenous west and French posts in An-ishinaabewaki. But what he really offered the French was the possibility of connecting New France to one of the most powerful social formations in North America—the vast alliance network of Dakota-Yankton/Yanktonai-Lakota oyate that dominated the northern Great Plains of the indigenous west.

The Anishinaabeg from La Pointe, similarly, represented the possibility of a deeper connection between New France and the western interior. First, however, Frontenac needed to pull these wayward children more firmly into the alliance. To do this the governor asserted his status as father and he emphasized the exchange relationship that underpinned the French alliance system. After recognizing the Dakota as his children, Frontenac spoke to the Anishinaabe ogimaa. "My son Cheingouabé," he began, reminding the war leader of his place at council. Frontenac then told Zhingobiins that he appreciated the gratitude of his people for the French traders sent to live among them. "I am well at ease," he declared, "that you feel the advantage that you derive from the commodities that they bring you, and to see your family now dressed like my other children, instead of the bearskins you were dressed in previously."[77]

Just as with Tiyoskate, Frontenac entered into a subtle negotiation with a potential ally about identity, social obligation, and political power. From the governor's remarks it would seem that the Shagwaamikong Anishinaabeg wore animal skins until the recently arrived French traders outfitted them in cloth garments. Winter bands that focused on dressing skins for trade did not spend their time and resources converting skins into clothing.[78] If the doodemag of La Pointe were not dressed like children of Onontio, that meant they were not participating in the French fur trade to any significant extent.

When Frontenac told Zhingobiins that it pleased him to see all of his children dressed in trade cloth he named the relationship, and sense of mutual obligation, that the French expected to maintain with the people of his village. The doodemag of Shagwaamikong, he suggested, had stepped outside of that relationship, becoming western Indians rather than children of the alliance. Frontenac expected his allies to exchange animal pelts for trade goods. It was, after all, the generalized reciprocities of the French fur trade that framed the mutual obligations between Onontio and his children. The abundance of the upper Mississippi valley, however, enabled the Anishinaabeg and their Dakota allies to live well whether or not they traded with the French. They were not indifferent to the French fur trade, but they wanted to engage French traders and the children of Onontio on their own terms. For them the council meeting was an attempt to refashion their relationship with New France in order to increase their power in the west. In other words, this was not simply a negotiation about access to trade goods. It was about power.

Frontenac understood power, and he understood that French power in the pays d'en haut worked through mediation. By linking the Shagwaamikong Anishinaabeg to a Sauteur identity rooted in the French fur trade, and by extension the French alliance, he could hold Zhingobiins accountable as a child of Onontio. In this way, he also linked mediation of Anishinaabe problems in the west to their participation in the alliance. "Listen well to my voice," he admonished Zhingobiins, and then he informed the warrior that he expected his people to be obedient children. They should follow the orders that he would pass along to Le Sueur, the new commandant at La Pointe, "and dream only of making war on the Iroquois." And he warned Zhingobiins: "Do not embarrass yourself in new quarrels, and do not meddle in those the Sioux have with the Foxes, Mascountens and others." In return, the governor promised that he would "find the means" to redeem the Dakota taken into captivity during the past year. Finally, Frontenac brought the council to an end by distributing presents to the ogimaag assembled before him.[79]

This final ritual exchange should have signaled a consensus between Onontio and his children concerning their mutual obligations to one another. Zhingobiins accepted his gift, but then he addressed the council a final time to offer an alternative understanding of what, exactly, this exchange meant. "It is not with us as with you, my father, when you command all the French obey you and go to war," he said. Then Zhingobiins bluntly informed the governor: "I will not be similarly heard and obeyed by my nation." Instead, he explained, "I will tell you that I answer for myself and those who are properly speaking my Allies or relations." He pledged, nevertheless, "I will make your will known to all of the Sauteurs."[80] Zhingobiins would not promise the impossible, which is to say he promised nothing.

Zhingobiins knew that no leader, no one ogimaa spoke for the Sauteurs. Zhingobiins was a Gichigamiing Anishinaabe, but his home territory was not at Sault Sainte Marie, and he was not the "Chief of the Sauteurs." He was from the country at the bottom of Lake Superior (Fond du Lac to the French), and he was a man of the west. Zhingobiins, the Little Balsam Fir, and relatives bearing his name would be leaders among the western Anishinaabeg for the next 150 years. Zhingobiins would forge relationships with British and American traders in the eighteenth and nineteenth centuries. Descendants bearing his name would lead this community in rejecting the ideas of American missionaries, and would sign treaties, or touch the pen, with the United States in 1837, 1842, and 1854 for the doodemag at Fond du Lac. But on all of these occasions, as in 1695, Zhingobiins the ogimaa spoke only for his village, not for all of the Anishinaabe peoples.

Zhingobiins might have, in good faith, attempted to make it known among the Anishinaabeg that Onontio desired an end to the warfare with the Mesquakie. But surely Le Sueur and the other voyageurs at this council knew how many different kinds of Anishinaabe peoples could be counted as Sauteurs. And yet, remarkably, the council records indicate no response from the governor to the caveat offered by Zhingobiins, that he could speak only for his immediate relations. The limited noncoercive nature of authority among Anishinaabe leaders, however, was a constant source of tension between the French and their Native allies. The governor called on Zhingobiins to act as an alliance chief, to convince the Sauteurs to listen to the voice of Onontio, and heed his commands. In response, Zhingobiins, like Tiyoskate, proposed a renewed alliance that reflected the reality of the indigenous west—an alliance that operated in place at the level of autonomous social units like the tiyospaye, doodem, or band, rather then abstractly at the level of a singular nation. Wide-scale cooperation was certainly possible, as with the inland trade, fish harvests, or the buffalo hunt, but the Anishinaabeg and the Dakota were multipolar social formations, not singular Indian nations.

From the perspective of the French in 1695, this council may have appeared as a step toward the incorporation of the Sioux and their territory into the French Empire. From the perspective of the Mdewakanton and Anishinaabeg, however, accepting Onontio as an itancan/ogimaa was a means of ensuring French cooperation in trade relations—including the expectation that Onontio would police his children, and put an end to their encroachments and incessant raiding. Relationships between the French and Native peoples in Anishinaabewaki had been built upon misunderstandings such as these. But in order for the Dakota to enter the world of the alliance, the children of Onontio would have to accept them as kin.

Defiant Trading at Hudson's Bay

Incorporation of the Dakotas into the French alliance system, however, would prove to be problematic. The alliance required constant mediation, and in the west the French remained divided and weak. The minister of marine wanted the trade regulated, but Frontenac had long been entangled with illicit trading operations. French officials in Canada did little, in fact, to control the coureurs de bois, and New France faced competition from the newly established French colony Louisiana, as well as from French and English posts at Hudson's Bay. Of course, even licensed traders like Nicolas Perrot moved between Anishinaabewaki and the indigenous west to trade with peoples like the Dakotas, creating resentment and anger among many French-allied Indians. The result, for the agents of New France, was a diplomatic chaos that made their alliance increasingly ungovernable and the region between the western Great Lakes and the indigenous west increasingly volatile.

Frontenac's intervention at Montreal gestured in the right direction, but ultimately failed to bring stability to the west, or result in any real expansion of French power in the region. Neither the French nor the Dakota were able to translate the ritual of their alliance ceremony into a working relationship. Tiyoskate fell ill and died within weeks of his council with the governor. He never returned home. Le Sueur chose not to return to his posts, but instead set sail for France in search of a license to mine for copper in the west. This scheme was widely regarded as a brazen attempt to create a cover for an illegal fur trading operation. Worse still, Le Sueur's departure severed the only direct connection linking Onontio to the Dakota and the Anishinaabeg in the west. Presumably the Dakota slave redeemed at Michilimackinac returned home with Zhingobiins, though French records offer no direct evidence as to her fate. This absence, along with Tiyoskate's death and Le Sueur's defection, suggests the inability of Onontio to make his voice heard in the indigenous west.

Zhingobiins's conditional response to Frontenac's gift, similarly, revealed the limitations of French power in the region. The absence of a strong French father not only left the Dakota outside the French alliance network but also made it easier for Anishinaabeg in the west to detach from the French fur trade. During the summer of 1695, while Zhingobiins and Tiyoskate made their way to Montreal, another party of Anishinaabeg made their way to the Hudson's Bay Company post at the mouth of the Albany River. The governor of that post made note of their visit in his account book: "Brazil tobacco presented some strange Indians called Ka-chi-ga-mein (alias) the Great Lakes Indians to feast among the rest of their tribe when they return to their country." He also noted that "they were never here nor had any commerce nor saw any English men before."[81] Ka-chi-ga-mein, or Gichigamiing, was the designation for the Great Lakes in Anishinaabemowin, though it is often used to specifically designate Lake Superior, and the visitors at the Albany post would have been identified as Sauteurs by the French.

The presence of people that the French thought of as Sauteurs at Hudson's Bay Company posts was not new. As Zhingobiins suggested, Anishinaabe doodemag exercised a great deal of independence in terms of creating alliance-and-exchange relationships with one another and with other peoples. Many of the Ojibwe-speaking bands that lived along the

northern shorelines and in watersheds to the north of the Great Lakes periodically visited Sault Sainte Marie but also traded with the English at Hudson's Bay. The self-identified Gichigamiing Indians who arrived at Albany
in 1695, however, most likely came from the same region as Zhingobiins.
As early as 1669, when the Ottawas and Huron-Petun took refuge from the
Iroquois at La Pointe, Jesuits identified la Nation des Kitchigamins as living
inland from the mission—at Fond du Lac or the bottom of the lake. Two
centuries after this initial identification by the French, the Ojibwe scholar
William Warren observed that Anishinaabeg who lived "on the immediate
shores of Lake Superior" referred to themselves as *Ke-che-gum-mewin-in-e-
wug*, which he translated as "Men of the Great Water." Various forms of this
designation consistently appear in European records as a self-identification
applied to Anishinaabe doodemag from the western lakeshore and immediate interior of Gichigamiing throughout the eighteenth and nineteenth
centuries.[82]

The Gichigamiing people treated to Brazil tobacco at the Albany post
in 1695 arrived at the Hudson's Bay Company post in the company of Native peoples who traded there regularly. They came to trade, apparently at
the invitation of Muskekowuck-athinuwick people who lived upriver from
the post. The English governor, in an attempt to facilitate this pattern of
cooperation, had earlier given tobacco to two leading men identified as
"Moose River" Indians, suggesting that they were Moosu Sepee Lowland
Cree. The Albany post account book describes these men, a father and
his son, as "captains." The father, identified as Noah—presumably a name
given to him by the English—and his son Miskwaamad (He is Red)," were
presented with tobacco "to feast the southern Indians . . . to invite them
down here."[83]

To attract "Southern Indians," that is people trading with the French, the
English at the Albany post worked to expand the alliance network of their
trading partners just as Radisson had done with the Penesewichewan Sepee.
In addition to the Gichigamiing, the governor at Albany presented Brazil
tobacco to "a capt of a tribe of Indians up Moose River very near halfway
to Canada called Ta Mish-ka-main." This was a phonetic approximation of
Dimiigamiing/Temiscamiing, an Anishinaabe dialect word signifying a deep
body of water that described just such a lake that had formed as part of the
Ottawa River. This watershed, called Temiskamingue by the French, provided
access to the Albany River and Moose River watersheds and their tributaries in the north, and connected Lake Nipissing to the waters around Mani-

toulin Island and Sault Sainte Marie in the south. French traders identified these Ojibwe-dialect-speaking Indians as Gens des Terres, frequent visitors to the Anishinaabe villages in the upper Great Lakes. In the summer of 1695, however, a captain or ogimaa from Timiigamiing joined Native traders from Gichigamiing and the Moosu Sepee in trading with the English at their post in the mouth of the Kastechewan River basin. Hudson's Bay Company traders called the Kastechewan, or the Muskekowuck-athinuwick, of this watershed Albany River Indians.[84]

Gift exchange and the opportunity to trade for English goods brought the Gichigamiing Anishinaabeg to the Albany post again in 1696. The Albany post account book provides a unique record of this second visit. The governor gave "powder and net line" as a present to "the Upland Capt of the Great Lake, His sister, and the young Capt his son." The account also records a gift of powder to another "leading upland Indian," and more Brazil tobacco presented to other "strange upland Indians" that claimed never to have seen Englishmen or traded with them.[85] The gifts themselves represented gestures of alliance. The tobacco was a sacred medicine offered to establish a relationship, and to induce the recipient to return to the post in the future; the powder was not an object used for hunting but a gift for warriors to ensure their strength against enemies; and finally, net line, like an awl or a brass kettle, was a household object given to kin to help sustain them.

The account book also provides a sense of how these objects worked in the world. The powder and line given to the Gichigamiing Anishinaabe "captain" was clearly meant to be distributed among his family—the sister and son (also a "captain") traveling with him. A second leading man received powder, and the other Anishinaabeg tobacco. This trading party was, in effect, a doodem. It was an extended family lead by a senior male, the ogimaa or "captain," accompanied by his son and more likely than not other male relatives, the other "leading upland Indian" probably being a brother or cousin. This was exactly the kind of social unit, seasonally mobile, flexible, and—like the Dakota tiyospaye—adept at integrating socially with other bands to create large-scale alliance networks that facilitated trade, hunting, and warfare.[86] It was this sense of autonomy among the Anishinaabe doodemag that made Zhingobiins tell the governor of New France that he could only speak for his relations.

Europeans like Perrot and Le Sueur, or the English governor at Albany, exercised some influence but very little control over indigenous alliance networks in the western interior. Moreover, the fluid nature of these networks meant that collective action needed to be negotiated constantly as the internal composition of the alliance changed. Perrot found himself vulnerable when French-allied Mesquakie and Mascouten bands attacked the Dakota near his post in 1694. The governor of the Albany post found himself in a similar situation in 1696. With the Gichigamiing Anishinaabeg once again at his post he learned that the French had captured York Fort on the Nelson River. This news was delivered by "northern Indians," most likely the Penesewichewan Sepee, to a council that included Gichigamiing Anishinaabeg, Moosu Sepee, Kastechewan, and Naskapi peoples. According to the governor, the council met to decide "for whom they should be if the French come, whither for us or for them." Finding the bands divided he distributed Brazil tobacco and gave "a large feast of pease . . . to draw them unanimously to our side."[87]

The French never attacked the Albany post, and so the allegiance of the Hudson's Bay Company's Native trading partners was never tested. The governor implied that the bands at his post, even the Gichigamiing Anishinaabeg with their connections to the French, chose to side with the English. Perhaps they did, although the more likely explanation is that the Gichigamiing Anishinaabeg made a strategic decision to preserve their access to English trade goods. In this sense, the council at the Albany post in 1696 mirrored the council between Zhingobiins, Tiyoskate, and Onontio at Montreal in 1695. In both instances, Anishinaabe ogimaag from the indigenous west negotiated access to the global market economy of the Atlantic World. Less clear, however, was their status within either empire. The English never mobilized their trading partners inland from Hudson's Bay for warfare the way they had been able to engage the peoples of the Haudenosaunee. It seems doubtful, though not impossible, that the Gichigamiing Anishinaabeg would have agreed to fight against invading French forces. On the other hand, the French proved increasingly incapable of holding Anishinaabe peoples in the west accountable to the alliance.

The attempt to attach the Dakota to the French Empire was severely disrupted by a radical change in the trade policy of New France. By the time Tiyoskate made his way to Montreal the French market for furs was completely glutted. While the value of beaver pelts plummeted, the Jesuit missions warned the Crown that the trade in brandy threatened to destroy the empire's Native allies. In 1696, after fierce lobbying by the Jesuits and the intendant of the colony, Louis XIV decided to abolish the congés, which licensed trade in the west. The market, they hoped, would be restored and the Jesuits would replace fur traders as the primary agents of influence among the allies. French soldiers in the west rebelled. They claimed that they could not sustain their garrisons without the trade, and withdrew to Lower Canada.[88]

Within a year of the decision to curtail the trade an open state of war existed between the Anishinaabeg and their Dakota allies and the children of Onontio at Green Bay. Adding to the chaos of this conflict, the Anishinaabe doodemag of the northwest raided French-allied Indians with impunity. When Frontenac called his allies to council in 1697, the Sauteurs refused to send their ogimaag to Montreal. Their relatives among the French-allied Indians called on Onontio to lament this transformation. An Odawa ogimaa named Longekam begged Frontenac to act like a father. He spoke for all of the Odawaag, as well as the Boodewaadamii, Mesquakie, and Wyandot. The ogimaa informed his father that the "inland nations" had raided them, and he asked for mediation. Then he declared, "Father! You have rebellious children; there is the Sauteur who has raised his tomahawk against the Miami, and is going to kill him." The Dakota and the Anishinaabeg from Shagwaamikong had, in fact, attacked the Miami in a series of raids to avenge the attacks that brought Tiyoskate to Montreal. The allies of Onontio worried that this conflict would soon boil over, and engulf all of the peoples of Anishinaabewaki.[89]

The world of the alliance was slipping away, however, and the power of the French to influence the politics of the Native New World was rapidly diminishing. This was Zhingobiins's world, and by the end of the seventeenth century the people of Shagwaamikong and the Anishinaabeg in the western interior were no longer part of the French alliance or the social world of the middle ground. Many Anishinaabe peoples would remain on the middle ground attached to important villages like Detroit, Sault Sainte Marie, and Michilimackinac associated with the inland trade and the French Empire. Here they would constantly negotiate the terms of their alliance with New France. This was particularly true for the Odawaag, who were masters of the diplomatic maneuvering and cultural misappropriations and reinventions that made up this hybrid social world connecting the Atlantic and Native New Worlds. Zhingobiins and the doodemaag of Shagwaamikong, however, were increasingly detached from the alliance with New France and oriented toward the west, where the peoples of the Native New World were beginning to reimagine Native social identity. As the eighteenth century progressed the same would be true for all of the doodemag that the French identified as Sauteurs. This process of reimagination would take peoples like the Dakota, Yankton/Yanktonai, Lakota, Anishinaaabeg and Nehiyawa-athinuwick and many other Native peoples deeper into the west, and farther away from the influence of the Atlantic New World.

CHAPTER 6

The Great Peace and Unraveling Alliances

In the summer of 1701 the peoples of Anishinaabewaki gathered at Michili-mackinac. They came together for an event that for many would be the most spectacular moment of their lives. A fleet of approximately two hundred canoes set off for New France. The warriors and ogimaag of Anishinaabe-waki paddled through the waters of their homelands, leaving the lake country for the Ottawa River, and descending the Saint Lawrence to Montreal. They traveled in canoes loaded with beaver peltry, wampum, and slaves taken during the last decade of brutal fighting with the Haudenosaunee. The peoples of Anishinaabewaki came to Montreal to put an end to this warfare. The things they carried represented the seeds of a great peace. They represented hope—the promise of an end to the violence that frequently saw entire villages destroyed or enslaved. This would be perhaps the largest ceremonial gathering since the Feast of the Dead forty years earlier. And like that long ago ceremony, the Great Peace of Montreal was designed to refashion the patterns of kinship and belonging that defined the social and physical boundaries of Anishinaabewaki and the French Empire.

When Onontio called for his children to make peace with the Iroquois many, at first, refused. Too much was at stake. Too much loss and suffering was not yet accounted for. It took more than three years of diplomatic work by emissaries of the governor to create a widespread consensus about the need for peace.[1] Several prominent ogimaag—Koutaoiliboe and Outoutaga of the Odawaag, and especially Kondiaronk of the Wyandot—worked to per-suade many reluctant communities to come to the council, and to give up the prisoners they had taken from the Haudenosaunee and adopted into their families. Imagine their frustration when, on the eve of their departure, ru-mors began to circulate that "la maladie" was ravaging Montreal.

Worse still, imagine the sense of horror these ogimaag must have ex-

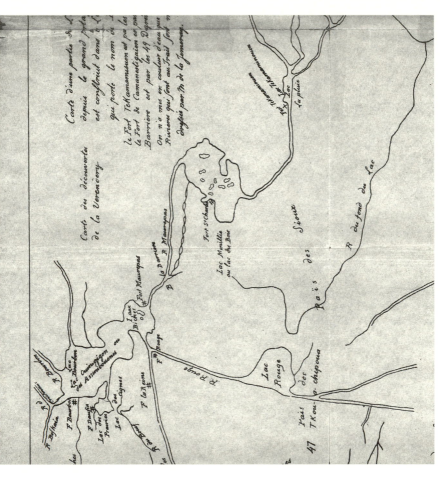

Figure 6. From *Journals and Letters of Pierre Gaultier De La Verendrye and His Sons*, ed. Lawrence J. Burpee (Toronto: Champlain Society, 1927). This map provides a cartographic sketch of the forts established by La Verendrye and another representation of the northern borderland between the Dakota and the Western Cree, Assiniboine, and the Anishinaabe doodemag fighting to control the inland trade.

perienced as they descended the river to Montreal and discovered that the rumors were true. At the opening of this grand council called by Onontio, Kondiaronk (the Muskrat) spoke of these challenges. He remarked on the perils they endured: "The falls, the rapids, and a thousand other obstacles seemed to us not too difficult to surmount because of the desire we have to see you." They came in spite of the devastation of la maladie. "We have also found our brothers dead along the rivers: our spirit has been made sick," Kondiaronk informed the council. As they descended through this landscape of death they watched birds tear at the remains of bodies left to rot in the open when survivors abandoned their village sites, and their dead, following the outbreak of disease. "However," Kondiaronk proclaimed, "we made ourselves a bridge of all these bodies, on which we have firmly walked."[2]

For the peoples of Anishinaabewaki the bodies of the dead held particular significance. They were venerated, and in ceremonies like the Feast of the Dead, the bodies of their ancestors gave meaning to the lives of the living. Joined ritually with the remains of other peoples, they created a shared history—a way of binding people together in the present. Their past, their history as distinct peoples, literally came together with the bones of their ancestors interred in a common grave. How did the bodies of the dead killed by "la maladie" and left in the path of the peoples of Anishinaabewaki give meaning to the living? Kondiaronk suggested that they were not an obstacle, but a bridge. Passing through villages abandoned to the dead, the allies crossed a threshold. They came to make peace with the Iroquois. They walked over the corpses of their deceased relatives to bring an end to more than a half century of death and suffering.

Following the remarks of Kondiaronk, select ogimaag spoke to Onontio on behalf of the allies. The Odawa Outoutaga presented the governor, Frontenac's replacement, Louis Hector de Callières, with a gift of four packets of beaver skins. He too remarked on the hazards of the journey they had undertaken, and he told Onontio, "We come to beg you to open the trade, nothing should be hidden from us in the shops of the merchants."[3] Outoutaga then apologized for the poor quality of the beaver peltry he offered the governor. Onanguisse, a prominent Boodewaadamii ogimaa, speaking for his people and for the Ho-Chunk, Mesquakie, Mascouten, Menominee, and Amikwas, asked the governor "to have pity on them, and give them good prices on merchandise, because they had few beavers."[4] Chichicatalo, speaking for the Miami, similarly asked Onontio "to have pity on us," and declared "we are not happy since the French are not among us."[5] With trade in the upper country officially banned the allies announced their desire to trade during the peace conference. And speaking over gifts of beaver peltry, the ogimaag established the conditions for this exchange. The region between Lake Erie and Michilimackinac had been overhunted. This was in fact a principal source of the conflict between the Iroquois and the peoples of Anishinaabewaki. With their gifts they demanded that Onontio take pity on them. The ogimaag sent a clear signal to the governor that in addition to peace with the Iroquois they expected him to act like a father, and ensure that the merchants of Montreal met their needs.

This interconnection of trade and diplomacy was at the heart of the alliance between New France and its Native allies. It was also the central issue driving the conflict between the French and their allies and the peoples of the Haudenosaunee. French records of this historic peace conference clearly demonstrate the relationship between the fur trade, warfare, and political alliance making. Because French colonial officials were focused on creating a lasting peace between their Native allies and the Iroquois Confederacy, it is all too easy to gloss over the other important theme to emerge in the council meetings of the Great Peace of 1701—the interconnection between trade, diplomacy, and violent conflict in the west. The French had formally, technically, put an end to trade in the region they thought of as the upper country. An illegal trade flourished, however, and this trade increasingly took place in the west beyond the hunting territories of most of the peoples of Anishinaabewaki, and beyond the missions and permanent posts of the French Empire.

The Great Peace was negotiated during a series of council meetings held in July and August, and while negotiations focused on ending the violence between the Iroquois and the allies of New France, Onontio failed to use this gathering to adequately address the problem created by his "rebellious children" acting out in the west. The Gichigamiing Anishinaabeg from Shagwaamikong did not send an ogimaa to Montreal. Zhingobiins stayed at home, and their Dakota allies were similarly unrepresented. In fact, while Frontenac claimed the Dakota as his children in 1695, Callières made no such declaration in 1701. Onanguisse, after asking Onontio for a bon marche, presented the governor with two packets of beaver peltry. Speaking for the Sauk and Boodewaadami, the ogimaa sought to cover the death of a French man "that a reckless young man from our nation killed in a clash with the Sioux." Indicating some degree of ongoing political dissension among his people, Onanguisse noted that one of the more prominent leaders of his village had refused to make the journey fearing punishment. "However as you are a good father," he added, "I have risked presenting myself before you."[6] Onontio accepted the peltry, offering his pardon, and in response Onanguisse presented him with a young slave, and declared, "Here is a little flesh we offer you, we took it from the country where the people go on horse. We wipe the mat stained with the blood of this Frenchman."[7] Another man named Coluby, speaking for the Sauk, also presented the governor with a slave, "this living flesh, that is a little boy that we present in place of the dead Frenchman."[8]

Accepting these slaves, the governor reaffirmed his alliance with the peoples of Green Bay, but the origin of these children suggested how conflicts in the west had become entangled with conflicts within the alliance. These slaves, taken from Native communities in the western interior, were given to Onontio to cover the death of a Frenchman caught up in the violence sparked by the ongoing French trade among the Dakota. Following Onanguisse, another leader from Green Bay, Noro (the Porcupine), speaking for the Mesquakie, called on the governor to intervene in yet another western conflict. "The Sauteur has killed me," he told Onontio. "My young men wanted revenge and had been stopped when you invited us to come hear you." Lamenting the departure of the French, Noro then asked for a black robe and a blacksmith to be sent to his village. With the French living among them, he declared, "the Sauteurs would not be bold enough to come to insult them, we ask for Nicolas Perrot."[9]

The French could not untangle the fur trade from their diplomacy with Native people and thus, even though they wanted to focus on peace with the Iroquois, violence in the west remained a central and unresolved issue. Callières asked for Waabange (He Sees), the Anishinaabe ogimaa from Bowe-ting (Sault Sainte Marie), to answer for the "Sauteurs." The ogimaa replied that the Mesquakie too often complained about his people. "The Outagami had not been killed by the people from his quarter," Waabange declared. He admitted "that there had been in the past a great quarrel," but he said "that they had ceased all acts of hostility for a longtime; that had been made by the Sauteurs of Chagouamikon."[10]

A debate then ensued between Noro and Waabange about what exactly had happened. The Sauteur asserted that it was known that the Outagami had killed a man from Shagwaamikong. The young men from this region wanted revenge, but their elders prevented them from taking it. One "scatterbrained" young man, however, raised a war party and left surreptitiously to strike at the Outagami. Noro countered that his people had not struck at the Sauteurs in the first place. Instead they had sent a raiding party against the Sioux, killing forty people including the Sauteur who was living among them. He concluded by saying that the Outagamis had not retaliated against the Sauteurs, even after they mistakenly killed one of his people. Waabange backed down. He said, "The Outagami was right." According to La Potherie, he even went so far as to disavow the Outagamis' responsibility for the killing. Apparently changing his story, Waabange asserted that the Outagami did not make the arrow that killed the Sauteur living with the Dakota.[11]

It seems likely that Waabange learned about this recent conflict from his relatives in the west who chose not to attend the conference. Their absence spoke to their increasing detachment from the alliance, and the persistence of this particular pattern of violence suggested a growing attachment to the Dakota. Time and again raiders from Green Bay struck at Dakota bands in the upper Mississippi valley only to find that they had killed and enslaved Anishinaabeg who had been living among their enemies. Both Perrot and Du Lhut had redeemed "Sauteur" captives from the Mesquakie. And both men promised they would stop the Anishinaabeg from joining Dakota raiding parties only to fail in this endeavor as well.

But what to make of Waabange? Why did he change his story and absolve the Mesquakie? The obvious answer is because that is what they had gathered together to do. All of the peoples allied to the French came to Montreal to reaffirm their alliance with Onontio, and expand it to include the Iroquois. In truth, however, Waabange could not speak for the people of Shagwaamikong. He was apparently from Bow-e-ting, having signed the treaty by drawing a crane, the principal doodem at this village. Although selected to speak for his people at the conference, Waabange may not even have been an ogimaa. He may have been an orator, chosen to represent the consensus among the people of his village in favor of peace. More importantly, although Waabange had been chosen to speak for the people of his village, he could not, would not, presume to speak for Anishinaabeg from a different doodem and different village unless he had been asked to do so. There is no record that this was the case, and Waabange never claimed to speak for all the Gichigamiing Anishinaabeg.

This was the underlying problem at the Great Peace of Montreal. Anishinaabewaki was a multipolar social formation. The doodemag and villages within this social world simply did not operate with the same degree of political unanimity as those of the Haudenosaunee. The Anishinaabeg shared a collective identity, but they also imagined themselves as an extended family comprising autonomous social units. They were not a single nation, but a community of related peoples whose social identity was defined by their kinship with one another, but also by the relative autonomy of the doodemag—the core social units that determined place and belonging in villages and hunting territories, as well as in trade and warfare. The Anishinaabeg frequently incorporated outsiders like the Wyandot, Muskekowuck-athinuwick, Dakota, and French into their social world. But doodemag, and even smaller winter lodge groups, periodically engaged in warfare and diplomacy on their own in order to create an advantageous position for themselves within the inland trade—the constantly changing exchange networks circulating goods between the Atlantic coast and the western interior.

The Anishinaabeg did not recognize the right of a single ogimaa to speak for all of the peoples of Anishinaabewaki. Waabange knew this reality. As did the far more influential Onanguisse, the Boodewaadamii ogimaa who spoke for all of the peoples of Green Bay, as well as for the peoples of the Illinois country. During a subsequent council meeting he complained to the governor that French trade with the Dakota made it difficult for him to advocate for the cause of peace. He noted that he listened to the governor's agent, le Sieur Coutremanche, and stopped attacking the Iroquois because Onontio made peace with the confederacy. He complained, however, "turning from this side for that of the Sioux, who struck me, he asked that I suspend this, but all the nations I speak for want to make war on them." Onanguisse then told the governor, "We regard these strikes as if they were from the people of Le Sueur."[12] Pierre-Charles Le Sueur, the man who escorted Tiyoskate and Zhingobiins to Montreal, had returned to the west via Louisiana, and was actively trading among the Dakota and Yankton-Yanktonai. Onanguisse made it clear that this trade, which "carried munitions" to their enemies, was unacceptable.

At the conclusion of the conference Callières gestured only vaguely to the idea of halting this trade among the Dakota. He addressed the issue of warfare between the Mesquakie and the Anishinaabeg more directly. Designating the Mesquakie by the French word for Fox, Callières commanded, "that you Renards, and Sauteurs, follow my example and forget what has passed between you."[13] He had earlier met with Noro and Waabange, and covered the dead Mesquakie. And in a council session he had both men smoke the calumet to reestablish their alliance. According to La Potherie, "All of the chiefs of the other nations smoked as a witness to this reunion," and in this fashion the governor hoped that the children of Onontio would hold these men accountable for maintaining the peace.[14] He placed an additional burden on Waabange, "you are charged with making known . . . to your brothers at la pointe du Chagouamigon that my intention is that all these quarrels must end with the Renards."[15] With no one to represent either the doodemag of Shagwaamikong or the Dakota, and with coureurs de bois continuing to trade in the west, this conflict would not be so easily brought to an end. On the other hand, neither would it cause the peace negotiations at Montreal to collapse.

The issue of captives posed a more immediate threat to the successful conclusion of the peace conference. For both the peoples of Anishinaabewaki and the Haudenosaunee the return of their family members taken into captivity provided one of the principal motivations to seek peace.[16] The peoples of Anishinaabewaki delivered thirty-one prisoners, a small fraction of the people who had been taken during years of fighting. The Odawa ogimaa Chingouessi bluntly told the governor, "I did not bring any Iroquois because I ate all those that I took." He purchased a slave, however, to give to the Iroquois in order to make his father happy.[17] The return of thirty-one captives did not appease the Iroquois, who desperately wanted to recover from devastating population losses suffered from a combination of epidemic disease and decades of aggressive fighting to expand their control over hunting territories and trade routes.[18]

Not only would the Haudenosaunee continue to press the children of Onontio to hand over additional captives in the years following the Great Peace, but they also brought only two captives to the conference. Kondiaronk expressed the frustration voiced by all of the allies when he said at council that "he was so sad to see himself be the dupe of the Iroquois who had not brought any prisoners from his nation."[19] The Iroquois orators responded by claiming "that those they have adopted they regarded as their children."[20] Governor Callières rejected their plea, asserting, "I can not accept your excuse for not having brought any of their prisoners," and he chastised the Iroquois delegates for not taking the necessary actions to remove the captives from their adopted families. In the end, however, both sides swallowed their anger and accepted the promise of a future redemption for their people who remained in captivity. They made this sacrifice to bring an end to the animosity and warfare that had plagued the peoples of the Haudenosaunee and Anishinaabewaki since the founding of the European settler colonies in North America.

It took adept negotiating on the part of the governor, and alliance chiefs such as Kondiaronk, Onanguisse, and all of the Odawa ogimaag, to convince the children of Onontio to accept this sacrifice and agree to "touch the pen." Following the language and custom of alliance making shared by both the Iroquois and the people of Anishinaabewaki, they would now eat from the same bowl.[21] Chichikatalo, speaking for the Miami, expressed the idea of peace as a shared meal. At the moment that wampum was ritually exchanged to ratify the peace, he declared, "So it is today that the sun shines, and that the land is going to be united, and we will not have any more quarrels. When we meet one another, we will regard each other as brothers, and we will eat the same morsel together."[22] People who were related, inawemaagen, fed one another, sharing whatever sustenance they had when they met. The children of Onontio, who now included the peoples of the Haudenosaunee, would live together in peace, bound to one another as members of the same extended family.

In addition to the spoken word and ritual performance that traditionally accompanied Native alliance making, the delegates to the 1701 peace conference signed a written treaty. Thirty-seven Native delegates signed the treaty by drawing a figure to represent their doodem or village, along with the governor and intendant of New France, who wrote their names on this document. This event was made all the more extraordinary by this artifact—a document that was, in effect, coauthored by Native and European peoples. The Treaty of 1701 was inscribed with a narrative account of the new relationship forged between Onontio and the peoples of the Native New World. The social world of the alliance, the middle ground, now included the peoples of the Haudenosaunee. Callières, speaking as the French father, described this new relationship at the conclusion of the conference. "Having one and all placed your interest in my hands," he told the signatories, "I gather up again all your hatchets, and other instruments of war, which I place with mine in a tomb so deep that no one can take them back to disturb the tranquility that I have re-established among my children." The governor made himself the sole arbiter of this peace. "If it so happens that one of my children struck another," he declared, "the one who was struck will no longer seek revenge, neither he nor any of his people, but he should come find me so that I can make it right by him."[23]

The Peace of 1701, like the Feast of the Dead, represented an attempt to refashion the social world of Native North America. With this conference New France created a new political imaginary, one that joined Canada and the Native peoples who resided in the colony with the peoples of Anishinaabewaki and the Haudenosaunee in alliance. The successful conclusion of this conference represented the high point of French political power and influence in North America. Making themselves the arbiter of a peace between the peoples of Anishinaabewaki and the Haudenosaunee, the French achieved a strategic advantage in any future conflict with the English colonies. The economic advantages of the peace were more ambiguous as a more stable relationship between the Anishinaabeg and the Iroquois increased the probability of losing at least some traffic in furs to English traders. Nevertheless, the Treaty of 1701 united two of the most important Native social formations east of the Mississippi River in an alliance relationship that would be brokered and maintained by the political leadership of New France.[24]

On the ground, however, this new relationship would lead to the gradual unraveling of the French Empire in the west. The immediate impact of the peace between the peoples of Anishinaabewaki and the Haudenosaunee was to shift the agents and resources of the French Empire to the borderland between these two social formations. From the moment the Great Peace concluded until the defeat of New France at the hands of British forces, the French in Canada would spend all of their energy and influence fighting to protect and preserve peace and stability in this region. At the same time this borderland became an increasingly complex political space as peoples left old village centers in the Upper Country and Iroquoia and relocated into the Ohio country below Lake Erie. A no-man's-land during the ferocious period of fighting leading up to the Treaty of 1701, this region attracted hunters who wanted a new life, and greater autonomy from the politics and obligations of the French alliance and the Iroquois confederacy. This was particularly true for the refugees and captive/adoptees that made up a significant segment of both social formations.[25]

The simultaneous closing of French trading posts in the west resulted in a collapse of the middle ground in this region, and the growing dominance of the politics and social formations of the Native New World. The inland trade would continue to thrive in the western interior, and in the pays d'en haut. Accordingly, this pattern of exchange and interaction with the Atlantic World economy would continue to act as a catalyst for change among the peoples of the Native New World. But trade in the west would become increasingly detached from empire, or at least detached from the politics and influence of the settler colonies on the eastern seaboard. It would become instead the impetus behind the expansion of power and political autonomy among the Native peoples of the western interior.

Even when the French began to reestablish licensed trade at posts in Anishinaabewaki between 1712 and 1720 they could not resurrect the power and influence of the old alliance. This was, in part, a matter of military weakness. When they reoccupied their posts the governor complained about how few soldiers he was able to deploy. In 1715 he sent twenty soldiers to Michilimacki-nac, ten to Detroit, and ten to the Illinois country. These numbers remained consistent up to the outbreak of war with the British colonies. At the time he made these deployments, the governor also noted that approximately one hundred coureurs de bois had passed unchecked through Michilimackinac making their way into the west, where they expected to join other French traders already established on the Mississippi River.[26] There had always been a small number of soldiers to support the claims of possession made by the French Empire. Similarly, there had always been large numbers of unlicensed traders who undermined French diplomacy and trade policy. After 1701, however, these small contingents of French military forces in Anishinaabe-waki would never be more than the caretakers of an illusion of empire.

The military weakness of the French in the west had always been bol-stered by their political strength. The treaty of 1701, however, redirected French power to the east and left the empire significantly weaker in the upper Great Lakes and Mississippi valley. This weakness would translate into a loss of political control that resulted in an escalating series of conflicts with and between the Mesquakie, the Dakota, the Zhagwaamikong and other west-ern Anishinaabeg, Muskekowuck-athinuwick, Nehiyawa-athinuwick, and Nakoda peoples (or in French and English records the Fox, Sioux, Sauteurs, Cree, Western Cree, and Assiniboine). The outcome of these conflicts was that the politics of the Native New World completely supplanted the politics of the middle ground and the old alliance. By the time of the Seven Years' War, posts in the Anishinaabewaki were politically and militarily inconse-quential in terms of supporting New France. The French Empire in the pays d'en haut existed only in the minds of colonial officials, and did not corre-spond to reality on the ground.

This loss of power meant that the agents of New France would become little more than a token imperial presence at the chain of French forts strung out across the landscape of Anishinaabewaki. The middle ground that men like Daniel Du Lhut and Nicolas Perrot had been able to call into existence would disappear, but the hybrid world of the old alliance would survive among the Métis communities that emerged alongside these faded French posts. This was where the new power and influence would emerge, among the people who were themselves an embodiment of the connections between the Atlantic and the Native New Worlds. These communities would control the gateways linking the cosmopolitan social worlds of the indigenous west and the burgeoning world system dominated by the empires of the Atlantic

World. Unlike Perrot and Du Lhut, but perhaps not unlike Pierre Radisson, the Métis would find it easy to shape-shift—keeping the trade alive while shifting their political allegiance between French, British, American, and Canadian colonial regimes.[27] They would simultaneously facilitate the cultural and political transformation of many of the peoples of Anishinaabewaki into western Indians. Already connected to or living in the interior, many of these peoples moved even deeper into the west for hunting and trading, removing themselves from the obligations of any permanent relationship to European empires, and in many cases reinventing themselves as a people.

The Treaty of 1701 and the Politics of Anishinaabewaki

In spite of their claims, the French had never really extended the sovereignty of their empire into Anishinaabewaki. Forty soldiers, a comparable number of licensed traders, and a handful of Jesuit missionaries hardly constituted a military force or institutional presence sufficient to establish French rule. Indeed, these representatives of New France were not even capable of enforcing French laws among the colony's habitants who traveled through French posts to trade illegally in the west. At best, the alliance worked when influential traders and priests used their personal influence to drag the peoples of Anishinaabewaki onto the middle ground, or when the Anishinaabe ogimaag compelled the French to join them within this hybrid social world where they negotiated with one another until they reached a consensus about how to best preserve and advance their mutual interests.

In 1701, after decades of bitter struggle, the French persuaded the peoples of the Haudenosaunee to join Onontio and his children on the middle ground. This was not so much an expansion of the alliance as it was an attempt to expand the social mechanisms of the alliance to include the Iroquois. While the confederacy entered into a relationship with New France, the Haudenosaunee did not promise to fight for a French father. Rather, they pledged neutrality in any conflict with the English colonies, and they accepted the governor of New France as the arbiter of any disputes or conflicts they had with the Native allies of the colony. This, in effect, was the outcome of the Treaty of 1701.

To regard the Treaty of 1701 as an expansion of French sovereignty would be to misread the political consequences of the peace it created. Similarly, to understand this new arrangement of power as the creation of French hegemony over sovereign indigenous nations would be to misconstrue both the nature of Native identity and the nature of French political influence.[28] The peace created by the Treaty of 1701 provided a process for bringing an end to violence between the peoples of Anishinaabewaki and the Haudenosaunee. It failed to secure peace in the west, however, precisely because the social formations that dominated this region were not organized as nations, and the French had allowed the middle ground to implode in the west while they concentrated on the Iroquois in the east.

The Anishinaabeg did not imagine themselves collectively as a nation. They were instead a people comprising related but distinct and autonomous communities who performed/enacted their identity via a lived relationship on the land. Anishinaabewaki was the landscape created by this lived relationship. Within their social world both collective identity and political authority were directly tied to membership within a kinship community. Because kinship could be created socially as well as biologically, Anishinaabewaki was infinitely expandable. The alliance relationship created by the Shagwaamikong Anishinaabeg and the Dakota expanded Anishinaabewaki into the upper Mississippi valley. The overlapping territory created by this relationship, however, was unstable because Anishinaabewaki was a multipolar social formation. There were multiple centers of power among the doodemag of the Anishinaabeg at places like Michilimackinac, Sault Sainte Marie, Keweenaw, Shagwaamikong, Green Bay, and after 1701 at Detroit.[29] By the time of the Great Peace, Green Bay had emerged as a political outlier within this constellation of village centers.

For the most part, the cultural, political, and kinship ties between the peoples of Shagwaamikong and the doodemag of Keeweenaw, Michilimackinac, and Sault Sainte Marie were strong enough to sustain the inclusion of the Dakota within the political orbit of the westernmost village of the Anishinaabeg. There had been opposition, particularly among Cree and Anishinaabe doodemag who resided primarily in the bush country north of Gichigamiing. But violence between the village communities themselves had been largely contained. This was not the case at Green Bay, where some Anishinaabe doodemag had taken refuge along with the Huron and other Algonquian peoples with origins as far away as New England. Originally occupied by both Algonquian- and Siouan-speaking peoples, the villages of this region, like Shagwaamikong to the north, had long been connected to the Mississippi valley and the western interior. Relations between the villages of Green Bay and the Dakota had been adversarial at least since the arrival of refugees in this region in the mid-seventeenth century. The fact that the Dakota had no formal relationship with New France, and therefore were regarded politically as outsiders by the majority of the peoples of the bay, only added to this animosity. This was particularly true for the Mesquakie and their close allies the Sauk, Mascouten, and Kickapoos. All of these people came to Montreal in 1701 not only to make peace with the Iroquois but also to ask for a resolution of their conflict with the Shagwaamikong Anishinaabeg and their Dakota allies. As part of this resolution the peoples of Green Bay asked the French to repudiate the Dakota, stop trading with them, and designate them as political outsiders.

The failure of Governor Callières to make this repudiation created growing instability in the west that signaled the gradual unwinding of French power and influence in this region. The illegal trade continued to flourish after the peace conference, greatly antagonizing Onontio's children at Green Bay. In October, a few short months after the treaty was signed, the Odawa returned to Montreal to complain to the governor about Le Sueur, who "had traded for beaver with the Sioux." They warned that he would be pillaged for taking the trade to them.[30] The governor subsequently discovered Le Sueur's wife preparing to send a cargo of two hundred rifles to her husband's post among the Dakota. Callières made her exchange these weapons for other merchandise, but noted in his report to the minister that these goods must pass through villages that remained at war with the Dakota. He also noted that French-allied Indians had pillaged other traders traveling this route, inland through Green Bay and into the west via the Fox and Wisconsin Rivers to the Mississippi.[31] Le Sueur merited special attention from the governor only because he so openly flouted the Crown's policy to end the fur trade. His story, however, was not an isolated incident but rather reflected a widespread problem. Not only were the merchants of Montreal outfitting unlicensed voyageurs to trade in the Mississippi, but so too were the merchants of the newly formed French colony of Louisiana.[32]

From the perspective of their allies at Green Bay the French appeared unwilling to halt this trade with the Dakota. Even more insulting, this illicit trade passed through their villages. In the summer of 1702, one year after the conference at Montreal, the west became engulfed in a familiar pattern of violence as a result of this traffic. The Dakota and their Anishinaabe allies were at war with the people of Green Bay. Five French men had been caught up in this conflict and killed. On this occasion the Anishinaabeg held two Sauk captives, but there was no Nicolas Perrot or Daniel Du Lhut to march into their village and demand that they obey the will of their French father and spare their prisoners for the sake of the alliance. Instead the Odawa of Michilimackinac traveled to Montreal to seek an audience with Callières, calling on him to be a father to his children. The governor informed this delegation that he was aware of this new conflict in the west, and that he was waiting for the Sauk and the Sauteurs to come to Montreal so that he could bring an end to this rift in the alliance.[33] The summer passed, however, and the Shagwaamikong Anishinaabeg stayed away from Lower Canada. Finally the Odawa ogimaa Longekam sought another audience with Callières. He told the governor: "We know that not any Sauteurs will come even when you send a canoe expressly to tell them." He then asked Callières "to make them give us back two little Sakis they have, or they will once again drink the broth of these two with the Scioux."[34]

On similar occasions in the past Nicolas Perrot's defiance—his command that his children eat his own flesh and spare their prisoners—had shown his allies strength and a political will that compelled them to accept the protocols of the French alliance. Now, in the face of this exact same kind of crisis, Governor Callières merely appeared ineffectual. His children at Shagwaamikong refused to present themselves for an audience with their French father. The governor reassured Longekam, "I learned last year from my children who came here for the peace of the strikes that the Sauteurs made on the Fox and the Saki," and he added, "this peace accommodated all of their differences." Callières then told the ogimaa that the absence of the Shagwaamikong Anishinaabeg from this conference explained their aberrant behavior. "I am persuaded," he said at council, "that if they had been at the general peace that I made between all my children that they would not have made this last strike."[35]

The governor promised that he would make the Anishinaabeg come to him and cover the deaths of the Sauk and Mesquakie they had killed. In response Longekam said that during the past winter the Sioux had also raided a Mesquakie village. He warned his father that the Mesquakie, along with the Miami and Huron, planned to launch a counterraid against them. Callières replied that he was not surprised at "the treason that you say the Sioux have wanted to make since they are always at war." But, he argued, "It is necessary to lead them into the peace that I have made between all of my children and the Iroquois." Callières, in effect, repeated the proposition that he made in Montreal in 1701—that the peace treaty should be extended to include the Dakota.[36]

Another Anishinaabe ogimaa addressed the governor after Longekam, however, and his testimony underscored the diplomatic complexity of the conflict in the west. This man, Piamaola, spoke for the Amikwas doodem. He informed the governor that when the Amikwas returned to their village after their winter hunt, "a canoe arrived from Sault Sainte Marie . . . that reported that the Renards and Saki had made a strike on the Sauteurs and that they had killed an Amikois, a Sauteur, a Cree, and two Gens des Terres who were found with them." Callières again pledged weakly that he would make the Sauk and Mesquakie cover the dead, and he promised that as soon as they joined him at council "the Sauteurs and the Sakis will find themselves at ease with one another."[37] In a letter to France, however, he worried: "Our allies in the upper country were not by all affairs in a good situation by the growing war between the Sioux and by the differences coming on the part of the Saulteurs against the Renards and the Sakis. . . . It is feared by these alliances that all of the upper nations have . . . taken one side or the other and that they are thrown into a great war."[38]

In order to restore French influence Callières asked the king to restore the trade licenses and grant an amnesty to the coureurs de bois to draw them back to the colony. "These same licenses would be useful," he argued, "for the maintenance of peace, and to reunite the nations when they have problems with each other, as occurred recently between the Fox and the Sakis who were at war with the Sauteurs." This conflict, he lamented, "endures more and more." Restoring the licensed trade, he asserted, "would not disturb the commerce of the colony, on the contrary it would increase the proportion from the savages of Lake Superior carrying their peltries to the English of the North Bay."[39] Callières recognized that without traders operating in the villages of Anishinaabewaki, the French exercised very little political influence among their allies. And so in spite of the diplomatic success of 1701, the French could only stand by and watch the dismantling of their alliance in the upper country.

The summer councils of 1702 and the governor's letter calling for a return of the licensed trade reveal how quickly French political influence in Anishinaabewaki and the western interior faded after the Peace of 1701. Not only was Onontio unable to bring an end to the violence between the peoples of Green Bay, the Dakota, and the Gichigamiing Anishinaabeg, he was also unable to persuade them to sit at council with him at Montreal. As Callières' letter suggested, the peoples of Lake Superior had shifted their trade entirely to the English posts at Hudson's Bay. Not only was New France deprived of this commerce, but it also forfeited any ability to shape or influence the complex political alliances and exchange networks that governed the inland trade.[40] This weakness also placed the Mesquakie at an added disadvantage. Striking at the Shagwaamikong Anishinaabeg, they inadvertently killed individuals from three additional Anishinaabe doodemag. As a result, the Mesquakie and their close allies the Sauk, Mascouten, and Kickapoos were increasingly politically isolated from all the Anishinaabe peoples.

The Shrinking Social World of the Middle Ground

Political leadership among the peoples of Anishinaabewaki, however, was also becoming fractured. After 1701 the French tried to force their allies in the upper country to relocate to Detroit so they could better manage their relations with the Iroquois. The commandant of this post, Antoine Laumet le Sieur de Cadillac, also convinced the governor that the presence of French traders at this location would stop their allies from going to the English at Albany and at Hudson's Bay.[41] In the summer of 1703 the Huron called on a new governor, Philippe de Rigaud de Vaudreuil, to reaffirm their alliance. Their council session revealed the ineffectiveness of Cadillac's plan to make Detroit into a center of French power. They informed the new governor that the Mohawk had invited the Huron and the Miami located at Detroit to join them at Albany in New York where they could trade furs for English goods. They then requested permission to trade with the English. They also declined to locate at Detroit and instead requested permission to settle at the Miami River in the Ohio country. Finally, the Huron asked Vaudreuil to protect them at this new location, and to "permit them to make war against the Scioux."[42] The governor informed the Huron that the French and English were once again at war, and he encouraged them not to trade at Albany, but rather to settle near Detroit as directed by Cadillac. He also told them, "as regards the Scioux, they were included in the peace like the rest, but if they attacked his nation, they would promise to defend him." At this same council Miami warriors also spoke, telling the governor that they too had "come to tell him that their fathers are dead, that the Sioux had killed them." Implying that the Dakota struck and killed political leaders at their village, these young men demanded the warriors' right of revenge. Again Vaudreuil responded conditionally, "if the Scioux waged war against them, he does not prevent them from defending themselves."[43]

Within months of these councils, in October 1703, the Odawaag returned to Montreal to call Vaudreuil to council and demand that he focus on the growing disorder in the west. The Odawa ogimaag, perhaps the staunchest and most effective advocates for the treaty settlement of 1701, resisted French pressure to relocate to Detroit. Instead, over a gift of beaver pelts they informed the governor that the elders of Michilimackinac would not move to Detroit, and "begged their father for a French commander." Over another package of beaver pelts the Odawa orators pleaded with the governor. "The elders," they reported, "are astonished to see that their brothers the Sauteurs, the Sakis, the Folles Avoins, and the Outagamis are killing themselves again." The Odawa "sent presents to appease this disorder," but they feared they too might soon be drawn into this war. Vaudreuil responded, "I will give the order to those I send to Michilimackinac to stop their anger and oblige them to conform to the treaty made at the general peace."[44]

Neither the Dakota nor the Shagwaamikong Anishinaabeg had signed this treaty, however, and Vaudreuil soon abandoned any hope of making them a functional part of the new alliance. The following year, in 1704, Odawa warriors attacked an Iroquois trading party at Fort Frontenac. The Onondaga, Keepers of the Central Fire, called on Vaudreuil at Montreal on behalf of the confederacy. They were furious at this violation of the peace, and demanded once again that the peoples of Anishinaabewaki provide them with prisoners to raise their dead. Vaudreuil said that he would send soldiers to Michilimackinac, "to oblige them to make satisfaction to you." When the Odawaag arrived at Montreal to make restitution the following summer they appeared contrite. They first smoked the calumet with the Seneca whose young men they had killed. Then they covered the dead with presents at council and declared, "Our warriors in the name of all of those from our country bring you the calumet all red with the blood of your enemies." They asked the Seneca to smoke with them "to forget the pain of your dead." And they promised to go "search among the Sioux" for slaves to replace the people they had lost.[45]

The Odawaag tried to drag Vaudreuil back into the old world of the middle ground, but with his hands tied by the king's policy he could not reestablish a formal French presence among the villages of Anishinaabewaki. Instead he tried to forge a new middle ground at Detroit, situated along the borderland with the Haudenosaunee.[46] Rooted in the east, this new alliance of Iroquois and Algonquian peoples would sacrifice the political influence of the French Empire in the west in the hope of blocking English influence with the confederacy. Vaudreuil explained his strategy to the Crown following these councils with the Iroquois and Odawaag. "My Lord," he wrote, "In regard to the continuation of the peace with the Iroquois as the principal affair of the country." He reported that he had sent an officer to Michilimackinac to retrieve prisoners taken by the Odawaag for the Iroquois. He also sent an officer among the Seneca, but he warned, "the partisans of the English were engaging everyone among the young men to revenge this blow that the Outtauois had made on them."[47]

Vaudreuil stressed the importance of Detroit for blocking trade with the English, and preventing their allies from abandoning New France. He feared that with access to English traders through the Iroquois the peoples of Anishinaabewaki might be persuaded to take up arms against the French. "You will see my Lord," he wrote, "the difficulty of maintaining all these different nations in peace." To prevent this defection he sacrificed the Dakota. "I have been obliged," Vaudreuil reported, "to allow them the liberty of making war on the Scioux, in the end giving them this occupation and turning by this means the upper nations from making war on the Iroquois, which I regard as the only nation that it is important that I conserve."[48] The following year he reported that "this necessity of reuniting the spirit of all these savages made us take . . . the resolution to send a canoe to Michilimackinac to oblige the Outtaouaise to give the prisoners that they have taken to me." These people, he noted, were "living slaves, that is to say prisoners, that they made among the far nations to replace the dead Iroquois that they have killed." Vaudreuil added that while he had "permitted several small parties of our savages to recommence the war . . . I am persuaded My Lord that this will have a good effect."[49]

Encouraging or even condoning raids in the west to meet the demands of their new Iroquois allies in the east led only to increasing political instability. The allies became entangled in a web of violence that, without mediation, demanded violent retaliation in return. In 1706 the Odawaag called out their father for failing to meet his responsibilities at a council held at Detroit. Raiding into the west for slaves brought them into a series of conflicts with western peoples—both within the alliance, and marginal to it. A prominent ogimaa that the French called Le Pesant informed Etienne Venyard le Sieur de Bourgmont, the commandant of the French fort during the temporary absence of Cadillac, "We have come down to ask to go to war." He said the Odawaag were sick at heart because so many of their people had been killed. Their father had failed to raise the dead; "he always tells us to wait and that he wants to be the master of these affairs." Le Pesant then stood before Bourgmont and recited a list those who had taken Odawa lives. "The Sioux have killed us," he continued, and "we carried our complaints to the Governor and told him that the young people want to revenge these deaths he told us again to wait." Since that time Waabange, the treaty signer from Bow-e-ting, had been killed in fighting with the Dakota. Le Pesant then said that the Gens des Terres, the Outagamis, and the Illinois had all taken Odawa lives and he expressed great frustration that all of these deaths remained unanswered.[50]

In response to Odawa anger the French at Detroit only offered them more of the same counsel, keep the peace. "Breaking heads . . . to revenge death," Commandant Bourgmont replied, "that was the cause of the war that you had with the Iroquois." Then he reminded them that they had been allowed "to go to war against the Sioux." Bourgmont concluded his remarks, however, by cautioning the Odawaag not "to go stirring up the land," and he added that Cadillac was to return to Detroit soon, "and he would enlighten all the nations."[51] With nothing more than the promise of future enlightenment, Odawa warriors left Detroit to raid in the Dakota country. On the war road they learned of an alleged plot by the Huron and Miami to attack their people during this absence. The Odawaag resolved to strike first. They ambushed a party of Miami outside their village near Detroit, and then began to attack the Miami settlement. The people of this village sought refuge in the French fort, and when soldiers fired on the advancing Odawa warriors a full-fledged confrontation broke out that pitted the Odawa peoples against a combination of French, Huron, and Miami forces.

The Odawaag quickly abandoned their siege of the French fort at Detroit and withdrew to Michilimackinac. By the time they departed, however, over eighty people were dead, including three Frenchmen and a prominent Odawa warrior who had just been recognized as an ogimaa. Desperate to preserve Detroit as a viable village and the locus of French political power, Cadillac initially sided with the Miami and Huron. He pledged the destruction of all the Odawa doodemag. In the meantime, the brother of the slain Odawa war leader began to circulate among the different Anishinaabeg at Michilimackinac (the Ottawa, Sauteurs, and Amikois by French reckoning). At the same time two of the more prominent women among the Odawa who lost relatives in the clash at Detroit began to actively call for the Anishinaabeg to raise a war party to raise their dead. In the midst of this escalating conflict, the Iroquois approached the governor and volunteered to lead an assault on the Odawa at Michilimackinac.[52]

Governor Vaudreuil, recognizing the fragility of the French position at Detroit and in the upper country, accepted reconciliation as his only course of action. The restoration of the Odawaag to the alliance unfolded through a dramatic and entirely staged surrender of the ogimaa Le Pesant to Cadillac at Detroit. This was to be a public showing of Odawa submission to French authority. After walking into the French fort to accept his punishment Le Pesant, a fat old man, promptly escaped from French custody. The idea behind this bit of stagecraft concocted by Cadillac and the Odawa ogimaag had been to restore order to the alliance by demonstrating the relative status of the French and their Native allies—as a father and his children. The result, as usual, was an impromptu battle of wits over the authority, obligation, and conditions of mutual responsibility attached to these social personas. In the end, this conflict and its dramatic resolution only demonstrated the weakness of the French. In reality, they exercised very little political control and limited military power—even within the confines of their own fort. It also underscored the relative power of the Anishinaabeg within this new alliance. In his letter to the Crown explaining this affair, Vaudreuil reported, "I can not consent, My Lord, to allow the destruction of a nation that has been faithful to us in the last war and in what has happened at Detroit has been perhaps more bad luck than bad will."[53]

In truth, the Anishinaabeg greatly outnumbered the other Native peoples allied to New France. Equally important, the new spatial configuration of the alliance left the principal villages of the Anishinaabe peoples both physically and socially outside of the sphere of French political influence. The new middle ground was, for all practical purposes, reduced to Detroit and focused almost entirely on managing relations with the peoples of the Haudenosaunee. In addition to addressing the issue of Odawa fidelity, Vaudreuil's letter also suggested that the alliance would not, in fact, survive their estrangement. "My Lord, the real reason I responded like this," he wrote, "is that I consider that if the Huron, the Miami, and the Iroquois would be united, they would have finished the Outtauois, destroying them or forcing them to abandon Michilimcakinac." If this happened, he predicted, the Iroquois would turn on the French "making a bloody war against us." The Odawa doodemag, he wrote, "would take refuge in Lake Superior and arm themselves from the English at the bottom of Hudson's Bay."[54] They would melt into that undiscovered infinity of nations that haunted the dream of a French Empire in North America. The Odawaag might lose their power within the alliance, but then they would shape-shift, preserving their status as part of Anishinaabewaki. Vaudreuil knew that this other New World loomed at the edge of the French Empire, and he had even less power to influence this alliance and the social world it had created than he did the Iroquois and what was left of the pays d'en haut, now largely confined as a social space to a peninsula of land between Lake Huron and Lake Erie.

In 1708 the Crown ordered an inspection of the French posts in Canada. This report, like the fighting two years earlier at Detroit, revealed the lack of French influence within the political world of the Native peoples allied to the colony. It also suggested a corresponding loss of trade to the English at Hudson's Bay and in New York. While the king's agent was at Fort Frontenac on the edge of the Iroquois country, two different parties identified as "canoes of Mississaguas and Sauteurs" arrived seeking permission to go the village of the Onondaga. These people came from Lake Saint Clair above Detroit. Miami traders living south of Detroit came to the fort a few days later and made the same request. The post commander barred the passage of these parties of French-allied Indians into the country of the Haudenosaunee, but it was obvious to the king's agent, le Sieur d'Aigremont, that a significant amount of peltry was going to the English through the Iroquois settlements east of Lake Erie.[55]

The situation at Detroit was perhaps even more disturbing. Aigremont reported that Cadillac, the post commander, was widely disliked both among the French habitants and the Natives living near the fort. There were sixty-three French settlers, but very little permanent housing or farming was evident, suggesting that the majority of the inhabitants traded illegally in the interior. The commanders, both Cadillac and Bourgmont, wanted to unify the peoples they identified as Huron, Miami, Fox, Kickapoos, Sauteurs, and Ottawas at Detroit by sending them "to war against the Sioux their common enemies." Aigremont, however, questioned the wisdom of drawing so many different peoples together at the French post. This fear would prove quite prescient.[56]

To dissipate these tensions and restore the French trade that animated all of the political relationships between the peoples of the Great Lakes and with Onontio, Aigremont called for the restoration of licensed trade and the reestablishment of Michilimackinac. "It is certain my Lord," he wrote, "that the commerce from the north of Lake Superior is the only good one in Canada by the good quality of the peltries." Aigremont argued that the Odawa doodemag would never abandon Michilimackinac, which could provide the French with access to the peoples and resources of Lake Superior. He also asserted that beaver skins traded through this village routinely passed south though Detroit and east to the English. Although this traffic was troubling, Aigremont observed that "since there are no more French at Michilimackinac the great part of the pelts are brought to the English at Hudson's Bay." He provided a brief description of the river systems from Kaministiquia and Nipigon in the west to Temiscamiing in the east that connected the north shore of Lake Superior to the watersheds that drained into the bay. More importantly, he argued, "this trade can not be made by the Outaois for two reasons. The first is that the savages of the north are extremely timid and they very much fear those who have without right pillaged them. . . . The second is that the Outaouis do not have enough of an economy to furnish them with merchandise."[57]

The timidity of the peoples of the north was, perhaps, exaggerated. During this time, Anishinaabe doodemag identified as Sauteurs, Nipissing, Mississaugua, Monsoni, and Gens des Terres routinely traveled up north through Temiscamiing to trade with the English at Hudson's Bay.[58] And as Aigremont reported, these bands even ventured into the villages of the Haudenosaunee to trade for English goods. Hudson's Bay Company records confirm the fact that French-allied Indians traded with the English to the north and with western Indians in the interior. These records also indicate that coureurs de bois, most likely operating out of Michilimackinac, traded in these same watersheds. The man in charge of the English post at the mouth of the Albany river heard a rumor in the summer of 1706 that the French, "with a great many Indians are coming to burn down our factory and cutt our throats and to this end they have wintered at a lake up Ruperts River."[59] He would hear these same rumors again the following summer. And he learned from a Lowland Cree man "that they had had wars that way and severall Indians had been killed and likewise some French men."[60]

During both the 1706 and 1707 trading seasons the Hudson's Bay Company post at Albany River traded with Moose River Indians, "Cristeens," and unidentified "Uplanders," who would have been some combination of Anishinabe doodemag, Nehiyawa-athinuwick, and Assiniboine. The Anishinaabe peoples, a variety of bands identified in French records as Ojibwe speakers with various names (Gens des Terres, Zhiishiigwe, and Monsoni for example), as well as the Western Cree and Assiniboine lived in the region northwest of Lake Superior and shifted their trade between French and English posts. This shifting of exchange networks was frequently violent. By the end of May 1707 twelve canoes of "Uplanders" told traders at the Albany River post that "all the Cristans that way are gone to the wars and therefore no more

would come and trade here this year."[61] This warfare among "Uplanders," that
is, the Western Anishinaabeg, Cree, and Assiniboine, most likely involved
fighting and competition for trade and hunting territory with the Dakota
and Yankton/Yanktonai peoples in the upper Mississippi valley and northern plains, although these "wars" could also have referred to conflict with
the Gichigamiing Anishinaabeg over trade and hunting territories among the
watersheds of the north shore of Lake Superior.

Native peoples who traded with the French at places like Detroit and Fort
Frontenac also traded with French coureurs de bois, with nonallied western
Indians, and with the English up and down the western shore of Hudson's
Bay. In 1714, York Fort in the Hayes-Nelson watershed reported that "many of
the Indians has great friendship for the French here," even though they also
clearly traded with the English. This post, home to the Peneswichewan Sepee,
recorded trade with unspecified "Upland Indians," a variety of named Western or plains Cree bands, parkland and plains Assiniboine bands, and Ojibwe
speakers from the northern shore of Lake Superior and the northwestern interior between Lake Superior and Lake Winnipeg.[62]

The configurations of trade alliances that brought these people to the
Hudson's Bay coast changed frequently. In May 1716, for example, post traders reported that five canoes of "Uplanders . . . reports that as those Indians
had made a peace w 4 nations that lyes between the SW & the Wst they are
people as never had any trade or commerce with any Europeans." Later that
summer they reported that three canoes of "Mountain Indians," or northern
Assiniboine from the parkland above the Assiniboine River, arrived at York
Fort. The post commander wrote in his journal that "I am more concerned
for these as any has been here as they come from the farthest and border upon
the worst sort of Indians in this country that are their enemys." He noted that
he sent presents "to invite some of the remotest Indians to come down here."
And he noted that "Mountain Indians" told him that they had traded the last
several years at the Hudson's Bay post in the Albany River. The commander
at York also noted, "they could have gone to the lake as they call it wch lyes
at the south from their country where there are svll settlements of the French
wood runners." In other words, these people, who traded at York and Albany
posts, also had access to coureurs de bois operating out of the Lake Nipigon
and Kaministiquia region—traders who passed through the villages of Michilimackinac and among the children of Onontio.[63]

Obviously, exchange in the western interior, the inland trade, involved
constant diplomacy. It did, however, also frequently involve pillaging and

even armed conflict. This could and did prove problematic for the French when the Native traders and raiders involved in these conflicts also asserted their status as children of Onontio. They might seek French sanction and arms for retaliatory raids to force the empire to support their trade practices. They also actively sought French mediation, or indirectly forced the French to seek conciliation on their behalf in order to preserve a general peace among their allies in the interest of trade and the defense of the colony. This had been the case when Le Pesant demanded that the French allow the Odawa to raise their dead, and then drew them into an internecine conflict with the Huron and Miami.

In the years following Aigremont's critical report, similar explosions of violence once again threatened to rapidly unravel the alliance in the upper country, and collapse what was left of the licensed French fur trade. The first conflict occurred in the year after Aigremont's inspection when, according to Vaudreuil, "the Saulteurs had attacked the Poutaoutamies." He worried "that was going to cause a war among the nations of the lakes where the Outouais would be enveloped."[64] It is difficult to know which doodem or village made this strike, as the French sent an official to all of the Gichigamiing Anishinaabe communities to try to reestablish peace.[65] As the French worked to prevent this violence from spreading, another man identified as a Sauteur killed two Iroquois who came to Fort Frontenac to trade. Vaudreuil feared that unless these deaths were covered the Iroquois would begin to attack "all the savages of the lakes and declare war on this colony."[66]

Once again Vaudreuil focused on resolving the conflict with the Iroquois, rather than spending his diplomatic capital in the west. He dispatched an officer to Fort Frontenac and to the Onondaga village to cover the dead. The Iroquois assured the French and Mississauga at this location that "their hatchet was in the hands of their common father at Montreal."[67] Vaudreuil, however, worried about his ability to make proper restitution. Following European notions of justice, he promised to turn the murders over to the Iroquois. This, he felt, was better than allowing them to take revenge following Native custom, which would involve the Iroquois attacking and enslaving prisoners from any of the Anishinaabe peoples that they encountered. This, he rightly feared, would rapidly spread the conflict throughout Anishinaabewaki. In his report to France this incident became one more reason to reestablish Michilimackinac. "This affair, My Lord, is so much more delicate," the governor wrote, "as there is no one in the upper country capable of inducing the savages of the lakes to deliver up these murderers to me." Vaudreuil concluded by empha-

sizing "how important it is to have a commandant with some soldiers and a
certain number of voyageurs at Michilimackinac."[68] What little power men
like Daniel Du Lhut and Nicolas Perrot had possessed was no longer available
to the agents of the French Empire.

The Fox Wars

In his correspondence to the king and his ministers in France, Vaudreuil most
urgently expressed fear that the Iroquois would abandon the protocols of the
Great Peace of 1701 and turn on the French. Underlying this seemingly all-
consuming fear, however, was a corresponding fear that his allies would defect to the British. Specifically, Vaudreuil worried that the children of Onontio
would abandon their father who was failing to "meet their needs" by curtailing
French participation in the fur trade. This fear was not unfounded. The coureurs de bois, and especially the British traders at Hudson's Bay and among the
Iroquois, played an increasingly important political and economic role within
the inland trade, and they were not a stabilizing force in the western interior.

Although Vaudreuil most often gave voice to fears that the Iroquois would
abandon their neutrality, he also repeatedly worried about the defection of
the Odawa peoples. He seemed to realize that they were the most powerful
political force within the new alliance created by the Great Peace.[69] This fear
about the defection of the Odawa doodemag took two forms. Vaudreuil expressed concern that they would get "enveloped" in the politics of Anishinaabewaki, and be dragged into the interminable wars of the Native New World.
This led to a second related fear that if unduly threatened the Odawa peoples
would withdraw from Detroit, and disappear into the infinity of nations of
the Lake Superior country.

The political leadership of the Odawa doodemag had been perhaps the
most adept of all the children of Onontio at manipulating their father. The
withdrawal of the French from the upper country placed the Odawaag simultaneously at an advantage and a disadvantage. On the one hand, the weaker
French presence increased their political influence within the new alliance.
On the other hand, this added influence increased their political exposure. At
the same time, Odawa leaders also found themselves partnered with a weak
French father, making their diplomacy all the more difficult.

For example, the Odawa leadership had worked consistently to address
the issue of violence in the west only to find French leadership that was un-

interested in resolving these problems or unable to do so. In particular, the Odawa ogimaag had struggled to create reconciliation between their closest relatives, the Gichigamiing Anishinaabeg, and the peoples of Green Bay. Other than trade with the Dakota, this had been the most persistent source of political and social instability in the Great Lakes since the Treaty of 1701. It had been, perhaps, as much of a problem within the French alliance as conflict with the Iroquois in the decades leading up to the Great Peace. Following the signing of this treaty, the periodic flash of violence between the children of Onontio and the Iroquois drew a rapid response from the governor and his agents at Detroit. The steady and ongoing conflict between the Gichiigamiing Anishinaabeg and the peoples of Green Bay, in contrast, remained an open wound that had been allowed to fester. The decline in the French trade, and the related collapse of Onontio's political influence in Anishinaabewaki, created a political vacuum in the west that made this festering wound particularly dangerous. The Odawa stepped in to fill that void and resolve this problem. The result was a massive escalation of violence that would haunt the alliance until its collapse.

This conflict, typically called the Fox Wars by historians, pitted the Mesquakie and the closely related Sauk, Mascouten, and Kickapoos peoples who were their allies against the Anishinaabeg and all the other allies of New France. This conflict had its origins in the west, in the warfare between the Shagwaamikong Anishinaabeg and their Dakota allies on one side and the Mesquakie and their allies at Green Bay on the other. A cycle of raiding and slaving between these two sets of allies resulted in an ongoing conflict that periodically expanded to include other peoples in both Anishinaabewaki and the west. The parties to this conflict had overlapping alliances with New France and with Native social formations of the western interior, and that meant that violence sometimes traveled along these connections like electrical current along a wire.

In 1712 this conflict jumped currents from the Native New World and the politics of the west to the middle ground and the politics of the east. The reasons behind this move are at once obvious and obscure. The obvious part was that everyone involved in this conflagration shared a long history that included both political accommodation and betrayal. The curious thing about this warfare was how it moved from being locally specific to a region-wide conflict. This movement into a bigger arena had everything to do with the diplomatic miscalculations of the Odawa ogimaag and the weakness of the French within their new alliance.

When fighting erupted at Detroit in 1712, the Mesquakie and their closest allies at Green Bay had been engaged in a grueling on-again, off-again conflict with the Shagwaamikong Anishinaabeg for at least thirty years. This history of bitter conflict left the Mesquakie poorly positioned within the French alliance. Perhaps that was why approximately a thousand Mesquakie, called "Outagamis" by the Anishinaabeg and "Fox" by the French, moved to Detroit at Cadillac's request. In relocating to this post they relocated to their original homeland, and so they claimed a right to hunt in an already overhunted territory where land-use privileges were disputed between the Iroquois and more recent arrivals. They also gained direct access to the Iroquois and British traders, and may have calculated that this would enhance their political power within the alliance. Surely all of these things factored into the decision of the Mesquakie to relocate to Detroit, but this move created the sort of complicated political circumstances that Governor Vaudreuil had feared would result in an alliance-wide conflagration.

For reasons that are not entirely clear, the war leader Sakima, a man of mixed Odawa and Boodewaadamii ancestry from Michilimackinac, began to call for an attack on the Mesquakie. He circulated a red wampum belt among the Boodewaadamii at the Saint Joseph River "with the intention of destroying the Outagamis." Toward this end, he enlisted the help of the Boodewaadamii ogimaa Makisabe, and he asked that together they "begin with the Maskoutin who were their allies, making a broth of those who were among them." The Boodewaadamii brought the Miami and Illinois peoples into this conflict, and warriors from all four communities attacked the Mascouten village at Saint Joseph.[70] The survivors fled toward Detroit, seeking French protection. The fighting, however, quickly escalated. The warriors of Saint Joseph also turned on the Kickapoos "because they were the same as the Outagamis," and began to kill and enslave the peoples of this community. As the refugees streamed toward the French fort at Detroit the post commander learned that the Mesquakie living near his post "had been defeated by the Saulteurs."[71] This conflict erupted everywhere that the Mesquakie, Mascouten, Sauk, and Kickapoos lived, from the villages at Green Bay to the eastern shore of Lake Michigan and in the villages surrounding Detroit. Sakima and Makisabe were apparently very effective advocates for war against the Mesquakie. The attacks had obviously been coordinated among all of the children of Onontio.

This fact should have suggested to the French commander at Detroit that his allies had engineered this conflict. As the violence swirled around him, however, the French commander was duped into seeing a Fox-led conspiracy to overthrow the French, destroy their allies, and hand his fort over to the Iroquois. The end result of this gullibility was a brutal application of military force against people who suddenly found themselves surrounded by enemies who had once been their allies.[72] The fighting was vicious and left approximately a thousand dead among the Mesquakie, Mascouten, Sauk, and Kickapoos. The Gichigamiing Anishinaabeg, the people identified as Sauteurs by the French, took large numbers of captives during the conflict to redress past grievances that remained unresolved.[73] All of this death and captive taking left a legacy that guaranteed conflict would remain ongoing between the Anishinaabeg and the Mesquakie and their allies for the foreseeable future.

The fighting with the Mesquakie that began in 1712 culminated in a French-led military expedition to restore peace in 1716, with the reestablishment of a French garrison at Michilimackinac. The commander in charge of the French forces in this campaign, le Sieur de Louvigny, recognized the futility of any attempt to crush his opponents militarily.[74] After all, when the French regarrisoned Michilimackinac, they merely added twenty additional troops to the posts they operated with comparable numbers at Detroit and in the Illinois country. This was hardly a daunting military presence.[75] The military power of the French in the upper country lay with their allies. More to the point, the Mesquakie had seen the Dakota mount raids against them that placed over eight hundred warriors in the field. They knew who was capable of wielding real military power in the west and who was not. In fact, their dramatic reversal of fortune prompted some Mesquakie to seek refuge in the west among the Dakota, their longtime rivals. The Dakota were powerful enough militarily to shelter them from both the French and the children of Onontio.[76] Equally important, the French had no political influence among these former enemies.

Louvigny seemed to be aware of all these factors, and so he mounted an expedition to bring an end to the fighting, and to try and restore order and political stability to the alliance. The children of Onontio wanted to destroy the Mesquakie as a people, and were furious when Louvigny quickly came to terms with them after only a brief show of force at Green Bay. The French commander believed that to continue the assault would only undermine French power and authority, while fueling future conflict. Both he and the Mesquakie people wanted an end to the conflict, and so the Fox were restored to the alliance. In truth, however, this latest round of fighting with the Anishinaabeg and the other allies had opened wounds so deep that they would never fully heal. From this moment on, the Mesquakie relationship with both

Onontio and his children would always be tense and prone to outbreaks of violence.[77]

It is difficult to ascertain the motivations of Sakima and Makisabe, but after the Mesquakie moved to Detroit in large numbers the Odawaag seemed to feel some apprehension toward them. Their aggressive behavior and diplomatic outreach to the Iroquois and the English may have caused the Odawa leadership to fear that growing political power of the Mesquakie might eclipse their own. In this case, it would have been appropriate for war leaders like Sakima and Makisabe to advocate for a military assault against this threat. But what makes this particular conflict difficult to understand is that there should have been more push back from the civil leadership of the Anishinaabe peoples. Instead, there seemed to be a uniformly aggressive determination to destroy the Mesquakie by use of force. When this war heated up again in the 1720s and 1730s there was enough bad blood, uncovered dead, and unredeemed captives to secure the active participation of all the children of Onontio. This time, however, civil leaders pushed back against the overzealous response by their French father, and they demanded that the governor broker a reconciliation.[78]

The French were never a powerful military presence in Anishinaabewaki, but conflict with the Mesquakie allowed them to indulge in the fantasy that they were. Governor Vaudreuil and his commander in the west, Sieur Louvigny, grasped the limited nature of French political influence and advocated for a negotiated settlement whenever conflicts demanded their intervention. And they realized that within the social world they had created with their allies, the lives of the children of Onontio had become so intertwined that to encourage violent retribution would only create political chaos. But other colonial officials from Commander Joseph Guyon Dubuisson at Detroit to Vaudreuil's successor, the Chevalier de Beauharnois, saw the opportunity to punish the Fox as a way to demonstrate French power. As Richard White has argued, "The French always retained the hope of reducing their allies to subjects."[79] They imagined a world where the might of the French Empire allowed them to dictate the terms of the alliance to the children of Onontio. After the Treaty of 1701, however, the French Empire in Anishinaabewaki was only an illusion and its power consisted of a waning political influence rather than military power.

The real power of New France in Anishinaabewaki was their alliance, and this power existed only when the French worked to preserve their relationships with Native peoples. Their power to destroy Native peoples in the west was nonexistent. The French were strongest when they resolved conflict, when they helped to raise and cover the dead, when they helped to heal the painful wounds caused by the social disruption of North America's colonization. This required that they accept the social meanings and cultural practices that their allies attached to events far more than they would like. But it also meant that their allies had to make concessions to the ways that the French interpreted social meaning and cultural practice as well. More to the point, the French simply did not possess the military power to rule by force, or even to force a social acceptance of French sovereignty as the political basis for their relationship with the peoples of Anishinaabewaki. The terms of this alliance were determined by cooperation, not dictated by force. This cooperation was often an ugly thing based on cultural misappropriations and political compromises that left everyone dissatisfied, but it allowed the French influence within Anishinaabewaki. This was the middle ground—a hybrid creation of the Native New World and the Atlantic New World.

After 1701, the middle ground began to change. The violence of the Fox Wars was not just a result of the collapse of the social world of the old alliance. More significantly, this conflict represented a swing of the pendulum as the politics of the middle ground began to give way to the politics of the Native New World. This conflict represented a change in the diplomatic relationships between Native peoples in Anishinaabewaki and the western interior and the peoples and empires of the Atlantic World. This was an instance of Native peoples dictating the terms of their political relationship with Europeans. The end result of this new arrangement of political power was violent and disruptive, allowing the French to push back against their allies and force them back onto the middle ground, but that space was fast disappearing.

A Struggle for Power in the West

Following their campaign against the Mesquakie, the French attempted to restore their influence in the west. They reopened the trade in the upper country and made Louvigny commandant of the west. The commandant and the governor would find, however, that the west had changed significantly during their absence. The licensed French trade may have been dramatically curtailed, but the fur trade thrived. In addition to competition from the Hudson's Bay Company posts, the French had to contend with the coureurs de bois. In 1714, at the height of the warfare with the Mesquakie, the French estimated that there were no less than two hundred illegal traders operating out of Michilimackinac. Trade in brandy and rum as well as English manu-factured goods and trade cloth made its way into the west from traders oper-ating out of the villages of the Haudenosaunee and Albany.[80] French traders from Louisiana were beginning to make their way up the Mississippi River in growing numbers to trade with western Indians, a practice that left Onontio's children at Green Bay angry and vulnerable. In short, the French now faced considerable competition. They would never effectively restore the monopoly for licensed traders, and they would find the politics of the Native New World increasingly dominating both the inland trade and their relations with Native peoples in Anishinaabewaki and the western interior.

Established to curb English trade in the upper country and manage re-lations with the Iroquois, Detroit proved largely ineffective in advancing French influence. It also continued to be a hot spot for political infighting among the allies. In the spring of 1717 an Anishinaabe man named Waatawaa-giizhig arrived at Detroit with a keg of rum and a wampum belt. According to the post commander, "he carried a collar on the part of the English to all the nations from here." With these gifts he brazenly called on the people of the fort to come trade among the English.[81] Later that year Governor Vaudreuil reported that one of his officers in the west encountered a party of Odawa traders "from Michilimackinac, from Detroit, and from Saginaw going to Or-ange," the English fort at Albany in New York. This same man encountered a second party of fourteen canoes from Detroit at the Niagara portage on their way to the English. The officer, Sieur de Tonty, chastised his allies. "It is absolutely necessary that you change your thoughts because you can not have two fathers," he told them. "The English," he complained "have never done anything for you, on the contrary they always excite the Iroquois to make war on you."[82] The French commander managed to divert only a few of the canoes he encountered, and these successes required him to ignore Crown policy and trade brandy.

French authority and political influence in Anishinaabewaki had all but disappeared. With so many different Europeans moving through the Great Lakes and into the western interior post commanders found their diplomatic efforts constantly undermined. This made the task of resolving the smolder-ing conflict with the Mesquakie all the more difficult. Louvigny brought an end to open warfare between the allies, but that was only a beginning. In order to restore the Mesquakie to the alliance he made them turn over six people, three chiefs and their children, to accompany him as hostages while

he ratified the peace in Montreal. Three of these people, including one prominent war leader, died of smallpox in the French settlements. The survivors
were sent back to their village along with ten French men to explain these
deaths. This party of soldiers included Louvigny, who later wrote that "their
young men had been carried away by the sight of the merchandise which
several French canoes had bought them." Trade had been restored, the Mesquakie dead had been covered, and the peace ratified by Onontio. After the
calumet ceremony had been performed reaffirming peace and alliance with
the French, the commandant of the west reported that he "made known to
them the death of our Great King as well as to all the nations of the lakes,
who are to come down next year and cover the death of the King and to
ask his August successor for his protection." Louvigny concluded, somewhat
prematurely, that with the Mesquakie militarily subdued and politically re-
united with Onontio and his children he had forged "a peace among all of the
peoples with whom the French trade."[83]

While Louvigny treated with the Mesquakie he sent another officer to
Shagwaamikong. Vaudreuil reported that along with the commandant, "I
made follow Sieur St. Pierre, a captain of the company of troops that I have
sent to la pointe du Chaqouamigon to inform the Sauteurs of the assembly
of nations coming to Montreal and to come there themselves." Unlike the
Great Peace of 1701, when the ogimaag of Shagwaamikong refused to attend the council, the governor demanded the people of this community send
representatives to Montreal, although he made no effort to bring their Dakota allies to the assembly.[84] The following summer the Mesquakie and the
Sauk sent a total of eight representatives to the gathering at Montreal. The
day after their arrival the ogimaag "of the Sauteurs of Chagouamigon and
of Keoeouenan of Lake Superior arrived with the Sieur de St. Pierre."[85] The
Kickapoos and the Mascouten, who had become entangled in a conflict with
the Illinois, stayed away. When the ogimaag assembled at council, Governor
Vaudreuil addressed the Mesquakie and "declared to them that, as they had
come to show me their submission and to conclude peace with me and all my
children, I wanted to receive them well as good children." He then made their
restoration to the alliance conditional upon the return of prisoners, specifically a Huron and two Sauteurs. Vaudreuil further ordered the Mesquakie,
Kickapoos, and Mascouten "to bring some slaves next year to replace our allies because of their people who had been killed during the war."[86]

The governor recognized that declaring peace at Montreal meant very
little in the west where the political influence of Onontio had been so greatly

diminished. To correct this situation Vaudreuil sent St. Pierre "with some soldiers, to go establish a post at la pointe de Chag8amigon on Lake Superior." In spite of the peace conference, he reported, "the savages of the nation of the Suateurs, who live there and those of the same nation who are at Kioueouenau [Keeweenaw] loudly threatened the nations of the bay to go and avenge the deaths of their chiefs killed in the Fox war."[87] Vaudreuil also sent a trader named La Noue to reoccupy Du Lhut's old post at Kaministiquia, northwest of Lake Superior. This man reported, "the savages of his post were greatly pleased with his establishment and promised to attract all of those who were accustomed to go make their trade at Hudson's Bay." Like Du Lhut, he would try to forge a peace with the people of this region and the Dakota. Through one of the soldiers at La Pointe, La Noue had written "to a chief of the Sioux nation that he hoped to succeed in making peace between this nation and that of the Christinaux."[88]

The efforts of Vaudreuil, Louvigny, and La Noue proved to be too little too late. Events rapidly overtook their efforts to reestablish French influence in the western interior. The Western Cree, Assiniboine, and Anishinaabe doodemag undoubtedly welcomed the return of the French to their old post at Kaministiquia. The Native peoples of this region, however, had never traded exclusively with the French. During the era of Du Lhut—a time when the power of New France reached its zenith in the west—these peoples still traded at Hudson's Bay. In part, this was a practical consideration, as the French could not adequately supply the numerous peoples of this region, the undiscovered infinity of nations, with a sufficient quantity of goods to keep them from making the trip to the coast. This continued to be the case.

For the peoples of the western interior, however, dividing their trade between the French and the English was also a strategic decision. Shifting their trade in this way provided a means of preserving their social connections throughout the inland trade. By extension, this practice helped them to maintain their economic and political autonomy. In 1719, the same year that they welcomed La Noue at Kaministiquia, the Western Cree and Assiniboine also traded at York factory. They informed the post commander that "the French wood runners are very brief up in the lakes and that they invited some mountain Indians to come and trade with them." But they also complained that the Indians who accompanied them from Lake Superior, most likely the people of Shagwaamikong, had attacked their people. They also indicated that they continued to fight with their enemies in the west—a reference to their ongoing conflict with the allied Dakota, Yankton/Yanktonai, and Lakota peoples.[89]

The following year the Dakota attacked the inland peoples, identified as the Western Cree and Monsoni, living inland from the French post at Kaministiquia. In doing so they ignored French enquiries about making peace. Seventeen people were killed in this raid. Surprisingly, La Noue reported, "This has strongly alarmed the Sauteurs of Chagouamigon among who they began to sing for war against the Sioux." The people of Shagwaamikong apparently interpreted the attack as a threat against the French, and in turn, as a threat to their position within the inland trade. The French sent officers to the Dakota country and asked them "to make satisfaction to the nation that had been attacked." They returned to Kaministiquia with the news that the Dakota had rejected the requests of their council. They were also convinced that the Mesquakie had been working to turn the Dakota against the French. The inland peoples were divided about how to respond. One village, La Noue reported, "had taken the resolution to continue the war." But "the other villages," he wrote, "wanted to have no part in this war and they wished for peace."[90]

This conflict between the Dakota and their allies and the Western Cree and the Assiniboine had long been a consistent pattern within the inland trade. The addition of so many new points of connection to the trade goods of the Atlantic World, however, began to set in motion another reconfiguration of the alliance networks that made this trade possible. In a report about the new western posts Vaudreuil wrote: "one of the things that contributes the most to the arrogance of the Sioux and the Fox is the ease they have of always being furnished with powder, shot, arms, and other merchandise by the means of the coureurs de bois of Canada who removed themselves into the government of Louisiana, they make the trade and remount the Mississippi until the Sioux country with licenses that the officers who command all of the Illinois country give them."[91]

Vaudreuil also claimed that the Louisiana coureurs de bois traded at Green Bay, and with the people of Shagwaamikong "by a river which connects the Mississippi to Lake Superior," and even among the Cree and Assiniboine.[92] This trade, he concluded, along with the English posts at Hudson's Bay, constituted a threat to the colony of Canada. Vaudreuil demanded a new post at Timiigamiing to interdict the trade going to Hudson's Bay. And he demanded that the Louisiana traders stop "going out of the boundaries that have been given to this government following the letters patent of the King."[93] The governor, however, was asking for the impossible. The boundaries that the agents of empire imagined for New France in the west had never really been functional. More to the point, the soldiers and licensed traders sent west to make up for Onontio's absence from the upper country found that they had been absent too long to assert any real political influence. They returned only to witness a further evolution of the Native New World. The middle ground created by their old alliance was no longer in existence.

Expansion of French and English trade into the west, largely detached from the institutions of empire, allowed the indigenous social formations of Anishinaabewaki and the western interior to change the ways that they related to one another. The patterns that had defined the inland trade were being reconfigured on a large scale. A significant recovery of population among the Native peoples of the Great Lakes added to this dynamic. The French noted this expansion, and they also began to understand the expansive nature of Anishinaabewaki as a social space. A report about the restored French posts in the mid-1720s noted, "The Saulteaux are one of the most considerable and most numerous nations of this country." Where past records described these people as residents of Sault Sainte Marie, and suggested those found in the west were refugees, by the middle of the eighteenth century the French understood the Sauteurs as Gichigamming Anishinaabeg, that is, as the people of Lake Superior. This report, of course, did not rely on Anishinaabemowin to reframe Sauteur identity. It did, however, describe the "Sauteurs" as residents of villages at Toronto, Michilimackinac, Michipicton, Lake Nipigon, and Kaministiquia, as well as Sault Sainte Marie, Keeweenaw, and Shagwaamikong. And it noted that "the Outouais and the Saulteaux, the language of these people is perhaps regarded as the mother language, it is the same from the upper country until the Sioux."[94] The Sauteurs of Anishinaabewaki were an expansive political power who dominated both the northern and southern shores of Lake Superior as well as the territory inland from this body of water. Perhaps more important, the Gichigamiing Anishinaabeg were increasingly disconnected from the French Empire and oriented toward life in the western interior.

In an attempt to gain control over the fur trade in the west, and recover some measure of power within their alliance, the French tried to reestablish a formal presence in the interior beyond the Mississippi. They quickly found themselves entangled in a series of conflicts with and between Native peoples scattered across this region. For the most part the French would try to mediate and resolve these disputes. Time after time they would, nevertheless, find themselves pulled into the violent politics of the Native New World. Political turmoil at Green Bay and in the Illinois country made the traffic of goods and traders into the west up the Mississippi River a hazardous business. Once again the Mesquakie emerged at the center of this violence. Initially, they managed to forge an alliance with the Dakota, who joined them in raids against the Illinois. Their attempts to block or otherwise control trade into the Dakota country, however, caused this new alliance to quickly fall apart. In 1728 French soldiers and traders built Fort Beauharnois at Lake Pepin on the Mississippi River. This was a reestablishment of Nicolas Perrot's post among the Dakota, and it effectively crushed the nascent alliance between the Dakota and Mesquakie. At the same time, French troops were able to rally their allies in a series of conflicts with the Mesquakie that broke the militant resistance of all the Green Bay villagers to French trade in the Dakota country. This renewed warfare also pushed the Mesquakie politically to the margins of the alliance.[95]

The Dakota appeared happy to see the French rebuild a post in their country, but they did not like the fact that the French brought conflicts from the upper country into their territory. Apparently, the Dakota had migrated onto the prairies west of Lake Pepin as more and more oyate began to adapt to a plains lifeway. The governor reported that with the establishment of the French post "they had been obliged to come back to their old village," and he noted their wariness at being "surrounded" by the peoples of the French alliance at this location. The Dakota occupied this village, however, to secure steady access to the French trade goods that would make them the most dominant military power on the plains and prairies west of the Mississippi. Even though they returned to their old village site in the east, they maintained contact with their allies in the west. The Iowa, as well as "a band of around sixty men . . . who were from the nations that are called the Sioux of the Prairies," visited the village of ninety-five Dakota cabins camped around Fort Beauharnois. The tiyospaye of this village dispersed into the west to hunt for the winter, but remained in periodic contact with the French post. The Jesuit father attached to the fort noted "that they were not very far away and there were always some to be seen during the winter."[96]

Just as they maintained contact with their allies in the west, the Dakota also remained in contact with their enemies. The violent conflict with peoples from Green Bay and the lower Mississippi was largely contained, but the Dakota and their allies remained at war with the Western Cree, Assiniboine, and Monsoni bands to their north and northwest. These doodemag, in addition to trading at Hudson's Bay, actively traded with the French. The

French had reestablished Du Lhut's old posts northwest of Lake Superior at Kaministiquia, Lake Nipigon, and Rainy Lake. As in the past this conflict periodically enveloped the Gichigamiing Anishinaabeg. Dakota raids into the north shortly after these posts were reoccupied had disturbed the peoples of Shagwaamikong. In spite of this tension, however, they maintained close enough ties to the Dakota that when the Cree raided the Dakota in the upper Mississippi valley in 1728, they killed seventy Anishinaabeg.[97]

The following year the French would become involved in this cycle of violence. Their involvement would quickly spiral out of control, leaving the French powerless to defend their posts throughout the west, collapsing the Dakota-Shagwaamikong alliance, and witnessing the birth of a vast new alliance of Anishinaabeg, Nehiyawa-athinuwick, and Nakoda peoples that would rival the Dakota-Lakota allies for dominance of the west. French posts west of the Mississippi would be abandoned or destroyed in this fighting, and the soldiers and traders of New France would retreat from the west to their old posts in the major villages of Anishinaabewaki. Garrisoned with a small number of traders and soldiers these posts would serve as the caretakers of the illusion of a western empire for New France. The posts themselves would lose political and military significance, but the villages surrounding them would become the engines for a revitalized western trade dominated by Métis and European traders working for a number of international trading enterprises with headquarters in Montreal, New York, and London. This trade would empower the Anishinaabeg to turn away from the world of empire, and focus instead on their place and power in the Native New World.

The events that would set off this massive and radical transformation would begin with the sadly quixotic attempt by the French, once again, to find the Northwest Passage. In spite of a growing knowledge about the geography of the western interior of North America that suggested this water route was unlikely to exist, the governor of New France sent a man into the country northwest of Lake Superior to search for it. Charged with the task of finding the way to the Western Sea (the Pacific Ocean), Pierre Gaultier de Varrennes le Sieur de La Verendrye pushed west from the Grand Portage into the region west of Lake Winnipeg, and ultimately traveled out onto the northern plains on a visit to the Mandan. He built five posts, Fort Bourbon and Fort Dauphin on the west side of Lake Winnipeg, Fort Maurepas on the southeast shore of the lake, Fort Saint Charles on the western shore of Lake of the Woods, and Fort Saint Pierre on Rainy Lake. In 1729 he wrote that "this entire region is occupied by the Cris," with the country south of the lakes being occupied by the Assiniboine and Lake of the Woods region by the Ojibwe-speaking Monsoni.

Immediately following his arrival La Verendrye stopped the Cree, Assiniboine, and Monsoni peoples from launching a raid against the Dakota and the people of Shagwaamikong. He also accepted a wampum belt from the Cree who told him "that now they make one and the same body with us."[98] La Verendrye also claimed that peoples who lived in the territory of the French posts asked to be counted among the children of Onontio. And while they most likely used the linguistic conventions of the French alliance, they clearly interpreted this new relationship as the sort of political cooperation characteristic to the inland trade. For example, all of these new allies continued to openly trade with the English. In part this was because the French could not bring enough supplies to these remote posts to satisfy the demand for goods. But this was also a matter of maintaining ties with the peoples at the Hudson's Bay coast, including the English.[99]

During the first four years at these posts, however, La Verendrye managed for the most part to bring an end to the violence that connected his new allies to the Dakota and Shagwaamikong Anishinaabeg. In the early summer of 1733 he halted a large Cree-Monsoni war party only to learn that a party of Dakota and Shagwaamikong raiders was preparing to attack the Cree and Monsoni villages. After a brief skirmish both parties agreed to end the fighting on the basis of their mutual alliance with the French. La Verendrye believed "that the Sioux and the Saulteurs have from time immemorial waged war against the Monsoni, the Cristinuax . . . and the Assiniboine."[100] The Sioux-Sauteur alliance, of course, was approximately fifty years old, and this relationship really included only the people of Shagwaamikong, not all Gichigamiing Anishinaabeg. Equally important was the fact that there had long been close ties among Cree and Anishinaabe doodemag in the northwest, and with many of the people the French called Sauteurs at villages like Sault Sainte Marie, Michilimackinac, Keweenaw, Michipicton, and Timiigamiing, and even at Shagwaamikong. The following year, in 1734, La Verendrye learned that the Cree and Monsoni planned to raid the Dakota, but would refrain from attacking the people of Shagwaamikong with the apparent goal of splitting up this alliance and alienating the Dakota from the French.[101]

The Cree and Monsoni together sent La Verendrye a wampum belt and asked him to come to them for a war council. This was not the behavior of obedient children seeking their father's pity and protection. La Verendrye answered the call, and he came bearing lavish gifts. At council he presented the war leaders with wampum and said, "peace is proposed, yet you seek to trouble the land. You want to strike the Saulteur and the Sioux? You need not leave the fort, here they are." He then pointed to the French traders, implying that a strike against either the Dakota or Shagwaamikong Anishinaabeeg was the equivalent of an attack on his people. Then he suggested that the Cree and Monsoni raid the Mandan if they must go to war. The war chiefs accepted La Verendrye's gifts and promised to return in the spring.[102] Like Nicolas Perrot, La Verendrye offered to sacrifice his own body to spare the children of Onontio, and the alliance itself. But this was a different era, and these were a different kind of children. They would return only to demand that Onontio prove his willingness to sacrifice his body if he wanted to preserve his alliance with them.

The following spring four hundred Monsoni warriors arrived at La Veredrye's post among the Cree, armed and ready for battle. They called a war council and presented the French commander with beaver robes and wampum. The leader of this war party rose, and after asking his father to have pity, said: "Here we are at your post, at whom are we to strike?" Without waiting for a response, and gesturing toward his warriors, he said, "I am chief, it is true, but I am not always the master of their will." Then the war chief demanded that La Verendrye's oldest son join the war party. "If you refuse," he said, "I can not answer for where the blow may fall." He finished by asserting that many among them remained bitter at heart because of past conflict with "the Sioux" and "the Saulteurs."[103] La Verendrye panicked. "I was agitated," he wrote, "and cruelly tormented by conflicting thoughts." In his journal he wrote: "On the one hand, how was I to trust my eldest son to barbarians whom I did not know, and whose name I scarcely even knew, to go and fight against other barbarians of whose name and whose strength I knew nothing? Who could tell whether my son would ever return?"[104]

This was a startling confession for the man who claimed to be the voice of Onontio. It was a candid admission that the French did not really know the names of many of the Native peoples they claimed as the subjects of their empire. Who were these people that asked for the life of his son? What did it mean to be Cree or Monsoni? In a memoir detailing his discoveries La Verendrye noted that the people he called the Monsoni spoke "Sauteux," as did the people who lived on the eastern shore of Lake of the Woods that the French called Cree. The people who lived on the northwest side of the lake, also called Cree by the French, spoke "a corrupted Cristinaux," as did the people who lived on the Winnipeg River, although the latter, according to

La Verendrye, spoke the language of the Sauteurs properly. He identified the people who lived on the western shores of Lake Winnipeg as speakers of "true Cristinaux," as he did the people living north of the Assiniboine River, whom the French called the Bois Fort or Strong Woods Cristinaux. Was there a Cree nation? Was there a Sauteur nation? And if these nations existed, how were their national identities and boundaries defined? (see Figure 6).[105]

Who was Cree, who was Monsoni, and who was Sauteur, increasingly identified in the Lake of the Woods region as Sauteux, the plural form of the French word? What did it mean to claim a Cree or a Sauteux identity, and how did this explain the conflict between the people the French identified as Cree, Gens des Terres, Sauteurs/Sauteux, and Sioux? La Verendrye did not know the answers to these questions, and yet he was powerless to do anything other than obey the request of the warriors at his post if he wanted to remain their allies. This was the same choice that Daniel Du Lhut had asked Achiganaga to make in 1684. Sacrifice your son if you want to remain a part of this alliance. At this moment the French had come full circle. If the French hoped to have any influence or power in the west they would have to enter into the politics of the Native New World. In truth, Du Lhut had risked his own life when he demanded that the Anishinaabeg join him on the middle ground, and he had a partner in the Amikwa ogimaa Oumamens. In a complete reversal of political fortune, La Verendrye was asked to gamble the life of his son by entering into a world of Native politics and warfare where the French had very little standing, and even less understanding.

La Verendrye's son would join the raiding party, and the consequences for him and his father would be tragic. The consequences of this raid would also prove tragic for New France as well. La Verendrye armed the war party, and reminded them not to attack "the Saulteurs and the Sioux." He told them, "I entrust to you my eldest son who is my dearest possession, consider him as another myself."[106] The party of over six hundred Cree and Monsoni warriors, as they had intended from the beginning, left their village with Jean-Baptiste La Verendrye and raided the Dakota. They counted on the fact that the Dakota would consider La Verendrye's son to be another version of himself, implicating the French in their attack. They succeeded. The following year a party of one hundred Dakota and Lakota warriors raided the Lake of the Woods country in retaliation. They came in search of Jean-Baptiste, and they found him with twenty-one Frenchmen, one a priest camped on an island in Lake of the Woods. The Frenchmen were all killed, and their heads were cut off and wrapped in beaver skins. The body of Jean-Baptiste outfitted entirely in Native regalia was mutilated. The Dakota hacked his body with postmortem knife wounds, and a drove a stake into his side.[107] One account suggests that there were Shagwaamikong Anishinaabeg warriors with this party who did not participate in the massacre.

The Cree, Monsoni, and Assiniboine bands from the country west of Lake Winnipeg to Kaministiquia held war councils when they learned of Jean-Baptiste's death. These bands all sent emissaries to their French father, placing their warriors at his disposal to avenge the death of his son. In the fall of 1736, they gathered for a region-wide council at Lake of the Woods. A man speaking for all the Nehiyawa-athinuwick bands addressed La Verendrye: "My father, we have already sent you word many times that we were sick at heart." As he spoke all of the people at the council wept profusely. "We are here now to invite you to lead us," and he declared, "if you can not walk we will carry you."[108] He concluded by reporting that they had assembled eight hundred warriors to attack the Dakota. The following day La Verendrye made his reply. He said "We must not avenge French blood by shedding it anew." La Verendrye expressed his sadness and his desire to lead them in battle, "but I am held back," he concluded.[109] Then he asked them to wait until he could ascertain the wishes of the French governor. This incident revealed how much the world of Native diplomacy had changed from the time of Du Lhut—Native allies called in French fathers to sacrifice their sons to preserve their relationship.

As La Verendrye made his way to Montreal, he must have felt shock and horror that he had lost his son for the sake of an alliance with an infinity of nations whose real names he did not know. Like Achiganaga he had overestimated his ability to control his allies and paid a dear price. Governor Beaharnois instructed La Verendrye that he needed to prevent retaliatory raiding against the Dakota and work to restore peace. In a letter to the minister the governor explained that "the connections he has established with the nations of the continent there can only procure great advantages for the colony especially if it becomes evident . . . that they are truly attached to the French." The French would learn that these people were truly attached to the French so long as the French served their political interests.[110] In this same report the governor also wrote that he had instructed Sieur de la Ronde at the La Pointe post "to calm down a war which is clearly beginning to be kindled between the Saulteur of his post and the Sioux."[111]

When La Verendrye returned to the west he found that significant political changes were under way. When he arrived at Kaministiquia he learned that all the warriors from this region were raiding in the Dakota country. The French identified the people at this post as Sauteurs, and the people came from the same doodemag as the people of Shagwaamikong. La Verendrye chastised them for going to war. At Rainy Lake he learned that all of the Cree and Monsoni ogimaag waited for him at the Lake of the Woods post. They were stunned at the decision to attempt a reconciliation with the Dakota. A Cree war leader that La Verendrye called La Colle said they had not stopped weeping for his son and the other Frenchmen, and he lamented, "the lake was still red with their blood." He declared their intention to be obedient children, but concluded that he was "still hoping that you would later take vengeance."[112]

La Verendrye carried this message to every French post between Lake Superior and the Assiniboine River. At Lake Winnipeg he found two Cree war chiefs among the people camped by the French post. He sent for these men in order to relay the call for peace, and to tell them that he had been informed at Michilimackinac that they traded with the English at Hudson's Bay every year. One of these men replied that he had not been to the bay in years. He also reassured La Verendrye that "the Englishman is quiet and does not talk of the Frenchman." Then he said, quite candidly, "As long as the Frenchman remains in our lands we promise you not to go elsewhere." Both men knew that traders from all of the bands in this region routinely went to the English.[113] The war chief allowed La Verendrye to save face: I do not go to the English anymore, he said. But he was also direct: bring us goods and we will have no need to go elsewhere. Do not worry about the English because they do not want any trouble. As for peace with the Dakota, the war leaders said, "We will keep quiet as he desires, and let the Sioux do the same." Then one of these men casually informed La Verendrye that "I have already been at war once to avenge him." He killed ten cabins of Dakota, an entire tiyospaye.[114] Both he and La Verendrye must have known that these deaths would not go unanswered.

Everywhere La Verendrye went the people told him they would obey their father. Everywhere he went he heard that there had already been raiding. He also learned that the people of Shagwaamikong were now openly conspiring with the Cree and Anishinaabe peoples of his post to wage a war against the Dakota. And he learned that the French had abandoned their fort in the Dakota country as this conflict spread like a wildfire throughout the western interior. The French had become expendable pawns in a Native power struggle for dominance of the western interior of North America, and La Verendrye had given up his son as part of a power struggle he could not fully understand, and that had been in the making for nearly a century.

The Dakota did seek an answer for the lives taken by the Cree and Anishinaabe raiders from the Lake of the Woods and Lake Winnipeg region. They turned first against the French, and then against their longtime allies from Shagwaamikong. Both it seems were implicated in the raiding into the upper Mississippi valley following the massacre at Lake of the Woods. The raiders from their north entered the Dakota country armed with French weapons. Even without the politically disastrous decision to send Jean-Baptiste de La Verendrye raiding with a prominent Cree war leader, supplying weapons to enemies was a serious breach of the protocols of alliance. This did not escape the attention of the Dakota, who found themselves the targets of well-armed raiders from their north who had skillfully drawn the French into their long-standing conflict.

In the months before La Verendrye made his way west carrying a message of peace, the Dakota delivered a different kind of message to the French at Fort Beauharnois. In May 1736, fifty-four warriors gathered near the fort "and danced the scalp dance, for four days, without saying which nation they had killed."[115] The post commander later learned from the Ho-Chunk living near his fort that the Dakota had killed and scalped two French traders in the Illinois country. These deaths went unaccounted for due to the political vulnerability of the French. In August two canoes from Shagwaamikong arrived at the fort with the news of the massacre at Lake of the Woods. A month later a party of ten Dakota men presented food, dressed deerskins, and two slaves, young girls, as gifts to the post commander, the Sieur de St. Pierre. They claimed they had nothing to do with the deaths of the French at the other western posts, and they said that they wanted the French to maintain their post among the Dakota. Their gifts were a gesture signaling the desire for the French to remain in their country.

The Dakota, however, seemed to be divided over the value of having a French post in their country, just as they had been during the time of Nicolas Perrot. They valued French goods, but they had access to European merchandise from the many coureurs de bois and voyageurs circulating throughout the west. In addition, the post brought the trespassing children of Onontio onto their territory and hunting grounds. Many warriors also seemed to have only disdain for French officers who insisted they were fathers to the Dakota. The day after one itancan asked the French to stay, another arrived with a more hostile message that reflected this division among the oyate. Accompanied by three warriors this man entered the fort wearing a silver coin suspended from his ear like a pendant. St. Pierre recognized the coin as a war trophy taken from the massacred French traders. He asked the warrior where he found the French coin. "He said nothing to me and began to laugh," he said. St. Pierre reported that he ripped off the medallion, taking the man's ear along with it.[116]

Tensions continued to escalate following this incident, but the real problem the French faced was the mounting conflict between the Dakota and the coalition of Anishinaabe, Cree, and Assiniboine peoples to their north. The Anishinaabeg of Shagwaamikong began to fight alongside their relatives from these western doodemag, and this created significant instability in the region between Lake Superior and the upper Mississippi valley. In the winter of 1737 the Dakota set fire to the Ho-Chunk settlement near the French fort, sending a message that they would no longer tolerate intruders onto their territory. They also demanded credit from the post traders, and threatened to pillage French stores when the post commander turned them down. Toward the end of winter a Dakota war party found an extended family from Shagwaamikong alone in their hunting territory inland from the lakeshore. They killed and scalped everyone in the lodge. The warriors of Shagwaamikong raised a war party and came to Fort Beauharnois looking for revenge against the Dakota. For the next few days the Dakota fought the Anishinaabeg and Ho-Chunk in a series of skirmishes in the immediate vicinity of the fort. After three days of fighting the Dakota warriors slipped away into the west, and the Anishinaabeg and Ho-Chunk withdrew from the vicinity of fort. St. Pierre held a council with the resident missionary and his second in command. "They told him," St. Pierre reported to the governor, "that there was nothing else to be done but to abandon the post, burn the fort, and escape, because they ran the risk of being any day massacred by the Sioux."[117] The French burned their fort to the ground and left the Dakota country, never to return.

The Dakota drove the French from their country, a territory New France had claimed as part of their empire since the late 1600s. This was the truth of the French Empire in the west: to the extent that it existed at all, it was built on political relationships with powerful and autonomous Native social formations. Perhaps a more accurate assessment of the reasons for the French withdrawal would be that the violence and political instability surrounding the breakup of the Anishinaabe-Dakota alliance had destroyed the conditions that supported the illusion of empire in this region. The French worked to restore the relationship between these former allies, but they would fail time and time again because the politics that had created their alliance had changed.

The unraveling of this political relationship proceeded from both sides of the alliance. The Dakota oyate remained in the east in the region around Mde Wakan and Lake Pepin, but there were fewer and fewer numbers each year. They continued to be divided about restoring their relationship with their longtime allies the Anishinaabeg and with the French. In 1738 a Dakota, Yankton, or Lakota war party from the plains killed thirty people from Shagwaamikong. The commandant at La Pointe, Sieur de La Ronde, wrote that Dakota "sent two Sauteur women that they had made prisoners to ask for peace." The French commander believed they wanted to repair the damage caused by their attacks during the previous year. Apparently, the Anishinaabeg signaled their rejection of this offer by attacking the Dakota. La Ronde reported "when I arrived at Chagouamigon I strongly blamed the Sauteux for having struck the Sioux of the lakes since it was the Sioux of the prairies who killed their chief and had more over killed their other relatives." The leaders of Shagwaamikong said this was true, but they asserted that they acted out of a desire to avenge the twenty-two Frenchmen killed at Lake of the Woods. The post commander concluded by asserting, "I have no doubt that I shall be able to restore peace."[118] The people of Shagwaamikong, however, told him otherwise. In their response to the attack, they signaled a realignment of Native power in the west. Just as the Dakota were increasingly joining their relations on the northern plains, the people of Shagwaamikong were rebuilding their alliance with their relations in the northwest interior.

The remaining French posts in the western interior actually facilitated this transformation. The posts under the command of La Verendrye provided the political infrastructure for the expansion of a new collective identity among Anishinaabe peoples. In 1742 the governor learned of planning for a coordinated attack against the Dakota that sketched the outline of this revitalized alliance. The Jesuit at Kaministikuia visited the French post at Grand Portage, where he found that the "Saultuers" of his post "came to hold council with a savage chief of that place who possesses much influence." It seems the Sauteurs of Shagwaamikong, under the pretext of a political reconciliation, would lure the Dakota into an ambush involving "the peoples of Nipigon, Kaministikwia, Tecoumamiouen [Rainy Lake], the Monsoni, Cree, and Assiniboine."[119] The French may have imagined that the preservation of these posts signified the expansion of their empire, but in truth they were allowed to operate in these western villages because it was politically expedient. These posts were the inland equivalent of the English posts at the Hudson's Bay coast.

After the collapse of Fort Beauharnois, the French posts in the western interior operated as part of the inland trade. These forts were decidedly not the outposts of empire in the same sense as the French garrisons at Detroit, Michilimackinac, Prairie du Chien, and St. Louis. They represented the next phase in the evolution of the inland trade when traders began to move inland to establish makeshift posts associated with the seasonal round of Native hunters. There was no pretense that the infinity of Nations in the northwest interior would ever be mobilized to fight for their French father against the British colonies. There was not even the notion that they might be utilized in the upper country to fight potential Native enemies like the Iroquois or the Mesquakie. When there was violence directed toward English traders at the bay, this was not a military assault, but rather the kind of fighting that the coureurs de bois engaged in in the early 1700s. In other words, the Anishinaabeg in the west engaged in violence not on behalf of any imperial power, but solely to secure an advantage for their doodem in the trading of goods and pelts. If anything, these French posts would serve to facilitate Anishinaabe expansion into the west as people from villages in the Lake Superior region began to make multiyear sojourns onto the prairie parkland, with many bands remaining on the plains permanently and adopting a bison-equestrian political economy.

Some of the peoples of Anishinaabewaki would be pulled southeast into the Ohio country along with the disaffected refugees and hunters from the villages of the old alliance. These people sought independence from the leadership of a now moribund middle ground. Following on the heels of these disaffected relatives some of the peoples of Anishinaabewaki would be sucked into the cauldron of the first world war, called the French and Indian War in North America. They would fight for their French father and bring him victory in a brief rebirth of the old alliance, until a petulant military command dismissed its Native forces, contemptuous of Indian fighting tactics. Without the military support of their Native children New France would fall. First Fort Duquesne would give way, revealing that French posts in the interior were nothing more than rotting empty structures without the support of the Native communities that surrounded them. The loss of Quebec and New France followed quickly. British American settlers, soon to become Americans, would stream into the backcountry, and make it once again a cauldron of violence. But they would not penetrate into the heart of Anishinaabewaki. They would settle instead in the more temperate territories in the hinterlands of this region—places that would become the Ohio, Kentucky, Indiana, and Illinois Territories.

This is a familiar story where America almost cannot stop itself from becoming America. Its population is too explosive, its economy too dynamic to be contained in the east. And yet until the middle of the nineteenth century, America, like New France, would be the caretaker of an illusion of empire in the upper Great Lakes. Anishinaabewaki would remain, socially and demographically, a Native space. This is the other story of a dynamic and expansive North American social formation—this one indigenous, a Native New World that emerged around the thinly garrisoned forts in the village centers of Anishinaabewaki. This was the social world that would greet Americans and Canadians when they moved into the northwest at the head of newly formed composite nation-states with newly forged North American national identities. This was the social world that the missionary William Boutwell would stumble upon while traveling west with Henry Schoolcraft. Boutwell was stunned not to find a wilderness populated by savages waiting to be changed by civilization. Instead he discovered the Native New World, a fully formed social world that had been changing and adapting since the Eastern Hemisphere first collided with the Western Hemisphere at the end of the fifteenth century.

PART IV

Sovereignty

The Making of North America's New Nations

IN THE FIRST half of the nineteenth century America was engaged in a national conversation about the place of Indian peoples in the republic. Did they belong in the United States? Could they leave the wilderness behind and make the transition to civil society? James Fenimore Cooper answered these questions in his novel of 1826 *The Last of the Mohicans*. His response took literary form in a showdown between the good and bad Indians who inhabited America's backcountry during the time of the Seven Years' War. Like Henry Wadsworth Longfellow's *The Song of Hiawatha*, Cooper's fictional Indian landscape was a literary creation, and a product of the mythology of Europe's discovery and conquest of North America. The novel answers the question about the fate of Native peoples in the New World through a cascading series of events that place the future of Anglo-America in the hands of his Indian protagonists. Their struggle, in effect, becomes a metaphor about the fate of the new American nation.

The birth of the United States is the narrative end point of Cooper's story, which unfolds as a story about the Seven Years' War, and the triumph of Anglo-America. In many ways, America's historical memory of this conflict mirrored the national debate about the place of Indians in civilized society. The Seven Years' War concluded with the British claim of conquest over the majority of North America east of the Mississippi. This epic struggle, however, was identified by a different name among the Anglo-American colonists on their way to becoming citizens of the New World's first republic. They called it the French and Indian War. As the name suggests, this conflict was remembered as a battle against a French Empire that willingly encouraged its savage allies to terrorize Anglo-American settlements in the backcountry.

The Seven Years' War provided the ideal setting for a novel about the meaning of the American experiment, and what it took to make a new civilization in the wilderness of North America. This idea that the founding of a New World on this continent involved a clash between civilization and savagery is fundamental to the ideology of European discovery. It survives to this day in arguments about the significance of the frontier in American history. And it explains the enduring popularity of works like *The Song of Hiawatha* and *The Last of the Mohicans*. Cooper's novel, like Longfellow's poem, suffered a great deal of criticism, even mockery. And yet both works made their authors famous and wealthy.

The Last of the Mohicans, even more than Longfellow's poem, stands out as a reflection about the founding and meaning of America in the popular imagination. Cooper's book has never been out of print since its publication in the early nineteenth century. It has been made into a movie multiple times, in multiple countries and languages; it is an enduring signifier of the twinned meanings and attributes associated with American Indians and the United States of America. Perhaps most important, Cooper was explicitly interested in writing a distinctly American national narrative. Cooper's vision of America was essentially conservative, a privileging of the white elite in the new society created by the republic. This vision, however, was also crossed by a streak of romantic primitivism that allowed the author to identify with the noble savages who sometimes appeared in stories about the discovery of the New World. Although Cooper's text is fiction, it is important to understand that his work fits within an existing tradition of polemical writing about Indian wars and the founding and development of Anglo America.[1]

The Last of the Mohicans is not only a tale about the creation of a new civilization in North America, it is also a story about the battle between the good and bad Indians who inhabited the continent. The idea that there were two kinds of Indians—good and bad, noble and bloodthirsty—was a common element in narratives of discovery. Cooper's plot, however, also centers on the ways in which discovery and conquest had created a shared history for Natives and newcomers in the New World. *Last of the Mohicans* takes up this narrative thread through the story of Alice and Cora Munro and their escort, Major Duncan Heyward. Indians attack the trio on their way to the battle of Fort William Henry in the Lake George region of New York. They are then rescued by the Mohicans Uncas and his father, Chingachgook, but abducted yet again by the leader of their Indian attackers. The novel essentially unfolds as a variation of the captivity narrative, the earliest and most popular literary genre in colonial America. True to form, the narrative revolves around a series of journeys with the sisters either fleeing from their Indian tormentors, or undergoing a forced march at the hands of Indian captors.[2] During the course of these journeys the fate of Cora and Alice Munro becomes intertwined with that of Uncas and Chingachgook, just as in Cooper's imagination the fate and future of Anglo-America became intertwined with that of Native America.[3]

In this fashion, the journeys undertaken by the novel's heroes and heroines foreshadow the fate of all of the peoples of colonial America. En route to the fort on the eve of the battle between the British and French forces, the Munros learn too late that their Indian scout Magua has betrayed them. Magua, who lost his family at the hands of their father, Colonel George

Munro, is the epitome of the bloodthirsty savage. He finds glory in violence, revenge, death, and self-destruction. Magua is Cooper's bad Indian, the narrative counterpoint to Uncas and Chingachgook. It is the good Indians, the Mohicans, and their companion Hawkeye, who disrupt Magua's attempt at revenge. The character Hawkeye is another uniquely American archetype—the white Indian. This literary figure, like the real life persons George Rogers Clark, Daniel Boone, and Davy Crockett, appropriated some Native customs and practices in order to survive on the frontier. In American popular culture, the figure of the white Indian takes on elements of both the bloodthirsty savage and the noble savage. This adaptation was seen as a necessary response to life on the frontier, which during the Seven Years' War, and at the time Cooper wrote his novel, was seen as a dangerously Indian place.

The people who adopted the persona of a white Indian often styled themselves as Indian fighters. They were unofficial agents of the republic clearing the continent of Indian opposition to American settlement—precisely what was at stake in *The Last of the Mohicans*. The novel functions as a narrative microcosm of the epic struggle for the settlement and possession of North America that asks the reader to contemplate who survives, who will inherit the continent, and most important who should assume the mantle and legacy of Cooper's good Indians—"the unchanged race" of noble savages who imparted their character onto the American landscape.[4]

Like Longfellow, Cooper imagined a time when Indians would vanish from the continent, leaving behind only their legacy. Even more than the poet, however, Cooper makes it clear that this legacy had two faces—one noble, the other vicious and bloodthirsty. Both kinds of savage were destined to vanish, but in appropriating the legacy of the noble savage Americans could stake their claim to a cultural heritage rooted in North America's beautiful and untamed wilderness. Equally important, in killing off Magua's savage kind of Indian, Americans could claim the continent by right of conquest. In making this connection to Native America, Cooper's novel anticipated Longfellow's epic poem about the vanishing of Indian peoples and triumph of the people of morning and light.[5] And yet he offered a strikingly different interpretation of the fantasy of the vanishing Indian than the romantic poet.

In both texts the Indian protagonists see the end of their time in North America, and they embrace their fate. But where Hiawatha retreats into the west to preserve the memory of his nobility, Uncas and Chingachgook stand and fight. The Mohicans refuse to accept a quiet death in the west. Uncas fights and dies honorably against Native savagery, proving the fitness of his lineage as one of the Native founders of America. Equally important, in granting his protagonist an honorable death, Cooper is able to draw upon an established American literary tradition that Phil Deloria has called "the Indian death speech." *The Last of the Mohicans* was published in 1826, and by this time there was already a "last of . . ." genre in American letters. One of the first and most famous of these death speeches was attributed to a Cayuga chief, identified as Logan by Anglo-Americans. After a frontier war that saw his family killed, Logan supposedly gave a speech lamenting his fate as the last of his race: "There is not a drop of my blood in the veins of any living creature. Who is there to mourn for Logan?—Not one."[6] While Logan was a real person, the speech attributed to him was an American literary creation recycled in various forms of cultural production during the eighteenth and nineteenth centuries. In this same tradition, Longfellow's Hiawatha vanishes quite literally, fading from sight and history as he paddles into the sunset. Cooper's Uncas is killed, a more permanent kind of vanishing, and one from which it is impossible to return. Both vanishing acts, like Logan's speech, give voice to the fantasy that there will come a time when all the Indian peoples disappear from the face of the earth, their bloodlines extinguished, their spiritual and political legacy up for grabs.

The figure of the vanishing Indian in both Cooper and Longfellow's work gave expression to an ideology that justified American expansion into Indian country. This was an ideology, Deloria argues, "which proclaimed it foreordained that less advanced societies should disappear in the presence of those more advanced."[7] Longfellow tells us rather vaguely that the future belongs to the people of "morning and light." Cooper, in contrast, gives us a more intricate analysis of what the future holds for all the peoples of North America. His analysis is shaped both by the political purposes of his moment (Indian removal), and by his inability to comprehend the Native New World that continued to exist in the western interior claimed by the United States. Instead, Cooper's novel offered his reader a New World history that reflected the fantasy of European discovery and conquest as a way of explaining the triumph of Anglo-America. In *The Last of the Mohicans* Cooper offers his reader a tale about the time of Native America, a vision of the end of this era, and a glimpse of the beginning of a new one—the time when North America's new nation would stake its claim to the continent.

Cooper's narrative asks and answers a series of questions about the meaning and responsibilities of settler colonialism in North America. What does it mean to be a New World power? By what right have Anglo-Americans come to see themselves, their imagined community, as the legitimate occupants of North American territory? How are settler societies to justify, or not, the seemingly inherent violence of the colonial experience? What does it mean to be a New World nation, and what does this new kind of nation signify for indigenous people?

America's French and Indian War provides a perfect framework to ask and answer these questions. At the conclusion of this conflict the British found themselves with claims over (if not possession of) the greater part of the continent of North America. Struggling to come to grips with the political implications of these claims British North America faced a rebellion, and suffered the loss of thirteen colonies. These former colonies declared themselves to be part of a new social formation, an American nation-state, a republic that by its very nature mobilized political power and structured social relations in a new way. The United States would be a new kind of settler colony, one that would disavow its colonial roots, and declare itself to be the continent's first indigenous republic.

This new social formation would mythologize its own creation as the transformation of the North American wilderness into an Anglo-American civil society. Cooper's *The Last of the Mohicans* is part of that mythology, as is Longfellow's *Hiawatha*. Cooper wrote his novel at a time when the United States faced the same questions the British Empire had faced in 1763. With the success of the Revolution, Americans claimed possession of an immense western territory populated almost exclusively by Indian peoples. Were they part of the American nation? What would be the basis for the relationship between Native peoples and American citizens? Native peoples in the Great Lakes had not, in fact, been conquered and dispossessed. What did this say about the nature of American political sovereignty in the west? Cooper's story is a meditation on the Native origins of the New World. It was also a meditation on the meaning of that origin for the peoples of the new republic. With this novel, Cooper suggests that for the American republic to fulfill its promise, its destiny, the old New World of empires and Indians had to come to an end.

CHAPTER 7

The Counterfactual History
of Indian Assimilation

In the early years of the republic, American political figures saw themselves as the creators of a new New World. This would be the era of republican nations. There was no place in this new and reimagined America for retrograde social formations, whether they be monarchial empires or Indian tribes. Within three decades of the American Revolution the political leadership of the republic openly called for the expulsion of Native peoples, and the extinction of Native title, on lands claimed by the United States east of the Mississippi River. The call for removal signaled the direction of American ambitions—they lay in the west, in Indian country. President James Monroe, in his second annual address to Congress in 1818, said, "Experience has clearly demonstrated that independent Savage communities cannot long exist within the limits of a civilized population. The progress of the latter has almost invariably terminated the extinction of the former. . . . To civilize them, and even to prevent their extinction, it seems to be indispensable that their independence as communities should cease, and that the control of the United States over them should be complete and undisputed."[1]

The capacity for national expansion was embedded in the core ideals of the American republic. Republican government called for a transformation at a societal level—a reconfiguration of social relations that transferred political power to the people. In this sense, it was a fulfillment of the politics of the Glorious Revolution in England that transferred the ultimate authority of government—sovereignty—from the monarch to Parliament. The founders of the United States believed that this transformation would become fully realized in North America. Political leaders like President James Madison and his mentor President Thomas Jefferson believed this new system of government required territorial expansion. These men also believed that this expansion would necessarily bring an end to the independent political self-determination of Indian peoples.

For the British Empire, the emergence of a new American nation posed a direct threat not only to Native peoples but also to their remaining colonies in North America. The young republic to the south of Canada represented a new and rather unsavory kind of civilization –a bastardized nation born of British culture and political tradition mixed with the homespun culture and political lawlessness of the American backcountry. In choosing inde- pendence over loyalty, the rebellious citizens of the United States gave in to their baser and more selfish impulses. Nowhere was this more evident than in the west, in Indian country, and on the hotly contested boundary between the two Anglo-American settlements. Here the ruthless frontier rabble of the United States fought viciously to expand their territory without any consid- eration for the rights of the indigenous population, or of the prerogatives of the British Empire. This, at least, was the vision of North America and the struggle for its future that the Canadian author John Richardson penned for his readers in the novel *The Canadian Brothers; or, The Prophecy Fulfilled: A Tale of the Late American War.*[2] Published in 1840, Richardson's novel was written as an explicit challenge to James Fenimore Cooper and his vision of the American republic as the spiritual and political heir of a vanishing Native North America.

The war of 1812 and the fighting in and around Detroit and Lake Erie pro- vided the setting for *The Canadian Brothers*. Richardson's novel, however, was published in the immediate aftermath of two failed rebellions in the Upper and Lower Canadian provinces in 1837 and 1838. These conflicts as much as the War of 1812 informed the author's thinking. The rebellions represented a struggle over self-governance and colonial rule in British Canada. In the wake of these events, Richardson emerged as a supporter of Lord Durham, the man who was appointed governor general and tasked with the responsi- bility of resolving the political tensions that had produced civil strife in Great Britain's Canadian provinces. Durham called for political reform as a means of keeping the provinces loyal to the monarchy. Specifically, he authored a re- port advocating the need to make Canada function more like a representative democracy. As part of this reform process, Durham called for the merger of Upper and Lower Canada into a single administrative unit, and for the cul- tural and political assimilation of the Francophone population. Many French Canadians believed such reforms would weaken their political influence, and threaten their language and culture, as Canada's Anglo subjects constituted a significant majority in both provinces. The reform measures advocated by Lord Durham, they believed, would benefit Anglophone Canadians politically and culturally at the expense of Francophone Canadians.[3] Written during this atmosphere of intense and divisive political dissension, *The Canadian Brothers* imagined a unified national future in which all Canadians—Anglophone, Francophone, and Native—fought to preserve their collective place in North America as loyal subjects of Great Britain.

For these reasons the War of 1812 offered the story line for Richardson's novel, much as the French and Indian War had in Cooper's narrative. In the War of 1812 Great Britain and the United States rejoined the battle for control of the North American continent that began during the Seven Years' War and culminated in the American Revolution. For Canadians the War of 1812 resulted in a national awakening—a moment when the subjects of the British colony began to see themselves as a distinct people and society. From either a British or Anglo-American perspective this series of conflicts could also be seen as wars fought in defense of an American homeland. The Rebellions of 1837–38 similarly marked a moment of crisis related to this long-term struggle within Anglo-America in that British Canadians were once again fighting over issues of representation, home rule, and republican versus monarchical government.[4] Like Cooper, Richardson was self-consciously attempting to create a national literary tradition that spoke to these experiences, and through this history laid claim to the continent.[5] But where Cooper evoked the past to explain the present, Richardson wrote about the past in order to imagine the future.

In *The Canadian Brothers* John Richardson used a moment in the past (the War of 1812), with echoes in the present (the Rebellions of 1837–38), to present two possible futures. The first part of the novel recalled the British colony's early successes in the war, which occurred when all of the Crown's subjects—Canadian-born Francophone and Anglophone soldiers, Canadian- and British-born officers, and most importantly their Native allies—fought together for king and country. This was one possible future. This story line also stridently warned about the avaricious nature of an American republic populated by bloodthirsty backwoodsmen greedy for land. This was Richardson's call to arms—Canadians must embrace reforms and accept unity, as well as their Native allies, if they wanted to preserve a national future in North America. The novel also contained a parallel plot twist that warned rather darkly of fratricide, and the dangers of being seduced by the idea of the United States. This was the other possible future imagined by the novel—a dark world where Canadians, enticed by the succubus-like myth of the American republic, sacrificed their honor and abandoned their national destiny. In short, Richardson's novel, as his title suggests, was a prophecy about the fate of Canada as an imagined community in North America.

Much like Cooper's *Last of the Mohicans*, Richardson's novel represented the fate of British Canada as intertwined with the fate of the continent's Native peoples. *The Canadian Brothers*, however, does not imagine a time when Indians would vanish from North America. Instead he imagines a future where selfishness, disloyalty, and fratricide threaten the survival of Canada. In this imperiled future Native peoples represented a last line of defense against an expansive and rapacious United States. By standing steadfastly together, Canada and its Native allies would preserve one another. Richardson saw a future for Native peoples, and he saw it in Canada where the British Empire's loyal Anglophone and Francophone settlers clung to their Native allies for dear life in order to fend off the land-hungry republicans to their south.

In fact, British support for Native peoples in the Great Lakes region was a source of great political frustration, as well as a cause for alarm, in the United States. When the United States declared war in the summer of 1812 after years of escalating conflict with Great Britain this issue was at the forefront of America's grievances. Like the restrictions imposed on American merchants trading with France, or the forced impressment of American citizens into the British navy, this issue centered on the question of sovereignty. From an American perspective, such actions reflected attempts to undermine the political integrity of the republic.[6] From a Canadian perspective, of course, America's aggressive and expansive settlement policies threatened to overwhelm both Native and Canadian territory in the west. At the time war broke out America's western ambitions, while not insignificant, were nevertheless undermined by the weakness of the republic's political hold on much of its western territory and the corresponding strength of Canada's Native allies. This was particularly true for the Upper Great Lakes, that part of the Northwest Territory that remained largely unsettled by Europeans. Identified as the "Michigan Territory" by the United States, this region was, in reality, still Anishinaabewaki, or Indian country (Figure 7).

William Hull, the governor of Michigan Territory, was acutely aware of the discrepancy between the political and territorial claims of the United States and the reality on the ground. In theory he was the chief executive of a sovereign

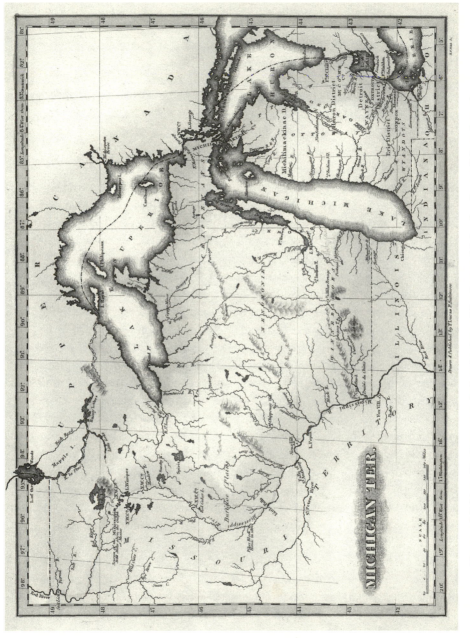

Figure 7. Michigan Territory map during the time of the Cass and Schoolcraft expeditions through Anishinaabewaki. Courtesy William L. Clements Library, University of Michigan.

territory of the United States—a region that would eventually encompass the states of Michigan, Wisconsin, Iowa, and Minnesota. Organized politically as a territory under the Northwest Ordinance, this space contained fewer than six thousand U.S. citizens.[7] The Native peoples who occupied the majority of this country, however, were also organized politically into a transregional alliance network with long-standing ties to British Canada. Hull was also painfully aware that the United States, in stark contrast with the Canadians, had a troubled and violent history with the Native peoples living within the borders of the territory he claimed to govern (Figures 8–10). Understanding these facts, when war was declared with Great Britain, Hull assumed that the peoples of Anishinaabewaki would turn against the United States.

Indeed, the United States and the Native peoples to their west had been on a collision course even before the republic came into existence. The settler colonists in the territories that became the United States had been propelled toward revolution because the mother country tried to restrict their expansion onto Indian lands. The revolutionaries gained their independence, but they had been largely unable to make good their claims to this coveted land base. Even though the Treaty of Paris ceded the Great Lakes to the republic, British military forces continued to occupy the posts that had been first established in this region by the French. The United States fought for and won control of Indian-occupied territory in the Ohio country, but it could not establish even a veneer of political sovereignty in the remainder of the Northwest Territory until it negotiated the Jay Treaty with Great Britain in 1794.[8] With this settlement the British withdrew from their posts and agreed to enter into arbitration to reach a peaceful settlement about the location of the U.S.-Canadian border. In reality, however, British forces did not withdraw from this region; they simply crossed to the other side of the water boundaries at places like Detroit and Sault Sainte Marie and built new posts at Amherstburg and on Drummond Island.[9] From these locations they continued to dispense gifts and trade goods. Native peoples came from locations throughout Anishinaabewaki to the new posts to reaffirm their relationship with British Canada. When war was declared in 1812 the precise location of the border remained undetermined. More to the point, the boundary was politically inconsequential. Neither the United States nor Canada could force Native peoples to respect any sort of national territorial boundary in this region. For that matter, neither could they force their own citizens to respect any notion of a boundary, as citizens and subjects of these two polities engaged in a brisk and illegal trade.[10]

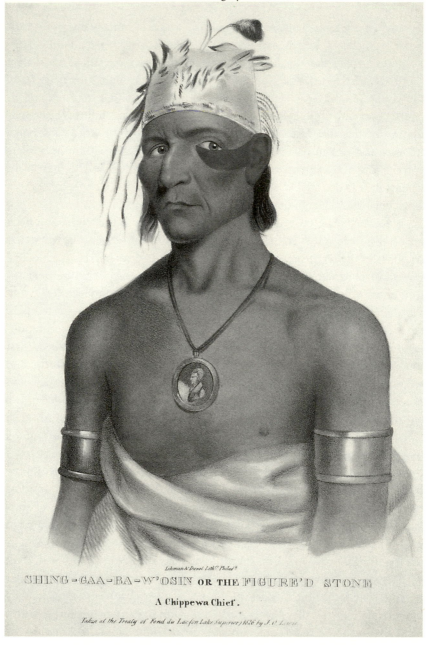

Lehman & Duval Lith. C Philad.ª

SHING-GAA-BA-W'OSIN OR THE FIGURE'D STONE

A Chippewa Chief.

Taken at the Treaty of Fond du Lac (on Lake Superior) 1826 by J. O. Lewis

Figure 8. Shiga-B'wassin. Anishinaabe ogimaa from Sault Sainte Marie who negotiated with Governor Cass at Sault Sainte Marie in 1820 and at Prairie du Chien in 1825. Courtesy William L. Clements Library, University of Michigan.

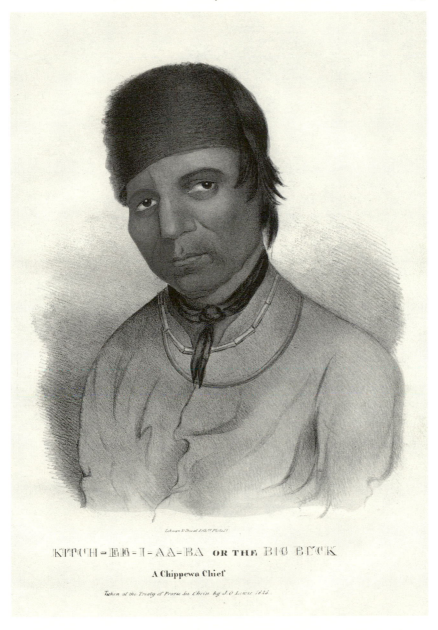

KITCH-EB-I-AA-BA OR THE BIG BUCK

A Chippewa Chief

Taken at the Treaty of Prarie du Chein by J O Lewis 1825.

Figure 9. Kitchi-Iamba. Anishinaabe ogimaa from Keweenaw who negotiated with Governor Cass regarding the surrender of warriors accused of killing American traders on the Mississippi River. Courtesy William L. Clements Library, University of Michigan.

WAA-BIN-DE-BA
or the
WHITE HEADED EAGLE
A Chippeway Chief
Painted by J. O. Lewis

Figure 10. White Head Eagle. Anishinaabe ogimaa from Lac du Flambeau involved in the murder of American traders who defied Governor Cass. Courtesy William L. Clements Library, University of Michigan.

In other words, Governor Hull had good cause to be concerned about the relationship between the peoples of Anishinaabewaki and Canada. But he was more than concerned; he was terrified. Perhaps his fear came from living in Indian country, and knowing that he was living what was, in truth, a lie. On paper he was the governor of a vast territory encompassing the Upper and Lower Peninsulas of Michigan and the country west along the southern shore of Lake Superior to the headwaters of the Mississippi River. In reality, he was the governor of a small outpost in southeast Michigan, a few other trading posts in the interior, and their attached populations. Each of these posts was, in turn, attached to a larger and politically autonomous Native village community. Many of the citizens of Michigan Territory living in the vicinity of these posts were actually Canadians by birth and or mixed-blood, or Métis fur traders.[11] Hull was governing people who were only nominally American. Moreover, he was literally surrounded by Indians, and they were not vanishing.

The fact of these Indians, and their alliance with British Canada, clearly worried the governor. Shortly after war had been declared Hull led a modest military force across the Detroit River and took the small Canadian town of Sandwich without firing a shot. After this easy victory Hull circulated a pronouncement that indicated his profound fear of Native-Canadian collaboration: "If the barbarous and savage policy of Great Britain be pursued, and the savages are let loose to murder our citizens and butcher our women and children, this war will be a war of extermination. The first stroke of the Tomahawk, the first attempt with the scalping knife, will be a signal of one indiscriminate scene of desolation. No white man, found fighting by the side of an Indian, will be taken prisoner—instead death will be his lot."[12] Days after Hull's easy victory at Sandwich, the Americans at Fort Mackinac surrendered to a combined force of approximately six hundred Canadian regulars, militia, and Native warriors. This post, formerly called Michilimackinac, was far more isolated than Detroit and when an army that included four hundred warriors appeared outside its walls the commander quickly surrendered. A month later Hull surrendered Detroit to Canadian forces without a fight. It seems his fear of fighting the Native allies of the Canadians unnerved the governor, causing him to surrender to an army half the size of the one under his command.[13]

The relationship between British Canada and its Native allies was central to the plot of *The Canadian Brothers*. Richardson's novel addressed the fear of Indian savagery expressed by Governor Hull, as well as the implied critique that it was politically and morally unethical for Canada to fight alongside Native allies. The novel turns this criticism on its head, however, and accuses the United States of being the perpetrators of frontier savagery. Richardson's villains are not bloodthirsty Indians, but rather duplicitous, hyperaggressive, land-hungry, Indian-hating Americans. This literary perspective was undoubtedly a reflection of the author's connection to Native North America. He was born in Upper Canada, and not only grew up among Native peoples but also shared their heritage. His mother was the child of the Detroit-based British Canadian fur trader John Askin and his Anishinaabe wife. Richardson's multicultural identity was no aberration—rather it reflected the reality of life in Upper Canada.[14] Settler colonists and European empires had been woven into the fabric of Native life in this region for over two hundred years. This relationship was fundamental, even constitutive, to the new national identities created by the encounter between Native and European peoples in the New World. Both Richardson and Cooper recognized the importance of this encounter, and made it a central theme in their novels. They diverged quite dramatically, however, in their interpretations of the cultural and political legacies of this history. Cooper imagined Native peoples who disappeared in the face of American progress. Richardson, in contrast, imagined Canadian nationalism as a phenomenon that Native peoples and Anglo settlers had forged together in defense of the British Empire, and their shared homeland in Upper Canada.

The Social Contract and the State of Nature

For John Richardson colonization placed a burden on the imperial power to bring order to the wilderness of North America so that Natives and newcomers could live together, in peace. This was the lesson to be learned from the history of Upper Canada in general, and the War of 1812 specifically. In this regard, Canada was the guardian of a unique social compact, forged by the encounter between empires and Indians in the New World. Loyalty to one another was paramount to the preservation of this compact, because on the other side of a rather porous frontier there was a maniacal villain named America. In his novel *The Canadian Brothers*, that villainy is personified in the character of Jeremiah Desborough—a ravenous lunatic skulking about in the Canadian woods and the American backcountry, driven by greed and an uncontrollable need for blood vengeance. A recent American immigrant to Upper Canada, Desborough maintained ties to the republic, and operated as a smuggler during the War of 1812. His nefarious and disloyal activities eventually result in the death of his son, an American soldier, at the hands of Canada's Indian allies shortly after the outbreak of the war. Following his son's death, Desborough descends into madness. He begins to roam the woods of Upper Canada and the American backcountry killing and cannibalizing Native warriors fighting as British allies.

Richardson's disturbing narrative gives expression to the devastating impact of American expansion into places like the Ohio, Indiana, and Kentucky Territories. What is Desborough, after all, if not the embodiment of American settler colonialism? His character, in gruesome fashion, performs the horrors of U.S. expansion. He is the American republic, a cannibal-settler consuming Native America with a vengeance, then gnawing on the bones of the Native New World while casting hungry glances at the Canadian west.

In Richardson's gothic tale the citizens of the United States, personified by Jeremiah Desborough, have abandoned civilized society. Rebelling against empire and pushing their way into Indian territory, American settlers entered a primitive social world. This was the backcountry, or frontier, a lawless space with no recognized or commonly acknowledged authority, governed solely by violence. American settlers who entered this space, like Jeremiah Desborough, were savage, antisocial beings locked in an all-or-nothing struggle to take possession of the western interior of the continent. Their success could end only with the destruction and dispossession of the Native peoples of North America, and the New World they had created in partnership with the British Empire.

Canada was the manifestation of this threatened New World, and the heroes of Richardson's novel, the Canadian-born British officers Gerald and Henry Grantham, were its literary (and political) representation. The brothers are presented as the literal and literary antithesis of Desborough. They are British loyalists committed to the crown and rule of law. Their tragic demise, the narrative end point of Richardson's story, comes when Gerald forsakes duty to country in pursuit of his personal and romantic self-interest. In the end, his selfish actions result in the deaths of both brothers, and the extinction of their family line. In their death we see one possible future for the Canadian nationalism that emerged during the War of 1812, and we glimpse the ominous lesson offered by the Rebellions of 1838–39. This lesson and Richardson's warning were not subtle—accept loyalty to Britain or face the death of Canada.

In Richardson's imagination Canada represented the imperial transformation of North America, and the culmination of the history of European discovery and conquest. His New World was not a savage wilderness waiting for transformation by hordes of colonial settlers striking out on their own in a new land. On the contrary, it was the wilderness and its inhabitants—both indigenous and immigrant—that gave meaning and purpose to the British Empire. In Richardson's national narrative, Canada is the embodiment of the social compact between the British Crown and its North American subjects. In this sense, the empire brings civilization to nature, not to tame it and transform it, but to rule over it. Properly ruled Indians are not a menace to Canadians, only to their lawless neighbors to the south who are a looming threat to the imperial order of the New World.

American liberty, born of greed and an insatiable hunger for Native land, represented the inevitable chaos that comes with the dissolution of this New World social compact. In Richardson's interpretation of the republican experiment, the Anglo settlers' dream of a new American nation had resulted in a nightmare of regression, turning men into savages, and the wilderness into a place of unending war. Gerald Grantham, as a literary figure, suggests the need for Canadians to discipline their appetites less they succumb to the chaos and violence of the American republic. Adhering to the rule of law and the constitutional prerogatives of the British Empire, Canadians (Anglophone, Francophone, and Native) function collectively as the agents of a sovereign monarch fighting those who would challenge their right to rule over the continent. This is the fantasy of empire embedded in the narrative of Richardson's gothic tale.

The story of Canada in this national narrative was the story of the social contract as articulated by the English political philosopher Thomas Hobbes. One of the first political thinkers to articulate this idea, Hobbes argued that the natural condition of man "is a condition of warre or everyone against everyone."[15] People entered civil society to bring an end to this state of nature where "the life of man," Hobbes wrote, was "solitary, poore, nasty, brutish, and short."[16] In civil society individuals transferred their natural rights to a single individual or assembly of men, recognized by all as the sovereign power in society, "to the end he may use the strength and means of them all, as he shall think expedient for their Peace and Common Defence."[17] This was the social contract that formed the basis of Britain's constitutional monarchy, and established the relationship between the sovereign and subjects in the British Empire. Hobbes's *Leviathan*, the most forceful expression of these concepts, was written during the English Civil War. In this text Hobbes asserts that once a people entered into a covenant with a sovereign power, they could not reject this authority without returning to the chaos and violence of their natural condition. Richardson's narrative, in effect, reflects the logic of Thomas Hobbes. Jeremiah Desborough and Gerald Grantham offer object lessons about the consequences of rejecting or failing to honor their social covenant with the British monarchy. This was the purpose of empire—to provide subjects with the rule of law and prevent them from descending into the chaos and violence of their natural condition. America, which likes to imagine itself as a new Eden, was nothing more than a Hobbesian jungle.

Reading John Richardson's text alongside James Fenimore Cooper's *Last of the Mohicans*, we see two different understandings of the nature of political power and national identity in North America. Cooper's tale of vanishing Indians is, in effect, a manifestation of Thomas Jefferson's imperial fantasy of Native assimilation into the body politic of the United States. Writing to the American Indian agent Benjamin Hawkins in 1803, President Jefferson admonished him "to promote among the Indians a sense of the superior value of a little land, well cultivated, over a great deal, unimproved." Once Native peoples made this mental shift, he predicted, "the ultimate point of rest & happiness for them is to let our settlements and theirs meet and blend together, to intermix, and become one people. Incorporating themselves with us as citizens of the United States, this is what the natural progress of things will of course bring on."[18]

Jefferson's dream of Indian assimilation reflected his understanding of the nature of political power in human societies. The president, like most of the political leadership of the United States, was deeply influenced by the thinking of the English political theorist John Locke, and his concept of natural law. For Locke America represented the world as it was at the dawn of time, "in the beginning," he famously wrote, "all the world was America."[19] He theorized that the New World existed in a "state of nature," that is, it had not been incorporated into a settled and civilized society of human beings. In other words, the Americas remained part of the natural world. The idea that the New World was unsettled territory, or *res nullis* (empty thing/space) derived from Roman law, and provided the logic behind the European claims of discovery and possession of lands occupied by Native peoples.

Europeans did not claim the New World was literally empty of human occupants. But they did imagine that Native peoples were uncivilized and therefore exercised no claims or rights over the land on which they lived. For

Europeans, and especially for the English, civilization was explicitly tied to particular land-use practices. According to John Locke, "God when he gave the world in common to all mankind . . . commanded him to subdue the earth, i.e., improve it for the benefit of life, and therein lay out something upon it that was his own."[20] Laboring to cultivate the earth created property. Locke argued that according to natural law, anything that a man removed from a state of nature by his own labor became his by private right.[21] "As much land as a man Tills, Plants, Improves, and can use the product of," he wrote, "so much is his property."[22] By extension, any lands not so improved were de facto unpossessed. Following this circular reasoning, land not encompassed by any property regime recognizable to the English was, from their perspective, unsettled land.

Unsettled land existed in a state of nature. Under these conditions human beings created property, and became invested with power over their creation. But when they transformed this individual power into a collective power— turning their individual rights and personal authority into rights and privileges shared equally within a community—they left behind the state of nature and entered into civil society. This was the Lockean version of the social contract— the recognition of a common authority representing the collective rights and political self-determination of a people who came together to form what Locke described as "one Body Politick under one Supreme Government."[23] This marriage of private property and political rights created a particular form of political self-determination understood by the English and Anglo-Americans as sovereignty, which invested mankind with dominion, or supreme authority within a fixed territory. Following this logic, land use, social development, political rights, and the legitimate exercise of power were explicitly linked. This political philosophy also allowed men like Thomas Jefferson to imagine North America as a wilderness occupied by uncivilized people who had neither improved the land nor formed a sovereign government.

By framing collective political self-determination around culturally specific ideas about land use, Americans could imagine western expansion as the establishment of legitimate sovereign government on unsettled land. This political philosophy made it possible to imagine the western expansion of the American nation-state to be synonymous with the advance of human progress across an empty wilderness. It also simultaneously divested Native peoples of their land rights and political self-determination by inscribing them as people who lived outside of civil society. Unlike his political protégée James Monroe, Thomas Jefferson believed that Indian peoples could and should participate in the expansion of American progress. Native peoples would, he believed, stop being Indian/uncivilized when they were incorporated into the American nation-state as citizens. This social transformation from Indian into citizen would also result in and from a transformation of unsettled wilderness into private property. When Native peoples entered civil society they would give up the hunting way of life and become farmers. And since yeoman farmers required significantly less land than nomadic savages, there would be surplus lands available for development by fellow citizens of the republic. Of course, many Native peoples already relied on farming for their subsistence, but the construct of natural law as applied to North America required a willing suspension of disbelief. Indians were savages and their land-use practices were uncivilized. They lived outside of historical time, in a state of nature.

Assimilation into the American republic would require Native peoples to leave this state of nature. More importantly, taking their place in civilized society would require Native people to undergo a cultural death as Indians. Thomas Jefferson may have imagined a place for Native peoples, suitably transformed, within the United States, but he also feared Native savagery. Like the fictional U.S. army officer Major Montgomerie in John Richardson's novel, the president accused the British of enticing Native peoples to commit atrocities against American settlers during the War of 1812. This fear of Native savagery, however, could also be interpreted as an implicit recognition of the inherent violence of American settler colonialism. Richardson's character, Major Montgomerie, explains to a Canadian officer in the novel that conflict was inevitable because, "the Indians being anxious to check, we to extend our dominion and power as a people; the causes existing now, were in being nearly a century ago, and will, in all probability, continue until all vestige of Indian existence shall have utterly passed away."[24]

Richardson's Montgomerie articulats not only the logic behind America's Indian policy but also the vanishing Indian fantasy embedded in Cooper's novel and Thomas Jefferson's dream of assimilation. The western expansion of the United States required the death and dispossession of Native peoples. This was the ugly truth behind Jefferson's vision of American progress—it was predicated on the destruction and consumption of Native North America. Richardson's cannibal settler Jeremiah Desborough represented a fictional recognition of this reality. The Indian policy of Thomas Jefferson and his political successors was the moral and political equivalent of cannibalism in that it was a plan to kill off and consume the indigenous peoples and lands of the Native New World.

The Anishinaabeg Refuse to Vanish

Lewis Cass, appointed governor of Michigan Territory in 1813, was under no illusion about the possibility that Indian peoples might be assimilated into the body politic of the American republic. Like many of America's founders, he too believed that the western expansion of the United States was part of God's plan to bring civilization to North America. "There can be no doubt ... that the Creator intended the Earth should be reclaimed from a state of nature and cultivated," he wrote in 1828, toward the end of his time as governor. In the tradition of writers like Thomas Jefferson, James Monroe, and even John Locke, Cass described the founding of America as the transformation of an unsettled wilderness into a modern civil society: "The new race of men, who landed on these shores, found that their predecessors had affixed few distinctive marks of property in the forests where they roamed. There were none of those permanent improvements, which elsewhere by universal assent become the evidence and security of individual appropriation."[25] Cass asserted that Native people possessed the right to provide for themselves on this unimproved territory, but argued that "this right can not be exclusive, unless the forests which sheltered them are doomed to perpetual unproductiveness."[26]

Like Thomas Jefferson, Cass believed that Native peoples lived in a state of nature, on unimproved lands, without a properly constituted sovereign government. Unlike Jefferson, the governor believed Native peoples could not be incorporated into the republic as citizens. In fact, he argued, they stood in the way of American progress. "The peculiar character and habits of the Indian nations," Cass claimed, "rendered them incapable of sustaining any other relation with the whites, than that of dependence and pupilage."[27] Native peoples, in other words, were both unwilling to become civilized and incapable of it. Writing in a periodical with a national circulation two years after the publication of *The Last of the Mohicans*, the governor of the Michigan Territory echoed James Fenimore Cooper's conclusion that the Native New World was coming to an end. "Experience has shown," he wrote, "that Indians are steadily and rapidly diminishing."[28] America's Indian policy, the policy of civilizing and assimilating Native peoples, was failing. "It has been shown," he concluded, "that our efforts to stand between the living and the dead, to stay this tide which is spreading around them and over them, have long been fruitless, and are now hopeless."[29] North America's remaining Indians were, like Cooper's Chingachgook, "a blazed pine in the clearing of the palefaces."

For Lewis Cass the solution to America's Indian problem was removal to territory west of the Mississippi River. Governor Cass became a leading advocate of this policy, which essentially called for a process that people in the late twentieth century would recognize as ethnic cleansing. The logic of removal, however, was the same logic behind Cooper's narrative in *The Last of the Mohicans*, and Thomas Jefferson's Indian policy—contact with white people resulted in the physical and cultural death of Native people. When Anglo-America inevitably expanded, as the creator intended, the world of Native North America would vanish. The thing that made Cass an effective public advocate of this ideology was his considerable direct experience with Native people. He gained this experience, and his credibility as an expert on Indians, by being the governor of the Michigan Territory—a space that remained demographically Indian throughout his entire time in office. Apparently the ironic juxtaposition of this reality with the ideology of removal was lost on the American public, which continued to believe what their politicians, Indian experts, and popular literary figures told them—that Indians were dying off and would soon cease to exist altogether.

The writings of Lewis Cass reflect the ideology of American settler colonialism, which presumed the inevitable demise of Indian peoples, and asserted the cultural and social superiority of Anglo-America. And yet, Governor Cass found that this ideology functioned rather imperfectly on the ground. In fact, he spent his time in office engaged in a largely failed attempt to extend American sovereignty onto the peoples and territory of Anishinaabewaki. A decade after the War of 1812, only 8,675 Americans resided in Michigan, a far cry from the 60,000 white male citizens required to form a state under the provisions of the Northwest Ordinance.[30] The government estimated the Native population to be more than three times the number of whites, and most Native people lived on lands to which they retained legal title.[31] The first attempts to survey public lands in Michigan Territory to make them available for sale ended in failure. Daunted by miles of wetland and harassed by Indians, American surveyors abandoned their task. Rather than creating a new landscape, surveyed and divided according to the Land Ordinance of 1785, they produced a map that labeled all of southern Michigan an "interminable swamp."[32] The Native peoples of Anishinaabewaki, in other words, were not vanishing in the face of American progress. Rather, American progress had stalled in the interminable swamp of the Native New World. The metaphor of the swamp, as well as the existence of so much un-improved land, signified the extent to which America had failed to recreate itself in the northwest interior. As late as the early nineteenth century—during the time of Reverend Boutwell's expedition to the Mississippi, and when Cooper and Longfellow were writing *Mohicans* and *Hiawatha*—the American republic found itself unable to impose its sovereignty onto Anishinaabewaki. Cass may have written breathlessly about Native peoples being swept away by the tide of civilization, but he could not even successfully survey the territory he governed.

Determined that progress should at long last come to Michigan, Governor Cass organized and led an expedition to explore the southern shore of Lake Superior and the upper reaches of the Mississippi River Valley in the summer of 1820. This was the second official U.S. visit, and the first such expedition since Zebulon Pike's visit with Flat Mouth. Unlike the more famous expeditions of Pike, and Lewis and Clark, this was not a voyage of discovery. The Cass expedition was not designed to bring the Great Lakes into the public imagination as American territory. It was instead a rather explicit exercise in nation building. Cass traveled into America's inland empire with the specific goal of extinguishing Native title to tracts of land at Sault Sainte Marie, Prairie du Chien, and Green Bay. "At each of these points," he wrote to Michigan's congressional delegate, "it is important with a view to their progressive growth in population, strength and resources, and to the future security and defense of this exposed frontier, that this cession of Indian title should be procured, and the land brought into market as speedily as practicable."[33]

At Sault Sainte Marie Governor Cass planned to terminate Native title and solidify American possession with the creation of a military post. The Saint Mary's River served as a border dividing American territory from British Canada. The geologist attached to the Cass expedition, future Indian agent, author, and Indian expert Henry Rowe Schoolcraft, described this stretch of river as the place by which "all the fur trade of the northwest is compelled to pass, and it is the grand thoroughfare of Indian communication for the upper countries."[34] The governor was also aware of the strategic importance of the portage located along the rapids of this river. And he knew that the Anishinaabe village at this location facilitated the flow of people and goods between the heartland of the continent and the Canadian and American cities on the east coast. At the outset of this expedition he informed the secretary of war that, in addition to extinguishing Native title, "I think it very important to carry the flag of the United States into these remote regions, where it has never been born by any person in a public station."[35] The British, however, were also aware of the strategic importance of this location, and they dispensed presents annually from the Canadian side of the Saint Mary's River on Drummond Island.[36]

In order to stake his claim to American possession of Sault Sainte Marie, Governor Cass first had to get there. The Cass expedition, however, was incapable of navigating the lakes, rivers, and marshes of Anishinaabewaki on its own. A crew of French Canadian mixed-bloods, or Métis, and a party of ten Anishinaabeg brought the expedition to the village on the American side of the river on June 15, 1820. The Americans arrived in the early evening, interrupting a Midewewin, or curing ceremony, that had brought representatives from all of Anishinaabewaki to Bow-e-ting, the place that Europeans referred to as Sault Sainte Marie. Cass, through his interpreter, called the ogimaag of the Anishinaabe doodemag attending the ceremony to a council in the morning. Then the governor passed the night unable to sleep, listening to the drumming and singing of the Mide ceremony that lasted till dawn—a tangible reminder that he was a foreigner (meyaagizid) in the territory claimed by his government. Any fantasy about vanishing Indians that Cass may have clung to in 1820 confronted the very real Indians dancing in large numbers just outside of his tent—just as they would in 1832 when Schoolcraft brought Boutwell to Fond du Lac on the west end of Gichigamiing (Lake Superior) in the hope that religion would pacify the Native peoples who so stubbornly refused to vanish from American territory.

The Anishinaabe ogimaag arrived the next morning at the governor's tent, outfitted in British trade cloth, wearing British silver and medals, and carrying British guns. They lit their calumet, smoked, and passed it to Cass, who took his turn at the pipe and then announced the purpose of his visit. Sault Sainte Marie, he claimed, had been ceded by their ancestors to the French "to whose national rights and prerogatives the Americans had succeeded." Cass asked for their "assent to its reoccupancy."[37] The Anishinaabe ogimaag demurred, asserting that they would be unable to stop their young men from pillaging an American garrison built on Anishinaabe land. In a pique of anger at this rejection, Cass told the ogimaag that he planned to establish a post "whether they renewed the grant or not."[38]

The brash challenge issued by the governor was greeted in kind by Sassaba, war leader of the Crane clan, the Anishinaabe doodem that claimed to be the first human inhabitants of Bow-e-ting. Wearing the crimson jacket of a British general, Sassaba (the Wolf) rose to his feet, thrust his lance into the ground, and stormed out of the tent. Sassaba then marched to his lodge and promptly raised a British flag. Cass ordered his men to arm themselves, and then instructed his interpreter to follow him. He walked into the Indian camp and confronted Sassaba, telling the war leader that in raising the British flag he had insulted the United States. He tore down the offending flag, and warned Sassaba that if the Anishinaabeg attempted to raise another British flag on American soil "the United States would set a strong foot upon their necks, and crush them to the earth."[39]

One has to wonder what Cass thought he was doing. He was a corpulent man with a handful of soldiers surrounded by thousands of angry Indians. There was a certain nation-backed confidence in his gesture, a belief that he represented a powerful new country, the United States of America. There was some truth in this sentiment. At this time and place, however, that confidence reflected the same misplaced certainty that would cause Boutwell to reflect during his 1832 expedition that the Anishinaabeg must feel comforted by the paternal care extended to them by the U.S. government. Cass was confident that Indians would fade from history before the coming tide of American civilization. He was confident that the power of a mighty nation-state backed his power play against Sassaba. In truth, however, it would be the internal politics of Anishinaabewaki that saved his expedition, and prevented him from learning that the United States was incapable of either enforcing its laws or using military force anywhere in Anishinaabewaki except at its few scattered military posts. In fact, Cass would soon learn that even those posts were not immune from the possibility that Native people would simply reject any form of American authority.

With both camps armed and preparing for battle a prominent Anishinaabe woman, Ozhaawshkodewikwe (Green Prairie Woman), worked to restore calm and forge a peace with the Americans. Ozhaawshkodewikwe, the daughter of the prominent civil chief from Fond du Lac named Waabojiig, lived on the American side of the river where her husband, the British-born John Johnston, based his fur trade operation. She dispatched her Métis son George to find Shingwaukonse (the Little Pine), a war leader and rival of Sassaba. Together they built a consensus among the civil leadership of the Anishinaabeg around the idea of accommodating an American presence at Bow-e-ting. After meeting in a separate council throughout the day, the ogimaag agreed to meet with Governor Cass a second time in the house of Ozhaawshkodewikwe. At this second council they consented to sell the Americans four square miles along the Saint Mary's River. The treaty signed by the ogimaag, however, stipulated that the Anishinaabeg retained hunting and fishing rights on this territory in perpetuity, and provided financial compensation for the sale of their land.[40]

The treaty process imposed on the Anishinaabeg at Sault Sainte Marie reflected the cultural logic of America's western expansion. The United States asserted an American title to Native land in a place that was pivotal to the political economy of the inland trade and the western interior of the entire continent. And yet this treaty also reflected the cultural logic of the Anishinaabeg. They retained the right to use the land as they always had. At the same time, the ogimaag created a relationship with the Americans. The United States, just like the British in Canada, represented a source of tremendous power that existed at the edge of the Anishinaabewaki. It was the responsibility of the ogimaag to foster a benevolent relationship with any external source of power that might exert an influence over the lives of their people.[41]

In 1820 the Anishinaabeg at Bow-e-ting faced the Americans from a position of strength, but they also recognized the potential power of the American state. Governor Cass threatened to crush the Anishinaabeg, but he also described the United States as "their natural guardians and friends." As a military threat the Americans were hardly overwhelming. They required Native guides and Métis transport to make their way from Detroit to Sault Sainte Marie. They had lost Detroit and Mackinac to the British in the recent war, and even after establishing a military garrison at Bow-e-ting they proved powerless in stopping Anishinaabe doodemag from crossing the border at will, and even accepting annual gifts from the government of British Canada in addition to their American annuities. Conceding even a token degree of American sovereignty at Bow-e-ting, however, affirmed the status of mixed-blood relatives of the Anishinaabeg as important cultural brokers and as American citizens. And this twinned status, potentially, translated into American support for the independent traders competing against the Canadian Hudson's Bay and Northwest Companies for the fur trade in the interior country west of the Great Lakes.

This, at least, was the future that Ozhaawshkodewikwe hoped to secure for her mixed-blood children. Her son George prospered as a trader under the American regime, and eventually became an Indian agent at La Pointe on the west end of Lake Superior. The eldest daughter of Ozhaawshkodewikwe, Jane, would marry Henry Schoolcraft—the geologist who accompanied Cass, and stayed on to become the Indian agent at Sault Sainte Marie, and led American expeditions to the Mississippi River valley in 1830 and 1832. In this fashion, the agents of American empire learned that in order to maintain a presence at Sault Sainte Marie, the hub of the North American fur trade, they—like their British and French predecessors—would need to accommodate themselves to the social world of the Anishinaabeg. Anishinaabewaki had been created as a social formation through the forging of these sorts of accommodations. Incorporating outsiders, claiming their manidoo for the people, was a long-standing practice among the Anishinaabeg. In the end, American expansion would overwhelm and largely subsume Anishinaabe political power. In 1820, however, neither the ogimaag nor Cass could reasonably see an end to Anishinaabe political hegemony in this region. No matter what the governor wrote about Indian cultural death and the need for removal, he never experienced anything but Native cultural and political dominance the entire time he claimed to govern Anishinaabewaki on behalf of the United States. The Americans lacked any means of projecting power into this territory, and the only compelling economic opportunities in this region involved the fur trade—which required Indians to continue to live as Indians.

Indian Citizens and the Chippewa Nation

Mixed-blood Anishinaabeg like the Johnstons, however, paid a high price for their new identity as American citizens. They would be forced to guard and preserve this status by denying their indigeneity. In 1825, five years after the Cass expedition, the territorial government of Michigan questioned the right of Sault Sainte Marie's mixed-blood citizens to vote in federal elections. John Biddle, a political confidant of Henry Schoolcraft and Democrat candidate for territorial delegate to Congress, won election to office by a seven-vote margin. He secured his victory by winning all but two votes cast at Sault Sainte Marie. Biddle's opponent protested that the election was a fraud precisely because the people of Sault Sainte Marie had been allowed to vote in the first place. Biddle's supporters at the Sault, according to his Whig opponents, were "Half-breeds," mixed-blood Indians "assimilated entirely to Indians of the full blood, and had no habits in common with the white population."[42]

The protest triggered a controversy that resulted in the creation of a special commission by the Michigan territorial government. The secretary and the treasurer of the territory examined the voting returns for each county, took depositions pertinent to alleged voter fraud at Sault Sainte Marie, and submitted a report on their findings to the Congress of the United States. This bipartisan commission divided along party lines and produced an inconclusive report. Both officials agreed that the congressional act of February 16, 1819, authorizing the election of a delegate from Michigan Territory reserved the franchise for free white men, but they disagreed as to whether or not people of Indian descent might fit into this category. Robert Abbot, Whig politician and treasurer of Michigan Territory, argued that "It is puerile to suppose that Congress could have intended to confer upon a Wyandot or Chippewa Indian a right to vote at our elections, or in any wise to intermeddle with our political affairs. Without any reference to the actual color of the skin—let it approach more or less closely to pure white, we presume that the expression "white citizen" was used as a generic term and was meant to describe those whose descent could be traced to a pure European origin. Influenced by this train of thought, one member of this board is of opinion that no one, having any Indian blood in his veins, can be entitled to vote."[43]

The Democrat commissioner, however, accepted the cultural logic that had made the American treaty at Sault Sainte Marie possible in the first place. That is, he accepted the fact that the Métis held important social and political positions throughout Michigan Territory. The distinction, according to the Democrat supporters of John Biddle, was that "the half breeds (so Called) . . . are not in their habits like wandering Indians, but on the contrary many of them are owners of comfortable houses, speak English or French, and dress like white men."[44] Such a person, the Democrat commissioner concluded, ought to be allowed to vote. Ultimately, the Committee of Elections for the Nineteenth Congress of the United States agreed with the Democrat commissioner. The committee produced a congressional report concluding that if an individual "by his manner and place of abode, was assimilated to and associated with, the great body of the civilized community; had never belonged to any tribe of Indians, as a member of their community, no good reason is perceived against such a person being considered as a qualified elector."[45]

The cost of American citizenship with the franchise for the Métis was, at least in theory, disassociation from the tribal communities of their relatives. In practical terms, the idea that the Métis, the majority of whom were fur traders, held no ongoing association with their tribal communities was absurd. It was this very association that had allowed Governor Cass to avoid conflict and secure a treaty extinguishing Native title at Sault Sainte Marie. Accommodating American notions of citizenship and civilization, however, forced the mixed-blood people of Michigan Territory to reimagine their relationship with their Anishinaabe relatives. The Great Lakes Métis understood their identity as part Indian, not only in a biological and cultural sense, but also in the sense of being indigenous in origin—that is, as being a part of Anishinaabewaki. In other words, like their Indian relatives, the Métis asserted a Native title to the land on which they lived. Their social identity as Anishinaabe people derived from the lived relationships forged on the shared landscape of Anishinaabewaki, or Indian country.

Lewis Cass was determined to extinguish Native title to this same territory claimed by the United States. The governor sought to carry out President Monroe's mandate—that is, to bring civilization to the Michigan Territory by subordinating the region's Native inhabitants, and making their land available for purchase as private property by U.S. citizens. But at Sault Sainte Marie he quickly discovered that any attempt to implement this policy hinged on the cooperation of the Métis, and would require a restructuring of the relationships between the Native communities that still dominated politics, trade, and diplomacy in the western interior. Thus, while the territory's political parties struggled with the question of mixed-blood voters in 1825, Cass found himself engaged in a comparable struggle to define the boundaries of U.S. civil society and political authority throughout the territory that he claimed to govern.

American officials in Michigan Territory, like Governor Cass, wanted to use the treaty process to transform Anishinaabewaki from a multipolar social formation into discrete and politically subordinate tribal entities with limited territorial claims. Toward this end, Cass called another treaty council at Prairie du Chien at the confluence of the Wisconsin and Mississippi Rivers with the goal of bringing an end to any ongoing or future warfare between Native peoples in the northwest interior. Writing to the secretary of war, Cass claimed the treaty would "stop the hostilities, which have been carried on among those tribes for several generations."[46]

In a published essay outlining the tenets of America's Indian policy, Cass described the importance of this treaty as an instrument of peace, and he claimed that only the power of the United States could prevent the Indians of the west from destroying one another. "That the Indians might not vanish as the snow melts before the sun beam," he wrote, "commissioners were appointed to meet the various tribes . . . and to conclude a peace among them." And he described the origins of these conflicts as rooted in the savage nature of Indian identity. "During many generations," he claimed, "a war had been waged between the Chippewas and the Sioux. Its origin is lost in the depths of time, and no other motive for its prosecution has existed, since these tribes have been known to us, then the thirst for revenge, and the necessity of having some enemy, from whom trophies of victory might be won."[47] Using faux Indian speech and the metaphor of the United States as the rising sun (recall

Longfellow's land of light and morning), Cass articulated the idea of the vanishing Indian and asserted the benevolent nature of American expansion.

In August 1825, the year of Michigan's disputed election, the governor negotiated a treaty with the Chippewa, as well as with people identified as the Sioux, Sac, Fox, Iowa, Menominee, Pottawatomie, and Ottawa at Prairie du Chien. At council General William Clark of the Saint Louis Superintendency spoke to the assembled peoples using ritual language inherited from the French by way of the British. "Children," he declared, "your Great Father has not sent us here to ask anything from you—we want nothing not the smallest piece of your land not a single article of your property." Clark called for peace, and echoing Cass he described the conflict between the Chippewa and the Sioux as an ancient rivalry with no political basis that frequently flared into a region wide-conflict. "Your hostilities," declared Superintendent Clark, "have resulted in a great measure from your having no defined boundaries established in your country." He suggested that because the assembled tribes did not know the limits of their own territory they chased game onto the territory of their neighbors. Conflict resulted when different tribes found themselves in competition over disputed territory. Cass and Clark proposed to remove this source of conflict "by the establishment of boundaries which shall be known to you and which boundaries we must establish at this council fire."[48]

Instead of extinguishing title to Native lands, the treaty concluded at Prairie du Chien purported to establish fixed boundaries between the bands of the treaty signers. The first article confirmed "a perpetual peace between the Sioux and the Chippewas," and also between the Sioux and the Sac, Fox, and Iowa. Subsequent articles laid out the political boundaries between the territories of all the tribes at the council. Perhaps most importantly, the treaty at Prairie du Chien claimed American sovereignty in these newly delineated territories. Article 10 declared: "All the tribes aforesaid acknowledge the general controlling power of the United States, and disclaim all dependence upon, and connection with, any other power." The article also recognized the land claims of the "half breeds" at Prairie du Chien, Green Bay, and Saint Peters, as well as unspecified settlements on the Mississippi and Wisconsin Rivers. The commissioners than made the United States the guarantor of these boundaries, while reserving the right to renegotiate the limits of each tribal territory at a future date.[49]

It is impossible to know what the Native treaty signers understood when they recognized the "general controlling power" of the United States. At a minimum they would not have recognized American political power as sovereignty, that is, as the supreme power within a fixed territory that was formerly their homeland but was now part of the United States. More likely they simply recognized the manidoo or wasicun of the republic. The treaty process acknowledged this power and signaled the creation of a relationship with the ogimaag of the Gichi-mookomaanag. The commissioners, acting on behalf of the United States, promised to use the manidoo of the republic to facilitate peaceful exchange among the peoples of Anishinaabewaki and the west. With very limited resources and no real military force, American officials quickly found this promise impossible to keep. In fact, it was the failure of the United States to exercise this power, and fulfill its treaty obligations, that led to the angry confrontation between Eshkebugikoozhe/Flat Mouth/Gueule Platte and Indian agent Henry Schoolcraft (Nawadaha) at Leech Lake in 1832, less than a decade after the signing of this treaty.

At least one Anishinaabe ogimaa at Prairie du Chien in 1825 saw the futility of this treaty as a political process. Shiga-B'wassin (the Spirit Stone) thanked the commissioners for their efforts, but warned them, "I am afraid it will not be good. The young men are bad and hard to prevent." Kisk-ketawak (the Cut Ear), speaking for the warriors from the Anishinaabe village at the Saint Croix River, however, told the commissioners, "My Father, in my section of the country there is no harm I hope to find or find here—I am for peace." But most of the ogimaag spoke with more of a sense of ambivalence. Flat Mouth showed a reticence that would later turn to anger when he told the commissioners, "I have not much to say. I have listened to what you have said and put it in my mind." Wabasha (the Leaf), identified as speaking for the Sioux, smoked the pipe at council and said: "When the peace is made I hope it will be a lasting one." [50] At best, the council speeches of the treaty signers signaled a cautious willingness to allow the United States a greater diplomatic role in the region. They did not, however, accept peace on American terms, but rather required Americans to adapt to Native protocols.

This moment looks like American power, and it is, but it is far from an absolute or even controlling kind of power. The treaty was a fiction that looked forward to a future American power, rather than a reflection of reality. The American government had no means of enforcing the recognition of national borders around or between Native peoples in Anishinaabewaki or in the northwest interior. In an important sense, however, this negotiation and the treaty of 1820 at Sault Sainte Marie were eerily prescient in that these documents would become legally and socially productive of those "tribes" of the late nineteenth century that found themselves circumscribed by a restrictive political sovereignty tied to a significantly reduced land base. There would come a time when Americans would have the power to force Native peoples onto Indian reservations as an alternative to removal. In 1825, however, the Native peoples at Prairie du Chien could sign this treaty and still imagine themselves as independent communities with their own indigenous sense of political self-determination. Moreover, even at this moment—in the middle of what Cass hoped would be a successful geopolitical strategy for establishing U.S. political power in Indian country—Indians required Americans to adapt to their understandings of place and identity.

For example, at Prairie du Chien the commissioners tried to make the Anishinaabe ogimaag acknowledge that they spoke for all of the Chippewa people. They even designated Shingaba' wassin as the "the first chief of the Chippewa nation." They gave the ogimaa this title in part because he was a prominent civil leader at Sault Sainte Marie, a village of enormous political, spiritual, and cultural importance to the Anishinaabeg. But they also wanted to simplify the complex leadership patterns and social relationships that defined Anishinaabewaki in order to make it governable. The treaty document itself, however, suggests that the Americans failed to politically reconfigure Anishinaabewaki. Article 12 stated in part, "The Chippewa tribe being dispersed over a great extent of country, and the Chiefs of that tribe having requested, that such portion of them as may be thought proper, by the Government of the United States, may be assembled in 1826, upon some part of Lake Superior."[51]

In other words, the Anishinaabe ogimaag assembled at Prairie du Chien forced Cass to concede that he could not treat with the Ojibweg as a singular nation, with a single paramount leader. Rather, the United States needed to work to create relationships with all of the Anishinaabe doodemag. And so less than a year after signing this treaty the governor found himself explaining to the secretary of war why he needed to hold yet another treaty council. He reminded the secretary of article 12 and its provision for a council in 1826. And as Cass explained to the secretary, the ogimaag at Prairie du Chien had insisted on a separate council for the Gichigamiing doodemag. "The Chippewa tribe," he wrote, "extends from Lake Erie to the heads of the Mississippi and Lake Winipeek, and they are so widely separated that they have no common authority, which can exercise any general control." The United States, Cass argued, needed to hold a council "at some central point of their country."[52]

After Prairie du Chien, Cass realized that he would need to hold this additional council if he had any hope of subordinating the Anishinaabe doo-demag to American political authority. The independence of these bands, he believed, was the primary obstacle to the expansion of U.S. influence in the northwest interior. Cass informed the U.S. secretary of war: "It is also impor-tant that the power and authority of the United States should be displayed upon Lake Superior. This region is subject to British influence, and the many murders recently committed there, and the hostile attitude assumed by the Indians evince the necessity of exhibiting the physical force of the govern-ment." The United States had never deployed troops in the Lake Superior country, and he noted "the character of the American people is only known through the reports of the traders."[53] In other words, the majority of the An-ishinaabeg had no contact with or knowledge of any of the persons or in-stitutions representing the sovereign authority of the United States. For all practical purposes they were not, in fact, part of the republic.

Wicked Chippewas

Interwoven within this larger story of borders, treaties, and assertions of American sovereignty there was a murder, and a failed attempt by Gover-nor Cass to punish the Native perpetrators of this crime under American law. The murder was an undercurrent running through all of the governor's negotiations with tribal leaders, and all of his correspondence with Indian agents and cabinet secretaries. This story is important not only because it was emblematic of America's lack of political authority in Anishinaabewaki but also because it reminds us of the ongoing struggle between the Anishinaabeg and the Dakota for control of the transcontinental trading system that shaped the daily lives of everyone, Native and non-Native, in the western interior of North America from the seventeenth century until the later part of the nine-teenth century.

In the summer of 1824 a war leader named Keewaynoquet (Passing Cloud) led a party of approximately forty warriors from his village on the southern shore of Gichigamiing into the Dakota country. When they arrived on the Gichi-ziibi (the Mississippi River) they encountered a small party of American traders. The Americans carried their national flag, and they were heavily armed. One of the traders spoke Anishinaabemowin and acted as in-terpreter for the two parties, which decided to camp together. In the middle of the night the Ojibwe warriors rose and attacked the Americans, killing and scalping four of them. They seized the provisions and trade goods from the Americans who had been on their way to trade in the Dakota country. The war party made their way home, pausing to dance the scalps and stolen flag at every Anishinaabe village between Green Bay and the Keweenaw Peninsula on the southern shore of Gichigamiing.[54]

The news of these killings reached Governor Cass in a letter written to him by his Indian agent at Sault Sainte Marie, Henry Schoolcraft. John Holliday, a trader for the American Fur Company, brought the details of the attack and of the subsequent celebrations of this victory throughout Anishinaabewaki to Sault Sainte Marie. The initial American response to these killings came in the form of a letter from Captain Clarke, the military commander at the Sault Sainte Marie agency, to Holliday. Clarke asked Holliday to read a translated version of this letter to the peoples of the Keweenaw village, where he lived as a trader. The letter named the murderers Keewaynoquet, Can Can bee Shaw, and Can wan de baw, and declared that "the blood of these whites call loud for the punishment of these wicked Chippewas." Asserting that he spoke on behalf of the president of the United States, Holliday said on behalf of Captain Clarke, "Your Great Father is unwilling to believe that this wicked act is sanctioned by the good and true men among his red children of the Chippewas."[55]

The Ojibweg of Keweenaw, in turn, asked John Holliday to deliver their response to Captain Clarke and the president of the United States. The trader assured the American authorities that the people at Keweenaw disapproved of the killings on the Mississippi River, and that they promised to help apprehend those responsible. But in a letter that they asked Holliday to write for them they also explained that their assistance would be limited. "'Father if any of the murderers belonged to my village," said Gichi Iamba, the principal ogimaa, "I would not hesitate one moment or trouble you with so long a talk, but would tie him and give him up to you immediately, but father as they are quite another band I must take another plan, by insisting on their coming out by fair words." Gichi Iamba and all of the ogimaag of his village then made their mark next to their names written on this letter.[56]

The events surrounding these killings offer a perfect example of what Governor Cass meant when he complained to the secretary of war that the Ojibweg, or Chippewas, knew nothing of American power and authority but that which was communicated to them by fur traders. Cass had demanded the surrender of the murderers at the council meeting he called at Prairie du Chien in the Green Bay in 1825. The ogimaag of the Anishinaabeg did not comply with this demand. But after the council Cass met with limited success. The murderers turned themselves over to American authorities at Michilimackinac. When they learned that Cass actually intended to prosecute them for murder, however, they made their escape, apparently with help of the Métis inhabitants of Mackinac.[57] This escape posed a significant political problem. When Native prisoners, who turned themselves in voluntarily, escape from your island fortress at will—it becomes difficult to sustain the claim to be the sole political authority in Michigan Territory.

Governor Lewis Cass regarded these murders, and his inability to apprehend and punish the murderers, as an affront to American sovereignty. In truth, however, they were a reflection of the fact that this sovereignty did not yet exist in Anishinaabewaki. The American traders died near the junction of the Mississippi and Chippewa Rivers, a water route used by traders and warriors since the mid-seventeenth century. Violence, but also alliance and peaceful exchange, had shaped the social relationships between the Dakota and the peoples of Anishinaabewaki for more than two centuries by the time this small party of American traders found themselves at the wrong place at the wrong time. Their story was but an echo of past stories from Nicolas Perrot's redemption of an Anishinaabe captive held at Green Bay to the murders punished by Daniel Du Lhut at Michilimackinac to the loss suffered by his successor, le Sieur de La Verendrye, at Lake of the Woods. Like these similar acts of violence, the murder of American traders in 1824 was not a random crime on a lawless frontier. Instead, these murders represented a minor tactical maneuver in the epic struggle waged between the Dakota oyate and the Anishinaabe doodemag for control of a vast inland trading system. From this vantage point it was the larger struggle, the Indian struggle in the western interior, that had the longer history and the greater consequence. American claims to govern this territory were no more than a nuisance, the illusion of empire.

For Governor Cass, however, the murders represented a defiance of American political authority. The failure of Ojibwe leaders to capture and surrender the guilty signaled the absence of properly constituted government among the Native peoples of the Michigan Territory. The governor explained the need for a second treaty council with the Anishinaabeg in 1826 as a necessary affirmation of American sovereignty in this political space. "The reapprehension of the escaped murderers," he wrote to the secretary of war, "is essential, not merely to the preservation of our influence, but to the peace of that frontier."[58] The United States, he argued, needed to make a show of force.

"We are compelled to transmit our messages & speeches to the Indians by means of the traders. The government should be felt through its own agents," Cass concluded.[59] At this moment Cass seemed to realize that what had been anticipatory, like ripping down the British flag of Sassaba, had to be put into practice at moments like this. In killing the traders the Anishinaabeg were calling his bluff to place his foot on their necks, and Cass had to prevent that from happening. He had pretended the strength of American sovereignty, and now he had to prove it—and he had to do so without any of the institutions of the American nation-state.

As a consequence, in 1826 Lewis Cass once again called on the Anishinaabeg to enter into treaty negotiations with United States, to cede territory, and recognize American sovereignty. And once again, his ability to carry out these negotiations would depend entirely on Métis fur traders and Indian agents married into the very communities with whom he negotiated. The American delegation made a show of force—soldiers, Indian agents, and representatives from the War Department made their way to Fond du Lac at the west end of Lake Superior—transported to the treaty council entirely on Métis boats. The assembled Anishinaabe ogimaag made their marks on a treaty document that read, in part: "The Chippewa tribe of Indians fully acknowledge the authority and jurisdiction of the United States, and disclaim all connection with any foreign power, solemnly promising to reject any messages, speeches or councils, incompatible with the interests of the United States." As a supplement to this treaty the "Chippewa tribe" agreed to hand over the accused murderers to American authorities at Sault Sainte Marie in the summer of 1827.

In addition to securing compensation in the form of an annual annuity for the Anishinaabe bands of Lake Superior, this treaty pledged compensation for the Métis. The treaty negotiated by Governor Cass granted 640 acres to each of the "half-breeds and Chippewas by descent . . . in consideration of the affection they bear to these persons . . . to be located, under the direction of the president of the United States, upon the shores of the St. Mary's River." The same mixed-bloods who had secured their right to vote by demonstrating their civilized character, and their detachment from their Indian relatives, were now included in a negotiation that recognized the Anishinaabeg and their mixed-blood relatives as a distinct, independent, and politically autonomous social entity with a legal claim to territory that was simultaneously claimed by the United States. As a part of this treaty, Ozhaawshkodewikwe was given a grant of 640 acres as was each of her mixed-blood grandchildren.[60] Lewis Cass negotiated this document with the assistance of his former geologist, Henry Schoolcraft, America's Indian agent at Sault Sainte Marie, the son-in-law of Ozhaawshkodewikwe.

As they did in 1820, the Anishinaabeg negotiated the terms of their relationship with the United States from a position of strength, and with the assistance of relatives who could claim U.S. citizenship. They received trade goods and cash money for conceding American sovereignty in a place where Americans were incapable of exercising any real power. The representatives of the American state could not even travel through the country of the Anishinaabeg unless escorted by Native guides. They gave up title to a small amount of land on which Americans had shown absolutely no interest in settling, and on which they retained the legal right to hunt, fish, and harvest rice. And finally, the United States recognized the Métis as indigenous and deserving of compensation for the extinction of Native title to lands now claimed as part of the American republic. With respect to the negotiation of this treaty Lewis Cass informed Secretary of War John Calhoun, "there is no Indian agent superior to Mr. Schoolcraft."[61]

And indeed, Henry Schoolcraft, in superb Anishinaabe fashion, made certain that the treaty he helped to negotiate in 1826 served the interests of his new family. This family included Ozhaawshkodewikwe and her husband, John Johnston, who benefited from the treaty directly. It included Waabojiig, a signer of both the 1825 and 1826 treaties, and an important political leader with roots in the Shagwaamikong region at Fond au Lac, and at Sandy Lake in the upper Mississippi valley.[62] In spite of Schoolcraft's success at knitting together the interests of his country with his new family, all parties to the treaty would be disappointed with their fellow participants' unwillingness to live up to its terms. The U.S. Senate ratified the 1826 treaty with the "Chippewa Indians" only after removing article 4, which contained the mixed-blood land grant.[63]

The Anishinaabeg, for their part, declined to turn over the murder suspects as demanded by American authorities. Cass went so far as to insert this condition as an article in the treaty. The murderers, however, lived at Lac du Flambeau, a village inland from Shagwaamikong where American forces could not travel without becoming hopelessly lost. Thus, even though American authorities knew the identity of the murders they were powerless to arrest them without the cooperation of the Métis and their Native kin.

The year following the La Pointe treaty the ogimaag of Fond du Lac sent a letter to Governor Cass declaring a resolution to the problem of the 1824 murder of four American citizens. They sent four strands of white wampum (as a gesture of healing and signification of their peaceful intent) to be delivered to the president of the United States via the Métis Indian agent George Johnston.[64] They remarked that protocol dictated that they deliver this wampum in person, but they demurred, claiming they did not want to leave their families for such a lengthy trip. With their wampum they asked George Johnston to carry these words from the murderers: "Listen Father! We cannot resolve to deliver ourselves up. We have not the resolution to go to prison. Your arm is strong and heavy. Your punishment too severe."[65] And with this gesture, they informed the governor that the affair had been put to rest. They were not interested in submitting themselves to the authority of the United States. They would cover the dead, albeit not in person as tradition dictated. Governor Cass, it seemed, had less authority and control in Anishinaabewaki than Daniel Du Lhut had exercised in 1684. The "middle ground" was long gone, surviving only in embodied form in the persons of the Métis, and they served the interests of the American fur trade rather than the nation-state. Even during a time when the nations of North America were beginning to exercise a degree of power over people and space that exceeded the power of empires, the United States could not make good on its claim of sovereignty in Anishinaabewaki.

In spite of signing treaties that granted a "controlling power" and recognized the "authority" and "jurisdiction" of the United States in their territory, the Anishinaabeg remained politically autonomous. In effect, their political self-determination in Anishinaabewaki remained intact even after they entered into a formal relationship with the United States. The Métis, however, were the greatest losers in this new relationship—from the perspective of the American nation-state, they were not white enough to win the franchise outright and they were not Native enough to claim an indigenous title to the land of their Anishinaabe ancestors. On the other hand, the Native peoples of the Upper Great Lakes were never removed from their territory. Neither did they fade away, or cease to exist as independent communities. During an era that saw the right to vote linked to whiteness and male privilege, and that defined Indian peoples as unfit for citizenship or even residency in American territory, the Native peoples of Anishinaabewaki—both mixed-blood and tribal members—made a space for themselves within the social and political boundaries of the American republic. Through confrontation, treaty, and negotiation they deftly preserved their place in a distinctly Native New World. As the American republic approached the middle of the nineteenth century, political officials like Lewis Cass and Henry Schoolcraft found themselves largely powerless in a world controlled by men like Flat Mouth and Waabojig and women like Ozhaawshkodewikwe.

At the same time, however, the peoples of Anishinaabewaki began down the path of a relationship with the United States that would ultimately lead to their political subordination. It is important to note that the Anishinaabeg successfully fought for their culture. They kept alive a way of being—an imagined community—that to this day is distinctly indigenous. In the face of horrendous policies like Indian removal, the Dawes Act, and boarding schools, Native peoples resisted the cultural death that U.S. Indian policy demanded. The treaties negotiated by Governor Cass, however, created the legal mechanisms that would eventually erode their political independence. These documents succeeded in establishing the right of the United States to extinguish Native title to lands claimed by the republic. More importantly, they also secured recognition of American political authority in Indian country.

These treaties did not establish the political hegemony of the United States in Anishinaabewaki at the time of their signing. They did, however, provide a legal precedent that would allow Americans to claim such an authority in the future. In other words, these treaties began a process that would restructure Native social relations by linking indigenous political power to the concept of sovereignty. Native sovereignty, in turn, was linked to a steadily diminishing land base. Political self-determination is not necessarily sovereignty. This term evolved in the context of English and Anglo-American history and political philosophy. In this sense, it is a means for creating political power and authority within an autonomous social formation. It is not, however, the only way to organize social relations and political power.

Political power and social identity within Anishinaabewaki did not take territorial form as a sovereign nation, wherein the body politic exercised supreme authority within a fixed and bordered land base defined by individual property rights. Among the Anishinaabeg, social identity and political autonomy derived from lived relationships forged across a shared and infinitely expandable landscape. Politics and place were relational, and power was multipolar within Anishinaabewaki. Political power manifested itself in a variety of cultural forms, which were adapted to create optimal social relations of production in specific physical locations, environments, and social settings. The multipolar nature of Anishinaabe political power created a fluid and flexible social formation that changed form and function in reaction to cyclical changes linked to political economy and the ritual calendar. This social and political adaptability enabled the Anishinaabeg to take maximum advantage of the inland trade, which depended on seasonal hunting, and fluctuated in response to changes in the market, tribal and imperial politics, and conflict.

Treaty making with the United States, however, began a process that tied Native political power to a land base legally situated within the sovereign territory of the American nation-state. When the United States developed the infrastructure that made it possible to integrate the non-Native population of the upper Great Lakes and prairie west into the political economy of the republic, settler colonialism began to flourish in these regions that had remained an "interminable swamp" since the days of empire. The United States, however, had to work hard to colonize Anishinaabewaki. It took over fifty years to develop an infrastructure and institutional presence sufficient to begin to put demographic pressure on the indigenous population. Once the demography and political economy began to change, however, the United States was able to leverage its treaties with the Anishinaabeg to alter the boundaries of Indian country. The United States would never achieve Thomas Jefferson's dream of fully incorporating Native America into the body of the republic, but it would alienate the vast majority of the Anishinaabe land base. And equally important for Anishinaabewaki, it would change the nature of political power by linking Native self-determination to a restricted land base defined by property rights. No longer would Anishinaabe peoples mobilize political power by creating use rights across a shared and infinitely expandable land base. Native peoples would learn to mobilize their political power as sovereign nations in the twentieth and twenty-first centuries. Native national sovereignty would, in time, emerge as an important counterweight to U.S. and Canadian settler colonialism. But this form of indigenous power would only be a faint echo of the power of Anishinaabewaki during the first two centuries after the arrival of Atlantic World empires in North America.

The history of Anishinaabewaki during those two centuries remains invisible, or largely unknown to the majority of the inhabitants of North America. And yet there was a time when at least a literary version of this history was known to most of the non-Native peoples of North America. In the days of the early republic Americans eagerly appropriated the symbolic virtues and the iconic imagery and even the imagined history of American Indians. In so doing they laid claim to their spiritual and political heritage over the North American landscape. Ironically, the fact that Native peoples still occupied this landscape in large numbers seemed to escape their attention. This invisibility occurred in large measure because of cultural production about Native peoples like *The Song of Hiawatha*, *Last of the Mohicans*, and *The Canadian Brothers*.

To read these texts alongside the writings of men like Thomas Jefferson and Lewis Cass is to realize that no matter their literary merit, they express with stunning clarity American beliefs about the fate and future of the Native peoples who shared their continent. Politicians and authors alike believed that Native North America was destined to come to an end. It had to, unless the United States was to be contained and confined to the eastern seaboard. After the War of 1812 most Americans, and certainly the political descendants of Thomas Jefferson, did not believe this was possible. Perhaps more to the point they believed that any attempt to preserve Native peoples and culture as they existed would be politically regressive and morally flawed. Canadians apparently understood American ambitions, and if John Richardson is any indication they feared (with good reason) that the country's appetite for settling new lands extended to territories claimed by British Canada. They chose to combat this threat by maintaining alliances with the autonomous peoples of the Native New World in the first half of the nineteenth century, but their tactics would change. By the time of confederation, when the colonies of British North America came together to form the modern Canadian nation-state, their Indian policy would closely resemble the Indian policy of the United States. From the time when Europe founded its first colonies into the early nineteenth century, however, the thing that shaped the historical development of North America as profoundly as any non-Native social formations was the power of Anishinaabewaki and the existence of the Native New World.

Louis Riel, Native Founding Father

During the summer of 2002, I was in Winnipeg, Manitoba, doing research for this book. Taking a break from the archives I decided to take a riverboat tour of the city. Winnipeg is located at the junction of the Red and Assiniboine Rivers, and the trip takes tourists through the heart of the old city, which includes a French enclave and a restored Hudson's Bay Company trading post.

I picked a bad time to take my tour. The Red River had swollen to record levels and all of the waterfront attractions were inundated with water and mud. The river smelled like dead fish, and the person who sold me the ticket kept talking nervously about currents. But after fourteen straight days in the Provincial Archives of Manitoba, I decided to take my chances, and found myself on a boat with two high school history teachers from Minnesota and a very lonely tour guide. He gave us a personalized tour, comparing Winnipeg to Chicago and talking about the development of the American and Canadian west.

The tour ended at the provincial government building, directly in front of an enormous bronze statue of a man. The guide pointed at the statue and said, "That's Louis Riel. He's the George Washington of Manitoba." I pointed out that the government of Canada had executed Louis Riel not too long after he formed the province's first "provisional government." The guide seemed surprised. He said, "yeah, but they've changed their minds about that."

In Canadian history Louis Riel is a figure comparable in many ways to Nat Turner or John Brown. He was an insurrectionist, a race rebel, and a martyr who believed that he spoke directly to God. Riel led a coalition of Métis, Native peoples, and French Canadians from the Red River settlement in open rebellion against Great Britain and the newly formed Dominion of Canada in 1869. Riel was himself Métis, a person of mixed Cree-Ojibwe Indian and French Canadian ancestry.[1] He created the modern province of Manitoba, formed explicitly to guarantee representative government and claim aboriginal title for the indigenous peoples of the Canadian Northwest.

Riel's most radical step was to assert, simultaneously, an indigenous social status and rights for the Métis, and the right of self-government for all Native peoples. The Red River rebels stood conventional notions of race and citizenship on their head. They were not asserting their whiteness as evidence of their right to political self-determination. Rather, they asserted their indigeneity. Being Indian gave them a right to constitute a representative government in the west that Anglo-Canadian immigrants, as outsiders, did not possess. Canada's immigrant settlers, they decided, could eventually become naturalized citizens in a state built to preserve Native land rights, and religious and linguistic freedoms. The Red River rebels, in effect, offered a radical reinterpretation of nation building in the west—one that envisioned the rebirth, rather than the death, of Native identity in the form of a genuinely indigenous New World nation-state.[2]

The first prime minister of the Dominion of Canada, John A. Macdonald, disagreed with Riel's project. Macdonald forged a coalition government that united eastern and western (Upper and Lower) Canadian political interests. This coalition, according to Macdonald, believed that "the future interests of British North America" required "the immediate establishment of a strong government" in the Northwest. And he publicly proclaimed his intentions to deal equitably with the "aborigines." Macdonald also asserted that the Native peoples of the western interior were "incapable of the management of their own affairs."[3] In effect, the prime minister believed the Métis and their Native relatives to be incapable of self-government, and he believed that the lack of a proper European settlement left the region vulnerable to American ambition. "It is quite evident to me," he wrote to a political confidant, "that the United States Government are resolved to do all they can short of war, to get possession of the Western territory and we must take immediate and vigorous steps to counteract them."[4]

Macdonald dreamed of creating a united Canada out of the disparate colonies of British North America, linking Upper and Lower Canada, Quebec, and the Maritime Provinces. This vision also included the incorporation of the vast territory of Rupert's Land and the Red River colony, claimed by the Hudson's Bay Company. In short, Macdonald imagined Canada as a transcontinental nation-state, a rival power to the United States. To fulfill this ambition the Dominion of Canada purchased Rupert's Land from the Hudson's Bay Company in 1869, renamed this region the Northwest Territory, and appointed William McDougall as the lieutenant governor of the new province. McDougall was a member of the Clear Grit Party, liberal reformers prominent in the west of Upper Canada who advocated universal male suffrage and western expansion, and expressed hostility toward the perceived privileges granted to the Francophone population by the preconfederation colonial regime.

In short, the leadership of the Canadian government had a plan for the integration of Rupert's Land into their new country, and it was sharply at odds with the vision of the Red River rebels. While Lieutenant Governor McDougall shared the prime minister's vision of making Canada into a transcontinental nation, he proved to be a rather inept politician, too easily provoked by what he regarded as the unlawful pretensions of the Métis to self-government. His attempt to take control of the Red River colony met with immediate opposition that quickly escalated into violent conflict between the newly formed dominion and the people of the Red River settlement. This conflict would end badly for Louis Riel. Before Canada turned Riel into a founding father, it banished him from his homeland, and then executed him as an enemy of the state.

In spite of this failure, Louis Riel and the Red River rebels captured a rather compelling moment in North America's history. The rebellion represented an attempt by the Métis to hold on to an indigenous homeland in North America. This, of course, was not unique as Native peoples throughout the Americas waged similar struggles. Understood as the Native inverse to stories of the European discovery and conquest of the New World, tales of Indian resistance and defeat are tragic, and seemingly inevitable. What makes Red River so fascinating is that it provides such an effective counterpoint to this sort of teleological narrative. The rebellion serves as a reminder of the fact that there was a Native New World that was just as dynamic as the Atlantic New World. This was what Riel and his fellow rebels fought to preserve. They were not trying to preserve some timeless version of a premodern Native social world. The Red River rebels reimagined what it meant to be indigenous. They adapted their place and identity in the Native New World to match the new social formations that were emerging as dominant political powers in nineteenth-century North America. They fought to preserve the place that Native peoples had made for themselves as part of modernity.

I want to explore this argument by examining the imagined community that the Red River rebels fought to create, because I think their struggle raises important questions about the complex relationship between race, nation, and the claim to an indigenous identity in North America. There is perhaps nothing more quintessentially American than the idea that migration and the resulting ecological and social adaptation formed the cornerstones of the modern American identity. And yet this process of transformation and adaptation killed Louis Riel, which raises an intriguing question. What had to happen for Louis Riel to be transformed from a mixed-race savage destined to fade from history into the George Washington of Manitoba?

The answer is that Riel became a New World martyr. Perhaps Louis Riel never really talked to God. But his vision of creating a Métis/indigenous nation-state was strangely prescient. He could see the coming destruction of the Native New World. The engine of this destruction would be the new nations of North America—settler colonies reimagined as multiethnic, racialized nation-states with a continental as opposed to an imperial origin. In truth, Riel did not need to talk to God to see this coming destruction. He merely had to look to the south where he could watch as the United States, at long last, found the right combination of politics, demography, and infrastructure to overwhelm the Native peoples who refused to vanish from the shorelines of the Great Lakes and the prairies and woodlands of the upper Mississippi valley. Like the Canadian soldier and novelist John Richardson, Louis Riel watched as the United States cannibalized Native North America with the same ruthless ferocity that the fictional character Jeremiah Desborough killed and ate his Native victims. Riel knew that to survive, the peoples of the Native New World needed to reimagine themselves as nations capable of exercising political power as nation-states. Fighting for this transformation cost Riel his life.

Riel's martyrdom also made him into a politically desirable figure. He became the kind of Indian that nineteenth-century Americans and Canadians most admired—a dead Indian. What's more, he died heroically, resisting his inevitable conquest. In other words, Riel performed the most important act nineteenth-century Americans and Canadians asked of their Native founding fathers—he vanished. He became a figure like James Fenimore Cooper's Uncas or Henry Wadsworth Longfellow's Hiawatha. Like his literary counterparts Riel set the stage for the arrival of a new power, the North American nation-state, and then he vanished. Like Uncas's, Riel's vanishing act would be the permanent kind of departure—a real death that Canadians could appropriate symbolically as a founding moment. More significantly, with this postmortem appropriation they too could claim native status in North America. Like their American neighbors, nineteenth-century Canadians would now claim to be native citizens of a New World nation-state.

Adopting Riel as a founding father, the citizens of the province of Manitoba, and the Dominion of Canada, claimed a founder with an even more powerful legacy than the fictional Uncas. Historian François Furstenberg has argued that republican ideology in early America linked freedom to resistance. This linkage created a racial divide that marked some people as worthy or capable of self-government, and others as social and political dependents. Women, of course, fell into this category of domestic dependents, but so too did people of African descent. While the dependence of women in a patriarchal society seemed natural, imposing this condition on black men required explanation.

According to Furstenberg, republican ideology deemed people of African decent unworthy of citizenship precisely because slavery rather than freedom was their natural condition. This ideological caveat, he asserts, grounded "slavery in an act of individual choice—consent, even—. . . thereby legitimating slavery on principles consistent with the American Revolution." In effect, America's republican ideology and popular culture necessarily marked slaves as unfit for participation in America's emerging civil society. Quite simply, the existence of so many enslaved Africans revealed them to be unworthy of citizenship because of their willingness to be enslaved. Conveniently, this circular logic also absolved Anglo-Americans of moral culpability for the existence of the peculiar institution.[5]

Just as the enslavement of black people signaled their willing forfeiture of freedom, the defeat of American Indians fighting for their way of life signaled their love of freedom. It also, sadly, signaled their need to be conquered because freedom loving or not, in fighting conquest they rejected civilization. This is how republican ideology (even in its Canadian form) adapted and borrowed from the ideology of European discovery—and it is the means by which all of North America's New World nations would come to lay claim to Native founders and to a Native status for their American- and Canadian-born citizens—although the Mexican nation went even further, openly embracing a Mestizo/a national identity.[6]

Louis Riel and the Red River Métis demonstrated the irony of American and Canadian Indian policy. They proved that the expansion of the democratic nation-state did not have to be predicated on the cultural death of Indian peoples. The Red River rebels show the power of Indians to define themselves in a multitude of ways, and the power of Native identity and culture to adapt to social and ecological changes, to the arrival of new peoples, even to the emergence of new North American nations. Indians were part of modernity. They always had been. The problem for Riel and for Indian peoples, however, was that by the time of the Red River Rebellion the cultural and political space for this sort of multidimensional Indianness was gone. Treaty making and the link between western expansion, immigration, and racialized categories of citizenship had the effect of reinventing Indians. There was room only for the likes of Uncas and Hiawatha, not for living and breathing Indians who insisted on taking their place in the New World . . . as Native people.

Indians became traditional people, socially and culturally primitive beings incapable of participating in a democratic society, or becoming part of a new nation. Like the descendants of America's African slave population, they became definitively nonwhite, and noncitizens. Even stranger, Indians, at least when they were dead or considered to be on the verge of disappearing, came to represent something quintessentially American. This association has left Indian peoples, historically and at present, in a peculiar category—as people from another time and another place when they are really people who have been integral to the development of national identities and the nation-state in North America, a process that unfolded over the centuries since the peoples of the Eastern and Western Hemispheres rediscovered one another.

The Red River Rebellion, in effect, was a struggle over the meaning and nature of political self-determination in the northwest interior. In an important sense the rebellion was an amplified version of the political struggles that took place in the Michigan Territory during the 1820s and 1830s. The issues at stake in the rebellion at Red River reflected the national debate in the United States about the place of Indian peoples in the republic. The questions of race and citizenship that resulted in the contested election in the Michigan Territory in 1825, and the negotiations over sovereignty and Native title to land in the treaties of 1825 and 1826, played out in Canada's Red River Rebellion.

The parallel nature of the political struggles in Michigan Territory and Red River derived from the fact that even though these territories had long been claimed by settler colonies in the east, they actually formed part of the Native New World. Any claim of sovereignty in Michigan or Red River by the American and Canadian nation-states required a restructuring of social relationships and political power in these territories. The conflicts over race, the franchise, and land rights were the result of this power struggle. It is important that we understand the expansion of the American and Canadian nation-states into these territories as closely related historical experiences, rather than as part of discrete national historical trajectories.

In fact, the struggle by the United States to create self-replicating settler colonies in the northwest disrupts the larger narrative of America's western expansion. There are parallel issues with U.S. expansion in the southwest in that the question of race, citizenship, and the place of Indian peoples in the republic became part of a national debate about the nature of American civil society. But in the northwest, issues of law and race—specifically property rights and citizenship—were not defined by blackness and slavery. Similarly, Indian removal was not a political possibility. People of mixed race were so thoroughly integrated into both social worlds—the Native New World and the emerging settler colonies—that they could not be disenfranchised as easily as free blacks or enslaved peoples. Indeed, as the experience of Governor Lewis Cass of Michigan demonstrated, the expansion of settler colonies depended on the cooperation of Métis citizens. Equally important, the region's political economy depended on the fur trade, which meant that these western states and provinces needed both Indians and their mixed-race relatives. And they needed them to continue living as indigenous peoples.

Canada's colonization of Red River, however, does offer one striking difference in comparison to the American experience in the northwest. The Michigan Territory, or Anishinaabewaki, was surrounded by places that had been effectively colonized by the United States—Kentucky, Ohio, Indiana, Illinois. There was no Canadian equivalent to this success. Upper Canada had long been a part of British Canada, but in much the same way that Michigan had been part of the United States. There were small towns like Sandwich and military posts at places like Amhurstberg and Drummond Island but Upper Canada was still an Indian space. Even as the demography changed, more densely populated cities like Toronto were not contiguous with the territory of the Red River colony in the way that Michigan shared an established border with Ohio, Indiana, and Illinois. In 1867 the British North America Act that created the Dominion of Canada renamed Upper Canada Ontario, and in 1869 after the purchase of Rupert's Land the dominion claimed this space as the Northwest Territory. When Lieutenant Governor McDougall wished to enter Canada's new province, however, he had to travel through the United States because western Ontario was so remote and undeveloped that it was impenetrable to non-Native travelers.

McDougall had to come to terms with the fact that, like Cass, he had been appointed governor of a territory that was effectively still a Native space. Like Cass he could not travel into this territory without Native guides. For all practical purposes Red River was part of the Native New World. Accordingly, social constructs familiar to most settler colonists—such as race, land tenure, and political sovereignty—did not function at Red River in the same way as they did in Canada's other provinces. Race at Red River, for example, had little to do with skin color and everything to do with a more concrete series of cultural associations. The residents at Red River, Native, European, and mixed-blood, identified themselves by their connections to one another. These peoples did not think of race in terms of phenotype and color lines. Instead a person's social relationships constituted his or her identity.

These relationships allowed for a certain degree of flexibility. The social networks that tied the Métis to their Cree and Ojibwe relatives allowed individuals to associate themselves with either community. Social practices distinguished one group from the other. The Métis, for example, dominated the trade in buffalo hides, practiced a syncretic form of Catholicism, and maintained permanent residences at the Red River settlement. But there were people who were biologically Métis living within Native communities as Cree and Ojibwe people. Similarly, Métis ties to a Catholic Francophone culture rooted in the fur trade allowed French Canadians to assume the persona or social role of a Métis, or to become Cree or Ojibwe band members, even if they were biologically European in origin. The term "half-breed" operated in this same fashion for Anglophone people of mixed race connected to the English and Scottish traders associated with the Hudson's Bay Company, Northwest Company, and other British-based trading outfits.[7] The point here is that the social structure of Red River society mirrored the social practices and cultural constructs of the Native New World. Identity formed as a result of lived relationships—meyaagizid (foreigner) and inawemaagen (relative) were the categories that imparted social meaning to a person's being, not the European construct of race.

From the time of first contact with European empires until the era of formal relations with the United States and Canada, the agents of empires and nation-states struggled to make sense of the shifting categories that marked identity, and defined political and cultural boundaries in the Native New World. From 1640 to the nineteenth century, for example, the Anishinaabeg appear in historical documents as Sauteurs, Saulteaux, Ojibwe, Chippewa, Bungi, Monsoni, Muskegoe, Nakawewuck, Zhiishiigwe, Noquet, Marameg, Amikwas, and several other designations. They have been confused with or connected to Indian peoples identified as the Ottawa, Pottawatomie, Mississauga, Nipissing, Gens des Terres, Cree, and several other Native peoples, some of whom they were related to linguistically, and others to whom they were related only politically.

Louis Riel, Native Founding Father   367

In the seventeenth century, Anishinaabeg in the west were all but invisible to the French. More than one colonial official wrote that the interior west was populated by "an infinity of nations" which remained "undiscovered."[8] As the French fur trade expanded Anishinaabe, doodemag (clans) in the interior increasingly identified themselves as Sauteurs, a collective identity that placed them within the French alliance and trade system. As a consequence they became increasingly visible to the French. As traders and colonial officials pushed deeper into the west they encountered these Sauteurs time and again at Green Bay, at the western edge of Lake Superior, in the upper Mississippi valley, at Rainy Lake, at Red River, and still farther west on the northern prairies. The French assumed that the Sauteurs, like themselves, were migrating.

I have described this process as shape-shifting. And it is important to note that the Cree, Ottawa, Sauteur, and other Anishinaabe shape-shifters reborn in the west through this process of migration and seasonal movement are at once Native and immigrant.[9] They are connected by kinship, by trade, through their origin stories, and by treaty to the Great Lakes and to the northern prairies. They are connected similarly to the Algonquian culture of the eastern woodlands, to the plains culture of the Assiniboine and the Dakota, to the French, the English, the Americans, and the Canadians. They are people perpetually in the process of recreating themselves in the sense that the Anishinaabeg have always been adept at incorporating new people and new spaces within their social world.

For this reason the social formations of the Atlantic World, empires and nation-states, found Anishinaabe identities to be elusive and even ephemeral. Empires wanted subject nations who could submit their people and territory to the authority of a sovereign ruler. The New World nation-states claimed sovereignty over North American territory on behalf of their people, but then made race and gender into social categories that determined who, in fact, could exercise the franchise and hold political office. Power among the Anishinaabeg, in contrast, shifted between various social and cultural forms that ranged from the most intimate to the most abstract of connections—family, doodem, village, the people. This social fluidity allowed the Anishinaabeg to create an infinite number of lived relationships in a great diversity of settings—on the plains, in the swamplands and river valleys that drained into lakes and the seacoast, in large multiethnic lakeshore villages, and even in the cities of European settler colonists.

For this reason the Anishinaabeg elude easy categorization. They are shape-shifters, adapting identity to physical and social environment. They are, in effect, experts at reinventing the self, and in this sense they are a pro-totypical New World people. This process of migration and reinventing one's identity has always defined the New World in the popular imagination.

The Métis identity needs to be understood in this context. The Métis, in effect, represented a social identity comparable to Cree, Ottawa, and Sauteur identities. That is, the Métis identity was not a sociopolitical designation linked to a national identity and national territory. It was, more accurately, a situational identity that existed within a larger indigenous social forma-tion. French-speaking Métis and English-speaking "Mixed-bloods" (or half-breeds in nineteenth-century terminology) connected European trading companies and their agents to the western interior through their community at Red River, and at other villages that were integral to the inland trade. The exchange practices that governed the fur trade in the west derived from the social world created by the kinship and exchange networks of the Anishi-naabeg, and closely related Nihiyawa and Muskekowuck-athinuwick. For the Métis, hybrid European-Anishinaabeg-Nihiyawa/Muskekowuck-athinuwick peoples, their niche role as cultural brokers during the early contact era, and later their more specialized occupational role in the fur trade, offered a point of contact and influence within the multiethnic, indigenous, and autonomous Native New World that formed in the western interior of North America.

The Métis emerged in this milieu moving between the Native and Atlantic New Worlds, and they became an important link to an interior west coveted by the United States and Canada in the nineteenth century. They were, in effect, the physical embodiment of the older kinship, exchange, and alliance systems created by the French and the English and their Native allies and trading partners. A hybrid indigenous/European identity allowed the Métis to claim a place in the settler society enclaves in the east and in the Native New World in the west. Riel tried and failed to transform this indigenous situational identity into a national identity. He tried proactively to create a bordered national space for the Métis before the competing national iden-tities and institutions of Canada and the United States swallowed up their homeland in the Red River valley. These new North American nation-states, in turn, used the Métis to access the interior, but then reified indigenous identity as antimodern, and inherently outside of the civil societies that con-stituted North American national identities. Indigenous peoples, so pivotal to the evolution of modern North America, were coercively refashioned as cultural outsiders in the very world that they had helped to create.

The Red River Rebellion speaks powerfully about the ways in which the ideologies of discovery and republican revolution created a justification for Native conquest so powerful that it masked the long history of Native peoples who managed not to succumb to either for more than two centuries. The Red River story also ensures that we consider the role of Canada in this multifaceted narrative of national expansion. The revolution in Texas and the Mexican-American War guarantee that the U.S. and Mexican national narratives are seen as intertwined. The northern borderland, however, had a similar history where the attempt to impose national boundaries onto a contested space had the effect of reifying categories such as race, nation, citizenship, and sovereignty among a population that had lived for centuries in a social world where these things did not exist. The challenge for any historian of North America is to recognize the existence of this other space, this Native New World, and to account for its significant impact on the historical development of the modern world in which we live.

GLOSSARY OF NATIVE TERMS

The history of the Native New World needs to be considered in terms of indigenous politics, social categories, and where possible language and meaning. The latter can be problematic. Incorporating the Ojibwe language, Anishinaabemowin, into an English-language text presents a challenge. Until recently this was an oral language with many mutually intelligible spoken dialects. Even more important, the Ojibwe language consists mostly of verbs, whereas the English language is dominated by the use of nouns. Accordingly, I often used words such as *inawemaagin* (relative) as the signifier of a noun or category where it would more properly be used as a verb. Where possible I tried to use a standard contemporary orthography, although in some circumstances I am forced to use older transcriptions for clarity. In spite of these differences, however, we can still see how these linguistic and social categories shaped how the Anishinaabeg understood the world in which they lived.

Terms

adaawewininni	traders
athataion	Feast of the Dead
calumet	pipe, showing peaceful intent
doodem (pl. doodemag)	clan
inawemaagen	relative, insider
itancan	leader of a Dakota band
manidoo	power, esp. beyond normal human abilities
meyaagizid	foreigner, outsider
ogimaa (pl. ogimaag)	leader, a person skilled in diplomacy, warfare, trade, or hunting—someone with access to manidoo and the willingness to use such power and resources on behalf of the people of the leader's community
oyate	people
tákukic 'iyapi	a people "related to each other"
tiyospaye	winter band, lodge group

| wasicun | similar to manidoo, anything with sacred or extraordinary power |

Names of places

Anishinaabewaki	homeland of the Anishinaabeg
Bow-e-ting	Sault Sainte Marie
Gaazagaskwaajimekaag	Leech Lake
Ga-mitaawaa-ga-gum	Sandy Lake
Gichigamiing	Lake Superior
Gichi-ziibi	Mississippi River
Makoumitikac	the bears' fishing place
Miskwaawaak-zaaga'igan	Red Cedar Lake
Odaawaa Zaaga'igan	Ottawa Lake, which goes by its French equivalent, Lac Courte Oreilles
O-Mush-ko-zo-sag-ai-igum	Elk Lake
Penesewichewan Sepee	Hayes River; *see also under names of people*
Pikousitesinacut	the place where shoes are worn out
Shagwaamikong	La Pointe du Chequamegon

Names of people or groups

Achipoes	Loon
Anishinaabeg	Real or Original people, self designation used by speakers of Anishinaabemowin, including the Ojibweg, Odawaag, Boodewaadamiig, as well as people designated by the French as People of the North and Gens des Terres.
Assiniboine	phonetic transcription of the Anishinaabemowin *assini-pwa-n*, or stone enemy
Athinuwick	*see* Muskekowuck-athinuwick
Ayoes	Iowa
Boodewaadamiig	*see* Pottawatomie
Bwaanag	Ojibwe designation for the Dakota
Christinos	Cree
Eshkibagikoonzhe	Flat Mouth
Gens des Terres	French designation for People of the North
Gichi-manidoo	the greatest of spirit beings
Gichi-mookomaanag	Long Knives/Americans

Haudenosaunee	People of the Longhouse (Iroquois Confederacy)
Ho-Chunk	People of the First Voice, Winnebago
Iroquois	*see* Haudenosaunee
Malamechs	Catfish
Mesquakie	Red Earth People
Monsoni	Moose and Marten
Moosu Sepee	Lowland Cree inhabitants of the Moose River
Muskekowuck-athinuwick	Lowland Cree
Nawadaha	Henry Rowe Schoolcraft, U.S. Indian agent
Nehiyaw-athinuwick	Upland Cree
Ni-ka	Goose
Noquets	Bear
Oceti Sakowin	The seven council fires, the designation for the Dakota-Yankton/Yanktonai-Lakota peoples who also referred to themselves as the allies or the Dakota/Lakota. *See also* Sioux
Odawaag	Anishinaabe peoples also identified as the Ottawa peoples by the French
Onontio	governor of New France (Native title for)
Otagami	Ojibwe designation agaaming signifying across the lake and used to identify the Mesquakie people identified as the Fox by the French and the United States
Penesewichewan Sepee	Lowland Cree inhabitants of the Hayes River
Pottawatomie	French designation for the Boodewaadamii Anishinaabeg, Keepers of the Fire
Sauteur	French designation for the Anishinaabe peoples residing at Sainte Marie du Sault, and applied to the Ojibwe peoples in general
Sioux	Nadoneceronons, na-towe-ssiwak Nadouessioux, commonly shortened to Sioux
Tiyoskate	Plays in the Lodge
Washeo Sepee	Severn River Cree
Wemitigoozhig	French
Wyandot	Wendat, Huron Dakota
Zhaaganaashag	British
Zhingobiins	Little Balsam Fir

NOTES

Prologue

1. For an Ojibwe account of the Pike expedition to Leech Lake, see William Warren, *History of the Ojibway People* (1885; repr. St. Paul: Minnesota Historical Society Press, 1984), 349–50.

2. *Schoolcraft's Expedition to Lake Itasca: The Discovery of the Source of the Mississippi*, ed. Phillip P. Mason (East Lansing: Michigan State University Press, 1993), appendix A, Henry Rowe Schoolcraft to Elbert Herring, February 13, 1832, 130.

3. Elbert Herring to Henry Rowe Schoolcraft, May 3, 1832, in Mason, *Schoolcraft's Expedition*, appendix A, 138.

4. Letters and journal of Lt. John Allen, in Mason, *Schoolcraft's Expedition*, 207.

5. Boutwell diary, July 17, 1832, 45.

6. Ibid., 45–46; and "Schoolcraft's 'Narrative of an Expedition Through the Upper Mississippi,'" in Mason, *Schoolcraft's Expedition*, 54.

7. "Schoolcraft's 'Narrative,'" 55.

8. Allen, letters and journal, 210.

9. Henry Wadsworth Longfellow, *The Song of Hiawatha* (Boston: Ticknor and Fields, 1855), 285.

10. Ibid., 287.

11. Ibid., 283.

12. For an example of this sort of narrative, see *The Capture of Old Vincennes: The Original Narratives of George Rogers Clark and His Opponent Gov. Henry Hamilton*, ed. Milo M. Quaife (Indianapolis: Bobbs-Merrill, 1927).

13. Robert F. Berkhofer, *The Whiteman's Indian: Images of the American Indian from Columbus to the Present* (New York: Vintage, 1979); Philip J. Deloria, *Playing Indian* (New Haven, Conn.: Yale University Press, 1998), 64–65.

14. Christoph Irmscher, *Longfellow Redux* (Urbana: University of Illinois Press, 2008), 108; Alan Trachtenberg makes a similar argument, writing that "Longfellow and Schoolcraft agreed that 'true nationality' derives from a nation's 'singular folk tradition,' and that in the absence of a 'folk,' the United States had its Indians, sadly 'vanishing' but gladly rich in accessible lore." Trachtenberg, *Shades of Hiawatha: Staging Indians, Making Americans, 1880–1930* (New York: Hill and Wang, 2004), 65.

15. Irmscher, *Longfellow Redux*, 111.

16. Henry Rowe Schoolcraft, *Oneota, or the Characteristics of the Red Race* (New York: Wiley & Putnam, 1845), 14.

17. For an example of Schoolcraft's use of his wife's literary production, see *Schoolcraft's Ojibwa Lodge Stories: Life on the Lake Superior Frontier*, ed. Phillip P. Mason (East Lansing: Michigan State University Press, 1997).

18. Report of Expedition of 1831, Henry Rowe Schoolcraft to Elbert Herring, appendix A in Mason, *Schoolcraft's Expedition*, 126–27.

19. For Hiawatha and the Law of Peace, see Daniel K. Richter, *The Ordeal of the Longhouse: The Peoples of the Iroquois League in the Era of European Colonization* (Chapel Hill: University of North Carolina Press, 1992), 30–49.

20. For an explanation of the name *Anishinaabeg* by a scholar who was an Ojibwe mixed-blood, see Warren, *History of the Ojibway People*, 37, 56.

21. The borderlands of the American southwest have seen the most innovative scholarship in this regard. See James Brooks, *Captives and Cousins: Slavery, Kinship, and Community in the Southwest Borderlands* (Chapel Hill: University of North Carolina Press, 2002); Ned Blackhawk, *Violence Over the Land: Indians and Empires in the Early American West* (Cambridge, Mass.: Harvard University Press, 2006; Pekka Hämäläinen, *Comanche Empire* (New Haven, Conn.: Yale University Press, 2008); Karl Jacoby, *Shadows at Dawn: A Borderlands Massacre and the Violence of History* (New York: Penguin Press, 2008); and Brian DeLay, *War of a Thousand Deserts: Indian Raids and the U.S.-Mexican War* (New Haven, Conn.: Yale University Press, 2008).

22. James Merrell, "The Indian's New World: The Catabwa Experience," *William and Mary Quarterly*, 3rd series, 41, no. 4 (October 1984), 538.

23. The quotation comes from the intendant of New France in the 1680s, Jean Talon, in Archives National de France, Archives des Colonies, Series C11 E, Des limites des Postes, AN C11 E 1 Mémoire sur la domination des Francois en Canada, July 1687, f 210.

Part I. Discovery

1. See, for example, Thomas D. Dillehay, *The Settlement of the Americas: A New Prehistory* (New York: Basic Books, 2000).

2. Stephen Greenblatt, *Marvelous Possessions: The Wonder of the New World* (Chicago: University of Chicago Press, 1991), 14.

3. Ibid., 60.

Chapter 1. Place and Belonging in Native North America

1. *Anishinaabeg* can be translated as "human beings" or "original people"; *Anishinaabe* is the singular form of this word. This term is significant as a self-referent used by multiple groups of Algonquian peoples that were identified by Europeans in the seventeenth century as distinct Indian nations such as the Sauteurs, known as the Ojibwe in the nineteenth century, the Ottawas, Pottawatomie, Nipissing, Mississauga, and several other named Native groups. As my focus here is on Ojibwe-speaking peoples inhabiting the western Great Lakes and northwest interior, I am using a Western Ojibwe orthography. John D. Nichols and Earl Nyholm, *A Concise Dictionary of Minnesota Ojibwe* (Minneapolis: University of Minneapolis Press, 1995), vii. See also Richard A. Rhodes, *Eastern Ojibwa-Chippewa-Ottawa Dictionary* (Berlin: Mouton, 1985); and Warren, *History of the Ojibway People*, 56–57. In a similar fashion I am using Native self-designations for Wyandot, identified as Huron by Europeans (see William C. Sturtevant, gen. ed., *Handbook of North American Indians* [Washington, D.C.: Smithsonian Institution, 1978], hereafter *HNAI*, vol. 15, *Northeast*, ed. Bruce Trigger); the Muskekowuck-athinuwick, the swampy or lowland people, identified as the Cree by Europeans (see David H. Pentland, "Synonymy of the West Main and Western Woods Cree," in *HNAI*, vol. 6, *Subarctic*,

ed. June Helm [Washington, D.C.: Smithsonian Institution, 1981], 226, 269); and the Dakota, identified as the Sioux by Europeans (see *HNAI*).

2. Linguist Richard Rhodes observed that "there are only two general terms in Ojibwa for categories of people with respect to membership in Ojibwa society: *inawemaagen* 'relative', and *meyaagizid* 'foreigner.' . . . Notably absent are separate categories of unrelated cultural insiders which would correspond to English 'friend' and 'stranger.'" See Richard A. Rhodes, "Ojibwa Politeness and Social Structure," in William Cowen, ed., *Papers of the Nineteenth Algonquian Conference* (Ottawa: Carleton University, 1988), 172–73.

3. For the origin and significance of the Feast of the Dead see Harold Hickerson, "The Feast of the Dead Among the Seventeenth Century Algonkins of the Upper Great Lakes," *American Anthropologist* 62, no.1 (February 1960); and Richard White, *The Middle Ground: Indians, Empires, and Republics in the Great Lakes Region, 1650–1850* (Cambridge: Cambridge University Press, 1991), 102–4.

4. In the Great Lakes and northern plains, territory was seldom, if ever, the exclusive domain of a single Native community. This fact necessitated frequent interaction between Native communities with the result that social boundaries remained porous and flexible. Given this situation, Donald Hardesty has argued: "As long as the social boundaries between groups are loose, 'owned' physical space becomes more a theoretical concept than an expression of actual behavior. Consequently, resources or land belonging to one group can be used by others if the social relationships are sufficiently close to make the outsiders practicing, if not actual, members of the group." See Donald L. Hardesty, *Ecological Anthropology* (New York: John Wiley and Sons, 1977), 186. In an extension of this argument, Patricia Albers and Jeanne Kay argue that historical analysis of Indian territoriality in the Great Lakes and northern plains requires a regional perspective. This is explicitly not a nation-state or national model of territoriality, but rather a call for a "theoretical framework in which varied relations between members of different tribal groups are understood as interdependent facets of geographically far-ranging and ethnically mixed systems." See Patricia Albers and Jeanne Kay, "Sharing the Land: A Study in American Indian Territoriality," in Thomas E. Ross and Tyrell G. Moore, eds., *A Cultural Geography of North American Indians* (Boulder: Westview Press, 1987), 57.

5. For quote see Benedict Anderson, *Imagined Communities: Reflections on the Origin and Spread of Nationalism,* rev. ed. (London: Verso, 1991), 4. Anderson explored how nation and nationalism came into being as a mode of political and social organization in human communities. In time Europeans would come to read this national idea onto Native communities in North America, and indigenous peoples themselves would adopt this self-designation as a means of asserting their sovereignty. But as Anderson argues so lucidly in *Imagined Communities*, the nation did not fully emerge as a type or category of social formation until the end of the eighteenth century. This does not, however, alter his argument that all communities are imagined. More to the point, this ceremony underscores the importance of trying to understand Native peoples in terms of an indigenous political imaginary.

6. Albers and Kay argue, "what distinguished and separated the actual land use of various groups was not some abstract territorial claim or boundary across the landscape, but rather the relationships among groups who lived in proximity to each other." Albers and Kay, "Sharing the Land," 56. These relationships, which I articulate here as structured by the categories meyaagizid and inawemaagen, created a multiethnic social space that linked the northern plains to the marshlands and lakeshore villages of the Great Lakes.

7. Radisson subsequently wrote narratives for two journeys into the interior from Hudson's Bay in 1682–84. The narratives of all six voyages were published in English in Pierre Esprit Radis-

son, *The Voyages of Peter Esprit Radisson: Being an Account of His Travels and Experiences Among the North American Indians, from 1652 to 1684*, ed. Gideon D. Scull (Boston: Prince Society, 1885), quote on 209.

8. The manuscript of Radisson's first four voyages likely received little circulation until 1686, after Charles II had granted the Hudson's Bay Company title to territory in North America. At this point they, along with the narratives of the fifth and sixth voyages, became important evidentiary material in the conflict between France and England for right of possession of Hudson's Bay and the western interior. Radisson's experience in the west described vividly in the first four narratives, however, is what made the voyageur and his brother-in-law influential in the establishment of the company in 1671. For the history of Radisson's manuscript and the publication and circulation of *The Jesuit Relations*, see Germaine Warkentin, "Styles of Authorship in New France: Pierre Boucher, Settler and Pierre Esprit Radisson, Explorer," *Papers of the Bibliographical Society of Canada* 37, no. 2 (Fall 1999).

9. Anthony Pagden has labeled this process of cultural erasure and territorial appropriation "the principle of attachment," which he describes as follows: "The sequence attachment, recognition, naming constitutes the process of carrying back, the route by which the discoverer 'enters into' what he has discovered. It is also, like every process of discovery, one which ends with an act of possession." He concludes that "from Columbus to Humboldt the principle of attachment served to make the incommensurable seem commensurable, if only for so long as it took the observer's vision to adjust, in Humboldt's metaphor, from the geology to the flora and fauna of the world he had come to inhabit. Attachment allowed for the creation of an initial (if sometimes troubling) familiarity. It also allowed the discoverer to make some measure of classification. Above all it allowed him to name, and by naming to take cognitive possession of what he had 'laid eyes on.'" See Anthony Pagden, *European Encounters with the New World* (New Haven, Conn.: Yale University Press, 1993), 34, 36. See also Greenblatt, *Marvelous Possessions*, 23–24, 60–61.

10. Edward Said, writing about the development of scholarly expertise as an aspect of European colonization of the Middle East or Orient, has argued that "such texts can create not only knowledge but also the very reality they appear to describe." This is not to suggest that the western interior of North America, like Said's Orient, is the textual creation of European scholars, but these discovery narratives did provide a description and explanation of the continent that simultaneously provided a rationale for its colonization. It was a place empty of civilization, and full of unclaimed wealth. See Edward Said, *Orientalism* (New York: Vintage Books, 1979), 94.

11. Radisson, in *Voyages*, 174.

12. For the Wendat/Huron and Wyandot, see *HNAI*, 15: 368–74, 398–402.

13. For the origins and development of the Haudenosaunee or Iroquois, see Elizabeth Tooker, "The League of the Iroquois: Its History, Politics, and Ritual," in *HNAI*, 15: 418–41. See also Richter, *The Ordeal of the Longhouse*; and Jose Antonio Brandao, *Your Fyre Shall Burn No More: Iroquois Policy Toward New France and Its Native Allies to 1701* (Lincoln: University of Nebraska Press, 1997).

14. When he sailed up the Saint Lawrence River in 1609 to reestablish the French Empire in territory identified as la Canada, Champlain met Huron leaders who, in his words, "desired vengeance" against the Iroquois, and who had "come to meet us for the purpose of making an alliance." Champlain assured them "that I had no intention other than to make war." For the establishment and consummation of this alliance through an attack on the Huadenosanee, see Samuel de Champlain, *Les Voyages du Sieur Champlain, 1567–1653* (Ann Arbor: University Microfilms, 1966), 206–10; and Francis Jennings, *The Ambiguous Iroquois Empire: The Covenant Chain Confederation of Indian Tribes with the English Colonies* (New York: W. W. Norton, 1984), 41–43.

15. Patricia Seed argues that the idea that "unimproved land" was "wasteland," that is, land not properly utilized and therefore subject to appropriation, was unique to the English. Improvement represented a culturally subjective and fetishized category of land use. Specifically, this term implied the practice of commercial agriculture defined by the accumulation and deployment of capital resources within a fixed (fenced) and privately owned space designed to produce surplus revenue in the form of merchantable commodities. This idea, the labor theory of property best articulated by John Locke, allowed the English to assert that improving land removed it from "the state of nature," where it existed as part of a universal commons. By extension, any lands not so improved were de facto unpossessed. Following this circular reasoning, land not encompassed by any property regime recognizable to the English was, for all practical purposes, unoccupied land. For the labor theory of property, see Patricia Seed, *American Pentimento: The Invention of Indians and the Pursuit of Riches* (Minneapolis: University of Minnesota Press, 2001), 14–23; and for English definitions of wasteland, 29–40. See also William Cronin, *Changes in the Land: Indians, Colonists, and the Ecology of New England* (New York: Hill and Wang, 1989). Anthony Pagden's work suggests that Seed overstates the case for the uniqueness of English ideology in this regard. The French Empire relied on a parallel argument that claimed occupancy did not confer property rights. Native peoples possessed usufruct rights, but due to the nature of their society (barbaric and or nomadic), they had failed to exercise sovereignty over the territory they inhabited. See Pagden's chapter "Conquest and Settlement" in *Lords of All the World: Ideologies of Empire in Spain, Britain and France, c. 1500–1800* (New Haven: Yale University Press, 1995).

16. This concept of unsettled land derived from an idea in Roman law known as res nullis, which defined unoccupied lands as the common property of all humankind. The idea of res nullis was used by the advocates of settler colonialism to rationalize European claims to sovereign possession of alien land in North America, and required the specious argument that Native peoples occupied their territory without exercising the rights of possession and sovereignty. For an exploration of how European jurists and thinkers deployed these concepts, see Pagden, *Lords of All the World*, 66–86. For the most developed articulations of the concepts of the state of nature and natural law from a French perspective, see Emeric de Vattel, *Le Droit des gens, ou, principes de la loi naturelle, appliqués à la conduite & aux affaires des nations & des souverains*, 2 vols. (Leiden: M. de Vattel, 1758); and from an English perspective, John Locke, *Two Treatises of Government*, rev. ed. (Cambridge: Cambridge University Press, 1960).

17. The term *Algonquian* describes an extensive language family. See Leonard Bloomfield, "Algonquian," in Harry Hoijer, ed., *Linguistic Structures of Native America* (New York: Johnson Reprint, 1971). Algonquian languages were spoken throughout North America, from the eastern seaboard to the Great Plains. The French recognized this language family to be divided into related dialects, which did not correspond to a singular political or cultural identification. Nevertheless, they generally used the term *Algonquian* as a designation associated with speakers of the Ojibwe dialects of the Algonquian language family from the region they called the pays d'en haut or upper country. For the clearest articulation of a French ethnographic reading of this linguistic community, and an explanation of how the term was applied by the colonists of New France, see Rueben Gold Thwaites, ed., *The Jesuit Relations and Allied Documents* (Cleveland: Burrows Brothers, 1898), hereafter cited as *JR*, 42: 221–23, 44: 239–45.

18. *JR* 18: 218–19.

19. For the story of this anonymous Anishinaabe woman, see *JR* 18: 218–221.

20. For an explanation of mourning wars, see Daniel Richter, "War and Culture: The Iroquois Experience," *William and Mary Quarterly*, 3d ser. (October 1983).

21. *JR* 23: 205.

22. *JR* 23: 205–7.

23. As the anthropologist Regna Darnell has suggested, "Hunters and Gatherers appear random or disordered in their social and political organization only as long as their seasonal round of subsistence practices is not taken into account." This intimate relationship with the plant and animal populations of a given territory, rather than any essential "nomadic consciousness," explains migration patterns and social structure, and how the two are interconnected. See Regna Darnell, "Rethinking the Concepts of Band and Tribe, Community and Nation: An Accordion Model of Nomadic Native American Social Organization," in David H. Pentland, ed., *Papers of the 29th Algonquian Conference* (Winnipeg: University of Manitoba, 1998), 98.

24. Darnell makes this argument quite forcefully and descriptively. "I want to suggest," she asserts, "that the basic model of Algonquian social organization is not one of random movement on land but of an accordion, a process of subsistence-motivated expansion and contraction of social groups in relations to resource exploitation. . . . Ties to land are foundational, but the particular piece of land to which they are tied can change; ties to new land require that individuals forge relationships to a particular local environment, continuing a pattern of mutual entailment between the social and natural worlds." Darnell, "Rethinking Band and Tribe," 91.

25. *JR* 23: 209–17.

26. *JR* 23: 221.

27. For the Jesuits' use of gift giving, see *JR* 23: 212–13, quote on 223.

28. *JR* 23: 225.

29. For *The Relation of 1640* see *JR* 18: 231; for Bow-e-ting and its significance to the Anishinaabeg, see Warren, *History of the Ojibway People*, 80–81.

30. *Anishinaabe*, as a signifier of identity, connected individuals to other peoples speaking Anishinaabemowin, the Ojibwe dialects of the Algonquian language family spoken with regional variations across the northern Great Lakes and northwest interior "*Anishinaabemowin*," the linguists John Nichols and Earl Nyholm argue, "is not spoken in a single standard from but varies from place to place in sounds, vocabulary, and grammar." Nichols and Nyholm, *A Concise Dictionary of Minnesota Ojibwe*, vii. See also Rhodes, *Eastern Ojibwa-Chippewa-Ottawa Dictionary*; and Warren, *History of the Ojibway People*, 56–57.

31. For the significance of doodemag, or clan identities, among the Anishinaabeg, see Heidi Bohaker, "Nindoodemag: The Significance of Algonquian Kinship Networks in the Eastern Great Lakes Region, 1600–1701," *William and Mary Quarterly* 63, no. 1 (2006); for a more dated but still important analysis of band and clan identities among the Ojibwe of Sault Sainte Marie, see Hickerson, "The Feast of the Dead"; and Harold Hickerson, *The Chippewa and Their Neighbors: A Study in Ethnohistory* (New York: Holt, Rinehart, and Winston, 1970), 37–50.

32. For the Native identifications in *The Relation of 1640*, see *JR* 18: 229, for the Cree, 231 for the Dakota, and 233 for the Mandan trade fairs.

33. *JR* 23: 225.

34. For the departure of the Wyandot from their homeland and their migration to Anishinaabewaki, see Nicolas Perrot, *Mémoire sur les moeurs, coustumes et religion des sauvages de l'Amérique Septentrionale*, ed. R. P. J. Tailhan, editions Elysee Montreal (Quebec: Bibliothèque natonale du Quebec, 1973), 83–104. In Darnell's accordion model formulation, the largest unit, summer villages, could include bands from "unrelated tribes." Darnell, "Rethinking Band and Tribe," 98. See also White, *The Middle Ground*, 8–10; Helen Hornbeck Tanner, *Atlas of Great Lakes Indian History* (Norman: University of Oklahoma Press, 1987), 30–34; and Gilles Havard, *Empire et métissages: In-*

diens et Français dans le pays d'en Haut, 1660–1715 (Paris: Presses de l'Université de Paris-Sorbonne, 2003), 126–30.

35. For the governor, see Radisson, in *Voyages*, 174–75.

36. Claude Charles Le Roy, Bacqueville de la Potherie, *Histoire de l'Amérique Septentrionale: Relation d'un séjour en Nouvelle France*, 4 vols., (1753; repr. Paris: Editions du Rocher, 1997), 2: 272.

37. *JR* 40: 211.

38. *JR* 40: 213–15.

39. *JR* 41: 77.

40. *JR* 41: 79.

41. *JR* 40: 211.

42. *JR* 40: 215.

43. *JR* 42: 221. Dreuillettes made a similar statement in *The Relation of 1656–58*. Speaking about the peoples of the pays d'en haut he said, "anyone who learns the Algonquin language will soon readily understand them all." *JR* 44: 239.

44. *JR* 44: 239.

45. See Gabriel Dreuillettes, "Chemins a la Mer du Nord," in *JR* 44: 238–45; and "De l'Estat du pais des Algonquins & de quelques nouvelles découvertes," in *JR* 45: 216–39. For a detailed account of Native traders participating in the inland, see the record of a voyage that began in the French settlements, headed west beyond Lake Superior, traced the watersheds from the lake to the north to Hudson's Bay, and then went back to New France, "On the Condition of the Algonquian Country and of Some New Discoveries," in *JR* 45: 216–39.

46. Darnell distinguishes between four functional units of social organization among Algonquian communities like the Cree and Ojibwe: the lodge group composed of 10–20 individuals, consisting of two to three extended families; the winter band made up of 35–75 people (two to three lodge groups) living together for the hunting season; the named band comprising 150–300 people linked by kinship and marriage; the nuclear core from which winter bands are derived; and the summer group, a larger village community of approximately 1,500 people, including several named bands. These were the social units that Lalemont referenced when he complained that the Nipissing "continually divide themselves up." And although he read this division as a sign of barbarity, Darnell notes that "this accordion-like system has a considerable advantage under stress conditions because it can regenerate complexity from any component part." See Darnell, "Rethinking Band and Tribe," 98–99.

47. *JR* 42: 219.

48. *JR* 42: 219–21.

49. This sort of exchange, characterized by the anthropologist Marshall Sahlins as "generalized reciprocity," established social conditions that facilitated the movement of goods and people between different social groups, across a jointly occupied territory. See Marshall Sahlins, *Stone Age Economics* (Chicago: Aldine-Atherton, 1972), especially 168, 193–95, 302–3.

50. "Onontio" was the name given to the first titular governor of New France, Charles Huault de Montmagny, by his Huron allies. Because the governor's name signified a mountain, the Huron called him "Onontio," which meant mountain in their language. Richard White argues that the figure of Onontio served as a political centerpiece that linked the French Empire to a vast array of autonomous Native allies. "Distant groups," he writes, "were united within the French alliance not so much by their real and metaphorical kinship relations with one another as by their common standing as children of Onontio, who was the representative of the French King." In this formulation, Native peoples were not political subordinates but partners bound by a complicated, and

often fragile, relationship of mutual dependency. For a summary of the evolution of the role and significance of Onontio, see White, *The Middle Ground*, 40. Gilles Havard offers a similar argument but with a slightly different emphasis. He contends that while the French were the driving force that structured the alliance, "il ne faut pas occulter le fait que cette alliance prolonge des reseaux anciens." Thus, the alliance was in part the product of colonial New France, but also represented a rebirth of existing social networks that defined the village world of the Great Lakes. See Havard, *Empire et métissages*, 142–43.

51. Anthony Pagden argues that Europeans understood executive power within their societies according to Roman law concepts that constructed the royal persona as a distinct political identity, a category separate from personhood. Political authority derived from this persona, and rights within the empire were determined by the royal subject's relationship to the king. This system, Pagden argues, was embedded within a model of the Roman family that gave parents absolute power over their children and created a language of personalized dependency. Although the governor never exercised absolute power over his allies, his desire to do so was a source of constant tension and negotiation. More to the point, however, this model would have easily fit within the idea of a father-child relationship imagined (albeit differently) by Onontio and his children. See Pagden, *Lords of All the World*, 140–46. The experienced voyageur Nicolas Perrot observed that elders were called father by the young men of their village, and he noted: "The most considerable and well-off chiefs go hand in hand with the poor. . . . They support and undertake warmly the cause of one another between allies, and when there are disputes they use a lot of moderation. . . . If there is anyone who merits a reprimand it is made with a lot of gentleness." For elaboration on the role of an Anishinaabe father, see Perrot, *Memoire*, 72.

52. *JR* 50: 285. For pity, unequal power in social relationships, and Ojibwe concepts of spiritual power, see Mary Black-Rogers, "Ojibwa Power Belief System," in Richard Adams and Raymond Fogelson, eds., *The Anthropology of Power* (New York: Academic Press, 1977).

53. For an examination of manidoo and pity in relation to the French fur trade and diplomacy, see Bruce White, "Encounters with Spirits: Ojibwa and Dakota Theories About the French and Their Merchandise," *Ethnohistory* 41, no. 3 (Summer 1994). See also Christopher L. Miller and George R. Hamell, "A New Perspective on Indian-White Contact: Cultural Symbols and Colonial Trade," *Journal of American History* 73 (September 1986).

54. *JR* 42: 227–29.

55. *JR* 42: 231.

56. *JR* 42: 233; throughout this ordeal Gareau lay wounded on the floor of the Mohawk fort, stripped naked and without food or water. Eventually, the Mohawk delivered Gareau and Dreuillettes to Montreal along with two presents—one to express their sorrow for the incident, a second to console the French for their loss. Gareau died shortly after his arrival. For Gareau's return, see *JR* 42: 237–39.

57. Dale Russell, citing Grace Lee Nute, questions whether or not Radisson participated in this voyage. Russell is concerned with establishing the fact of Cree occupation in territory northwest of Lake Superior, and thus offers a thorough examination of the origins and development of the inland trade both from New France and later from Hudson's Bay. See Dale Russell, *The Eighteenth Century Western Cree and Their Neighbors*, Mercury Series (Ottawa: Canadian Museum of Civilization, 1991), 48; and Grace Lee Nute, *Ceasars of the Wilderness* (New York: Appleton Century, 1943; repr., St. Paul: Minnesota Historical Society, 1978).

58. Radisson, "Third Voyage," in *Voyages*, 136–37.

59. Ibid., 147–48.

60. Ibid., 149. Radisson's identification of the Sauteurs is presented in a confusing fashion, but most clearly on page 154, where he identifies them as the people of Bow-e-ting.

61. Taking at face value assertions by French traders and missionaries that the Sauteurs moved west as refugees, the ethnohistorian Harold Hickerson has argued that the Anishinaabeg moved west following the French trade and became middlemen facilitating trade with western peoples. In his account, their migration is not seasonal and they enter the region as outsiders moving west with the trade due to a dependency on European technology. See Hickerson, *The Southwestern Chippewa*. Most monographs focusing on the nineteenth-century Anishinaabeg or Ojibwe in the Great Lakes and Upper Mississippi follow this argument concerning the eastern origin and western migration. See, for example, Gary Clayton Anderson, *Kinsmen of Another Kind: Dakota-White Relations in the Upper Mississippi Valley, 1650–1862* (St. Paul: Minnesota Historical Society Press, 1997); and Melissa L. Meyer, *The White Earth Tragedy: Ethnicity and Dispossession at a Minnesota Anishinaabe Reservation* (Lincoln: University of Nebraska Press, 1994).

62. Radisson, "Third Voyage," 149.

63. Ibid., 155.

64. For Radisson's description of the Anishinaabeg-Cree-Dakota conflict, see Radisson, "Third Voyage," 154. Estimates of the Dakota population living east of the Mississippi River in the seventeenth century are vague at best. Radisson estimated the population of the village at Mille Lacs in the upper Mississippi valley as seven thousand. See Radisson, "Fourth Voyage," in *Voyages*, 220. Dreuillettes, who would have relied on informants such as Radisson and Des Groseilliers as well as Native informants, claimed the Dakotas had forty villages; see *JR* 42: 221. During this time Louis Hennepin, who lived briefly in captivity among the Dakota, estimated their population at eight thousand to nine thousand men. Louis Hennepin, *A New Discover of a Vast Country in America*, ed. Reuben G. Thwaites, 2 vols. (London, 1698; repr. Chicago: A. C. McClurg, 1903), 1: 226. See also Raymond J. DeMallie, "The Sioux Until 1850," *HNAI*, vol. 13, ed. Raymond J. DeMallie and Douglas R. Parks (Washington, D.C.: Smithsonian Institution, 2001), part 2, 722–37. With the numbers suggested above, total population among the Dakota-Yankton/Yanktonai-Lakota peoples would be approximately 25,000 to 30,000.

65. Radisson, "Third Voyage," 154. Nicolas Perrot also described the warfare against the Dakota during this time; see Perrot, *Memoire*, 90–92.

66. Radisson, "Third Voyage," 155.

67. Ibid. The singular form of the term is *na-towe-ssi*, which the French spelled phonetically as Nadouessioux, using the French plural *-x* as a substitute for the Ojibwe plural *-ak*. See Raymond J. DeMallie and Douglas R. Parks, "Sioux, Assiniboine, and Stoney Dialects: A Classification," *Anthropological Linguistics* 34 (1992): 233–55. There is disagreement about the meaning of this word. William Warren, for example, described this as an Ojibwe dialect word from the precontact era signifying "adders," or snakes, which implied an enemy. This term, he suggested, was applied to the Iroquois as well as the Dakota. Warren, *History of the Ojibway People*, 82. DeMallie and Parks, however, show there is little evidence to suggest that this term had such a meaning. See also DeMallie, "The Sioux Until 1850," 749. For quote, see Radisson, "Third Voyage," 155.

68. Radisson, "Third Voyage," 157.

69. Radisson, "Fourth Voyage," 175. Although it makes sense that Radisson would need to partner with the one-eyed Sauteur in order to attend this ceremony, the latter is conspicuously absent from most of the narrative. He is clearly identified, however, as the "chiefest captain" and "that blind" on 201.

70. For the ambush, see ibid., 179–83.

71. For the encounter with the Confederated Indians, see ibid., 189; for the Cree, 193. *American Pentimento.*

72. This assertion was more than hubris as the royal procession of the king into the major cities of the realm, according to Patricia Seed, signaled a public affirmation of the transfer of power from the subject to their ruler. And the king's gift giving, again mirrored here by Radisson marked the subsequent dispensation of privileges by the king. See Patricia Seed, *Ceremonies of Possession in Europe's Conquest of the New World, 1492–1640* (Cambridge: Cambridge University Press, 1995), 52–53.

73. Radisson, "Fourth Voyage," 198–99.

74. Ibid., 200.

75. Ibid., 201.

76. Regarding the rituals of the Dakota, the Jesuits noted: "Their have extraordinary ways," which included the ritual feeding of their guests, but the missionaries asserted "they mainly adore the calumet." Perrot made a similar observation and noted that the calumet was "a great mark of distinction practiced among them. Because it made a child of the nation of the one who had this advantage, and naturalized him as such." Like gift giving, the calumet ritually established a social connection generally recognized as a kinship bond. For the Jesuits, see *JR* 42: 190; for Perrot, *Memoire*, 99.

77. For the Dakota calumet, see Radisson, "Fourth Voyage," 207, quote on 208.

78. Ibid., 210–11.

79. Ibid., 213.

80. Ibid., 214–15.

81. Ibid., 216.

82. Ibid., 216–17.

83. Ibid., 219.

84. Benedict Anderson described the evolution of the nation as a category of collective social identity as rooted in the search for "a new way of linking fraternity, power and time meaningfully together." This was exactly the effect of the Feast of the Dead ceremony, which used the concepts of manidoo and inawemaagen (power and kinship) to alter the meaning of the past (time). See Anderson, *Imagined Communties*, 36.

85. Radisson, "Fourth Voyage," 220.

86. *JR* 50: 249.

87. *JR* 50: 253.

88. *JR* 50: 266.

89. *JR* 50: 273.

90. This village community was reconstituted seasonally in different locations around Chequamegon Bay. Toward the end of the seventeenth century, French traders relocated their post from the end, or point, of the Chequamegon Peninsula to an island offshore of this location. The island, called "Mon-ing-wun-a-kuan-ing," or "place of the golden-breasted woodpecker" by Ojibwe speakers, became La Pointe until the late nineteenth century when, under American control, it was renamed Madeline Island. For Nanabozho and the Cequamegon Peninsula see Warren, *History of the Ojibway People*, 102, and for origins of La Pointe, 96. For another version of this story, see *JR* 54: 201–3. For the significance of Nanabozho in Anishinaabe origin stories, see Christopher Vescey, *Traditional Ojibwa Religion and Its Historical Changes* (Philadelphia: American Philisophical Society, 1983); for the Jesuit mission at this village, see *JR* 50: 273–77, 297–305. See also Hamilton Nelson Ross, *La Pointe: Village Outpost on Madeleine Island* (Madison: State Historical Society of Wisconsin, 2000), 40–43.

91. *JR* 50: 297.

92. *JR* 50: 301.

93. *JR* 54: 164.

94. *JR* 54: 167.

95. *JR* 54: 191.

96. *JR* 54: 167.

97. *JR* 54: 191–92.

98. *JR* 54: 193.

99. *JR* 54: 167.

100. *JR* 54: 195.

101. For the Illinois, see *JR* 51: 47–49; for the Pottawatomi, see *JR* 51: 27–29; for the Sauk and Fox, see *JR* 51: 43–45.

102. Village elders, for example, asked Allouez "to stay the hatchets" of their young warriors as soon as he arrived at La Pointe; *JR* 50: 279–81. The Jesuits also circulated presents throughout the region to secure their right to travel and to keep the mission open to visitors, many of whom had a history of conflict with one another. See, for example, *JR* 54: 191–95.

103. For the description of this episode, see Perrot, *Memoire*, 99–104.

104. For the reestablishment of the Odawa and Wyandot at Michilimackinac, see *JR* 55: 157–67.

105. For the abandonment of Saint Esprit, see *JR* 55: 171.

Chapter 2. The Rituals of Possession and the Problems of Nation

1. For Dablon, see *JR* 55: 107. In the original French version of this text it is said of St. Lusson, "Il fit d'abord convoquer les peuples d'alentour," which I have translated as "he summoned the surrounding peoples." The English translation of the *Jesuit Relations* edited by Reuben G. Thwaites gives this same sentence as "he summoned the surrounding tribes." The difference is significant in that the word *tribe* as used here imposes a nineteenth-century racialized spatial category onto seventeenth-century Native peoples.

2. *JR* 55: 104.

3. For the significance of the region northwest of Lake Superior to New France, see "Extrait d'une Lettre de Jean Talon au Roy," October 10, 1670, in Pierre Margry, *Découvertes et établissements des Français . . . de l'Amérique Septentrionale, 1614–1698*, 6 vols. (Paris: Maisonneuve, 1879; repr. New York: AMS, 1974), 1: 82–83. For the northwest interior and the search for the northwest passage, see "Second Extrait de l'Addition au Mémoire de Jean Talon au Roy," November 10, 1670, in Margry, *Découvertes* 1: 87–89. For Intendant Jean Talon's belief in the significance of discovering the Northwest Passage, see La Potherie, *Histoire*, 2: 294–95. For Talon on the French dependence on Indian allies for access and control of region northwest of Lake Superior, see "Premier Extrait d'une Lettre de Jean Talon à Colbert," November 10, 1670, in Margry, *Découvertes*, 1: 83–84; and "Extrait d'une Lettre de Jean Talon au Roy," November 2, 1671, in Margry, *Découvertes*, 1: 92–93.

4. "Premier extrait d'une letter de Jean Talon à Colbert," November 10, 1670, in Margry, *Découvertes*, 1: 84.

5. Ibid.

6. *The Royal Charter for Incorporating The Hudson's Bay Company* (London: Hudson's Bay, 1670).

7. AN C 11E 2 Mémoire général sur les limites de la Baye d'Hudson. The French made a similar

argument about the territories they claimed in South America, linking the possession of territory to the formation of a consensual alliance with Native peoples. As Patricia Seed suggests, "Indigenous willingness to participate in an alliance signaled that the French had not conquered the land, but rather had been able to persuade the natives voluntarily to ally with the crown of France." See Seed, *Ceremonies of Possession*, 64–65.

8. David Harvey, *Justice, Nature and the Geography of Difference* (Malden, Mass.: 1996), 111–12. For a more extensive discussion of mapping and colonization, see also J. Brian Harley, "Rereading the Maps of the Columbian Encounter," *Annals of the Association of American Geographers* 98, no. 2 (June 1992): 522–44; William Boelhower, "Inventing America: A Model of Cartographic Semiosis," *Word and Image* 4, no. 2 (April 1988): 475–97; and José Rabasa, "Allegories of the Atlas," in Francis Barker, Peter Hulme, Margret Iverson, and Diana Loxely, eds., *Europe and Its Others*, vol. 2 (Colchester: University of Essex, 1985).

9. Alfred Korzybski developed this concept that the map is not the territory as part of a semantic analysis about the nature of abstract representation and reality. Korzybski, "A Non-Aristotelian System and Its Necessity for Rigor in Mathematics and Physics," paper presented at the meeting of the American Association for the Advancement of Science, New Orleans, 1933, reprinted in *Science and Sanity* (New York: Harper & Row, 1970).

10. "Procès-verbal de la prise de possession des pays situés vers les lacs Huron et Superieur," June 4, 1671, in Margry, *Découvertes*, 1: 98.

11. See David Bell, *The Cult of the Nation in France: Inventing Nationalism, 1680–1800* (Cambridge, Mass.: Harvard University Press, 2001), 6–7.

12. *JR* 55: 109–11.

13. Gichi-manidoo, unlike a host of related other-than-human beings in Ojibwe cosmolgy, does not have anthropomorphic or animal attributes. Neither did this being play a role in the creation of the universe, although missionaries appropriated this term as a representation of the Christian God concept. Some scholars argue that existence of Gichi-manidoo was, in fact, a response to exposure to Christian missionaries, although this idea is rejected by the Ojibwe themselves. For Gichi-manidoo, and the spirit beings identified as grandfathers, see A. Irving Hallowell, *The Ojibwa of Berens River Manitoba: Ethnography into History* (Fort Worth, Tex.: Harcourt Brace, 1992), 67–68, 72–73.

14. For Allouez, see *JR* 55: 110–11. For manidoo and the appeal to spirit beings as grandfathers, see A. Irving Hallowell, "Ojibwa Ontology, Behavior, and World View," in *Culture in History*, ed. Stanley Diamond (New York: Columbia University Press, 1960), 22; and Bruce M. White, "Encounters with Spirits: Ojibwa and Dakota Theories about the French and Their Merchandise," *Ethnohistory* 41, no. 3 (Summer 1994), 380.

15. *JR* 55: 112–13.

16. For the construction of monarchial power and a national religious-cultural identity in France through violence and ritual as characterized the between Catholics and Protestant Huguenots during the sixteenth century, see Denis Crouzet, *Les Guerriers de Dieu: La violence au temps des troubles de religion*, 2 vols. (Paris, 1990). For a history of the idea of bodily resurrection and the early church, see Caroline Walker Bynum, *The Resurrection of the Body in Western Christianity, 200–1336* (New York: Columbia University Press, 1995); for discussion of the Eucharist and the survival of a spiritual identity that survives the earthly changes of the body, see 27–43.

17. For the concepts of person and self and the ritual of raising the dead, see Richard White, "'Although I Am Dead, I Am Not Entirely Dead. I Have Left a Second of Myself': Constructing Self and Persons on the Middle Ground of Early America," in Ronald Hoffman, Mechel Sobel, and

Frederika J. Teute, eds., *Through a Glass Darkly: Reflections on Personal Identity in Early America* (Chapel Hill: University of North Carolina Press, 1997); for the significance of ritual adoption as a response to demographic change, see Richter, "War and Culture."

18. For a description of the role of manidoo in living a healthy life, see Black-Rogers, "Ojibwa Power Belief System," 168, 193–95.

19. A. Irving Hallowell has written, "to the Ojibwa, persons are capable of metamorphosis by their very nature." He asserted, in fact, that "this is one of the distinctive generic attributes of persons in Ojibwa thought. So far as outward appearance is concerned, no hard and fast line can be drawn between an animal form and a human form because of this possibility." See Hallowell, *The Ojibwa of Berens River*, 66–67. For an example of human beings in Anishinaabe communities claiming direct descent from animals, see *JR* 51:33; and Perrot, *Memoire*, 5–7; and for analysis of this phenomenon and of the stories related to Nanabozho, see Vescey, *Traditional Ojibwa Religion*.

20. *JR* 55: 94.

21. *JR* 55: 94–96.

22. By the eighteenth century this marriage of map and travel narrative became a standard convention of European exploration. Most analysis of this practice has focused on maritime exploration, notably that of James Cook and George Vancouver. See, for example, Paul Carter, *The Road to Botany Bay: An Essay in Spatial History* (London: Faber and Faber, 1987); and Daniel W. Clayton, *Islands of Truth: The Imperial Fashioning of Vancouver Island* (Vancouver: University of British Columbia Press, 2000). Clayton argued that by fashioning Vancouver Island as a "cartographic shell," that is, represented as a space emptied of any social meaning outside its discovery by Europe, "Vancouver contributed to an imaginative geography that recontextualized the Northwest Coast [of North America] from imperial vantage points." The Jesuits in North America, in a sense, operated as inland explorers. Their intimate association with Native peoples, however, resulted in maps and cartographic texts with a unique emphasis on the outcome of colonial discovery and encounter— savage communities opened to proselytism, land opened to travel and trade, etc.—that provided a contextual understanding of the North American interior as a colonial possession of Europe. See also Harley, "Rereading the Maps of the Columbian Encounter."

23. *JR* 51: 21.

24. *JR* 54: 127.

25. For the definition of trader and an explanation of verb and noun construction, see Nichols and Nyholm, *A Concise Dictionary of Minnesota Ojibwe*; for another explication of this word and the Odawa identity, see Warren, *History of the Ojibway People*, 31–32.

26. *JR* 55: 97.

27. *JR* 55: 100, 101.

28. *JR* 55: 103.

29. For Talon, see "Premier extrait d'une lettre de Jean Talon à Colbert," November 10, 1670, in Margry, *Découvertes*, 1: 83–85.

30. *JR* 55: 98.

31. *JR* 55: 96.

32. *JR* 54: 134.

33. *JR* 23: 204.

34. For Radisson, see "The Third Voyage," 148–49; and "The Fourth Voyage," 191–93. For the Cree and northerners or Gens Des Terres at Sault Sainte Marie, see *JR* 54: 133. For Cree and Gens des Terres at Tadoussac, Montreal, and Quebec, see "Memoir in Proof of the Right of the French to the Iroquois Country and to Hudson's Bay," in *Documents Relative to the Colonial History of the*

State of New York; Procured in Holland, England, and France, ed. E. B. O'Callagahn (Albany, N.Y.: Parsons, Weed, 1853–87), 9: 304–5, hereafter cited as *NYCD*; *AN* C11E 1 Mémoire sur les domination des Francois en Canada, July 1687; *AN* C11E 1 Reponse au Mémoire présenté par Messieurs les Commissionaires du Roy d'Angleterre, March 7–17, 1689; and *AN* C11 E1 Mémoire sur les limites de la baye d'Hudson; for Cree at Hudson's Bay see "Second extrait de l'addition au mémoire de Jean Talon au Roy," November 10, 1670, in Margry, *Découvertes,* 1: 87–89; for the Cree and Monsoni at Montreal, see *JR* 54: 133.

35. La Potherie, *Histoire,* 2: 252.

36. For the best summary of the early contact history of the Assiniboine and their alliance with the Cree, see Russell, *Eighteenth Century Western Cree,* 172–86. For analysis of the migration of Dakota speaking peoples into the west, see Ray DeMallie, "Teton Dakota Kinship and Social Organization," Ph.D. diss., University of Chicago, 1971, 100. There is also linguistic evidence that Dakota-speaking bands were in contact with the Mandan by 1500, which supports a time line of western migration that has Dakota-dialect bands moving as far west as the Missouri River before 1700. See James W. Springer, and Stanley R. Witowski, "Siouan Historical Linguistics and Oneota Archaeology," in Guy Gibbon, ed., *Oneota Studies* (Minneapolis: University of Minnesota, 1982), 69–83.

37. At present Cree people only use the name Cree as a self-referent when speaking English; in their own language they use a self-identification that combines place and the word for original person or human being as in Winipeg-athinuwick or Muskekowuck-athinuwick. For the Ojibwe origins of the term Cree, see John Honigmann, "West Main Cree, Synonymy," *HNAI,* 6: 227.

38. Hudson's Bay Company trader James Isham recorded this word as *A'thin new,* or plural form *Athinuwick.* Both he and fellow trader Andrew Graham translated this term as "Indian" rather then original people, which is how most Ojibwe-speaking traders translated the word *Anishinaabe.* Graham and Isham produced the most thorough descriptions of Cree people in the early contact period, and both wrote that the Lowland Cree were divided between bands residing in the coastal tundra zone—the Winipeg-athinuwick—and bands residing in the marshlands further inland— the Muskekowuck-athinuwick. In addition, bands designated as Upland Cree, and residing in the prairie parklands region of contemporary Manitoba and Saskatchewan, made their way to the bay to trade. These Cree peoples called themselves *Ayisiyiniw* rather than *Athinew,* but spoke essentially the same dialect as their lowland relatives. See Nancy Le Claire and George Cardinal, *Alberta Elder's Cree Dictionary* (Edmonton: University of Alberta Press, 1998). See James Isham, *James Isham's Observations in Hudson's Bay, 1743 and Notes and Observations on a Book Entitled a Voyage to Hudson's Bay in the Dobbs Galley,* ed. E. E. Rich (London: Hudson's Bay Record Society, 1949), 12: 5; and Andrew Graham, *Andrew Graham's Observations on Hudson's Bay, 1761–1791,* ed. Glyndwr Williams (London: Hudson's Bay Company Record Society, 1969), 91, 192.

39. Adolph M. Greenberg and James Morrison, "Group Identities in the Boreal Forest: The Origins of the Northern Ojibwa," *Ethnohistory* 29, no. 2 (Spring 1982), 86. Greenberg and Morrison cite the Ojibwe writer and intellectual George Copway to argue that this term represented a pejorative epithet meaning a "hick" or "backwoodsman." They offer this interpretation as part of perhaps the most thorough published analysis of the names and terminology used to describe Ojibwe- and Cree-speaking people in the early contact period. For a description of the Ojibwe-, Cree-Ojibwe-, and Cree-speaking bands and analysis of territorial identities in the Lake Superior region, as well as the country to the north and northwest of the lake, see "Details of the Names and Distance of Each Nation, both to the north of Lake Superior, and on the Lands recently discovered and established in the West" by le Sieur de La Verendrye, Public Archives of Canada, MG 18 (Pre-Conquest Papers) B 12; see also AN C11 E 1 Mémoire sur la domination des Francois en Canada, July 1687.

40. For northern dialect variations of the self-designation *Anishinaabe*, see Richard Rhodes and Evelyn M. Todd, "Subarctic Algonquian Languages, Synonymy," in *HNAI*, , 6: 241.

41. I am using the term *political economy* to describe the structural relationships of production and consumption that allow a community to sustain itself. In this sense I am not using the concept of political economy to describe an ideological system, but rather as a framework for analysis of beliefs and actions that must be explained in order to examine economic behavior, ideas, and concepts. For this approach to the idea of political economy, see Charles S. Mayer, *In Search of Stability: Explanations in Historical Political Economy* (Cambridge: Cambridge University Press, 1987), 3–6.

42. The "Outoulibis" and "Tabitibies" identified as Gens des Terres who traded with the French by La Potherie, for example, had earlier been identified by the Jesuits as Cree because they traded with the Nipissing at Hudson's Bay. These names appear to be phonetic approximations of the Ojibwe designation *apittipi anissina pe* or Blue-water people, and refer to a band speaking a mixed Cree-Ojibwe dialect that hunted and traded in the various tributaries of the Moose River system, which begins in north central Lake Superior and drains into Hudson's Bay. See La Potherie, *Histoire*, 2: 251; *JR* 44: 249; John Honigmann, "Regional Groups, West Main Cree," in *HNAI*, 6: 228–30; Greenberg and Morrison, "Group Identities in the Boreal Forest," 86–87.

43. This is the structural relationship between people and landscape, specifically Algonquian seasonal migrants, that Regna Darnell describes as an accordion model social formation; see Darnell, "Rethinking Band and Tribe," 91. See also Albers and Kay, "Sharing the Land." For a similar analysis of Algonquian land use practices and territoriality where individuals exercise kin connections to hunt in multiple territories, see Janet E. Chute, "Frank G. Speck's Contributions to the Understanding of Mi'kmaq Land Use, Leadership, and Land Management," *Ethnohistory* 46, no. 3 (Summer 1999): 481–540.

44. *JR* 54: 132, 134. It is worth noting that the historian David Bell has suggested that "nation" was a category commonly used to describe the provinces of France. But in France "nation" used in this manner signified the body of institutions, rights, and privileges held by the "nation" or province and not the social identity of the region's inhabitants. Dablon may well have understood the relationship between the various Indian "nations" at the Sault in this sense, given that he clearly understood these communities both as territorial units and as subjects of the king. See Bell, *The Cult of the Nation in France*, 74–75. Similarly, Anthony Pagden argues that France and England conferred "a form of ill-defined *de jure* nationhood" onto indigenous peoples who occupied and controlled territories claimed by their respective empires at the end of the Seven Years' War. The Indian nations of the Great Lakes, in effect, stood in relation to the British Crown "as the states of Milan and Naples stood to the Castilian." The inclusion of Native peoples within the imperium of either colonial power as nations, he asserts, was a convention adapted from the Roman Empire. The political territories of non-Christian peoples were brought into the world of Christendom, and claimed as part of the empire of a Christian monarch. This appropriation, however, was more fiction than fact in the Great Lakes and western interior of North America. It was, essentially, an abstract representation of space rather than an accurate map of the social world of Native peoples and their European trading partners. See Pagden, *Lords of All the World*, 20–25, 82–86, quote on 86.

45. For Dablon and his description of the Sauteurs and Sault Sainte Marie, see *JR* 54: 129–35; and Michael Witgen, "The Rituals of Possession: Native Identity and the Invention of Empire in Seventeenth Century Western North America," *Ethnohistory* 54, no. 4 (2007); for discussion of the totemic organization of the Sauteurs, see Hickerson, "The Feast of the Dead," 84; and Hickerson, *The Chippewa and Their Neighbors*, 42–50. For an analysis of the record of the Catfish doodem in this region, see Greenberg and Morrison, "Group Identities in the Boreal Forest," 87–88.

46. For Warren and the origin of these two important Anishinaabe villages, see Warren, *The History of the Ojibway People*, 86–90. As Greenberg and Morrison note, *Awasse* was a synonym for *Marameg*, and both words meant "Catfish"; see "Group Identities in the Boreal Forest," 87–88.

47. In the wake of treaty negotiations that created reservations, and use rights for off-reservation resources, the nation has become the operative political category for Native communities in the United States and Canada. But this is a designation used to mobilize and express Native sovereignty, as opposed to a concept intrinsic to Ojibwe social organization or language. The Ojibwe linguist and historian Anton Treuer has suggested that this distinction is reflected in the fact that the word for reservation in Anishinaabemowin is *ishkonigan*, which means "leftovers." In this sense, the reservation is not designated as "national territory"; it is rather what is left of Anishinaabewaki, or Indian country, in the aftermath of Euro-American colonization (personal communication, 2005). See also Nichols and Nyholm, *A Concise Dictionary of Minnesota Ojibwe*; and Friedric Baraga, *A Dictionary of the Otchipwe Language* (Minneapolis: Ross and Haines, 1966), first published in 1878 and 1880 in Cincinnati and Montreal.

48. For the relationship between the fisheries and Algonquian social structure, identity, and village communities, see Charles E. Cleland, "The Inland Shore Fishery of the Northern Great Lakes: Its Development and Importance in Prehistory," *American Antiquity* 47, no. 4 (October 1982), in particular, 779–80.

49. For the shifting composition of winter bands and their varying patterns of dispersal onto hunting territories, see Darnell, "Rethinking Band and Tribe," 98–99. For an excellent example of how usufruct rights were determined, and how winter bands formed among seasonal Anishinaabe migrants in the eighteenth-century western interior, see John Tanner, *The Falcon: A Narrative of the Captivity and Adventures of John Tanner* (1830; repr., New York: Penguin Books, 2000), 69–75.

50. For analysis of doodemag and collective identity at Sault Sainte Marie, see Greenberg and Morrison, "Group Identities in the Boreal Forest," 90; and Edward Rogers and Mary Black-Rogers, "Who Were the Cranes? Groups and Group Identity in Northern Ontario," in Margaret Hanna and Brian Kooyman, eds., *Approaches to Algonquian Archaeology* (Calgary: University of Calgary Press, 1982).

51. "Extrait d'un memoire d'Aubert de La Chesnaye sur le Canada, 1697," in Margry, *Découvertes*, 6:6.

52. For this argument about the relationship between seasonal migration patterns and Anishinaabe identity, see Witgen, "The Rituals of Possession"; and Greenberg and Morrison, "Group Identity in the Boreal Forest."

53. Perrot, *Memoire*, 127.

54. La Potherie, *Histoire*, 2: 291–92.

55. For Dakota trading at La Pointe during this period, see *JR* 51: 56; and *JR* 54: 167, 191–93.

56. *JR* 55: 202, 204.

57. Quote on *JR* 54: 224; for the conditions at Green Bay and the threat of Dakota raids, see "Of the Mission of Saint François Xavier on the Bay of Stinkards," in *JR* 54: 197–237.

58. "Keepers of the Fire," in fact, was a designation indicating their alliance with the Ojibwe and Odawa peoples, and suggests the extent to which their identity as a people evolved from this relationship. The Boodewaadamii, who also identified themselves as *Nishinaabek*, a cognate of *Anishinaabeg*, were closely related linguistically, through intermarriage, and by alliance with Odawa and Ojibwe peoples. See David R. Edmunds, *The Potawatomis: Keepers of the Fire* (Norman: University of Oklahoma Press, 1978).

59. For Perrot at Green Bay, see Perrot, *Memoire*, 127–28.

60. Perrot, *Memoire*, 127–29; La Potherie, *Histoire de l'Amérique Septentronale*, II: 291-3.

61. "Procès-verbal de la prise de possession des pays situés vers les lacs Huron et Superieur," June 4, 1671, in Margry, *Découvertes*, 1: 97. For William Warren's description of N-ka and Muskegoes, and their connection to the Anishinaabe peoples identified by the French as Sauteurs, and subsequently known as Ojibweg, see Warren, *History of the Ojibway Nation*, 45. See also Greenberg and Morrison, "Group Identities in the Boreal Forest," 84–85, for a thorough analysis that traces the connection of these doodemag to territories in the west, and simultaneously to an evolving Sauteur or Ojibwe national identity.

62. "Premier extrait d'une lettre de Jean Talon à Colbert," November 10, 1670, in Margry, *Découverts*, 1: 84; and AN C11E 1 Mémoire sur la domination des Francois en Canada, July 1687, f. 182.

63. AN C11 E 1 f. 186 Mémoire sur la domination des Francois en Canada, July 1687.

64. *JR* 56: 154.

65. *JR* 56: 154, 156.

66. For the Mistassini, see Toby Morantz, *An Ethnohistoric Study of Eastern James Bay Cree Social Organization, 1700–1850* (Ottawa: National Museums of Canada, 1983) 12; and Edward S. Rogers and Eleanor Leacock, "Local Groups, Montagnais-Naskapi," in *HNAI*, 6: 186.

67. John Honigmann, "Synonymy, Attikamek," in *HNAI*, 6: 227–29.

68. For the Papinachois, see Frank Speck, "Montagnais-Naskapi Bands and Early Eskimo Distribution in the Labrador Peninsula," *American Anthropologist* 33, no. 4 (1931), 558; and Greenberg and Morrison, "Group Identity in the Boreal Forest," 86–87. For evidence of a north-south distinction among speakers of Cree and mixed Cree-Ojibwe dialects, see Morantz, *Eastern James Bay Cree Social Organization*, 14. For archaeological evidence that placed Cree- and Ojibwe-speaking peoples as occupants, respectively, of the northern and southern regions of the Moose River watershed, see John Pollock, "Algonquian Cultural Development and Archaeological Sequences in Northeastern Ontario," *Canadian Archaeological Association*, bulletin no. 7 (1975): 1–53.

69. *JR* 56: 174.

70. *JR* 56: 176.

71. *JR* 56: 190.

72. *JR* 56: 192.

73. *JR* 56: 195.

74. *JR* 56: 196.

Part II. The New World

1. For La Malinche, see Thomas Nicholson, *The Pleasant Historie of the Conquest of the West India, now called New Spain, achieved by the worthy Hernando Cortes, most delectable to reade* (London: Henry Bynneman, 1578), a translation of *Historia de la conquista de Mexico* by Francisco Lopez de Gorma; for a history of Pocahontas and a deconstruction of the myth surrounding this historical figure see Camilla Townsend, *Pocahontas and the Powhatan Dilemma* (New York: Hill and Wang, 2004).

2. D. W. Meinig, *The Shaping of America: A Geographical Perspective on 500 Years of History*, vol. 1, *Atlantic America, 1492–1800* (New Haven, Conn.: Yale University Press, 1986), 65.

3. Ibid., 74.

4. For this analysis, see ibid., 258–67. Kathleen DuVal, in contrast, argues that the heartland of North America was a distinctly Native space, a Native ground. She argues that this Native ground

"had its own cores and peripheries, borders and borderlands." See DuVal, *The Native Ground: Indians and Colonists in the Heart of the Continent* (Philadelphia: University of Pennsylvania Press, 2006), 28.

5. White, *The Middle Ground*, chapter 2.

6. Hämäläinen, *The Comanche Empire*, 5.

Chapter 3. The Rebirth of Native Power and Identity

1. For French recognition of the importance and autonomy of the western interior, see AN C11 A 6 M. de la Barre au Ministre, November 3, 1683, f. 138; AN C11 E 1 Mémoire de la Compagnie du Nord en Canada, February 1685; and "Extrait d'une Lettre du Marquis de Denonville au Marquis de Seignelay," August 25, 1687, in Margry, *Découvertes*, 6: 52.

2. Kathleen DuVal makes a comparable argument, tracing the development of autonomous Native social formations in the Arkansas River valley and the indigenous social world of the midcontinent. She argues that in postcontact North America indigenous peoples created a Native Ground. DuVal describes this Native space as a place "where Indians of the Arkansas Valley held sovereignty according to both their own ad European definitions," by adapting their economic, military, and cultural practices to incorporate both European and Native immigrants into their social world. See DuVal, *The Native Ground*, 7. As an interesting point of contrast, Pekka Hämäläinen makes a cogent argument that the Comanche peoples of the southwest evolved into an indigenous empire. This was not a European-style empire created to establish settler colonies, but it was "a deeply hierarchical and integrated intersocietal order that was unmistakably imperial in shape, scope, and substance." Rather than expel rival powers they developed policies to keep them in place as part of a dependent hinterland that supported Comacheria. See Hämäläinen, *The Comanche Empire*, especially 1–17.

3. Here I am drawing from Henri Lefebvre's notion of the production of space. Lefebvre argues that "social space is produced and reproduced in connection with the forces of production (and with the relations of production). And these forces, as they develop, are not taking over a preexisting, empty or neutral space, or a space determined solely by geography, climate, anthropology or some other comparable consideration." The social relations of production that animate social formations—that keep them alive as self-reproducing communities—also, simultaneously, make space. That is, the human self is produced via a lived relationship with the physical world. Human communities impose a spatial and temporal order onto the physical world producing, simultaneously, a shared social world (and identity) and a physically embodied place. In this sense, the social formations of the western interior were clearly indigenous, even though they incorporated persons and material artifacts of European culture. To read empires onto this social world in the seventeenth and eighteenth centuries would be to empty this space of its sociocultural meaning. It would, in effect, be an ahistorical act of erasure. The institutions and social structures of European empire simply did not extend into the west interior of North America until the second half of the nineteenth century. See Henri Lefebvre, *The Production of Space*, trans. Donald Nicholson-Smith (Oxford: Blackwell, 1991), 70–79, quote on 77.

4. This formulation borrows from Immanuel Wallerstein's conceptual scheme of a modern world system consisting of a core and peripheries that developed as a result of the emergence of a global market economy. For the concept of a core and periphery as the defining elements of a capitalist world system, see Immanuel Wallerstein, *The Modern World-System: Capitalist Agriculture and the Origins of the European World Economy in the Sixteenth Century* (New York: Academic

Press, 1974), 102–3, 129. Wallerstein's critics contend that he grants too much power to the European core and takes too little account of the social structures in the so-called periphery. The concept of a Native New World recognizes the transformative power of the emergent world economy, but also recognizes the relative power and autonomy of Native social formations that dominated the North American interior. For a critique of Wallerstein's Europe-centered paradigm and the argument that the capitalist world system was limited in its capacity to subjugate and render dependent the American periphery, see Steven J. Stern, "Capitalism, and the World-System in the Perspective of Latin America and the Caribbean," *American Historical Review*, 93, no. 4 (October 1988).

5. There were no French posts or missions in this region until the French erected the makeshift Fort St. Antoine. This solitary post was never permanently occupied and was abandoned after little more than a decade. See La Potherie, *Histoire*, 2: 327–29; and Louise P. Kellogg, *The French Régime in Wisconsin and the Northwest* (Madison: State Historical Society of Wisconsin, 1925), 231–42, 248. For the significance of the *coureurs de bois* and the trade in the west, see AN C11 A5 Mémoire pour faire connoistre à Monseigneur les nations sauvages desquelles nous tirons nos pelteries, de Intendant DuChesneau à Minstre, November 13, 1681.

6. The raid and its outcome are described in La Potherie, *Histoire*, 2: 306–9, 314–18.

7. La Potherie does not identify the Anishinaabeg as being from La Pointe; however, it was this village community that had made peace with the Dakotas from the Mde Wakan or Mille Lacs region of the upper Mississippi valley in 1679. The correspondence of Daniel Greysolon Du Luth and René Robert Cavalier le Sieur de La Salle with the governor of New France clearly identifies Sauteurs from La Pointe as seasonal residents in the Dakota country. See "Lettre du Sieur DuLhut à M. Le Comte de Frontenac," April 5, 1679 in Margry, *Découvertes*, 6: 28–32; and La Salle letter, August 22, 1682, in *Collections of the State Historical Society of Wisconsin*, ed. Lyman Draper and Reuben Thwaites (Madison: State Historical Society of Wisconsin, 1855–1911), 16: 107–10, hereafter cited as *WHC*.

8. For the mission Saint Xavier at Green Bay and the description of this location as a resort for refugees fleeing the Iroquois, see *JR* 54: 197–237; and *JR* 55: 183–219. In 1671 the Jesuits counted the Winnebago, Pottawatomi, Sauk, Fox, Menominee, Mascouten, Miami, and Kickapoos as residents of the bay, some living in mixed villages and others with their own village sites. Other Native peoples passed through this community during the course of the seventeenth century including the Sinago, Sable, and Kiskakon Odawaag, the Wyandot, and bands of Abenaki and Mohican Indians from the Connecticut River valley. For the significance of Green Bay as a refugee center and its importance to French diplomacy in the Great Lakes, see also White, *The Middle Ground*, 11, 14, 19, 24; and Havard, *Empire et Métissage*, 142–45. For the Fox, see Charles Callender, "Fox," in *HNAI*, 15, 636.

9. La Potherie, *Histoire*, 2: 306–7; for the Abanaki, see Evan Haefali and Kevin Sweeney, "Revisiting the Redeemed Captive: New Perspectives on the 1704 Attack on Deerfield," *William and Mary Quarterly* 52, no. 1 (January 1995), 13–14.

10. For Algonquians, addressing a murder meant compensating the victim rather than punishing the murderer. Kin "covered the dead," that is, they gave gifts so that the victim's death was no longer a source of grief for the family. Or, toward the same end, they "raised the dead." They replaced the lost person with another human self, usually a slave, who assumed the life and social position of the victim. Alternately, if the murderer was not kin the family of the victim raided another community, usually though not necessarily the offenders, and captured or killed a person of comparable stature to the deceased. For murder, revenge, and raiding, see White, "'Although I Am Dead,'" 412–15; and Havard, *Empire et métissages*, 153, 157–58.

11. For the shifting composition of winter bands among Ojibwe- and Cree-speaking peoples, and their varying patterns of dispersal onto hunting territories, see Darnell, "Rethinking Band and Tribe," 98–99. For an excellent example of how usufruct rights were determined and how winter bands formed among seasonal Anishinaabe migrants in the eighteenth-century western interior, see Tanner, *The Falcon*, 69–75.

12. Dakota winter bands, or tiyospaye, comprised five to six extended families because this was the optimal size for hunting beaver and deer and harvesting wild rice in the marshlands at the head of the Mississippi. Thus Dakota bands corresponded in size and function to the bands of the Western Anishinaabeg hunting the same territory. The political economy of hunting buffalo in the west, however, made larger bands—from ten to twenty families—the optimal social unit for the Dakota peoples hunting on the northern Great Plains. For the Dakota tiyospaye, see Perrot, *Mémoires*, 85–91; for the Western Sioux, see DeMallie, "Teton Dakota Kinship and Social Organization," 118–19.

13. The historian Ned Blackhawk has described this process as "the displacement of violence." Blackhawk described the impact of the expansion of trade and the acquisition of European weapons in the Great Basin north of Spanish New Mexico. "With each passing year," he wrote, "Spanish technologies, particularly metals, spread to more distant peoples and transformed their manufacturing, trading, and military capacities." These transformations were usually violent as Native peoples with access to European weapons encroached on the territory, resources, and human capital of communities without access to this trade. See Ned Blackhawk, "The Displacement of Violence: Ute Diplomacy and the Making of New Mexico's Eighteenth Century Borderlands," *Ethnohistory* 54, no. 4 (Fall 2007), 725.

14. See Chapter 1, n. 50, on Richard White's argument on the nature of the Native-French alliance. The generative force behind the alliance was Onontio's willingness to serve as a father to the various peoples of the pays d'en haut. See n. 50 in Chapter 1 also on Gilles Havard's argument on the nature of the alliance. The alliance was in part the product of colonial New France, but also represented a rebirth of existing social networks that defined the village world of the Great Lakes.

15. Generalized or positive reciprocity, according to Sahlins, established social conditions necessary for such movement. Sahlins conceptualized exchange as operating along a continuum of reciprocities between peaceful (generalized reciprocity) and violent (negative reciprocity). Generalized reciprocity created a social relationship that allowed for balanced exchange—the direct trading of goods considered to be of equivalent value. See Sahlins, *Stone Age Economics*, especially 168, 193–95. For a cogent analysis of how exchange reciprocities and social obligations changed as the fur trade evolved, see Bruce White, "Encounters with Spirits."

16. Patricia Albers has described the social nexus of exchange relations in Native North America as "a chain of social connections through which an interdependence was realized in the production and exchange of specialized goods." Albers argues that each of the categories of exchange described by Marshall Sahlins—generalized, balanced, and negative reciprocity—"emerged under relationships based on war (competition), merger (cooperation), and symbiosis (complementarity)." Warfare, she argues, could take place even between interdependent native peoples, or between native peoples and European traders. The diplomacy of exchange relationships (violent or peaceful), therefore, became deeply intertwined with the creation and negotiation of kinship boundaries and obligations. See Patricia Albers, "Symbiosis, Merger, and War," in John Moore, ed., *The Political Economy of North American Indians* (Lincoln: University of Nebraska Press, 1993), 99.

17. For a description of this alliance, which was negotiated over the course of two years, see "Lettre du Sieur Du Lhut à M. le Comte de Frontenac," April 5, 1679, in Margry, *Découvertes*, 6: 26–34, quote on 28.

18. See, for example, AN C11 A 6 "Lettre de La Durnataye la copie de la letter qui precede," April 22, 1684, f. 521–22; "Extrait de la Relation des événements passé en Canada de 1694 à 1695," in Margry, *Découvertes*, 6:56–58; Archives Nationales, Archives des Colonies, Series F, Collections de Moreau-St. Mery, F3/8 Parolles de Ottawas, July 29; AN C11 A 19 Commissioners de la Compagnie au Ministre, October 9, 1701; AN C11 A 20 de Calliers et Beauharnois au Ministre, November 3, 1702; AN F3/8 Parolles de Outaouoies, July 5, 1702; AN F3/8 Parolles de Longekam de Michilimackinac, July 23, 1702; AN C11 A 12 Calliers au Ministre, November 4, 1702.

19. According to Richard White, the middle ground emerged because the French and their Algonquian allies "had to arrive at some common conception of suitable ways of acting." They needed to find a way to understand and interpret the social identities enacted by the many different peoples of the alliance. See White, *Middle Ground*, 50. Gilles Havard argues similarly that the colonization of New France was made possible because of the economic and military collaboration and cultural accommodation between Native peoples and French colonials. He argues that White's middle ground is, in fact, a frontier that functions as a zone of exchange. This juxtaposition of two spaces, he contends, produced an intermediary space, which he calls a milieu, or middle space, as opposed to a middle ground. Havard describes this milieu not so much as a mixture, or hybrid space, but as the outcome or culmination of a dynamic process of exchange. While I agree that the village world of the alliance constituted a new social formation, as well as an intermediary space between the parallel social worlds of the Atlantic and Native New Worlds, I also think that the middle ground adequately encompasses these concepts. Havard's description of the milieu/middle ground as a frontier, however, is problematic. Describing the pays d'en haut as a zone of contact and cultural encounter, and therefore a frontier, imposes a spatial logic onto this region that simply did not exist. In the indigenous west, and even on the middle ground, space was not bounded by social identity, or by the national structure of European political formations. Kinship, and its attendant obligations, determined access and exclusivity to the physical world—fish runs, animals, wild rice, etc.—and to spatialized social formations such as villages, hunting territories, trade routes, etc. The French Empire existed in the pays d'en haut because it conformed to this pattern of social relations. Moreover, frontier in the North American context implies a racial rather than cultural encounter. Otherwise the pays d'en haut would have been a frontier long before European empires came to North America as this was always a multiethnic social world where dominant social formations from the east and west encountered one another. Frontier, then, seems to imply that this encounter becomes distinct—that is, an encounter constitutive as a frontier—only when Europeans participate. In this sense, frontier implies racialized social categories that were not operative in this region in the seventeenth and eighteenth centuries. See Havard, *Empire et métissages*, 44–50. The utility of frontier as an analytic construct has been thoroughly explored and debated; see Patricia Nelson Limerick, *The Legacy of Conquest: The Unbroken Past of the American West* (New York: W. W. Norton, 1988); Richard White, "Trashing the Trails," in Patricia Limerick, Clyde A. Milner II, and Charles E. Rankin, eds., *Trails: Toward a New Western History* (Lawrence: University Press of Kansas, 1991); and the response to these critiques from Jeremy Adelman and Stephen Aron, "From Borderlands to Borders: Empires, Nation-States, and the Peoples in Between in North American History," *American Historical Review* 104, no. 3 (June 1999).

20. "To further its interests," White argues, "each side had to attain cultural legitimacy in terms of the other." The result of this cultural borrowing was often a reinvention of their partner's worldview or cultural practices, but in the end this process created a space in which the allies could speak to one another on mutually acceptable terms. See White, *Middle Ground*, 55.

21. *JR* 57: 202.

22. *JR* 57: 208.

23. *JR* 57: 214.

24. *JR* 57: 210.

25. *JR* 57: 218–20.

26. *JR* 57: 220.

27. For identification and location of the Zhiishigwe, see Greenberg and Morrison, "Group Identities in the Boreal Forest," 85–87.

28. *JR* 57: 220, 222.

29. *JR* 57: 222.

30. See Albers, "Symbiosis, Merger, and War," 129, n. 99.

31. *JR* 57: 20.

32. *JR* 57: 22.

33. *JR* 57: 22.

34. John Oldmixon, "The History of Hudson's Bay," in *The Publications of the Champlain Society: Documents Relating to the Early History of Hudson Bay*, ed. J. B. Tyrrell (Toronto: Champlain Society, 1931), 386.

35. Ibid., 386–87.

36. For the vocabulary lists, see ibid., 396. For identification of the Cuscudidah, see "Synonymy, Attikamek," 6: 215; and for Attikamek at lac St. Jean, see *JR* 56: 154–56.

37. Oldmixon, "History of Hudson's Bay," 388.

38. For Western Anishinaabe bands at St. Lusson's 1671 ceremony, see "Extrait d'une lettre de Jean Talon au Roy," November 2, 1671, in Margry, *Découvertes*, 1: 93; and "Procès-verbal de la prise de possession des pays situés vers les lacs Huron et Superieur," June 4, 1671, in Margry, *Découvertes*, 1: 97. For the loss of trade to the Hudson's Bay Company, see "Premier extrait d'une lettre de Jean Talon à Colbert," November 10, 1670, in Margry, *Découvertes*, 1: 84; and AN C11 E 1 Mémoire sur la domination des Francois en Canada, July 1687, f. 182–86. For English description of Upland Indians including Cree and Assiniboine, see Oldmixon, "History of Hudson's Bay," 376.

39. Oldmixon, "History of Hudson's Bay," 390; and *JR* 56: 154–56.

40. There are multiple variations of this name including Abitibi, Outabitkek, and Tabititibis; see JR 44: 249; Extrait d'une letter de Greysolon Du Lhut a M. De la Barre, September 10, 1684, in Margry, *Découvertes*, 6: 51; and Honigmann, "Regional Groups, West Main Cree," 6: 228–30. See also La Potherie, *Histoire*, 2: 48–49; *JR* 18: 229, and Greenberg and Morrison, "Group Identities in the Boreal Forest," 85–87.

41. Oldmixon, "History of Hudson's Bay," 390.

42. Ibid., 391. For the Shamattawa, see David H. Pentland, "Synonymy, Northern Ojibwa," in *HNAI*, 6: 242.

43. Oldmixon, "History of Hudson's Bay," 382.

44. In the interior west, however, the collective identities that ordered the middle ground became infused with other meanings. This often had the effect of creating social instability when peoples like the Anishinaabeg moved between the indigenous social world of the western interior and the social world of the French alliance that existed in the villages of the pays d'en haut. Henri Lefebvre described this phenomenon of distinct but overlapping social worlds as the "hypercomplexity of social space." Social space, according to Lefebrve, is not the empty container of Cartesian space, but more accurately resembles a *mille feuille* pastry—layer upon layer of social relationships that produce an "unlimited multiplicity" of social spaces. These spaces interpenetrate and superimpose themselves upon one another. The alliance network of the Anishinaabeg reflected this sort

of multiplicity rather than the more neatly contained and singular social space produced by the empires of the Atlantic World. See Lefebvre, *The Production of Space*, 85–92.

45. *JR* 58: 256.

46. *JR* 58: 256.

47. *JR* 58: 258.

48. The Jesuits noted that "some of the principal and most esteemed" people of the village died in the assault, which is described in *JR* 58: 256–58.

49. Converting an enemy insider into a cultural insider, even under conditions of violence and subordination, provided a possible bridge between different social formations. The historian James Brooks has argued that unlike chattel slavery, "borderland slavery found affinity with kin based systems motivated less by a demand for units of labor than their desire for prestigious social units." In the American southwest, he argues, captive women and children became important cultural brokers between the region's different social groups. While undeniably destructive, this sort of violence also produced enduring networks of social and economic exchange. See Brooks, *Captives and Cousins*, 34–37.

50. *JR* 58: 262.

51. The extent to which the French participated in a burgeoning slave trade, buying, selling, and incorporating Native peoples into their households as chattel property is often overlooked. See Brett Rushforth, "'A Little Flesh We Offer You': The Origins of Indian Slavery in New France," *William and Mary Quarterly* 60, no. 4 (2003).

52. "Lettre du sieur Du Lhut à M. le Comte de Frontenac, April 5, 1679," in Margry, *Découvertes*, 6: 27.

53. Ibid., 6: 28.

54. Ibid.

55. Ibid., 6: 29.

56. M. Du Chesneau to M. de Signelay, November 10, 1679, in *NYCD*, 9: 131.

57. AN C11 A 5 Du Chesneau à Ministre, November 13, 1681.

58. AN C11 A 5 Frontenac au Ministre, November 6, 1679; For coureurs de bois diverting trade to the English and the necessity of stopping this commerce, see AN C11 A 5 Extrait de la lettre Escrite au Roy par M. de Frontenac, November 6, 1679. For the construction of the post at Catarcoui and Frontenac's trading interests in the west, see W. J. Eccles, *Frontenac: The Courtier Governor* (Toronto: McClelland and Stewart, 1959), 80–82.

59. AN C11 A 5 Frontenac au Ministre, November 6, 1679; while he defended Du Lhut, Frontenac also assured the minister that "I would not want to trade with persons who were rebelling against the orders of the King." For Randin, see George Brown, ed., *Dictionary of Canadian Biography* (Toronto: University of Toronto Press, 1966), 1: 565. Randin did not produce a written account of his voyage to Sault Sainte Marie, and the Jesuits did not record his presence at the village surrounding their mission. There is no evidence that he had any contact with the Dakota, and given the massacre that occurred a year before his arrival, the only Dakota he was likely to encounter would have been slaves. Even if his diplomatic mission failed, however, the gifts and the message he carried from Onontio must have encouraged the faction among the Anishinaabeg who wanted peace.

60. "Du Lhut à M. le Comte de Frontenac," April 5, 1679, in Margry, *Découvertes*, 6: 29.

61. "Mémoire du Sieur Greysolon Du Lhut adresse à Monsieur le Marquis de Seignelay," in Margry (ed.), *Découvertes*, 6: 22.

62. "Du Lhut à M. le Comte de Frontenac," April 5, 1679, in Margry, *Découvertes*, 6: 30.

63. Ibid., 6: 32.

64. "Lettre de Cavelier De la Salle, au Fort Frontenac," August 22, 1682, in Margry, *Découvertes*, 2: 252.

65. Ibid.

66. Ibid., 2: 254. According to La Salle, Du Lhut had persuaded La Salle's interpreter to desert his post at Fort Frontenac at Catarcoui and join Du Lhut at these councils between the Anishinaabeg and Dakota. And then, according to La Salle, "seeing that he had nothing to fear and that he could increase the number of his castor, he sent Faffart (the interpreter) by land with the Nadouesioux and the Sauteurs who were returning together." According to La Salle, it was the interpreter, not Du Lhut, who traveled to the Dakota village.

67. Ibid., 2: 252.

68. Ibid.

69. La Potherie, *Histoire*, 2: 258.

70. The ethnohistorian Harold Hickerson described the Dakota-Sauteur alliance as "a peace established in the interest of the fur trade." Hickerson argued that the alliance evolved as an extension of French commercial expansion. The Sauteurs, he argued, moved west as middlemen. They provided the Dakotas access to French goods in exchange for the privilege of hunting in the Dakota territory. Hickerson's thesis overlooks the extent to which both the Dakotas and Sauteurs were involved in an elaborate and long-lived attempt to renegotiate their kinship and alliance networks in order to accommodate the new peoples and things—including trade goods, Europeans, and Indian immigrants—that were already flowing through their villages and hunting territories. See Hickerson, "The Southwestern Chippewa," 65–66; see also Hickerson, *The Chippewa and Their Neighbors*. Gary C. Anderson has similarly argued that Du Lhut and the French initiated the Dakota-Sauteur alliance. He suggested further that the Sauteurs cooperated with Du Lhut to end the ongoing conflict between the Dakotas and Cree because such feuding was "a major detriment to commercialism." Anderson, like Hickerson, ascribed an economic or commercial motive to Sauteur diplomacy and patterns of migration. Both scholars presented the Sauteurs as a cohesive, national political unit and omit discussion of the presence of Anishinaabe bands in the west prior to the alliance. Similarly, both scholars failed to elucidate the fact that the Sauteurs and other Anishinaabeg had a history of hunting and trading in the interior west before the arrival of Du Lhut. See Gary Clayton Anderson, *Kinsmen of Another Kind*, 32.

71. For Dakota buffalo hunting territory and conflict with other native peoples, see DeMallie, "The Sioux Until 1850," 13: part 2, 719–20.

72. "Du Lhut à M. le Comte de Frontenac," April 5 1679, in Margry, *Découverts*, 6: 30–31.

73. Ibid., 6: 31.

74. "Mémoire du Sieur Greysolon Du Lhut adresse à Monsieur le Marquis de Seignelay," in Margry, *Découvertes*, 6: 22.

75. The term *itancan* is often translated as "chief," but more accurately means "leader." The model for this form of leadership derives from the head of a lodge group or extended family where the head of this unit can be identified as itancan. In the same fashion individuals could be designated as itancan at the band level given that these social units represented an extended family or kinship network. See DeMallie, "Teton Dakota Kinship and Social Organization," 112–15.

76. The man, Father Louis Hennepin, claimed that he called out the following phrase in the language of the Algonquians and the Iroquois: "Comrades we are men of wooden canoes," which even if accurate was apparently not understood by the Dakota. See Louis Hennepin, *A New Discovery*, 1: 228.

77. For the calumet ceremony, see Donald Blakeslee, "The Calumet and the Origin of Fur Trade Rituals," *Western Canadian Journal of Anthropology*, 7 (1977); and White, *The Middle Ground*, 20–23.

78. For a narrative description of this encounter, see Hennepin, *A New Discovery*, 1: 227–33.

79. Ibid., 1: 234.

80. Ibid., 1: 235. La Salle expressed skepticism about whether or not Hennepin and his companions, Michel Accault and Antoine du Gay, were ever in danger. "They were not treated as slaves," he argued. And he asserted that "Du Lhut was wrong to boast that he had taken them from slavery." Hennepin, he added, "will be sure to exaggerate everything: that's his character." See "Lettre de Cavelier de La Salle," August 22, 1682, in Margry, *Découvertes*, 2: 257, 259.

81. Hennepin, *A New Discovery*, 1: 247.

82. For wakan, see Raymond J. DeMallie Jr. and Robert H. LaVenda, "Wakan: Plains Siouan Concepts of Power," in Fogelson and Adams, *The Anthropology of Power*, 156–59; for wasicun, the weeping ritual, and the Dakota understanding of trade goods and fur trade exchange, see Bruce White, "Encounters with Spirits."

83. For the adoption, see Hennepin, *A New Discovery*, 1: 252.

84. Ibid., 1: 263.

85. Ibid. For the Issati, see DeMallie, "The Sioux Until 1850," 13: part 2, 751–52.

86. Literally "those who sit at the Council Lodge," the otiyotipi was the core institution of social control composed of all the influential men of a composite social unit such as the village at Mde Wakan. See DeMallie, "Teton Dakota Kinship and Social Organization," 125.

87. For clay pots, see Hennepin, *A New Discovery*, 1: 258, 268; and for guns, 1: 235.

88. Ibid., 1: 293.

89. "Mémoire du Sieur Greysolon Du Lhut adressé à Monsieur le marquis de Seignelay," in Margry, *Découvertes*, 6: 23.

90. Ibid., 6: 23–24.

91. Hennepin, *A New Discovery*, 1: 298.

92. Du Lhut wrote that "each stain was exonerated in the council but their excuse did not prevent me from saying to Reverend Louis that it was necessary to come with me to the coast of the Outagamie." In other words, he made the decision to return after admonishing the Dakota for their bad behavior, and after allowing them to ritually exonerate themselves at council. See "Mémoire du Sieur Greysolon Du Lhut adressé à Monsieur le marquis de Seignelay," in Margry, *Découvertes*, 6: 24.

93. Hennepin, *A New Discovery*, 1: 300.

94. La Potherie, *Histoire*, 2: 315.

95. Ibid., 2: 307.

96. Ibid., 2: 307–9;

97. Ibid., 2: 315.

98. Ibid., 2: 316.

99. Ibid., 2: 318. There is a storm that threatens to destroy the Fox in this version of the story, but here La Potherie presents the storm as a fact, an event that occurred and which the Fox themselves attributed to the power of Nicolas Perrot. In both cases the emphasis of the author's storytelling is on the ability of the French to manipulate their Native allies through both metaphoric and real displays of French power.

100. For the definition of *Dakota* and allied terms, see DeMallie, "Teton Dakota Kinship and Social Organization," 107–13; and DeMallie, "The Sioux Until 1850," 13: part 2, 718. The term *oyate*

is sometimes glossed as "nation" in Dakota-English dictionaries, but Ray DeMallie argues that this is an inappropriate translation. "Nation," he contends implies a political coherence that is inconsistent with the composite nature of the *oyate*. He argues instead that linguistically this term is a designation that means "people." DeMallie contends that *oyate* might be more properly glossed as "tribe," which he defines as a voluntary social organization comprising biologically and socially constructed kinship units. In the eighteenth century, as well as in the present day, the Dakotas considered themselves descendants of the Seven Council Fires people who formed a single winter camp at Mde waken, present-day Mille Lacs in the headwaters region of the Mississippi. As time passed the peoples or oyate of the Oceti Sakowin dispersed into the west but remained connected as allies or Dakota. The internal composition of the seven oyate changed considerably during the seventeenth and eighteenth centuries.

101. See DeMallie, "Teton Dakota Kinship and Social Organization," 107–8.

102. See n. 12 in this chapter on Dakota winter bands, which applies to the Mdewakanton tiyospaye. For the Mdewakanton tiyospaye, see Nicolas Perrot, "Mémoires on the Manners, Customs, and Religion of the Savages of North America," in Emma H. Blair, ed., *The Indian Tribes of the Upper Mississippi Valley and Region of the Great Lakes* (Lincoln: University of Nebraska Press, 1996), 1: 166; for the Western Sioux see DeMallie, "Teton Dakota Kinship and Social Organization," 118–19.

103. As a semantic domain, *wótakuye*, or kinship, did not distinguish between biological and social kinship. Both categories of social relations were expressed by the term *mitakuyepi*, or "my relatives," a general category of kinship that signified "relatives with whom I live," or "close relatives." Raymond J. DeMallie, "Kinship and Biology in Sioux Culture," in Raymond J. DeMallie and Alfonso Ortiz, eds., *North American Indian Anthropology: Essays on Society and Culture* (Norman: University of Oklahoma Press, 1994), 136.

104. Dakota ethnographer Ella Deloria wrote a history of the evolution and significance of kinship in Dakota society in the early twentieth century, and she argued that "Dakota life stripped of accessories, was quite simple: one must obey kinship rules; one must be a good relative." In describing this worldview Deloria wrote: "To be a good Dakota, then, was to be humanized, civilized. And to be civilized was to keep the rules imposed by kinship for achieving civility, goods manners, and a sense of responsibility toward every individual dealt with." Deloria, *Speaking of Indians* (New York: Friendship Press, 1944), 25. This sense of Dakota identity representing some essential humanity specific to a linguistic and cultural group is suggestive of social categories such as Anishinaabeg, which also provided a framework for fictive or social kinship among migratory bands.

105. For summary analysis of the western migration of Dakota-speaking bands, the Dakota-Yankton/Yanktonai-Lakota, see DeMallie, "Teton Dakota Kinship and Social Organization," 99–102. For precontact history of the Sioux, and the prairie west as a region, see Guy Gibbon, "Cultures in the Upper Mississippi River Valley and Adjacent Prairies in Iowa and Minnesota," in Karl H. Schlesier, ed., *Plains Indians, A.D. 500–1500: The Archaeological Past of Historic Groups* (Norman: University of Oklahoma Press, 1994), 128–48; Guy Gibbon, *The Sioux: The Dakota and Lakota Nations* (Malden, Mass.: Blackwell, 2003), 17–38; Elden Johnson, "The Seventeenth Century Mdewakanton Dakota Subsistence Mode," in Janet Spector and Elden Johnson, eds., *Archaeology, Ecology and Ethnohistory of the Prairie-Forest Border Zone of Minnesota and Manitoba* (Lincoln, Neb.: J&L Reprint, 1985); Elden Johnson, "Cultural Resource Survey of the Mille Lacs Area," University of Minnesota, Minneapolis, report prepared for the Minnesota Historical Society, St. Paul (1984).

106. For descriptions of the social relations of production for the summer buffalo hunt, see Hennepin, *A New Discovery*, 1: 271–72, 279, 290. Ray DeMallie has argued that the nonlineal kin-

ship system of the allies provided a flexible social identity designed to provide coherence and stability to communities formed from a shifting and interchangeable number of small groups or tiyospaye. Thus, while band divisions occupied specific hunting territories, the tiyospaye, the core element of Dakota social life, was not a territorial unit. See DeMallie, "Teton Dakota Kinship and Social Organization," 11–12, 42.

107. For the bison and Great Plains ecology, see Dan Flores, "The Great Contraction: Bison and Indians in Northern Plains Environmental History," in Charles E. Rankin, ed., *Legacy: New Perspectives on the Battle of the Little Big Horn* (Helena: Montana Historical Society Press, 1996); John R. Bozell, "Culture, Environment, and Bison Populations on the Late Prehistoric and Early Historic Central Plains," *Plains Anthropologist* 40, no. 152 (May 1995); and Brad Logan, "The Protohistoric Period on the Central Plains," in Jack L. Hoffman, ed., *Archaeology and Paleoecology of the Central Great Plains* (Fayetteville: Arkansas Archaeological Survey, 1996).

108. Frank Raymond Secoy, *Changing Military Patterns of the Great Plains Indians*, Monographs of the American Ethnological Society 21 (Locust Valley, N.Y.: J. J. Augustin, 1953; repr.: Lincoln: University of Nebraska Press, 1992); Richard White, "The Winning of the West: The Expansion of the Western Sioux in the Eighteenth and Nineteenth Centuries," *Journal of American History* 65 (September 1978); Gary Clayton Anderson, "Early Dakota Migration and Intertribal War: A Revision," *Western Historical Quarterly* 11, no. 1 (January 1980); Tim Holzkam, "Eastern Dakota Population Movements and the European Fur Trade: One More Time," *Plains Anthropologist* 28, no. 101 (August 1983); James H. Howard, "Yanktonai Ethnohistory and the John K. Bear Winter Count," *Plains Anthropologist* 21, no. 73, pt. 2 (August 1976).

109. French colonial official Le Moyne d'Iberville reported that Pierre Charles Le Sueur, who lived among the Sioux in 1694–95 and 1700–1702, estimated the population at four thousand families. Even by a conservative estimate of six people per family this would amount to a population of approximately twenty-four thousand people. Pierre Radisson in 1660 and Louis Hennepin in 1680 offer comparable figures of seven thousan men and eight thousand to nine thousand men respectively. See Pierre Le Moyne d'Iberville, "Mémoire sur l'établissement de la Mobile et du Mississipi," 1702, in Margry, *Découvertes*, 2:47–53; Pierre Esprit Radisson, *The Explorations of Pierre Esprit Radisson*, ed. Arthur T. Adams (Minneapolis: Ross & Hanes, 1961), 142; and Hennepin, *A New Discovery*, 1: 226. For the population of New France, see Yves F. Zoltvany, *De Rigaud de Vaudreuil: Governor of New France, 1703–1725* (Toronto: McClelland and Stewart, 1974), 17.

110. For a description of this process, see Gary Clayton Anderson, "Early Dakota Migration and Intertribal War"; and Richard White, "The Winning of the West."

111. For the dominance of the Mdewakanton in the fur trade, see "Extrait du mémoire de M. Le Chevalier de Beaurain sur la Louisiane," 1700, in Margry, *Découvertes*, 6: 80–81; "Truteau's Description of the Upper Missouri, 1796," in *Before Lewis and Clark: Documents Illustrating the History of the Missouri*, ed. Abraham Nasatir, 2 vols. (Lincoln: University of Nebraska Press, 1990), 2: 382; and DeMallie, "The Sioux Until 1850," 13: part 2, 719–32. For the evolution of the Eastern Sioux bands as specialists in fur trade hunting and diplomacy, see DeMallie, "Teton Dakota Kinship and Social Organization," 81–89.

Chapter 4. European Interlopers and the Politics of the Native New World

1. AN C11 A5, M. Du Chesneau, Mémoire Concernant l'estat présent du Canada et les mesures que le peut prendre pour la securité, November 12, 1685. Scholars focusing on the economics and

ethnohistory of the fur trade make a similar argument. See, for example, Harold A. Innis, *The Fur Trade in Canada* (repr., Toronto: University of Toronto Press, 1999), 48–49; E. E. Rich, *The Fur Trade and the Northwest* (Toronto: McClelland and Stuart, 1967), 38–41; and Arthur J. Ray, *Indians in the Fur Trade: Their Role as Trappers, Hunters, and Middlemen in the Lands Southwest of Hudson's Bay, 1660–1870* (repr., Toronto: University of Toronto Press, 1998), 12–13.

2. AN C11 A5 M. Du Chesneau, Mémoire Concernant L'estat du Canada et les mesures que le peut prendre pour la securité, November 12, 1685.

3. AN C11 A5 M. Du Chesneau à M de Seignelay, November 14, 1679.

4. AN C11 A5 Du Chesneau, Mémoire Concernant l'estat présent du Canada, November 12, 1685.

5. Ibid., quotes on ff. 307–8.

6. Ibid., quote on f. 315.

7. Ibid.

8. The debate over the rights to the trade and territory of inland Indians continued until French withdrawal from North America. After the Treaty of Utrecht granted the English possession of Hudson's Bay in 1714 this argument morphed into a debate over the determination of a boundary between the bay and interior, linked to the trade and territory of Native peoples. See, for example, AN C11 E1 Mémoire sur la domination de Francois en Canada, 1680; AN C11 E1 Copie de la Replique Remise par Mssrs. par les Commission Anglois, July 21, 1687; AN C11 E1 Copie de la Réponse au dernier mémoire de la compagnie francoise de Canada, touchant les droites de la compagnie Angloise de la Baye d'Hudson, August 12, 1687; AN C11 E1 Mémoire de la Baye d'Hudson, August 1697; AN C11 E2 Extrait de la Réponse, October 26, 1719; and An C11 E2 Mémoire sur la Baye d'Hudson, January 1720.

9. Tensions within the company derived from the opposition between the Catholic, absolutist Duke of York, a shareholder in the Hudson Bay Company (HBC) and the Earl of Shaftesbury, appointed executive director in 1673. Shaftesbury actively supported the Test Act, which required all public officials to swear allegiance to the Anglican Church, designed in part to remove the Duke of York from English public life. For the rivalry between the Duke of York and Shaftesbury and its effect on the HBC, see Fournier, *Pierre-Esprit Radisson*, 194–205. For Radisson's description of his treatment by the HBC, see Radisson, *Explorations*, 161–62. Martin Fournier argues that Shaftesbury not only distrusted Radisson and Des Groseilliers as Catholics but also wanted to focus company resources on colonization rather then trade. See Fournier, *Pierre-Esprit Radisson*, 207–8.

10. In 1681 Charles Aubert de La Chesnaye had secured a charter for La Compagnie de la Baie d'Hudson, and retained the services of Radisson and Des Groseilliers, the only voyageurs in New France with experience trading at the bay. La Chesnaye's company was chartered, but this enterprise was of questionable legality. As a consequence, Radisson was expected to take his cargo of peltries directly to France, bypassing the taxes that would be levied in North America. For Radisson's account of this agreement, see Radisson, *Explorations*, 165–67. For Frontenac, La Chesnaye, and colonial trade policy, see Rich, *The Fur Trade and the Northwest*, 42–44; W. J. Eccles, *The Canadian Frontier* (rev. ed., Albuquerque: University of New Mexico Press, 1983), 113–15; and Fournier, *Pierre-Esprit Radisson*, 218–22.

11. Radisson and Des Groseilliers's return to New France coincided with the removal of Governor Frontenac from office and his replacement by Denonville. Frontenac deftly used his political position to expand and develop the fur trade through posts and trading licenses in the pays d'en haut. He benefited financially from this effort, as did many merchants and habitants who engaged legally, and illegally, in this expansion of the fur trade. Colbert, in contrast, wanted to concentrate colonial settlement and Crown resources on the development of Lower Canada. He also wanted to

protect French claims to the interior west, and discover an inland waterway to the Pacific Ocean. French posts in Hudson's Bay represented a possible means of implementing these policies. Colbert tried to restrict the sale of trade goods to coureurs de bois, in effort to limit trade in the west; see AN C11 A3 Lettre du Roy au Gouverneur Frontenac, June 5, 1672; *Rapport de l'Archiviste de la Province de Québec pour 1926–27* (Quebec: L. Amable Proulx, Imprimeur de Sa Majesté Le Roi, 1927), 9, Ordonnance de M. le Comte de Frontenac, June 5, 1672; and for Colbert's desire to restrict development of posts in the west, see AN C11 A9, Colbert à Talon, March 30, 1666; for the different ambitions of Frontenac and Colbert, see Eccles, *Frontenac*, 77–92.

12. Radisson, *Explorations*, 163.

13. See E. E. Rich, ed., *Copy Book of Letters Outward and Begins 29th May 1680 Ends 5 July 1687* (London: Hudson's Bay Record Society, 1948), 5: 11, 35–36.

14. Radisson, *Explorations*, 170.

15. Ibid.

16. Ibid., 171.

17. For the significance of river basins and band identity among the Lowland Cree, see Thomas Gorst, "Extract of Mr. Thomas Gorst's Journall in the Voyage to Hudson's Bay Begun the 31th [*sic*] day of May 1670," in Nute, *Ceasars of the Wilderness*, appendix 2, 286–92; Oldmixon, "The History of Hudson's Bay," 388–96; and Victor Lytwyn, *Muskeowuck Athinuwick: Original Peoples of the Great Swampy Land* (Winnipeg: University of Manitoba Press, 2002), 8–12. Hudson's Bay Company trader Andrew Graham compiled a list of trading Indians identified by residence and linguistic affiliation in the late eighteenth century. See Graham, *Andrew Graham's Observations*, vol. 26. This list, reworked and published in five different variations, drew from an earlier work by James Isham; see Isham, *James Isham's Observations*, vol. 12.

18. For place names and Cree identity, see Graham, *Andrew Graham's Observations*. According to linguist David Pentland, this term translates as "flows-down-the-bank-river"; see Pentland, "Synonymy of the Western Woods Cree," 6: 269.

19. James Isham recorded this word as *A'thin new*, or the plural form *Athinuwick*. Both he and Graham translated this term as "Indian." See Isham, *James Isham's Observations*, 5; and Graham, *Andrew Graham's Observations*, 192.

20. Graham and Isham described divisions among the Lowland Cree according to residence on the coastal tundra zone and residence in the marshlands further inland, the Winipeg-athinuwick and the Muskekowuck-athinuwick. Modern Plains Cree dictionaries record this world as *Ayisiyiniw*, rather than *Athinnew*; see, for example, Nancy LeClaire and George Cardinal, *Alberta Elders' Cree Dictionary* (Edmonton: University of Alberta Press, 1998); and Freda Ahenakew and H. C. Wolfart, *The Student's Dictionary of Literary Plains Cree*, Algonguian and Iroquoian Linguistics Memoir 15 (1998). David Pentland has recorded this term as *iniw*, and the plains dialect version as *Wyiniw*. See Pentland, "Synonymy of the Western Woods Cree," 6: 227. Cree, like Ojibwe, is not a standardized language but a chain of linked local dialects with differences in pronunciation and vocabulary. Historically, among inland bands these dialects have evolved with admixtures of both Cree and Ojibwe. See Freda Ahenakew, *Cree Language Structures: A Cree Approach* (Winnipeg: Pemmican Publications, 1987). For examples of mixed dialects, see La Vérendrye, PAC, MG 18 (Pre-Conquest Papers) B12, 36–41; and A. Irving Hallowell, "Notes on the Material Culture of the Island Lake Saulteaux," *Journal de la Société des Américanistes* 30 (1938).

21. For Des Groseilliers at Rupert River, see Oldmixon, "Early History of Hudson's Bay," 390–93; for a broader discussion of migration and Lowland Cree identity, see Lytwyn, *Muskekowuck Athinuwick*, 6–25.

22. For migration and social organization among Algonquian peoples, see Regna Darnell, "Rethinking Band and Tribe."

23. David Pentland translates *nehiyaw* as "those who speak the same language," and describes the modifier "bush-people" as used by speakers of the plains and woods dialects of western Cree. See Pentland, "Synonymy of the Western Woods Cree," 267–68.

24. Douglas R. Parks, "Synonymy, in Assiniboine," in *HNAI*, 13: part 1, 590–91.

25. For the location and migration patterns of Assiniboine and Upland or Western Cree bands, see Russell, *Eighteenth Century Western Cree*; for Dakota, Lakota, and Assiniboine identity, language, and migration in the prehistoric and protohistoric eras, see Gibbon, *The Sioux*, 30–46. For Anishinaabe migration and identity, see Witgen, "The Rituals of Possession."

26. Patricia Albers describes this range of raiding and trading relationships as a symbiotic interdependence. Raiding and gift giving, she argues, were alternate means of resolving short-term imbalances in the distribution of goods, and use of both strategies was practiced by plains bands that had access to multiple sources of trade goods, that is, access to both the French and English, for example. See Albers, "Symbiosis, Merger, and War," 100–10. For the relationship between upland and lowland bands associated with the fur trade, see Lytwyn, *Muskekowuck Athinuwick*, 55–57.

27. For a description of Lowland Cree ogimaag, spelled as Okimahkan in Hudsons Bay Company records, and explanation of requests that band leaders attract Upland Indians to trade, see Oldmixon, "Early History of Hudson's Bay," 382, 390–91.

28. Both the English and the French recognized the potential of an English post on the Hayes-Nelson watershed to significantly influence the relative strength of their empires in the west. For the significance of this post in terms of empire, see Eccles, *The Canadian Frontier*, 141–50; Innis, *The Fur trade in Canada*, 48–52; Rich, *The Fur Trade and the Northwest*, 41–44; and Witgen, "The Rituals of Possession."

29. Radisson, *Explorations*, 176; for Radisson's narrative description of his capture of the English, see 172–90.

30. Ibid., 191.

31. Ibid., 197. For the significance of food in defining the obligations of kinship in a multiethnic exchange network, see Bruce White, "The Trade Assortment: The Meanings of Merchandise in the Ojbwa Fur Trade," in *Habitants et Marchands vingt ans apres: Lectures de l'histoire des XVIIe et XVIIIe siècles, sous la direction de Sylvie Depatie* (Montreal: McGill-Queen's University Press, 1998), 115–37.

32. Radisson, *Explorations*, 197.

33. For this dialogue, see ibid., 197–98.

34. Ibid., 198.

35. For the changing patterns of participation in the fur trade among various upland peoples, particularly the Western Cree and Assiniboine, see Russell, *Eighteenth Century Western Cree*, 92–93.

36. For the hazards of balanced exchange within a multiethnic exchange network, see Sahlins, *Stone Age Economics*, 220–23; and for a critical reading of Sahlins and a discussion of the shifting modalities of exchange, see Albers, "War Symbiosis, and Merger," 105–10.

37. See Graham, *Andrew Graham's Observations*; and Lytwyn, *Muskekowuck Athinuwick*, 12–14.

38. Warren, *History of the Ojibway People*, 50.

39. See Warren, *History of the Ojibway People*, 44–45, 50–53.

40. For Monsoni and Lake of Woods Cree trading at Hudson's Bay, see "Lettre du Sieur Du-Lhut à M. le Comte de Frontenac," April 5, 1679, in Margry, *Découvertes*, 6: 30–31. Various Gens des Terres bands, as well as the more generically designated Upland Indians, all from the region

northwest of Lake Superior, were identified as trading at HBC posts in the mid-1670s; see, for example, Oldmixon, "Early History of Hudson's Bay," 390. Greenberg and Morrison also demonstrate that these allied bands traded at the bay continuously throughout the early eighteenth century at Nelson River and Albany River posts; see Greenberg and Morrison, "Group Identities in the Boreal Forest," 83–84.

41. For the writing and presentation of the fifth and sixth voyage manuscripts, see Fournier, *Pierre-Esprit Radisson*, 234–42.

42. The voyageurs arrived at Percé, a port city on the Gaspe Peninsula, according to their arrangement with Aubert de La Chesnaye, the principal merchant behind the La Compagnie de la Baie d'Hudson. They expected to transship their goods and sail for France, taking one quarter part of the peltries for themselves. Instead they were met by a representative of the Ferme générale de la Nouvelle France, and ordered to Quebec. The Ferme took one quarter part of all pelts traded out of New France, which served as revenue for the colony, and was used to pay colonial officials. For the fur trade and the monetary system of New France, see Louise Dechene, *Habitants and Merchants in seventeenth-centur Montreal* (Montreal: McGill-Queen's University Press, 1992), 67–70.

43. For Radisson's account of these events, see Radisson, *Explorations*, 20–25, 207–10; See also Fournier, *Pierre-Esprit Radisson*, 232–35; and Rich, *The Fur Trade and the Northwest*, 50–57, who argues that France's Ministre du Marine, M. de Seignelay acted to undermine Governor La Barre and to support Jean Oudiette, who held the monopoly at Tadoussac and also controlled the entire Canadian revenue system.

44. Radisson, *Explorations*, 222–23.

45. Ibid., 223.

46. Ibid., 223–24.

47. For the feast and murder, see ibid., 224, and for English deaths, see 222, 225.

48. For the second assassination attempt, see ibid., 226, and for trading with the English, 227.

49. Ibid., 226.

50. For the Assiniboine, see ibid., 227–28.

51. Ibid., 214.

52. Ibid., 215.

53. Radisson was married to the daughter of John Kirke, a Protestant of French ancestry who was an important partner in the Hudson's Bay Company. For the question of Radisson's shifting loyalties, see ibid., 163–66; and Fournier, *Pierre-Esprit Radisson*, 217–22.

54. The description Radisson provides of their migration to the coast is reminiscent of descriptions provided by later HBC traders at York Factory on the Nelson River. See, for example, Henry Kelsey, *The Kelsey Papers*, ed. Arthur G. Doughty and Chester Martin (Ottawa: Public Archives of Canada, 1929). For descriptions of Upland Cree bands and their territories, see also "Details of the Names and the Distance of each Nation, both to the North of Lake Superior, and on the Lands recently discovered and established in the West, by the Sieur de La Vérendrye," *PAC*, MG18 (Pre-Conquest Papers) B12; Graham, *Andrew Graham's Observations*; and Russell, *The Eighteenth Century Western Cree*.

55. Radisson, *Explorations*, 218.

56. Ibid.

57. Ibid., 196.

58. Ibid., 218; for a narrative of this encounter, see 217–20.

59. Ibid., 219.

60. Ibid., 230.

61. Ibid., 232.

62. The anthropologist Patricia Albers described this process as a cycle of symbiosis, merger, and war. See Albers, "Symbiosis, Merger, and War," 129–32.

63. Greg Dening has written about the significance of naming and social identity to the construction of indigenous space in the Marquesas. See Greg Dening, *Islands and Beaches: Discourse on a Silent Land: Marquesas, 1774–1880* (Chicago: Dorsey Press, 1980), 49.

64. AN C11 A 6. M. de la Barre au Ministre, November 3, 1683, f. 138; see also AN C11 A 6 Canada et Nouvelle France, 1684, f. 472, for a similar statement: "The colony is again attacked by the establishment that the English have made in the north from Québec in Hudson's bay from where they draw the beavers from the Ottawa nations." See also AN C11 E 1 Mémoire de la Compagnie du Nord en Canada, February 1685; and AN C11 A 6, de la Barre au Ministre, November 14, 1684, where La Barre writing to de Seignelay asserts that Radisson's first establishment at the Bourbon River made this space French by right of discovery and occupation, and also claims that Du Lhut's post at Nipigon would capture the interior trade for the French.

65. AN C11 E 16 Mémoire sur l'Établissement de Tékkamenesne et Detroit.

66. "Extrait d'une Lettre de Greysolon Du Lhut à M. De la Barre," September 10, 1684, in Margry, *Découvertes*, 6: 51.

67. For the Assiniboine and Cree at Radisson's post, see Radisson, *Explorations*, 218; for attempted alliance negotiated by Du Lhut, see "Mémoire du Sieur Greysolon Du Lhut adressé à Monsieur le Marquis de Seignelay," in Margry, *Découvertes*, 6: 22; for the history of the Assiniboine and Western Cree, see Russell, *The Eighteenth Century Cree.*

68. *Sapin* is the French word for fir tree, and *sapinière* is an evergreen or fir tree forest. For Warren, see Warren, *History of the Ojibway People*, 45, 85. Warren also linked the Bois Fort to the Lake of the Woods Cree, who were also identified as Muskegoes, or swampy people. For Du Lhut using the generic designation "gens du Nord" or "Les Sauvages du Nord," see "Lettre du sieur Du Lhut à M. le Comte de Frontenac," April 5, 1679, in Margry, *Découvertes*, 6: 28; and "Lettre à Monseigneur le Marquis de Seignelay," in Margry, *Découvertes*, 6: 35.

69. For the Marameg, the Ne-kah, and other doodemag from the region west and northwest of Lake Superior that attended St. Lusson's ceremony in 1671, including a band identified as Muskegoe, see "Procès-verbal de la prise de possession des pays situés vers les lacs Huron et Superieur," June 4, 1671, in Margry, *Découvertes*, 1: 97. For band identities among the northwest Ojibweg, see Warren, *History of the Ojibway People*, 44–45. See also Greenberg and Morrison, "Group Identities in the Boreal Forest."

70. For Gens des Terres bands, see La Potherie, *Histoire*, 2: 48–49; see also JR 18: 229 and JR 44:249. For trade at Hudson's Bay Company posts, see Oldmixon, "Early History of Hudson Bay," 390–93; Greenberg and Morrison, "Group Identities in the Boreal Forest," 85–86.

71. "Extrait d'une Lettre du Marquis de Denonville au Marquis de Seignelay," August 25, 1687, in Margry, *Découvertes*, 6: 52.

72. Here I am again drawing upon Henri Lefebvre's notion of the social production of space. Lefebvre argues that social space is both the precondition for and a result of social superstructures. "Social space," he argues, "contains a great diversity of objects, both natural and social, including the networks and pathways which facilitate the exchange of material things and information. Such 'objects' are not only things but relations." Thus the Penesewichewan Sepee was a River Valley with an identifiable physical form. But it was also what La Febvre describes as a "spatio-temporal configuration." That is, the Penesewichewan Sepee was at once physical form and at the same time the invocation of social relationships that joined human beings from the seacoast and the muskeg

representing a distinct "social form." This "social form" was the active creation of space, place, and identity. The social formations of the western interior were clearly indigenous, though they incorporated persons and material artifacts of European culture. More importantly, for most Europeans, the spaces where interior west Native networks were produced remained invisible. And the material production of indigenous space and spatialized identities—such as the Penesewichewan Sepee or the Muskegoes/Gens de la Sapinière/Lake of the Woods Cree—remained a mystery that was collapsed into more simple national categories that misrepresented Native social formations. See Lefebvre, *The Production of Space*, 77; for "social form," 78; and for social space, 68–85.

73. AN C11 A 15 Raisons qu'on a proposé à la Cour, 1687, f. 271.

74. AN C11 A 6 Extrait de la lettre du S. Du Lhut escrite à Michilimackinac, April 12, 1684. A version of this letter has been translated into English and published in *WHC*, 16: 114–25. This translation has several errors, including the fact that the phrase "fuy de Chaouamigon" (or fleeing from Chequamegon) is absent in the published text. Additionally, the manuscript identifies the family of Achiganaga as "estant Nocke" or No-Ka, the Bear doodem (f. 233). The English translation omits this distinction. Both of these omissions constitute crucial components of this story.

75. For a French description of the Sauteurs, see JR 54: 132–34. See also Chapter 2.

76. For the Makwa doodem, see Warren, *History of the Ojibway People*, 49.

77. AN C11 A 6 Extrait de Lettre du S. Du Lhut escrite à Michilimackinac, April 12, 1684, f. 234.

78. Ibid., f. 233.

79. Ibid., f. 234.

80. Ibid.

81. Ibid.

82. Ibid., f. 235. In other documents Du Lhut provided a phonetic approximation of the Ojibwe dialect phrase *nopaming daje inini*, or "Bush people" or "Inland people," as *les opemens d'Acheliny*; see "Extrait d'une Lettre de Greysolon Du Lhut à M. De la Barre," September 10, 1684, in Margry, *Découvertes*, 6: 51. Similarly the Ne-ka or Goose doodem of the Muskegoe Ojibwe was sometimes glossed as "Ouikaliny"; see "Extrait d'une mémoire d'Aubert de La Chesnaye sur le Canada 1697," in Margry, *Découvertes*, 6: 7.

83. AN C11 A 6 Extrait de Lettre du S. Du Lhut escrite à Michilimackinac, April 12, 1684, f. 234.

84. Ibid., f. 235.

85. Ibid., f. 236.

86. White, *The Middle Ground*, 80; AN C11 A 6 Extrait de Lettre du S. Du Lhut escrite à Michilimackinac, April 12, 1684, f. 236.

87. AN C11 A 6 Extrait de Lettre du S. Du Lhut escrite à Michilimackinac, April 12, 1684, f. 237.

88. Ibid., f. 238.

89. Ibid., f. 239.

90. For mourning war rituals and practices, see Richter, "War and Culture." For raising the dead and the cultural practices surrounding murder and punishment, see Richard White, "'Although I Am Dead, I Am Not Entirely Dead.'" For Perrot, see La Potherie, *Histoire*, 2: 307–18; for "The Frenchman is now Master of your bodies," see AN C11 A6 Extrait de Lettre du S. Du Lhut escrite à Michilimackinac, April 12, 1684, f. 234.

91. Brett Rushforth has argued that this murder trial exemplified "Dulhut's rejection of Indian captive customs" and signaled a refusal by the French to accept the cultural logic that made this practice integral to the preservation of political alliances in the Great Lakes. In making this argument he underestimates the extent to which the alliance between the French and their Native allies was predicated on the middle ground, that is, a hybrid social world created by an amalgamation of

culturally misappropriated French and Indian cultural practices. This trial, after all, ended with an elaborate series of rituals covering the dead, including the individuals executed by the French. See Rushforth, " 'A Little Flesh We Offer You.'"

92. AN C11 A 6 Extrait de Lettre du S. Du Lhut escrite à Michilimackinac, April 12, 1684, f. 239.

93. See Howard, "Yanktonai Ethnohistory and the John K. Bear Winter Count," 20. This winter count indicates a big battle, Wico Kicize Tanka, but does not specify the identity of the enemy. The translator of this text has identified the Cree as the protagonists in this conflict based on generic statements of conflict between the "Cree" and the "Sioux" in the publications of Perrot and La Potherie. The only documented attack against the Sioux peoples during the 1682–83 winter, however, was the one described by Du Lhut. This raid by the Makwa doodem and an unnamed Gens des Terres band (people often identified as Cree) seems to correspond to the winter count. It is worth noting that Hudson's Bay Company documents offer no record of a Cree or Assinboine attack against the Sioux for this period.

94. For Jesuits, see *JR* 46: 69; for Hennepin, see Chapter 3; for the significance of the Yanktonai in the diplomatic and trade relations of the Sioux alliance, see Robert W. Galler, Jr., "Sustaining the Sioux Confederation: Yanktonai Initiatives and Influence on the Northern Plains, 1680–1880," *Western Historical Quarterly* 39, no. 4 (Winter 2008).

Part III. The Illusion of Empire

1. Alan Taylor, *The Divided Ground: Indians, Settlers, and the Northern Borderland of the American Revolution* (New York: Knopf, 2006)

2. Adelman and Aron, "From Borderlands to Borders," 820.

3. Ibid., 822.

4. Richard White, *The Middle Ground*, 143–45; Jose A. Brandao and William Starna, "The Treaties of 1701: A Triumph of Iroquois Diplomacy," *Ethnohistory*, 43, no. 2 (Spring 1996); and Giles Havard, *The Great Peace of Montreal of 1701: French-Native Diplomacy in the Seventeenth Century* (Montreal: McGill-Queen's University Press, 2001).

5. Adelman and Aron, "From Borderlands to Borders," 816.

6. For population growth, see Jeanne Kay, "The Fur Trade and Native American Population Growth," *Ethnohistory* 31, no. 4 (Autumn 1984); for Ojibwe expansion, see Laura Peers, *The Ojibwa of Western Canada: 1780 to 1870* (St. Paul: Minnesota Historical Society Press, 1994).

7. White, *Middle Ground*, 268, 472–73.

8. For Nativists and the seekers of accommodation defined, see Gregory Evans Dowd, *A Spirited Resistance: The North American Indian Struggle for Unity, 1745–1815* (Baltimore: Johns Hopkins University Press, 1992), xx, 20–21.

9. Reginald Horsman, "American Indian Policy in the Old Northwest, 1783–1812," *William and Mary Quarterly*, 3rd ser., 18, no. 1 (January 1961), 46–47; and Dowd, *A Spirited Resistance*, 118–19.

10. Horsman, "American Indian Policy," 39, 42.

11. The British experience in the western interior was comparable to that of the United States. The British and the Hudson's Bay Company called their colony Rupert's Land. As late as the mid-nineteenth century, however, company and government officials could not agree about where their colony ended and Indian Territory began. Moreover, the British government effectively abdicated sovereign jurisdiction over the western interior because it could not do things like punish murderers, or even enforce the mercantile tax codes and trade laws that constituted the very raison d'etre of

the Hudson's Bay Company. See, for example, Hamar Foster, "Long-Distance Justice: The Criminal Jurisdiction of Canadian Courts West of the Canadas, 1763–1859," *American Journal of Legal History* 33, no. 1 (January 1990).

12. Letter of Nicolas Boilvin to President James Madison, July 28, 1809, Boilvin file 1809, Boilvin Papers, State Historical Society of Wisconsin, Madison.

Chapter 5. An Anishinaabe Warrior's World

1. La Potherie, *Histoire*, 2: 314.

2. Ibid., 2: 318.

3. Ibid., 2: 319.

4. Ibid..

5. The archaeological record and early encounters with Europeans support the oral history that recounts this migration. For the Ho-Chunk, see Nancy O. Lurie, "Winnebago," in *HNAI*, 15, 690.

6. La Potherie, *Histoire*, 2: 320.

7. For the Iowa, see Mildred Mott Wedel, "Iowa," in *HNAI*, 13: part 1, 432.

8. La Potherie, *Histoire*, 2: 321.

9. For the significance of the horse and the evolution of an equestrian political economy on the plains, see John C. Ewers, *The Horse in Blackfoot Indian Culture: With Comparative Material from Other Tribes* (Washington, D.C., 1955); and Elliot West, *The Contested Plains: Indians, Goldseekers, and the Rush to Colorado* (Lawrence: University Press of Kansas, 1998). For the Comanche, see Pekka Hamalainen, "The Western Comanche Trade Center: Rethinking the Plains Indian Trade System," *Western Historical Quarterly*, 29, no. 4 (Winter 1998). For the Sioux alliance, see Richard White, "The Winning of the West."

10. La Potherie, *Histoire*, 2: 322.

11. Ibid.

12. "Lettre du Pere Enjarlan à Le Fevre de la Barre, gouverneur de la Nouvelle France," August 26, 1683, in Margry, *Découvertes*, 5: 5.

13. AN C11 A6 Lettre de La Durantaye accompagnant la copie de la letter qui precède, April 22, 1684, f. 521–22.

14. AN C11 A6 De la Mission de St. Francois dans la Baye des Puants, April 23, 1684.

15. DeMallie, "Kinship and Biology in Sioux Culture,"130.

16. Ibid., 136.

17. Ella Deloria, *Speaking of Indians*, 29.

18. For the Dakota, the universal power, the equivalent of the Algonquian spiritual category Master of Life, was wakan tanka, or the "great spirits," and in both cases these entities were the source of power in the world. See DeMallie, "Kinship and Biology in Sioux Culture," 127–28.

19. Significantly, for the Sioux, kinship, or the proper way of relating to one's relatives, was a gift of wakan tanka. The Anishinaabeg called the universal power "kitchi-manitou," a term that Ojibwe linguist and scholar Basil Johnston translates as "the great mystery of the supernatural order." Kitchi-manitou is the creator of all things and the source of manidoo. In both cultures the universal power is associated directly with the order and establishment of the social relations of kinship. For the Sioux, see DeMallie, "Kinship and Biology in Sioux Culture," 127; and for the Anishinaabeg, see Basil Johnston, *The Manitous: The Supernatural World of the Ojibway* (New York: Harper Collins, 1995), 2–3.

20. DeMallie, "Kinship and Biology in Sioux Culture," 133. For the significance of kinship in the context of migration, see Gibbon, *The Sioux*, 50–53.

21. For the Seneca attack, see La Potherie, *Histoire*, 2: 324–26; and "Memoir on the present state of affairs in Canada, and the necessity of waging war, next year, against the Iroquois," November 8, 1686, *NYCD* 9: 298.

22. La Potherie, *Histoire*, 2: 325.

23. Epidemics in 1672 and 1682 exacerbated population decline among the Iroquois. For the correlation between population loss and warfare against the Miamis and Illinois, see Brandanao, *Your Fyre Shall Burn No More*, 72–80, 122–23. See also Richter, "War and Culture," 528–59; for Iroquois claims to this hunting territory and their willingness to use military force to advance these claims, see Brandao and Starna, "The Treaties of 1701."

24. Daniel Richter has argued that in addition to the fighting for control of the fur trade, renewed conflict with the allies of New France was driven by the internal politics of the confederacy and centered on the idea of warfare as a means of revitalizing the spiritual power of the Haudenosaunee. See Richter, *Ordeal of the Longhouse*, 155. For a firsthand description of this understanding of warfare as a means to revitalize Iroquois spiritual power and to assert their status in the covenant chain, see *JR* 54: 75. In this *Relation* the French Jesuit missionary to the Cayuga Iroquois wrote that "there is nothing more inimical to our missions then the victories that these people gain over their enemies." The non-Christian Iroquois relied on success in warfare, he argued, to increase their political power, resist conversion, and argue for the maintenance of traditional cultural practices. See also Brandao, *Your Fyre Shall Burn No More*, 122.

25. "Attaque et Pillage de sept canots Français par les Iroquois," in Margry, *Découvertes*, 2: 338–44.

26. For Nicolas Perrot's account of this campaign, see Perrot, *Memoire*, 132–38; see also Louis Armand, Baron de La Honton, *New Voyages to North America*, ed. Reuben Thwaites, 2 vols. (Chicago: A. C. McClurg, 1905), 1: 66–87; and Eccles, *Frontenac*, 169–72.

27. Peter Wraxall, *An Abridgment of the Indian Affairs* (Cambridge, Mass.: Harvard University Press, 1915), 13. For the trading expedition organized by the Governor of New York, see "M. de Denonville to M. de Seignelay," May 8, 1686, *NYCD* 9: 287; "M. de Denonville to M. de Seignelay," August 25, 1687, *NYCD* 9: 336; "Summary of M. Denonville's dispatch and M. de Seignelay's Remarks thereupon," 25 August, 1687, *NYCD* 9: 345–46; "Memoir on the present state of affairs in Canada in reference to the Iroquois war," October 27, 1687, *NYCD* 9: 346–49; and Kellogg, *The French Régime in Wisconsin*, 230–31. The French also believed that their allies were beginning to trade with the English at Albany through Iroquois intermediaries; see "Lettre de Cavelier de La Salle," August 22, 1682, in Margry, *Découvertes*, 2: 236–39.

28. For Iroquois complaints against Miami and Illinois hunters in the disputed territory, see La Honton, *New Voyages to North America*, 1: 41; for Denonville's recognition that French trade with the Illinois and Miami provoked the Iroquois, which resulted in raiding and pillaging of voyageurs and French-allied Indians, see "Memoir on the present state of affairs in Canada, and the necessity of waging war, next year, against the Iroquois," November 8, 1686, *NYCD* 9: 301. For this raid against the Odawa, see "M. de Denonvilee to M. de Seignelay," June 12, 1686, *NYCD* 9: 293–95; "Memoir on the State of Canada," January 1687, *NYCD*, 9: 319; and Brandao, *Your Fyre Shall Burn No More*, appendix D, "The Statistics of War: Iroquois Hostilities to 1701," table D.1.

29. For population statistics, see Richter, *Ordeal of the Longhouse*, 188. For the correlation between population loss and warfare against the Miamis and Illinois, see Brandanao, *Your Fyre Shall Burn No More*, 72–80, 122–23. See also Richter, "War and Culture," 528–59.

30. For Dongan's assertion of an English claim to territory in the west, see "Memoir on the present state of affairs in Canada, and the necessity of waging war, next year, against the Iroquois," 8 November, 1686, *NYCD* 9: 296–97; see also Eccles, *Frontenac*, 177. Dongan also vigorously asserted the Duke of York's title to lands in the east on the Maine coast, claims contested by New France and also by the New England colony; see Richard R. Johnson, *John Nelson Merchant Adventurer: a life between empires*, (New York: Oxford University Press, 1991), 39–40. For French claims to this region, see AN C11 E1 Memoir concernant le droit que les Francois ont sur toutes les terres de la Nouvelle France, dit Canada at de la nullité des pretentions des Anglois, 1687; "Memoir on the present state of affairs in Canada, and the necessity of waging war, next year, against the Iroquois," November 8, 1686, *NYCD* 9: 297; and an attached memoir titled "Memoir in proof of the Right of the French to the Iroquois country and Hudson's Bay," *NYCD* 9: 303–4.

31. La Potherie, *Histoire*, 2: 326.

32. Ibid., 2: 327.

33. Perrot, *Memoire*, 139.

34. For Perrot's narration of this encounter, see ibid., 139–40; for La Potherie's narration, see La Potherie, *Histoire*, 2: 327–28.

35. Perrot, *Memoire*, 140.

36. La Potherie, *Histoire*, 2: 328.

37. Daniel Richter has characterized this attempt to control disputed territory north of Lakes Erie and Ontario as part of the beaver wars, that is, an attempt to control the flow of valuable pelts from the northwest to European cities such as Montreal and Albany. Hunting pelts, he argues, was less a priority than acquisition by theft. Richter also contends, however, that mourning raids had become the most significant factor behind the warfare of the late seventeenth century. See Richter, *Ordeal of the Longhouse*, 57–58. Brandao and Starna, however, insist that control over this territory and its resources was of paramount importance for the Iroquois. In this context they argue that it was not just competition over furs but the spread of the French alliance-and-exchange network itself that directly threatened the confederacy. See Brandao and Starna, "The Treaties of 1701," 212.

38. For Port Nelson as the most significant threat to the French fur trade from the Hudson's Bay Company posts, see AN C11 E1 Mémoir *de* la Compagnie du Nord en Canada, February 1685; AN C11 A6 Extrait de la letter ecrite par M. Du Lhut au M. de La Barre, September 10, 1684; AN C11 E1 Memoire de la Baye d'Hudson, August 1697. Governor Denonville explicitly linked the Iroquois attacks, sponsored, he believed, by the English, and the threat posed by English posts at Hudson's Bay as an interconnected problem. See "Memoir on the present state of Canada, the measures to be adopted for the safety of the country," November 12, 1685, *NYCD* 9: 274–75; and "M. de Denonville to M. de Seignelay," May 8, 1686, *NYCD* 9: 288.

39. In a memoir to the minister of marine ,Governor Denonville lamented, "nations of our friends and allies are at war with one another, it is absolutely necessary to establish peace among them before making them in any way useful." See "Memoir on the present state of Canada, the measures to be adopted for the safety of the country," November 12, 1685, *NYCD* 9: 284. He also complained, "Our reputation is absolutely lost both with our friends and with our enemies," in "Memoir on the present state of affairs in Canada, and the necessity of waging war, next year, against the Iroquois," November 8, 1686, *NYCD* 9: 296.

40. For Perrot's account of the campaign, see Perrot, *Mémoire*, 138–43. See also Eccles, *Frontenac*, 180–81; and Richter, *Ordeal of the Longhouse*, 157–58.

41. The voyageurs trading for the English were captured by Denonville's army and executed; see AN F3 2 Receuil de ce qui s'est passé en Canada au sujet de la guerre . . . depuis l'année 1682.

42. For Denonville's account of the Seneca campaign, see "Expedition of M. de Denonville Against the Senecas," October 1687, *NYCD* 9: 358–69; see also "M. de Denonville to M. de Seignelay," August 25, 1687, *NYCD* 9: 336–41; "Memoir on the present state of Affairs in Canada in reference to the Iroquois war," October 27, 1687, *NYCD* 9: 346–50. For Iroquois raids, see *JR* 63: 286, 289; and "Relation of the events of the war, and state of affairs in Canada," *NYCD* 9: 388–91; see also appendix D, table D.1, in Brandao, *Your Fyre Shall Burn No More.*

43. For troop deployments and military state of the colony, see AN C 11 A 9, Denonville au Ministre, November 7, 1687; and AN C11 A9 Denonville et Champigny au Ministre, November 6, 1688. For disease in 1688, see "Memoir on the present state of Affairs in Canada, in reference to the Iroquois war," October 27, 1687, *NYCD* 9: 354; and Eccles, *Frontenac,* 188.

44. Daniel Richter has described these factions as Francophile and Anglophile; see Richter, *Ordeal of the Longhouse,* 138–61. See also Jennings, *Ambiguous Iroquois Empire,* 176–77; Daniel Richter, "Iroquois versus Iroquois: Jesuit Missions and Christianity in Village Politics, 1642–1686," *Ethnohistory,* 33 (1985): 1–16. Brandao and Starna, in contrast, assert that these labels misconstrue the nature of the factional differences that divided the Haudenosaunee during this period. Specifically, they assert that this internal dispute centered over which strategy to pursue vis-à-vis New France, diplomacy or war, and did not reflect an allegiance toward one empire over the other. See Brandao and Starna, "The Treaties of 1701," 237, n58.

45. La Potherie, *Histoire,* 2: 334; and for the financial details of Perrot's trade and estate, see appendix A in Blair, *Indian Tribes,* 252–53.

46. La Potherie, *Histoire,* 2: 335.

47. Ibid., 2: 336.

48. Ibid., 2: 335.

49. Ibid., 2: 336.

50. Ibid., 2: 337.

51. Ibid., 2: 338.

52. "Prise de Possession par Nicolas Perrot," May 8, 1689, in Margry, *Découvertes,* 5: 33–34.

53. For the winter count, see Howard, "Yanktonai Ethnohistory," 21; and Galler, "Sustaining the Sioux Confederation."

54. For Perrot's description of the massacre, see La Potherie, *Histoire,* 2: 383–84.

55. Ibid., 2: 384.

56. Ibid., 2: 384–85.

57. Ibid., 2: 385. The French word used to represent the mouth of the Mesquakie would more accurately translate as "a dog's mouth," implying a deeper insult.

58. Ibid., 2: 386.

59. Ibid., 2: 386.

60. Ibid., 2: 387.

61. Ibid., 2: 388.

62. For Le Sueur posts among the Anishinaabeg and Dakota, see "Extrait d'une Lettre de Champigny au Ministre," November 4, 1693, in Margry, *Découverts,* 6: 55–58.

63. AN C11 A14 Relation d'Evenements survenus en 1694 et 1695.

64. The French identified the Anishinaabe ogimaa as "Chingouabé," a phonetic translation of the Ojibwe word for *Zhingob,* or "Balsam Fir." The *-iins* ending is a diminutive suffix with the *ii* pronounced *ee* as in the English word *seen.* The *ns* signifies a nasalized vowel (the *ii*) with the *ns* omitted in pronunciation. To French ears this would have most closely approximated the *é* sound of a conjugated *-er* verb.

65. Although Du Lhut briefly maintained a post at Kaministiquia, on the northwest corner of the lake, there had been no licensed trader in the region since his departure in 1689, and no post or mission at La Pointe since 1671. For the abandonment of the French post, see *JR* 55: 169–71.

66. These council meetings are recorded in AN C11 A 14 Relation d'Evenemens survenus en 1694 et 1695; they are published in La Potherie, *Histoire*, 4: 583–88; and in "Narrative of the Most Remarkable Occurences in Canada 1694, 1695," *NYCD* 9: 609–13, although here the council speeches were edited to shorten their length; and Margry, *Découvertes*, 6: 55–58.

67. La Potherie, *Histoire*, 4: 584.

68. Ibid., 4: 584; for Michilimackinac and the Dakota slave, see also ibid., 2: 392.

69. Ibid., 4: 584.

70. Ibid., 4: 585.

71. Ibid., 4: 585; "Extrait de la Relation des événements passé en Canada de 1694 à 1695," in Margry, *Découverts*, 6: 56–57.

72. For Tiyoskate, see La Potherie, *Histoire*, 4: 585.

73. For Itancan and Dakota leadership, see DeMallie, "Teton Dakota Kinship and Social Organization," 116–19.

74. DeMallie has raised this issue, arguing that woodlands characteristics of the Dakotas represented an adaptation to the fur trade and exposure to Algonquian groups, in particular the Sauteurs, or Ojibweg. See ibid., 44–45, 61, 64–65, 81.

75. For Hennepin, see Hennepin, *A New Discovery*, 1: 300; for Perrot, see La Potherie, "Savage Allies of New France," in Blair, *Indian Tribes*, 2: 33–34.

76. For iron or trade goods as wasicun, see Bruce M. White, "Encounters with Spirits." The Dakotas routinely sought access to the spiritual power of wakan tanka through the intercession of powerful beings; see for example, Frances Densmore, *Teton Sioux Music*, Bureau of American Ethnology, bulletin 61, (Washington, D.C.: Smithsonian Institution, 1918), 65–66.

77. La Potherie, *Histoire*, 4: 586.

78. White, *The Middle Ground*, 131–40.

79. La Potherie, *Histoire*, 4: 586.

80. Ibid., 4: 587–88.

81. Hudson's Bay Company Archives (hereafter HBCA) B3 d 1694–95, Albany Account Book, September 1–May 1, 1695.

82. For the Jesuit identification of La Nation Kitchigamins, see *JR* 54: 133–35. For Warren see Warren, *History of the Ojibway People*, 38; for "Gichigamiing" as an indicator of Anishinaabe or Ojibwe identity tied to western Lake Superior, see Greenberg and Morrison, "Group Identities in the Boreal Forest," 87–88.

83. HBCA B3 d5, Albany Account Book, July 1, 1694, to June 30,1695, f. 16. The governor spelled "Miskwaamad" phonetically as "Mis-squa-mot." Phonetically, in Ojibwe and closely related Ojibwe-Cree dialects there is no distinction between the consonants *d* and *t*.

84. For the list of bands trading at the Albany post in the summer of 1695, see ibid.; for identification of Cree bands, their homelands, and the posts where they traded, see Graham, *Andrew Graham's Observations*; for identification of Anishinaabeg at Dimiigamiing/Temiskamingue, see AN C11 E13 Descriptions des differents postes du Canada vers 1723–25, f. 150.

85. HBCA B3 d7 1696, Albany Account Book, April 1–July 1, 1696, f. 14.

86. For the form and function of Ojibwe and Cree bands, see Darnell, "Rethinking Band and Tribe." Charles Cleland provides a concise description of the cultural logic of Anishinaabe patrilineal bands with relation to hunting and trading; see Charles Cleland, *Rites of Conquest: The*

History and Culture of Michigan's Native Americans (Ann Arbor: University of Michigan Press, 1992), 43–55.

87. HBCA B3 d7 1696, Albany Account Book April 1–July 1, 1696, f. 14.

88. For restriction of the congés and evacuation of the western posts, see "Louis XIV to Count de Frontenac and M. de Champigny," *NYCD* 9: 636–38; for a summary of this policy and the development of Detroit, see Zoltvany, *Vaudreuil*, 37–41. For the impact of this edict on the French alliance, see White, *Middle Ground*, 110–15.

89. "Northwestern Indians at Quebec; Frontenac's Policy Toward Them," 1697, in *WHC* 16: 167–68.

Chapter 6. The Great Peace and Unraveling Alliances

1. For the diplomacy required to set the stage for the peace conference at Montreal, see Havard, *The Great Peace of Montreal*, 94–107.

2. La Potherie, *Histoire*, 4: 666.

3. Ibid.

4. Ibid., 4: 668.

5. AN F3 8 Pour Parlez antre monsieur le Chevalier de Calliers governeur et leutenant general pour le Roy en Canada et les sauvages descendu à Montreal pour parvenir à la ratification de la paix, July 29, 1701, f. 263.

6. La Potherie, *Histoire*, 4: 669.

7. Ibid., 4: 670.

8. AN F3 8 Pour Parlez antre monsieur le Chevalier de Calliers governeur et leutenant general pour le Roy en Canada et les sauvages descendu à Montreal pour parvenir à la ratification de la paix, July 29, 1701, f. 264.

9. Ibid., f. 263.

10. La Potherie, *Histoire*, 4: 672.

11. Ibid.

12. AN F3 8 Pour Parlez antre monsieur le Chevalier de Calliers governeur et leutenant general pour le Roy en Canada et les sauvages descendu à Montreal pour parvenir à la ratification de la paix, July 29, 1701, f. 267.

13. Ibid., f. 270.

14. La Potherie, *Histoire*, 4: 691.

15. AN F3 8 Pour Parlez antre monsieur le Chevalier de Calliers governeur et leutenant general pour le Roy en Canada et les sauvages descendu à Montreal pour parvenir à la ratification de la paix, July 29, 1701, f. 270.

16. The Jesuits remarked on the importance of redeeming captives for the Anishinaabeg. "Our Outaouas from Detroit," Father Marest wrote, "fear that the Iroquois have not given back their slaves, which was the most essential article of the peace." See "Lettre du Pere Marest à Lamothe Cadillac," October 8, 1701, in Margry, *Découvertes*, 5: 216; see also Rushforth, "'A Little Flesh We Offer You.'"

17. La Potherie, *Histoire*, 4: 680.

18. For the significance of Iroquois population loss, see Brandao, *Your Fyre Shall Burn No More*, 74–77.

19. La Potherie, *Histoire*, 4: 676.

20. AN F3 8 Pour Parlez antre monsieur le Chevalier de Calliers gouverneur et leutenant general pour le Roy en Canada et les sauvages descendu à Montreal pour parvenir à la ratification de la paix, July 29, 1701, f. 265.

21. Havard argues convincingly that the metaphor of the shared dish in this instance referred specifically to conflict in the territory north of Lake Ontario, hunted by both the Iroquois and the peoples of Anishinaabewaki. Encounters with an enemy in this jointly occupied territory often resulted in violent conflict. Following the peace this would be a neutral space, and when hunters met one another they would interact as kin rather than as enemies. See Havard, *The Great Peace of Montreal*, 145–47.

22. La Potherie, *Histoire*, 4: 693–94.

23. AN C11 A 19 Ratification de la Paix, August 4, 1701.

24. Jose Brandao and William Starna, scholars whose work focuses on Iroquois history, argue that the Peace of 1701 was not a French victory. It was instead, they contend, as their subtitle indicates, "A Triumph of Iroquois Diplomacy." They assert that peace with the French and their Native allies recognized Haudenosaunee rights to hunting territory north and west of Lakes Ontario and Erie. More significantly, Brandao and Starna reject the idea that the confederacy was in any way compelled to seek peace, and argue that this new arrangement of power met Iroquois political objectives. Given the fact that the Haudenosaunee lost a staggering 50 percent of its population in a little over a decade prior to the peace, any description of the Treaty of 1701 as an "Iroquois triumph" seems like as a wildly optimistic interpretation of this event. Brandao and Starna cite these grim statistics, but seem overly determined to interpret this new arrangement of power as a victory for the confederacy. Brandao and Starna, "The Treaties of 1701."

25. For the emergence of independent Ohio villages, see White, *Middle Ground*, 159–75; see also Dowd, *A Spirited Resistance*, 23–47.

26. AN C11 A35 M. de Ramezaye et Begon au Ministre, November 1715.

27. For the evolution of Métis communities in the Great Lakes region, see Jacqueline Peterson, "Many Roads to Red River: Metis Genesis in the Great Lakes Region, 1680–1815," in Jennifer S. H. Brown and Jacqueline Peterson, eds., *The New Peoples: Being and Becoming Metis in North America* (Winnipeg: University of Manitoba Press, 1985).

28. The historian Gilles Havard, in contrast, argues that the peace established a "Pax Gallica in the Great Lakes region." Havard described the alliance that emerged after the treaty of 1701 as "an association of sovereign nations." The treaty, he argues, established New France as the arbiter of international relations within this association. Although Havard is careful to acknowledge that "there was nothing absolute" about the power of Onontio, he nevertheless asserts that the Great Peace resulted in French hegemony in the Great Lakes. The institutional and military weakness of New France, and the immediate and sustained outbreak of violence in the west, makes the idea of French hegemony implausible. The argument that New France incorporated Native peoples within its empire as subject nations is similarly problematic. This conception of Native identity is overly reliant on European social and political constructions. See Havard, *The Great Peace of Montreal*, 155–56.

29. Antonine Laumet La Mothe le Sieur de Cadillac convinced the governor to establish a post at Detroit in 1701 to block the illegal trade and manage affairs with the Iroquois. See "Memoire adresse au comte de Maurepas," in Margry, *Découvertes*, 5: 138–53; see also Zoltvany, *Vaudreuil*, 37–41. Posts in the Illinois country, like Saint Louis, were arguably part of the region that the French thought of as the pays d'en haut. After 1701, however, this region was incorporated into the political world of French Louisiana.

30. AN C11 A19 Champigny et Callières au Ministre, October 8, 1701; see also AN C11 A 19 Champigny et Callières au Ministre, October 5, 1701.

31. AN C11 A19 Extrait des Lettres du Canada L'annee 1701, October 3–31, 1701; and AN C11 A19 Callières au Ministre, October 31, 1701.

32. For Montreal merchants supplying coureurs de bois to trade in the Mississippi, see AN C11 A19 Vaudreuil au Ministre, October 1, 1701; for trade entering the Upper Mississippi through Louisiana via the Illinois country, see AN C11 A19 Champigny et Callières au Ministre, October 8, 1701; see also AN C11 A19 Champigny et Callières au Ministre, October 5, 1701; and on the problem of the burgeoning illegal trade, see AN C11 A19 Copie de la lettre écrite à M. Le Comte de Ponchatrain, November 4, 1701.

33. AN F 3/8 Parolles des Outauoies, July 5, 1702.

34. AN F 3/8 Parolles de Longekam, July 23, 1702, f. 312.

35. Ibid.

36. Ibid.

37. AN F 3/8 23 Parolles d'un canot Amikois descendre à Montreal, July 23, 1702.

38. An C11 A20 Callieres au Ministre, November 4, 1702, f. 157.

39. AN C11 A20 Callieres et Beauharnois au Ministre, November 3, 1702, f. 60; for fear that the English would profit from this conflict, see AN C11 A20 Extraits des Lettres de Canada L'anee 1702, November 3, 1702, f. 90. For a similar argument about the need to recapture the western trade from the English, see AN C11 A21 Mémoire que le Direction de la Compagnie de la colonie de Canada, April 26, 1703; AN C11 A19 Mémoire de la Sieur LaZeur Conseiller au Conseil Superior de Quebec, October 28, 1706; AN C11 A24 M. de Vaudreuil au Ministre, November 4, 1706, ff. 216–17; and AN C11 A26 Mémoire sur le Fort Bourbon, November 25, 1707.

40. AN C11 A22 M. Vaudreuil et M. Raudot au Ministre, November 7, 1705. A new governor, Philippe de Rigaud de Vaudreuil, wrote the minster of "the necessity of permitting the re-establishment of the conges if we are not to lose entirely our commerce with the upper nations who are our allies but also have all of them become our enemies"; and AN C11 A22 Mémoire de Sr. Raudot, March 10, 1705.

41. For Detroit, see "Mémoire adressé au comte Maurepas," in Margry, Découvertes, 5: 138–53.

42. "1703 Conferences of Indian Envoys with Governor de Vaudreuil," in WHC 16: 224.

43. Ibid., 16: 226.

44. AN C11 A21 Parolles des Outtaouois of Missiliamakina, October 2, 1703.

45. For the attack at Fort Frontenac, see AN C11 A22 Parolles de la Grande terre Chef Onontague, October 8, 1704; for the calumet, see AN C11 A22 Parolles des Sauvaes de Detroit, Hurons, Outaouas, Miami au Iroquois, July 30, 1704; for searching among the Dakota, see AN C11 A22 Parolles des Outaouais des Michilimackinac, August 23, 1705.

46. This strategy was rooted in a fear of losing the allies to English traders; see AN C11 A22 Lettre de M. de Vaudreuil et M. de Beaharnois au Ministre, August 19, 1705; and AN C11A22 Memoire de Sieur Radot, March 10, 1705.

47. AN C11 A22 Vaudreuil au Ministre, October 19, 1705, f. 236.

48. Ibid., f. 238.

49. AN C11 A24 Vaudreuil et Radot au Ministre, April 28, 1706, ff. 4–5.

50. AN F 3/2 Moreau-St. Marie, Conseil tenu au Fort Ponchatrain, March 8, 1706.

51. Ibid.

52. AN C11 A24 Parolles des Outauois de Michilimackinac à Monsieur le Governeur General, August 22, 1706; and AN C11 A24 Copie de la lettre écrite à Monsieur Le Marquis de Vaudreuil par de la Mothe Cadillac du Detroit, August 27, 1706. For the Odawa war party, see "Letter from Father Marest to Governor Vaudreuil," August 14, 1708, in WHC 16: 232–35; for the Iroquois, see AN C11

A24 Vaudreuil au Ministre, November 4, 1706. Richard White has described the episode with Le Pesant as a pivotal event in the reformulation of the middle ground following the peace of 1701, and he writes about this event as an expansion of the middle ground. I argue here, in contrast, that while the political fiction was more broadly accommodating than, say, the actions surrounding Du Lhut's murder trial, the end result was in fact a reduction of the social world encompassed by the alliance. See White, *Middle Ground*, 82–90.

53. AN C11 A24 Vaudreuil au Ministre, November 4, 1706, f. 216.

54. Ibid., ff. 216–17. For fears of the need to preserve the alliance at Detroit to prevent the defection to the English of both the Iroquois and the Algonquians, see AN C11 A22 Lettre de M. de Vaudreuil et Beauharnois au Ministre, August 19, 1705; and AN C11 A22 Mémoire du Sieur Radot, March 10, 1705.

55. AN C11 A29 L'etat des differents postes du Canada, November 14, 1708, f. 32.

56. Ibid., for Cadillac (f. 45–46) and for Sioux (ff. 48–49).

57. Ibid., ff. 85–87.

58. AN C11 G6 Mémoire pour Monseigneur le Comte de Ponchatrain en 1707; AN C11 G3 M. Radot, pere et fils, au Meme, October 1708; AN C11 G6 Mémoire sur le Poste de Temiskamingues, October 27, 1708; AN C11 G4 Réponse à la lettre, July 6, de M. Radot, November 1, 1709: AN C11 A31 M. d'Aigremont au Ministre, October 18, 1710.

59. HBCA B.3/a/1 Albany Post Journal; for rumors, see May 2, 1706, May 27, 1706; for news of fighting, see B.3/a/2, May 2, 1707.

60. HBCA B.3/a/2 Albany Post Journal, May 2, 1707.

61. HBCA B.3/a/2 Albany Post Journal, May 23, 1707.

62. HBCA B.239/a/2 York Factory Post Journal, May 27, 1716.

63. Ibid., for peace; for Mountain Indians, see June 15, 1716; for trade at Albany, see June 16, 1716; and for access to French wood runners, see August 3 and August 22, 1716.

64. AN C11 A31 Vaudreuil au Ministre, September 2, 1710.

65. AN C11 A32 Mémoire de M. de Vaudreuil pour servir d'instructions aux officiers et voyageurs pour faire detaches pour faire descendre à Montreal les sauvages des pays d'en haut, March 10, 1711; AN C11 A31 M. Daillebout et Argenteuil au Ministre October 3 and 10, 1710.

66. AN C11 A31 Vaudreuil au Ministre, September 2, 1710.

67. "Extract from letter of Governor de Vaudreuil to Count Ponchatrain," October 31, 1710, in *WHC* 16: 263–64.

68. Ibid., 16: 264.

69. Richard White measured Odawa influence by adding up the number of ogimaag who represented the Native peoples that sought an audience with the governor of New France. The Odawa doodemag dominated these meetings by a significant margin. See White, *The Middle Ground*, 153.

70. AN C11 A33 Parolles de Makisabes P8t8, August 17, 1712, f. 87; the French sometimes used the number 8 to approximate the "waa" sound common to Ojibwe dialects.

71. AN C11 A33 Lettre de Dubuisson au Ministre, June 15, 1712, f. 162.

72. For the account of Detroit's commander, see AN C11 A33 Lettre de Dubuisson au Ministre, June 15, 1712. For the Odawa perspective of these events, see AN C11 A33 Parolles de Makisabes, August 17, 1712; and C11 A34 Parolles des Sauvages qui descendent fu Fort de Ponchatrain de Detroit, November 7, 1713.

73. For captives, see AN C11 A 33 Parolles De M. le Gouverneur, July 28, 1712; AN C11 A 34 Vaudreuil au Ministre, August 7, 1713; AN C11 A 24 Vaudreuil au Ministre, September 16, 1714; and AN C11 A34 Copie d'une lettre du RP Marest, June 19, 1713.

74. For Louvigny's assessment of French power in the west, see AN C11 A35 Louvigny au Ministre, September 9, 1715; AN C11 A35 Louvigny au Ministre, October 20, 1715; and AN C11 A35 Louvigny au Ministre, October 30, 1715.

75. For reestablishment at Michilimackinac to preserve French influence and try to curb trade at Hudson's Bay, see AN C11 A24 Vadreuil au Ministre, September 16, 1714. Vaudreuil argued that without this post they risked losing all the allies in the upper country; see AN C11 A33 Vaudreuil au Ministre, November 6, 1712; and for blocking trade with English, see AN C11 A33 Lettre du Pere Marest, June 21, 1712; and AN C11 A34 Memoire sur ce qui concerne le commerce des Castors, ff. 193–98.

76. For Mesquakie among the Dakota, see AN C11 A 34 Copie d'une letter du R.P. Marest, June 19, 1713; AN C11 A34 Parolles des Sauvages qui descenent du fort Ponchatrain de Detroit, ;November 7, 1713; and AN C11 A34 Vaudreuil et Begon au Ministre, November 20, 1714.

77. For the military campaigns against the Fox, see AN C11 A35 Lettre de M. Ramezay et Begon au Ministre, November 13, 1715; AN C11 A35 M. de Remaezay au Ministre, November 3, 1715; "Letter of Ramezay and Begon to the Minister," November 7, 1715, in *WHC* 16: 327–40; and "Letter of Governor Vaudreuil to the council of the Marine," October 14, 1716, in *WHC* 16: 341–44.

78. For a similar assessment of the Fox Wars, see Richard White, *The Middle Ground*, 159–85. Brett Rushforth takes issue with White's interpretation of this conflict as one where the French learned that mediation rather than force was the key to maintaining political influence in the upper country. Instead, he argues: "Whereas French imperial officials sought to enlarge their influence in the west, connecting with an ever-growing number of commercial and military partners, those natives already attached to the French wished to limit this expansion, blocking their enemies' access to French goods and support." The Fox Wars, he concludes, resulted when French-allied Indians waged war to shape the alliance, "shunning their historical enemies." The problem with this reassessment is that the French had been in the west at Green Bay and allied to the Mesquakie for at least four decades when this conflict erupted in 1712. The Fox were not recent additions to the French alliance network. They had been a part of the alliance from its beginning, along with the other peoples living at Green Bay identified by the French as the Pottawatomie, Miami, Winnebago, and Menominee, as well as more temporary residents like the Odawa, Huron, and Illinois peoples, and their close allies the Sauk, Mascouten, and Kickapoos. Another problem with this reassessment is that while there is a concrete basis for calling the Mesquakie the "historical enemies" of the Gichigamiing Anishinaabeg (the Sauteurs), the Mesquakie had traded and fought alongside the other peoples of Green Bay as allies from the period of their migration up to the conflict in 1712. The only French-allied Indians they were consistently at war with were the doodemag of Shagwaamikong. See Brett Rushforth, "Slavery, the Fox Wars, and the Limits of Alliance," *William and Mary Quarterly*,. 63, no. 1 (January 2006).

79. White, *The Middle Ground*, 173.

80. For coureurs de bois and English trade in alcohol, see AN C11 A34 Vaudreuil et Begon au Ministre, September 20, 1714.

81. AN C11 A38 Extrait de la lettre de M. de Sabrevois à M. Marquis de Vaudreuil, April 8, 1717.

82. AN C11 A38 Vaudreuil au Mininstre, October 12, 1717, f 110–11.

83. AN C11 A37 Copie de la lettre de M. de Louvigny sur le second voyage à Michilimackinac, October 1, 1717, ff. 325–26 ; see also AN C11 A38 Compte au Conseil du Second Voyage, September 21, 1717.

84. AN C11 A38 Vaudreuil au Ministre, October 12, 1717.

85. AN C11 A39 Vaudreuil au Ministre, October 30, 1718, f 144.

86. Ibid., ff. 145–46.

87. AN C11 A40 Vaudreuil au Ministre, October 28, 1719.

88. AN C11 A39 M. Begon au Ministre, November 11, 1718.

89. HBCA B.239/a/5 York Post Journal. For account of the French and conflict with the Anishinaabeg, identified as Poetucks by the Lowland Cree, see June 2, 12, 13, and 20, 1719.

90. AN C11 A43 Conseil de Marin, January 14, 1721, ff. 100–101.

91. AN C11 A45, Vaudreuil au Ministre, October 11, 1723.

92. AN C11 A45 Vaudreuil au Ministre, October 11, 1723; see also AN C11 A43, Conseil de Marin, January 14, 1721, ff. 103–4; AN C11 A47 Begon au Ministre, October 31, 1725; and AN C11 A49 Beauharnois au Ministre, April 30, 1727.

93. AN C11 A43 Conseil du Marin, January 14, 1721, f. 104; for Temescamiing see AN C11 A44 Vaudreuil au Ministre, October 15, 1721; and AN C11 A46 Vaudreuil au Ministre, October 28, 1724.

94. AN C11 E13 Description des differents postes du Canada, vers 1723–25; for demographic changes, see Kay, "The Fur Trade."

95. For the Dakota raiding with the Mesquakie against the Illinois and for their emerging alliance, see AN C11 A45 Vaudreuil au Ministre, October 11, 1723; AN C11 A48 Copie de la letter écreite à M. de Lignery, June 15, 1726; AN C11 A48 Longeuil au Ministre, July 28, 1726. For blocking trade to the Dakota and killing French, see AN C11 A47 Longeuil au Ministre, October 31, 1725. For the post among the Dakota, see AN C11 A46 Vaudreuil au Ministre, November 2, 1723; AN C11 A48 Méemoire du Roy, April 22, 1727; and "Extrait de la lettre de M. de Beauharnois," May 29, 1728, in Margry, *Découvertes*, 6: 552–58. For conflict with the Fox, see "Lignery's Report of the Expedition," August 30, 1728, in *WHC* 17: 31–35; see also Gary Anderson, *Kinsmen of Another Kind*, 40–41.

96. For reoccupation of the village and interaction with the Iowa, see AN C11 A 51 Beauharnois au Ministre, July 21, 1729; for prairie Sioux, see "Extrait de la lettre à M. de Beauharnois par le R.P Guignas," May 29,1728, in Margry, *Découvertes*, 6: 558.

97. AN C11 A50 Extrait des lettres ecrites à M. de Beauharnois, September 13, 1728; for Dakota-Cree conflict see also "Extrait d'une lettre de M. Pachot," October 27, 1722, in Margry, *Découvertes*, 6: 513–15.

98. La Verendrye to Beauharnois, May 25, 1733, in *Journals and Letters of Pierre Gaultier de Varennes de la Verendrye and His Sons*, ed. Lawrence J. Burpee (Toronto: Champlain Society, 1927), 101.

99. Beauharnois to Maurepas, "On the Discovery of the Western Sea," in Burpee, *Journals and Letters*, 125–27.

100. Ibid., 117, 135–38.

101. Journal of La Verendrye from May 27, 1733, to July 12, 1734, in Burpee, *Journals and Letters*, 165.

102. Ibid., 168, 170.

103. Ibid., 174.

104. Ibid., 175.

105. CAN MG18 (Pre-Conquest Papers) B12 La Verendrye, "Details of the names the distance of each Nation, both North of Lake Superior, and on the lands recently discovered in the west."

106. Journal of La Verendrye from May 27, 1733, to July 12, 1734, in Burpee, *Journals and Letters*, 180.

107. "Report of the Sieur de la Verendrye, Lieutenant of the Troops and Commandant of the Posts of the West," June 2, 1736, in Burpee, *Journals and Letters*, 215; and "Affair of the murder of twenty-one voyageurs at Lake of the Woods," in Burpee, *Journals and Letters*, 262–73.

108. "Report of the Sieur de la Verendrye, Lieutenant of the Troops and Commandant of the Posts of the West," June 2, 1736, in Burpee, *Journals and Letters*, 228.

109. Ibid., 230.

110. Beauharnois to Maurepas, October 1, 1738, in Burpee, *Journals and Letters*, 281.

111. Ibid., 288.

112. Journal of La Verendrye from July 20, 1738, to May 1739, in Burpee, *Journals and Letters*, 295.

113. "Report of the Sieur de la Verendrye, Lieutenant of the Troops and Commandant of the Posts of the West, June 2, 1736," in Burpee, *Journals and Letters*, 256.

114. Ibid.

115. "Relation du Sieur de Saint-Pierre, Commandant au poste des Sioux," October 14, 1737, in Margry, *Découvertes*, 6: 576.

116. Ibid., 6: 577.

117. Ibid., 6: 579–80.

118. AN C11 A69 Extrait de deux lettres écrites par Le S. de la Ronde, June 28, July 22, 1738.

119. Beauharnois to Maurepas, October 12, 1742, in Burpee, *Journals and Letters*, 383–84.

Part IV. Sovereignty

1. See, for example, Amos Adams, *A Concise Historical View of the Difficulties, Hardships and Perils which attended the Plantings ad Progressive Improvements of New England* (Boston: printed for Edward and Charles Dilly, 1769); Johnathan Mayhew, *Two Discourses Delivered as a day of Public Thanksgiving for the Success of his Majestys arms more particularly in the reduction of Quebec, the Capital of Canada* (Boston: Richard Draper, 1759); Thomas Jefferson, "A Summary of the Rights of British America," in Thomas Jefferson, *Writings: Autobiography; A Summary View of the Rights of British America, Notes on the State of Virginia, Public Papers, Addresses, Messages, and Replies, Miscellany, Letters* (New York: Library of America, 1984), 103–22; Lewis Cass, "Remarks on the Policy and Practice of the United States and Great Britian in Their Treatment of the Indians," *North American Review* 55 (April 1827).

2. For captivity narratives, see Pauline Turner Strong, "Transforming Outsiders: Captivity, Adoption, and Slavery Reconsidered," in Philip J. Deloria and Neal Salisbury, eds., *A Companion to American Indian History* (Malden, Mass.: Blackwell, 2002).

3. For Cooper, see Alan Taylor, *William Cooper's Town: Power and Persuasion on the Frontier of the Early American Republic* (New York: Knopf, 1996), 406–27.

4. Comparing Cooper's *Last of the Mohicans* to Michael Mann's 1992 film adaptation of the novel, Phil Deloria argues that the plots of both versions "are built around a series of pairings: Cora/Alice; Uncas/Chingachgook; and Uncas/Magua, among others. Each of these twosomes is set in motion through the introduction of a third character, setting up a series of triangular tensions that are only resolved through complete reshufflings. The story ends with new pairings, which not only give the story its motion, but also explain Cooper's vision of America and its future." In other words, the protagonists who survive the novel reveal America's national future. See Philip J. Deloria, "Last of the Mohicans," unpublished essay.

5. American studies scholar Alan Trachtenberg argues that for both Cooper and Longfellow, "the aim was to make the white nation seem an outgrowth of red roots." Alan Trachtenberg, *Shades of Hiawatha: Staging Indians, Making Americans, 1880-1930,* (New York: Hill and Wang, 2004), 60.

6. Deloria, *Playing Indian*, 65.

7. Ibid., 64.

Chapter 7. The Counterfactual History of Indian Assimilation

1. President James Monroe, November 17, 1818, *Journal of the House of Representatives of the United States at the Second Session of the Fifteenth Congress in the Forty-Third Year of the Independence of the United States*, (Washington D.C.: printed by De Kraft, 1818), 16.

2. John Richardson, *The Canadian Brothes: or the Prophecy Fulfilled A Tale of the Late American War*, Donald Stephens, ed. (repr. Ottawa: Carleton University Press, 1992)

3. See John George Lambton, Earl of Durham, and Edward Gibbon Wakefield, *The Report and Dispatches of the Earl of Durham: Her Majestys High Commissioner and Governor General of British North America* (London: Ridgways, 1839); for Lord Durham's biography, see *Dictionary of Canadian Biography Online*, http://www.biographi.ca/009004-119.01-e.php?&id_nbr=4155. For the Francophone perspective, see Louis Joseph Papineau, *Histoire de l'insurrection du Canada*, by Hubert Aquin (Montreal: Editions Lemeac, 1968); and J. M. S. Carless, *The Union of the Canadas: The Growth of Canadian Institutions, 1841–1857* (Toronto: McClelland and Stuart, 1967).

4. Canadian studies scholar Oana Godeanu has argued that Richardson envisioned the narration of the Canadian nation from an "evolutionary perspective, as opposed to a revolutionary [one]," in order to preserve the British lineage of Canada as an imagined community, thus avoiding a national trajectory that began with a revolutionary birth. Oana Godenau, "Authority, Nature, and the Native Other on the 19th Century North American Frontier: The Novels of John Richardson and James Fenimore Cooper," paper presented at the American Studies Association annual conference, Philadelphia, October 2007. Historian Jane Errington has made a comparable argument about the national significance of the War of 1812 for Canada, writing that "out of the war there arose a sense of community, an awareness of being Upper Canadian, which encompassed all settlers." This conflict, she argues, marked an important moment when the British subjects of Canada began to see themselves in nationalist terms. See Jane Errington, *The Lion, the Eagle, and Upper Canada: A Developing Colonial Ideology* (Kingston: McGill-Queen's University Press, 1987), 102–3, quote on 86.

5. In 1839 Richardson wrote to the lieutenant governor of Canada, asserting that "I trust I shall not lay myself open to a charge of undue vanity, when I express a belief that the book which I am about to give the world, will live in this country long after its writer shall have been gathered to his forefathers. . . . I think I can perceive, through the vista of years, a time when the people of Canada having acquired a higher taste for literature than they now possess, will feel that pride in the first and only author this country has yet produced." See Donald Stephens, ed., editor's introduction to *The Canadian Brothers; or, The Prophecy Fulfilled: A Tale of the Late American War*, by John Richardson (Ottawa: Carleton University Press, 1992), xlvi.

6. Gordon Wood argues that the desire to force British recognition and acceptance of U.S. sovereignty drove the war hawks in Congress to declare war. See Gordon S. Wood, *Empire of Liberty: A History of the Early Republic, 1789–1815* (New York: Oxford University Press, 2009), 664. See also Reginald Horsman, *The Causes of the War of 1812* (Philadelphia: University of Pennsylvania Press, 1962), which contains a chapter on the west and the proponents of American expansion.

7. 1820 Census of Michigan, in *Michigan Censuses 1710–1830, Under the French, British and Americans* (Detroit: Detroit Society of Geneological Research, 1982).

8. For the significant role that conflict with American Indians played in shaping the historical development of the United States, see Peter Silver, *Our Savage Neighbors: How Indian War Transformed Early America* (New York: W. W. Norton, 2008). For the Jay treaty and its significance and that of the British presence in the Great Lakes, see Dowd, *Spirited Resistance*, 116; and Richard White, *Middle Ground*, 472.

9. For the impact of British posts and Native border crossing on America's Indian policy, see Janet Chute, *The Legacy of Shingwaukowse: A Century of Native Leadership* (Toronto: University of Toronto Press, 1998).

10. For the extensive smuggling and widespread social connections between Americans and Canadians in this region, see Errington, *The Lion, The Eagle, and Upper Canada*, 58–61.

11. See Peterson, "Many Roads to Red River."

12. For Hull's proclamation, see "Proclamation," in David Thompson, *History of the Late War Between Great Britain and the United States of America; with a Retrospective on the Causes from Whence It Originated; Collected from the Most Authentic Sources* (Niagara: T. Sewell, 1832), 103–5, quote on 104.

13. For the failed defense of Mackinac and Detroit, see Wood, *Empire of Liberty*, 670–82; and A. J. Langguth, *Union 1812: The Americans Who Fought the Second War of Independence* (New York: Simon & Schuster Paperbacks, 2006), 178–98.

14. For a brief biographical sketch of Richardson, see Stephens's introduction to *Canadian Brothers*.

15. Thomas Hobbes, *Leviathan*, ed. with an introduction by C. B. Macpherson (1651; repr., Middlesex, England: Penguin Classics, 1985), 189.

16. Ibid., 186.

17. Ibid., 228.

18. Thomas Jefferson to Benjamin Hawkins, February 18, 1803, in Jefferson, *Writings*, 1115.

19. John Locke, *Two Treatises of Government: A Critical Edition with an Introduction and Apparatus Criticus*, ed. Peter Laslett (Cambridge: Cambridge University Press, 1960), 343.

20. Ibid., 332–33.

21. Ibid., 330.

22. Ibid., 332.

23. Ibid., 368.

24. Richardson, *The Canadian Brothers*, 85.

25. Cass, "Remarks on Policy and Practice," 28.

26. Lewis Cass, "Considerations on the Present State of the Indians, and Their Removal to the West of the Mississippi," *North American Review* 66 (January 1830), 17.

27. Ibid., 19.

28. Ibid., 15.

29. Ibid., 15–16.

30. 1820 Census of Michigan.

31. Cass Papers, Lewis Cass, January 1830, "Estimates of Native Population," Clements Library, University of Michigan

32. Henry Rowe Schoolcraft, *Narrative Journal of Travels Through the Northwestern Regions of the United States Extending from Detroit Through the Great Chain of American Lakes to the Sources of the Mississippi River in 1820*, ed. Mentor Williams (repr., East Lansing: Michigan State University Press, 1992), 11.

33. Lewis Cass to William Woodbridge, January 29, 1820, in ibid., appendix B, 307.

34. Schoolcraft, *Narrative Journal*, 96.

35. Lewis Cass to John C. Calhoun, November 18, 1819, in ibid., appendix B, 304.

36. For the Anishinaabeg at Sault Sainte Marie, see Witgen, "The Rituals of Possession."

37. Schoolcraft, *Narrative Journal*, 78.

38. Ibid., 79. See also "The Journal of David Bates Douglas," in ibid., appendix E, 369–70.

39. Schoolcraft, *Narrative Journal*, 90

40. For an analysis of Shingwaukonse's role in the encounter, see Chute, *Legacy of Shingwaukonse*, 20–22.

41. For a cogent analysis of Anishinaabe concepts of power, see Bruce White, "Encounters with Spirits." See also Black-Rogers, "Ojibwa Power Belief System."

42. "A Report of the Proceedings in Relation to the Contested Election for Delegate to the Nineteenth Congress, from the Territory of Michigan . . .," in *The Territorial Papers of the United States*, vol. 11, *The Territory of Michigan, 1820–1829*, ed. Clarence E. Carter (Washington, D.C.: GPO, 1945), 742.

43. Ibid., 732.

44. Ibid., 748.

45. House Committee on Elections, Michigan Election, 19th Congress, 1st Session, Rep. No. 69, February 13, 1826, 7.

46. Lewis Cass to the secretary of war, March 30, 1824, National Archives, RG 75, M 234, Office of Indian Affairs, letters received, Michigan Superintendency, 1824–25, roll 417.

47. Cass, "Remarks on Policy and Practice," 39.

48. Journal of the proceedings that took place under the commission of General William Clark and Governor Lewis Cass at Prairie du Chien, June 20–August 22, 1825; Ratified Treaty No. 139, documents related to the negotiation of the treaty of August 19, 1825, with the Sioux Chippewa, Sauk and Fox, Menominee, Iowa and Winnebago Indians and part of the Ottawa, Chippewa, and Pottawatomie and Illinois Indians, http://digital.library.wisc.edu/1711.dl/history.IT1825no139.

49. "Treaty with the Sioux and etc.," August 19, 1825, in *Indian Affairs: Laws and Treaties*, ed. Charles J. Kappler, 2: 250–55.

50. Journal of the proceedings that took place under the commission of General William Clark and Governor Lewis Cass at Prairie du Chien, June 20–August 22, 1825, f. 177; it is worth noting that Flat Mouth is mistakenly designated "Gros Platte," a variation of "Gueulle Platte."

51. "Treaty with the Sioux," 250–55.

52. Lewis Cass to the secretary of war, May 19, 1826, National Archives, RG 75, M 234, Office of Indian Affairs, letters received, Michigan Superintendency, 1824–27, roll 419.

53. Ibid.

54. For the report on the killings, see Henry Schoolcraft to Lewis Cass, August 31, 1824, National Archives, RG 75, Office of Indian Affairs, letters received, Michigan Superintendency, 1824–25, roll 417.

55. Copy of letter from Captain Clarke to M. Holliday, Sault Sainte Marie, dated December 25, 1824, National Archives, RG 75, Office of Indian Affairs, letters received, Michigan Superintendency, 1824–25, roll 417.

56. Copy of letter from Mr. Holliday to Captain Clarke, acting Indian agent at Sault Sainte Marie, Anse Quewee me non, dated February 3, 1825, , National Archives, RG 75, Office of Indian Affairs, letters received, Michigan Superintendency, 1824–25, roll 417.

57. George Johnston to Henry Schoolcraft, November 2, 1825, and February 27, 1827, National Archives, RG 75, M 234, Office of Indian Affairs, letters received, Michigan Superintendency, 1824–27, roll 419.

58. Cass to the secretary of war, May 19, 1826.

59. Lewis Cass to the secretary of war, August 21, 1826, 1826, National Archives, RG 75, M 234, Office of Indian Affairs, letters received, Michigan Superintendency, 1824–27, roll 419.

60. "Treaty with the Chippewas," 1826, in Kappler, *Indian Affairs*, 268–73.

61. Lewis Cass to secretary of war, May 19, 1826.

62. Schoolcraft, *Narrative Journal*, 77.

63. For the ratification proceeding, see *Senate Journal*, 19th Congress, 2nd session, January 5—11, 1827, 307–9.

64. George Johnston to Henry Schoolcraft, May 25, 1827, National Archives, RG 75, M234, Office of Indian Affairs, letters received, Michigan Superintendency, 1824–27, roll 419.

65. Copy of a letter from Henry Schoolcraft, Indian agent, Sault Sainte Marie, to Lewis Cass, governor of Michigan, Superintendent of Indian Affairs, August 2, 1827, National Archives, RG 75, M234, Office of Indian Affairs, letters received, Michigan Superintendency, 1824–27, roll 419.

Epilogue

1. The Métis identity evolved specifically as a hybrid or bicultural identity. This growing sense of a distinct political and cultural self-consciousness emerged in the context of the fur trade and in the context of both the French alliance system and the Hudson's Bay Company trading system. These mixed-blood people, in both the English and French colonial regimes, served as cultural brokers, and facilitated the interethnic trade and diplomatic exchange that was crucial to the development of colonial North America. It is significant to note that the French-speaking Métis and the English-speaking Mixed-bloods came together at the Red River colony settlement in the early nineteenth century when the Hudson's Bay Company and the Montreal-based Northwest Company merged, consolidating the fur trade. There is an extensive literature on evolution of Métis society; see, for example, Jacqueline Peterson, "Prelude to Red River: A Social Portrait of the Great Lakes Métis," *Ethnohistory* 25, no. 1 (Winter 1978), 41–67; Peterson and Brown, *The New Peoples*; Jennifer Brown, *Strangers in Blood: Fur Trade Company Families in Indian Country* (Vancouver: University of British Columbia Press, 1980); Sylvia Van Kirk, *Many Tender Ties: Women in Fur Trade Society, 1670–1870* (Winnipeg: Watson and Dwyer, 1981); and Gerhard J. Ens, *Homeland to Hinterland: The Changing Worlds of the Red River Métis in the Nineteenth Century* (Toronto: University of Toronto Press, 1996).

2. For Riel's argument regarding Métis and Native rights, see in *Les Ecrits Complets de Louis Riel*, 5 vols., ed. George F. G. Stanly, Glen Campbell, Thomas Flanagan, Raymond Huel, Gilles Martel (Edmonton: University of Alberta Press, 1985): "Lettre à J. V. Grandin," July 9, 1884, 3: 25–27; "Pétition à votre excellence en conseil," July 9, 1884, 3: 27–29; and "Les Métis du Nord-Ouest," October 11, 1884, 3: 278–94.

3. For Macdonald, see J. M. Bumstead, *Louis Riel v. Canada* (Winnipeg: Great Plains Publications, 2001), 15–21. Macdonald's territorial governor, William McDougall, was associated with the Clear Grit movement in Ontario, which called for the annexation of the Northwest. He had also negotiated the Manitoulin Island Treaty with Anishinaabeg in Ontario. McDougall became notorious for his role in producing this treaty, which fraudulently extinguished Native title to vast tracts of land in western Canada. For McDougall, see Robert J. Surtees, *Treaty Research Report: Manitoulin Island Treaties*, Treaties and Historical Research Centre, Department of Indian and Northern Affairs, Ottawa, Ontario, 1986.

4. Sir John A. Macdonald to C. J. Brydges, esq., January 28, 1870, in *Selections from the Correspondence of the Right Honorable Sir John Alexander Macdonald, First Prime Minister of the Dominion of Canada*, ed. Sir Joseph Pope (Garden City, N.Y.: Doubleday, Page, 1921).

5. François Furstenberg, "Beyond Freedom and Slavery: Autonomy, Virtue, and Resistance in Early American Political Discourse," *Journal of American History* 89, no. 4 (March 2003), 1297.

6. For white appropriation of American Indian identity, see Philip Deloria, *Playing Indian*.

7. The Métis were the largest percentage of the population of the Red River settlement, accounting for 9,800 out of a total population of 11,400 in 1870. There were 5,720 French-speaking Métis and approximately 4,000 English-speaking Métis, who also used the terms "Mixed-blood" and "Half-breed" to identify themselves. By the 1870s, however, there was considerable intermarriage among the Anglophone and Francophone populations. Perhaps more significantly, there were a large number of Métis not counted in the census because they had migrated farther west onto the prairies in order to pursue the buffalo robe trade. These Métis remained connected to their kin at Red River and were a part of the Métis struggle against Canada as it unfolded during the course of the 1870s and 1880s. For census data, see Olive P. Dickason, *Canada's First Nations: A History of Founding Peoples from Earliest Times* (Norman: University of Oklahoma Press, 1992), 263; for intermarriage between Métis and Mixed-bloods, see Ens, *Homeland to Hinterland*, 123–38.

8. See, for example, "Memoir of M. De Denonville on the State of Canada," November 12, 1685, in *NYCD* 9: 286; and AN C11 E1 Mémoire à Ministre, July 3, 1687.

9. The anthropologist Regna Darnell characterized this pattern of mobility and adaptation as an essential component of Algonquian social structure; see n. 24 to Chapter 1. Darnell, "Rethinking Band and Tribe," 91. The idea of shape-shifting is prominent in Anishinaabe culture and metaphysics; see for example, Vescey, *Traditional Ojibwa Religion*, 59–63; see also Hallowell, *Ojibwa Ontology, Behavior, and World View*, 30; and Diamond Jenness, *The Ojibwa Indians of Perry Island: Their Social and Religious Life*, Bulletin National Museum of Canada, no. 78, Anthropological Series, no. 17 (Ottawa: J. O. Patenaude, printer, 1935), 27.

ACKNOWLEDGMENTS

===

While writing this book I have benefited from the kindness and support of many people. This support has taken every form imaginable, from financial assistance and intellectual mentoring, to emotional encouragement. Scholarship, at its best, is a collaborative enterprise, and I have been fortunate to spend my time at academic institutions that generously supported this project and fostered my intellectual development.

In the history department at the University of Washington I received generous financial and intellectual support. I am especially indebted to Alexandra Harmon, Richard Johnson, and Richard White, who served on my committee, all outstanding scholars with infinite patience and a deep intellectual engagement and commitment to my training as a historian. I am grateful for their mentorship. I owe a special thanks to Richard White. His work has been an inspiration for me as a scholar, and his incredible generosity through the years profoundly shaped my intellectual development. I also benefited from the support and engagement of an amazing cohort including Ned Blackhawk, Matthew Booker, Connie Chiang, Liz Escobedo, Roberta Gold, Matthew Klingle, Rachel St. John, Jennifer Seltz, Jay Taylor, and Coll Thrush.

While I got off to an excellent start at the University of Washington, I thoroughly revised and completed this book at the University of Michigan. The support and mentoring I have received at Michigan has been truly fantastic. This book evolved significantly during my time here thanks to the engagement of my colleagues in Native Studies, the Program in American Culture, and the Department of History. Geoff Eley and Mary Kelly were outstanding mentors as chairs in the history department, and Phil Deloria and Greg Dowd in the Program in American Culture. Phil has been a tremendous influence as a friend and scholar. I learned much of what I know about interdisciplinary scholarship by studying his scholarship, teaching with him, and through his work as a public intellectual. Phil tolerated me popping in to his office repeatedly, always unannounced, to discuss the minutia of this book project. In similar fashion Greg Dowd made himself available to discuss the book, and to help me to think through the biggest and the smallest of questions related to our shared interests in the history of the Great Lakes, and to American Indian and early American history in general. He has been a good friend, and a scholar who has profoundly influenced my thinking about the practice of history. Greg and Phil have both generously read and commented on multiple versions of this book, which has benefited enormously from their care and attention.

My colleagues in Native Studies, past and present, have been an inspiration for thinking about the fields of Native Studies and American Indian history. In addition to Phil and Greg, Tiya Miles, Joe Gone, Gustavo Verdesio (who served on my third year review and promotion committees), Andrea Smith, Barbra Meeks, Lincoln Fowler, Howard Kimewon, and Meg Nori have contributed to this project with tremendous intellectual support, and in creating a fantastic Native Studies program. My work with language in this book owes an enormous debt to Meg who always made herself available to help me with translations and to think through the most tortuous eighteenth-century French renditions of Anishinaabemowin. Gichi-miigwetch to you all.

I am grateful to the Ford Foundation, which provided me with a Post-Doctoral Fellowship that allowed me to complete the final stages of research for *An Infinity of Nations*. This fellowship brought me to the Minnesota Historical Society, a wonderful institution with marvelous collections for anyone studying the Great Lakes and Upper Mississippi Valley, as well as a fabulous archivist in the person of the Reference Specialist Debbie Miller. Before, during, and after my Ford fellowship I received tremendous support, kindness, and wisdom from Brenda Child and Jean O'Brien-Kehoe at the University of Minnesota. Another Gichi-miigwetch to Brenda and Jeani, I am a far better scholar because of their contributions to the field of Native Studies, and their support for my work.

The Program in American Culture at the University enabled me to complete the final stage of revisions for *An Infinity of Nations* through a generous manuscript workshop. Damon Salesa and Amy Stillman read my manuscript for this workshop and provided me with critical interventions that improved the book immeasurably. Daniel Richter, an amazing scholar and Early American Studies series editor at the University of Pennsylvania Press read through multiple drafts of this book and provided deeply insightful comments. In addition, I am indebted to Robert Lockhart from the press who participated in the workshop, and serving as an editor helped me to think through the development of the revised book project. His insight too proved invaluable. I am also deeply grateful for the editorial work of Noreen O'Connor-Abel, who helped to complete my final revisions. Finally, I want to thank the anonymous readers who read and commented on the manuscript for the press. From start to finish, the University of Pennsylvania Press has been a fantastic partner in this project.

During the manuscript workshop and other venues I also benefited from comments from colleagues in history and American Culture including Martha Jones, John Carson, and Rebecca Scott who prompted me to think about the relationship between Native North America and the Atlantic World. Maria Montoya, now at New York University, read portions of this book, and more importantly helped me to make an intellectual home for myself at the University of Michigan. I also benefited from the outstanding work of research assistants Alyssa Chen Walker and Aileen O'Toole.

All of my colleagues at the University of Michigan have been generous, but none more so than Kristin Hass. Kristin partnered with me as we revised our manuscripts for publication, taking the time to read draft after draft of this book. Her intellectual contributions to this book have been enormous, and the project evolved significantly as a result of comments and insights. I am deeply grateful.

I could not have written this book without the love and support of my family. As I completed final revisions my mother Lois Faye Witgen suffered a heart attack, and fought an epic battle to recover from this health crisis for four and a half months. In the end her body simply could not sustain the strength of her will to live, and she passed at far too young an age. For better or worse I will always associate the completion of this book with her death and with the life she lived, which is as it should be since she nourished in me a love of books and reading that I have never been able to shake. My father, Michael, and in-laws Peter and Eileen Cunningham have also contributed to whatever success comes of this book through their love and tremendous support during long years when it must have seemed like this project would never be finished.

If the years of writing this book were long, they were lived with joy and grace thanks to Kelly Cunningham and Kieran Meagher Witgen. Kieran has grown up with this book, and a great deal of it was written during summers when we were locked away together in my office with the dog. A documentary filmmaker since the age of four and an kid ornithologist (his words) since the age of three he has taught me so much about the world, and about how to tell stories. Kieran is my very own personal Nanabozho, and in trickster fashion he has taught me that everything in life is, potentially, a source of amusement and self-knowledge. He also forced me to learn to write and think no matter what is happening in the background. Finally, this book could not have been written without Kelly, who has listened to a spoken version of this book on a regular basis for the better part of ten years. She never let me forget why I am doing this work, and she helped me to see that I needed to write this story. Kelly is patience and love, generosity and wisdom. She made everything possible.